EDITED BY LINSEY YOUNG

WOMEN IN REVOLT! ART AND ACTIVISM IN THE UK 1970–90

TATE

In celebration and loving memory
of Gael Elizabeth Stuart 1955–2020

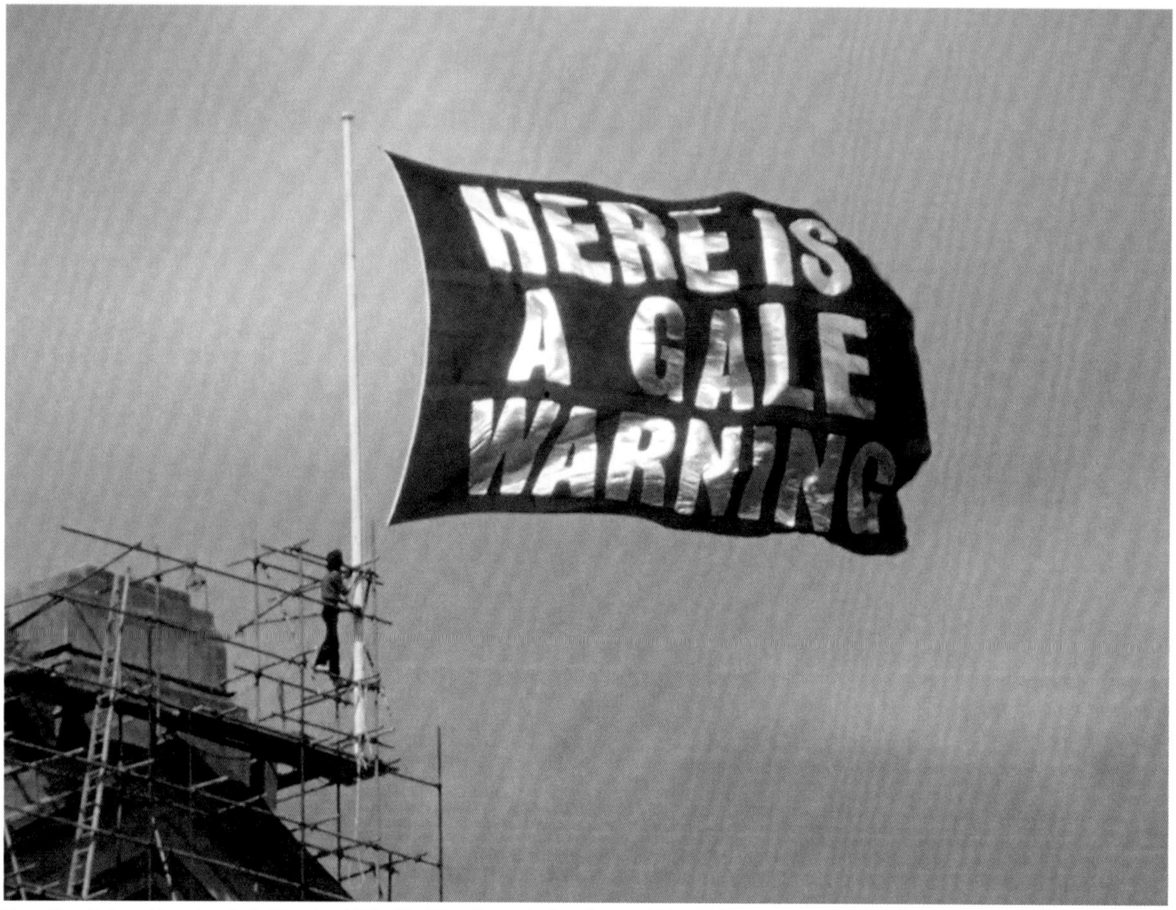

Rose Finn-Kelcey *Here is a Gale Warning* 1971. Black bunting and silver tissue. 114 × 209

First published 2023 by order
of the Tate Trustees by Tate Publishing,
a division of Tate Enterprises Ltd,
Millbank, London SW1P 4RG
www.tate.org.uk/publishing

on the occasion of the exhibition
*Women in Revolt!
Art and Activism in the UK 1970–1990*

Tate Britain, London
8 November 2023 – 7 April 2024

National Galleries of Scotland: Modern, Edinburgh
25 May 2024 – 26 January 2025

The Whitworth, The University of Manchester
7 March – 1 June 2025

Supported by
the Women in Revolt!
Exhibition Supporters Circle:
Lubaina Himid C.B.E.
Gillian Jason Gallery
Maria Sukkar

and Tate International Council,
Tate Patrons and Tate Members

With additional support on
Women in Revolt! film programme
from Action4Equality Scotland Ltd.

BRENDA AGARD
SAM AINSLEY
SIMONE ALEXANDER
BOBBY BAKER
ANNE BEAN
ZARINA BHIMJI
GINA BIRCH
SUTAPA BISWAS
TESSA BOFFIN
SONIA BOYCE
CHILA KUMARI SINGH BURMAN
SHIRLEY CAMERON
THALIA CAMPBELL
HELEN CHADWICK
JUDY CLARK
JENNIFER COMRIE
CAROLINE COON
EILEEN COOPER
SUE CROCKFORD
STELLA DADZIE
JOANNA DAVIS
POULOMI DESAI
VIVIENNE DICK
NINA EDGE
MARIANNE ELLIOTT-SAID

CATHERINE ELWES
ROSE ENGLISH
AILEEN FERRIDAY
ROSE FINN-KELCEY
FORMAT PHOTOGRAPHERS
CHANDAN FRASER
MELANIE FRIEND
CAROLE GIBBONS
PENNY GORING
JOY GREGORY
HACKNEY FLASHERS
MARGARET HARRISON
MONA HATOUM
SUSAN HILLER
LUBAINA HIMID
AMANDA HOLIDAY
BHAJAN HUNJAN
KAY HUNT
ALEXIS HUNTER
JANIS JEFFERIES
CLAUDETTE JOHNSON
MUMTAZ KARIMJEE
TINA KEANE
RITA KEEGAN
MARY KELLY

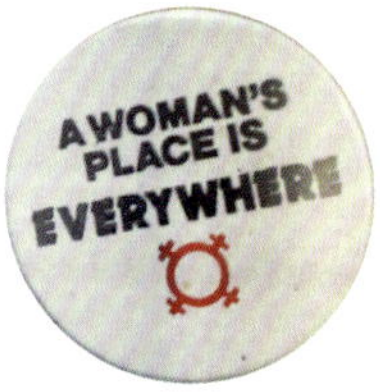

A catalogue record for this book
is available from the British Library
ISBN 978-1-84976-862-7

Distributed in the United States
and Canada by ABRAMS, New York
Library of Congress Control Number
applied for

Senior Editor: Emma Poulter
Production: Juliette Dupire
Picture research: Roz Hill
Designed by Roland Brauchli
Colour reproduction by DL Imaging Ltd, London
Printed by Graphicom SPA, Italy

The artists' biographies have been authored by
Hannah Marsh, Lucy Reynolds and Linsey Young.

Measurements of artworks are given
in centimetres, height before width

MIX
Paper | Supporting
responsible forestry
FSC® C013123
FSC
www.fsc.org

ROSHINI KEMPADOO
SANDRA LAHIRE
LORAINE LEESON
LENTHALL ROAD WORKSHOP
LINDER
ALISON LLOYD
LONDON WOMEN'S
FILM GROUP
ROSY MARTIN
RITA MCGURN
RAMONA METCALFE
JACQUELINE MORREAU
THE NEO NATURISTS
HOURIA NIATI
ANNABEL NICOLSON
RUTH NOVACZEK
MOWBRAY ODONKOR
HANNAH O'SHEA
PRATIBHA PARMAR
SYMRATH PATTI
INGRID POLLARD
JILL POSENER
ELIZABETH RADCLIFFE
FRANKI RAFFLES
SAMENA RANA

LIS RHODES
SU RICHARDSON
LIZ RIDEAL
ROBINA ROSE
MONICA ROSS
ERICA RUTHERFORD
LESLEY SANDERSON
MAUREEN SCOTT
SEE RED WOMEN'S WORKSHOP
GURMINDER SIKAND
SISTER SEVEN
MONICA SJÖÖ
VERONICA SLATER
PENNY SLINGER
MARLENE SMITH
JO SPENCE
MAUD SULTER
SUZAN SWALE
ANNE TALLENTIRE
SHANTI THOMAS
MARTINE THOQUENNE
COSEY FANNI TUTTI
SUZY VARTY
GEE VAUCHER
VERA PRODUCTIONS

SHIRLEY VERHOEVEN
CHRISTINE VOGE
DEL LAGRACE VOLCANO
WAGES FOR
HOUSEWORK CAMPAIGN
KATE WALKER
LAI NGAN WALSH
JILL WESTWOOD
CHRISTINE WILKINSON
NANCY WILLIS
W.I.T.C.H.
(BLACK WOMEN'S
MEDIA PROJECT)

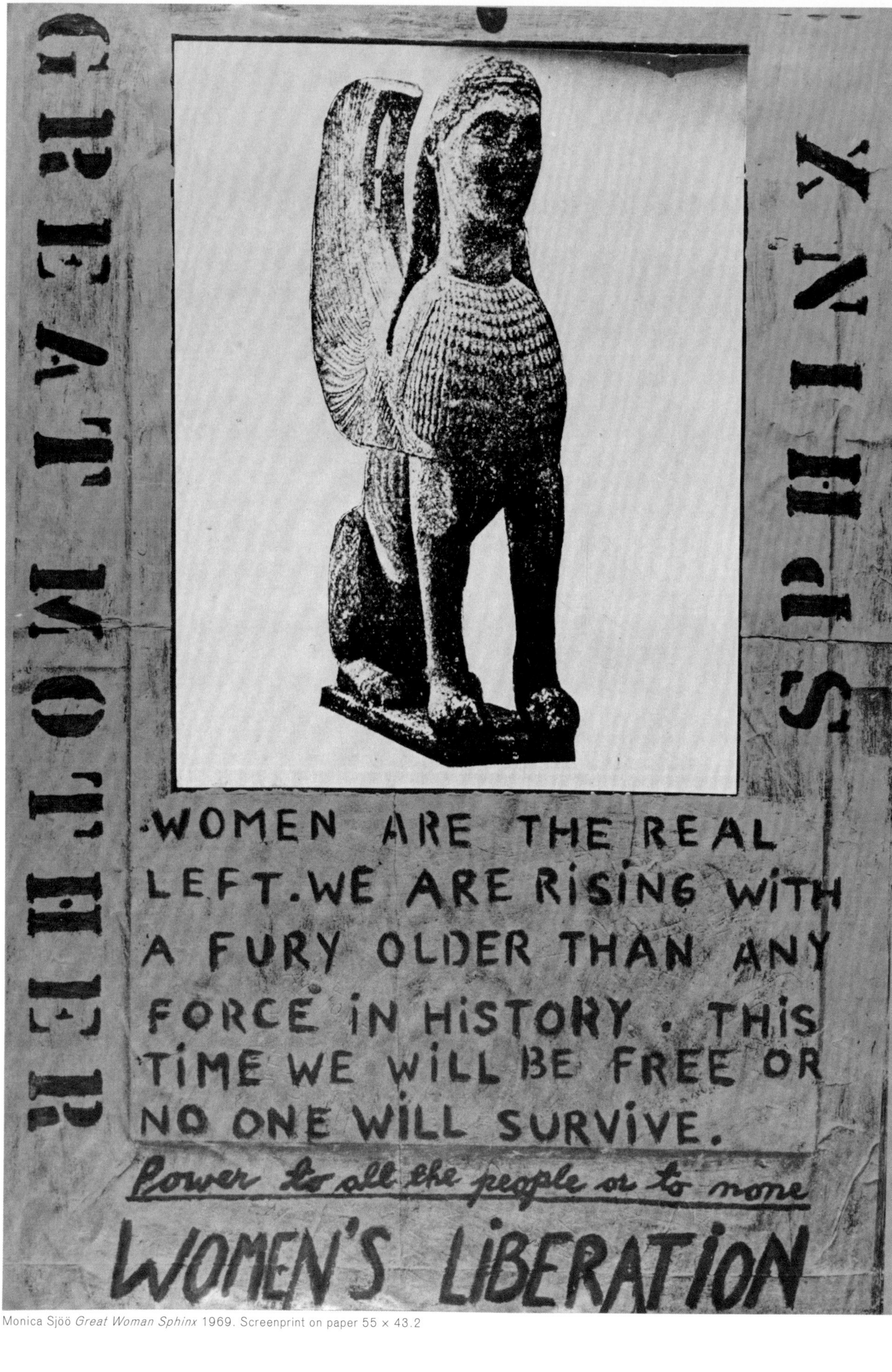

Monica Sjöö *Great Woman Sphinx* 1969. Screenprint on paper 55 × 43.2

FOREWORD

ALEX FARQUHARSON
DIRECTOR, TATE BRITAIN

This book, and the exhibition it accompanies, are devoted to surveying how work by women artists in Britain engaged with and contributed to the myriad struggles of second wave feminism across two decades, beginning in 1970. Unlike previous major feminist exhibitions, such as Cornelia Butler's pioneering *WACK! Art and the Feminist Revolution*, staged at the Museum of Contemporary Art Los Angeles (MOCA) in 2008, it focuses on the British experience through the work of over one hundred women artists working individually and in collectives. Featuring painting, drawing, performance, moving image, print-making, sculpture, photography and textiles, the selection is determined by the works' socio-political commitments, rather than a narrow range of artistic mediums. The title is taken from the highly influential 1970 text, *Women in Revolt: Patriarchal Attitudes* by Eve Figes.

The exhibition is structured chronologically around events and tendencies that variously defined the culture and politics of the women's movement in Britain: the 1970 Ruskin College conference and the beginning of the Women's Liberation Movement in the UK; policy changes such as the Equal Pay and Equal Opportunities Acts; women's domestic and maternal experiences; Punk and Rock Against Racism; Greenham Common and the anti-nuclear protests; women of the Black Arts Movement; the work of activist groups such as OWAAD, the Organisation of Women of African and Asian Descent; Section 28; and the AIDS epidemic. Many of the exhibition's themes explore how significant facets of the struggle against patriarchy were at the same time struggles against racism, class oppression, homophobia and nuclear weapons.

The exhibition and this publication are the outcome of an in-depth, five-year research project led by Linsey Young, Curator, Contemporary British Art, with passion, commitment and great care. Much of the research took the form of interviews with artists, who were very generous with their time and knowledge. Many of these women had little or no access to public institutions, private galleries, teaching posts or mainstream publishing, and as such their stories remain in large part obscured from British art history. Through this project we aim to help foreground and re-evaluate their contributions to British art in this period, as well as how they illuminate social change in this country.

The exhibition is curated and organised by Linsey Young, with curatorial colleagues Zuzana Flaskova and Hannah Marsh, supported by Inga Fraser and Laura Castagnini. The film selection is co-curated with Lucy Reynolds. The curatorial team has benefited greatly from the expertise and generosity of many advisors, most of all by the invaluable project advisors: Griselda Pollock, Professor, School of Fine Art, Leeds, and recipient of the 2019 Holberg Prize in recognition of her contribution to feminist theory; Marlene Smith, artist and curator, founding member of the Blk Art Group and lead researcher for the Black Artists and Modernism project with the University of the Arts London and the University of Middlesex; and Althea Greenan, Curator of the Women's Art Library, Goldsmiths.

We are grateful to Tate colleagues who have been tireless in their support of the project, in particular, Exhibitions Registrar Kiko Noda, our conservation and art handling teams, and Interpretation Curator Sam McGuire. The publication's project editor is Emma Poulter and the picture researcher is Roz Hill. Production aspects for the book have been handled by Juliette Dupire and the dynamic design is thanks to Roland Brauchli.

Our thanks also go to the essayists for their insightful contributions to this book: Alice Correia, Stella Dadzie, Amrita Dhallu, Zuzana Flaskova, Rachel Garfield, Juliet Jacques, Dorothy Price, Ash Reid, Amy Tobin and Linsey Young.

We thank the artists, institutions and private collectors who have kindly loaned works of art to the exhibition, enabling us to recount these art histories and lived experiences. Archive material has been sourced from private individuals and from organisations such as the Black Cultural Archives, Glasgow Women's Library, The Feminist Library, Women's Art Library, Goldsmiths and Bishopsgate Institute who have been the caretakers of these histories and extraordinarily generous with their holdings.

We also thank the Women in Revolt! Exhibition Supporters Circle, including Lubaina Himid C.B.E., Gillian Jason Gallery and Maria Sukkar, as well as Tate International Council, Tate Patrons and Tate Members for generously supporting this exhibition.

The exhibition aims to offer a UK-wide perspective on British art and the Women's Movement, so we are delighted that it will travel to the National Galleries of Scotland: Modern, with thanks to Simon Groom, Lucy Askew and Emma Gillespie, and to the Whitworth, The University of Manchester, with thanks to Poppy Bowers, Olivia Heron and Sook-Kyung Lee.

The exhibition has been made possible by the provision of insurance through the Government Indemnity Scheme. We thank HM Government for providing this, and the Department for Digital, Culture, Media and Sport and Arts Council England for arranging the indemnity.

A NOTE FROM OUR ADVISORS

ALTHEA GREENAN

GRISELDA POLLOCK

AND MARLENE SMITH

We want to salute this team of curators for wanting to know more about a critical moment in British art and culture – a time when contemporary art was fuelled by the energy, joy, wit, inventiveness, and sometimes anger, of so many artists, who made their art with a renewed, diverse and multi-faceted feminist consciousness sensitive to issues of class, race, age, ability, sexuality and economic precarity. It has been an enormous privilege to celebrate and contribute as advisors to this wonderful project. It has not just been a trip down memory lane for us as 'feminist veterans'. It has been a wonderfully creative dialogue with the team at Tate Britain led by Linsey Young. We have opened our archives – being, in a way, also living archives – and shared memories to deepen their fresh perspectives and supplement new research. It has been our pleasure to learn from Linsey's investigation into a past that we, as advisors, lived, each from our own different positions as artists, archivists, teachers and art historians.

Linsey Young's many visits to artists' studios and archives, her conversations and open questioning, have produced a revealing insight into an important chapter in the histories of British art and society. She and her curatorial colleagues bring a very different perspective on feminism to their exhibition, coloured by a different set of sensitivities emerging in this moment. The exhibition's long view, looking back over half a century, provides depth and breadth to questions in our present, and we have been able to share our continuous commitment to the transformation of our society, to challenging the injustice, hurts and wounds of racism, sex discrimination, sexual violence, homo- and trans-phobia, economic instability and cultural invisibilisation.

We also salute the incredible determination of the artists in this exhibition, in their singular resolve to keep making art, over lifetimes, and in their solidarity with each other. Some of these artists worked alone; others formed groups or collectives to challenge the institutional indifference to their new art. They dared to speak out and back to the world, often challenging each other's selectivity as much as institutional racism and sexism. They sustained art with wit, intellect, aesthetic invention and an unwavering commitment to revisiting forgotten histories and witnessing burdened presents.

The art these artists made, and continue to make, was never homogeneous. A dazzling array of voices from many cities and various communities and cultures across Britain is presented in this exhibition. These artists broke the boundaries of art in their many media, practices and locations, while fostering audiences that were themselves diverse. Their embrace of new materials, technologies and sites of art practice contributed to the radical expansion and complexity of what would be first termed 'postmodern' and later 'contemporary' art – notably in areas such as performance, film and video, installation and audience-engagement, as well as across drawing, painting, sculpture and photography.

What does it mean to revisit and, for the first time, acknowledge a major event in British art resulting from feminist creativity and critique during the 1970–90s? What can it tell us about Britain then and now, as seen through the eyes of women from our many communities? Why has it taken so long to recognise feminist energy and creativity as a historic force in British art and culture? What fault-lines did the work of artists from all areas and communities expose in Britain post-1970? And how shall we encounter the feminist artistic eruption in its complexity, differences and blind-spots, when many of the artists are still as creative as ever?

Feminism has often been understood too narrowly as only a political movement. However it was – and still is – also a cultural movement re-shaping art, literature and film – all of which have been challenged by feminism not only to end discrimination against all women, but to acknowledge the gross injustices around race, class and sexuality. These two forms of activism, political and cultural, became creatively entangled over two decades after 1970. This did not produce a new category of 'feminist art'. Rather, as this exhibition makes clear, these artists were making art for people other than the collectors, responding neither to the market nor to a curated supply chain of what is selectively considered 'contemporary'. They created with a sense of community that was urgent. It was about speaking to different communities, and also becoming a community of artists.

This exhibition joyfully, and critically, challenges a dereliction of duty by the museums, curators and critics, for not sharing with the British public what happened in British art in these decades. Museums and curators did not research, conserve or exhibit many amazing works by British artists, as their often shockingly inadequate history of acquisitions, notably of Black and South Asian women artists, suggests, even when these artists continued undeterred to produce and exhibit work with strong critical appreciation from many art writers. This willed indifference has created an incomplete history. We welcome, therefore a show that breaks that mould and commend Tate for welcoming the expanded history Linsey Young and her team have assembled that is enriched by the perspective of their present, with its own sensitivities and perspectives on British art and its histories.

The show is as art historically important as it is culturally significant. From 1968, side by side with movements for civil rights and decolonisation, lesbian and gay rights, demands for better working conditions, gender-specific health care and reforms, and disarmament in the face of nuclear threats, an intense moment of feminist activism erupted, intersecting with all the above. What was unique post-1968, however, was its flowering within the field of art just when art itself was changing so radically. What defined that moment was 'a conceptual turn' accompanied by artists' exploration of new media, such as photography, film and video, live performance and post-formalist institutional critique. While the demand for women's rights was on the political agenda, in cultural fields, artists, writers, filmmakers, dancers, cartoonists and architects were exploring the open question of what women could be and delving into histories and imagining futures through expanded art forms and practices.

This fuelled the self-empowering strategy encouraging women to assert their practices as artists by documenting their artwork. They enriched the archives we can access today – not only by photographing their work to produce 35mm slides and establishing slide registries, but also by producing or sharing artworks as part of a gift economy, with gestures of encouragement and solidarity cohering an alternative value system in which to practice and thrive. Slides are performative objects that could be duplicated and sent through the post, projected to an audience, reproduced in a print publication, and distributed as a teaching tool, and the Woman Artists' Slide Library initiated in the mid 1970s highlights the reproductive labour women artists undertook to educate and shift dismissive perceptions of women's art. Documenting practice was part of the process of self-professionalising that also enabled the peer-to-peer recognition that charged the 'margins' of the art world of this time with realising urgent socio-political change.

Women in Revolt! is not a culmination of these works' cultural impact, but more of an opportunity to see the museum exhibition as part of the continuum of the complex lives of these cultural objects. You are likely to experience déjà vu, as many of these practices are reflected by contemporary artists and researchers' experiences of these works through their makers' self-documentation, and are also increasingly collected, preserved and gaining institutional recognition as invaluable archives. They invite further personal research and question where the critical turning points of culture happen.

Above all, this is a moment to celebrate. As artists confront issues around sustainable living and the critical importance of social visibility, *Women in Revolt!* is an expressive space in which these works can be supported, understood and loved. The show will be a revelation for many about art, Britain, women, feminist creativity and insight. As advisors, we shall meet again dozens of artists whose work we have known, admired, learnt from and written about for decades. It is wonderful to be able to share that treasure now with wider and new audiences. We always knew there would be a hunger to see this work and once again, congratulate the team that has created this exhibition.

WE'RE NOT
BEAUTIFUL
WE'RE NOT
UGLY.
WE'RE
ANGRY

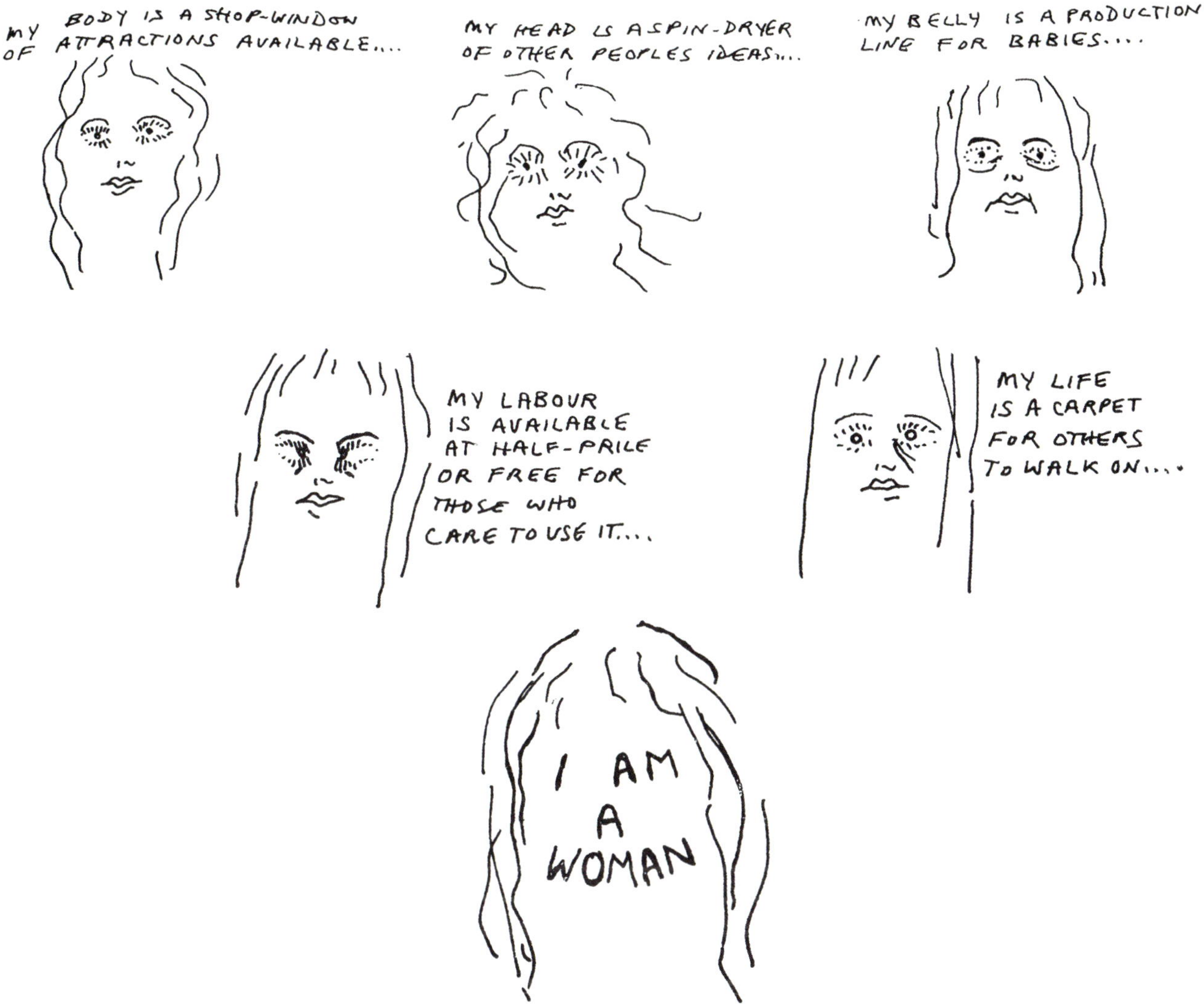

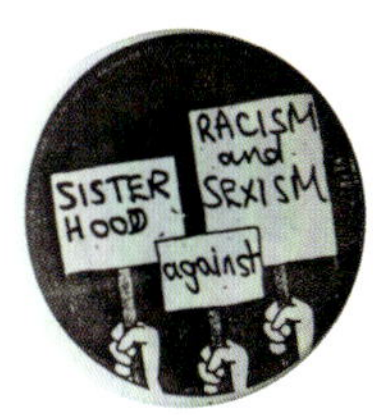

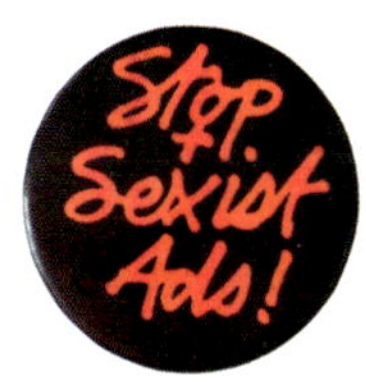

Above: Sarah Wilson b.1944 / *AM A WOMAN*, as reproduced in *Shrew*, June 1970. Ink on paper 21 × 29.7

Opposite: Slogan of Miss World Protest, London, November 1970. From the back cover of *Why Miss World?* Spring 1971. Lettering design by Jenny Fortune b.1949. Ink on paper 21.5 × 15.5

INTRODUCTION:

THE PERSONAL IS POLITICAL

LINSEY YOUNG

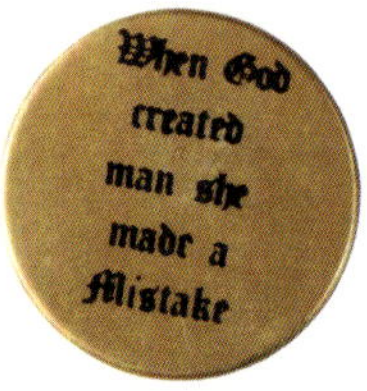

I have a photo of Gael Stuart, my mum, that was taken as we left for an oncology appointment. There we would be told, quite out of the blue, that her latest scan showed developments that might be 'very bad news'. They were very bad news.

In the picture Mum is smiling a true smile (I know the geography of them better than I know my own). She is standing in the sun, in front of the Glasgow tenement we had rented to live in together while she received treatment, and she is proudly wearing a jumper that reads 'fearless female'.

Mum once described herself to me as a 'reluctant feminist', someone who quite fancied what she imagined – having grown up in a loving, equitable household – as the simple, easy, domestic life, but ended up juggling a more precarious set of circumstances. She would often say to me, 'You've always been so interested in feminism. I don't know where you got it from.'

I got it from her! And how could she not see her impact? A woman who loved deeply and fiercely, who raised me single-handedly while working full-time as a nurse and still found time for fun. A woman who, in the late 1980s, when working in south London, refused to let homophobic colleagues anywhere near the AIDS patients in her practice, so that she could surround them with the love and respect they deserved. A woman who lived with a debilitating chronic illness, who cared physically and emotionally for her family, often to the detriment of her own health. A woman who was let down by the government's dismantling of the welfare state, who was humiliated by Personal Independence Payment assessments, but who, despite it all, was hilarious, glamorous, intellectual, left-wing, empathetic and loving, and without a single self-pitying bone in her body. A woman who, like so many of her generation, was underestimated because she chose to live quietly and humbly.

Two months after that oncology appointment, she lay calmly next to me in a hospice in Glasgow, asking for her nails to be painted bright red, telling stories about her family and love life, listening to audiobooks and receiving visitors (unless they were boring, in which case I got to deny admission on her behalf). A friend of mine and hers stalked into her room, looked straight at her and said, 'This is an outrage'.

It was, and so it remains. All I feel I can do to honour my mum is to make the exhibition I promised for her, for her generation of under-appreciated women who make everything brighter for the rest of us.

From the very beginning I wanted to approach the research for this show in a personal and intimate way: travelling to meet people, talking for as long as they could bear and, I hope, building relationships rather than simply extracting information. Balancing the demands of institutional working with a tentative attempt to apply a feminist methodology, while getting to grips with what that might mean. The first studio visit I undertook was with artist Margaret Harrison, who patiently listened to my lengthy and inarticulate attempt to describe the exhibition and responded, 'it's impossible, but that's no reason not to try'.

I have come to realise that she was, of course, right; an exhibition focused on the relationship between art and the women's movement in the UK, one that attempts to pin down a single definition of a feminist or womanist British art history, is impossible. This is partly because of the sheer amount of energy and creativity women artists in the 1970s and 80s brought to their daily lives. Working, caring, writing letters and journals, marching, making work, trying to get it shown, trying to find a fulfilling job; the list is endless and there is a huge range of perspectives, positions and objectives, many of which undermine or challenge the others. As writer Lola Olufemi has expressed:

> Feminists know all too well that rejecting the differences between us in the search for a binding universal is doomed to failure. Instead, we must roll with the messy, tangled desires of our community, embracing the myriad positions we take in our fight for equality.[1]

In its attempt to present the activities of a wide-ranging network of women practitioners, *Women in Revolt!* is the largest exhibition to be staged at Tate Britain by some margin. But despite its scale and ambition, and the years of love and attention that have been poured into it by a wide range of women, I already know that it is a failure. Rolling with the messy, I have chosen to focus attention on a large number of artists and the abundance of work they have created over many decades, a constellation of voices rather than a few individual stars.

I have sleepless nights about who has been excluded; some artists could just not be found, some have died prematurely, and a number of artworks have been lost forever because many women artists were not able to afford storage for their work, or simply found the effort of maintaining hope that someone would one day pay attention too exhausting. Of course, I have also had to edit and make selections, and the inevitable omissions and critical prejudices that play out across the galleries tell a story that for many will feel partial or inaccurate.

In an audio recording of the launch of Griselda Pollock and Rozsika Parker's groundbreaking publication, *Framing Feminism,* held at London's Institute of Contemporary Arts (ICA) in 1988, artist Lubaina Himid can be heard discussing the challenges of collating and communicating the complexities of artists' lived experience, stating that, 'As soon as you write a history it's a lie'. A written history is a lie, and it's also a dangerous thing if readers (or viewers) take a singular perspective as fact and don't criticise, question and agitate with their own truths. My truths lean towards those forced to the margins, the working class, the women of colour, the queers and the punks; this aims to be a trans-inclusive, intersectional, socialist-focused project that hopes to show the debt we owe to the women who came before us and to give a glimpse of how argumentative, fair, rigorous, empathetic, funny, disruptive, fraught and loving society might be if our dominant narratives were those written and visualised by women.

RISING WITH FURY

On 20 November 1970, the American comedian Bob Hope was broadcast to the nation on prime-time BBC1 as host of the infamous Miss World pageant. Comments Hope made included 'It's quite a cattle market, I've been back there checking calves' and 'I don't want you to think I'm a dirty old man, because I never give women a second thought. My first thought covers everything.' Happily, mere moments later, feminist activists began pelting him with flour bombs. What such comments and the feminist response tell us is that, despite a number of gains for women's liberation in the 1960s, Britain in the early 1970s

1 Lola Olufemi, *Feminism Interrupted: Disrupting Power*, London 2020.

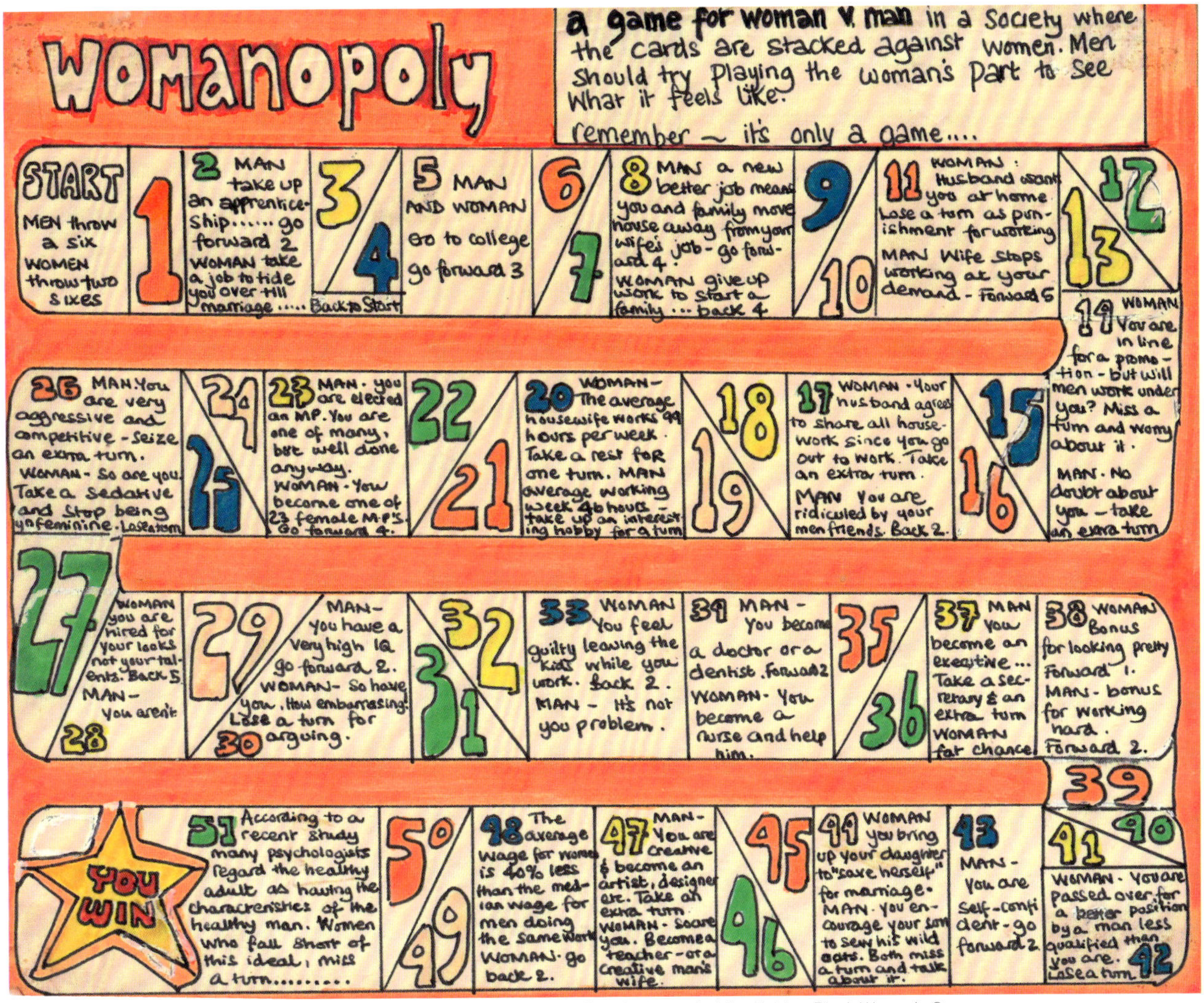

Stella Dadzie, 'Womanopoly' game, early 1970s. First published in *Speak Out*, the journal of the Brixton Black Women's Group.

was an environment in which women were firmly and aggressively designated as second-class citizens, fit only to serve or be looked at. Mainstream society, as exemplified by the media, viewed women (or rather straight, white women; they wouldn't even consider women of colour or queer or trans women) as one-dimensional and always less than their male counterparts, and many of those women had simply had enough.

It is easy to understand why: at the dawn of 1970 a heady list of injustices marred women's daily existence. Although the Equal Pay Act was passed in 1970, it would not be enacted until 1975. Statutory maternity pay was not a legal requirement, and there was no legislation protecting a woman against dismissal if she became pregnant. Nor was there any sex-discrimination protection in law, with jobs often advertised as being only for men or – for those open to women – specifically stating that candidates must be 'attractive'. Married women were classed as legal dependants of their husbands and were not entitled to claim benefits for themselves or their children in their own name, nor to secure a mortgage or loan without a husband or male family member as guarantor. Men's right to have sex with their wives, with or without their consent, was enshrined in law. There were no domestic violence shelters or rape crisis units, and women could not obtain a court order against a violent husband without divorce or separation proceedings. Meanwhile the first Race Relations legislation passed in 1965 did nothing to address systematic racism experienced in relation to employment and housing, and there was no Commission for Racial Equality, and no acknowledgement of the trans experience enshrined in law and little in the way of broader public consciousness.

The 1970 Miss World contest was held nine months after the first National Women's Liberation Conference in Oxford, an event widely recognised as the beginning of the Women's Liberation Movement (WLM) in the UK. A further seven conferences followed between 1970 and 1978, through which the formal demands of the WLM were set out:

- Equal pay now
- Equal education and job opportunities
- Free contraception and abortion on demand
- Free 24-hour nurseries
- Financial and legal independence
- An end to all discrimination against lesbians and a woman's right to define her own sexuality
- Freedom from intimidation by threat or use of violence or sexual coercion, regardless of marital status, and an end to all laws, assumptions and institutions which perpetuate male dominance and men's aggression towards women.

The WLM conferences were overwhelmingly attended by white women, but at the same time women of colour were coming together through organisations such as the socialist-feminist Brixton Black Women's Group (BBWG), co-founded in 1973 by Gerlin Bean, who had attended the first WLM conference; this was followed by the hugely influential Organisation of Women of African and Asian Descent (OWAAD), formed in 1978, and the Southall Black Sisters in 1979. While the BBWG did not have a formal manifesto, its newsletter *Speak Out* articulated concerns such as institutional racism, the effects of colonialism, sexist laws and practices, male domination in the home, racist labour practices and policies, the provision of safe and accessible contraception, and immigration laws.

The BBWG's proclamation of itself as a socialist group was very much in line with much of the wider network of women's groups and consciousness-raising circles. Throughout the research for this exhibition, an anti-capitalist, socialist approach to feminism has been raised again and again in interviews with artists, and might be said to be one of the defining features of British second-wave feminism. As feminist historian Sheila Rowbotham has described:

> The development of the socialist feminist networks and conferences within the women's liberation movement brought together women from differing left traditions. We came to trust one another by doing and thinking across boundaries, united by a desire to connect the emancipation of women to wider aspects of oppression in capitalism … we discovered the power of sharing ideas and of mutual help. Meetings were exhilarating learning experiences in which ideas formed collectively.[2]

2 Sheila Rowbotham, *Beyond the Fragments: Feminism and the Making of Socialism*, London 2013, p.10.

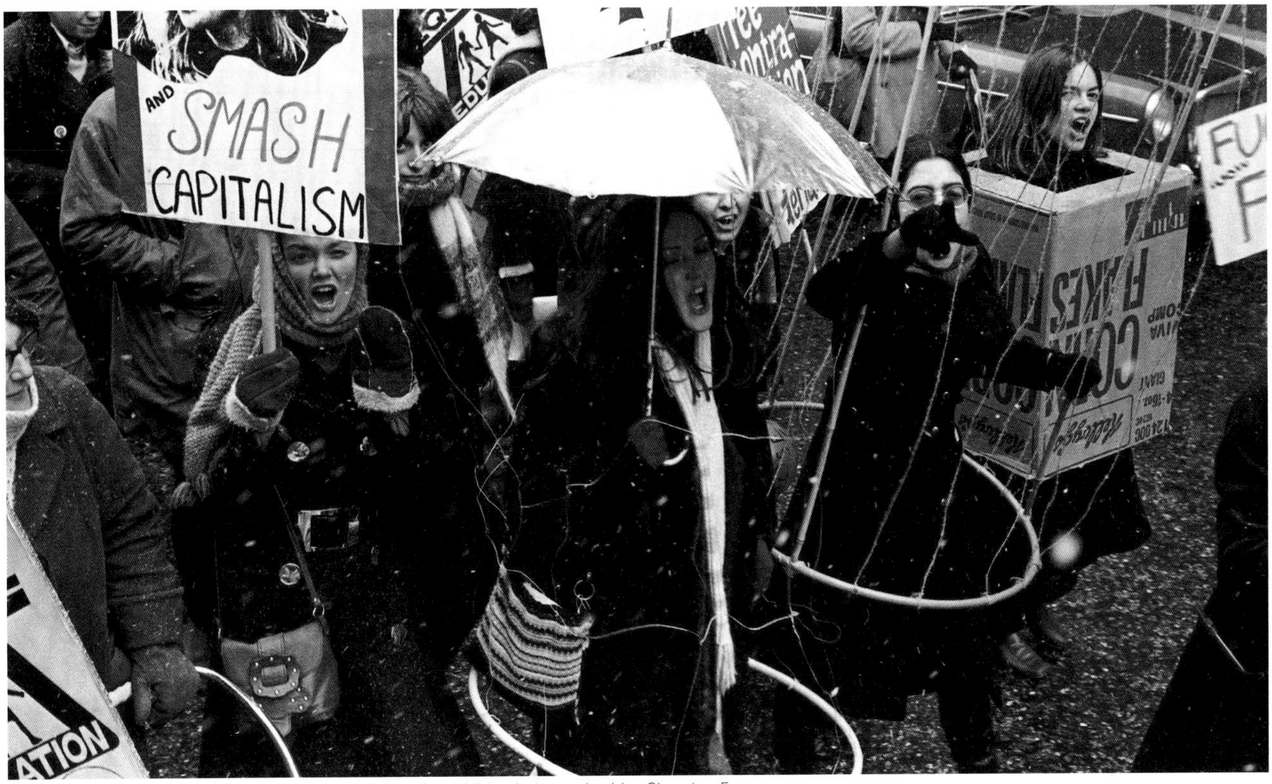

The first Women's Liberation Movement March, London 1971, photographed by Chandan Fraser.

Throughout the 1970s we see this grassroots, collaborative approach to activism playing into women's art- and exhibition-making strategies (as discussed by Amy Tobin, see pp.32–41). Alongside the emerging women's movement came a series of journals, exhibitions and events. The Women's Liberation Art Group, who performed at the Miss World protests, was formed in 1970 and held an exhibition at Woodstock Art Gallery in 1971. The Women's Workshop of the Artists' Union was founded in 1972 and in 1973 artist Monica Sjöö staged *Images of Womanpower* at Swiss Cottage Library in north London. In 1974, a group of artists and art historians who had met at anti-censorship protests at Sjöö's Swiss Cottage Library exhibition founded the Women's Art History Collective and the South London Art Group took over 14 Radnor Terrace in Vauxhall and created the large-scale installation *A Woman's Place*. In 1975, at a women's art history conference, Kate Walker made a call to expand the feminist *Postal Art Event* that she had started with her friend Sally Gollop, which would see women across the country making small artworks at their kitchen tables and posting them to each other (see pp.64–5). This grew into the major touring exhibition *Feministo: Portrait of the Artist as a Housewife*, with key members Su Richardson, Monica Ross and Kate Walker later collaborating on the travelling installation *Fenix* between 1978 and 1980 (see p.66).

These early feminist art pioneers bartered, negotiated, charmed and stole space. They made things happen with nothing and no prospect of making money through their efforts, communicating by letter and telephone chains, all while working multiple jobs and caring for children and parents. The art market of the 1970s and mid to late-1980s refused to acknowledge their existence, and so they found their own ways of making and sharing art: from exhibiting in domestic spaces and producing posters at feminist print workshops, such as

See Red Women's Workshop and Lenthall Road Workshop, to the creation of laminated panel exhibitions that could be reproduced and sent easily and cheaply on tour around libraries and community centres.

What might surprise a modern audience is the complete lack of commercial or institutional outlets for women's art in the early to mid-1970s. To take as one example the Tate, the national collection owned by and for the public. Between 1970 and 1990 the gallery held 344 exhibitions, presentations or displays, just seventeen of which were by or included women.[3] All bar one of these women were white. The exhibitions that did feature women tended to focus on subjects such as gardening, landscape or abstraction.

During the timeline covered by this exhibition, there was only one Tate Gallery (now Tate Britain), located on Millbank in central London. Tate curators were at the heart of a city bursting at the seams with alternative venues and publishers. Its nearest gallery neighbour was the ICA, which in 1976–7 alone staged the Cosey Fanni Tutti/COUM Transmissions exhibition *Prostitution*, Mary Kelly's *Post-Partum Document* and the Postal Art Group's *Feministo: Portrait of the Artist as a Housewife*. Yet despite being surrounded by feminist art activity, the national collection was barely showing – let alone collecting – women's work, and where Tate did collect women artists, they were almost exclusively those working within conceptual or abstract frameworks. The artwork featured in *Women in Revolt!* that looks at the overtly political, the domestic, the bodily or the social, the work that explores the experiences of lesbians and women of colour, was simply absent. With these facts and statistics in mind, it's not hard to see why women artists felt – and often continue to feel – hostility towards the artistic establishment or, to use a phrase from the time, 'the male artocracy'.

3 Looking at Tate's records from 1970–90 the projects listed in each year are broad-ranging, from solo and group exhibitions and collection displays to performances, film programmes, artist Christmas trees and 'birthday displays'.

THE MARXIST WIFE STILL DOES THE HOUSEWORK

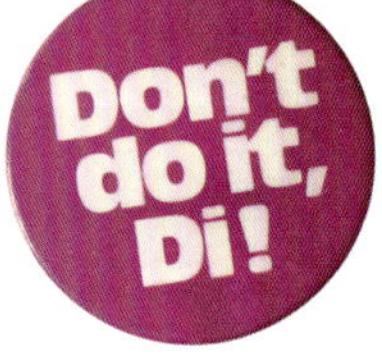

The social expectations placed on women in the 1970s were clearly defined (as explored by Zuzana Flaskova in relation to artists, pp.92–7). Despite their increasing role in the workforce following the Second World War, albeit largely in low-paid, insecure jobs, every section of social life – from government policy to media and marketing – made it clear that, to be accepted, women must be beautiful, get married, have and enjoy their children, and maintain the home. Women were projected as people who had no needs of their own and were content to serve, their labour not considered as such because surely, for a woman, to make a home and to care is a satisfying act of love? If she worked, it was most likely the kind of labour that would be replicated in the home: nursing, care-giving, cleaning. For Black women this landscape was further complicated by their ongoing experiences of racism in the workplace, as articulated by an interviewee in *The Heart of the Race:* 'At the new firm, they had to employ Black workers or they would get taken to court, so they employed two of us. They called us all sorts of names and even went on strike and brought in the union.'[4] International groups like Wages for Housework began to form. Founded in 1972 by Marxist feminists in Italy, they argued that capitalism could not be supported without the invisible domestic labour of maintaining families. The demand for a wage was a provocation, a way of demonstrating that the capitalist class

4 Beverley Bryan, Stella Dadzie, Suzanne Scafe, *The Heart of the Race: Black Women's Lives in Britain*, London 2018, p.27.
5 https://www.npeu.ox.ac.uk/assets/downloads/mbrrace-uk/reports/maternal-report-2021/MBRRACE-UK_Maternal_Report_2021_-_FINAL_-_WEB_VERSION.pdf.

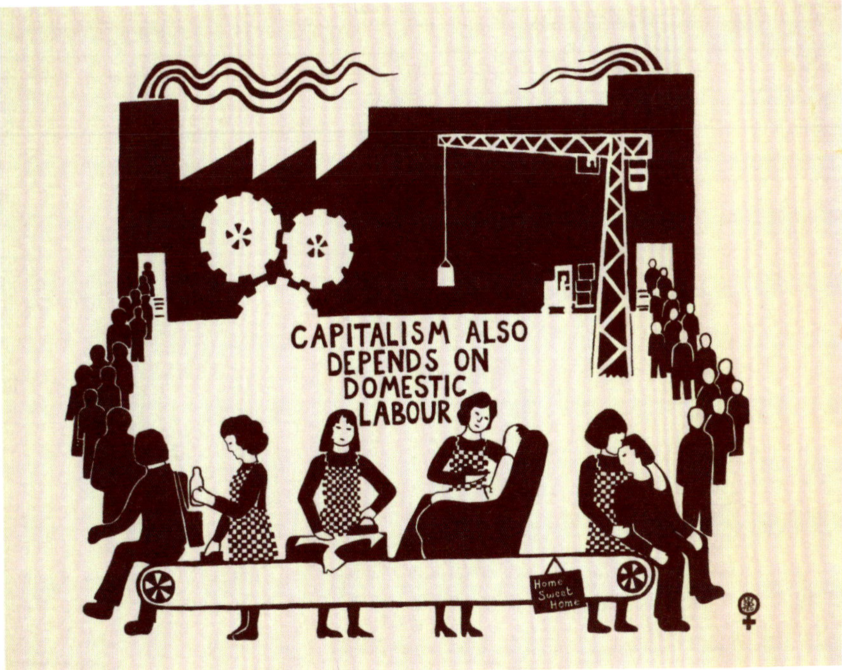

See Red Women's Workshop *Capitalism Also Depends on Domestic Labour* 1975. Screenprint on paper 53.5 × 69

could never afford to pay for all that women do, and that it is inherently exploitative to think that women will just get on and do this work because it is expected of them.

The domestic environment was explored by many artists of the time, with women subverting the contents and context of the home, reworking domestic scenes or objects through textile, sculpture and photography, or physically destroying and rebuilding it through photomontage. Much of this work is reflected in the increasing feminist questioning of the institution of marriage. In the late 1970s the YBA Wife campaign was founded to draw attention to the WLM's fifth demand for legal and financial independence for married women. With its usual humorous flair, the magazine *Spare Rib* launched the campaign 'Don't do it, Di!' in 1981, looking to use the impending marriage of Prince Charles and Diana Spencer to spotlight their cause.

Issues of childbearing and rearing were equally complex. The medical system, which we know to be built around the white male body and experience, was at this time dominated at a senior level by male practitioners, and where women's hospitals did exist they were regularly being closed or threatened with closure. In terms of mental health, as had played out in second-wave feminism in the United States, women were frequently medicated for depression, a condition that feminists often associated with dissatisfaction and unhappiness caused by the claustrophobia of women's lives, of being devalued at work or trapped in the home, and so in many cases had the potential to be alleviated by removing oppression and degradation inflicted by the patriarchy.

The 1967 Abortion Act made the procedure legal, but was faced with continuous right-wing legal challenges. Women campaigned tirelessly for an expansion of the bill to include abortion on demand, without the requirement for prior approval by two (almost certainly male) doctors, which was felt to keep women's lives under the control of patriarchal forces. Campaigns for fair access to abortion and contraception were highly visible, but often overlooked issues such as the over-prescription of the dangerous contraceptive injection Depo-Provera that most affected women of colour, who were disproportionately given the drug. In addition, women of colour were at four times the risk of dying in pregnancy than their white counterparts, and it continues to be a national scandal that this figure has not changed in nearly six decades.[5]

For trans women, whose experiences are explored in the essay by Juliet Jacques (pp.52–7), there was barely any serious mention of their lives in public discourse until Jan Morris's *Conundrum* was published in 1974.

Later in the decade the documentary *A Change of Sex*, broadcast on BBC2 in 1979, followed Julia Grant's gender confirmation surgery. Beyond these instances, any other mention of trans identity was confined to salacious and aggressive reports in tabloid newspapers that revelled in outing people they suspected may be transexual. Those brave enough to seek support from the medical profession were forced into humiliating psychiatric assessments and, for some, medically authorised aversion therapy.

6 Angela McRobbie and Jenny Garber, 'Girls and Subcultures' (1978), in Angela McRobbie (ed.), *Feminism and Youth Culture*, 2nd edn, Basingstoke 2000, pp.12–25.

OH BONDAGE! UP YOURS!

The 1970s are often described as drab, and those of us who weren't there hear about rubbish piled in the streets, an overarching sense of drudgery against the backdrop of strikes, the three-day week and calamitous financial markets. But beyond the mainstream, and at odds with the prim handbags of Conservative leader and later Prime Minister Margaret Thatcher or the stern reprimanding of 'moral campaigner' Mary Whitehouse, many women grabbed the opportunities opened up by movements such as punk, Rock Against Racism (RAR), post-punk and the industrial music scene. Across the country but particularly in London, new ways of living and creating were forged, from the punk and lesbian squats of the mid-1970s to the emergence of the New Romantics at clubs like Blitz in Covent Garden or The Fridge in Brixton, and queer spaces like the Belle pub in King's Cross or lesbian S+M club night Chain Reaction in Vauxhall.

In their essay 'Girls and Subcultures', Angela McRobbie and Jenny Garber write about the absence of women in analyses of subcultures, noting that the tropes of women in subcultures as defined by men, namely a passive cliquishness or aggression, have to be understood as a reaction to patriarchy: 'both the defensive and the aggressive responses are structured in reaction against a situation where masculine definitions (and thus sexual labelling, etc.) are in dominance' because 'girls are necessarily, more marginal on every dimension'.[6] Marginal perhaps, but women were there, in their droves. Beyond the recognisable figures of Vivienne Westwood and early punk icon Jordan, there was a broad-ranging community of women artists working alongside or influenced by punk and RAR (discussed by Rachel Garfield, pp.134–40).

As in the wider feminist movement, women working in and around music often utilised newsletters or fanzines to communicate. Three notable women-run punk fanzines were *Jolt* by Lucy Toothpaste (Lucy Whitman), *Moreon* by 'Crystal Clear' and 'Vinyl Virgin', and the beautifully titled *Apathy in Ilford* by Sharon Spike (Sharon Dunham). Lucy Toothpaste and her friend Ruth Gregory were also leading figures in the anti-racist RAR fanzine *Temporary Hoarding*. Emerging out of the punk movement, but covering a broad range of topics, was the feminist fanzine *Shocking Pink*, published between 1981 and 82. Made by and for young women, *Shocking Pink*'s articles, letters and cartoons included subject matter such as how to fight the National Front, young women's experiences

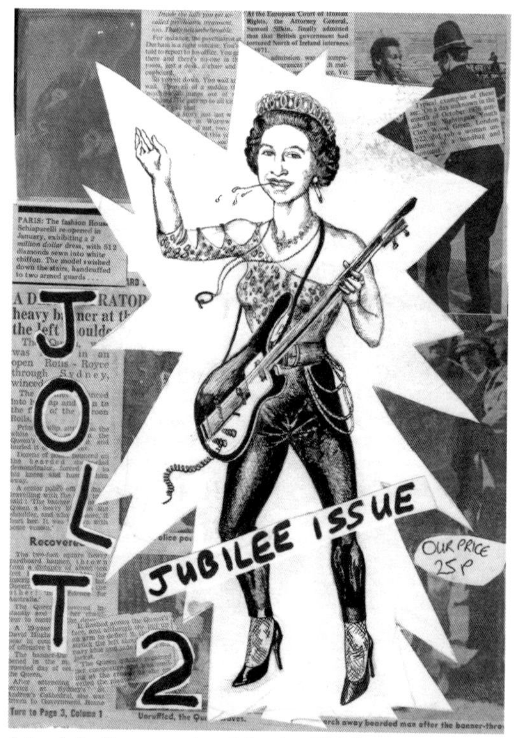

Artwork for the cover of punk fanzine *JOLT* #2, 1977.
Collage by Lucy Whitman. Drawing by Rosalind Whitman.

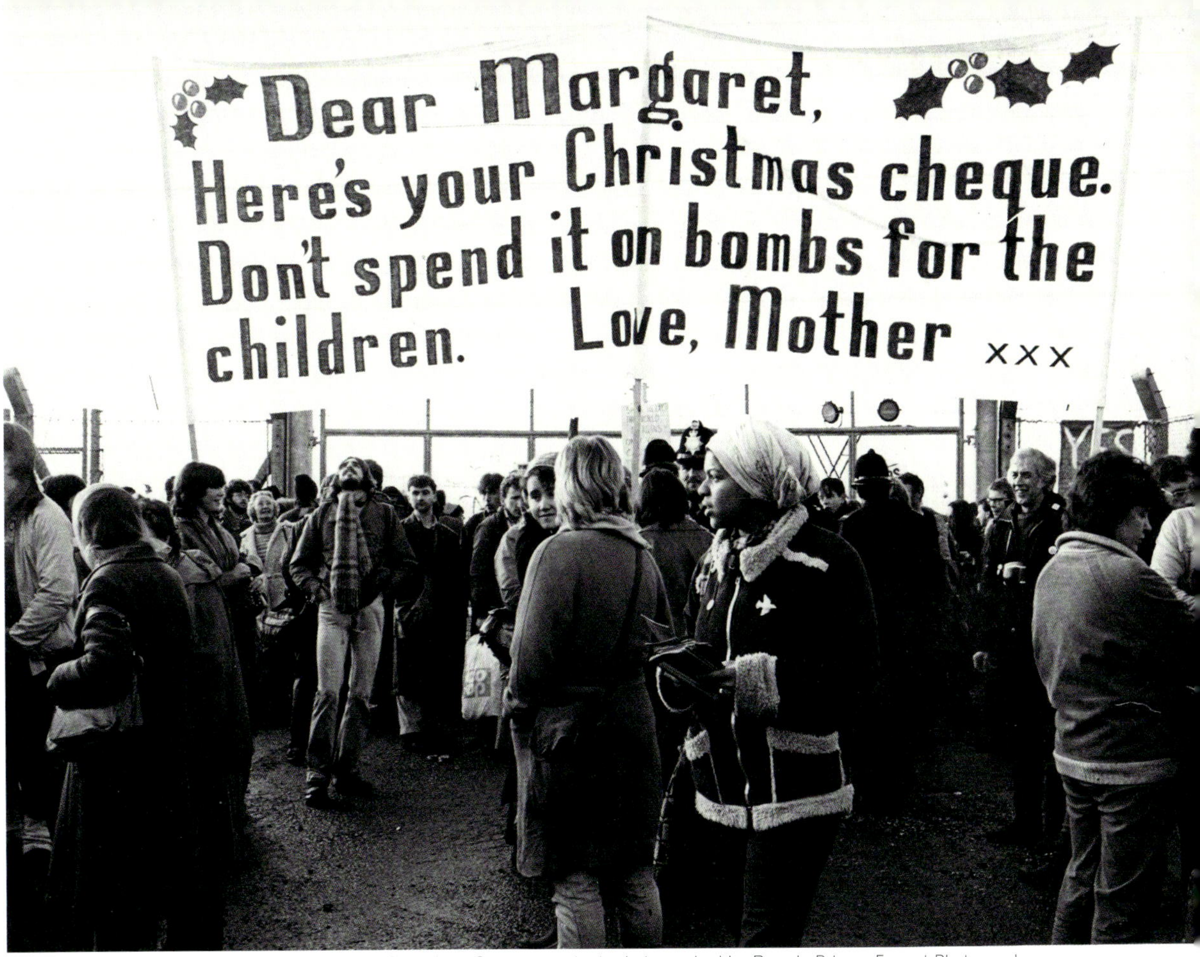

Embrace the Base, Greenham Common 1982. Greenham Common protest, photographed by Brenda Prince, Format Photographers.

of racism at school, lesbianism, masturbation, guidance for starting your own band and interviews with musicians.

The list of woman musicians and women-only or mixed bands who had an impact in the UK during this time is extensive: The Adverts, Au Pairs, The Bodysnatchers, Jayne County, Delta 5, Essential Logic, Cosey Fanni Tutti, Fistfuck, Girls at Our Best!, The Gymslips, Lene Lovich, Ludus, Marine Girls, Mo-dettes, Hazel O'Connor, Penetration, Poison Girls, The Raincoats, Rip Rig + Panic, The Selecter, Siouxsie and the Banshees, The Slits, Strawberry Switchblade ... I could go on. One of the most influential musicians of the period, Poly Styrene, was the lead singer of X-Ray Spex, whose debut album *Germfree Adolescents* was released in 1978. The record is a trail-blazing critique of patriarchal oppression, of the position of the working class and, notably, a scathing attack on consumerism and the encroaching plasticisation and commodification of society, themes that were unusual for the time beyond small groups of ecologists and radicals and a growing eco-feminist movement.

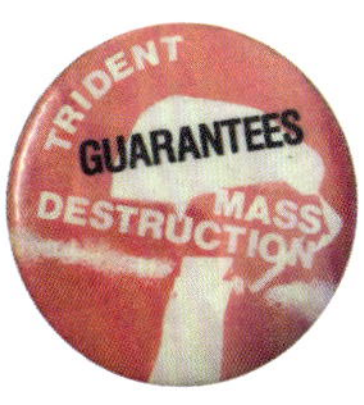

GREENHAM WOMEN ARE EVERYWHERE

For most people, the most visible and well-known manifestation of eco-feminism is the Greenham Common women's peace camp, which was occupied from 1981 to 2000. Its history is well known and heavily documented; on 5 September 1981 a group of women ended a march from Cardiff to the Greenham Common US Air Force base in Newbury, Berkshire, where American nuclear cruise missiles

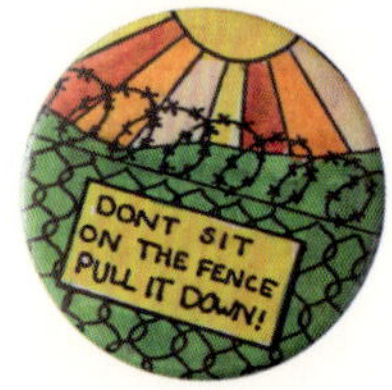

were to be housed. Between 1981 and 1983 the camp grew in size, quickly becoming a women-only space, with some people staying for months or years, and others (including a great number of artists featured in this exhibition) visiting on multiple occasions. While there were – and still are – active peace camps, like the one at Faslane Naval Base in Argyll and Bute, perhaps more than any other event, protest or network Greenham Common was a public beacon for the Women's Liberation Movement. The military camp represented the ultimate patriarchal space, and the peace camp, for those who lived there permanently, visited or simply knew of its existence, offered hope and potential to women eager for change. Many of the DIY methods of art-making that we see in women's artwork of the 1970s were present at Greenham, from the group singing and keening to knitting, decorating the fencing with objects, weaving spider-webs of yarn through holes in the fence and, of course, large-scale performative actions, like when an estimated 30,000 people came to Greenham in 1983 to hold hands, encircle its nine-mile perimeter fence and 'embrace the base'.

As no men were allowed, Greenham became something of a refuge for women who were politically engaged across the spectrum, and its way of life – camping, no running water, open communal cooking – offered an alternative to the domestic, heteronormative family structures so lauded by mainstream society and the media, a place in which they could reimagine a woman's role and relationships in society. However, as in the wider feminist movement, Greenham was dominated by white women, and while race and class were regular topics of discussion they were not always adequately addressed, let alone resolved. The Eurocentric nature of the feminist movement is highlighted in the foundational book *The Heart of the Race* by Beverley Bryan, Stella Dadzie and Suzanne Scafe:

> they can only see the anti-nuclear issue in terms of protecting their own backyards. It's as if they've just discovered imperialism, and they're only worried about it because it threatens their particular lifestyle. They say they don't like violence, but there are a lot of other forms of violence around which they've never bothered about before now.[7]

BLACK WOMAN TIME NOW

In the late 1970s and early 1980s, a small number of women-only and women-organised exhibitions began to spread into the institutional mainstream. Following feminist protest at the predominantly male sculpture show *The Condition of Sculpture* at the Hayward Gallery in 1975, women artists were asked to select the Hayward Annual in 1978, and in 1980 three breakthrough shows were staged at the ICA that were curated by and populated exclusively by women: *Women's Images of Men*, *About Time* and *Issues*. While these exhibitions (developed in part from the protest of an Allen Jones exhibition at the ICA) played a hugely important role in the visibility and accessibility of a politicised, women-led arts practice, one in particular had an indirect but arguably more lasting effect. *Women's Images of Men* was chosen by open call; one artist who was not selected, having submitted images of what she describes as her 'first feminist works', channelled her frustration into the organisation of three exhibitions that would

7 Anonymous interviewee in Beverley Bryan, Stella Dadzie and Suzanne Scafe, *The Heart of the Race: Black Women's Lives in Britain*, London and New York 2018, p.175.

in later years come to define British art in the 1980s. The artist was Lubaina Himid, with the exhibitions *Five Black Women* (1983), *Black Woman Time Now* (1983) and *The Thin Black Line* (1985).

Himid's exhibitions were developed through her active engagement with and encouragement of the community of artists around her; many remember receiving lovingly insistent letters encouraging submissions for the exhibitions. This was a large and growing community of a new generation of Black and Asian artists, most in their early twenties and beginning their lives as professional artists. Himid's *Five Black Women* opened in 1983, but arguably, the first feminist art exhibition by women of colour in the UK was staged two years earlier when, *Four Indian Women Artists*, curated by Bhajan Hunjan and Chila Kumari Singh Burman opened in London in 1981 (as discussed by Alice Correia, pp.200–8). Around the same time, artist Rita Keegan began her involvement with Brixton Art Gallery, established in 1983, where she would co-curate a series of hugely important exhibitions focused on intersectional feminist and queer visual art perspectives. Keegan would go on to found the Black Women Artists Index (later Women of Colour) at the Women Artists Slide Library.

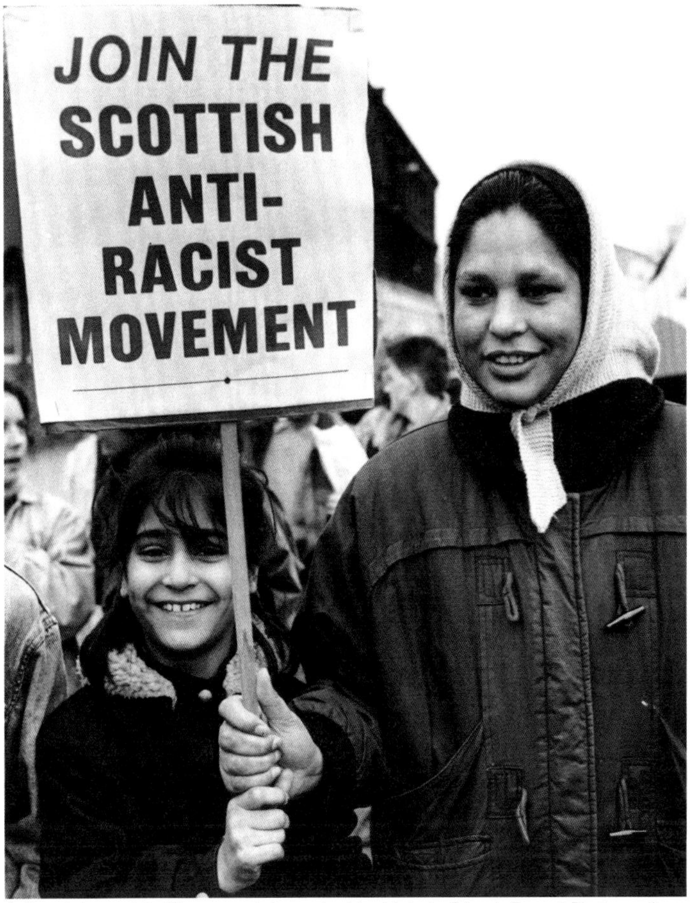

Anti-racist march in Glasgow, photographed by Melanie Friend, Format Photographers

OWAAD (the importance of which is discussed by Stella Dadzie, pp.44–51) held its first conference in 1979 and acted to consolidate and influence a surge in activist activity in the key areas of health, education, employment, immigration policy and policing. Members Beverley Bryan, Stella Dadzie and Suzanne Scafe later published the groundbreaking book *The Heart of the Race* in 1985, which through a series of interviews foregrounds the lived experiences of women of colour asserting their place in British socio-economic history.

The backdrop to this creative activity and activism is an extraordinarily violent and aggressive one. In the late 1970s it wasn't uncommon to see fascists marching on the streets of places like Southall in London, and organisations such as the intersectional feminist print studio See Red had their premises attacked by the National Front. Numerous highly public acts of racism were perpetrated on the Black community, including the so-called 'virginity testing' at Heathrow Airport in the late 1970s and in January 1981, thirteen Black children were killed at a house party in New Cross in a suspected arson attack. Black children were systematically let down by the education system, regularly siphoned into 'sin bins' or 'educationally subnormal' (ESN) schools. Outside, young Black people were at the mercy of the UK's racist SUS law, which gave police the right to apprehend people merely suspected of 'intent to commit an arrestable offence', a power that was wielded disproportionately and arbitrarily towards Black people as young as twelve, who could be detained for days for 'offences' such as waiting for a bus. The act was repealed in August 1981 following a three-year campaign led by activist Mavis Best, but not before the Metropolitan Police's 1981 Operation Swamp (named after Thatcher's assertion that Britain was being 'swamped by people of a different culture') led – along with localised concerns in regional cities and further acts of violence such as the shooting of Cherry Groce in 1985 – to uprisings in Brixton in London, Toxteth in Liverpool and Handsworth in Birmingham throughout the 1980s.

NO SUCH THING AS SOCIETY

Alongside the multiple uprisings that reshaped the streets of Britain in the mid-1980s, another – deadly – concern was fundamentally altering communities. In Pratibha Parmar's 1987 film *Reframing AIDS* (p.259), writer, art historian and AIDS activist Simon Watney describes the scale of devastation experienced by the lesbian and gay community in the face of the AIDS epidemic: 'straight people are rather like tourists, strolling through the Blitz. In my community there is a Blitz, the bombs have been falling for years and nobody seems to be taking a blind bit of notice.'

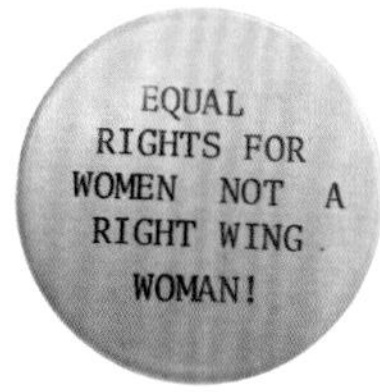

Where there was public or governmental focus it was largely on men, who were being infected in much greater numbers, but women were of course also affected by the virus, both directly and indirectly. The lesbian community worked alongside their male friends to provide practical and emotional support; magazines such as *Square Peg* published guides to safe sex for lesbians; and in 1987 the organisation Positively Women was set up by Sheila and Jenni, two women living with HIV who, finding no services available for women, took matters into their own hands by putting up hand-drawn posters in HIV/AIDS clinics and inviting other women to meet in their homes.

A year later, Section (or Clause) 28 would become another unifying moment for the lesbian and gay community, with Thatcher's Conservative government passing a series of laws that prohibited the 'promotion of homosexuality' by local authorities. This was a brutal piece of legislation that degraded and undermined lesbian and gay communities and denied many the ability to continue or set up support and educational groups, as well as fuelling homophobic violence across the country. Women took to the streets in a series of marches and protests. As artist Tessa Boffin states in her introduction to *Stolen Glances: Lesbians Take Photographs*: 'we were aware of the irony that, despite its attempts to repress us, Section 28 had given us more visibility in the mainstream media than ever before.'[8] Alongside campaigning, part of that visibility came from direct action. On 2 February 1988 lesbians Olivia Butler, Rachel Cox and Angela Nunn abseiled into the House of Lords on a washing line after a vote result in favour of the legislation. Then on 23 May, the night before the clause passed into law, another group of women invaded the BBC studios live on the *Six O'Clock News*.

In 1987, when feminist artists and activists in the UK had spent the past two decades making progress, carving out space and increasing their visibility

8 Tessa Boffin and Jean Fraser (eds.), *Stolen Glances: Lesbians Take Photographs*, Kitchener, ON 1991, p.9.

9 Griselda Pollock in conversation with Linsey Young, April 2022.
10 Juliet Jacques, 'Cultural Capital: The Greater London Council's Arts Policies, 1981–6', *Suite 212* podcast, Series 3, Episode 5 (soundcloud).

through collaboration, campaigning, exhibiting and supporting each other, Margaret Thatcher was interviewed for the mainstream women's lifestyle magazine *Woman's Own*:

> I think we have gone through a period when too many children and people have been given to understand 'I have a problem, it is the Government's job to cope with it!' or 'I have a problem, I will go and get a grant to cope with it!' 'I am homeless, the Government must house me!' and so they are casting their problems on society and who is society? There is no such thing! There are individual men and women and there are families and no government can do anything except through people and people look to themselves first.

This sentiment, reiterated by Thatcher later in the interview as 'there is no such thing as society', seems to sum up the free market intentions of the Thatcherite project. Griselda Pollock shared with me her perspective:

> No other movement of the time gained as many wins in terms of changing laws and attitudes than the feminist movement. Steadily throughout the 1970s and early 1980s things were changing but, as feminists built, Thatcher was working in tandem to demolish the socialist foundations on which they stood, and by the end of the 1980s the ground was crumbling beneath our feet.[9]

In the many conversations that formed the bedrock for this research I asked each artist why the production of artwork that we might consider to be aligned to a feminist perspective seemed to slow down in the late 1980s. I was often given similar answers that centred around emotional and physical exhaustion; the difficulty of obtaining well-paid, relevant work, in major cities; Thatcher's closure of the Greater London Council (GLC), 'one of the United Kingdom's most radical experiments in cultural policy'[10], which financially supported a huge range of left-wing creative projects. Cuts to the arts resonated nationwide, but one of the reasons consistently raised by artists was the emergence of a fiercely commercialised and commodified art market in the late 1980s, much of which is linked in the UK to the collector Charles Saatchi. With his brother Maurice, Saatchi ran the advertising agency Saatchi & Saatchi, creators of 'Labour Isn't Working', an advertising campaign for the Conservatives that is widely recognised as having played a significant role in Thatcher winning the 1979 general election (right).

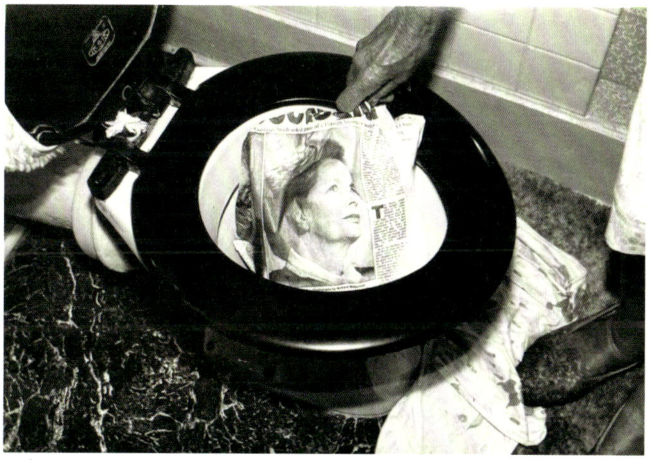

Jo Spence and Terry Dennett, untitled photograph, 1988.

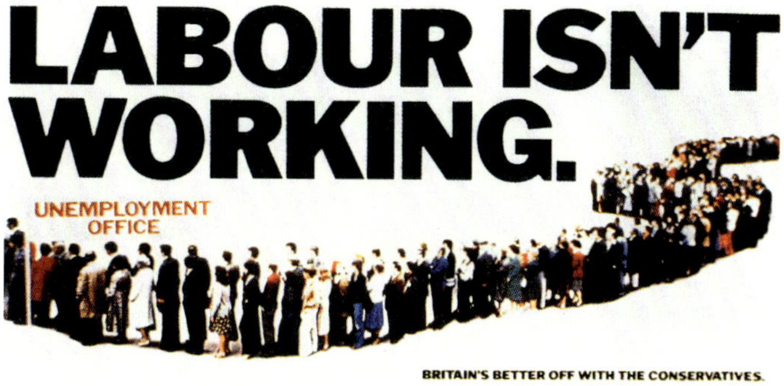

Conservative Party poster declaring 'Labour Isn't Working', 1979.

When the Young British Artists (YBA) exhibition *Sensation* opened (to much controversy) in New York in 1999, a *New York Times Magazine* profile noted that many of Saatchi's art world critics already viewed the show as only his 'latest effort to inflate the value of his holdings, the sly move of a man for whom art is mainly a speculator's game'. From its inception in the late 1980s, this speculation, the trading of artwork, and the marketing of artists as personalities had fuelled an emerging industry that fed into the legacy of the Conservative free market project, the effect of which was arguably not truly felt until the mid-1990s, the rise of New Labour and (almost inconceivably in 2023 Britain, after years of austerity and Brexit) the rebranding of the UK as 'Cool Britannia'.

In 2021 writer Isabel Waidner argued that:

> In hindsight, the YBAs were probably a disaster for British art because of the extent to which they dominated the 1990s discourse. The worst of it was XXL-sized white people art and pure posturing; the best of it was low-budget, raw video work. But even the YBA works that didn't cost a fortune to make cost a fortune to buy … Arguably, the YBAs contributed to the marginalisation of a generation of 1980s Black British artists – like John Akomfrah, Sonia Boyce, Chila Kumari Burman, Lubaina Himid, Isaac Julien, Keith Piper and Ingrid Pollard … or the art that developed in relation to the AIDS crisis.[11]

11 Isabel Waidner, 'An Alternative Art History of the 1990s', *Frieze*, no.220 (June–Aug 2021), https://www.frieze.com/article/isabel-waidner-alternative-90s-history-2021, accessed 10 May 2023.

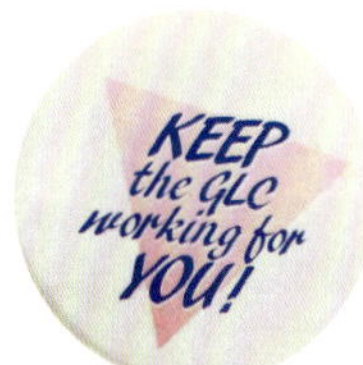

This is in no way to suggest that any of the artists associated with the YBAs set out to obscure their peers; but rather that, in the face of a powerful, financially backed wave of collectors, commercial galleries and art fairs, artists engaged in socially motivated practices, who questioned authority and challenged dominant narratives, had ever fewer opportunities to do so.

A NEW WORLD?

The commercialisation and privatisation of cultural life that began in the late 1980s snaked seamlessly into the neoliberalism of the 1990s and 2000s. Indeed, despite subsequent changes in leadership and then government, consumerism and individualism continue to rule, exemplified by our current reality, whereby feminist thought is often co-opted by big businesses that appropriate and monetise it. The term 'self care', a concept first defined in the late 1980s by American writer, philosopher and civil rights activist Audre Lorde, is now freely used by companies looking to sell beauty products, fashion chains with poor labour and ecological credentials sell 'Feminist' branded goods and social media platforms perpetuate narcissism disguised as community.

At the time of writing, it seems that women's lives are still in a desperate state: the welfare state is dismantling around us; the wage gap continues to grow and rape crisis centres are being closed. Trans women experience relentless violence, our access to abortion is threatened and women of colour continue to be four times more likely to die in childbirth than their white peers. All the while, queer spaces are turned into luxury housing, extortionate childcare keeps women away from the workplace and unpaid carers continue to prop

12 Lola Olufemi, *Feminism Interrupted: Disrupting Power*, London 2020, p.11.

up an underfunded healthcare system. However in tandem with this decline comes the emergence of a new inspirational generation of young artists and activists, holding much the same values as the radical women of the 1970s and 80s. Concerned with anti-capitalism, environmentalism, anti-racism, and trans inclusion, these people are continuing the fight and actively changing the physical and cultural landscape in which we live. My hope for this publication and the accompanying exhibition is that it makes accessible a version of British history that gives due attention and credit to those artists and activists who came before us and did the heavy lifting; who knew that community and not capital was the key to developing a truly equitable and inclusive society.

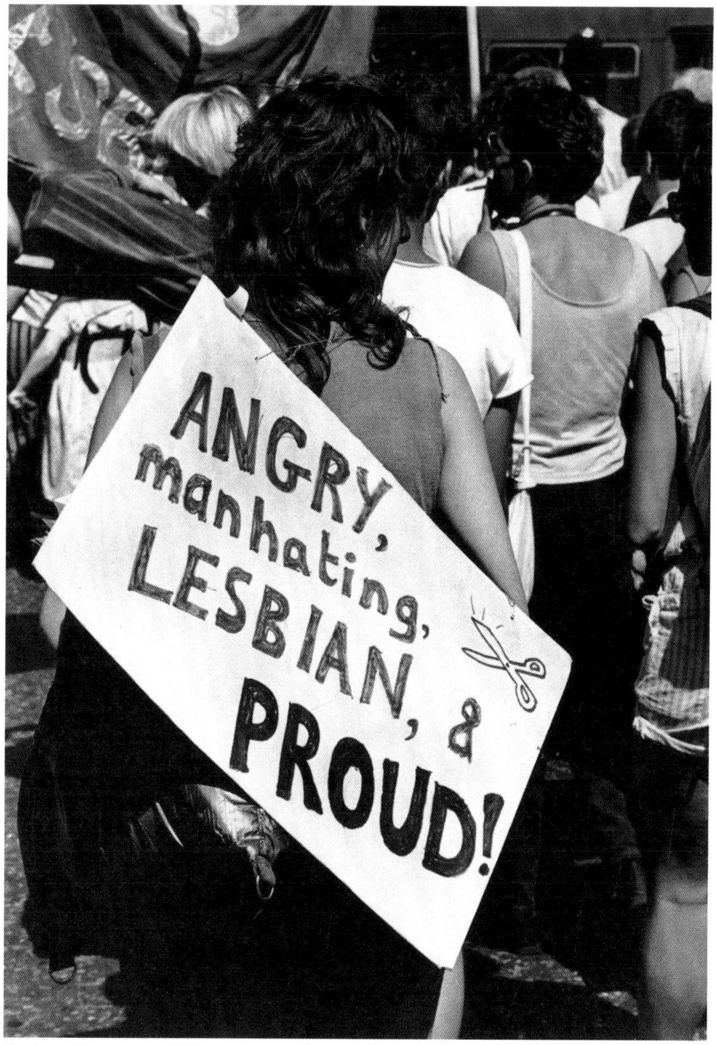

Section 28 protest, 1980s, photographed by Pam Isherwood, Format Photographers.

To return to Lola Olufemi's *Feminism Interrupted*:

> Black women's history travels in whispers and memories recalled around the dining table by mothers and grandmothers and it often dies when those voices leave us. The power of these stories is that they make us feel less alone and give us the courage to act by providing us with a blueprint. This is important for young feminists because there are forces acting on us at all times that tell us that revolution is impossible. These forces take a toll on our bodies, our minds, our sense of ourselves and our understanding of what is possible. History allows us to see that subversion and more importantly, resistance has always existed. Feminist activists have always pushed boundaries set by the state, by men, by the powerful, and in doing so, laid the foundations for a new world.[12]

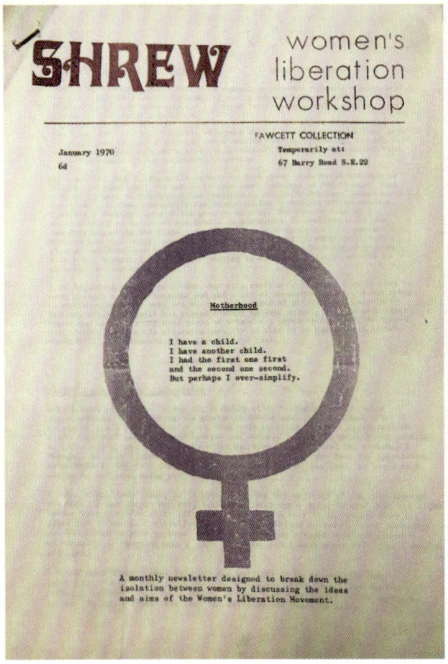

1

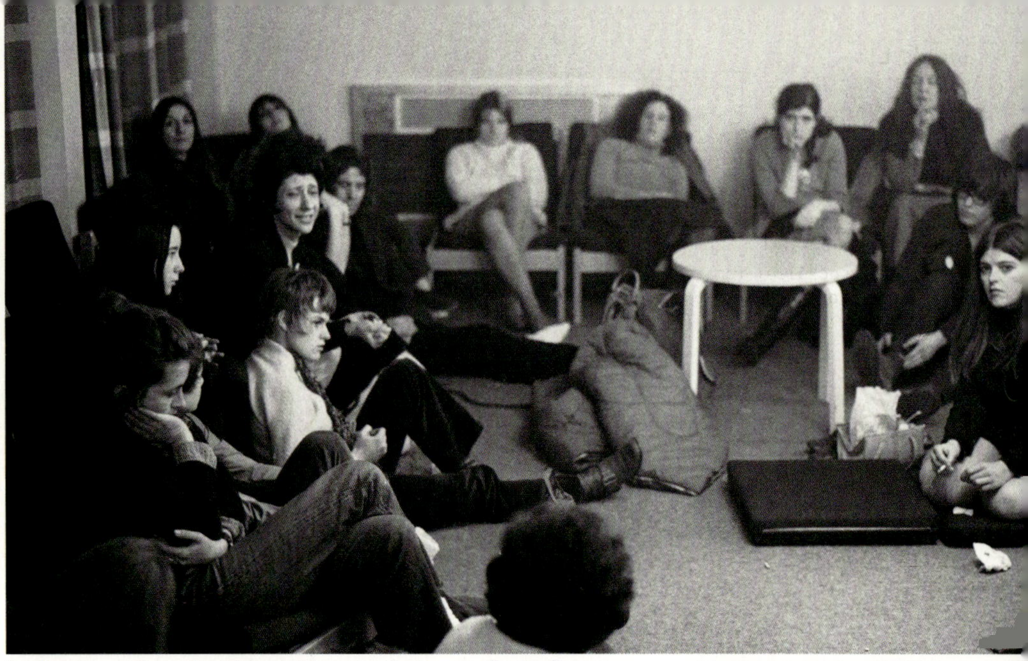

Small group meeting at the Women's Liberation Conference, Ruskin College, Oxford, 27 February – 1 March 1970. Photographed by Chandan Fraser.

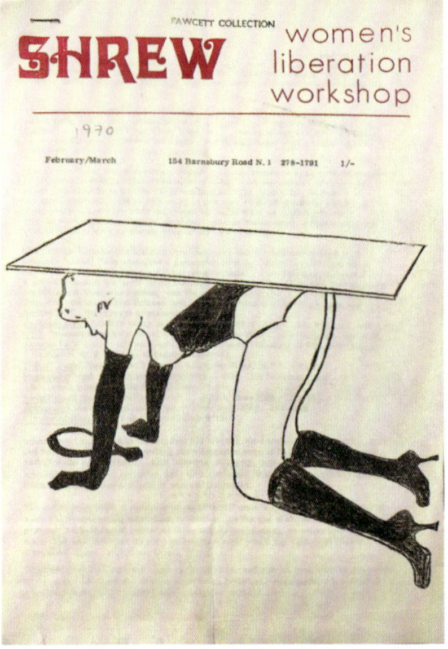

2

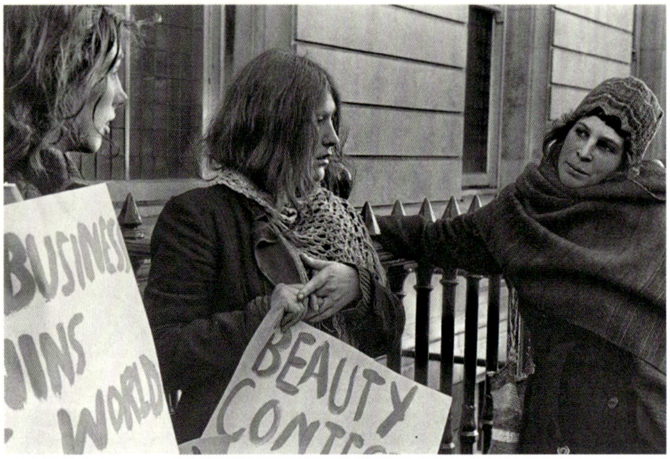

Miss World Trial: Anna Davin, Roberta Hunter-Henderson and Liz Merrington outside Bow Street Court, February 1971. Five women were arrested at the Miss World protest and tried in February 1971. After one night in Holloway Prison they were released with fines of £10 or £20 and £5 costs, which were paid by the Women's Liberation Workshop. Photographed by Chandan Fraser.

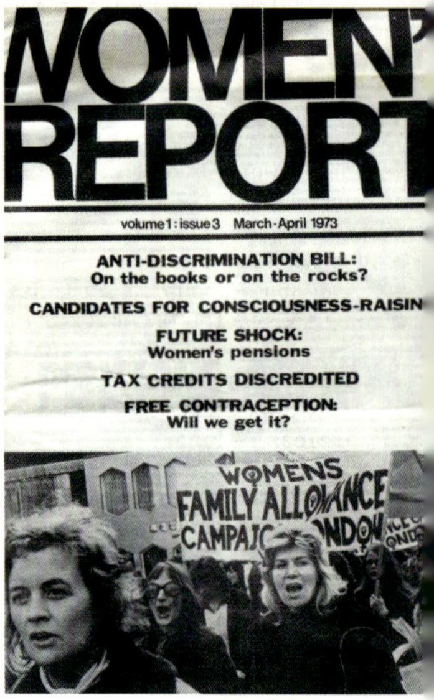

5

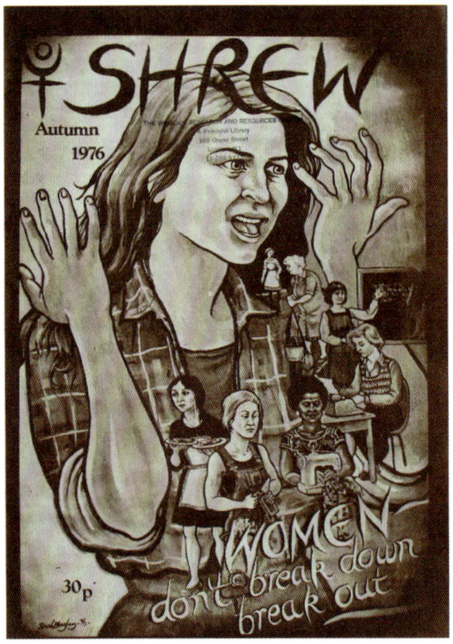

3

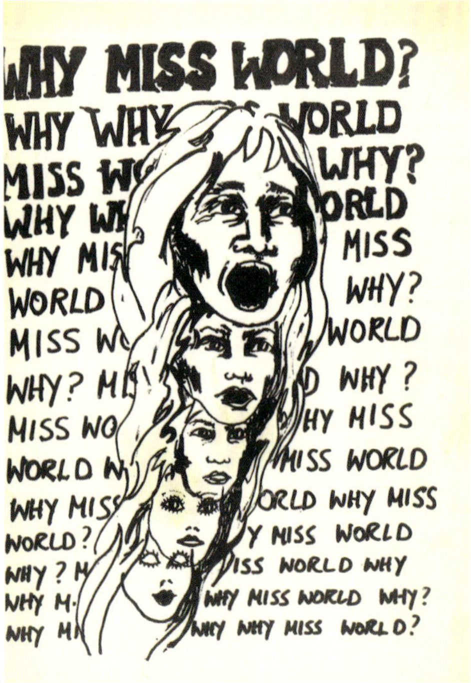

4

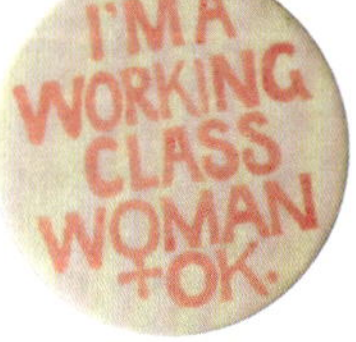

1 *Shrew*, publication of the Women's Liberation Workshop, January 1970.
2 *Shrew*, publication of the Women's Liberation Workshop, February/March 1970.
3 *Shrew*, publication of the Women's Liberation Workshop, Autumn 1976.
4 Front cover of *Why Miss World?* Spring 1971. Designed by Jenny Fortune b.1949. Ink on paper 21.5 × 15.5.
5 *Women's Report*, vol.1, no.3, March–April 1973. Active between 1972 and 1979, the *Women's Report* compiled news reports on health, economics, social issues, law and work that were relevant to women. It was run by a collective of women, including Anna Coote, Mandy Merck, Angela Phillips, Pat Kahn, Diana Kahn, Jill Rakusen and Griselda Pollock.
6 Ellen Adams, Janet Hadley, Carolyn Roth, Laura Stevens and Annie Freud at the first Women's Liberation Conference, Ruskin College, Oxford, 27 February – 1 March 1970. Photographed by Chandan Fraser.
7 Joanne O'Brien addressing the first Women's Liberation Conference, Ruskin College, Oxford, 27 February – 1 March 1970. Photographed by Chandan Fraser.
8 Selma James speaking at the Women's Liberation Conference, 1970. Photographed by Chandan Fraser.
9 *Banshee, Journal of Irishwomen United*, no.1, 1975.
10 *Edinburgh Women's Newsletter*, no.11, date unknown.
11 *Red Rag*, no.2, 1974. *Red Rag* was a magazine produced by a Marxist collective in the Women's Liberation Movement between 1972 and 1980.
12 *MAMA, Women Artists Together*, one-off publication produced by the Mama Collective in Birmingham, January 1977

Women's Liberation

The first National Women's Liberation Conference took place at Ruskin College in Oxford on the 27 February 1970. Organised by Arielle Aberson, Sheila Rowbotham and Sally Alexander it is widely recognised as marking the beginning of the Women's Liberation Movement (WLM) in the UK. The conference addressed issues such as patriarchy, sexuality, women's economics, and socialist feminism. It was heavily oversubscribed and eight further conferences were staged across the country between 1971 and 1978. Through these meetings a set of demands would be established:

- Equal pay now
- Equal education and job opportunities
- Free contraception and abortion on-demand
- Free 24-hour nurseries
- Financial and legal independence
- An end to all discrimination against lesbians and a woman's right to define her own sexuality
- Freedom from intimidation by threat or use of violence or sexual coercion, regardless of marital status and an end to all laws, assumptions and institutions which perpetuate male dominance and men's aggression towards women.

Alongside the conferences which were dominated by white women, equally vital and energetic work was happening within feminist communities of colour, including the work of Olive Morris, Beverley Bryan and Liz Obi, who co-founded the socialist feminist Brixton Black Women's Group in 1973; Jayaben Desai, who organised the Grunwick Strikes between 1976 and 1978; and Stella Dadzie, Olive Morris and Gail Lewis, who co-founded the Organisation of Women of Asian and African Descent (OWAAD) in 1978.

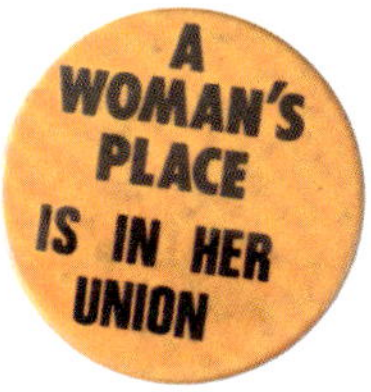

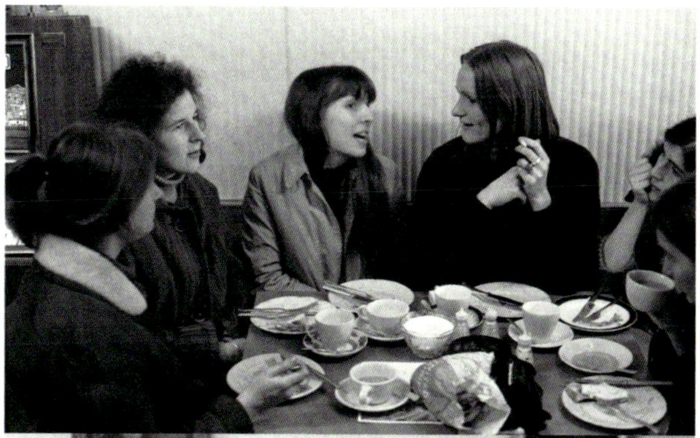

6

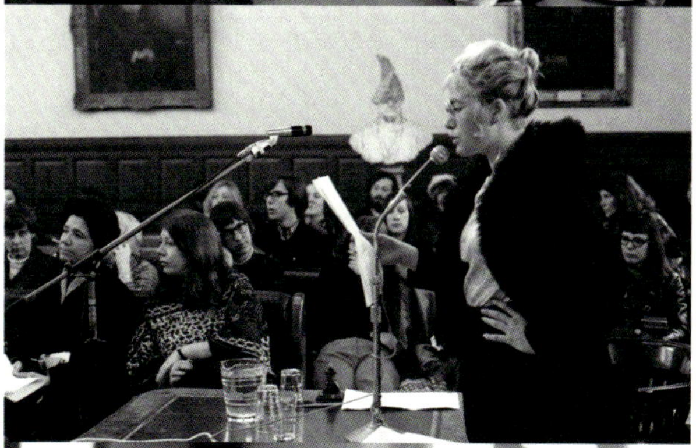

7

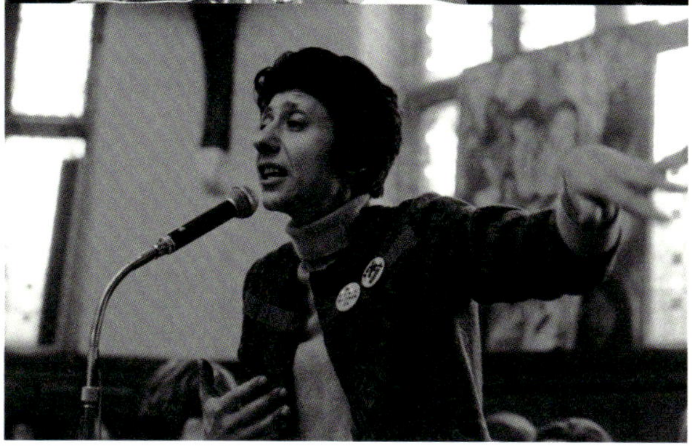

8

Plenary session at the first Women's Liberation Conference, Ruskin College, Oxford, 27 February – 1 March 1970. Photographed by Chandan Fraser.

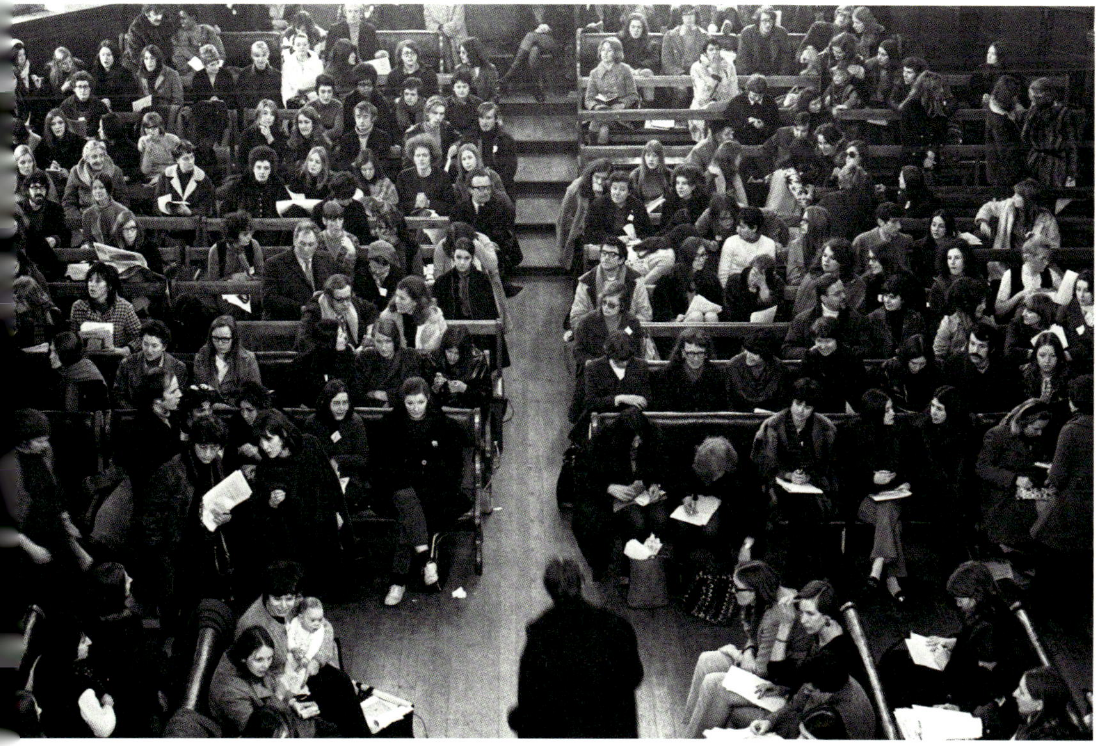

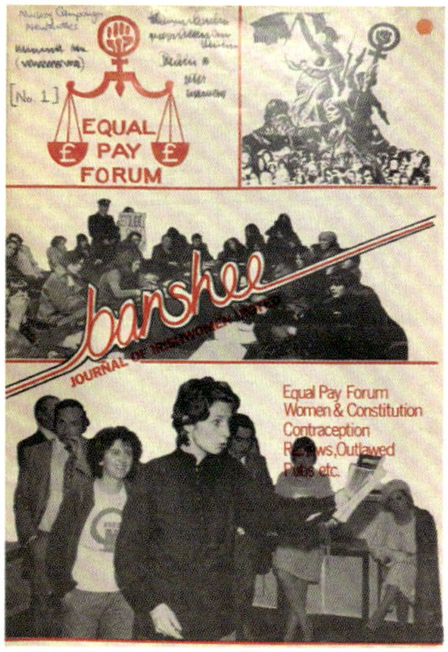

9

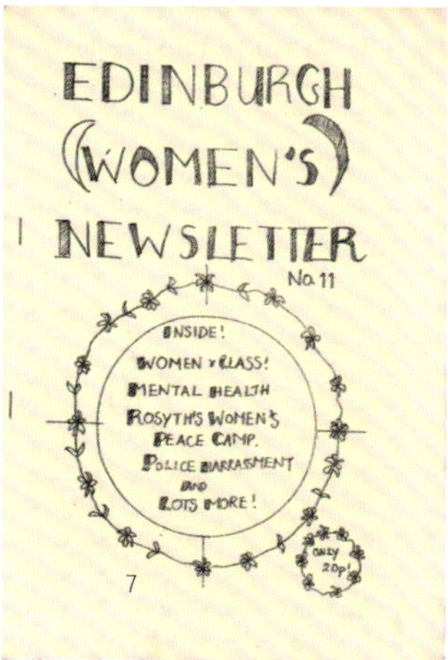

10

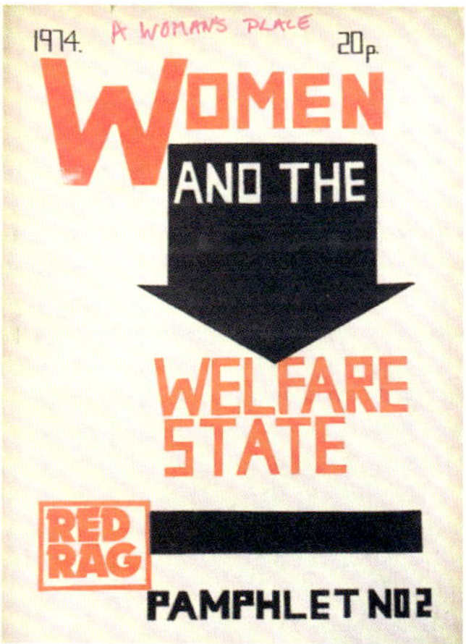

11

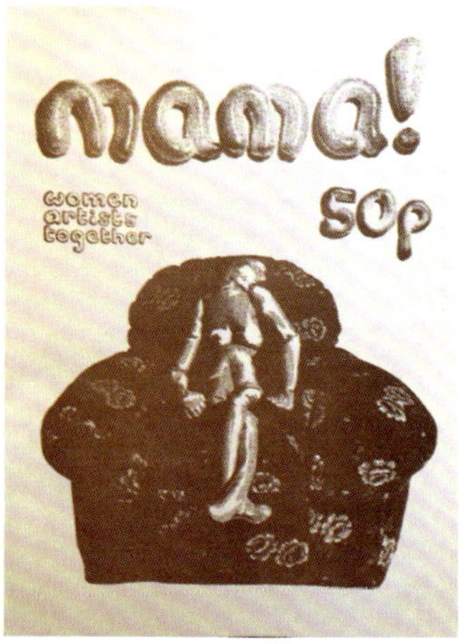

12

‘LITTLE CIRCLES’: ON GROUP WORK, FEMINISM AND ART BY WOMEN

AMY TOBIN

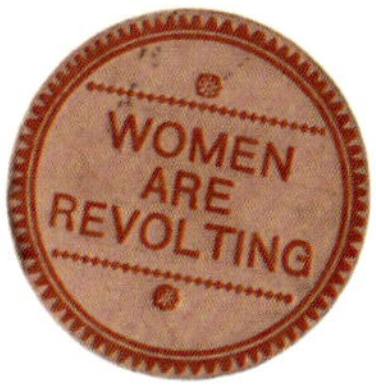

1 Kate Walker, 'How Not to Reinvent the Wheel', in *Women's Work: Two Years in the Life of a Women's Art Group*, London 1985, pp.1–4.
2 For two useful accounts of the women's art movement in Britain, see Margaret Harrison, 'Notes on Feminist Art in Britain 1970–77', *Studio International*, vol.193, no.987, March 1977, pp.212–20, and Rozsika Parker and Griselda Pollock (eds.), *Framing Feminism: Art and the Women's Movement 1970–85*, London 1987.
3 Walker 1985, p.4.

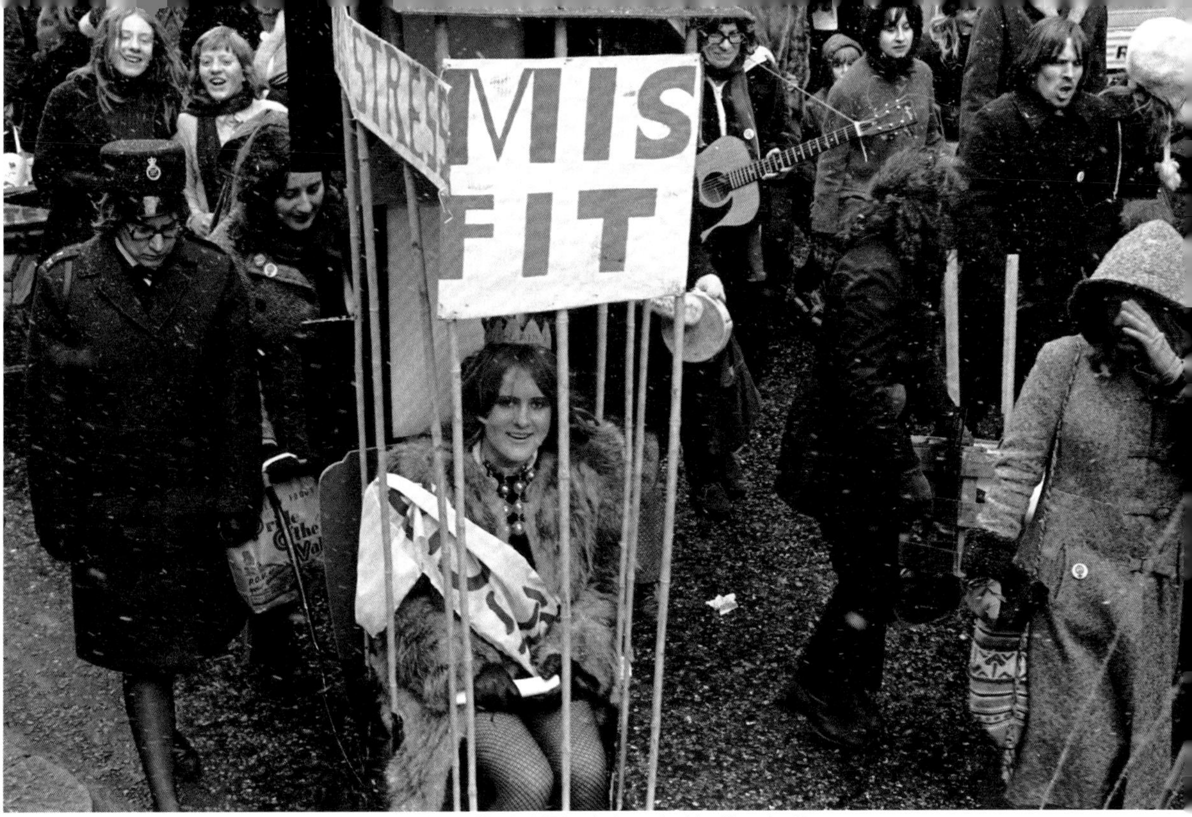

The first Women's Liberation Movement March, London, 6 March 1971, photographed by Chandan Fraser.

In 1985 the artist Kate Walker contributed an introduction to a publication about the 'Women's Work' programme at Brixton Art Gallery in south London.[1] Walker had been an active member of the Women's Liberation Movement (WLM) and the women's art movement in the previous decade: she was a constant collaborator, an organiser and a mother.[2] In her text, titled 'How Not to Reinvent the Wheel', she offers caution and advice to her reader. She laments the increasing divide between the 'Famous Feminist Few' and the 'Women's Ghetto of Great Unknowns', encouraging the Women's Work collective – a group of artists organising at Brixton Art Gallery – to stop the 'silencing' so that the women's art movement could go 'somewhere a bit faster' rather than making 'little circles'.[3]

For Walker, these 'little circles' – echoes of the decentralised and anti-hierarchical small groups and collective structures important to women's liberation organising in the 1970s – were self-fulfilling revolutions without propulsion. A focus on such group work, she suggested, risked forgetting to look outward, or back, to remember what had already been achieved. 'How Not to Reinvent the Wheel' encouraged women artists to maintain the structures of intimate support that constituted the women's art movement, while finding the means and the infrastructure to share that work publicly. For Walker this too was a collective endeavour that could not be left to the values of the institutional British art world. As she said of her 1974 work *Death of a Housewife* in the previous decade: 'here is a start, please carry on.'[4]

Around the time of her advice to Women's Work, Walker made *Art of Survival – A Living Monument* for a 1987 exhibition at Brixton Art Gallery (p.282). In the galleries, Walker installed herself on a plinth wearing a grey costume – complete with quilted sash and painter's palette – posing in the attitude of an allegorical statue. An inscription on the plinth tells us she is the personification of 'Art'. This reclamation of a neoclassical sculptural language was an act of feminist reintervention,

4 Kate Walker, 'A Woman's Place', in *MAMA: Women Artists Together*, Birmingham 1977, p.19. For more information on this project, see Amy Budd, Naomi Pearce and Amy Tobin (eds.), *A Woman's Place*, London 2017, and Amy Tobin, 'Breaking Down *A Woman's Place*', http://www.ravenrow.org/texts/75/, accessed 7 Feb. 2023.

with the typically young, ebullient virtue transformed into the living artist, who paints *and* quilts, merging the high and low procedures of fine art and craft.[5] Walker's act of giving herself a platform was also a claim to artistic identity; she was insisting on her stature as an artist and offering up a different image of success.

Along with her many collaborators through the 1970s – including Sue Madden, Sally Gollop, Phil Goodall, Monica Ross, Suzy Varty and Su Richardson – Walker had transformed art-making, motivated and informed by the emergent feminist politics of women's liberation. The *Art of Survival* was a statement of endurance and a living monument to the entwining of art and life. Walker's participation in shows organised by the Brixton Art Gallery collective – formed in 1983, in the wake of the earlier Brixton uprising – and the Women's Work group – whose artist members included Teri Bullen, Françoise Dupré and Rita Keegan – evidence the continued importance of group work, solidarity and support for artists into the 1980s, when those 'little circles' of practice took on new forms, both opening and closing as artists confronted difference and privilege.[6]

5 Walker was co-editor of a book on craft practices; see Gillian Elinor, Su Richardson, Kate Walker et al. (eds.), *Women and Craft*, London 1987.

6 See Françoise Dupré, 'Brixton Art Gallery, Brixton Artists Collective, Women's Work: A Personal Account', https://brixton50.co.uk/francoise-dupre, accessed 7 Feb. 2023, and 'Shark Moves, Soup, and Honouring our Artistic Journeys: Barby Asante in conversation with Rita Keegan', in Rita Keegan, Matthew Harle and Ego Ahaiwe Sowinski (eds.), *Mirror Reflecting Darkly: The Rita Keegan Archive*, London 2021, pp. 18–21.

7 This video is available online through the London Community Video Archive, https://the-lcva.co.uk, accessed 7 Feb. 2023.

ART AND POLITICS

Group work – encompassing collaborations, collectives, reading groups and cooperatives – was fundamental to the women's art movement, just as the process of small group consciousness-raising sessions, autonomous organisations and DIY practices were central to the broader Women's Liberation Movement. Working together provided a means for support at a moment when women's social and professional status was lower than men's, but it was also a means of challenging existing social structures – such as the family unit, in which many women felt isolated – and a context for sharing skills and resources. Artists used the group for many reasons, but collaboration also represented a particular kind of defiance against the romantic idea of the expressive, original, individual genius artist, so lionised in the history of art and particularly in the modernism of the previous half-century. To be sharing ideas, showing unfinished artworks, working together on projects and collaborating with non-artists were all forms of artistic revolt. The emphasis on mutuality, empathy, sociality and experiment opened the artwork to the world, rather than keeping it sealed in the controlled spaces of the museum or art gallery. Nonetheless, many artists also wanted their works to be exhibited in these spaces and fought for it. When they did so, and when they appear now, these works challenge these sites and their histories, offering new trajectories for imagining what art can be or do.

STRUGGLE

The early years of the WLM in Britain emerged through small groups, large gatherings and mass marches. Small groups were a vital site of politicisation in which women came to understand the social causes of personal problems through a process of giving testimony and active listening known as 'consciousness-raising'. The discussions in these meetings shaped the agendas of larger gatherings, such as the landmark Ruskin conference in Oxford in 1971 and the later annual National Women's Liberation Conferences, at which issues were debated and political demands articulated. Mass marches were also sites of resistance, where women could unite in public space, raise their voices and, by stopping traffic, disturb everyday habits and routines. These were all sites of the grassroots struggle for women's liberation.

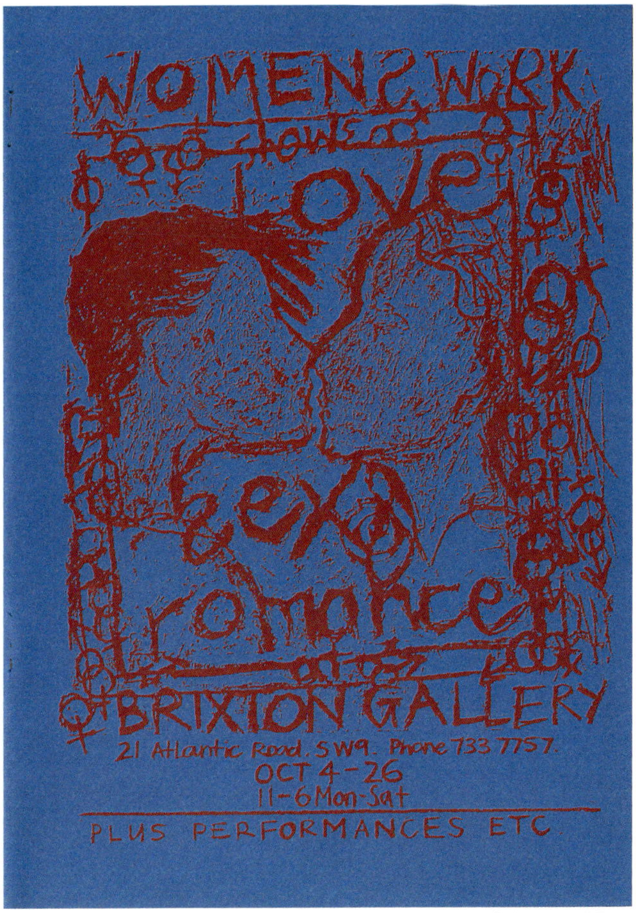

Poster for the exhibition *Love, Sex and Romance*, Brixton Art Gallery, 1985.

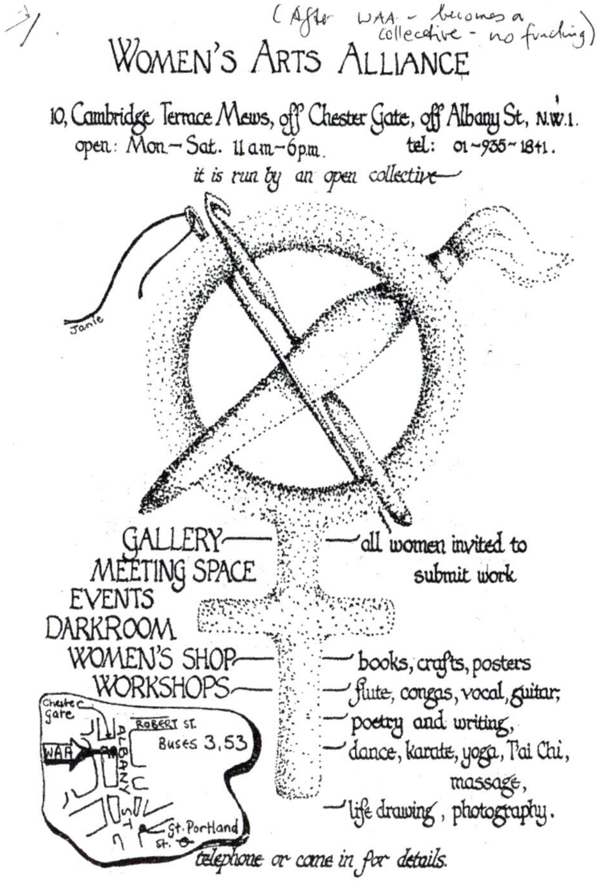

Women's Free Art Alliance poster, c.1975–8.

A video by the collective Liberation Films, made with the filmmaker Sue Crockford, documented the speeches and open discussions of the Ruskin conference and the first WLM march through London (p.81). The footage of the march shows a mass of women flooding the streets of the city.[7] Both an act of defiance and a celebratory festival, women appear walking the streets together, holding signs and banners, or skipping, or breaking pace for a dance routine. Others carried puppets or figures on palanquins dressed up as the unconventional beauty queens 'Mis Stress' or 'Mis Fit', a callback to the 1969 and 1970 protests of the Miss World pageants at the Royal Albert Hall, which included interventions by the London Women's Liberation Art Group.[8] As the crowd concentrated on Trafalgar Square, copies of the WLM publication *Socialist Woman* were distributed, proliferating cropped reproductions of Sandro Botticelli's *The Birth of Venus* 1485–6 on their covers.

Socialist Woman's Venus cover girl was a punning reclamation of the goddess of love. It played on the use of the Venus sign (a circle with a cross below) – usually associated with the female gender – as an emblem of women's liberation. In subsequent years this sign appeared in many iterations from pin badges to magazines, posters and t-shirts. It was adapted for different purposes, including on a Women's Free Arts Alliance poster (above), where it was crossed with a paintbrush, or multiplied into pairs and cadres referring to both women's collective power and lesbian rights, as the poster *Lesbian Spirit* 1975 by the See Red Women's Workshop poster collective demonstrates (see p.36). Over a decade later, a Women's Work poster for the 1985 exhibition *Love, Sex and Romance* at Brixton Art Gallery featured a thicket of multidirectional signs emphasising varieties of intimate joining and the complexities of erotic desire (above). For some women – particularly those associated with revolutionary

8 In 1969 and 1970, groups of women protested outside the Royal Albert Hall during the Miss World beauty pageant. In 1970 their protest also included a group of feminist seditionaries waiting inside the venue to disrupt proceedings with flour bombs. See 'Why Miss World?', *Shrew*, Feb. 1970, and Victoria Bazin, 'Miss-Represented? Mediating Miss World in Shrew Magazine', *Women: A Cultural Review*, vol.27, no.4, 2016, pp.412–31. The London Women's Liberation Art Group included Valerie Charlton, Alison Fell, Ann Colsell, Roslyn Smythe, Margaret Harrison and Sally Frazer. Harrison dressed up as 'Miss Loveable Bra' and Fell organised a 'Flashing Nipple' action for the event. Mary Kelly later made *WLM Demo Remix* 2005, citing this early action. For a discussion of these two works, see Catherine Grant, *A Time of One's Own: Histories of Feminism in Contemporary Art*, Durham, NC 2022.

feminism – the Venus sign collapsed differences between women in favour of biological sameness and the advocacy of separatism from other political struggles. For many others it was more mutable, standing in for a new focus on overcoming women's oppression, often in solidarity with parallel (if not intersecting) movements. For instance, *Socialist Woman* was associated with the International Marxist Group, a revolutionary socialist organisation, exemplifying the impact of leftist thought and organising on the early years of the movement.

Many women's liberation activists came from Marxist, left-wing and union movements, and while these politics shaped their feminism, group work around issues that uniquely affected women became a necessity. Unlike the centralised structures of other struggles, which were often more formal and comprised parties, committees and leadership, the network of small groups that made up the WLM aspired to be anti-hierarchical: every member was to have an equal voice. So even though the movement agreed on a series of political demands, it did not share a consistent ideology. This was more than an activist method; decentralisation and collectivity influenced a range of activities from pedagogy to film- and exhibition-making and editorial work.

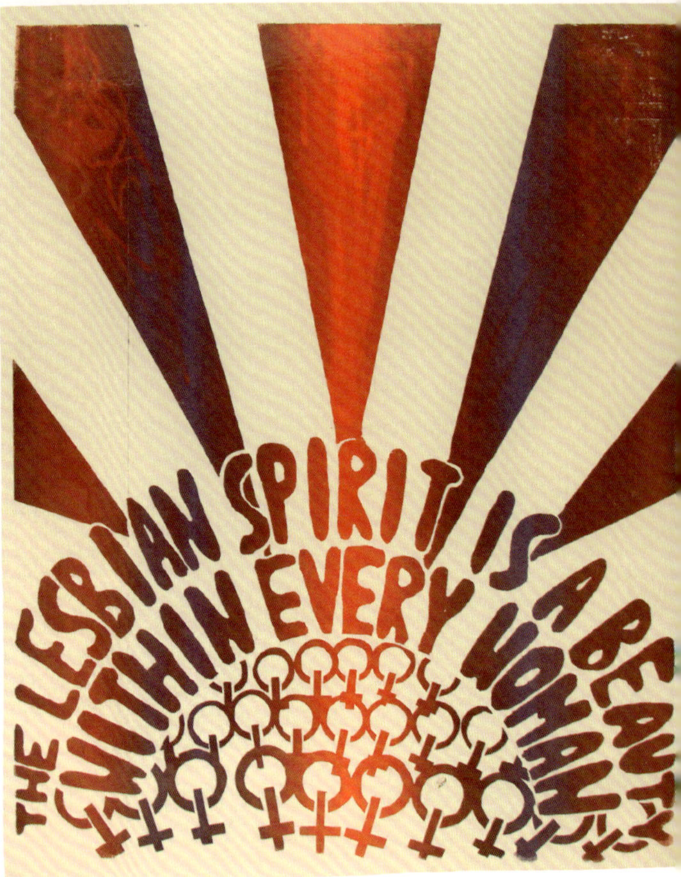

See Red Women's Workshop *The Lesbian Spirit* 1975. Screenprint on paper 65 × 54

Publications were a particularly important site for group work because they connected activists and organisations across large distances. Many magazines, journals and newsletters were made by collectives, representing varied interests and investments through reader submissions, while some, such as the magazine *Shrew*, were established so that each issue was produced by a different group, who then decided on a theme and worked up the content. These publications captured the diversity and extent of feminist struggle. But small group structures also had a political impact, by offering their members the opportunity to develop skills. Often collectives involved in creative or practical projects switched roles, shared specialisms and distributed decision-making. Sometimes the group took precedence over individual members, with no spokespeople and all contributions anonymised to retain the power of collective coherence.

The December 1970 issue of *Shrew*, produced by the History Group, appeared without members' names. It included texts reporting on Miss World protests, on politics in Lebanon and the work of Sigmund Freud, written by figures who would go on to be important voices in the Movement, including the theorist and psychoanalyst Juliet Mitchell, the historian Rosalind Delmar, the artist Mary Kelly and the filmmaker and writer Laura Mulvey. The History Group, later the Lacan Reading Group, provided the context that forged their early work, including Kelly's installation *Post-Partum Document* 1973–9, Mitchell's book *Psychoanalysis and Feminism* 1974 and Mulvey's essay 'Visual Pleasure and Narrative Cinema' 1975.[9] Mitchell said of her influential book that it 'sprang Athena-like' from this 'period of profound collectivity'.[10] The events that accompanied the first exhibition of *Post-Partum Document*

9 Juliet Mitchell, *Psychoanalysis and Feminism: Freud, Reich, Laing and Women*, London 1974; Laura Mulvey, 'Visual Pleasure and Narrative Cinema' (1975), in *Visual and Other Pleasures*, New York 1989, pp.14–28. Mary Kelly also published an artist book for *Post-Partum Document* in 1973.

10 Juliet Mitchell, 'Theory as an Object', *October*, vol.113, Summer 2005, pp.27–38, p.36.

at the Institute of Contemporary Arts (ICA) in London in 1975 presented the group's theories of sexual difference to a wider audience.[11] This commitment to understanding the complex ways that identity developed and was reasserted and reproduced across generations challenged the possibility or even the desirability of legal equality alone, which was a central demand of the British WLM.

Kelly was also a member of the Women's Workshop of the Artists' Union (WWAU), an autonomous interest group of the broader Artists' Union, set up to campaign for artists' rights as workers and particularly to support those whose practices fell outside the marketable objects preferred by the commercial art world. The WWAU was a women-only group of artists who considered how debates in the union impacted on women, but members also held prominent roles in the larger organisation – Kelly was elected chair and Margaret Harrison to the secretariat. Women artists' situation was not considered a separate issue, but one that required the focused attention of the smaller group. In the WWAU, the group split off into four further interest groups: one to organise a version of the 1972 Los Angeles installation *Womanhouse* in an empty London home; a second to collaborate with other unions to track the impact of the implementation of the Equal Pay Act on women workers; a third to address the provision of playgrounds; and a fourth to research the history of women artists.[12] These groups had numerous outcomes, including *A Woman's Place*, realised by the South London Art Group in 1974, and Margaret Harrison, Mary Kelly and Kay Hunt's *Women and Work: A Document on the Division of Labour in Industry 1973–75*, which traced women's working conditions at the Metal Box Factory in south London (see pp.82–3).

The WWAU also hosted a group exhibition of its members' work at the experimental organisation Arts Meeting Place in London in 1974. Titled *Hang Up, Put Down, Stand Up*, this group show connected the act of exhibiting and claiming artistic identity with the cessation of other duties and the embrace of a political stance. Throughout the 1970s, women artists fought for art-world recognition, whether they were campaigning for an exhibition of historic women artists at the Tate Gallery and the National Gallery (it never happened), protesting the absence of any women artists from the 1977 Hayward Annual (the 1978 Annual had a selection committee of five women artists but was not a woman-only show, and for some critics not a feminist one either), or disrupting an Allen Jones show at the ICA after a series of feminist exhibitions (the protests resulted in the Women's Cycle at the ICA in 1980).[13] At the same time, many artists found other spaces to exhibit in, from the foyers of libraries and theatres to alternative arts organisations such as Artists for Democracy – a space established to host artists working to support internationalist and Third World politics – and the Women's Free Arts Alliance, which, along with a gallery, ran 'Womanschool', a programme of classes in art, craft, music and self-defence.[14]

NOT PERFECT AESTHETICS: AN EVOLVING CONVERSATION

The emphasis on small, autonomous groups meant there was vital women's liberation activity beyond London's concentrated art world. Artists gathered and shared their work locally, as well as connecting with women in different communities nationally and internationally. The artists Monica Sjöö, Anne Berg, Liz Moore, Roslyn Smyth and Beverley Skinner toured their exhibition *Woman Spirit* across the UK, after Sjöö's work *God Giving Birth* 1968 (p.38), included in the earlier group show *Womanpower*, had been threatened with censure and an obscenity charge. For Sjöö, this attack on a painting

11 See Juli Carson, '(Re)Viewing Mary Kelly's *Post-Partum Document*', *Documents*, Fall 1998, pp.41–60, pp.48–53.
12 Amy Tobin, *Women Artists Together: Art in the Age of Women's Liberation*, New Haven and London 2023.
13 Catherine Elwes, 'A Parallel Universe: The "Women's" Exhibitions at the ICA, 1980, and the UK/Canadian Film and Video Exchange, 1998–2004', in Judith Rugg and Michèle Sedgwick (eds.), *Issues in Curating Contemporary Art and Performance*, Bristol 2007, pp.101–12.
14 See Fiona Anderson and Amy Tobin, 'Collaboration is Not an Alternative', in Meredith A. Brown and Michelle Millar Fisher (eds.), *Collaboration and its (Dis)Contents: Art, Architecture, and Photography since 1950*, London 2017, pp.158–78.

that reconnected maternity and spirituality was symptomatic of the cultural denigration of women that secured patriarchal power.[15] In her 'Images of Womanpower' manifesto, co-authored with Anne Berg, Sjöö argued for a new art that broke with the conventions of abstraction:

> WE SAY NO TO EMPTY ABSTRACTIONS, to the 'art for art's sake' philosophy of the privileged white middle-class male artworld. WE THE OPPRESSED cannot afford this empty play with words and forms, for us the important task is to convey to people to WOMEN – their dignity and strength and beauty – OUR PAST AND FUTURE [...] Art must be the expression of the total human world and only art fed by female and male views interacting can be vital. The time is now and it is overdue![16]

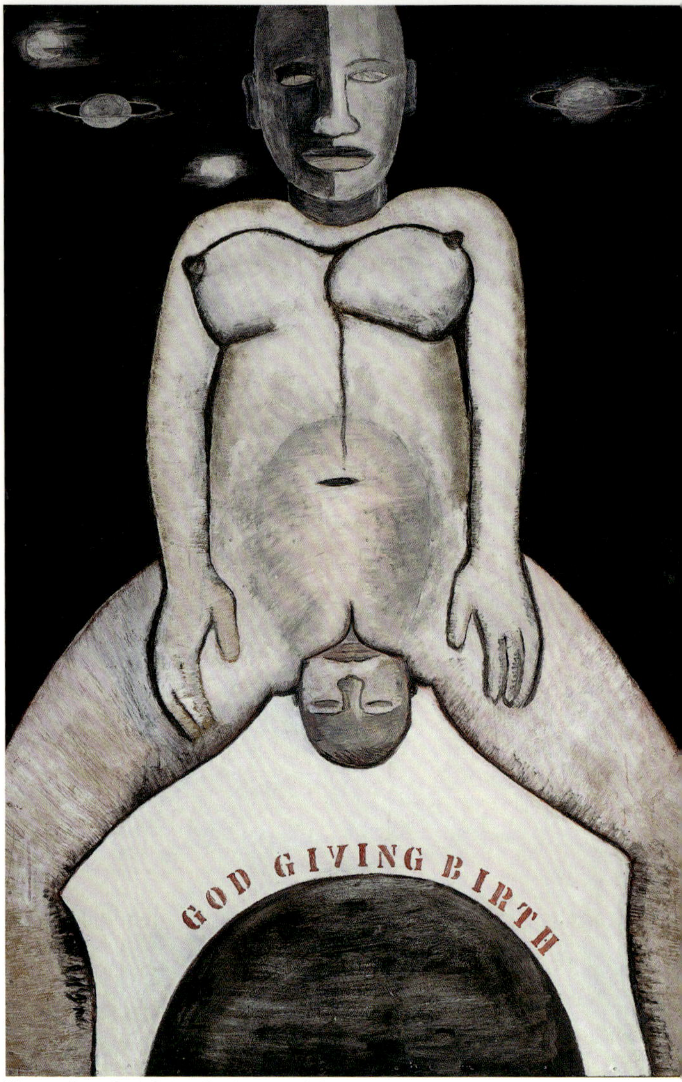

Monica Sjöö *God Giving Birth* 1968. Oil paint on board 183 × 122

The artists in *Woman Spirit* used figural painting and craft techniques to represent such a 'total human world', one that incorporated the spiritual and the material.[17] Although there were many debates over artistic co-option and success, as well as the degrees of aesthetic experiment or social impact, there was no agreed feminist style. Nonetheless, many artists sought a total break with modernist practices such as abstraction; their strategies ranged from using new technologies like film or video, or making temporary interventions and performances, to appropriating and transforming existing cultural forms to intervene in the material languages of painting and photography, or to retell canonical tales. Other artists expanded non-image-based conceptual art practices into social installations such as *Women and Work*, while others explored the potential of everyday craft to communicate the specificity of women's experience in the home.

The artists involved in the *Postal Art Event* 1975–7 experimented with making art amid the domestic responsibilities that unevenly fell to women. The event was a series of conversations between women spread across the UK, via artworks sent through the postal service. These works had to be small enough to mail and were therefore either assemblages of everyday things found around a typical family home or carefully crafted non-functional objects (see pp.64–5). They were often inexpensively made, things possible to realise on low household budgets that could be worked on between other caring responsibilities or paid work. While the network of correspondents in the *Postal Art Event* started off small, it quickly grew as participants sought the impetus both to make and to receive things from other women. For Kate Walker the event was akin to a political manifesto for feminist practice, and so it also went by the title *Feministo*. As the Birmingham-based artist Monica Ross said of the project, 'It is a non-stop process, new work constantly emerges as a visual conversation develops. The aim is communication, not perfect aesthetics.'[18]

15 See Monica Sjöö and Barbara Mor, *The Great Cosmic Mother: Rediscovering the Religion of the Earth*, New York and London 1991 (1st edn 1981), and Monica Sjöö, *The Spiral Journey*, St Agnes 2018.
16 Monica Sjöö and Anne Berg, 'Images of Womanpower 71 – Arts Manifesto', in *MAMA* 1977, p.5; reprinted in Katy Deepwell (ed.), *50 Feminist Art Manifestos*, London 2022, unpag.
17 Sjöö and Berg 1977, p.5.
18 Monica Ross, 'Portrait of the Artist as a Young Woman: A Postal Event', in *MAMA* 1977, pp.24–5.

19 Su Richardson in conversation with the author, July 2017.
20 See Siona Wilson, *Art Labor, Sex Politics: Feminist Effects in 1970s British Art and Performance*, Minneapolis 2015; Amy Tobin (ed.), *Linderism*, exh. cat., Kettle's Yard, Cambridge 2020; Laura Guy, 'Sex Wars, Revisited', *Aperture*, no.225, 2017, pp.54–9; and Flora Dunster, 'Lesbians Talk: British Lesbian Politics and the Sex Wars', in Sarah Crook and Charlie Jeffries (eds.), *Resist, Organize, Build: Feminist and Queer Activism in Britain and the United States During the Long 1980s*, Albany, NY 2022, pp.307–28.
21 Alexandra Kokoli, *The Feminist Uncanny in Theory and Art Practice*, London 2016.

Ross was one of the project's early proponents, along with her friend Su Richardson. They were both young mothers living in Birmingham, a stone's throw from the radical thought and scholarship emerging from Stuart Hall and Richard Hoggart's Centre for Contemporary Cultural Studies at the university, and on the periphery of the city's experimental Arts Lab, but it was the itinerant network of the *Postal Art Event* that gave them a space to make their work. Richardson had heard about the event during a panel on art and women's liberation. She recalls Walker standing up, frustrated with the proceedings, to ask the audience if there were any housewives and mothers among them who just wanted to make art.[19] From this intervention the network grew, catalysing a wave of isolated women, many of whom were working class, to make art.

After the first year of exchanges, contributors to the *Postal Art Event* devised a series of exhibitions of their objects. Beginning in Manchester, travelling to Birmingham and Edinburgh and ending in London, the sequence of installations transformed the logic of the exhibition from static, curated displays to holding spaces for accumulations of objects distributed through the mail and gathered up again. In each exhibition the objects had labels listing both their makers and recipients as a signal of their shared ownership, and, as the tour went on, the installations became increasingly dense, evidencing a feminist consciousness growing in complexity.

The ICA iteration in 1977, titled variously as *Portrait of the Artist as a Housewife* or *Portrait of the Artist as a Young Woman*, was installed in a domestic structure heavy with objects that explored entrapment, exhaustion, romantic pretence, boredom, disappointment, objectification and desire. Some artists employed brutal metaphors, like Cathy Nicholson's small sculptures of women bound and maimed on salad plates, while other objects teemed with humour, such as Richardson's crocheted sandwiches complete with insidious baby faces, flies or tongues. Kate Walker included her series *notoriously anonymous artistes of 1977*, comprising the exhibiting artists' biographies in the form of collectable cards (p.64), within a nightmarish kitchen dresser that encroached into the space via dense arrangements of pots, pans and plates hanging from the walls and ceiling.

The central installation at the ICA was pasted with hundreds of erotic, pornographic and sexualised images of women, transforming the bedroom into the 'rape room'. This equation of marital sex and pornography with abuse highlighted the threat of sexual violence within marriage at a moment when spousal rape was still legal (it would not be criminalised until 1991). Other objects celebrated sensuality and sexuality: from Richardson's body-part cushions to Walker's chocolate box of tits and smiles. These works were distinct from the pursuit of sexual freedoms and transgression in the work of artists such as Cosey Fanni Tutti or the appropriation of bondage by Linder and Tessa Boffin, nor did they align with some feminists' arguments against men and for gender separatism, which exploded at the National Women's Liberation Conference in London in 1978.[20] As Alexandra Kokoli has suggested – beyond the heated debates of the movement – *Portrait of the Artist as a Housewife* captured an enduring truth that violence and alienation were as evident in the home as in the world beyond.[21]

The *Postal Art Event*, with its accumulative logic, sustained different voices and politics under a mobile idea of feminism. The contingency of the 'event' purposefully disrupted the fixed term of a project, and as such the routines and regimes of care, waged and unwaged work. It allowed participants to keep their creative practice dynamic and open to change; this extended to international presentations of the event in Berlin and Australia. Other artists were also contending with the force of the status quo, with similar everyday disruptions. For instance, Cecilia Vicuña's *precarios*, small sculptures constructed from found and leftover materials, were made in London as emblems of resistance to Augusto Pinochet's 1973 coup in her homeland of Chile.[22] Vicuña exhibited a series of these works in a display at Arts Meeting Place in 1974. While Vicuña was in London, she brought women's liberation and women's art movement participants together with politically minded artists and anti-imperialist artists and activists to raise consciousness and protest the junta, resulting in the rally and exhibition Arts Festival for Democracy in Chile, held at the Royal College of Art in October 1974, which also hosted contributions by feminist artists including Tina Keane.

GREAT BLACK WOMEN ARTISTS

In 1985 the fourth edition of the Women's Work programme at Brixton Art Gallery was dedicated to Black women artists. *Mirror Reflecting Darkly* was an open exhibition that any woman who identified as Black – which in this political context also included people of East Asian, South Asian, South East Asian and Arabic descent – could submit their work to, in any creative medium. The poster described the impetus:

> This exhibition of black women's art at Brixton Gallery is a celebration of our creativity and until such time that we are able to come together with real sexual and racial equality, it will be important to have these points of autonomy to assert our visibility in all areas.[23]

As a 'point of autonomy', *Mirror Reflecting Darkly* articulated a space away from the 'mixed' shows and collectives at Brixton Art Gallery and beyond, where Black women were the focus. In her 1987 text 'There Have Always Been Great Black Women Artists', Chila Kumari Singh Burman (who participated in the exhibition) described the political impasse Black women faced as active contributors to both anti-racist and women's liberation struggles, which in confronting racism and sexism as separate struggles also marginalised them.[24] For Burman, Black women were caught between struggles that were uneven equivalents, because white women had the greater privilege over Black men, who had a harder time intervening in the British cultural elite, while Black women fought for visibility in either context. Burman's citation and transformation of Linda Nochlin's famous question, 'Why Have There Been No Great Women Artists?', contested this invisibility and attested to the presence of great Black women artists despite the pedagogic, institutional and political barriers to their acknowledgement. Often, the little circles of the women's art movement in the 1970s had very few participants of colour, and struggles were often organised around a white-dominated understanding of women's oppression that was taken to be neutral. The marginalisation of Black women in these movements incorporated tokenism in white-dominated spaces, and so autonomous organising was important, even within the relatively diverse space of Brixton Art Gallery.

While the opportunity to exhibit was an important factor in such group work, these exhibitions were also about creating a space of reflection to see, as the organisers of *Mirror Reflecting Darkly* wrote, 'the diversity within the concept black women'.[25] The title of the exhibition extended this conceit: 'To exhibit the differing perspectives expressed through our art and to challenge the way we have been encouraged to associate black and white and its derivatives with the negative/marginal.'[26]

22 For more on Vicuña's time in London, see Giulia Lamoni, 'Diario de Vida: Cecilia Vicuña's artistic practice in London (1972–1975) (A letter to Carla Macchiavello)', *Revista de Estudios Globales y Arte Contemporáneo*, vol.5, no.1, 2017–18, pp.87–119, and Jo Applin, Catherine Spencer and Amy Tobin (eds.), *London Art Worlds: Mobile, Contingent, and Ephemeral Networks, 1960–1980*, University Park, PA, 2018.

23 Exhibition statement printed on the poster for *Mirror Reflecting Darkly: Mixed Media Art by Black Women*, 18 June – 6 July 1985, at Brixton Art Gallery, London, and in *Mirror Reflecting Darkly*, exh. cat., Brixton Art Gallery, London 1985; see https://brixton50.co.uk/mirror-reflecting-darkly/, accessed 8 Feb. 2023.

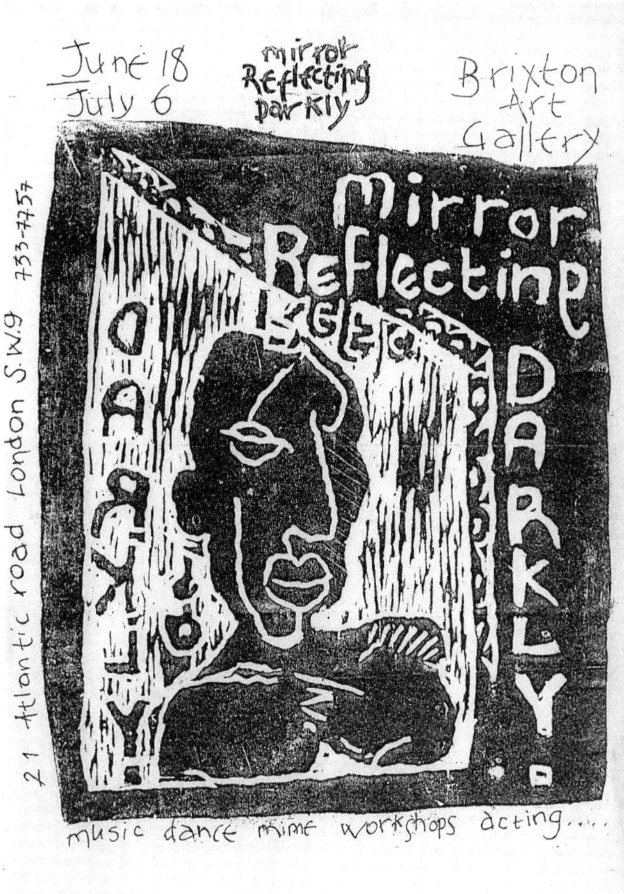

Poster for the exhibition *Mirror Reflecting Darkly*, Brixton Art Gallery, 1985.

With this, the exhibition was transformed into an arena for identification and recognition between Black women, in which they could see each other as artists and reflect on the great range and variety of issues, ideas, styles and media refracting Black women's experiences. The group extended beyond the limits of the exhibition, meeting regularly first under the name 'Mirror Reflecting Darkly' and then as 'Black Women in View'. A 1987 notice in the *Women Artists Slide Library Journal* describes their 'open access and flexible membership' policies, followed by a list of current participants: Carole Enahoro, Rita Keegan, Lorraine Luke, Ogu Nnachi, Susie Nottingham, Louise Owen, Elaine Somerville and Paula Williams.[27]

Keegan subsequently emphasised the importance of group work, saying it was the 'artist's responsibility' to be inclusive rather than exclusive because 'as a practitioner you don't work in isolation'.[28] To organise with others was to create a context. In the 1970s and 1980s it also meant working alternatively from – and sometimes against – the museums, galleries, clubs and commercial spaces that made up the established art world. These groups were not a stepping-stone to significance as defined art historically or monetarily, but a means of making and sharing art. Central to this, and particularly to Keegan's practice, was documentation. Posters, publications, photographs, videos and photocopied ephemera all served as traces of these activities, which may have been accompanied by artworks but also required different kinds of labour – from administration to bureaucracy and care – to sustain.[29] When Kate Walker lamented little circles and the reinvention of the wheel, perhaps we can detect her frustration with the limited impact of artists taking responsibility for their social and political part compared with the adulation of the 'Famous Feminist Few'. Keegan's words offer an important reminder that this is a matter of perspective. If we break with the idea of the isolated artist in their studio – a Victorian fantasy, Keegan says – and all the judgements around greatness, beauty, quality and apoliticism that follow from this, then what we determine to be artwork or who we consider an artist may change.[30] We can bring these relatively little circles of practice into view and recognise something far from diminutive in them. The variations on group work that emerged in relation (and antagonism) to women's liberation are just one strand in this alternative artistic ecosystem.

24 Chila Kumari Singh Burman, 'There Have Always Been Great Black Women Artists', *Women Artists Slide Library Journal*, no.15, Feb. 1987, pp.9–12; reprinted in Alice Correia (ed.), *What is Black Art?*, London 2022, pp.112–19.
25 *Mirror Reflecting Darkly*, exh. statement.
26 Ibid.
27 'Black Women in View', *Women Artists Slide Library Journal*, no.15, Feb. 1987, p.12.
28 Rita Keegan in *Journey to Here*, video produced for Genealogies of Black Curating in Britain, British Art Network, July 2021, https://britishartnetwork.org.uk/activity/conferences/genealogies-of-black-curating-in-britain-july-2021/rita-keegan-journey-to-here/, accessed 8 Feb. 2023. See also 'Actual Lives of Women Artists – Rita Keegan 1987: Painter Rita Keegan talks to Clare Rendell', *Women Artists Slide Library Journal*, no.19, 1987, pp.10–11.
29 See Ego Ahaiwe Sowinski, 'It Takes an Archival Village', and Naomi Pearce, 'Remember Me', in Keegan, Harle and Ahaiwe Sowinski 2021, pp.24–31 and 36–9.
30 Keegan in *Journey to Here*.

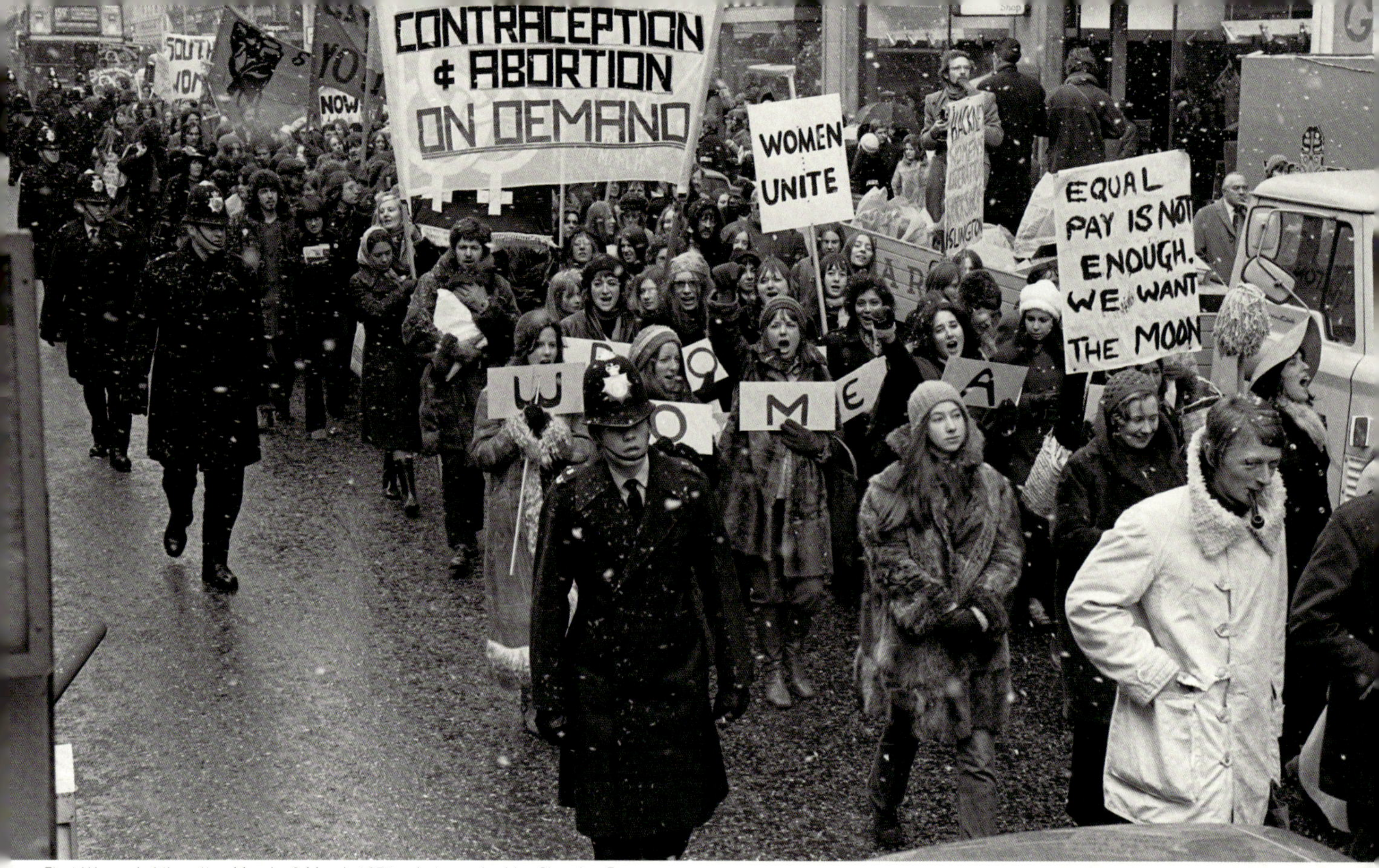

First Women's Liberation March, 6 March 1971, photographed by Chandan Fraser.

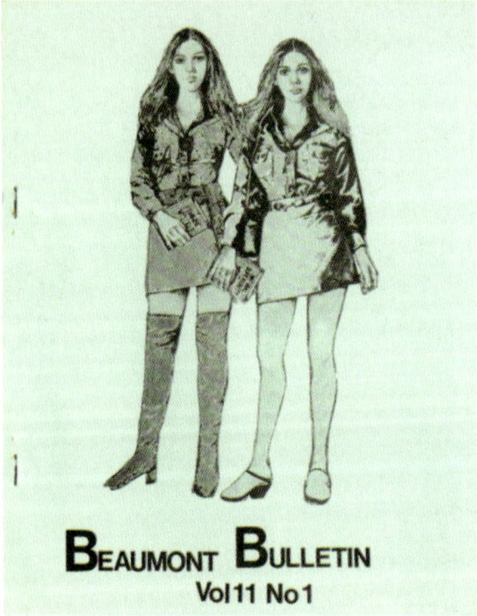

1

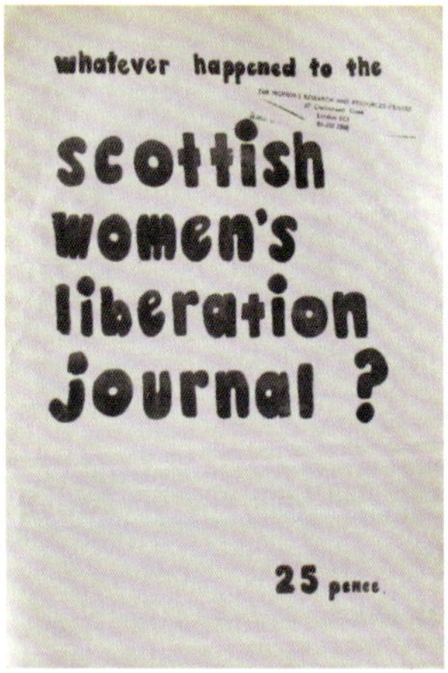

2

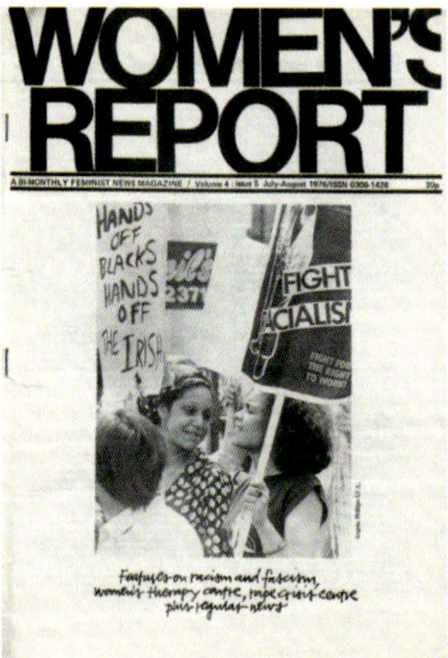

3

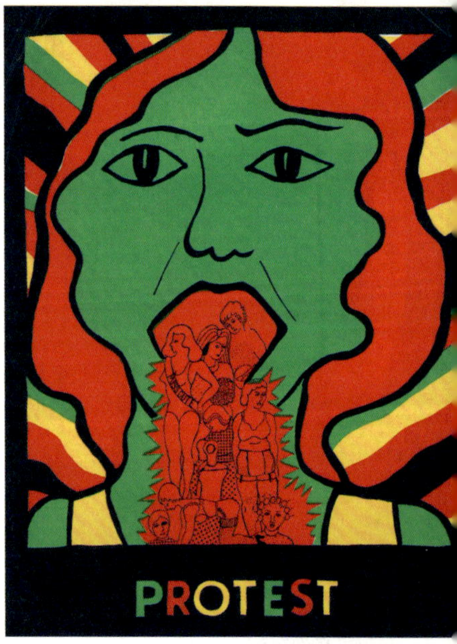

7

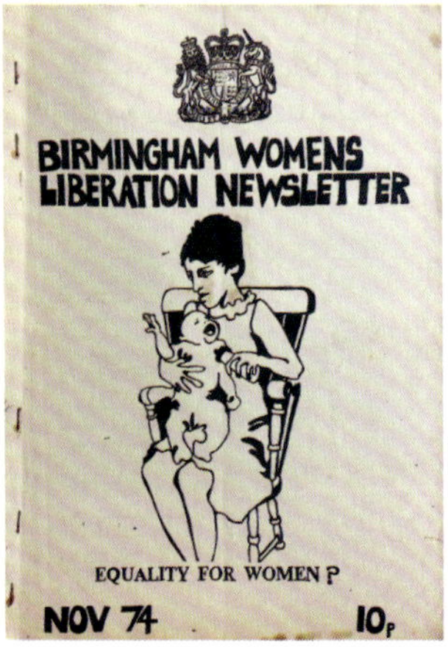

4

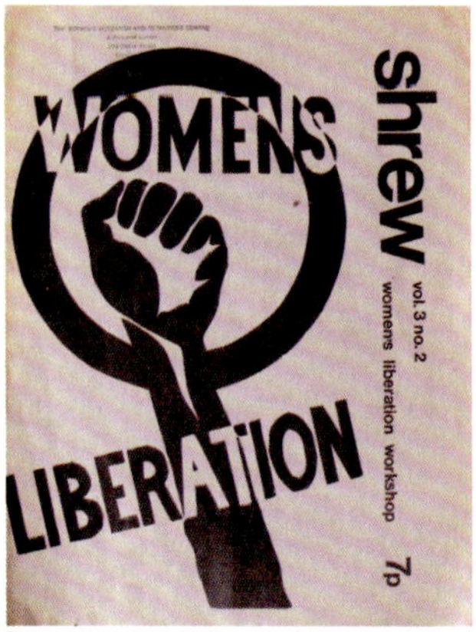

5

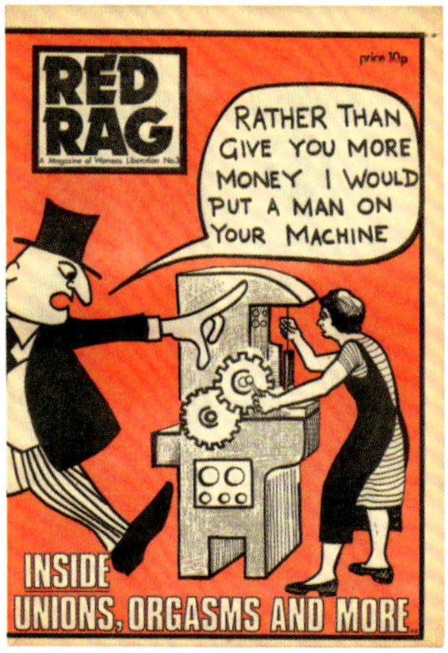

6

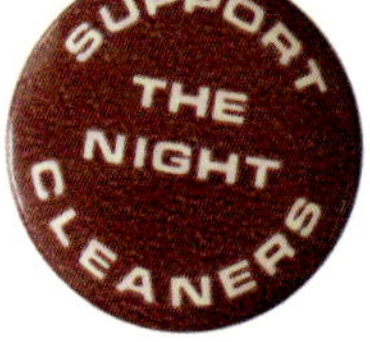

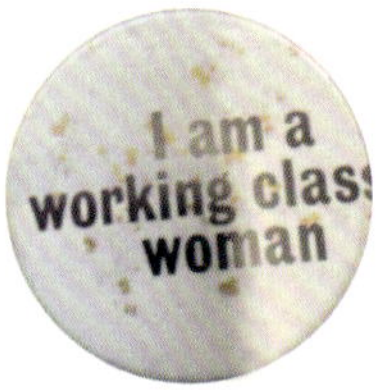

Rising with Fury: Women's March

On 6 March 1971, the first demonstration march of the British Women's Liberation Movement took place with 4,000 people marching through snow from Hyde Park to Trafalgar Square in London. Organisers and participants of the march ensured that spectators paid attention, or even joined them, by singing and dancing along to the deeply misogynistic song 'Keep Young and Beautiful', which was played from a gramophone being pushed in a pram. Other protesters dressed for a satirical beauty pageant as characters such as 'Mis Behave' and Mis Stress'. The march is documented in Sue Crockford's film *A Woman's Place* (p.81). This film and photographs by Chandan Fraser show some of the causes that women were fighting for and against, including: equal pay, free contraception and abortion on-demand, as well as free 24-hour nurseries.

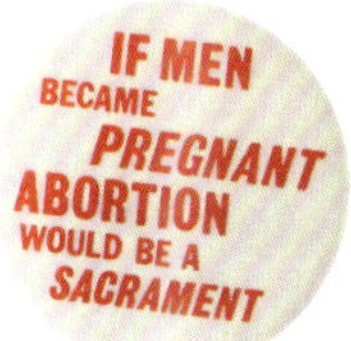

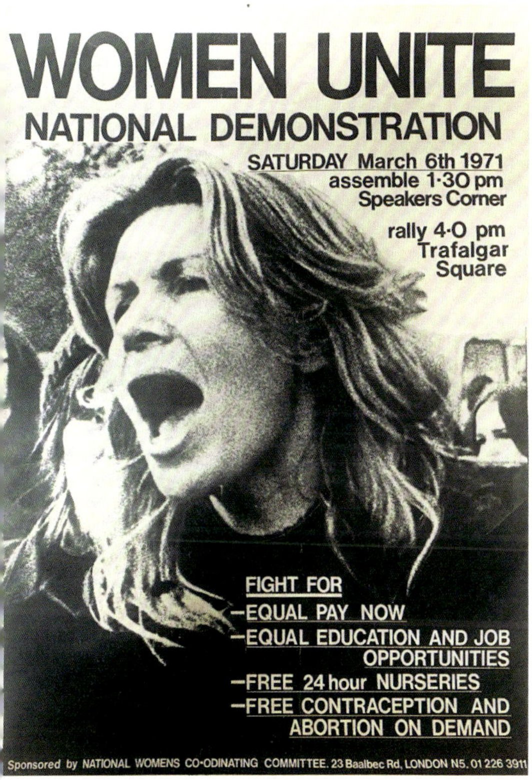
WOMEN UNITE
NATIONAL DEMONSTRATION
SATURDAY March 6th 1971
assemble 1·30 pm
Speakers Corner
rally 4·0 pm
Trafalgar
Square
FIGHT FOR
–EQUAL PAY NOW
–EQUAL EDUCATION AND JOB OPPORTUNITIES
–FREE 24 hour NURSERIES
–FREE CONTRACEPTION AND ABORTION ON DEMAND
Sponsored by NATIONAL WOMENS CO-ODINATING COMMITTEE. 23 Baalbec Rd, LONDON N5. 01 226 3911

8

1 *Beaumont Bulletin*, no.1. First published in 1970.
2 *Scottish Women's Liberation Journal?*, date unknown.
3 *Women's Report*, vol.4, no.5, July–August 1976. Active between 1972 and 1979, the *Women's Report* compiled news reports on health, economics, social issues, law and work that were relevant to women. It was run by a collective of women, including Anna Coote, Mandy Merck, Angela Phillips, Pat Kahn, Diana Kahn, Jill Rakusen and Griselda Pollock.
4 *Birmingham Women's Liberation Newsletter*, November 1974.
5 *Shrew*, publication of the Women's Liberation Workshop, vol.3, no.2, 1971.
6 *Red Rag*, magazine produced by a Marxist collective in the Women's Liberation Movement between 1972 and 1980.
7 See Red Women's Workshop *Protest* 1974. Screenprint on paper 65 × 51.
8 Poster for the Women's March on 6 March 1971.
9 *Women Artists Newsletter*, no,4, date unknown.
10 *Shrew*, publication of the Women's Liberation Workshop, vol.3, no.9, December 1971.

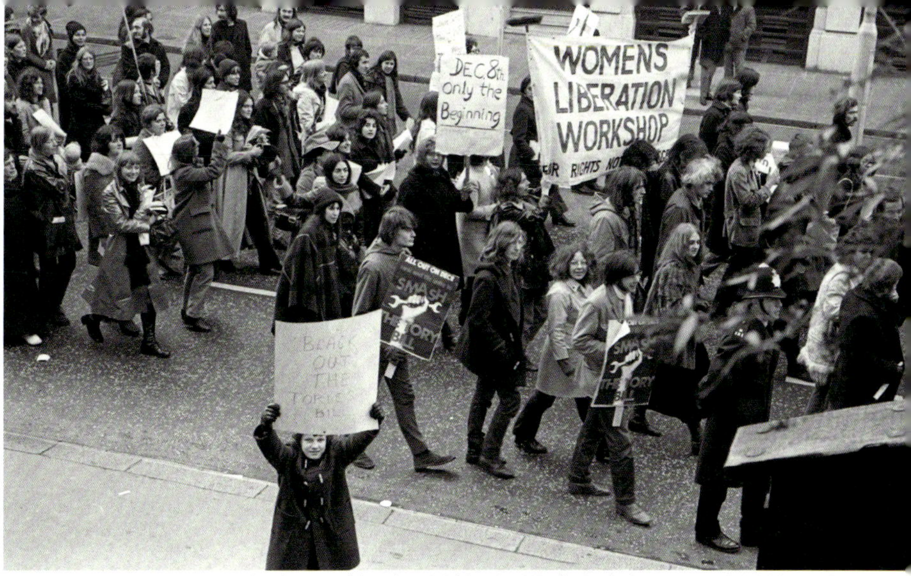

Women's Liberation March, 6 March 1971 (above) and 8 March 1971 (below). An estimated 4,000 people marched from Hyde Park to Trafalgar Square in London. Photographed by Chandan Fraser.

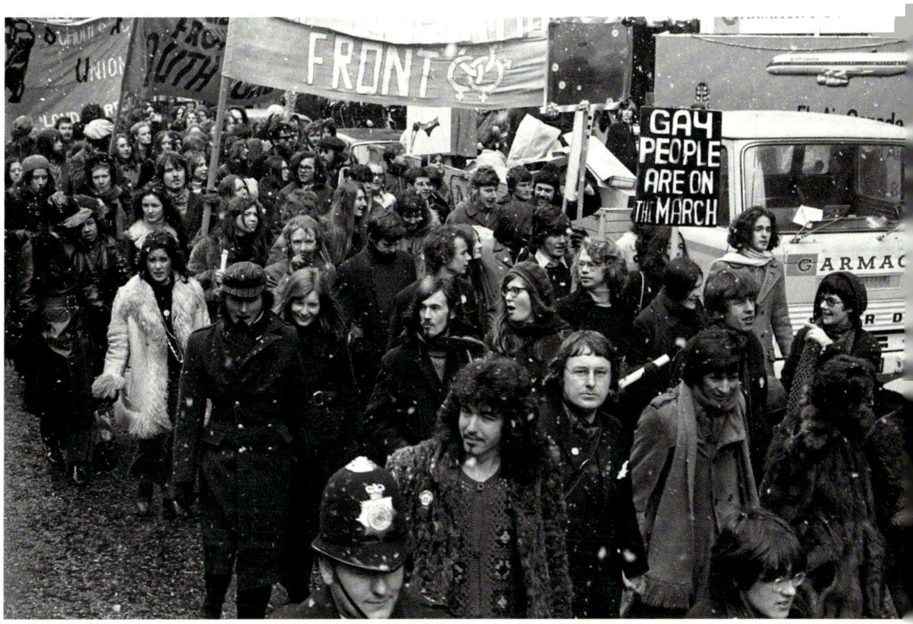

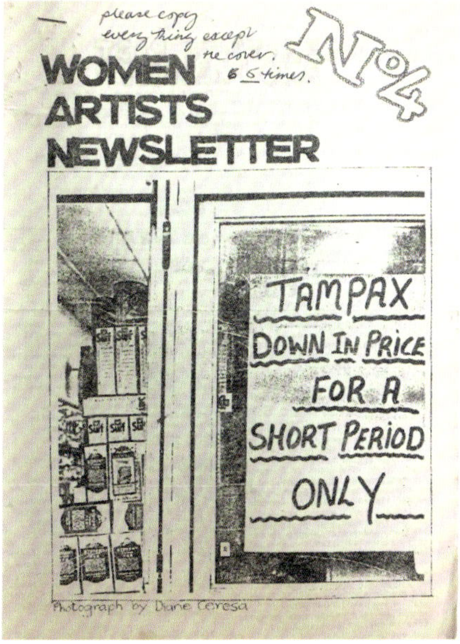

9

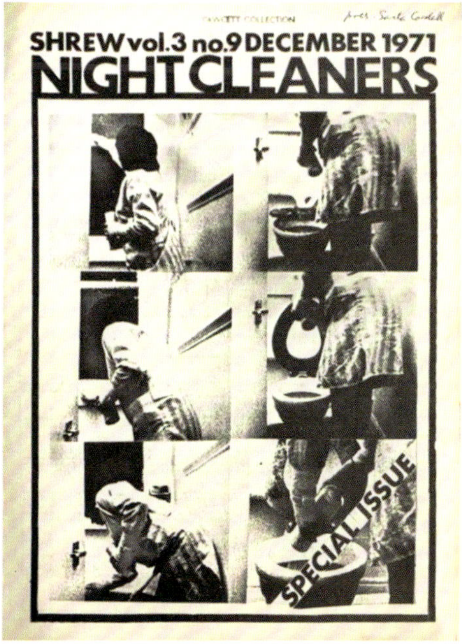

10

THE BLACK WOMEN'S MOVEMENT: FIGHTING ON ALL FRONTS

STELLA DADZIE

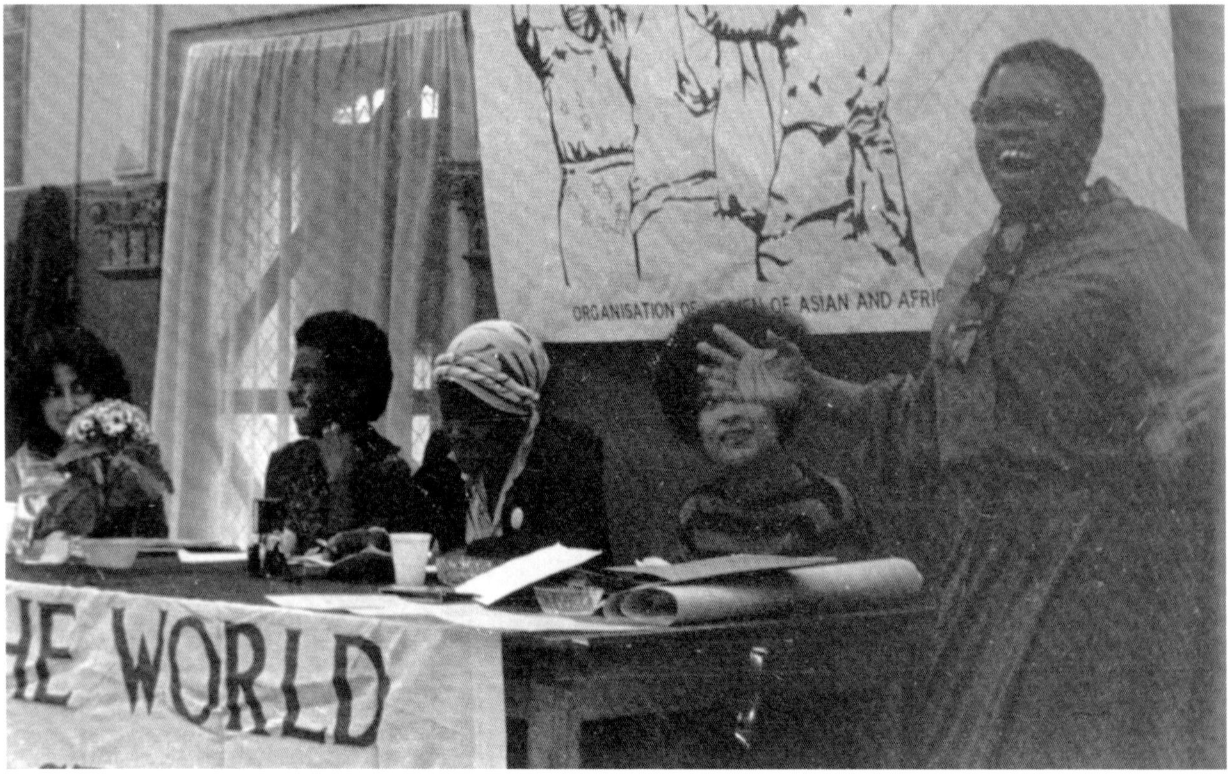

Here and opposite: The First National Black Women's Conference, Abeng Centre, Brixton, London 1979.

No one would disagree that the first National Women's Liberation Conference, held in Oxford in 1970, was an important milestone in the history of British feminism. But for Black British women, our watershed moment came a few years later at a conference in 1979, when around two hundred women of African, Caribbean and Asian descent converged on the Abeng Centre, just a stone's throw from Brixton Police Station. The contrast in venues speaks volumes.

The first National Black Women's Conference, set up by the Organisation of Women of African and Asian Descent (OWAAD),[1] was the culmination of months of hard work. With no social media, no mobile phones, no email, we relied solely on our existing networks, spreading details of the upcoming event via word of mouth. The organisers had jobs, children, studies or other commitments, all of which had to be juggled. We had no premises, no workers, no sponsors, no funding; everything was done on a shoestring, yet none of these obstacles deterred us in our determination to make it happen.

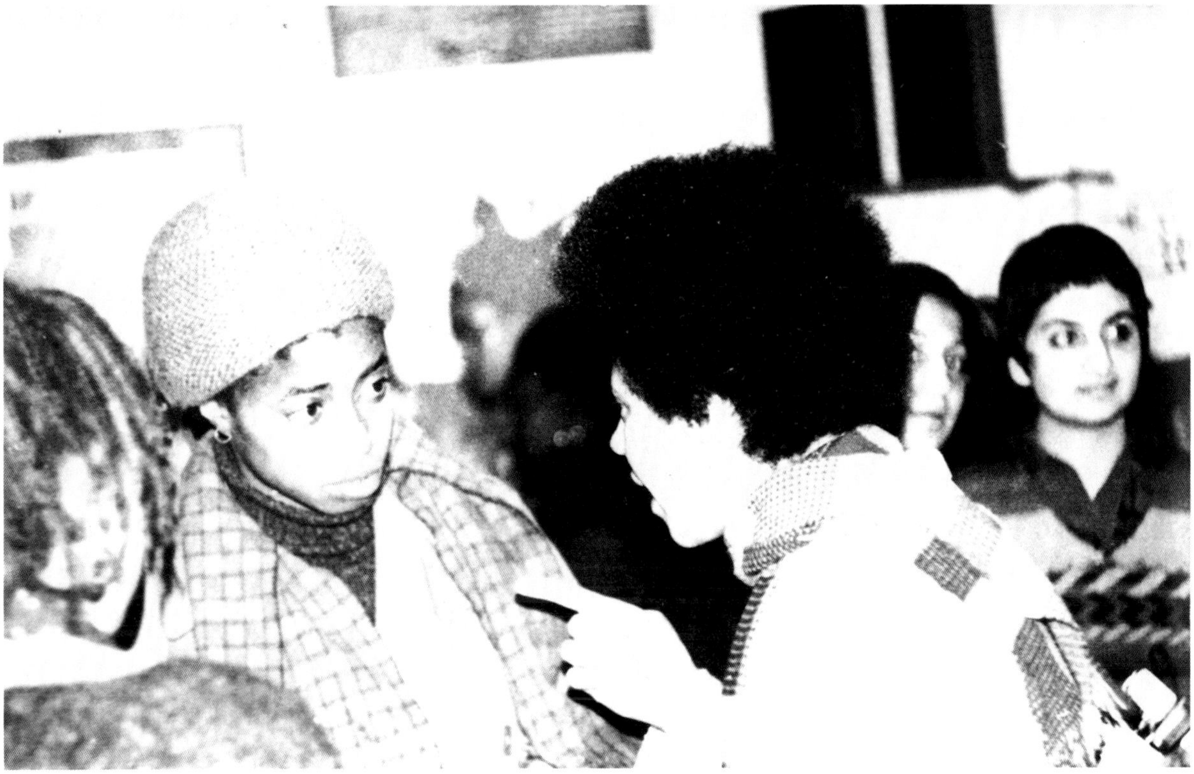

Those who attended remember the event as a hugely empowering experience, not least because it was the first time most of us had seen so many Black and Brown women gathered together under one roof. Asian sisters were in a minority in those early days when we were still forging links, yet they felt it too. As we listened to speeches and poetry, took part in discussion groups or browsed the bookstalls, we felt safe and strong and connected. During the plenary sessions, we explored the issues that mattered to us, with our experiences of education, employment and the welfare state high on the agenda. During the breaks, we played Judy Mowatt's 'Black Woman' on a continuous loop. '*Black woman, ooh, black woman ... Don't give up now, Just pray for strength now ... I know you've struggled long, To you I dedicate my song.*'[2] With our focus on building the strength to fight back, it seemed like the perfect sound track.

1 For more information about OWAAD, see chapter 4, 'Chain Reactions' in Beverley Bryan, Stella Dadzie, Suzanne Scafe, *The Heart of the Race: Black Women's Lives in Britain*, London 2018. The Black Cultural Archives in Brixton also holds many of OWAAD's original papers.
2 'Black Woman' by Judy Mowatt (Ashandan Records, 1979).

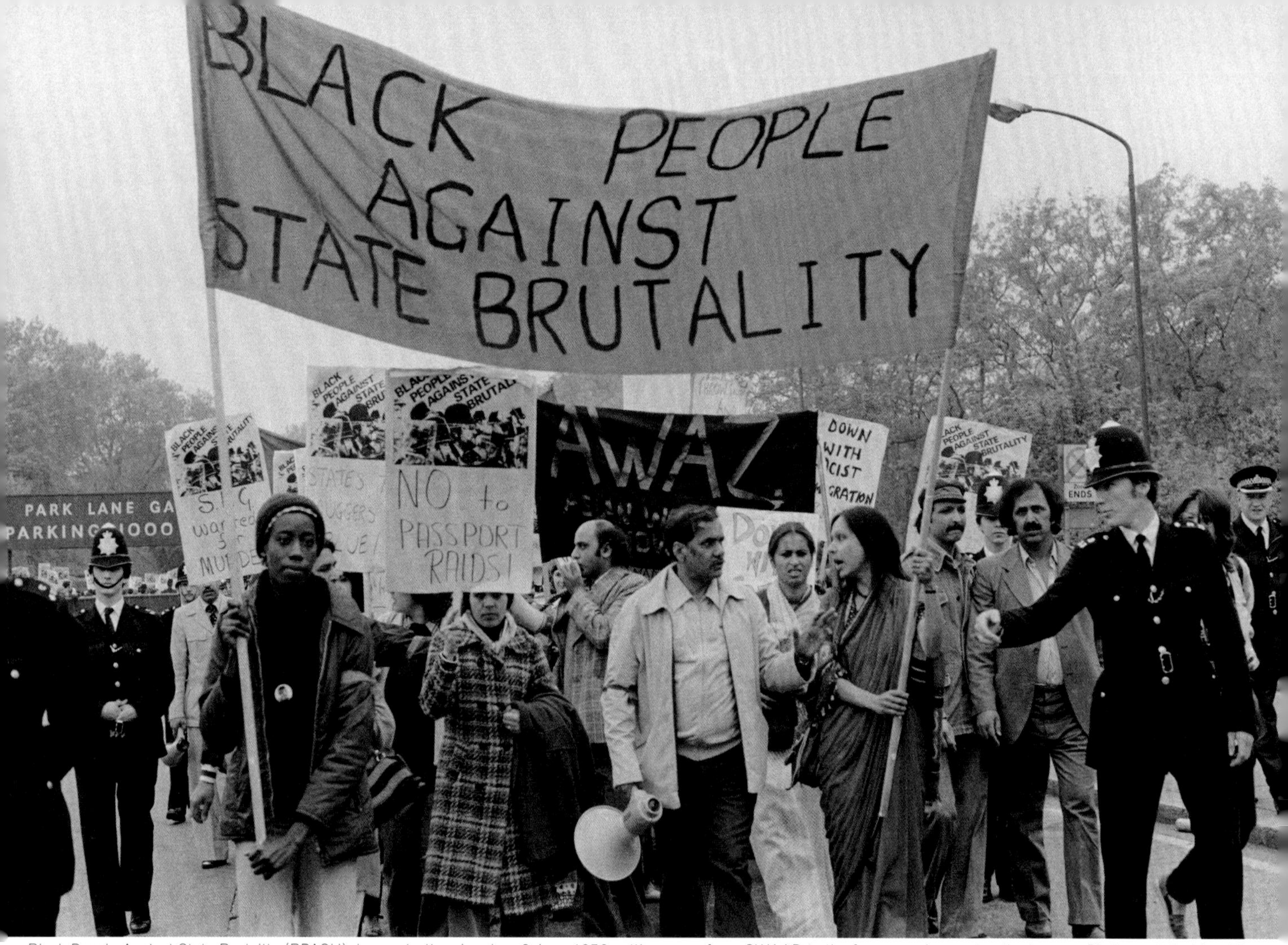

Black People Against State Brutality (BPASH) demonstration, London, 3 June 1979, with women from OWAAD in the foreground, carrying the banner. Photograph by Vron Ware.

The context of this historic event is worth recalling. The 1960s had spawned the rise of the US civil rights movement, along with its more militant expression, Black Power. Across the African continent, people were taking up arms in the fight to end apartheid or remove the yoke of decades of colonial rule. By the mid-1970s these struggles for Black liberation had witnessed a groundswell of support here in Britain. We'd seen our heroes and she-roes murdered, imprisoned or silenced. We had followed the marches, supported the boycotts and the protests, sent messages of solidarity. When Nelson Mandela was imprisoned for life, we joined the demonstrations. When Angela Davis was thrown into jail on a trumped-up charge, we supported the campaign to free her.[3] Some of us ditched the hot curling tongs and adopted her Afro hairstyle, which we wore as a proud statement – a visual declaration that we felt comfortable, at last, in our own skin.

Culturally, this sea-change was palpable. At our social gatherings, we danced and sang to music that celebrated these developments, absorbing its messages of Black pride and self-love – Nina Simone's 'Young, Gifted and Black', James Brown's 'Say It Loud, I'm Black and I'm Proud'. The demand for civil rights in America spoke to our experience here, but it had implications for people of African descent across the diaspora. Soul music articulated a new confidence, a new optimism: we could feel it in our bones. At blues parties and house parties, sound systems popularised the radical lyrics of reggae artists, bringing these messages home with a shuddering

3 When a gun allegedly belonging to Angela Davis was used in a raid on a courtroom, she was arrested and charged with conspiracy to commit murder. The campaign to free her spread far and wide, popularising the iconic image of her Afro. Later acquitted of all charges, she remains a vocal advocate of Black feminism. A powerful speaker and the author of numerous books, she continues to inspire Black women to this day.

bass, in a language we understood. *Babylon-a-go-burn. Here to stay, here to fight. No justice, no peace.*

Here in Britain, we had our own civil rights struggles to contend with. The offensive signs in landlords' windows – 'no Blacks, no dogs, no Irish' – were still visible in some areas, and members of the National Front were out cracking skulls. In 1979, at an anti-fascist demonstration in Southall, the police were accused of doing the NF's work for them when activist Blair Peach was killed, allegedly through a blow from a truncheon. Relations with the police had already come to a head, leading to violent confron-tations at the Notting Hill Carnival three years earlier. Meanwhile, politicians made fiery speeches about sending us all back to where we came from, ignoring the uncomfortable truth that many of us came from just up the road. Everywhere we turned, we found ourselves under siege.

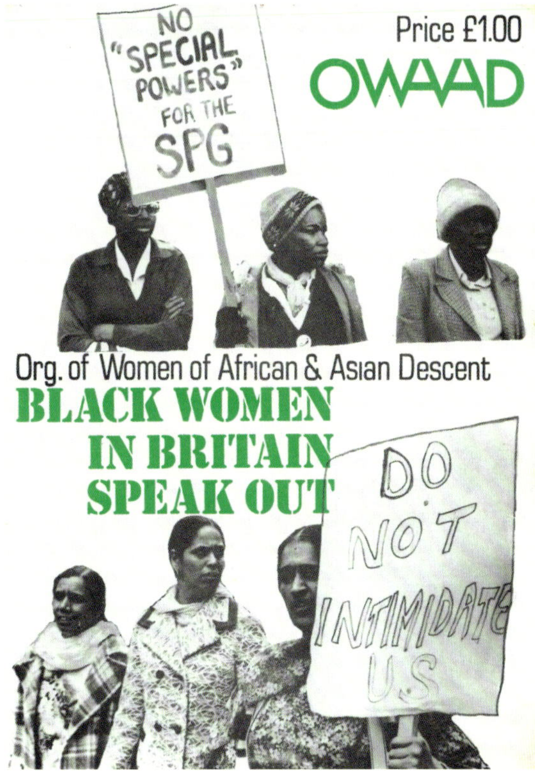

Front cover of OWAAD publication, c.1980.

The groups and campaigns that sprang up in our communities were a direct response to these realities. Women often formed caucuses within them, either to ensure our focus or our sanity. We were the note-takers and the tea-makers, whose contribution went largely unnoticed and whose priorities were often dismissed as secondary. Sisterhood in those male-dominated groups was beginning to make more and more sense. We had issues of our own and we wanted them addressed.

This was the precursor – the small, incremental steps that led us to something more defined and coherent. It was a gradual yet formative process. Throughout the 1970s, at the risk of being accused of 'splitting the struggle', Black women began forming groups wherever the need arose. In south London, members of the Brixton Black Women's Group started meeting as early as 1973, after some of its founder members grew tired of all the male posturing. We had Southall Black Sisters in west London; the United Black Women's Action Group in Tottenham; the Simba Black Women's Group in Woolwich; the Manchester Black Women's Co-operative (later re-named the Abasindi Co-operative) – all part of a growing network of Black women activists and community organisers who were fed up to the back teeth with the negative impact on our lives of race, sex and class oppression. OWAAD, formed as an umbrella organisation in 1978, brought these groups together with the aim of giving Black women a collective voice.

We had much to give voice to. As the members or offspring of that first generation of post-war immigrants who had arrived in the 1950s and 60s, some of us were here by invitation, lured by the promise of jobs and 'streets paved with gold'. Other women had arrived more recently, due to Africanisation policies that had led to a wave of expulsions – Asian sisters, born and bred in East Africa, who had experienced at first hand the life-shattering consequences of 'divide and rule'. Mixed-race women like myself had at least one parent whose family had lived in this country for generations. How we came to be here didn't seem to matter. We were all in it together.

To us, 'Black' was a political term, encompassing anyone who experienced racism. We recognised that, whatever our roots, African, Caribbean and Asian women shared a common experience of second-class citizenship. It began in the classroom with the casual racism of teachers, and continued through into the workplace or the dole office, the doctor's surgery, the housing office, the police station, the street and beyond. As women, we also had to contend with sexism and misogyny – the double day, the lack of maternity rights, forced marriages, domestic violence, and so much else besides. Cultural differences or sexual orientation may have shaped our experience, yet everyone had a story we could relate to.

We organised in the spirit of sisterhood, but our focus was never confined solely to feminist demands. In a context where economic disadvantage was almost a given, Black women mostly saw racism as the defining issue. But as women we had a uniquely gendered experience – one that placed us in the vanguard of campaigns and spontaneous protests, because we so often bore the brunt of the stereotypes and assumptions that blighted so many lives. When we took those issues of race and class and examined them through the prism of gender, it gave us a whole new perspective.

Through its conferences, newsletters and study days, OWAAD succeeded in casting a spotlight on the different ways race, class and gender inequalities impacted on Black women's lives – the 'SUS' law, for example, which allowed the police to arrest us simply on suspicion that we were *about* to commit a crime.[4] Or virginity testing, which gave immigration officers licence to insist on physical checks to determine whether would-be Asian brides entering this country were bona fide virgins. We campaigned against immigration laws that were splitting our families. We campaigned against the trialling of Depo-Provera, an injectable contraceptive which saw disproportionate numbers of Black and working-class women used as guinea pigs. We campaigned against unexplained deaths in police custody, against the miseducation of our kids, the criminalisation of our youth and the ghettoization of our communities. The list goes on and on.

Mothers, aunties, daughters, lovers – one way or another, all of us felt it. The many casualties deserve more than a footnote in the long and bitter struggle for our basic human rights – the right to family life, the right to a fair trial, the right to life. In 1976 Anwar Ditta, a British Pakistani woman, fought a lengthy campaign for the right to have her three young children join her here, a fight she eventually won thanks to huge community support. That same year, Jayaben Desai, a Gujarati woman, would become the face of Grunwick during a protracted two-year strike that mobilised her fellow Asian women workers and exposed trade union racism. Cynthia Jarrett died of a heart attack following a police raid on her home in July 1985, sparking the uprising on Broadwater Farm that resulted in the death of PC Blakelock. Cherry Groce, another African-Caribbean woman, was shot during a police raid on her home three months later, sparking the so-called 'Brixton riots'. Confined to a wheelchair, she died several years later as a result of her injuries.

Fast forward into the 1990s and the toll continued. The Jamaican mother Joy Gardner, here as a mature student, was asphyxiated when she was bound and gagged with thirteen feet of tape in a botched deportation attempt in 1993. That same year, Doreen Lawrence had to bury her seventeen-year-old son Stephen after a violent racist attack at a bus stop in Eltham. Her vocal criticism of the way the police handled the subsequent investigation resulted in Lord MacPherson's

4 A power dating back to the 1824 Vagrancy Act, which often led to arbitrary arrest.

5 Many of the responses described relied on women mobilising in their local groups or communities. For example, sisters from Simba were actively involved in supporting the families of victims and survivors of the New Cross Fire, and mobilising the community to take part in the Black People's Day of Action.

6 A collection of articles and papers produced by the Brixton Black Women's Group (BWG), was edited by Jade Bentil-Ojo, and published in *Speak Out: A Brixton Black Women's Group Reader*, London 2023. The book confirms the breadth and scope of some of these discussions. Members of Brixton BWG – women like Gerlin Bean, Olive Morris, Gail Lewis and Beverley Bryan – had a significant influence on OWAAD's politics and played a central role.

7 The term 'womanist' was coined by the American author-activist Alice Walker in 1982, in her book *In Search of Our Mothers' Gardens*.

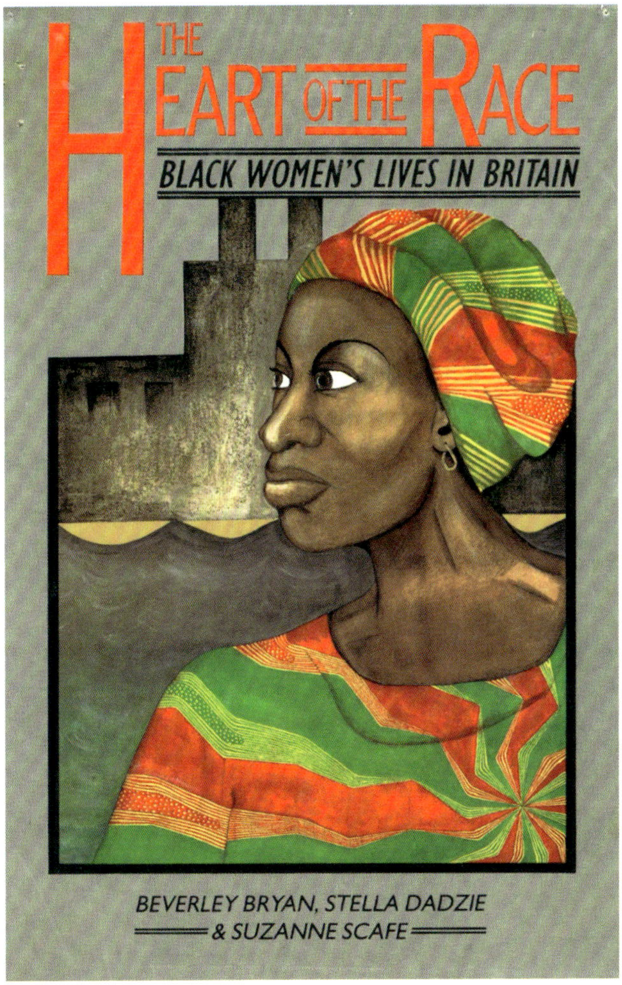

The Heart of the Race: Black Women's Lives in Britain, first edition, published by Virago in 1985.

landmark enquiry into institutional racism. Subsequent decades would reveal more of the same. After centuries of struggle, Black women remain on the front line.

Back in the 1970s and 80s, we responded with outrage, often in response to similar atrocities involving Black men. The deaths of thirteen Black children in a suspected arson attack at a house party in New Cross saw the largest demonstration of Black people this country had ever seen.[5] But demonstrations, sit-ins and spontaneous gatherings outside police stations were only part of the story. We also subscribed to a shared vision – the belief that we could help build a better society for our children. It is no coincidence that Black women were such key players in the Supplementary School movement, which offered an alternative to the Eurocentric curriculum they were taught in schools. Nor is it a coincidence that so many Black women found themselves embroiled in battles for employment rights at work, better childcare provision or decent housing. Every one of these issues impacted directly on our lives, sometimes with fatal results.

We were often required to respond in the moment – an arbitrary arrest, an unfair suspension from school, a groundless deportation – yet our responses could not be described as simply reactive. Many of OWAAD's members came armed with a socialist-feminist vision, the fruits of countless hours spent poring over key texts in study groups. We discussed Marxism and African socialism. We discussed imperialism, neo-colonialism, Garveyism and pan-Africanism. We discussed racism, sexism, chauvinism, lesbianism, womanism, feminism – a plethora of -isms, all of which got thrown into the mix when it came to articulating our political aspirations. The result was a uniquely Black female politics, grounded not only in our experiences here in Britain but also in our understanding of the legacies of slavery, colonialism and empire.[6]

This, above everything else, marked us out as different from the generic women's movement. It was Alice Walker who declared that 'Womanist is to feminist as purple is to lavender', and there were those who went on to embrace the term 'womanist' to signify this difference.[7] Black women were clear from the outset that our struggles could not be confined solely to gender inequality and patriarchy. To demand equal pay was all very well, but since we were typically confined to the lowest, most menial jobs, for us the starting point had to be the right to a living wage. To call for a woman's right to choose was fine by us too, but only if the demand took account of centuries of genocide, enforced breeding and unwanted sterilisations, denying us not only the right to abortion but also the right to have or keep our children. There was always a qualification, always a 'yes, but ...'. As for 'our bodies, ourselves', only an enlightened few grasped the importance of self-care or the need to rethink heteronormative assumptions about love, sexuality and marriage.

This is not to suggest that all Black women felt alienated. It's true, some dismissed the women's movement as too white, too middle-class, too self-absorbed, but others persevered, attempting to bring these critical perspectives into focus. We were present at every major conference, albeit in small numbers, yet we often felt unheard or unseen. Meanwhile, back in our own communities, we faced allegations that women who organised separately from men were 'just a bunch of lesbians'. As we grappled with notions of what it meant to be a feminist, some rejected the label out of hand. Others chose to qualify it. We were *Black* feminists. There's a difference.

Not all white women were blithely unaware of our concerns, far from it. Groups like Women Against Imperialism, for example, and women who supported the Chilean Solidarity Campaign, the Anti-Apartheid Movement or the liberation struggles waging across Africa were important allies. They knew that race, class and gender intersected. They understood the impact on the rest of the world of events in the so-called West, and vice versa. Like us, they were able to join the dots. Our allegiances and relationships with white feminists were complex and nuanced. Some got it, others didn't, yet it was rarely a straightforward case of Black or white.

OWAAD went on to hold three more national conferences, the last in 1982. The reasons for its eventual demise are hard to pinpoint. Some blame the dominance of African-Caribbean women in an organisation committed to African–Asian unity; others point to a failure to pay more attention to issues of gender and sexuality. For its founding members, there were constraints common to all women – the pull of young families or embryonic careers, which made this level of activism hard to sustain. Some women chose to return to Africa or the Caribbean to continue the struggle there. Others chose to refocus their energies – typically defence campaigns in the wake of the 1981 uprisings. Theories abound as to why the organisation folded, yet this much is undeniable: OWAAD was of its time. Like the civil rights movement, or more recently Black Lives Matter, OWAAD arose when it was needed. Its activists went on to fight other battles, but Black feminism didn't die. We took what we had gained from the experience into our homes, our workplaces, our communities and subsequent campaigns. OWAAD's most enduring legacy is that its message of Black female empowerment continues to resonate to this day.

Another of OWAAD's abiding legacies was the publication of *The Heart of the Race: Black Women's Lives in Britain* in 1985. Republished by Verso Books in 2018 as a feminist classic, it provides a permanent record of these events, using first-person narratives and analysis to explore the social and historical context out of which they arose. The image on its front cover, which I painted in 1984, depicts the African woman's journey, via the the turquoise seas of the Caribbean to the grey, unwelcoming shores of the 'mother country'. Her red, gold and green attire symbolises the historical baggage she carried with her – red for our bloodshed, gold for our stolen wealth, green for our stolen land. Just one example of the many ways Black feminist activism inspired or nurtured our creative spirit.

Black women were painting, writing, singing, dancing or finding other creative outlets throughout this period. Writers like Bernardine Evaristo and visual artists like Sonia Boyce forged their skills in a crucible that was distinctly Black and female. Our influences came from across the diaspora. From America's inner cities to the ghettoes of Kingston, Jamaica. From the townships of South Africa to the streets of Brixton, Toxteth or Solihull. Our creative artists have always found ways to give expression to our lived realities, revealing the soft underbelly of life in the margins, highlighting the pain and the joy.

However we chose to engage with the challenges, wherever we pitched our energies, Black women's creativity and activism have left an indelible mark. The official story of the women's movement often overlooks our contribution. To be frank, we've grown used to being airbrushed out of the picture. This exhibition confirms that Black women – or if you prefer, women of colour – were present at every step of the creative journey.

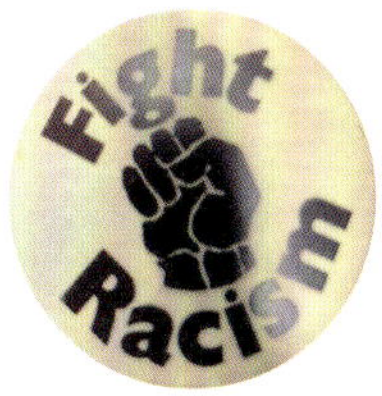

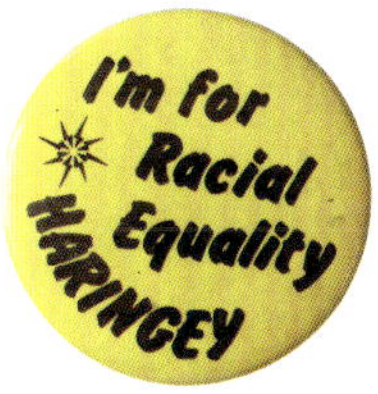

TOO MUCH TO DREAM?

TRANS PEOPLE AND THE ART OF THE 1970s AND 1980s

JULIET JACQUES

'The body is being used as an art language by an ever greater number of contemporary painters and sculptors ... who use widely differing art techniques, and who come from a variety of cultural and intellectual backgrounds'. So wrote Lea Vergine in her introduction to *The Body as Language*, first published in Italian in 1974.[1] A foundational critical study of the 'body art' movement of the 1960s and early 1970s, Vergine's original publication focused mostly on men; her case studies included Rebecca Horn, Joan Jonas, Gina Pane and just a handful of other women, barely anyone (with the notable exception of Gilbert & George) who might be identified as gay or lesbian, and no one who was openly transgender or transsexual. That last omission is unsurprising: only a tiny number of artists who might have identified as such had emerged by the mid-1970s. Those few who did express discomfort with being assigned a gender, such as French writer/artist Claude Cahun (who moved to Jersey in 1937) or British painter Gluck, did not describe themselves using terms like 'transvestite' or 'transsexual', and did not make the kind of 'body art' that Vergine anthologised.

Not only were openly trans artists not present within the body art movement, but they were also a conspicuous absence from British art of the 1970s and 1980s. This was a time when transsexual women such as actress/model April Ashley and travel writer Jan Morris were making their mark on British society. The BBC was broadcasting documentaries such as *A Change of Sex* 1979–80, which followed catering manager and performer Julia Grant through her transition, and one-off TV dramas such as *Even Solomon* 1979, about a young transsexual woman coming out to her mother and colleagues. Transsexual people were on the fringes of emerging feminist and gay/lesbian rights movements, and composers Wendy Carlos and Angela Morley were scoring high-profile films. In artistic works of the time, however, trans people were usually the subjects of photographers, be it Lisetta Carmi, Pierre Molinier or Nan Goldin, or starring in improvised, underground films by directors such as Jack Smith or Andy Warhol (with his trans 'superstars' Jackie Curtis, Candy Darling and Holly Woodlawn all appearing in Paul Morrissey's film *Women in Revolt* in 1971). In all these cases, none of them British, trans people weren't in control of their own representations, despite art being the perfect forum for exactly that and the art world traditionally being welcoming to outsiders. Why not?

Soon after the Second World War, transsexual people became a media phenomenon in which a handful of individuals came out to or were outed by the press – famously, ex-GI Christine Jorgensen, who became a global sensation after featuring in the *New York Daily Times* in 1952, but also Ashley, Roberta Cowell and Michael Dillon in the UK. During the 1960s they became an identifiable group, as sexologists codified the process of gender reassignment and set up Gender Identity Clinics (GICs) to manage their transitions, providing hormones and surgery to those few people who met their strict diagnostic criteria. In the US trans people formed communities, rioting in San Francisco's Tenderloin district over healthcare inequality and police raids on Compton's Cafeteria (their preferred hang-out) in August 1966, and playing an important role in the uprising at New York's Stonewall Inn in June 1969.[2]

1 'The Body as Language. Body Art and Like Stories', in Lea Vergine, *Body Art and Performance: The Body as Language*, 2nd edn, Milan 2000, p.7.
2 Screaming Queens', in Juliet Jacques, *Front Lines: Trans Journalism 2007–2021*, London 2022, p.161.

In the UK this happened slightly later, in the wake of the partial decriminalisation of homosexuality in 1967. Organisations such as the Beaumont Society (for heterosexual, cross-dressing men) and the Transsexual Action Group were formed in the early 1970s, along with transvestite/transsexual (TV/TS) support groups in London and Manchester; the first National Transvestite and Transsexual Conference was held in Leeds in 1974. The NHS Gender Identity Clinic was set up at Charing Cross Hospital in London in 1966; leading doctor John Randell's demands for transsexual women to conform to antiquated ideals of femininity became notorious among the community, especially after he featured, unnamed, as Julia Grant's domineering clinician in *A Change of Sex*.

Throughout the 1970s heated discussions took place in North American second-wave feminist groups about whether to allow transsexual women into women-only spaces and to let them be part of their organising. The decade ended with former nun Janice G. Raymond 'consolidat[ing] the many strands of anti-transgender [feminist] discourse into one grand narrative' in *The Transsexual Empire: The Making of the Modern She-Male*, published by the Women's Press in 1979.[3] Raymond characterised transsexuality as a plot, facilitated by the Gender Identity Clinics, to infiltrate feminist circles, calling it 'rape ... by deception' and concluding that 'the problem of transsexualism would best be served by mandating it out of existence'.[4] This treatment of trans people, and especially transsexual women, both by the GICs, who advised them to live in 'stealth' in their chosen genders and to keep their personal histories private, and by the transphobic elements of contemporary feminism, was not conducive to the emergence of trans people within boundary-pushing artistic and musical circles, some of which were closely aligned to feminist movements. While it is by no means indicative of their endorsement of such views, British feminist artist Linder, also lead singer of Mancunian post-punk band Ludus, introduced Smiths frontman Morrissey to Raymond's work,[5] and the liner notes for *The Mekons Honky Tonkin'*, a 1987 LP by Leeds post-punk/country group The Mekons, included a quote from *The Transsexual Empire*.[6] (This, incidentally, was where I first heard of it.)

One of the few openly trans people on the British music and art scenes of the period, American singer Jayne County, wrote in her autobiography *Man Enough to be a Woman* that plenty of people around the punk scene (including Julie Burchill, who was later to write some of the UK's most notorious anti-trans opinion pieces) were welcoming to her when she identified as a cross-dressing boy, but 'when I got tits and started looking like a woman ... it bothered people'.[7] County recalled that: 'There was a distinct cooling of attitude, even among the fans ... Some of them even said, "You've betrayed your sex". The papers were saying things like, "This week we have another guess-what-sex-Wayne-County-is gig", and I didn't feel the need to explain myself.'[8]

Outrageous costumes and make-up were acceptable, even welcomed, when they set out to shock Middle England, as seemed to be the case with the glam rock movement, or as part of a queer counterculture centred around events such as Andrew Logan's Alternative Miss World, first held in 1972. But when County came out as transsexual, she was met with hostility and intrusive questions,

3 Susan Stryker, *Transgender History*, Berkeley, CA, 2008, p.105.
4 Ibid., p.109.
5 'Picture Piece: Morrissey by Linder', *Frieze*, no.84, June–Aug. 2004, https://www.frieze.com/article/picture-piece-morrissey-linder, accessed 30 Aug. 2022.
6 The Mekons, *The Mekons Honky Tonkin'* (LP, Sin Recordings, London, 1987).
7 Jayne County, *Man Enough to be a Woman*, London 2021, p.172.
8 Ibid.
9 'Returning to the *City of Lost Souls*', in Jacques 2022, pp.165–6.

as *Clockwork Orange* composer Wendy Carlos had been earlier in the decade. The handful of British reviews of the queer musical film County starred in after moving to Berlin, Rosa von Praunheim's *City of Lost Souls* 1983, give an indication of contemporary attitudes: the *Guardian* and the *Observer*, Britain's biggest liberal broadsheets, complained that it seemed 'calculated to upset a heterosexual audience' and sneered at it as 'A sort of transvestite/transsexual cabaret'.[9] Only Derek Malcolm made any attempt to sympathise with its 'quite ordinary' trans characters, who were mostly playing themselves, but his efforts to understand the challenges that trans people faced, and his open-mindedness towards their artistic expression, were sadly rare.[10]

These cultural barriers functioned to hinder the presence of many trans people in British public life. After the documentary *A Change of Sex* ended, Julia Grant did not remain a spokesperson for the trans 'community', small and fragmented as it was, and no one else volunteered or was asked to step forward in her place. Again, this is hardly surprising: in a pamphlet entitled 'Divided Sisterhood' 1980, published in response to Raymond, sociologist Carol Riddell wrote that there were 'a few hundred trans-sexuals' in the UK, and that 'there seem to be two trans-sexuals' in the British feminist movement.[11] Certainly, there was little sense of the emergence of trans people as an identifiable demographic, either as an organised force in gay and lesbian politics (as they were usually designated at the time) or in their own right.

The 1980s were a disaster for the UK's radical feminist movement, as the first female prime minister crushed the trade unions and wider British socialism. It was also an incredibly hard time for the gay and lesbian community, as the HIV/AIDS pandemic killed more than 12,000 people by 1996, many of whom were LGBT+.[12] In 1988, amid an anti-gay moral panic led by the tabloid press, Thatcher's government passed the Local Government Act, including the notorious and widely protested Section 28, outlawing the 'promotion of homosexuality' – and, in practice, anything associated with it, including transsexuality – by schools, libraries and other public bodies. In this climate the microscopic numbers of open, politically active trans people posited by Riddell in 1980 were unlikely to rise much higher, even allowing for the potential of the circumstances to radicalise them into action. Indeed, Christine Burns's historical essay collection *Trans Britain* looks at 1970s support groups and the establishment of the GIC at Charing Cross Hospital, but does not feature civil rights activism or cultural currents before the end of the decade, with contributors focusing on how they, as individuals, navigated it.

The first stirrings of a trans rights movement or cultural renaissance in the UK or in North America were not felt until the early 1990s, and when they were, most of its forerunners were from the US. Sandy Stone's response to Raymond, entitled 'The *Empire* Strikes Back: A Posttranssexual Manifesto', written in 1987, was published in the anthology *Body Guards: The Cultural Politics of Gender Ambiguity* in 1991, and shared online. Stone directly refuted

10 Ibid., p.166.
11 Carol Riddell, 'Divided Sisterhood: A Critical Review of Janice Raymond's *The Transsexual Empire*', in Susan Stryker and Stephen Whittle (eds.), *The Transgender Studies Reader*, London and New York 2006, p.145.
12 Matt Cook, '"Archives of Feeling": The AIDS Crisis in Britain 1987', *History Workshop Journal*, vol.83, no.1, Spring 2017, pp.51–78, https://eprints.bbk.ac.uk/id/eprint/17900/3/17900.pdf, accessed 30 Aug. 2022.

some of Raymond's arguments (prompted by Stone's employment as a sound engineer at the women-only Olivia Records), but she began with a critique of transsexual memoirs such as Jan Morris's *Conundrum* (1974), which, she argued, did not adequately explore the space between ideas of 'male' and 'female' as their authors must have experienced them. She then asserted that 'post-transsexual' people had to ignore the GICs' demands to hide their histories and constitute themselves 'as a *genre* – a set of embodied texts whose potential for *productive* disruption … has yet to be explored'.[13]

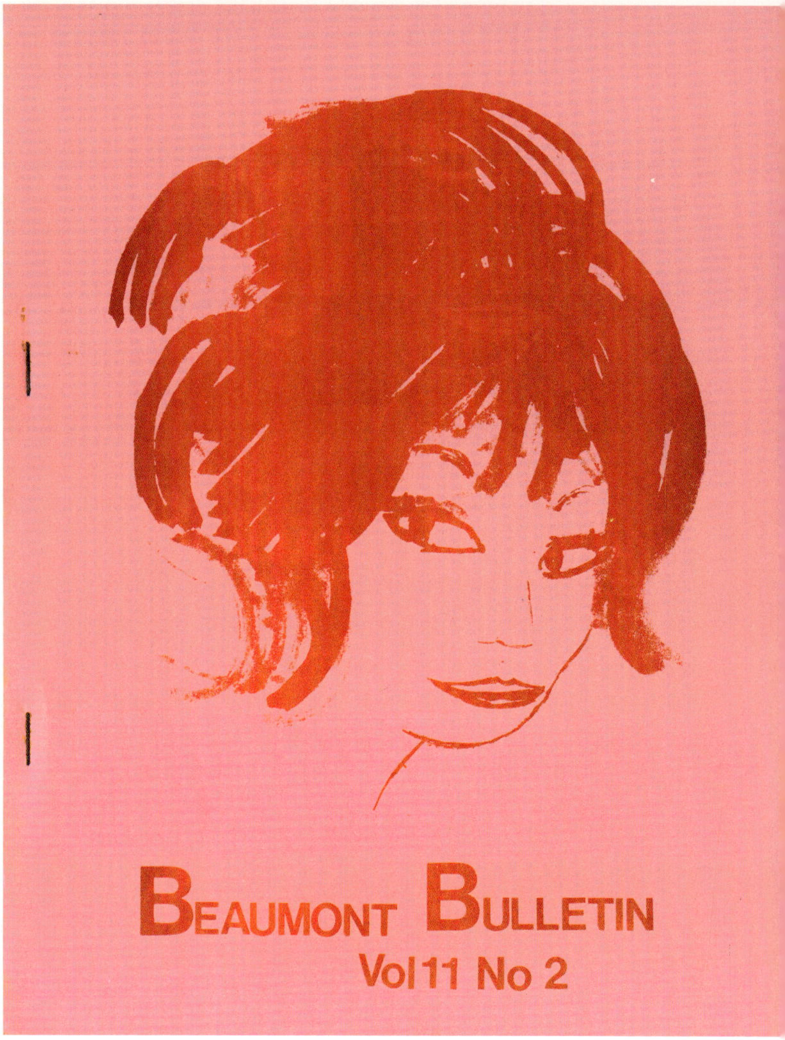

Beaumont Bulletin, vol.11, no.2. First published in 1970, the *Beaumont Bulletin* was the journal of the Beaumont Society, set up in 1966 to provide information and education on 'transvestism'. Today it is the UK's largest running support group for transgender people.

This call to arms was taken up by authors such as Kate Bornstein, Leslie Feinberg and Jack Halberstam, quickly turning into a sophisticated discourse that formed the basis of transgender studies. This led to a flourishing of different trans identities, as Stone has suggested, as well as a new wave of trans activism, academia and art on both sides of the Atlantic. However, the shared language and increasingly intertwined culture – even more so in the age of the internet and social media – has tended to mean North Americans have remained the dominant voices within each sector, as they were within the feminist and LGBT+ movements of the 1970s and 1980s, even if that gap has closed to some extent with the appearance of more British writers, actors, musicians and artists during the 2010s.

The progress made over the last few decades – however limited, faltering or frustrating – might have made it easier for artists from the 1970s or 1980s to come out as trans later in their lives, as Throbbing Gristle and Psychic TV musician Genesis P-Orridge did some years before dying in March 2020. I cannot think of, nor have I heard of, many other trans or non-binary artists whose works were not known in their lifetimes but were later rediscovered. One major exception is Erica Rutherford, who was born in Edinburgh in 1923, studied at the Slade School of Fine Art in London and transitioned after moving to Missouri in the mid-1970s, as documented in her autobiography *Nine Lives* (1993). Rutherford's rarely seen paintings from this period, which her widow calls her 'trans-hardedge series', chronicle her feelings of gender

13 Sandy Stone, 'The *Empire* Strikes Back: A Posttranssexual Manifesto', in Stryker and Whittle 2006, p.231.
14 Blake Morrison, 'Percy Kelly, the painter of hidden talent', *Guardian*, 25 February 2012, https://www.theguardian.com/artanddesign/2012/feb/24/percy-kelly-painter-hidden-talent, accessed 30 Aug. 2022.

dysphoria and her transition, often showing the artist in blue and red clothing with a fetishistic tinge. (pp.70–1) Stylistically, the paintings are a departure from her earlier abstract collages, clearly tuned into contemporary currents; their minimalistic use of primary colours and sharp lines recalling artists such as David Hockney and Bob Thompson. They could easily have been used as a cover for her book and remain striking examples of post-war graphic design; the knowledge that they were made by a trans artist adds an extra aesthetic layer that is not immediately obvious in their composition, and a compelling historical reason to explore her work further.

Rutherford's trans-hardedge series did not attract much attention during her lifetime, perhaps in part because she internalised the demand to live in 'stealth' that the GICs and wider society often made of transsexual people at the time. As for other artists whom we might put under the contemporary 'trans' umbrella, Percy Kelly, the cross-dressing painter who refused to sell works before dying in 1993, is one of the few to have garnered any coverage.[14] Body art and other performance-based forms tend not to throw up neglected artists later unearthed by historians – you really did have to be there – and I don't hold out much hope of trans painters, sculptors or filmmakers of the period coming to light. In any case, right now, the past is most important as a lesson. At a time when right-wing politicians are using anti-trans sentiment to shore up their crumbling support, with the two candidates in the 2022 Conservative leadership contest both promising to attack the community with new legislation akin to Section 28, implicitly or explicitly supported by 'gender critical' feminists who work in the same tradition as Janice Raymond, it is incumbent upon trans people to make art that will illuminate our lives and showcase our talents – and upon galleries and museums to support us.

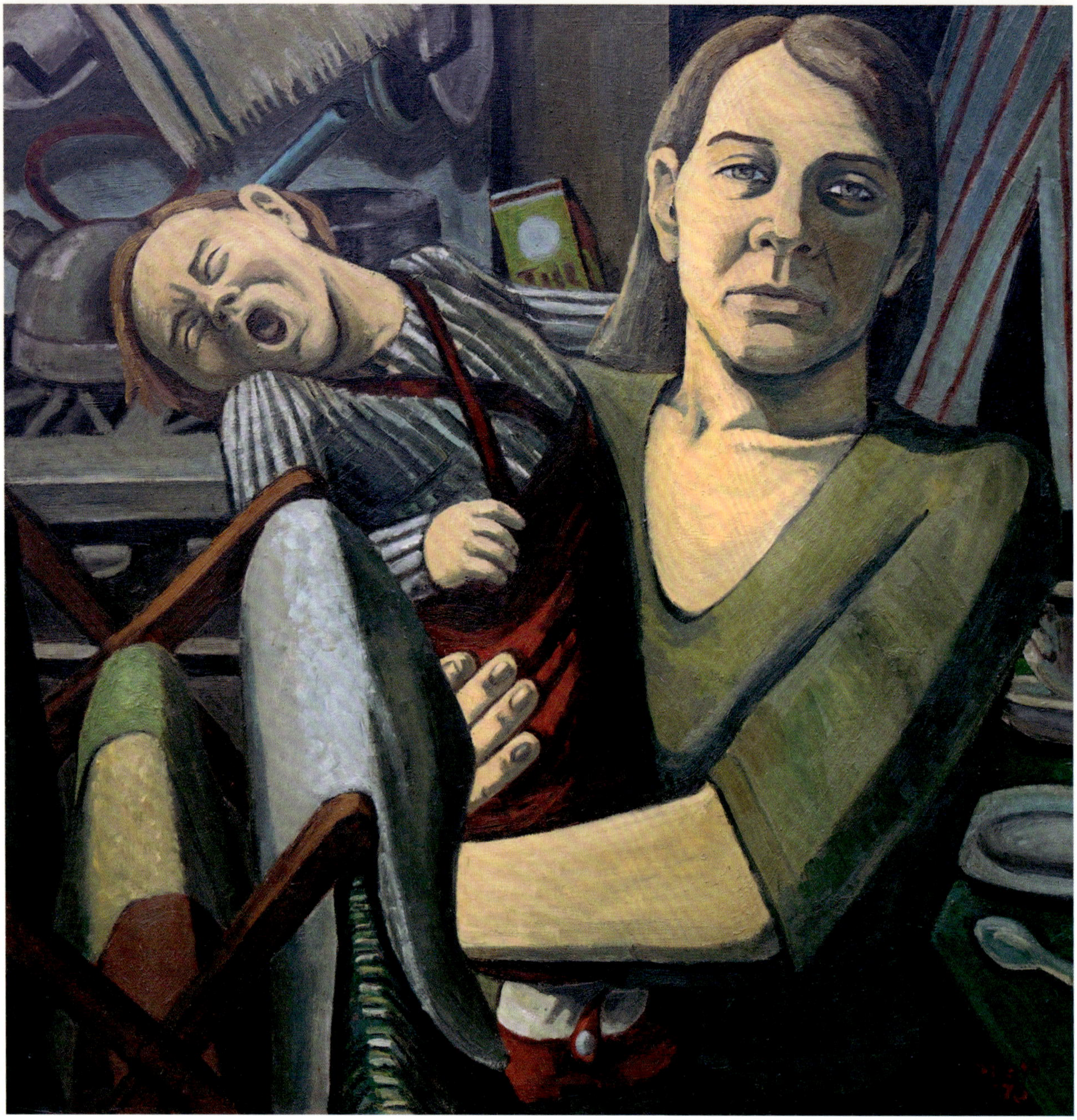

Mother and Child at Breaking Point 1970. Oil paint on board 91.5 × 91.5

MAUREEN SCOTT

Maureen Scott was born in Coventry in 1940. She studied fine art at Plymouth College of Art in the early 1960s, moving on in the 1970s to Goldsmiths College and Saint Martin's School of Art. Scott's practice as an artist was rooted in socialist concerns, demonstrating solidarity with socially oppressed groups including women. Although primarily a painter, she also worked across print and poetry. From 1971 Scott was a founding member of the League of Socialist Artists (LSA) and the Marxist-Leninist Organisation of Britain. Working in a socialist realist style, she created graphics and illustrations for the groups, including the posters 'Testament against War and Suffering – Last Hope of the Rich!' and 'To the Women of the Whole World'. Much of her work from the 1970s depicts scenes of parenting, a subject of much discussion in the Women's Liberation Movement. Her painting *Mother and Child at Breaking Point* shows a mother exasperated as she holds her crying toddler, a more realistic portrayal of the nuances of motherhood than those commonly seen at the time. She has lived and worked in London for over sixty years, but recently moved to Somerset to be closer to family.

Carole Gibbons (b.1935) studied at the Glasgow School of Art in the late 1950s and has lived and worked in the city for most of her life. In the late 1950s she was a member of the Young Glasgow Group, a collective of eleven artists who worked together to make opportunities to show their work. In the 1960s, Gibbons travelled across Europe where she was influenced by its painting traditions and mythological narratives, and consequently began to use bright colours on her canvases. Much of Gibbons' work sits between abstraction and representation.

Her still lives within domestic environments will often feature cats and her self-portraits have a symbolic quality that speak of a woman's experience of the home and studio. The painting *Goddess* (below) was inspired by the artist's memories of her mother and their separation during the First World War.

In 2012 Gibbons exhibited with the artist Lucy Stein and in 2023, the first major new publication on the artist was released.

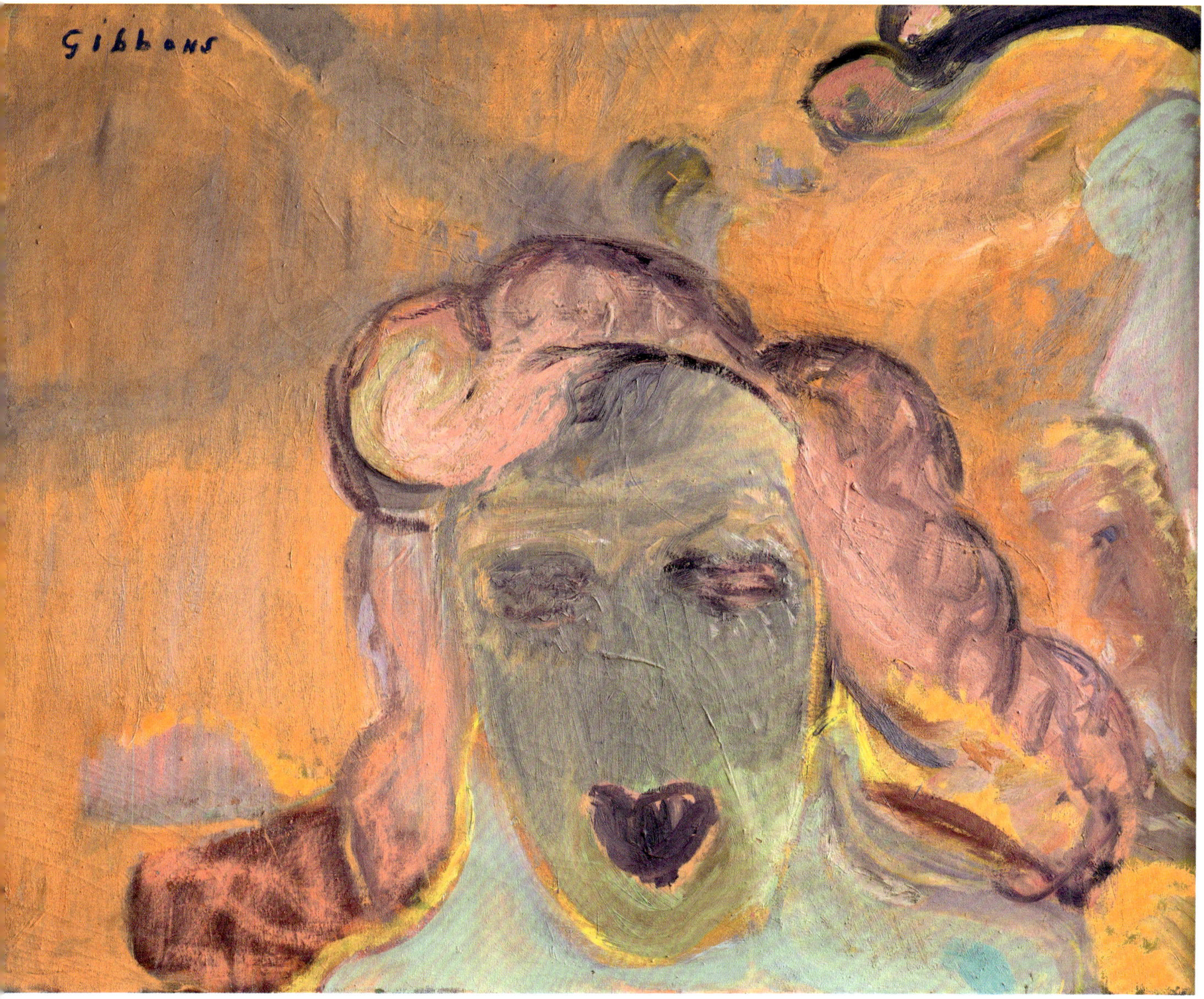

Goddess 1972. Oil paint on canvas 100 × 125

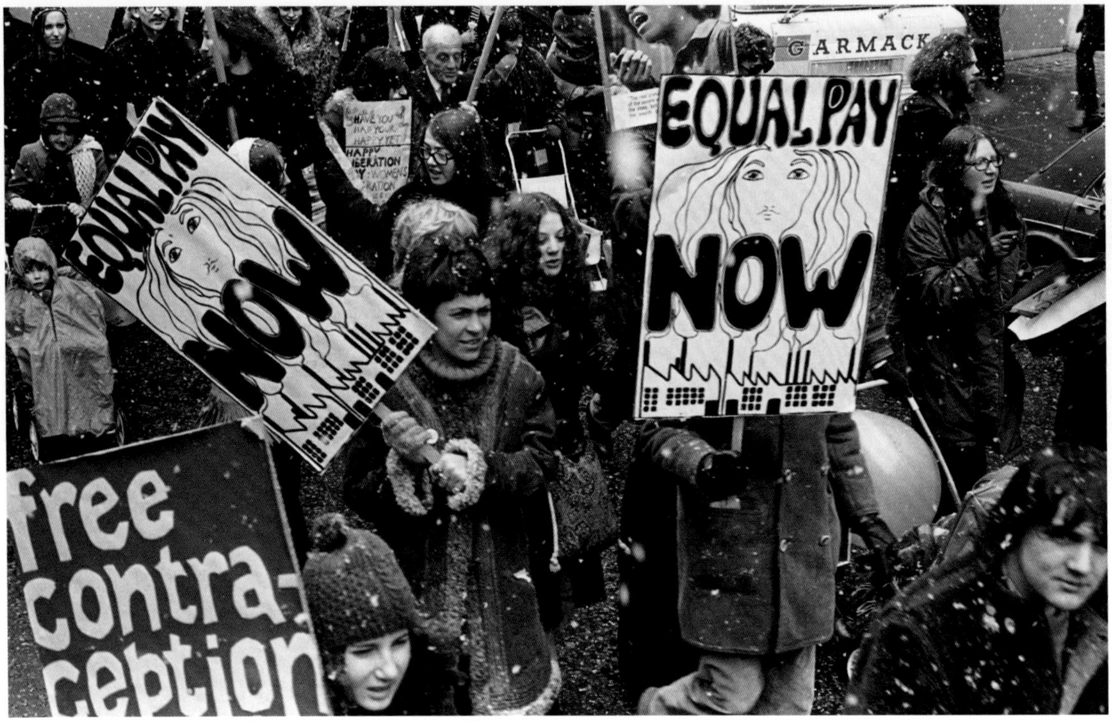

1971 Women's March 1971. Photograph on board 63 × 103

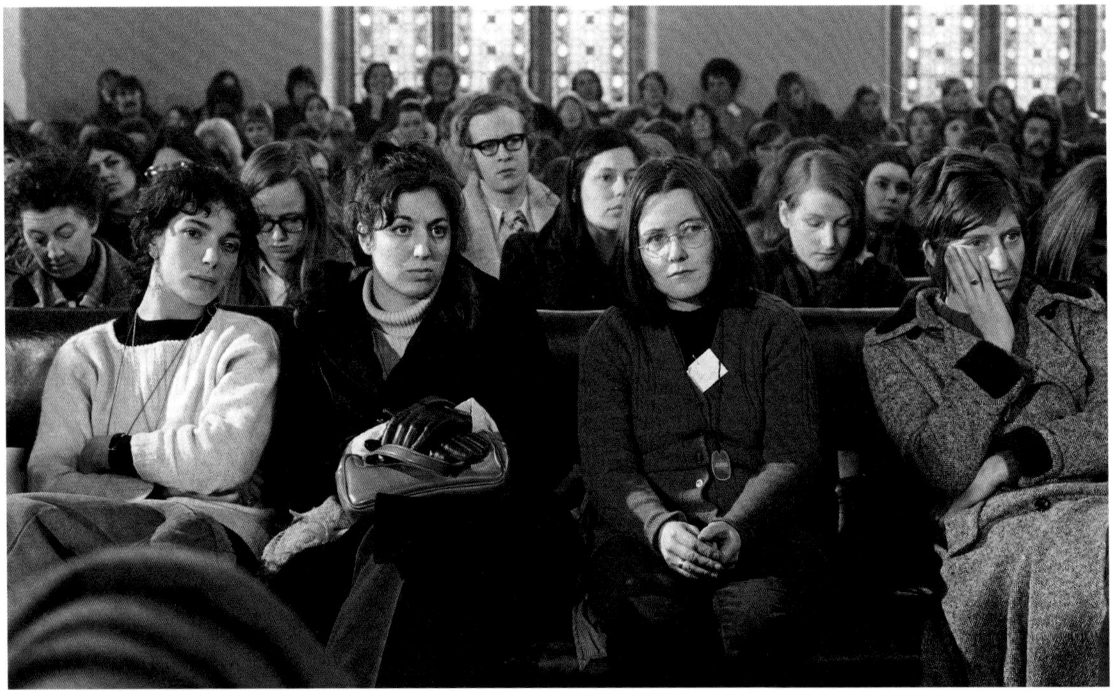
Women's Liberation Conference 1970. Photograph on board 35.5 × 60

Chandan Fraser (b. 1950) is a British photographer and feminist activist who documented events connected with the Women's Liberation Movement and the fight for social change in the 1970s. Attending the first Women's Liberation Conference in Oxford at the age of twenty, Fraser captured the event through the lens of an integral and avid participant, describing herself as a 'supporter first' and 'photographer second'. Fraser's images offer an insight into the conference for a contemporary audience, from the crèche that was run by men to photographs of Mrs Walsh, a member of the Committee for Civil Rights for Women and Children of Broken Families. She also photographed other landmark events relating to the movement, including the first ever Women's Liberation demonstration in London a year later (pp. 42–3).

In 2021 Fraser's work was exhibited at Photo Oxford, appropriately at Ruskin College, site of the first women's conference, and in London in 2022, at the Four Corners Gallery exhibition *Photographing Protest*. Fraser lives and works in France.

CHANDAN FRASER

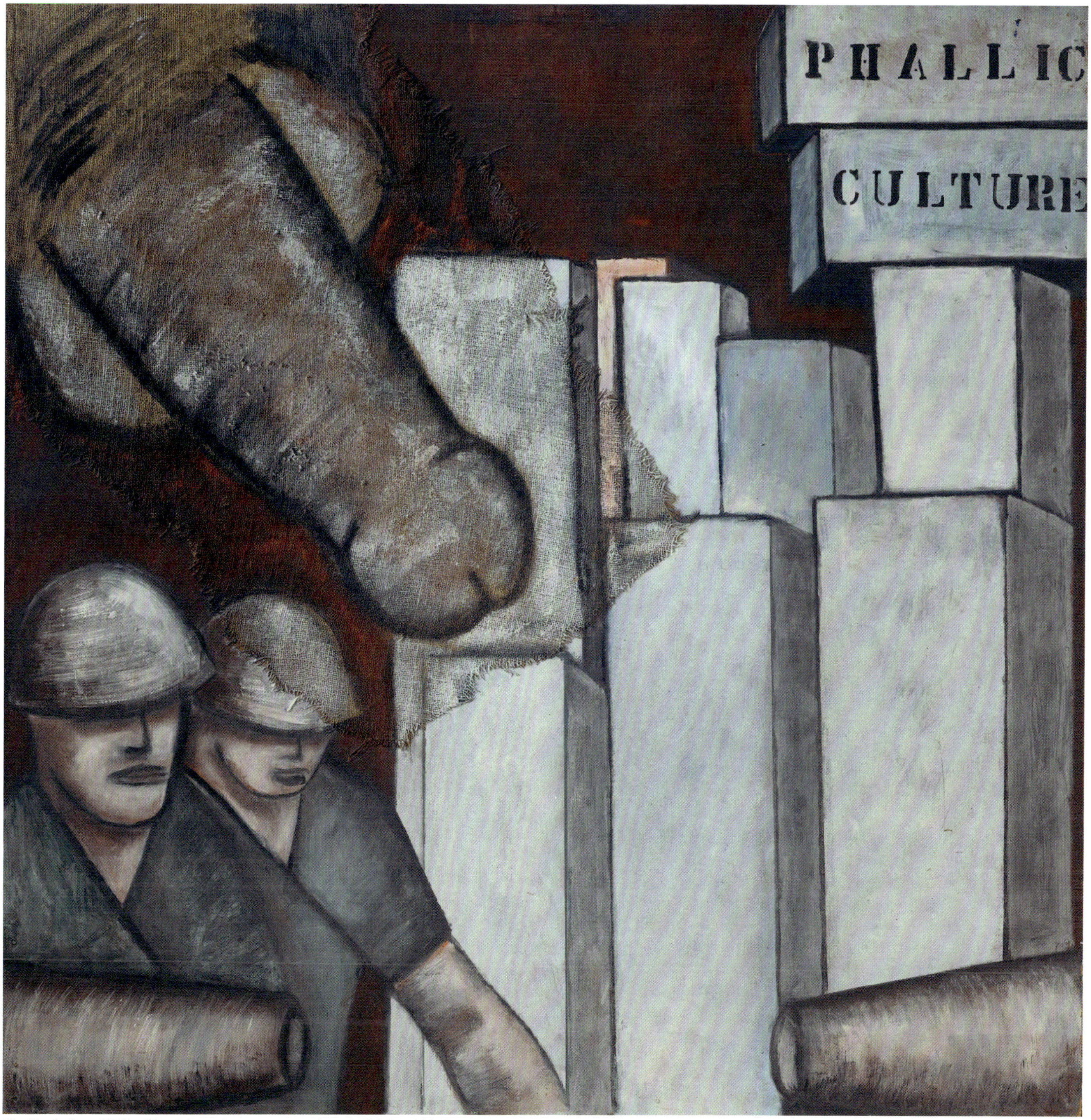

Phallic Culture 1970. Oil paint, part on canvas, on board 121.9 × 121.9

Moncia Sjöö (1938–2005) was a Swedish self-taught artist, writer, activist and radical eco-feminist. She moved to the UK in the 1950s and became one of the most active and well-connected members of the British feminist art community. Sjöö's art came to public attention in the UK in 1971, when her painting *God Giving Birth* 1969 (p.38), which depicts God as a woman, was removed by authorities from the St Ives Art Council Festival. Her direct and often confrontational style of painting came from a desire to express what she understood as a feminine experience – one that was physically, emotionally and spiritually rooted in the experience of living in a patriarchal society. Sjöö looked to a wide range of ancient sources to build a visual language in which matriarchal forces are dominant. Throughout her work we see references to Celtic, Greek and African ancient mythologies, which were intended to counter Western capitalist patriarchal ideas and structures.

Sjöö organised key early feminist art exhibitions such as *The First Feminist Art Show* at Woodstock Gallery, London, which opened in 1971, the same year in which she published *Images on Womanpower – An Arts Manifesto*. The exhibition *Images of Womenpower* opened at the Swiss Cottage Library, London in 1973. In 1987, Sjöö and Barbara Mor published *The Great Cosmic Mother: Rediscovering the Religion of the Earth*, a book that remains a central feminist text.

Solo exhibitions of Sjöö's work were held at Beaconsfield Gallery in London and in 2022, and at the Moderna Museet in Stockholm and Modern Art Oxford in 2023.

MONICA SJÖÖ

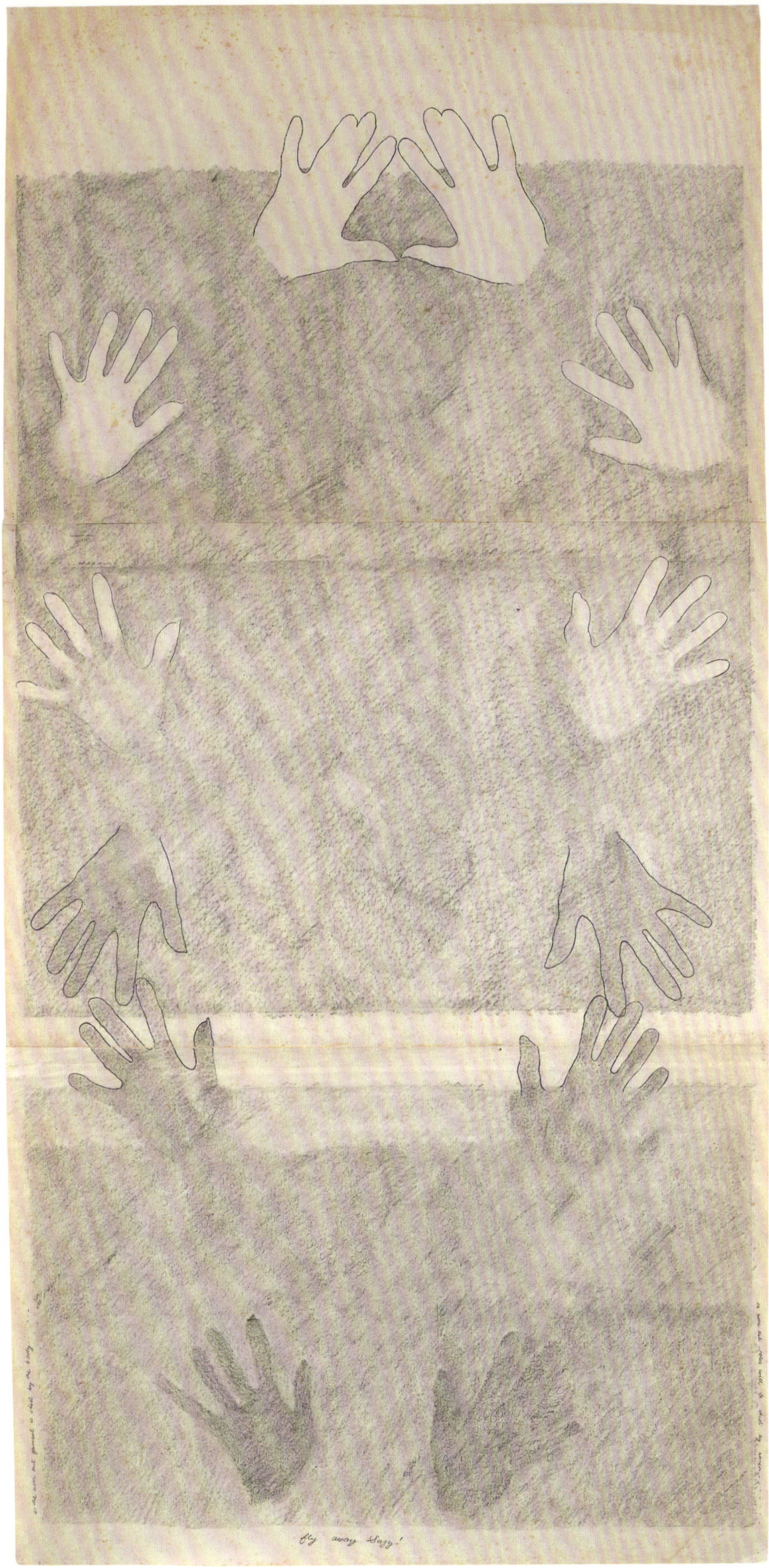

'fly away Susy!' 1976. Graphite rubbing on paper 148.5 × 76 (overall)

Monica Ross (1950–2013) was born in Lancashire and studied at the University of Reading. Working across multimedia, text and performance, her practice was underpinned by feminism and other movements for social, cultural and political change. Ross' work critiques patriarchal industrial capitalism and the social and political constraints imposed on working-class women through experimental and often collaborative art practice. It addresses how we experience events in the present and the cultural transitions which transform them, or not, into memory and history.

Ross played a significant role as a feminist organiser, co-founding the Women's Postal Art Event and Fenix with artists Su Richardson, Suzy Varty and Kate Walker, and later the women's art group Sister Seven. Her work with Fenix was included in the important feminist exhibition *Issue* at the ICA in 1980.

Alongside her art practice, Ross had a long career as an influential educator, teaching at Central Saint Martins from 1985 to 1998, and later at the University of Brighton and University of the Arts, Berlin. Following the artist's death in 2013, the Monica Ross Action Group was set up to enable new audiences to benefit from her legacy.

MONICA ROSS

Born in South Shields in 1947, Su Richardson studied graphic design before moving to Birmingham in the 1970s where, with artists Monica Ross, Phil Goodall and Suzy Varty, she formed the Birmingham Women's Art Group. Along with Monica Ross and Kate Walker, Richardson was instrumental in the creation of the Postal Art Event in (1975–7), through which women artists working at home began to make and exchange artworks in the post, resisting the patriarchal systems that made being an artist and a mother so difficult. The Postal Art Event would lead to the groundbreaking exhibition of Postal artworks: *Feministo: Portrait of the Artist as a Housewife* (ICA, 1977). In the late 1970s, with Ross, Walker and Varty, Richardson formed Fenix, a feminist art collective that exhibited a collaborative exhibition across the country. Work from Fenix was included in Lucy Lippard's show *Issue* (ICA, 1980).

Richardson contributed to a number of important recent feminist exhibitions including *Where does gesture become Event?*, Cooper Gallery, Dundee, 2016; *A Woman's Place*, Raven Row, London 2017 and *Women Power Protest* at the Birmingham Museum and Art Gallery, 2018. Richardson lives and works in Birmingham.

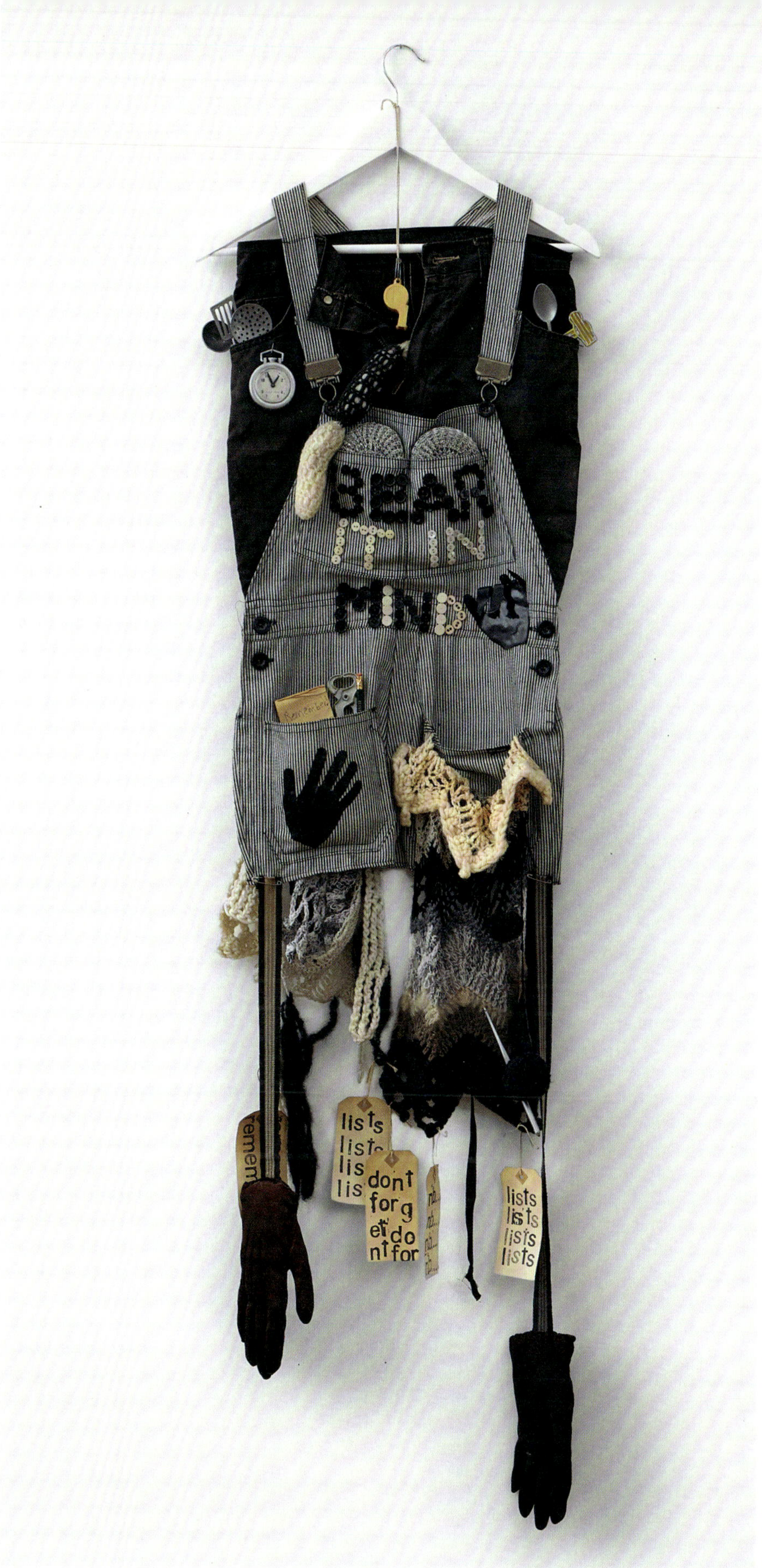

Bear it in Mind 1976. Dungarees, jeans, coat hanger, gloves, ink on paper and other materials 150 × 45 × 4

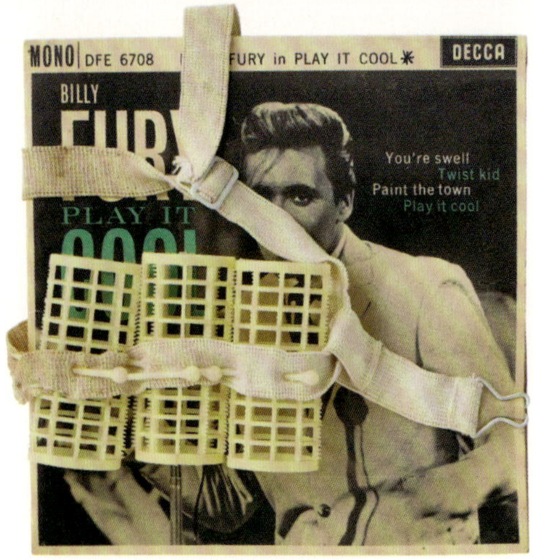

1

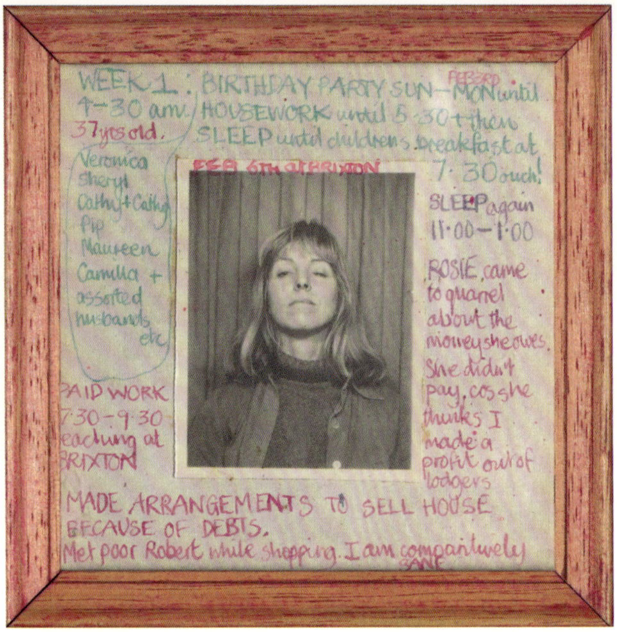

2

The Postal Art Event (1975–7), also known as the Women's Postal Art Event, was conceived by artists Sally Gollop and Kate Walker who had been neighbours in London. When Gollop moved out, they began posting artworks to each other that explored their domestic and emotional experiences and allowed them to continue to engage in consciousness-raising. At the 1975 Women's Art History Conference in London, Walker made an appeal for other women to join them. Su Richardson remembers that Walker said: 'Aren't there any housewives out here who want to make some art and who are fed up with this fine art business?'.[1] A number

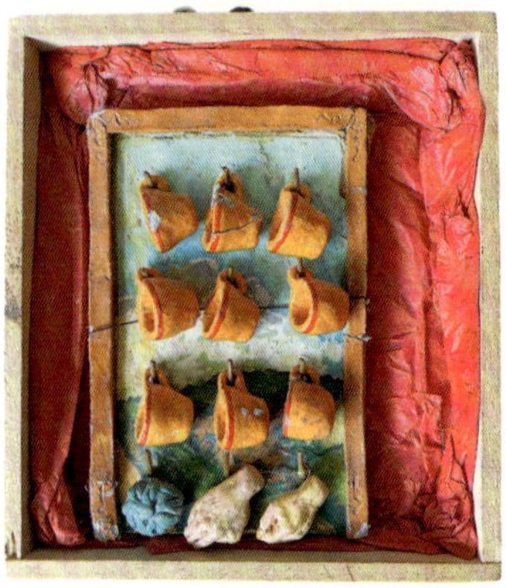

3

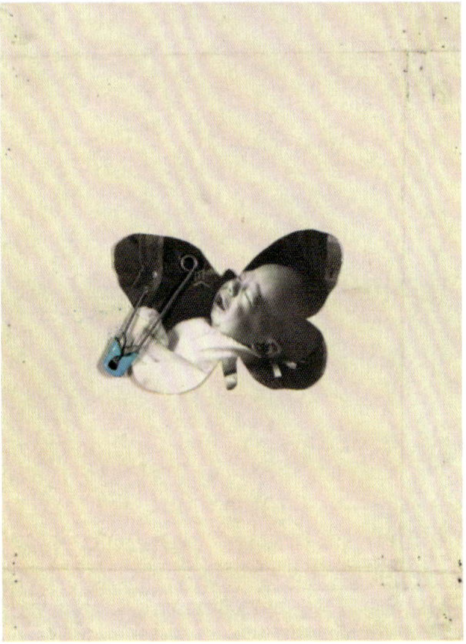

5

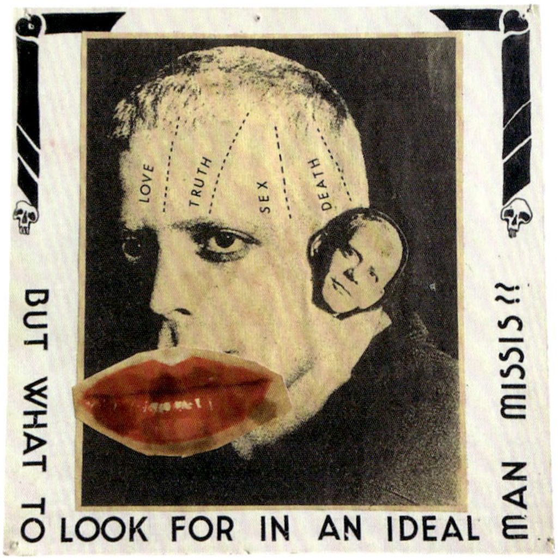

6

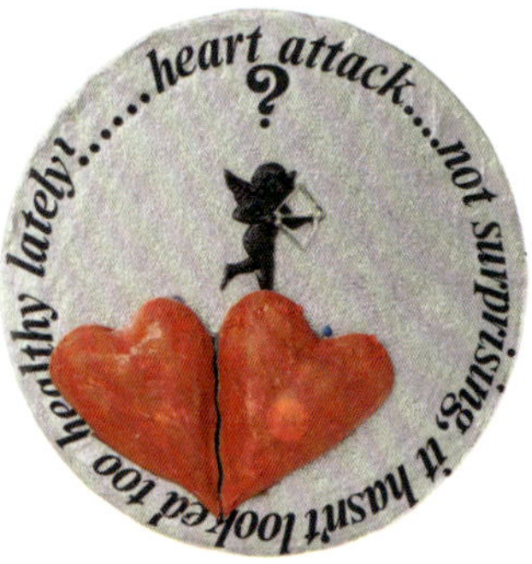

4

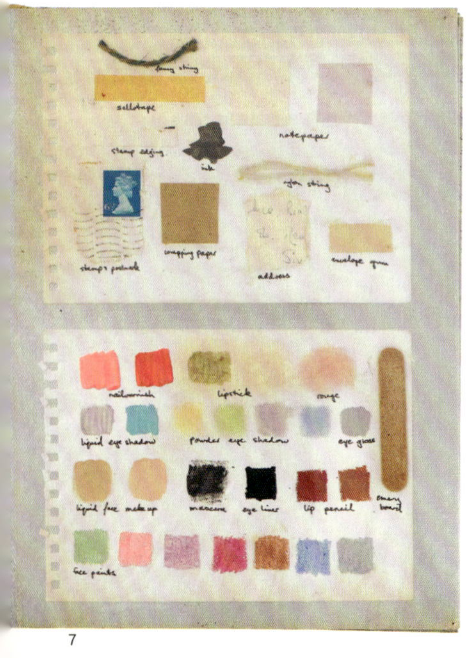

7

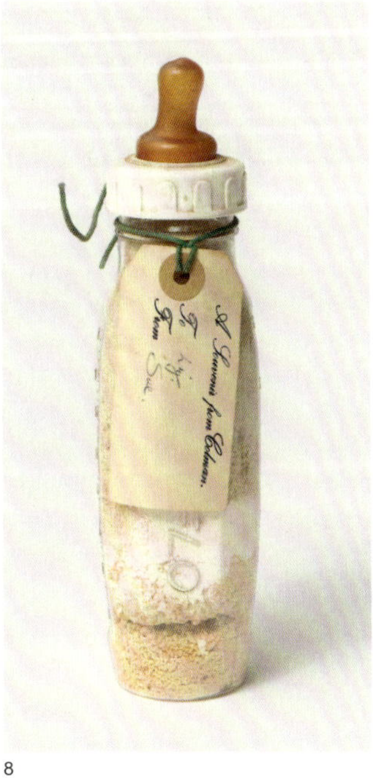

8

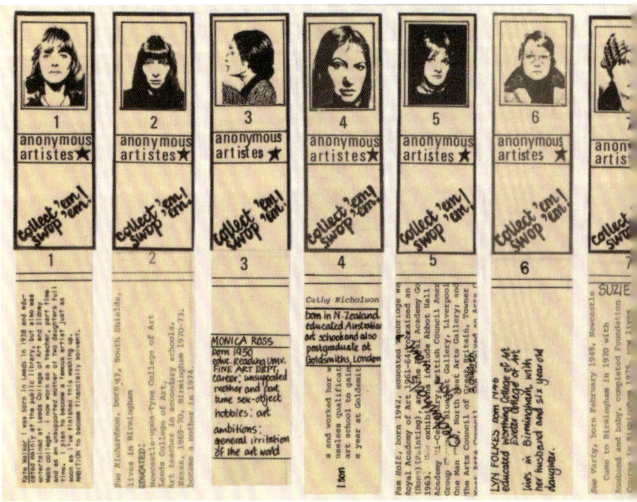

9

1 Su Richardson *Postal Art, Untitled (Who Was I Trying to Fool?)* 1975–6. Photograph with glitter, handwritten text inside a vintage record cover and elastic band holding three curlers.
2 Kate Walker *Postal Art Event (Kate Walker, aged 37, with diary notes)* 1977. Black-and-white photo-booth photograph, paper, wooden frame, glass 10.5 × 10.5 × 1.5
3 Kate Walker and Sally Gollop *Postal Art Event* 1975. Modelling clay, paint, wire, paper, wood 18.6 × 16.2 × 2.2
4 Su Richardson *Postal Art – Heart attack?...not surprising, it hasn't looked that healthy lately...* 1975–6. Facsimile cake

of women joined creating a network that spanned the country. Postal Art Event objects were by design small scale and lightweight, made with everyday household items and were often humorous in their challenges to the formal strategies of the patriarchal 'fine art business'. In 1977 the works were exhibited at the ICA in London before touring to Manchester, Birmingham, Liverpool and internationally. The exhibition is referred to variously as *Feministo*, *Feministo: Portrait of the Artist as a Housewife*, *Feministo Portrait of the Artist as a Young Woman* and *Feministo: Portrait of the Artist as a Young Housewife*.

1. Kate Walker quoted by Su Richardson in Alexandra Kokoli, 'Undoing "Homeliness" in *Feminist Art: Feministo: Portrait of the Artist as a Housewife* (1975–7)', *n.paradoxa: international feminist art journal*, vol.13: Domestic Politics, Jan. 2004, pp.75–83, p.77. See also Kathy Battista, *Renegotiating The Body: Feminist Art in 1970s London*, London and New York 2013, pp.108–10, which includes discussion of the Postal Art Event and commentary from Walker.

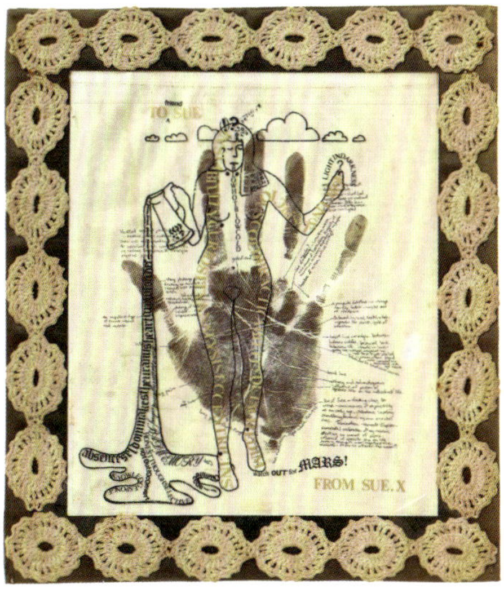

10

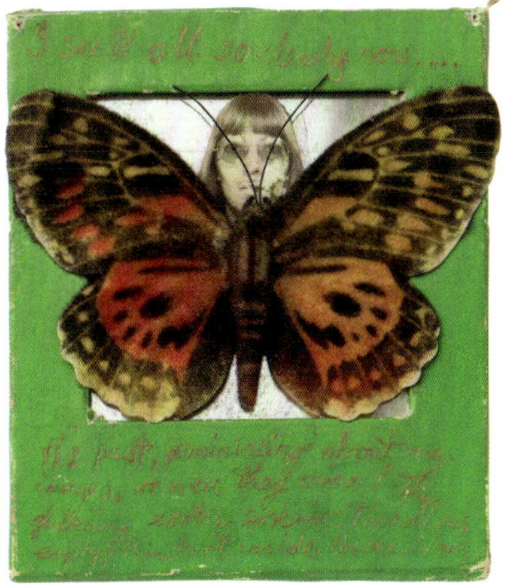

11

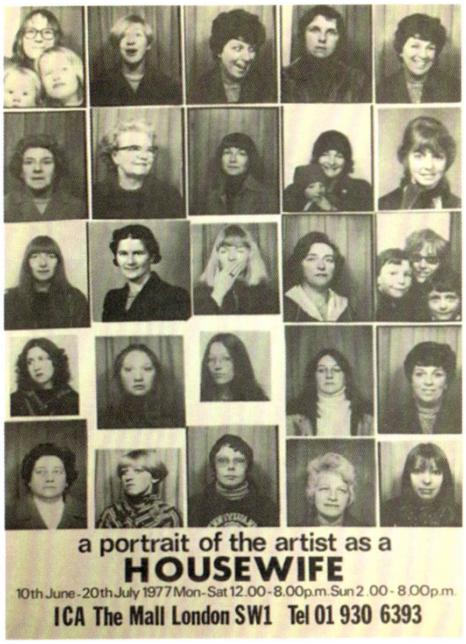

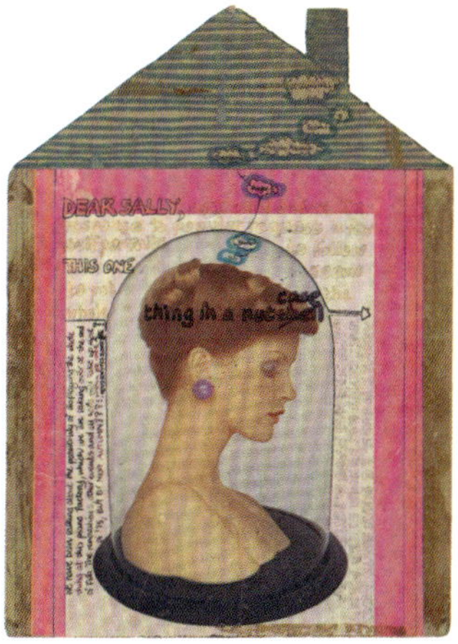

13

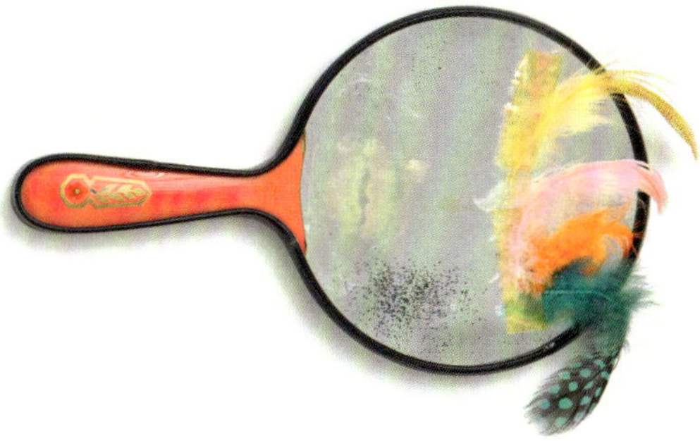

14

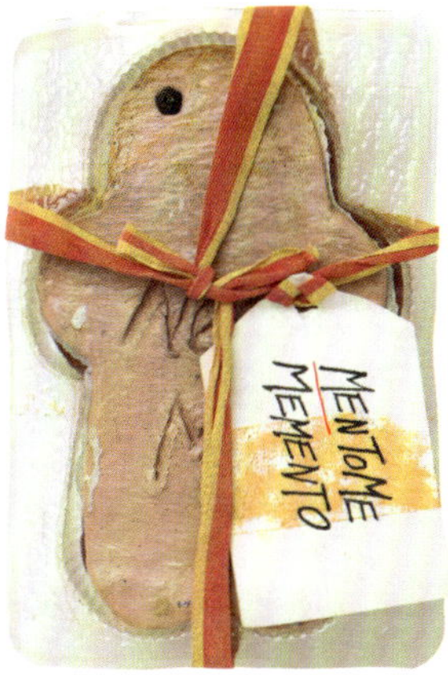

15

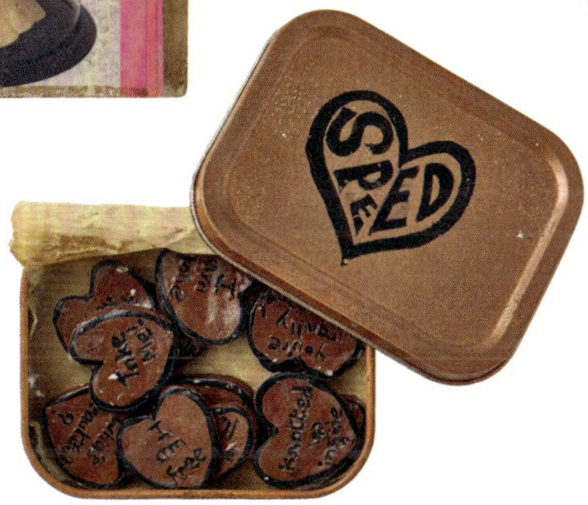

16

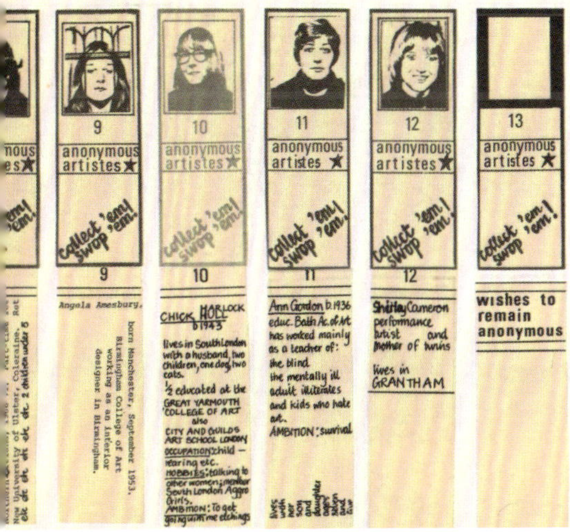

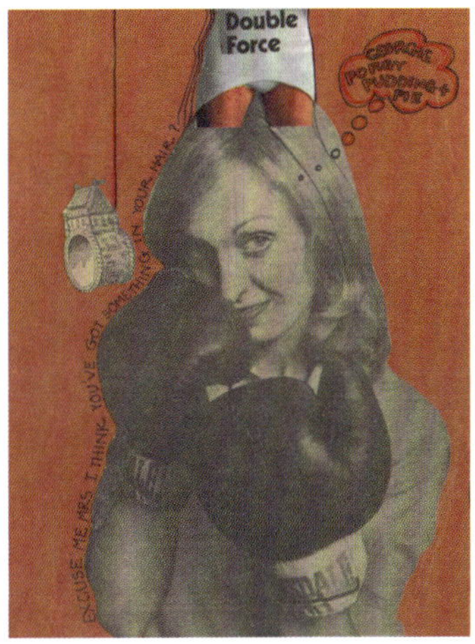

17

with hand-painted plaster and plastic pin on tin foil with printed text and handwritten text on the back 17.5 × 17.5

5 Su Richardson *Untitled, Postal Art* 1975–6. Collage and nappy pin on paper 25 × 19

6 Suzy Varty *But What To Look For In An Ideal Man*, August 1976. Felt-tip pen and printed papers on board 16.5 × 16.5

7 Su Richardson *Postal Art – Domestic Colour Charts* 1975–6. Archival typologies with samples taken from the domestic and the body including: spices, condiments, papers, make-up, body clippings 29 × 23.5 × 2

8 Su Richardson *Postal Art – Sand souvenir feeding bottle* 1975–6. Baby bottle filled with sand and a printed tag with hand-written text 20 × 5 × 5

9 Kate Walker *Anonymous Artistes, Collect 'em! Swap 'em!* 1977. Paper, card and sticky-back plastic 21 × 59

10 Su Richardson Postal Art - The Intuitive Palm + The Aquarius Woman 1975–6. Human handprint on paper, with handwritten notes covered in plastic with printed text and affixed to board covered in polyester and decorated with crochet cotton 34.5 × 30

11 Su Richardson *Postal Art – I see it all so clearly now...* 1975–6. Black-and-white photograph mounted on card with handwritten text in gold overlaid with facsimile butterfly in crochet pouch 11 × 9

12 Poster for *A Portrait of the Artist as a Housewife*, Institute of Contemporary Arts, London, 1977

13 Kate Walker *Postal Art Event ('...To put this whole thing in a nut shell/case...')* 1974. Card, paper, felt-tip pen 35 × 25.5 × 3

14 Su Richardson *Postal Art – Mirror Mask* 1976. Mirror, coloured feathers and lipstick 21 × 12

15 Su Richardson *Postal Art – Men-to-me, Memento* 1975–6 Hand-painted plaster 'gingerbread man' cookies in plastic with coloured ribbon tie and handwritten label 16 × 11 × 2

16 Su Richardson *Postal Art – Speed* 1975–6. Altered tin box and hand-painted plaster cookies 6.5 × 8.5 × 3

17 Kate Walker *Postal Art Event ('Excuse me Mrs...')* 1976. Paper and card 22.9 × 17.6

Fenix (also known as Phoenix) was a collaborative, touring exhibition project that grew out of the Postal Art Event. Fenix comprised of Kate Walker, Su Richardson, Monica Ross and, in its initial stages, Suzy Varty. The exhibition, which had the self-imposed rule of only including black-and-white works, was developed in situ in the four venues in which it was staged: Bluecoat Gallery, Liverpool (1978), Darlington Hall Gallery (1980), Bristol Arts Centre (1980) and at the ICA in London (1980) as part of *Issue: Social Strategies by Women Artists*, curated by Lucy Lippard. To accompany the exhibition, Fenix produced a publication in which they discussed their working methods:

'The concept of Collective artwork is related in Fenix to the process called Consciousness-Raising within feminist small groups and also to the progress of the women's art movement in Britain. This type of working procedure as a feminist strategy is best described by extracts from a dialogue (recorded in Birmingham, May 1979) between Ross, Richardson and Walker:

"The generation which this trio represents is the first in which working-class women have had access to art education. Some of these women are making a conscious collective attempt to combine motherhood with a professional career. Individual careerist 'solutions' such as we have seen throughout art history do not work in their interest."'

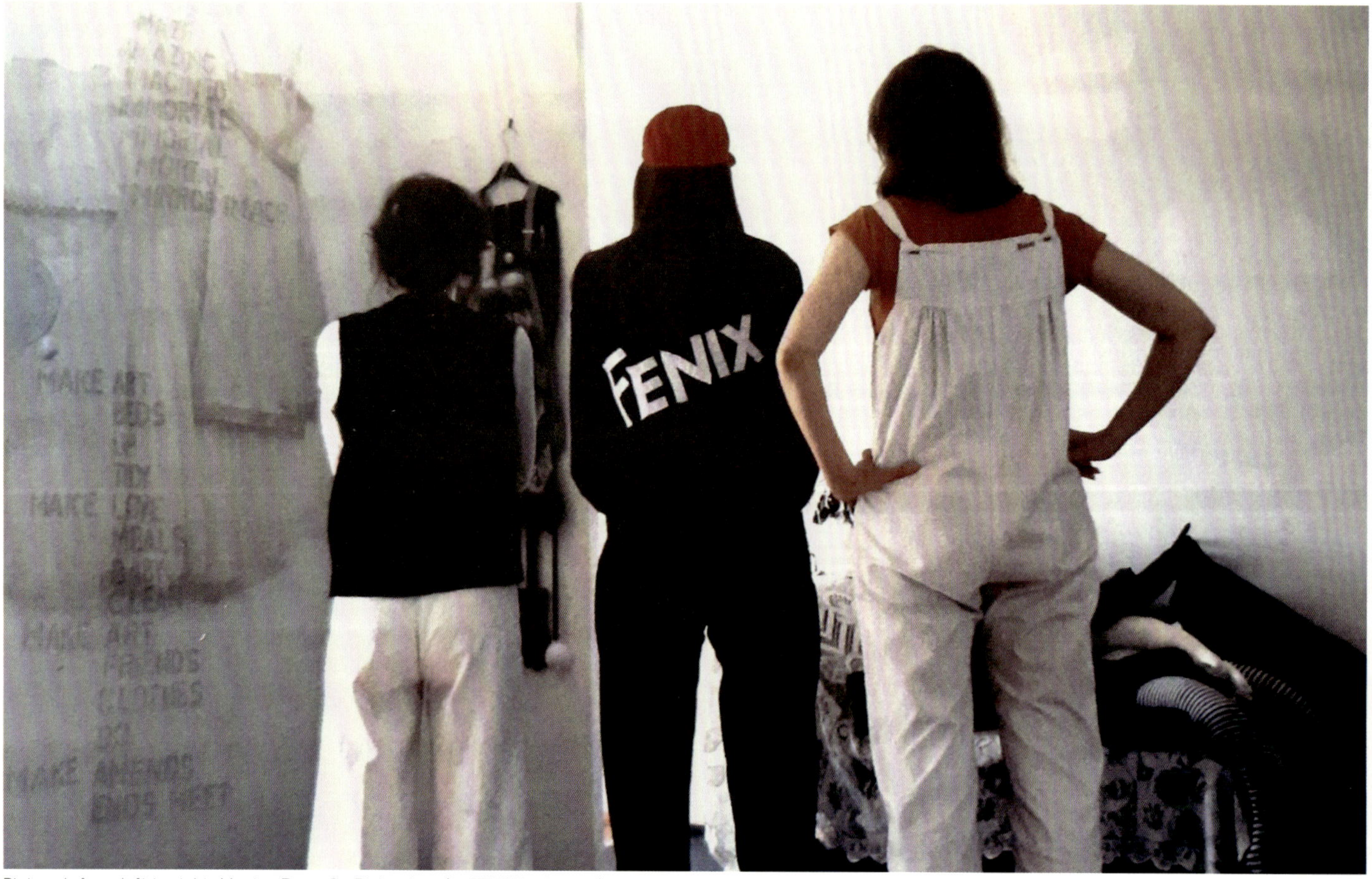

Pictured, from left to right: Monica Ross, Su Richardson (in FENIX boiler suit) and Kate Walker facing Richardson's MAKE screen, *Bear it in Mind* (p.63) and *Try These on For Size? – Legs, arms and pregnant belly cushion*, c.1978, location unknown.

Margaret Harrison was born in Wakefield in 1940 and studied at Carlisle College of Art, the Royal Academy Schools and the Accademia di Belli Arti di Perugia in Italy. Working across drawing, installation, collage and textiles, Harrison was a key figure in the feminist art scene of the 1970s and one of the founders of the London Women's Liberation Art Group and a member of the Women's Workshop of the Artists' Union. A 1971 solo exhibition by Harrison at Motif Editions in London displayed a series of drawings that sought to challenge the portrayal of women in popular culture. Some works depicted women with large pieces of food, suggestive of pornographic imagery and society's reduction of women to objects of consumption. Harrison intended the series to reclaim the depiction of women's bodies, describing it as 'anti-pornographic'. The exhibition was closed by the police on grounds of indecency. In 1973–5 Harrison collaborated with artists Kay Hunt and Mary Kelly to conduct a study of women's experiences working in a factory in Bermondsey, south London. This resulted in *Women and Work: A Document on the Division of Labour in Industry*, an installation which used the women's accounts to consider their working environment and the recent Equal Pay Act (pp.82–3). Harrison lives and works in Carlisle.

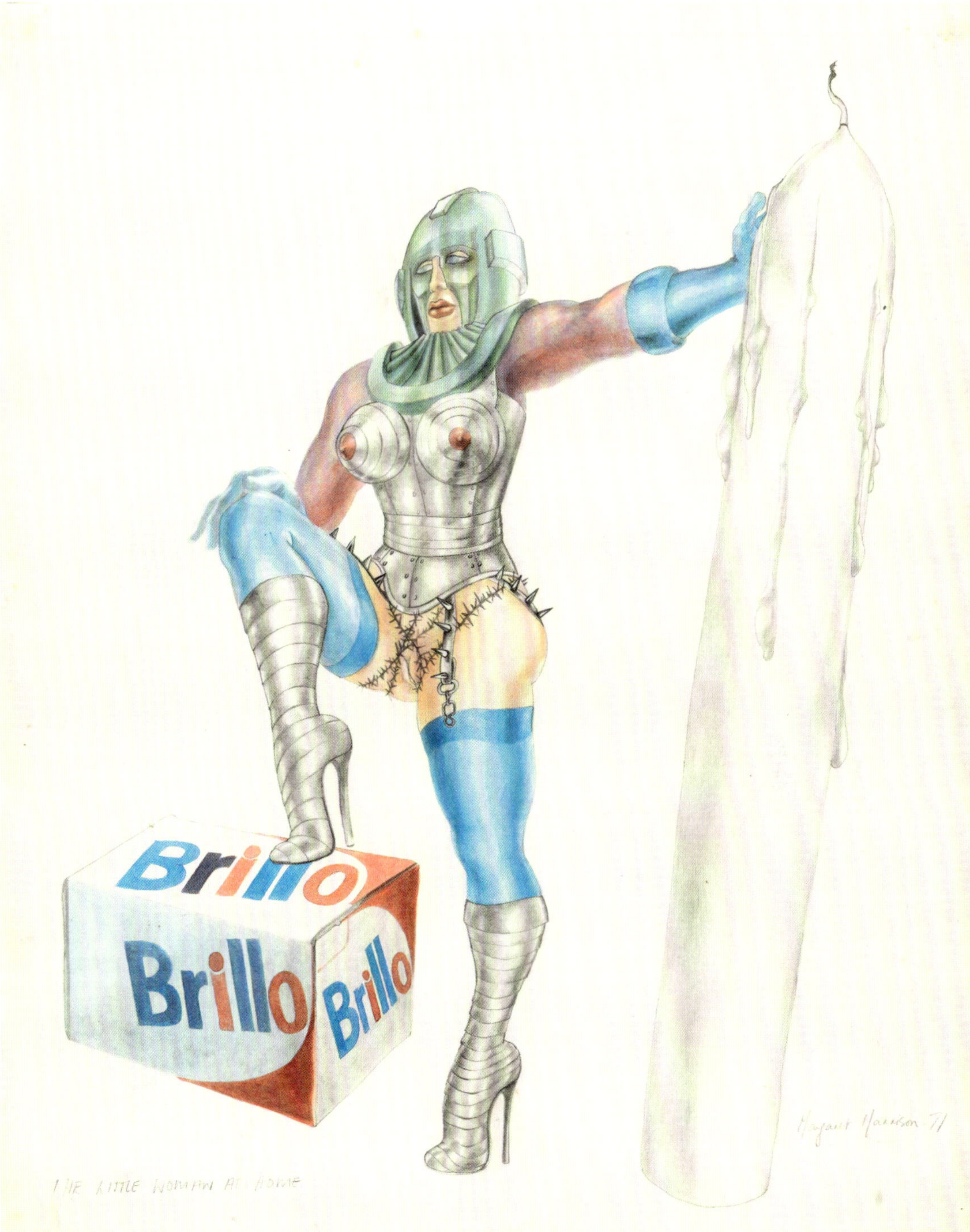

Little Woman at Home 1971. Graphite and watercolour on paper 63.6 × 51.8

MARGARET HARRISON

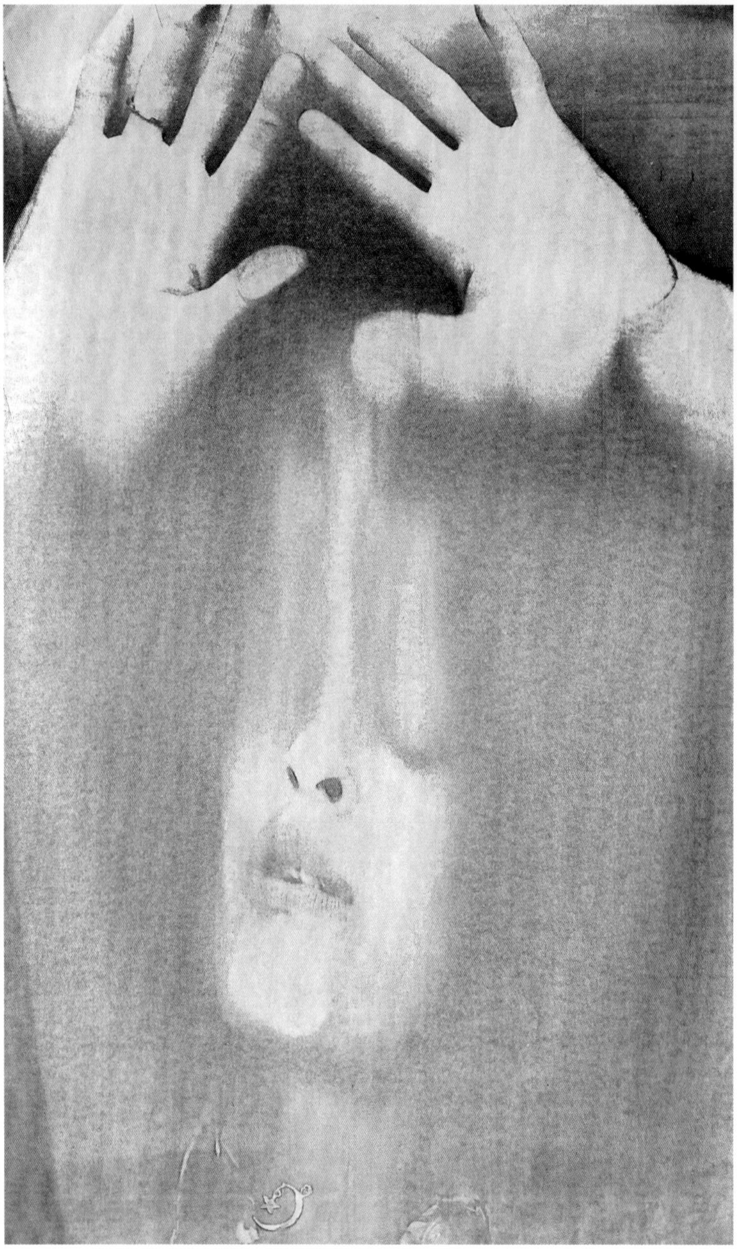

Spirit Impressions – 5 1974. Xerox print 48.3 × 29.2

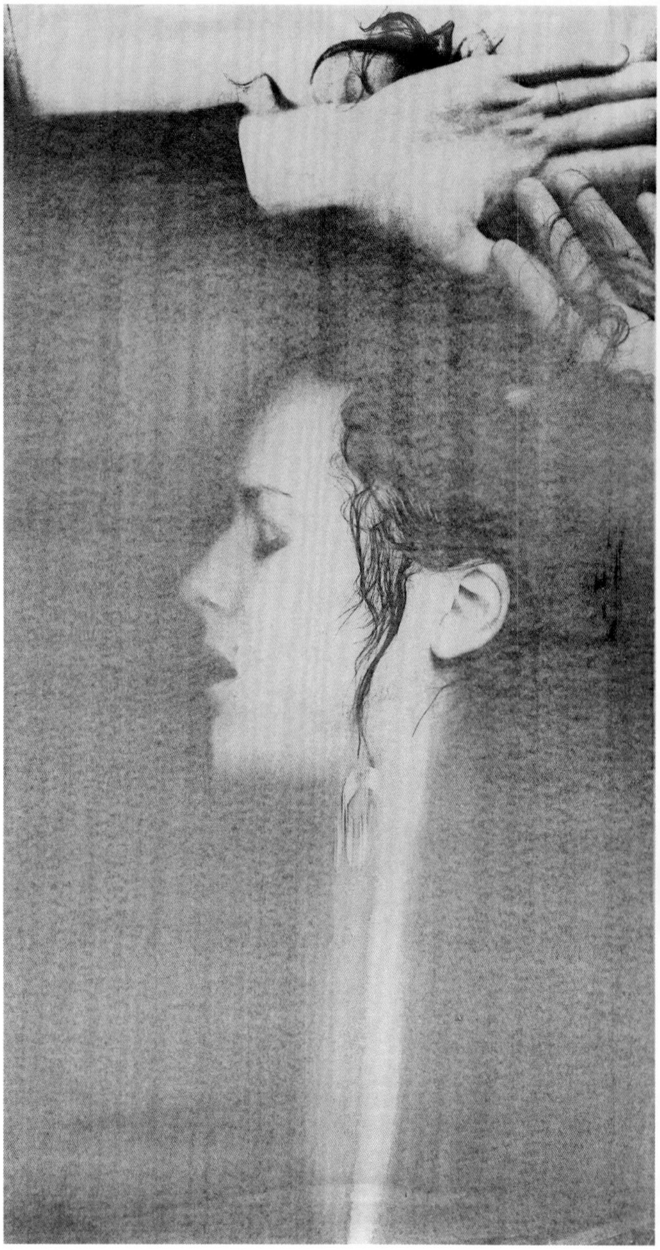

Spirit Impressions – 4 1974. Xerox print 48.3 × 29.2

Born in London in 1947, Penny Slinger began her art practice while studying for an art diploma at West Surrey College in 1966. She went on to receive a first-class honors degree in art and design from Chelsea College of Art, graduating in 1969. Rooted in feminism, her practice spans photocollage, drawing, xerography, painting, film, theatre and sculpture, with surrealist-influenced collages that use her own body to explore ideas around sex, desire, liberation and memory. In 1969, she produced her first book of photographic collage *50% The Visible Woman*. Her work of the 1970s challenged notions of male supremacy and the objectification of women in a male-dominated society. In 1973, in her solo exhibition *Opening*, at the Angela Flowers Gallery in London, Slinger exhibited her *Bride's Cake* series in which the artist is dressed as a three-tiered wedding cake in bridal whites, offering herself up for consumption. By aligning the experience of being a bride with the presentation of a slice of cake, Slinger critically assesses the idea that women exist to satisfy the desires of men. Slinger used the photographs to create a 'Bride's Book', a parody of the traditional wedding album.

Slinger lives and works in California. A survey of her tantric work was presented at Richard Saltoun Gallery, London, in 2019.

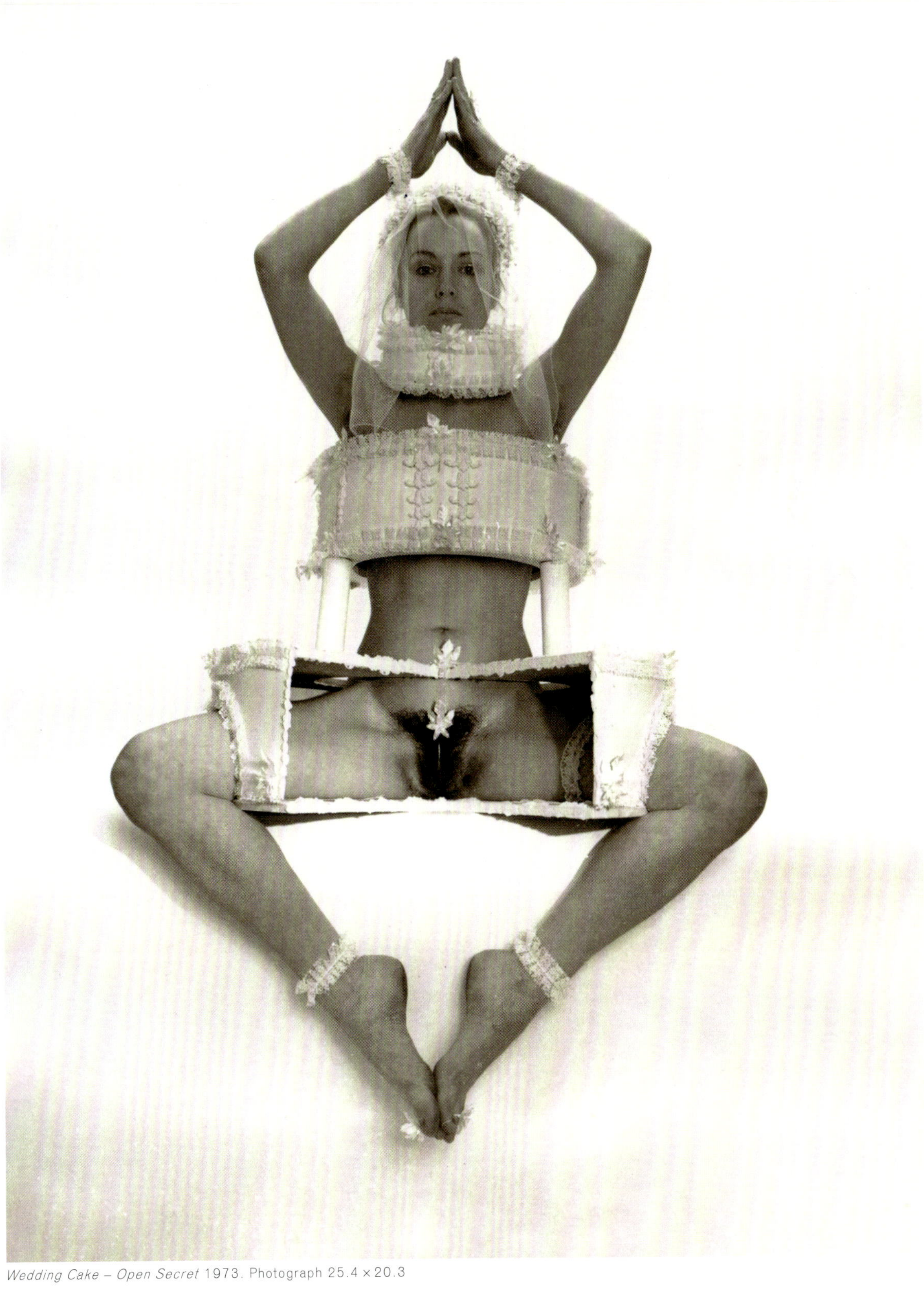

Wedding Cake – Open Secret 1973. Photograph 25.4 × 20.3

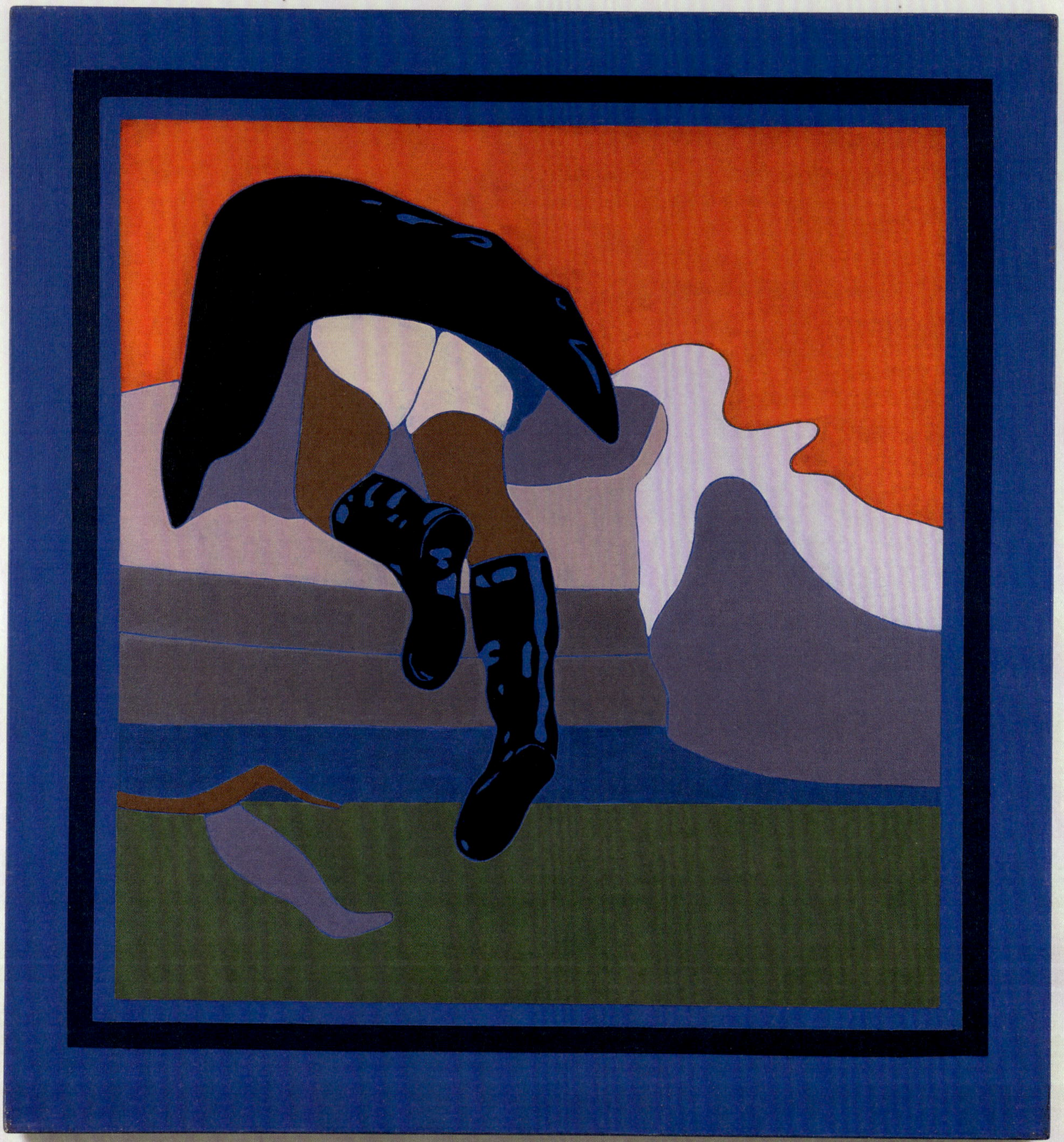

The Bed 1973. Acrylic paint on canvas 122 × 127.2

Born Eric Rutherford in Hawick, in the Scottish Borders, Erica Rutherford (1947–2008) attended Dartmouth Royal Naval College in 1937 before going on to a study a range of creative subjects including stage design, drawing and sculpture at the Slade School of Fine Art, and drawing at the Academie Julien in Paris. Rutherford's early work was largely focused on abstraction, however in the early 1970s there was a significant shift to a stylised pop figuration. Rutherford was also a prolific printmaker.

In 1976 Rutherford underwent gender affirmation surgery while living in the United States and around this time began creating a series of works that explored representations of her body in fashionable women's clothing. Works such as *The Coat* (*the Mirror*) were painted from self-portrait photographs taken by the artist.

In 1985 Rutherford moved to Prince Edward Island, Canada where she was very active in the cultural scene. She illustrated a number of children's books and in 1993 published *Nine Lives: The Autobiography of Erica Rutherford*. Rutherford was admitted to the Royal Canadian Academy of Arts in 1999 and is the subject of a retrospective at the Confederation Centre Art Gallery, in Charlottetown, Canada in 2024.

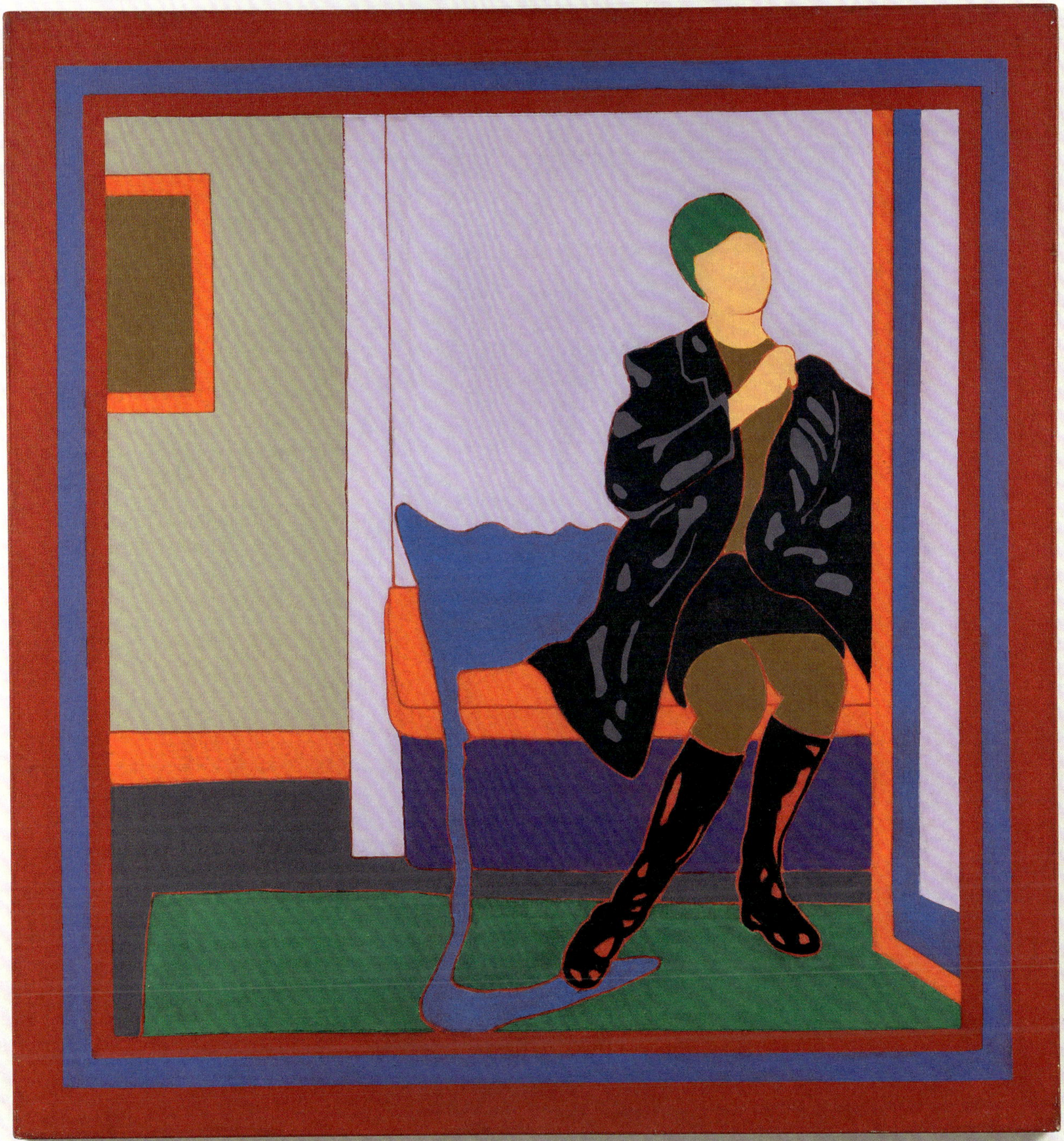

The Coat (The Mirror) 1974, Acrylic paint on canvas, 122 × 127.2

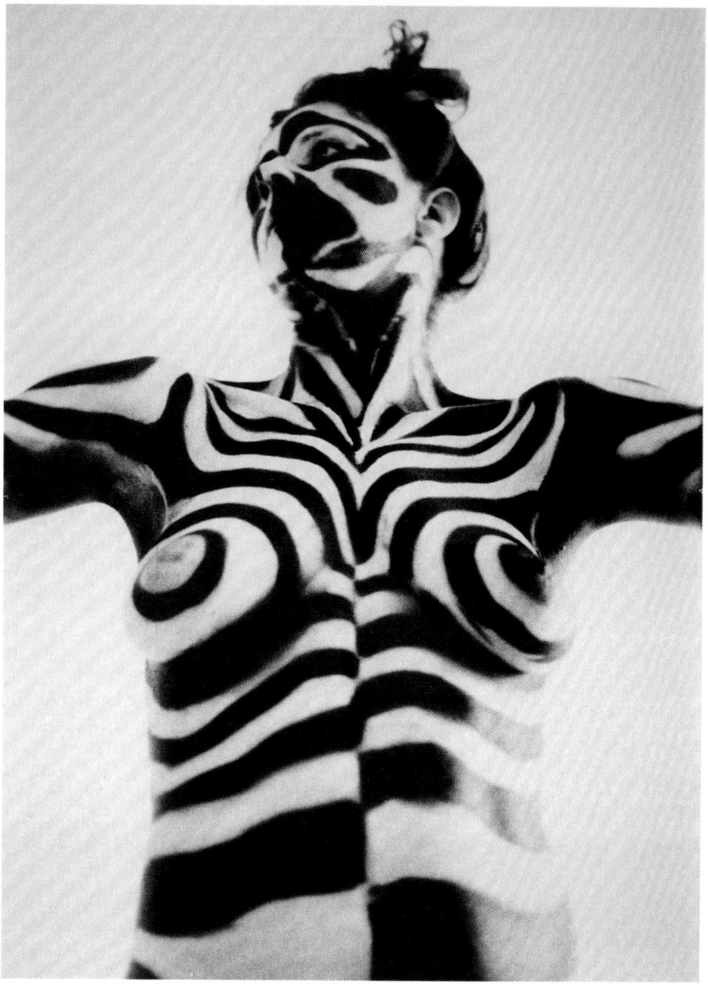

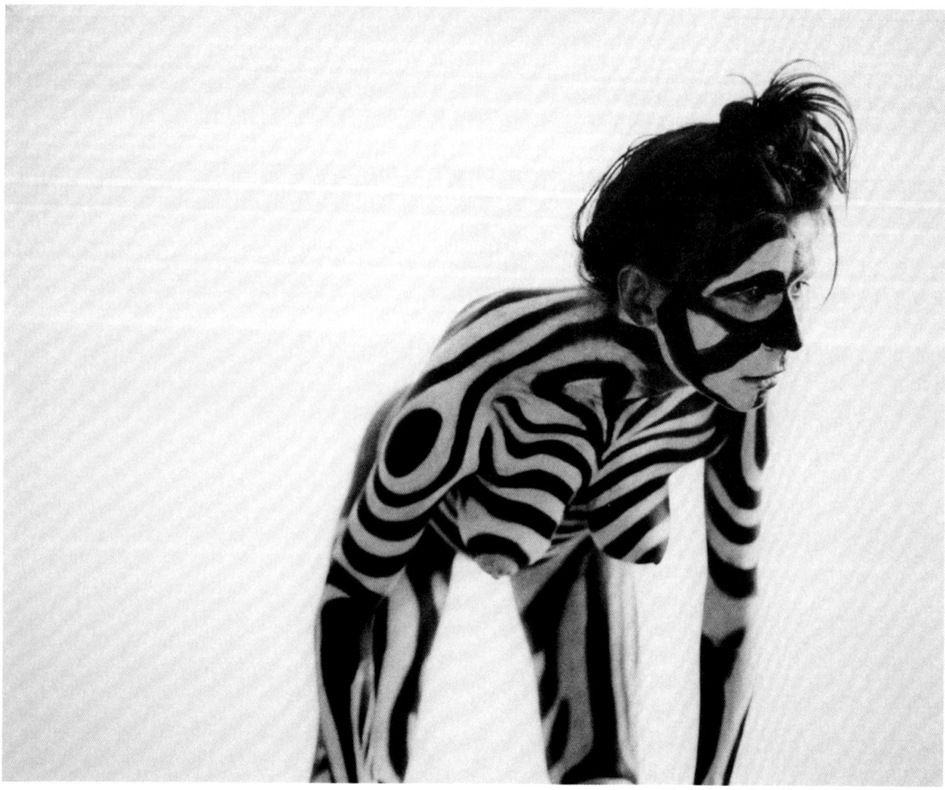

Hannah O'Shea (b.1939) trained in sculpture at Goldsmiths College in London in the 1960s, going on to explore performance and time-based media while studying at the Slade School of Fine Art. A member of the Women Artists Collective alongside artists including Rose Finn-Kelcey, O'Shea's practice in the 1970s was highly political, especially focusing on the concerns and ideas of the Women's Liberation Movement. Her film *A Visual Time Span* (*A Visual Diary*) brought together political themes, collaging imagery taken from women's demonstrations, queer rights demonstrations and her own performances. In 1976 O'Shea performed her iconic work *A Litany for Women Artists*, in which the artist chants the names of forgotten women artists to critique their absence from art history. The religious nature of the work's title was echoed by a thunder storm outside during the performance, which O'Shea claimed as a sign of God's rage.

In 2016 *A Litany for Women Artists* was restaged by the 12-Hour Action Group, hosted by the Cooper Gallery, Dundee. The artist lives and works in London.

Stills from 'A Visual Time Span' (A Visual Diary) c.1975.
Vintage silver bromide prints
51 × 38 (top image)
and 40.5 × 50.5

HANNAH O'SHEA

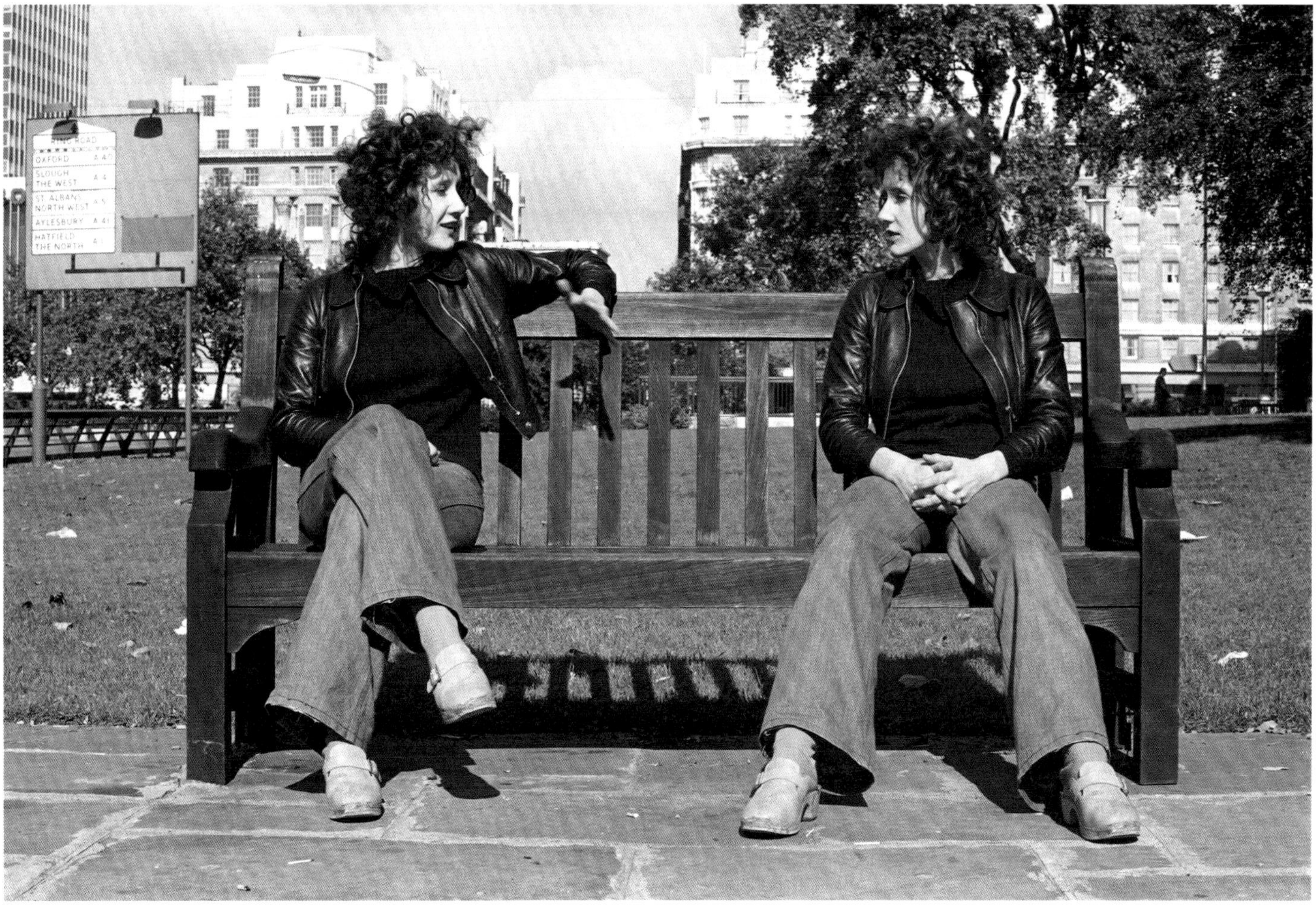

Divided Self (Speakers' Corner) 1974–2011. Gelatin silver print on aluminium 51.2 × 77.8

Rose Finn-Kelcey (1945–2014) was born in Northampton, and studied at Ravensbourne College of Art and Design and Chelsea College of Art. An important figure in both the feminist and conceptual art scenes in the UK, Finn-Kelcey worked across performance, sound, installation and sculpture to create socio-political statements that considered systems of power, public spaces, the self, agency and ideas around the subjective and the personal. Her work first attracted public attention in the 1970s when she installed a series of flags over London landmarks, including *Power for the People* 1972, which was flown over Battersea Power Station. Her work in the early 1970s aimed to challenge the institution of art and re-integrate art with life. In the photographic work *The Restless Image: a discrepancy between the seen position and the felt position* 1975, the artist is depicted carefully performing a handstand on a beach. The work's subtitle suggests a divergence between the lived experience of the subject and what is presented to the viewer.

Finn-Kelcey died in 2014. Despite her significance in the art world, no major public exhibition of her work was held until Modern Art Oxford presented a retrospective in 2017.

ROSE FINN-KELCEY

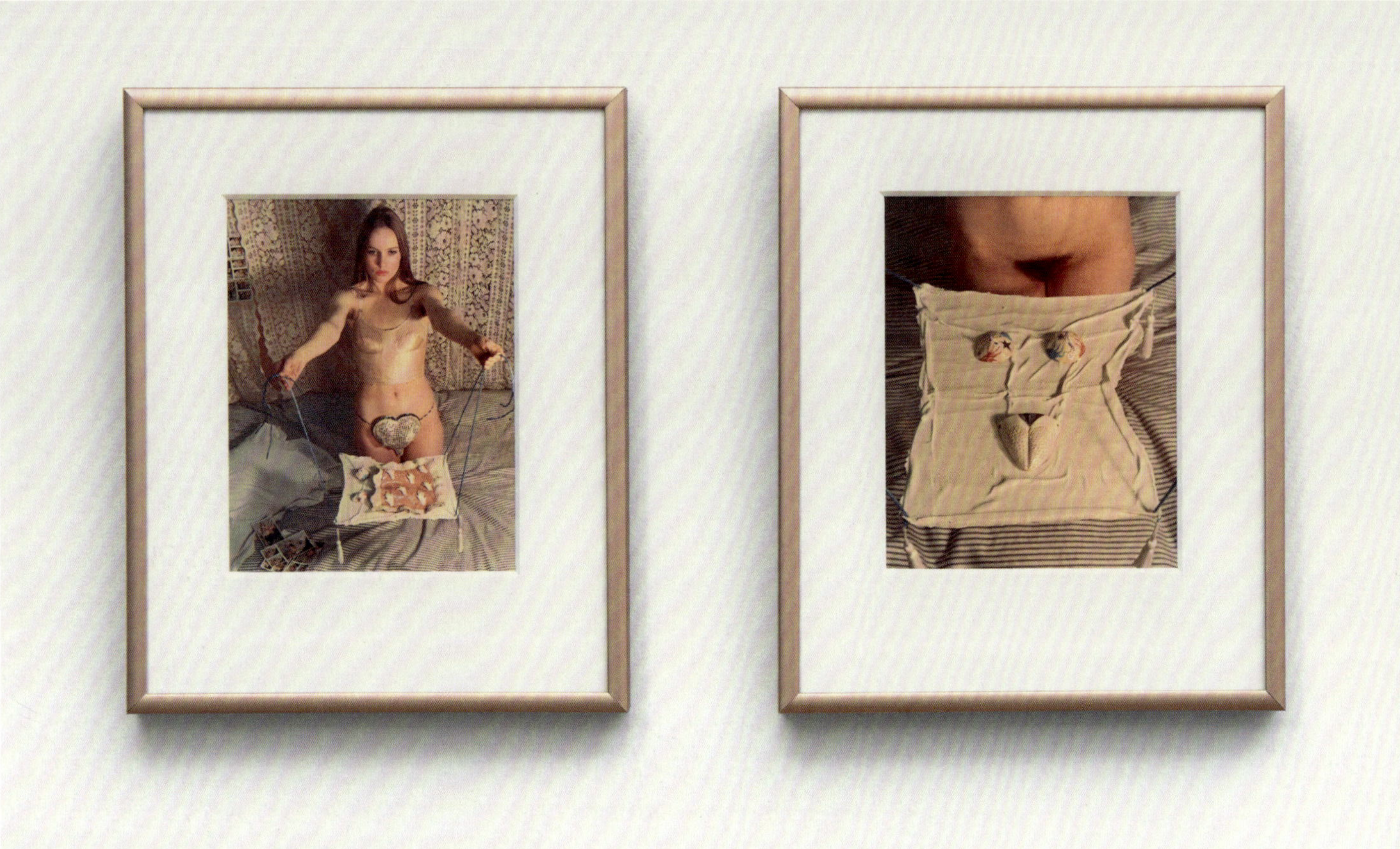

Study for a Divertissement: Jo and Porcelain sheet with breasts, yoni and coverlet with hands 1973. C-prints on paper 13.5 × 11 (each)

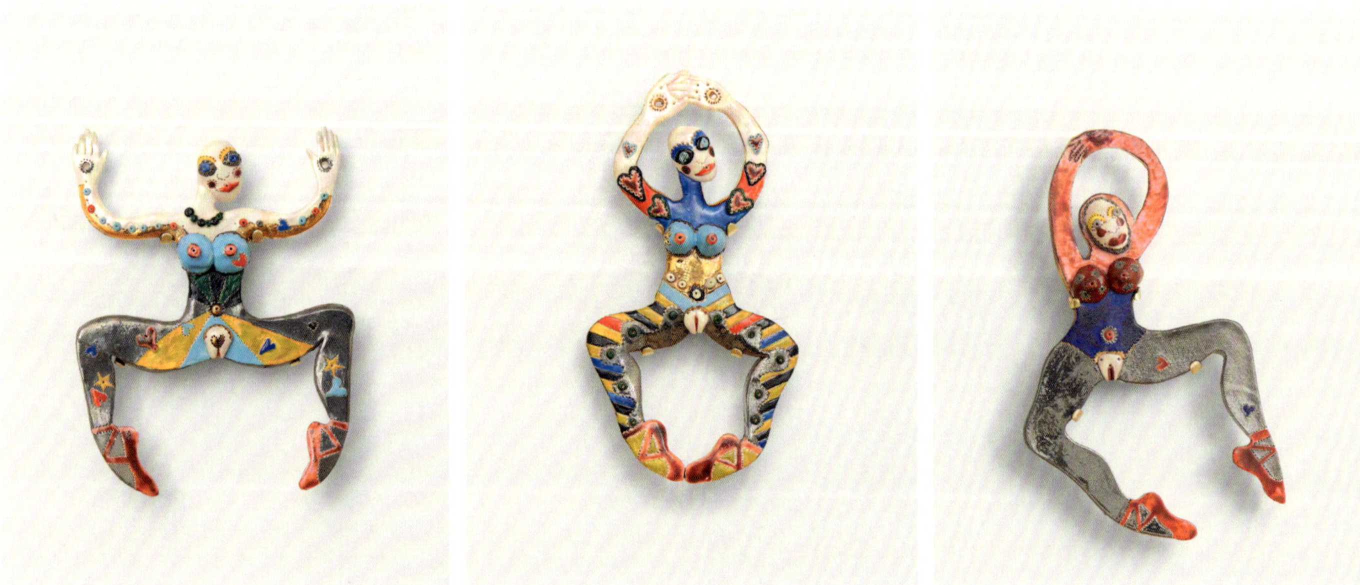

Study for a Divertissement: Porcelain Dancer 1 1973. Porcelain and enamel 22.9 × 17.8 × 2.5
Study for a Divertissement: Porcelain Dancer 3 1973. Porcelain and enamel 22.9 × 15.2 × 1.9
Study for a Divertissement: Porcelain Dancer 4 1973. Porcelain and enamel 22 × 11.5 × 2

Rose English was born in 1950 in Hereford and studied fine art at Leeds Polytechnic, graduating in 1973. Her interdisciplinary degree show combined ceramics and performance in an inquiry about aesthetics, form and feminism that became a hallmark of her work to come. Performance is, for English, a means of social commentary and critique. *Quadrille* 1975, which addresses the fetishisation and objectification of both women's and horse's bodies, is regarded as one of the most important performance works in feminist art history. It is held in the national collection at Tate. In 1975 English also exhibited in *Sweet Sixteen and Never Been Shown* at the Women's Free Art Alliance in London, now considered a key feminist exhibition of the period.

English went on to create groundbreaking solo performances in the 1980s, including *Plato's Chair* 1983 and *The Beloved* 1985. In the 1970s and 1980s, she collaborated with Jack Lansley and Sally Potter on performances including *Berlin* 1976 and *Mounting* 1977, and the film *The Gold Diggers* 1983. Her performance work from the 1970s was included in the 2007–8 highly influential show *WACK! Art and the Feminist Revolution*, and in 2019 a solo exhibition of her work was held at the Richard Saltoun Gallery. She lives and works in Stege, Denmark.

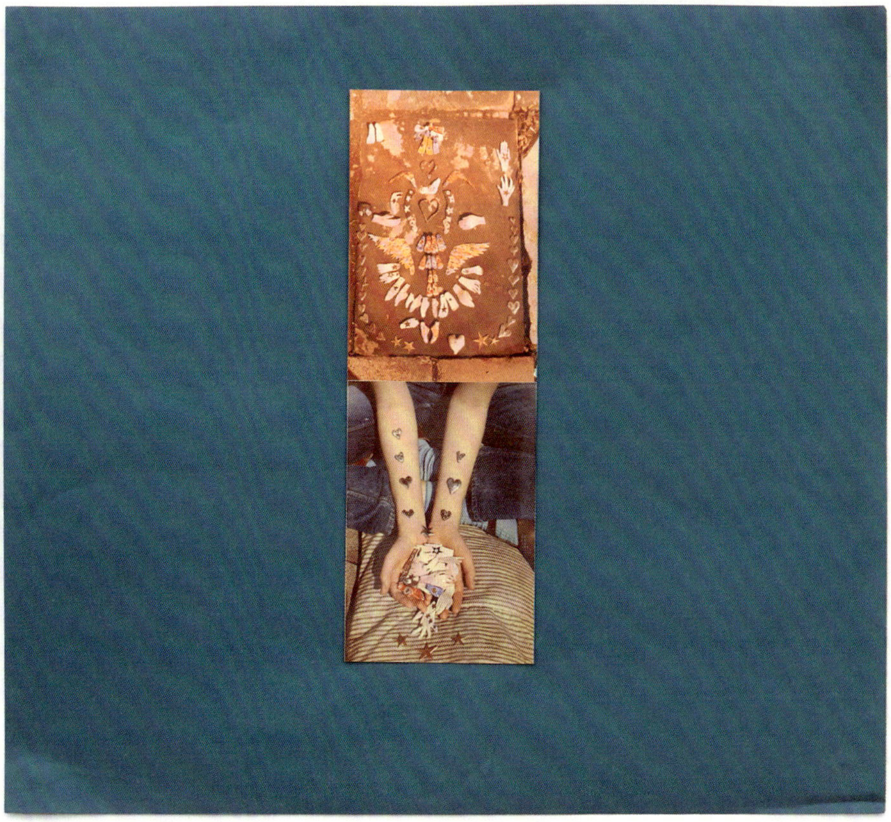

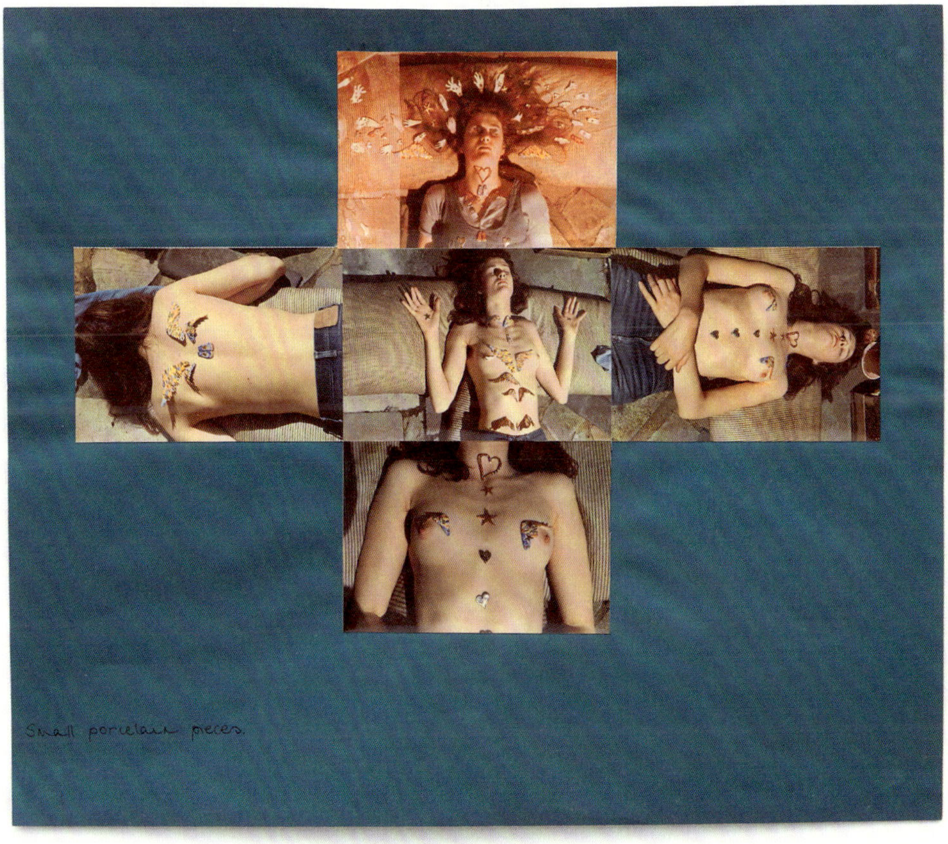

Small Porcelain Pieces (Collage) 1973. Two collages; C-prints on paper 35 × 40 (each)

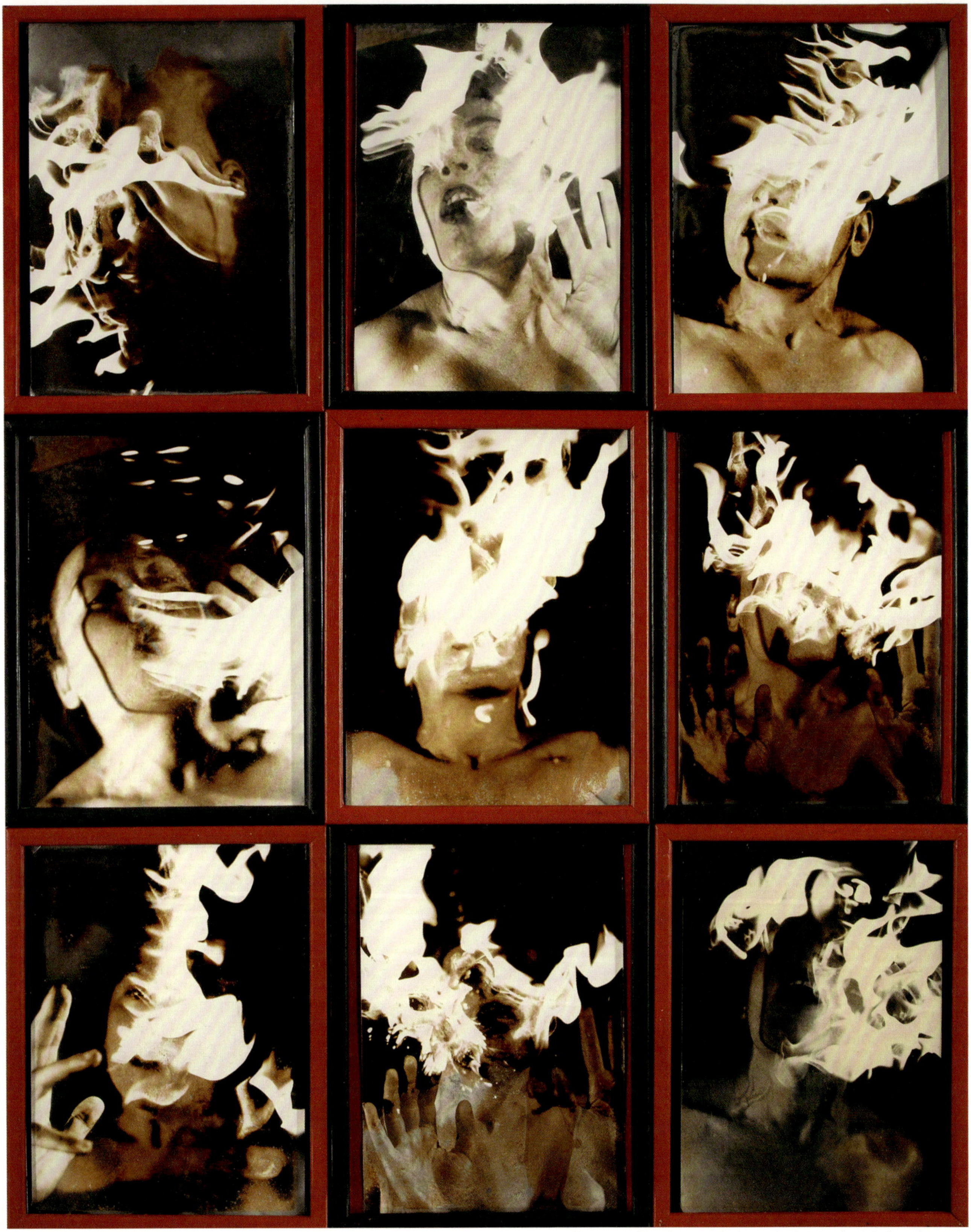

Heat 1974–7. 9 chemically altered and distressed gelatin silver prints from the performance *Elemental (Heat)*, on painted wood, glass and painted card
81.5 × 66.5 × 2.5 (overall)

Born in Zambia in 1950, Anne Bean studied art at the University of Cape Town in South Africa before moving to the UK in 1969, where she attended Reading University. She credits her arrival in England as an awakening, engaging with consciousness-raising, activism and alternative lifestyles. Bean's practice encompasses drawing, video, sound, slide projections and photography, but she is especially considered a pioneer of performance art in Britain, transgressing the boundaries between art and life. Her work often addresses identity, ideas of the self and the process of erasure, utilising a range of materials from weather balloons to wind, steam and honey, with a particular interest in materials that have a destructive potential. Bean's fearless performances from the 1970s sought to challenge and subvert societal norms by engaging with the elements of fire and water, testing her own endurance and placing her within a sphere of work that had been historically prohibited to women.

The artist's work has been presented in solo exhibitions with Matts Gallery in 2006, and with England & Co. gallery in 2019. Bean lives and works in London.

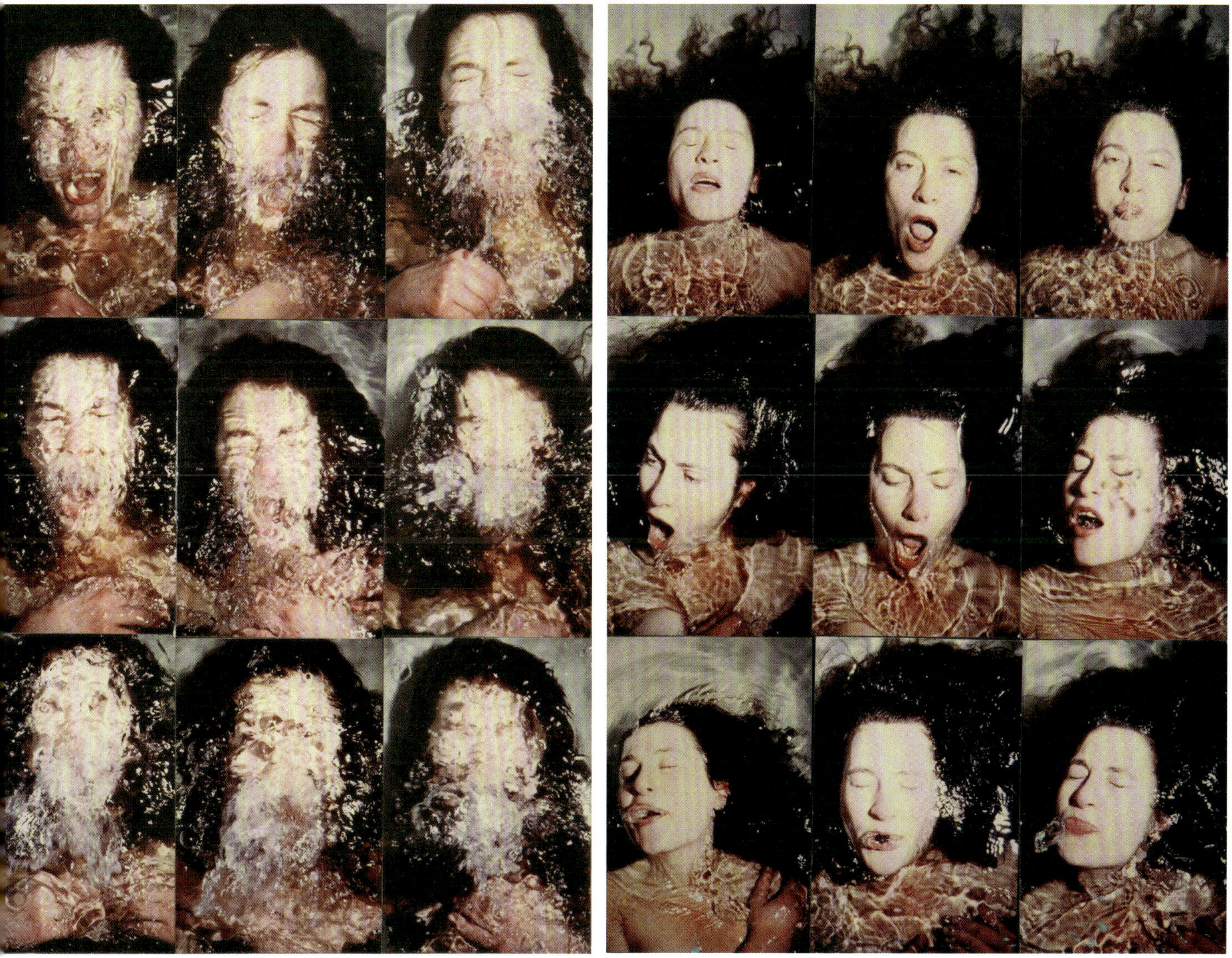

…ting 'Mortality' as I Drown 1977. Two sets of 9 photographs mounted on paper 39.5 × 27 (each)

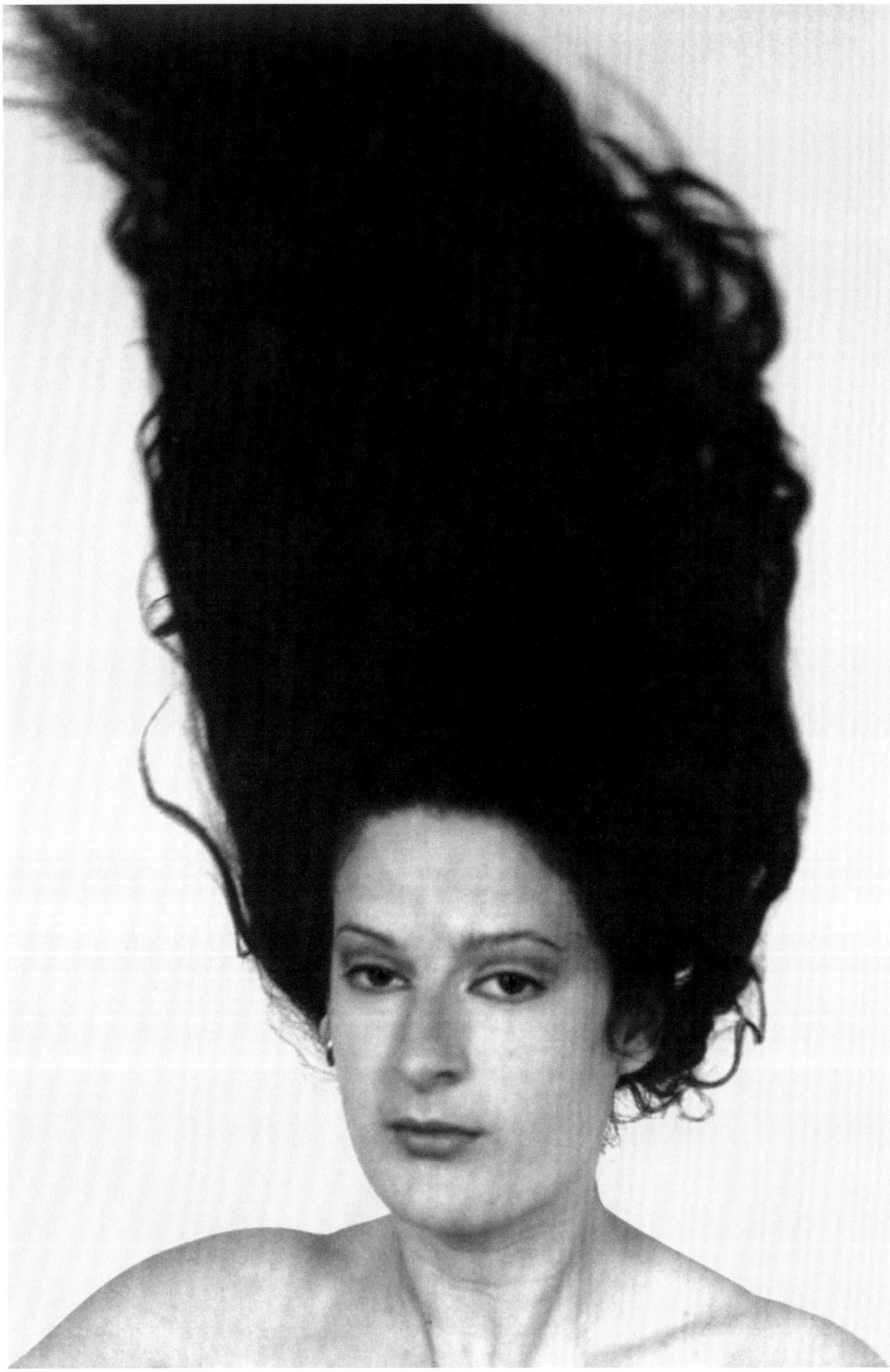

Chevelure 1977. Photograph 25.5 × 18

Catherine Elwes was born in France in 1952, and studied in London at the Slade School of Fine Art and the Royal College of Art, graduating from the latter in 1982. She worked as a painter and explored performance before specialising in video and video installation, becoming an early pioneer of video art. In the late 1970s, Elwes was a member of the Women Artists' Collective and Women's Art Alliance. For her performances *Menstruation 1 and 2* (p.100), Elwes isolated herself on a circular paper platform and in a glass-fronted chamber in the Slade School of Fine Art and free bleed for the duration of her period, using the time to explore the creative potential of the physical and psychological experience of menstruation. In 1980, she co-curated two groundbreaking feminist art exhibitions in the UK, *Women's Images of Men* and *About Time*, both presented at the ICA, London. Elwes worked as Professor of Moving Image Art at Chelsea College of Art. She was founding editor of the *Moving Image Review & Art Journal* (MIRAJ) and is author of *Video Loupe* (2000), *Video Art, A Guided Tour* (2005), *Installation and the Moving Image* (2015) and *Landscape and the Moving Image* (2022).

CATHERINE ELWES

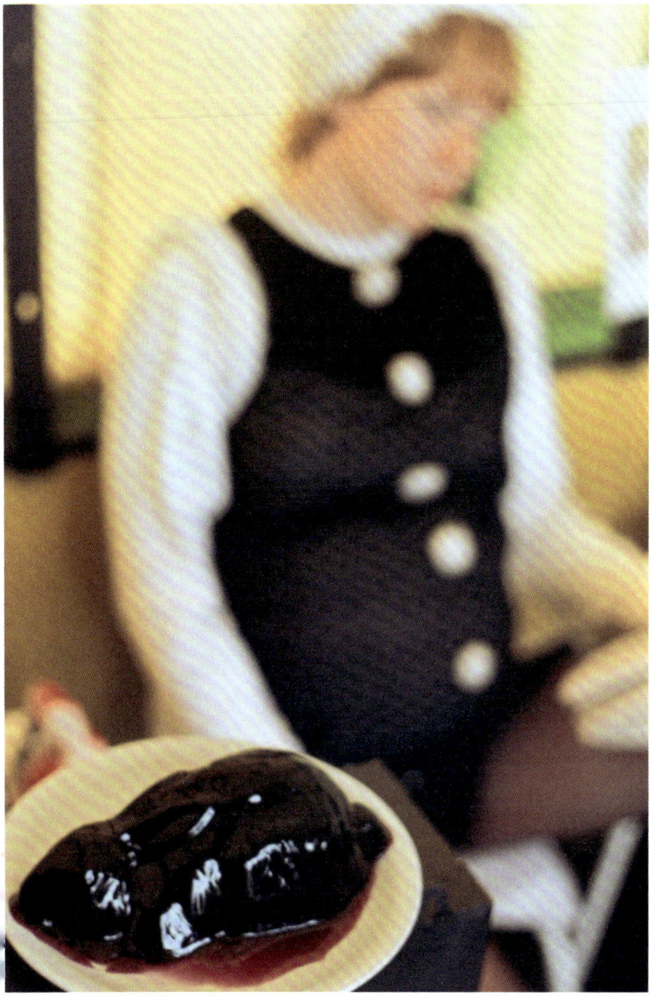

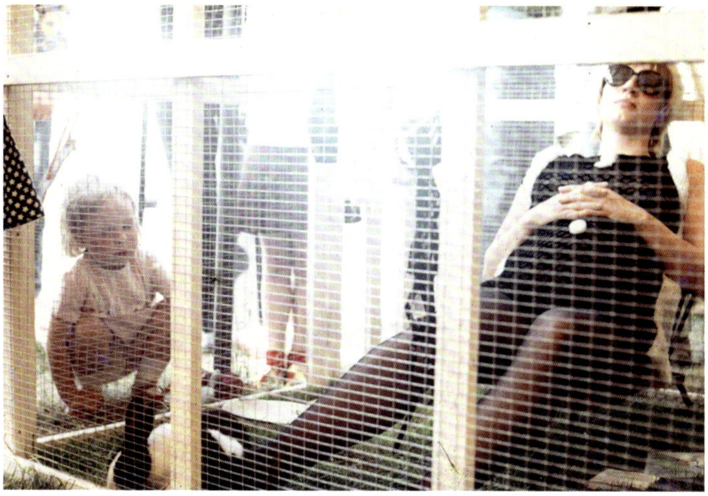

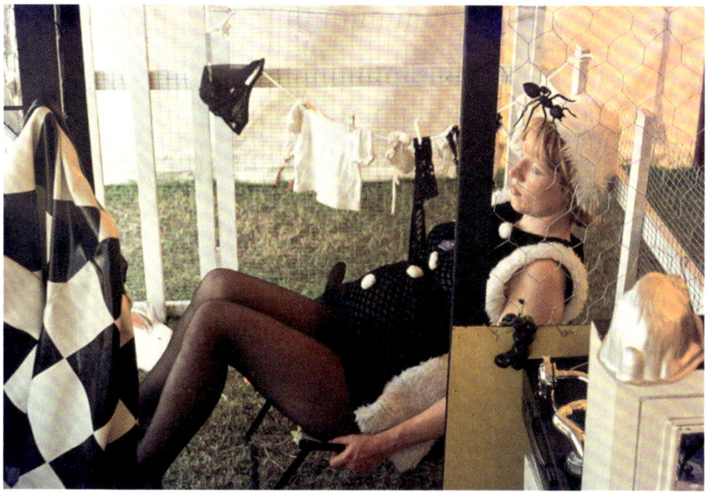

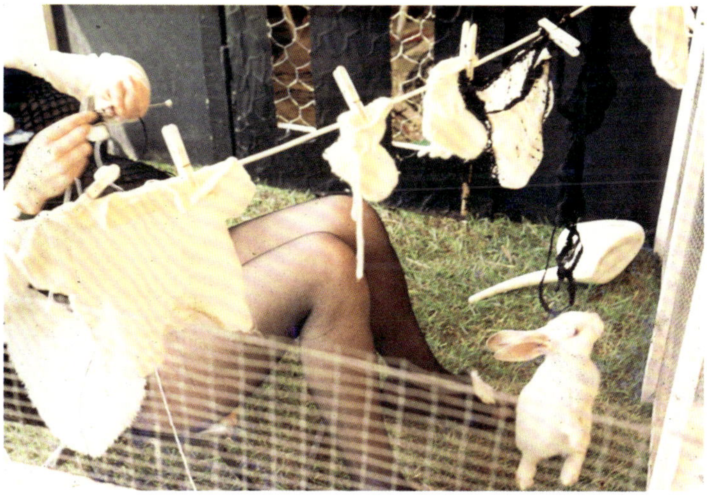

Rabbits – the Pregnant Bunny Girl, Mrs Rabbits and Woman as Animal 1974.
5 of 7 photographs 29.7 × 42 (each)

Shirley Cameron (b.1944) studied at Sutton Art Schools and St Martins Sculpture Department between 1962 and 1966, and lectured at Swansea Art College and Carmarthen Art College from 1970. She has worked as a sculptor, set designer, installation and performance artist. Through her performance work and sculpture, she was a key figure in the women's art movement of the 1970s and 80s and was involved in various groups and activities. She was part of the Feminist Art Group, a collective that adopted performance art specifically for its accessibility and the openness of its subject matter. She was also involved with the national touring network Sister Seven, a group of artists who sought to distribute anti-nuclear poster art and performances around the country, from shopping malls to colleges to art galleries (see pp.188–90). In *Rabbits – the Pregnant Bunny Girl, Mrs Rabbits and Woman as Animal* 1974, a humorous site-specific work which toured agricultural shows, the artist responded to expecting twins.

The importance of Cameron's performance work was acknowledged at the 1987 NAA Women's Conference in Birmingham. She lives and works in Sheffield and runs art classes in association with the WEA.

SHIRLEY CAMERON

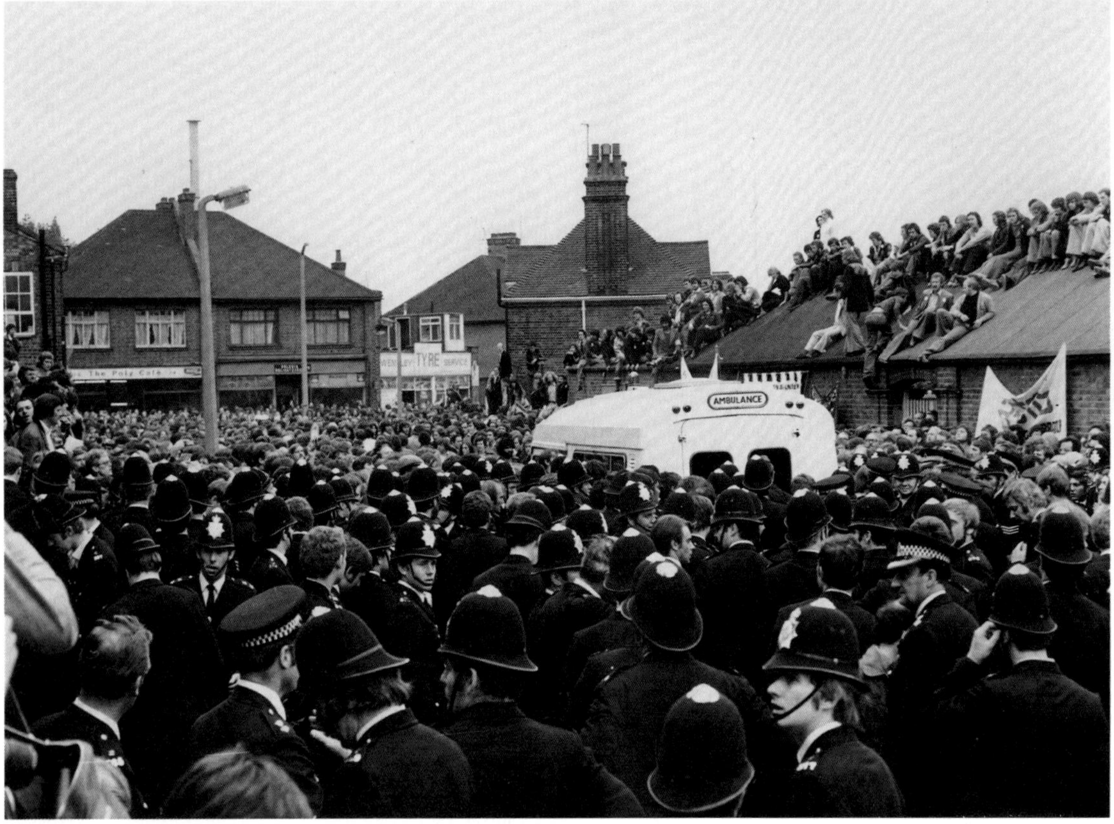

Val Wilmer *Police at the Trade Union Picket at Grunwick* 1976. Photograph 30.5 × 40.6

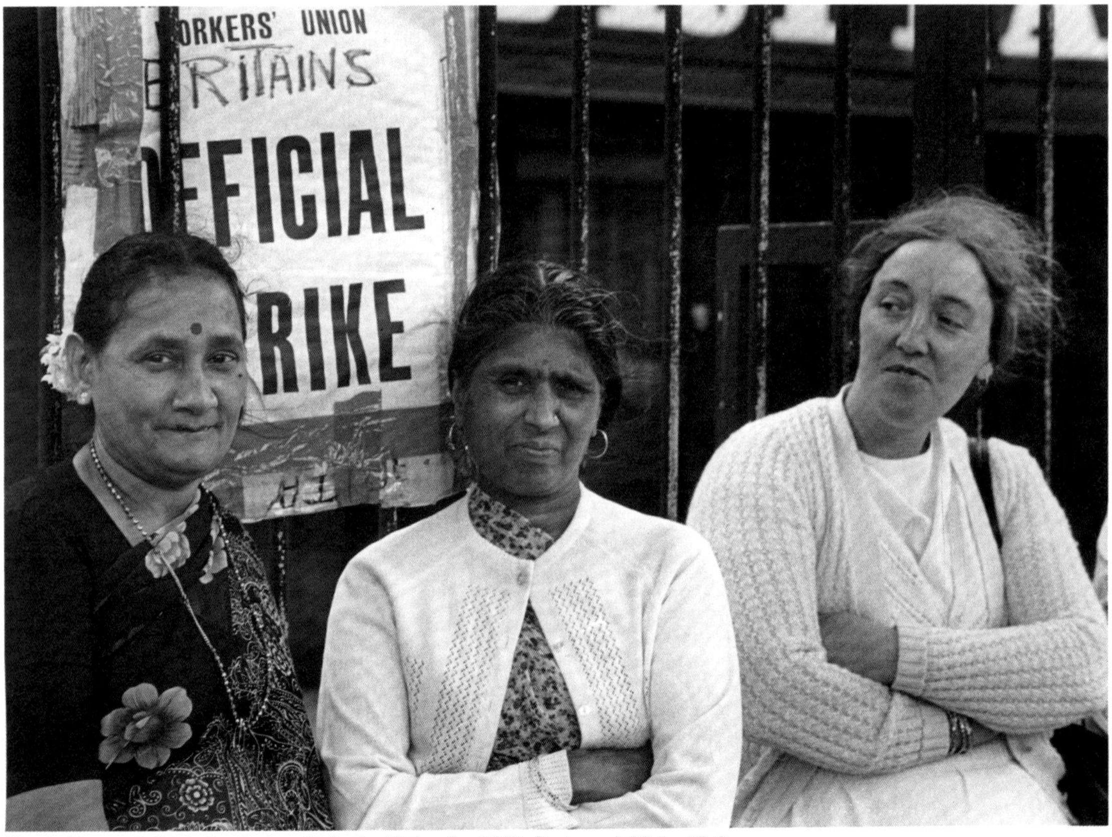

Maggie Murray *Britain's Toy Factory Strike for Higher Pay* 1983. Photograph 30.5 × 40.6

Format Photographers was founded in 1983 as a collective run by women photographers for women photographers. It offered members a route into the professional world, some control over how their work was used and support in developing their skills and creativity. The woman-only agency chose to focus on the representation of issues and individuals otherwise receiving little attention in the mainstream press of the day – such as anti-nuclear protests, LGBTQ+ campaigns, women's involvement in the miners' strike, anti-racism.

The agency was established by Maggie Murray, Val Wilmer, Joanne O'Brien, Jenny Matthews, Pam Isherwood, Sheila Gray, Anita Corbin and Raissa Page. Other prominent members included Brenda Prince, Melanie Friend, Judy Harrison, Roshini Kempadoo, Jacky Chapman and Mo Wilson. Format's photographs have been used across *Women in Revolt!* to ensure that the socio-political gaze of the exhibition is from a women's perspective. The agency disbanded in 2003 and their archive is now at the Bishopsgate Institute in London.

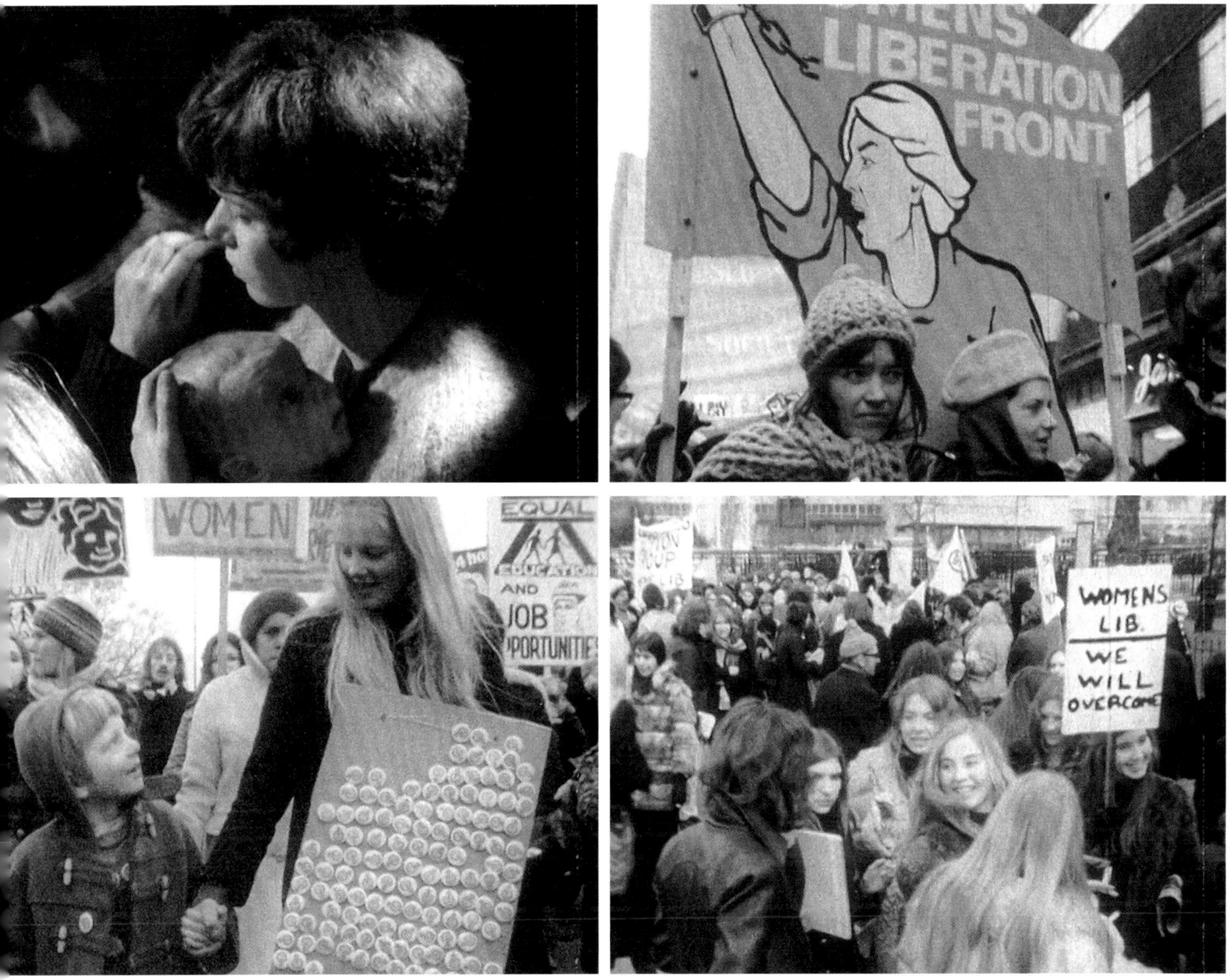

oman's Place 1972. 16mm film; shown as digital video; black and white, sound. 32 min, 24 sec

Sue Crockford (1943–2019) grew up in Coulsdon, Surrey. Following her studies in English and fine art at Leeds University, Crockford became immersed in the politically-engaged arts community of the late 1960s, through the Tufnell Park Women's Liberation Group, and Liberation Films, with whom she made *A Woman's Place* 1972. It was the first film to document the marches for equal rights on International Women's Day in 1971, and an emergent Women's Liberation Movement in Britain, filmed at the first national conference at Ruskin College, Oxford. Her commitment to the rights of women, children and young people can be seen across her subsequent career as a freelance filmmaker, during which she ran the Camden Town Youth Centre and worked as Assistant Commissioning Editor for Education at Channel 4, where she also developed the channel's programming for deaf people.

SUE CROCKFORD

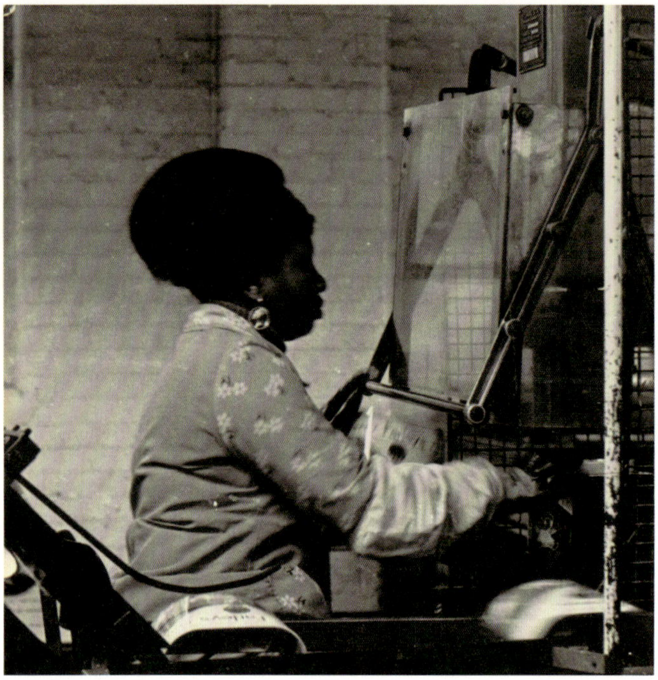

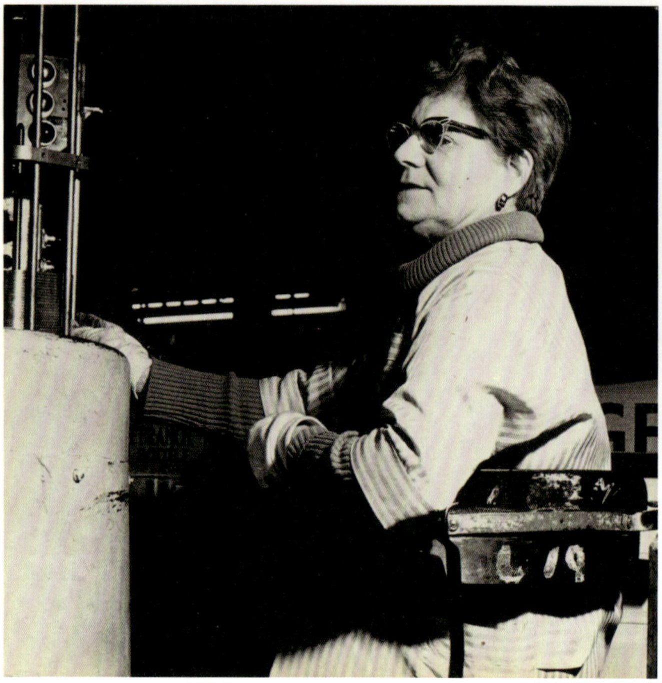

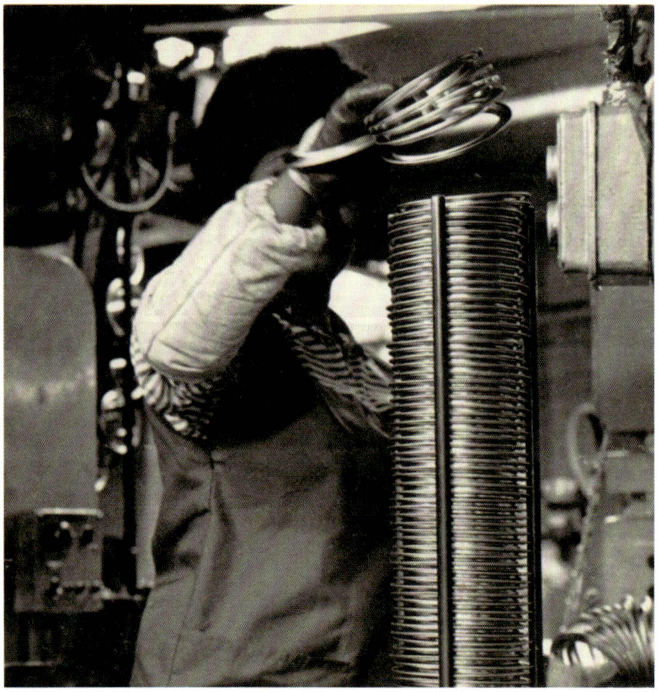

Margaret Harrison was born in Wakefield in 1940 and studied at Carlisle College of Art, the Royal Academy Schools and the Accademia di Belli Arti di Perugia in Italy. Working across drawing, installation, collage and textiles, Harrison was a key figure in the feminist art scene of the 1970s and one of the founders of the London Women's Liberation Art Group and a member of the Women's Workshop of the Artists' Union. A 1971 solo exhibition by Harrison at Motif Editions in London displayed a series of drawings that sought to challenge the portrayal of women in popular culture. Some works depicted women engaging with large pieces of food, suggestive of pornographic imagery and society's reduction of women to objects of consumption. Harrison intended the series to reclaim the depiction of women's bodies, describing it as 'anti-pornographic'. The exhibition was closed by the police on grounds of indecency. In 1973–5 Harrison collaborated with artists Kay Hunt and Mary Kelly to conduct a study of women's experiences working in a factory in Bermondsey, London. This resulted in the installation *Women and Work: A Document on the Division of Labour in Industry*, which used the women's accounts to consider their working environment and the recent Equal Pay Act (pp.82–3).

Harrison lives and works in Carlisle.

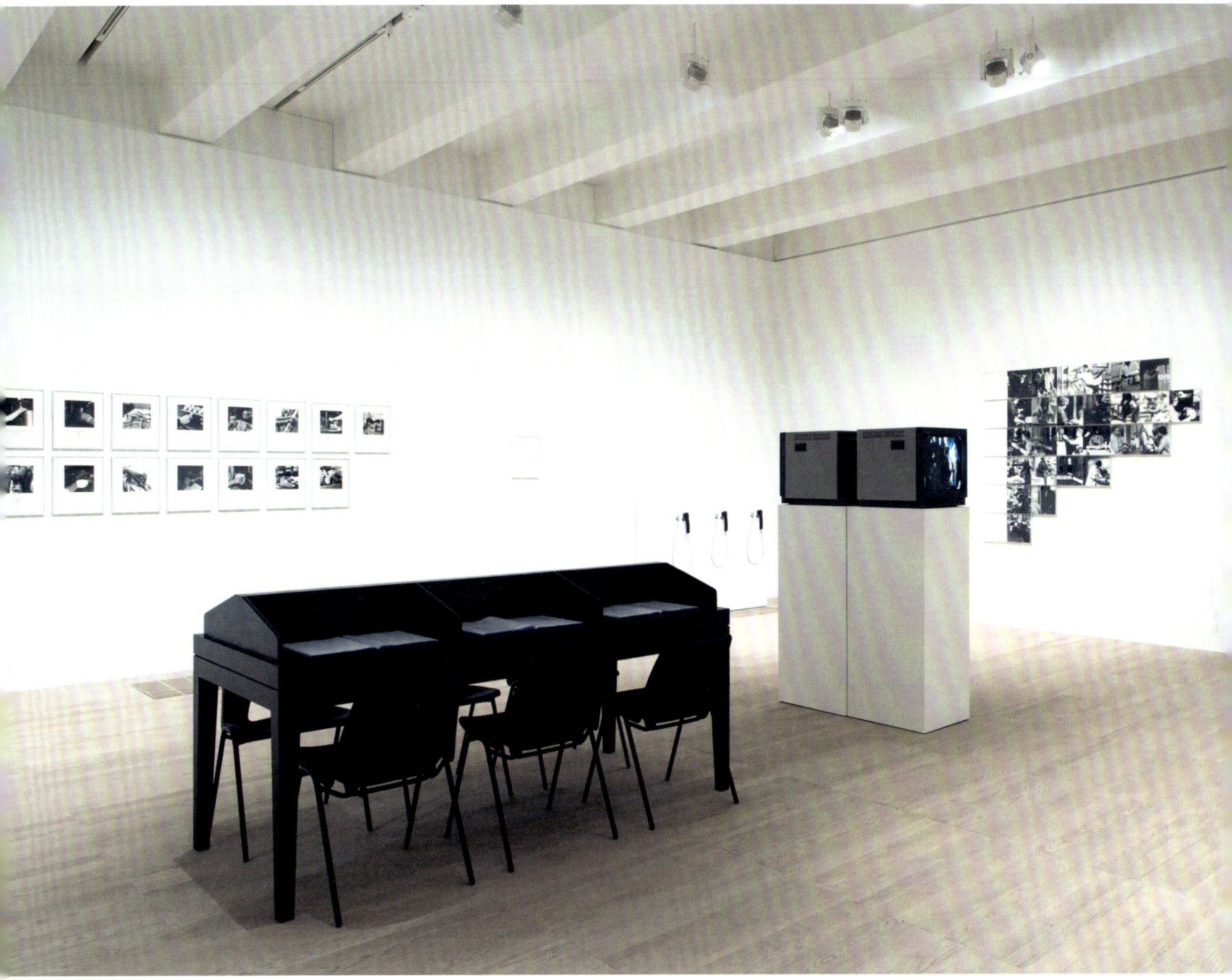

Women and Work: A Document on the Division of Labour in Industry 1973–5.
Video on 2 monitors, colour, audio; and photographs, gelatin silver prints on paper; and works on paper, ink. Dimensions variable

MARGARET HARRISON KAY HUNT MARY KELLY

Born in Fort Dodge, Iowa, USA, in 1941, Mary Kelly studied painting in Florence, Italy, before moving to the UK for postgraduate study at Saint Martin's School of Art in London in 1968. There she became involved with the Women's Liberation Movement and worked on key art projects that spoke to the movement's concerns and demands, including *Women and Work* 1973–5 with Margaret Harrison and Kay Hunt. Kelly is widely regarded as a prominent figure in feminist art history, with a profound impact on conceptual art and cultural politics. She was part of the Berwick Street Collective, contributing to the film *Nightcleaners* 1975, which sought to raise awareness of the lives of women who cleaned offices during night hours for minimal pay. In 1976 Kelly's work *Post-Partum Document* 1973–9 was presented in a solo exhibition at the ICA. It received notoriety in the tabloid press due to the inclusion of her son's soiled nappy liners. The work followed the film *Antepartum* 1973, in which the artist's pregnant abdomen at full term is seen rising and falling with each breath, the movements of the baby at times visible under the skin (p.103).

Kelly lives and works in Los Angeles.

Kay Hunt (1933–2001) was born in Bermondsey, London and attended Camberwell Art School, where she focused on sculpture. She taught at Camberwell and Farnham School of Art, where she was involved in the art school strikes of 1968, and went on to become active in various women's liberation groups. For many years Hunt led the Lina Garnade Foundation Course for the Unemployed, funded by the G.L.C., with the annual *Art on the Dole* exhibition of students' work held at the South London Gallery. She initiated the *Women and Work* project with Margaret Harrison and Mary Kelly, and selected the factory site.

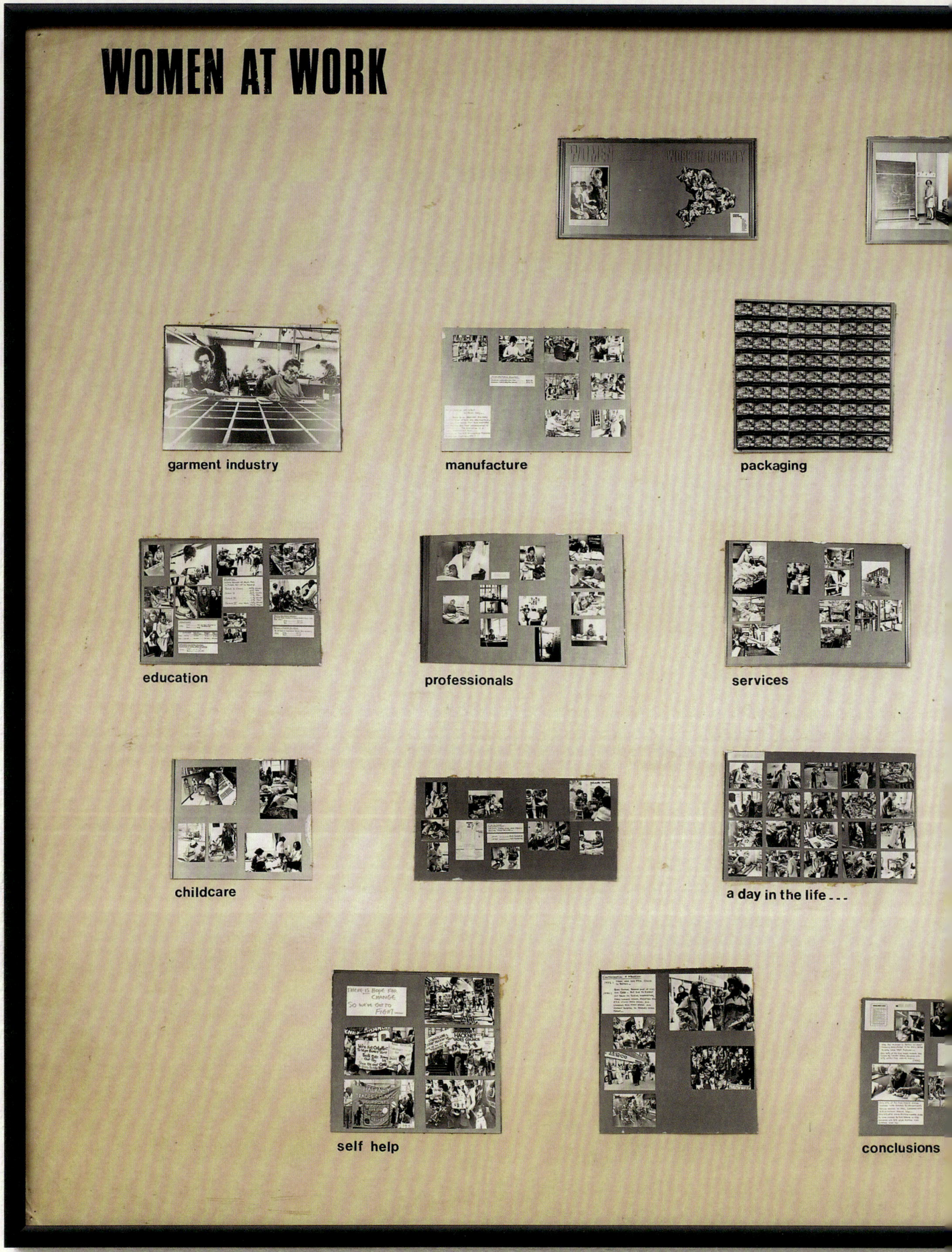

Women at Work 1975. 21 photographs mounted on board, 37.8 × 49.3

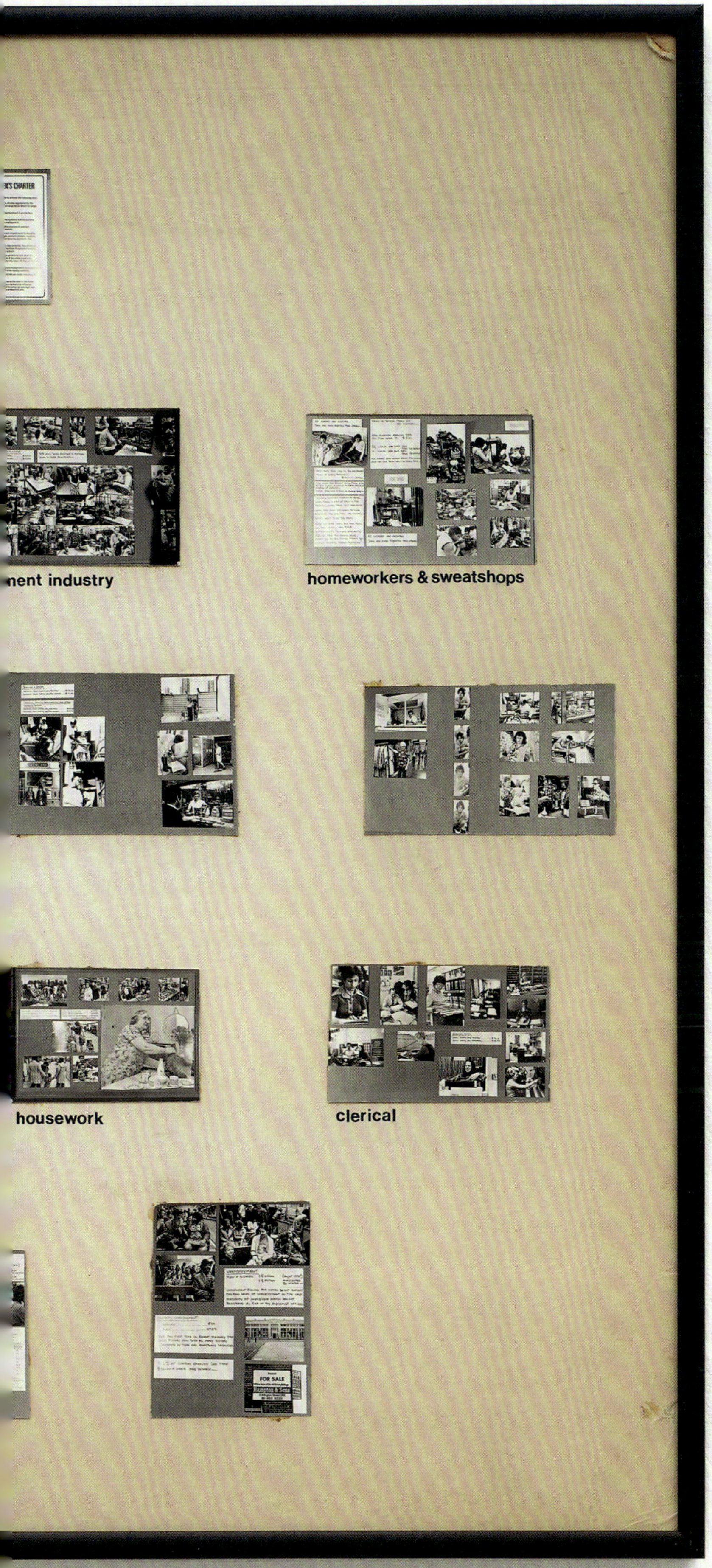

Active between 1974 and 1980, the socialist feminist women's agitprop collective Hackney Flashers focused their attention on the borough of Hackney in east London, home to some of the city's most severe poverty at the time. Their work was made for a purpose beyond the art gallery, intended to reach trade union events, women's liberation conferences and other forums dedicated to political activism and feminist action. The group members included An Dekker, Sally Greenhill, Gerda Jager, Liz Heron, Michael Ann Mullen, Maggie Murray, Christine Roche, Jo Spence and Julia Vellacott, but the work produced was always credited to the collective, without naming individuals.

Hackney Flashers produced two exhibitions, one of them travelling, *Women and Work* 1975 and *Who's Holding the Baby?* 1978. The latter addresses the importance of childcare, critiquing and highlighting the lack of government support, exploring the conflicting and impossible position of being both a mother and a worker in 1970s Britain. The collective stipulated that the installation could only be displayed at the Hayward Gallery if a public event about issues around childcare was laid on. In 2015 *Who's Holding the Baby?* (pp.122–3) was shown as a slide show in the Hayward Gallery exhibition, *History is Now*, curated by Hannah Starkey.

HACKNEY FLASHERS

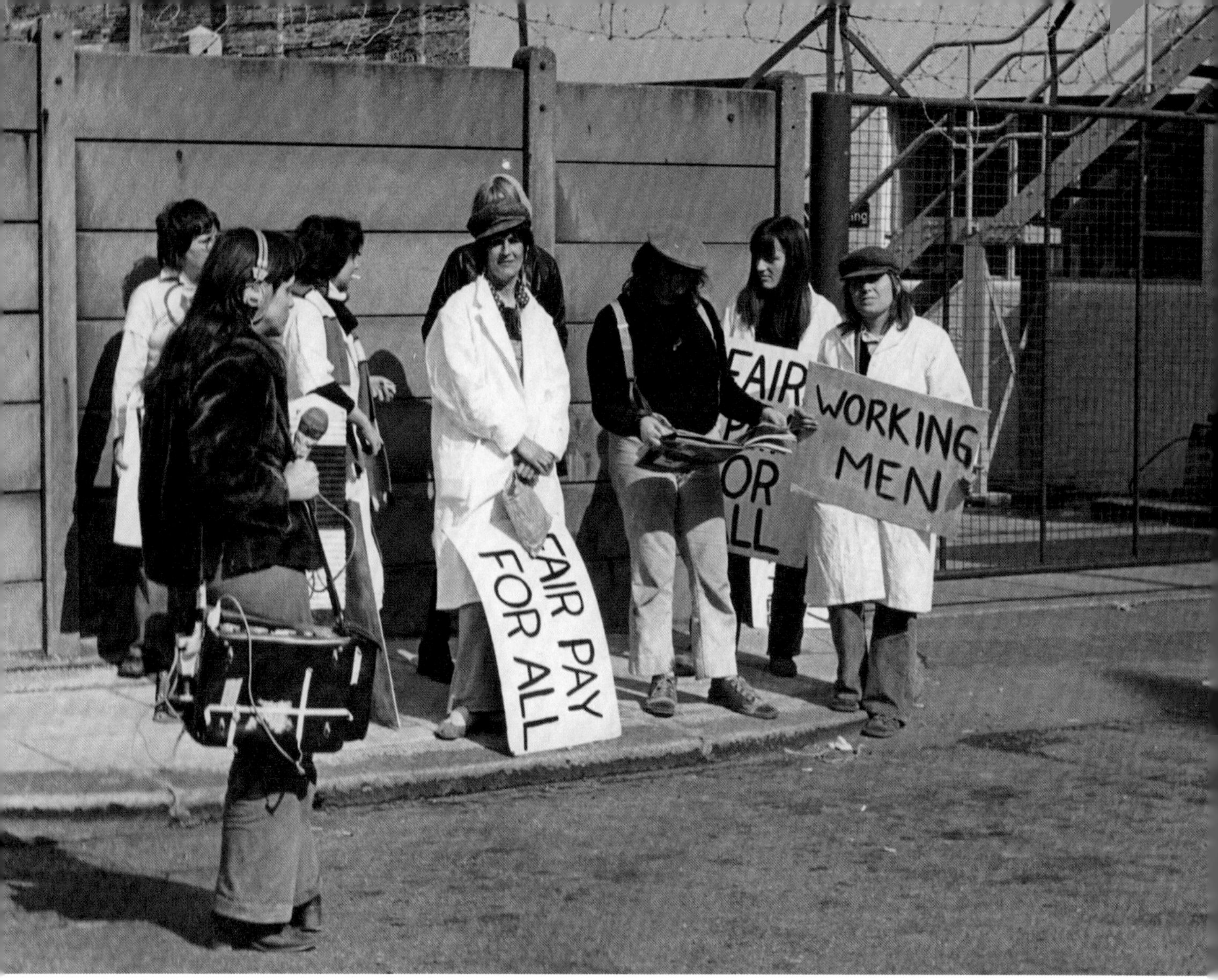

Amazing Equal Pay Show 1973–4. 16mm film, shown as digital video; black and white, sound. 48 min

The London Women's Film Group was formed in 1972 in response to the almost impermeable male-dominated film industry and culture of the time, along with the urgently felt need to put women's stories, told by women, on the screen. Made up of committed feminist filmmakers and theorists, the group produced a variety of films, both collectively and as individuals, including *Betteshanger, Kent* (1972), *Put Yourself in My Place* 1974, *The Amazing Equal Pay Show* 1974, and *Whose Choice?* 1976. Members included Linda Dove, Barbara Evans, Claire Johnson, Fran McLean, Esther Ronay, Susan Shapiro and Francine Winham, all of whom came together in response to a call to action by feminist filmmaker Midge McKenzie (*Shoulder to Shoulder* 1974.) Through their collaborative approaches to sharing practical filmmaking skills and radical evolution of ideas, the London Women's Film Group provided inspiration to other women who experienced the glaring lack of feminist expression in film.

LONDON WOMEN'S FILM GROUP

In 1974, upon seeing an advert in a radical women's liberation magazine asking for women interested in forming a group to explore and combat negative images of women in the media, three ex-art students formed the screenprinting collective See Red Women's Workshop. See Red (active 1974–90) set out to make posters that tackled sexist stereotypes and created positive and challenging alternatives, and spent the next sixteen years making some of the most powerful and instantly-recognisable protest posters of their time. See Red worked with over forty-five different women during this time, with four or five women in the workshop at any one time. Making posters that were accessible and affordable, all work was authored collectively with no hierarchy, and no one individual taking credit, and all tasks and skills were shared. Influenced by their members' respective interests, poster themes centred around childcare, housework, gender roles, identity, sexuality, class and race, and broadened out to include national and international themes supporting women's wider struggles for change. While mainly working on printing and selling their own posters, See Red also did service printing for the local community and LGBTQI+ groups to fund their work, focusing increasingly on this kind of work from 1984 to 1990.

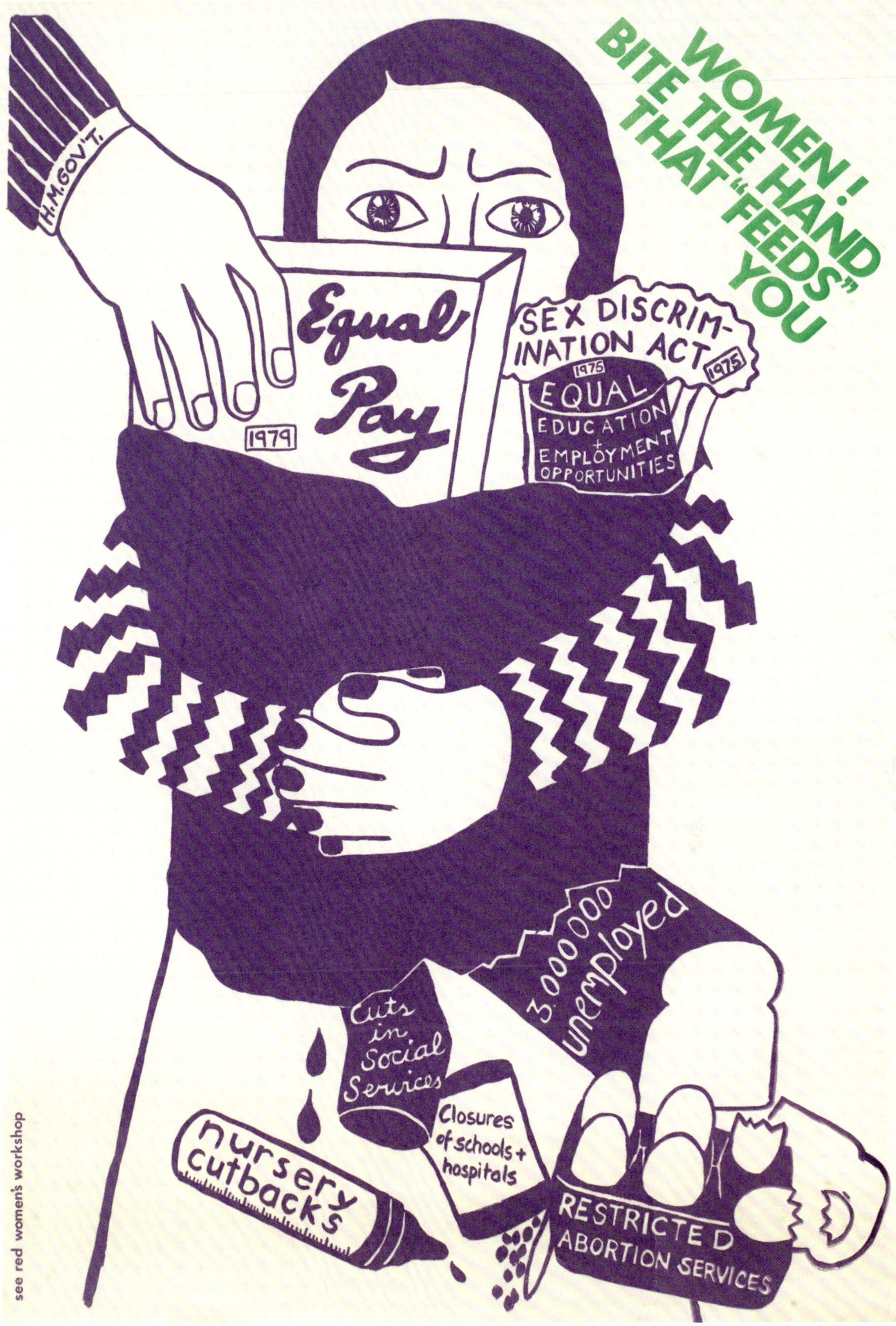

Bite the Hand 1978. Screenprint on paper 64 × 45

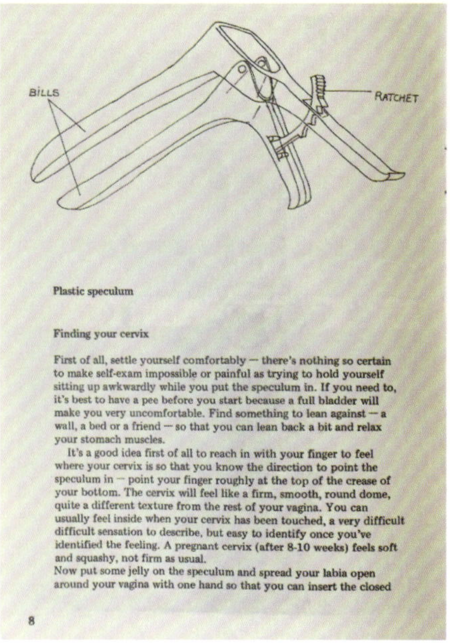

BILLS

RATCHET

Plastic speculum

Finding your cervix

First of all, settle yourself comfortably — there's nothing so certain to make self-exam impossible or painful as trying to hold yourself sitting up awkwardly while you put the speculum in. If you need to, it's best to have a pee before you start because a full bladder will make you very uncomfortable. Find something to lean against — a wall, a bed or a friend — so that you can lean back a bit and relax your stomach muscles.

It's a good idea first of all to reach in with your finger to feel where your cervix is so that you know the direction to point the speculum in — point your finger roughly at the top of the crease of your bottom. The cervix will feel like a firm, smooth, round dome, quite a different texture from the rest of your vagina. You can usually feel inside when your cervix has been touched, a very difficult difficult sensation to describe, but easy to identify once you've identified the feeling. A pregnant cervix (after 8-10 weeks) feels soft and squashy, not firm as usual.
Now put some jelly on the speculum and spread your labia open around your vagina with one hand so that you can insert the closed

8

1

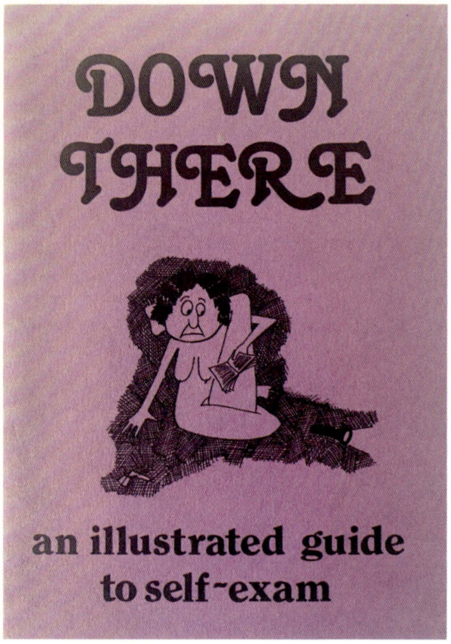

2

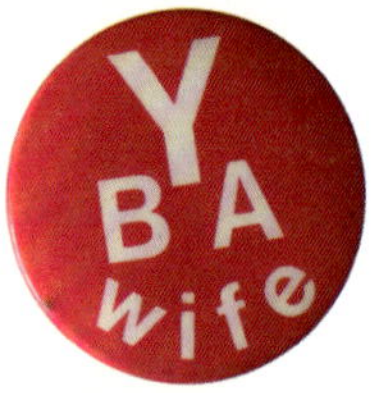

3

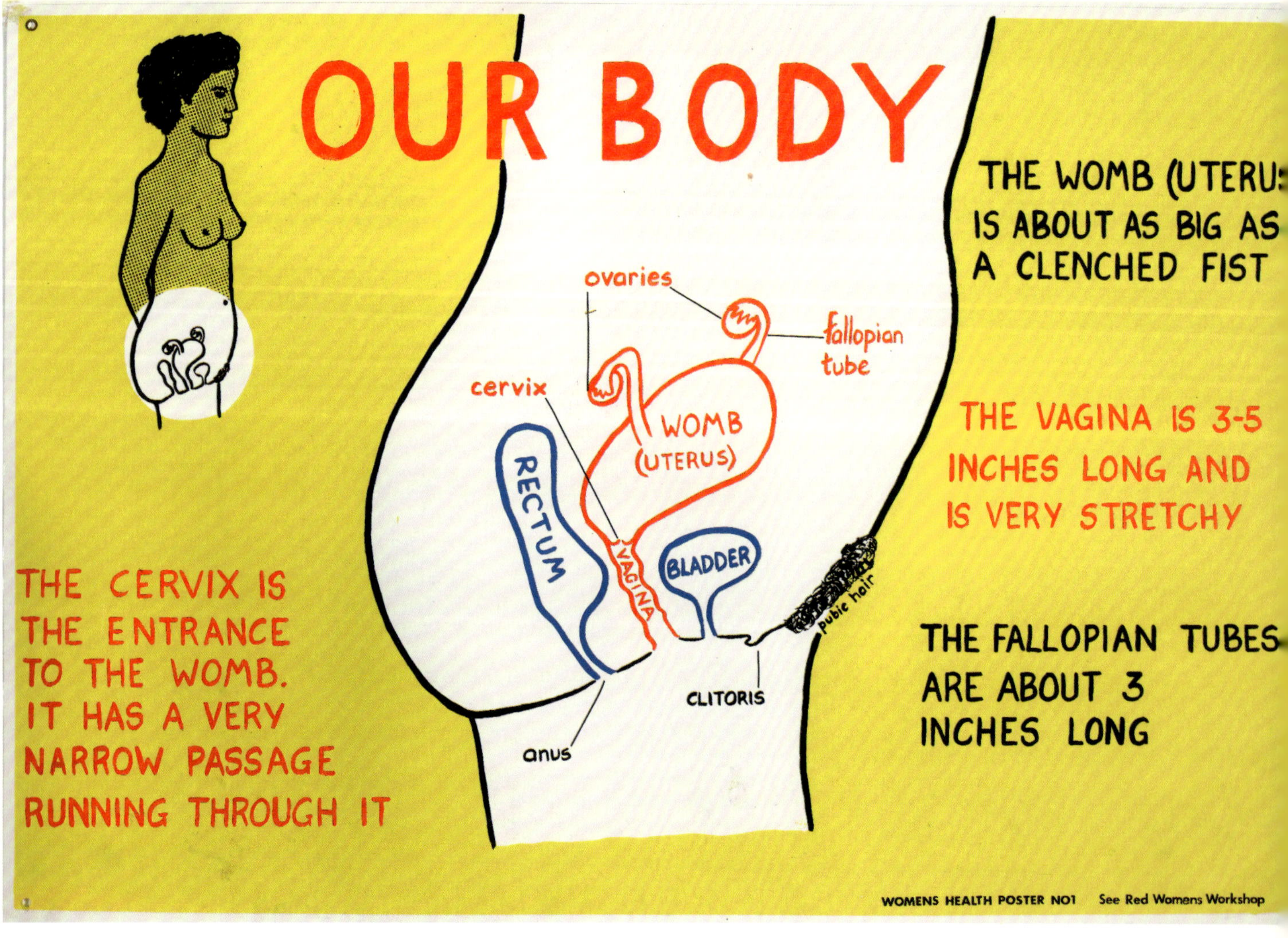

Women's Health

The contraceptive pill was introduced to the UK in 1961, but until 1967 it was only available to married women. In 1967, following the NHS Family Planning Act, it became available to unmarried women, allowing the majority autonomy over their reproduction for the first time – although a significant stigma remained and women were at the mercy of the mainly male doctors who needed to approve its use. In April 1974, all contraceptive advice and supplies became free on the NHS regardless of marital status. For women of colour engaged in the fight for access to family planning services, there was an additional battle to be fought around the provision of Depo-Provera, a contraceptive injection which was controversially tested on minority ethnic women, who were not given sufficient information of the potential risks and side-effects. The issue of safe childbirth was also one of critical importance for women of colour, as they were four times more likely to die during childbirth than white women in the 1970s, a statistic that has not changed in the intervening fifty years. Women's physical and mental health was often not taken seriously. Inspired by women's efforts in America, women's groups in the UK published guides and led workshops for gynaecological examination, and the issue of over-medication for depression, that many women thought was caused by domestic and political situations, became an urgent topic of conversation.

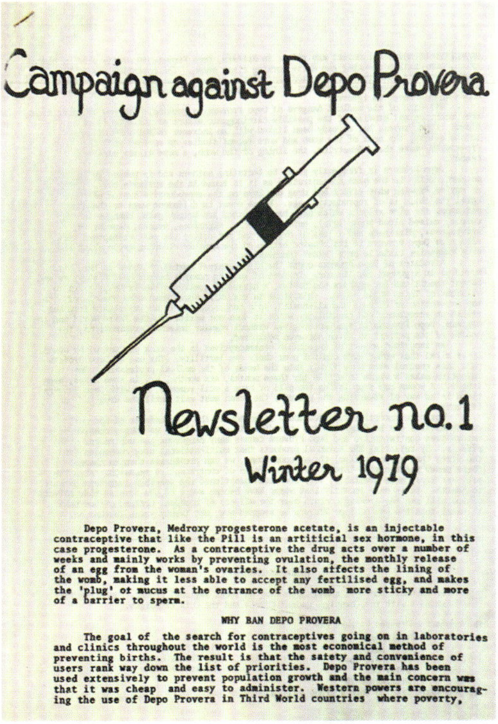

Campaign against Depo Provera

Newsletter no.1

Winter 1979

Depo Provera, Medroxy progesterone acetate, is an injectable contraceptive that like the Pill is an artificial sex hormone, in this case progesterone. As a contraceptive the drug acts over a number of weeks and mainly works by preventing ovulation, the monthly release of an egg from the woman's ovaries. It also affects the lining of the womb, making it less able to accept any fertilised egg, and makes the 'plug' of mucus at the entrance of the womb more sticky and more of a barrier to sperm.

WHY BAN DEPO PROVERA

The goal of the search for contraceptives going on in laboratories and clinics throughout the world is the most economical method of preventing births. The result is that the safety and convenience of users rank way down the list of priorities. Depo Provera has been used extensively to prevent population growth and the main concern was that it was cheap and easy to administer. Western powers are encouraging the use of Depo Provera in Third World countries where poverty,

4

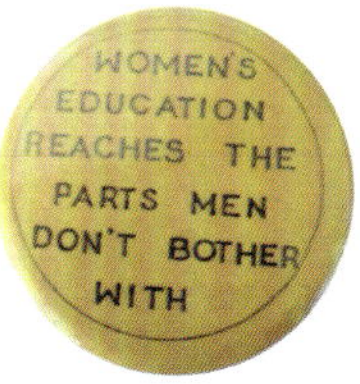

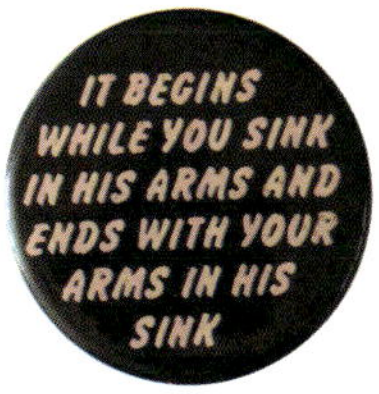

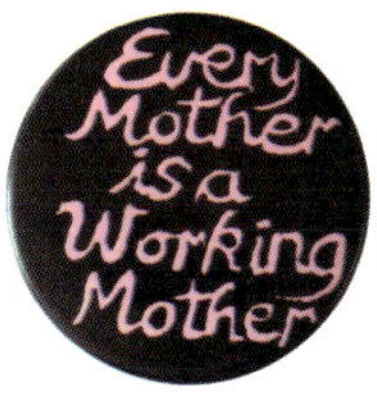

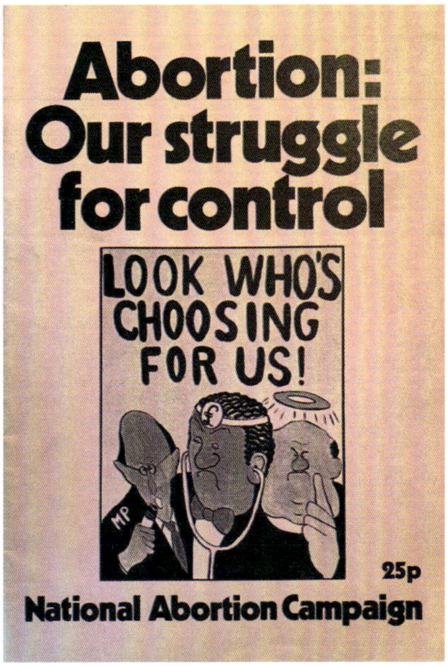

6

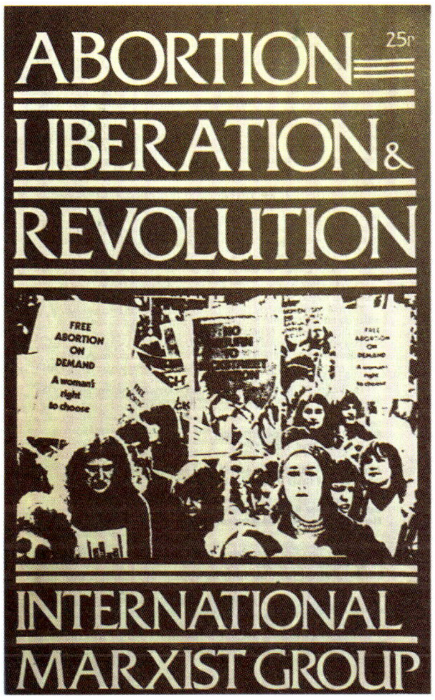

7

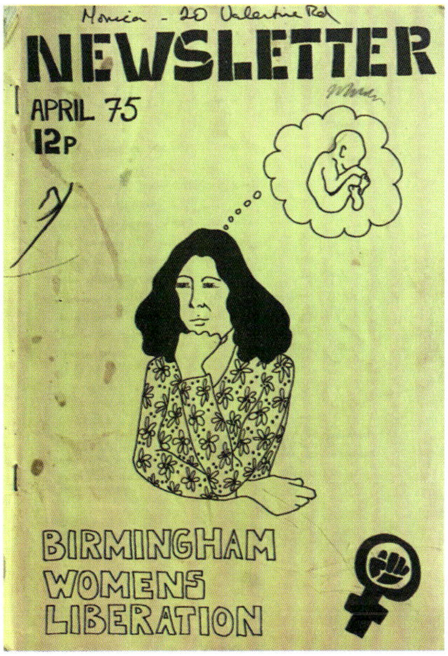

8

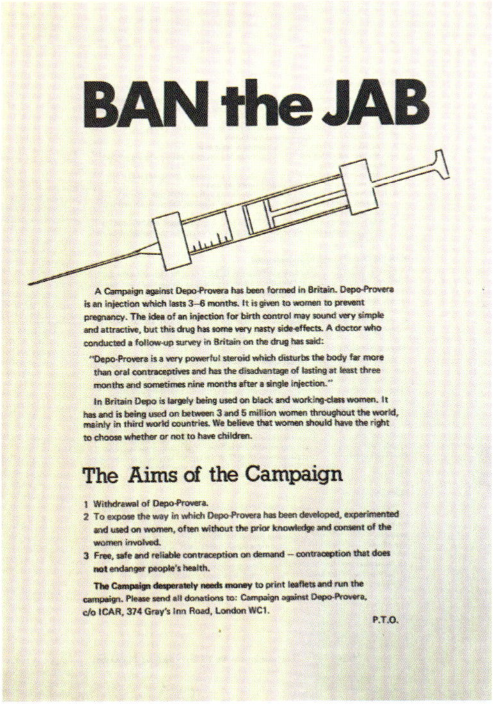

BAN the JAB

A Campaign against Depo-Provera has been formed in Britain. Depo-Provera is an injection which lasts 3–6 months. It is given to women to prevent pregnancy. The idea of an injection for birth control may sound very simple and attractive, but this drug has some very nasty side-effects. A doctor who conducted a follow-up survey in Britain on the drug has said:

"Depo-Provera is a very powerful steroid which disturbs the body far more than oral contraceptives and has the disadvantage of lasting at least three months and sometimes nine months after a single injection."

In Britain Depo is largely being used on black and working-class women. It has and is being used on between 3 and 5 million women throughout the world, mainly in third world countries. We believe that women should have the right to choose whether or not to have children.

The Aims of the Campaign

1 Withdrawal of Depo-Provera.
2 To expose the way in which Depo-Provera has been developed, experimented and used on women, often without the prior knowledge and consent of the women involved.
3 Free, safe and reliable contraception on demand – contraception that does **not** endanger people's health.

The Campaign desperately needs money to print leaflets and run the campaign. Please send all donations to: Campaign against Depo-Provera, c/o ICAR, 374 Gray's Inn Road, London WC1.

P.T.O.

5

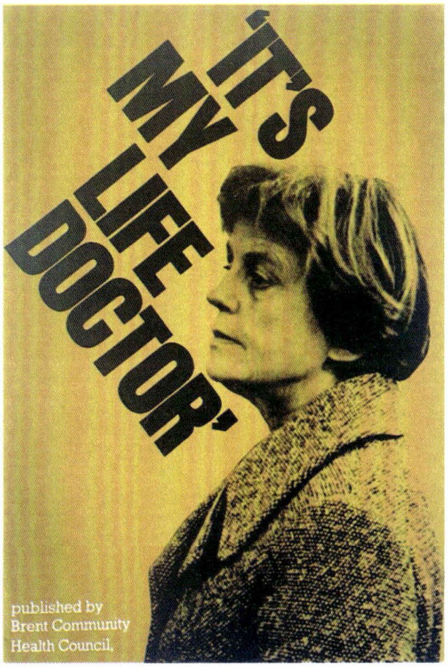

9

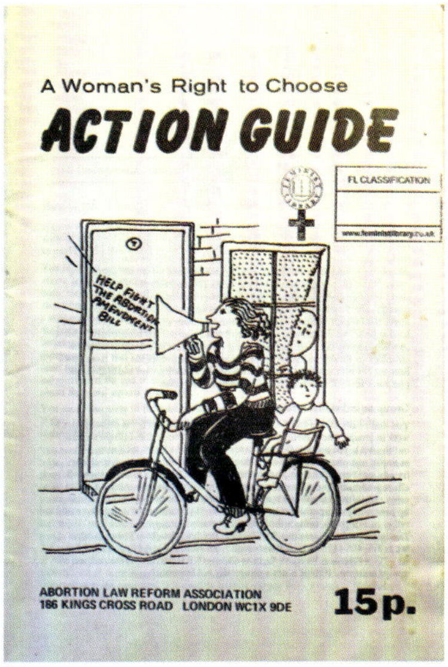

10

1–2 *Down There: an illustrated guide to self-exam*, published by Onlywomen Press Ltd, London 1981.
3 See Red Women's Workshop *Our Body* 1980. Screenprint on paper 51 × 76.
4 *Campaign Against Depo Provera, Newsletter*, no.1, Winter 1979.
5 'Ban the Jab' campaign materials, c.1979.
6 *Abortion: Our Struggle for Control*, published by the National Abortion Campaign, 1979.
7 *Abortion, Liberation & Revolution*, published by the Other Press (Relgocrest Ltd), London, 1979, for the International Marxist Group.
8 *Birmingham Women's Liberation Newsletter*, produced by the collective, including Su Richardson and Monica Ross, April 1975.
9 *It's My Life Doctor*, published by Brent Community Health Council, London, 1981.
10 *A Woman's Right to Choose Action Guide*, published by the Abortion Law Reform Association, Kings Cross, London, 1973.

A Marxist Wife Still Does the Housework

For many women in the late 1970s the home was a place of drudgery and sometimes violence: women may have had to contend with physical or psychological violence at the hands of a partner, or the emotional impact of living within others' expectations. Traditional gender roles were still in place, and it was rare to find any depiction of the home that did not include a woman undertaking all domestic and childcare duties, roles that were ingrained and perpetuated through the media and advertising. Despite the Sex Discrimination Act being passed in 1975, women were routinely refused mortgages and loans in their own right, only being granted them if they could provide details of a male guarantor. As such women relied on their male partners and family members for domestic security, regardless of whether or not that was something they wanted. In the 1970s the average age of marriage for a woman was twenty-four and the average age at which they became a mother twenty-six. Maternity leave was not legislated in the UK until 1975, and until 1990 only half of working women were eligible. The issue of childcare during this period was therefore prominent and a great many women were forced to sacrifice their careers to raise children. There were a number of childcare provision campaigns during this time, including within communities of colour a fiercely fought campaign against the racist policies surrounding 'pupil referral units' or 'Sin Bin' schools that were disproportionally populated with young Black children who were deemed 'threatening' or 'aggressive'.

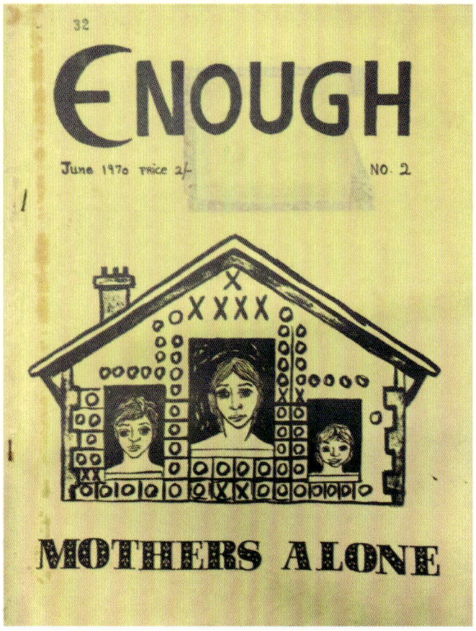

1

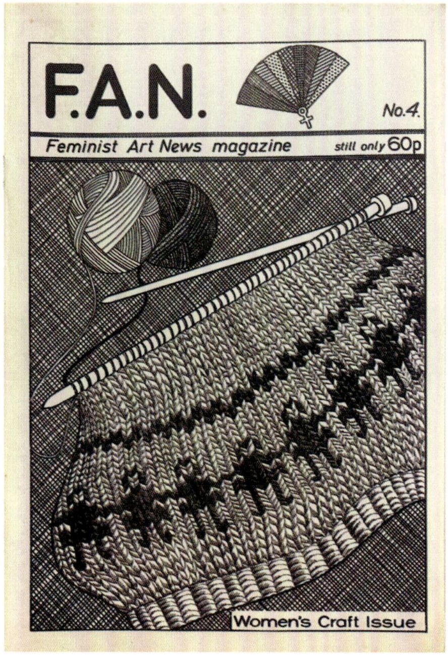

2

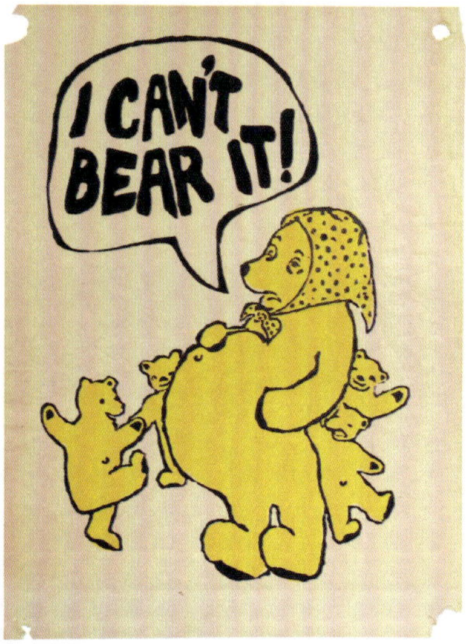

3

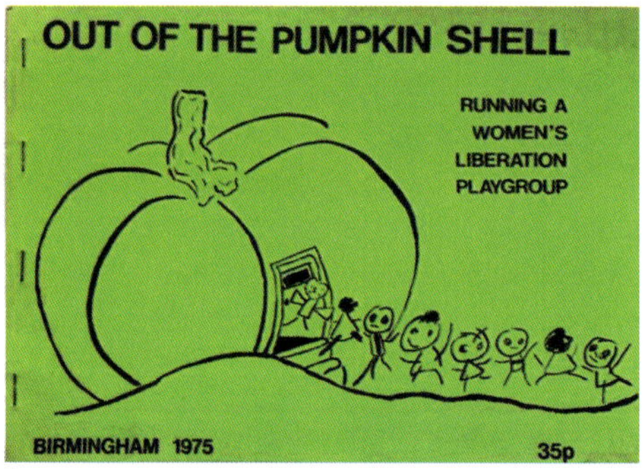

4

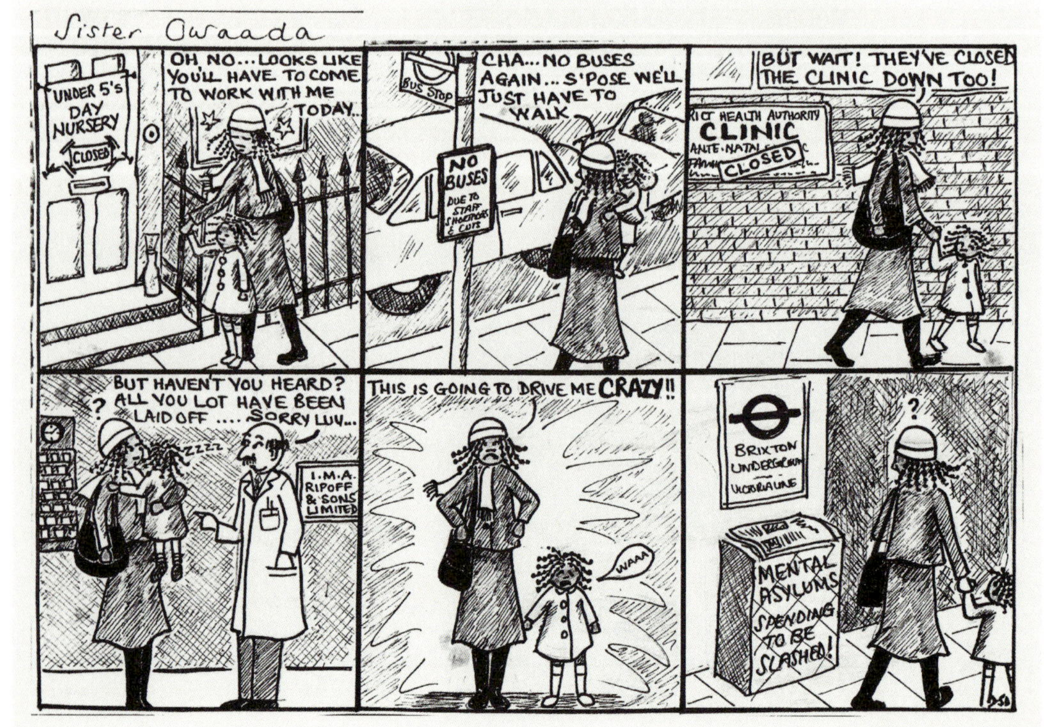

5

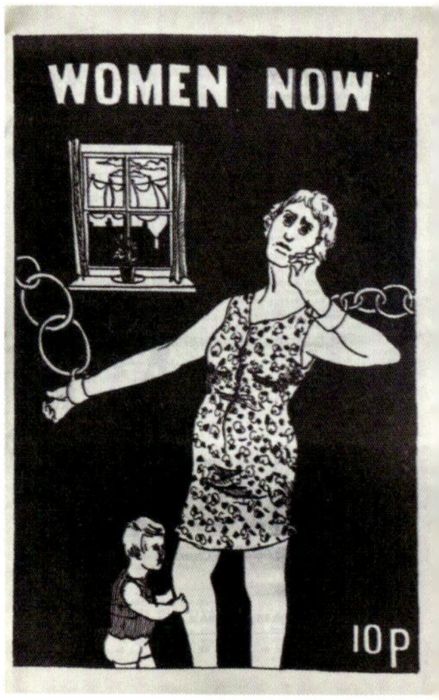

6

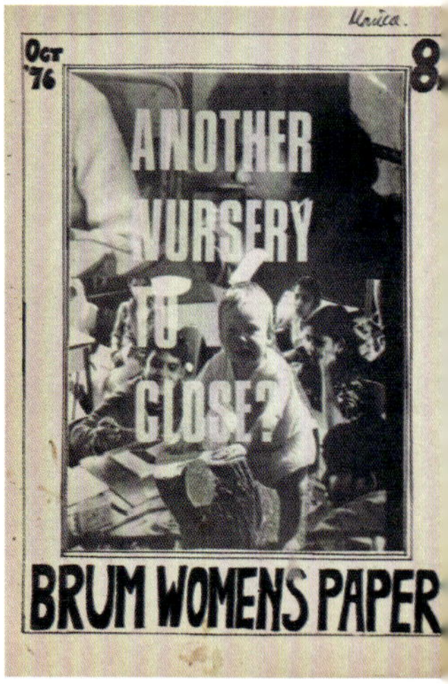

7

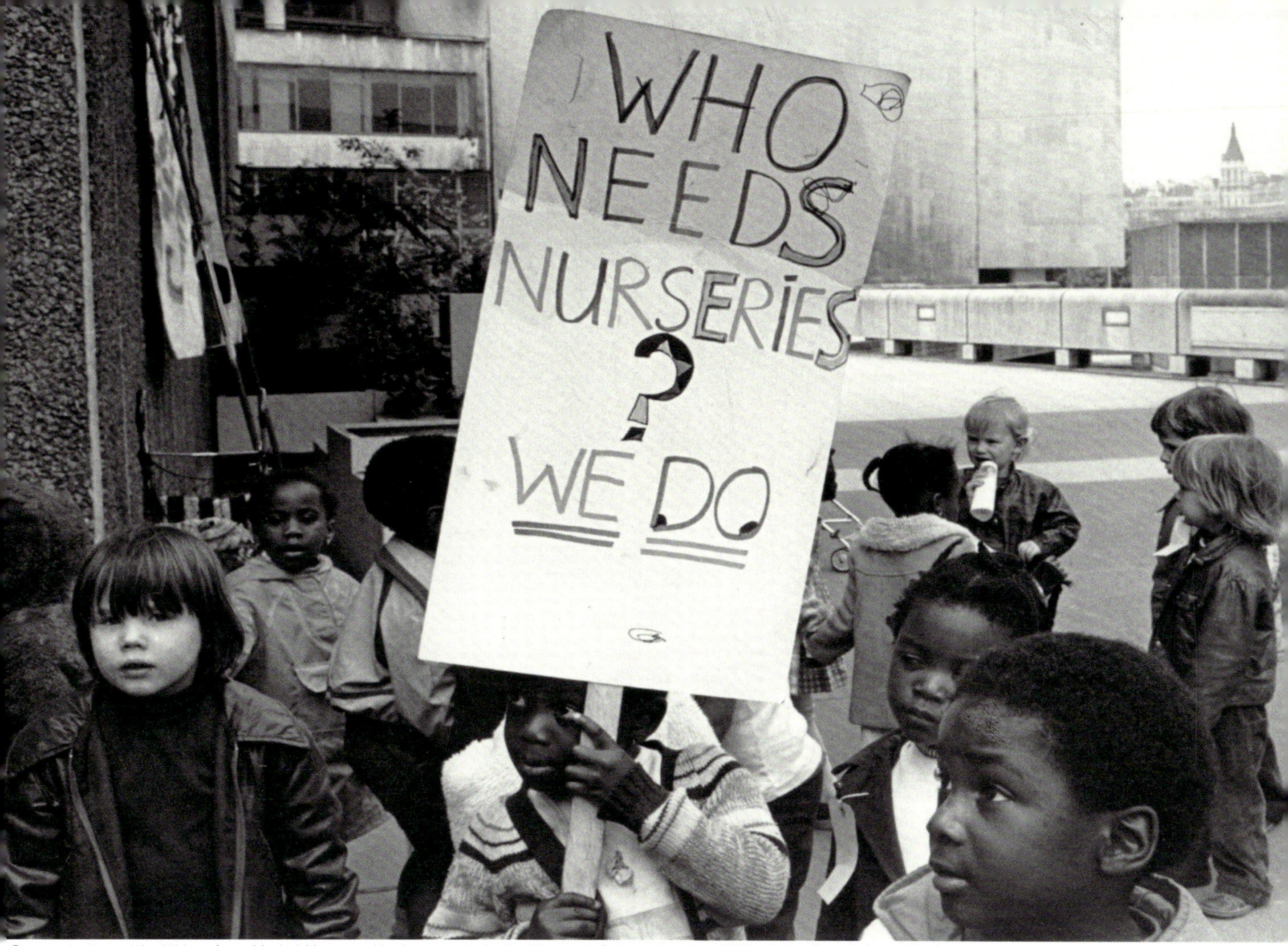

Demonstration with children from Market Nursery, Hackney, outside the Hayward Gallery, London 1979, during the Hackney Flashers' exhibition, *Who's Holding the Baby?*, their controversial contribution to the Arts Council show, *Three Perspectives on Photography*. Photographed by Maggie Murray, Hackney Flashers.

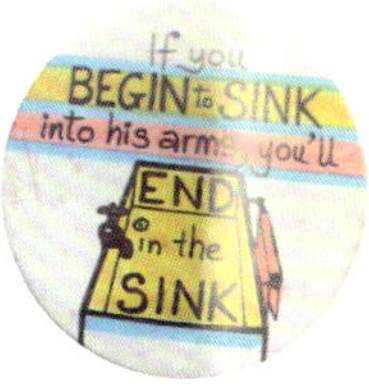

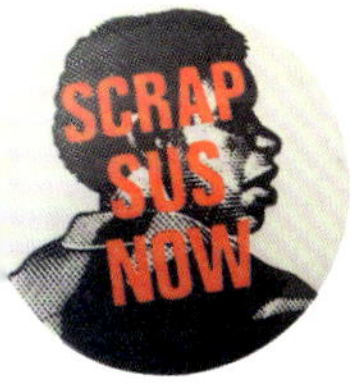

1 *Enough* journal, no.2, June 1970.
2 *Feminist Art News Magazine*, no.4. Women's Craft issue, produced by the F.A.N collective that included Kate Walker, Sol Jorgensen, Gill Elinor, Monica Ross and Sue Scott.
3 Unattributed feminist poster.
4 *Out of the Pumpkin Shell: Running a Women's Liberation Playgroup*, published by Birmingham 1975.
5 Sister Owaada cartoon for *FOWAAD!*, 1979.
6 *Women Now* magazine, c.1970.
7 *Brum Womens Paper*, October 1976.
8 *FOWAAD! Newsletter of the Organisation of Women of Asian & African Descent (OWAAD)*, no.3, November 1979.
9 *FOWAAD! Newsletter of the Organisation of Women of Asian & African Descent* (OWAAD), no.7, November 1980.

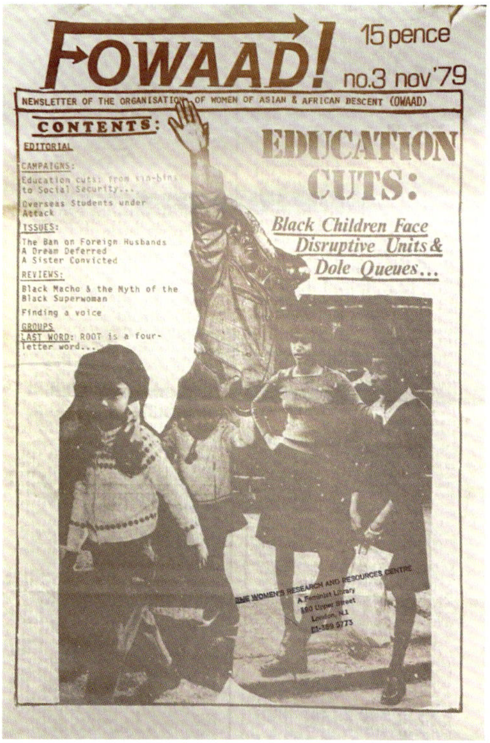
FOWAAD! 15 pence no.3 nov '79

NEWSLETTER OF THE ORGANISATION OF WOMEN OF ASIAN & AFRICAN DESCENT (OWAAD)

CONTENTS:

EDITORIAL

CAMPAIGNS:
Education cuts: from sin-bins to Social Security...
Overseas Students under Attack

ISSUES:
The Ban on Foreign Husbands
A Dream Deferred
A Sister Convicted

REVIEWS:
Black Macho & the Myth of the Black Superwoman
Finding a voice

GROUPS

LAST WORD: ROOT is a four-letter word...

EDUCATION CUTS:

Black Children Face Disruptive Units & Dole Queues...

8

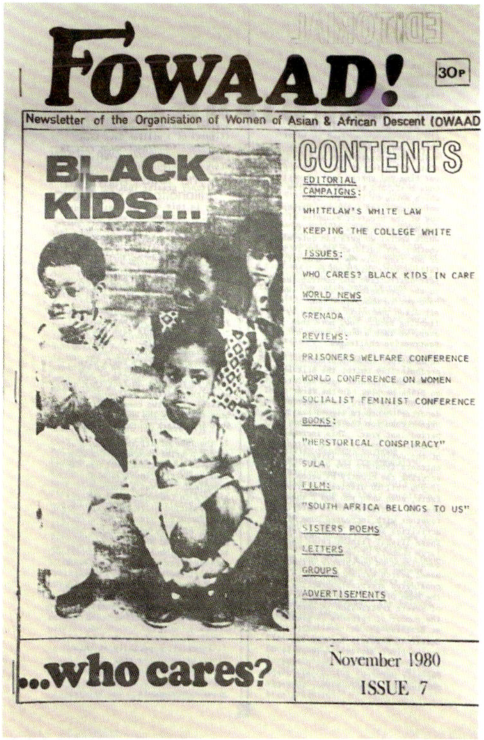
FOWAAD! 30P

Newsletter of the Organisation of Women of Asian & African Descent (OWAAD)

BLACK KIDS...

...who cares?

CONTENTS

EDITORIAL

CAMPAIGNS:
WHITELAW'S WHITE LAW
KEEPING THE COLLEGE WHITE

ISSUES:
WHO CARES? BLACK KIDS IN CARE

WORLD NEWS
GRENADA

REVIEWS:
PRISONERS WELFARE CONFERENCE
WORLD CONFERENCE ON WOMEN
SOCIALIST FEMINIST CONFERENCE

BOOKS:
"HERSTORICAL CONSPIRACY"
SULA

FILMS:
"SOUTH AFRICA BELONGS TO US"

SISTERS POEMS
LETTERS
GROUPS
ADVERTISEMENTS

November 1980
ISSUE 7

9

THE LONG LENS OF MOTHERHOOD: THE ART OF GIVING AND SUSTAINING LIFE

ZUZANA FLAŠKOVÁ

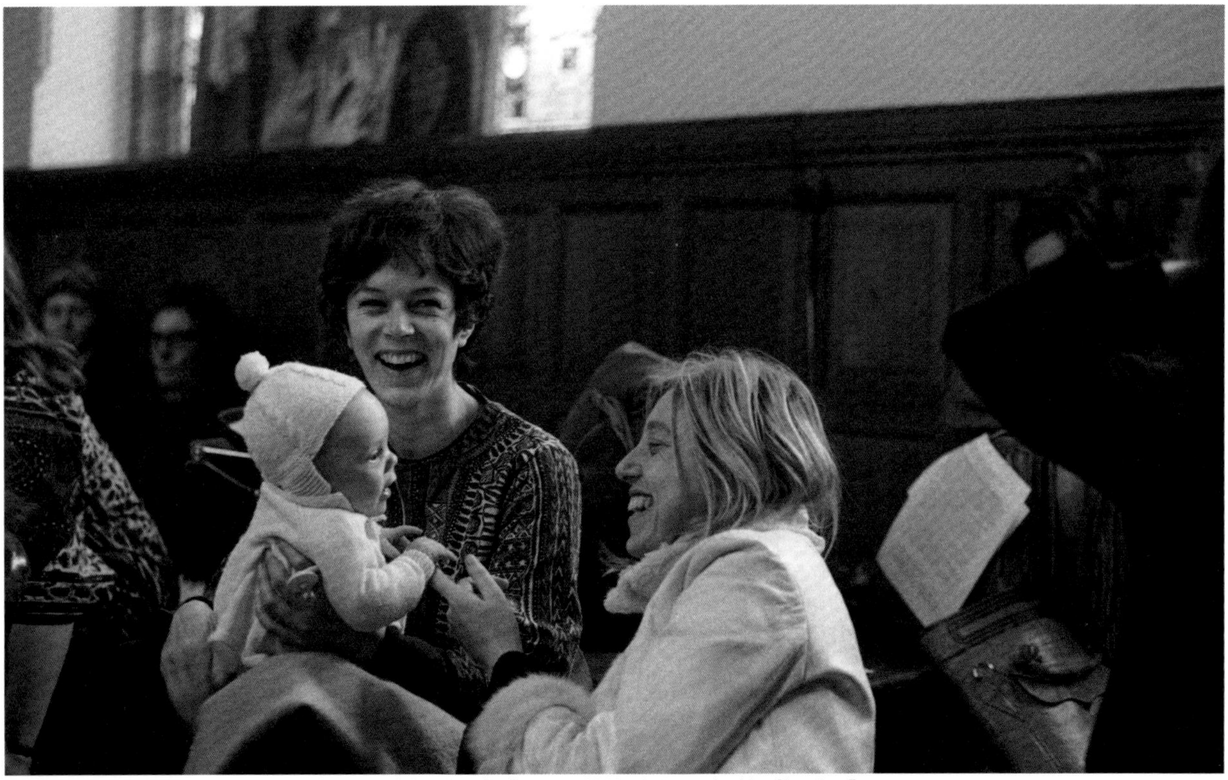

Sue Crockford and Juliet Mitchell at the Women's Liberation Conference, 1970, photographed by Chandan Fraser.

1 Tina Keane, 'Shadow Woman' (1977); reprinted in Richard Dyer, Jean Fisher and Peter Wollen, *Electronic Shadows: The Art of Tina Keane*, London 2004, p.14.
2 See Maud Perrier, *Childcare Struggles, Maternal Workers and Social Reproduction*, Bristol 2022.
3 See British Library, Timeline of the Women's Liberation Movement in Women's Histories, https://www.bl.uk/sisterhood/timeline, accessed 7 Feb. 2023.
4 See Margaret Iversen, Douglas Crimp and Homi K. Bhabha, *Mary Kelly*, London and New York 1997, p.15.
5 See Liz Heron, 'Hackney Flashers Collective: Who's Still Holding the Camera?', in Jo Spence and Terry Dennett (eds.), *Photography/Politics: One*, London 1979, p.124.

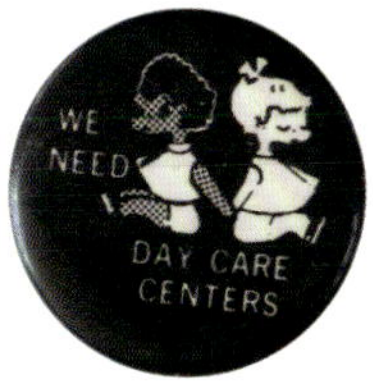

The shadow of my daughter
becomes the shadow of life
As I will become the shadow of hers
as my mother
grandmother and
great grandmother [1]

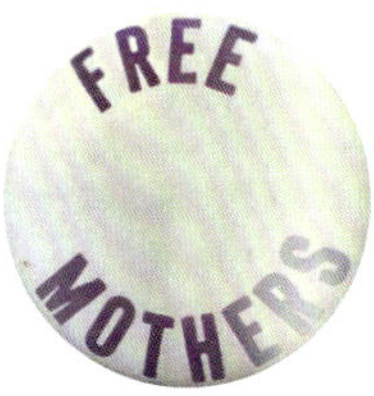

The circular pattern of continuity of life, looking after children, looking after parents, looking after grandchildren. As the world is recovering from, or perhaps adapting to, the consequences of the Covid-19 pandemic, here in the UK the issue of care work has become much more palpable than ever before. Or perhaps it has just finally come to the fore, moving from the private to the public. Despite social reproduction being the primary building block of the economy, and of society at large, reproductive labour – such as care work, domestic and maintenance labour, and the labour of childcare, as well as care for the ill or elderly – stays firmly assigned to the private realm of individual responsibility.[2] And while the public sphere, though traditionally a domain of male patriarchy, is slowly but steadily moving towards gender equality thanks to a greater degree of transparency and scrutiny, the realm of the private sphere is still by and large maintained by women.

Childcare, in the form of provision of free 24-hour nurseries, was one of the four core demands discussed at the first National Women's Liberation Conference in Oxford in 1970.[3] The other three were equal pay, equal educational and job opportunities, and free contraception and abortion on demand.

The installation *Women and Work: A Document on the Division of Labour in Industry* 1973–5 by Margaret Harrison, Kay Hunt and Mary Kelly, was based on an in-depth study of women's work experiences at a metal-box factory in Bermondsey, London (pp.82–3). Planned to coincide with the implementation of the Equal Pay Act, it is telling that, with regard to the stories of over 150 working women who participated in the project, Kelly later remarked that many of them barely spoke about 'the workplace' and instead elaborated on their work at home.[4]

Domestic labour, combined with the lack of childcare provision and the concomitant pressures on women as the default care providers in the absence of support, was the starting point for the portable panels installation fittingly entitled *Who's Holding the Baby?* 1978 (pp.122–3), created by members of the Hackney Flashers collective (1974–80). The collective evolved from the radical Photography Workshop when Jo Spence and Neil Martinson sought photographers to contribute to a project on 'Women and Work' for Hackney Trades Council, acknowledging the invisible contribution women made to the economy. For their second project, focused on childcare, An Dekker, Sally Greenhill, Liz Heron, Michael Ann Mullen, Maggie Murray, Christine Roche, Jo Spence and Julia Vellacott produced twenty-nine panels reflecting the circumstances of working mothers in the London borough of Hackney.[5] A montage of documentary photography, illustration, advertising, collage and graphics, it was employed as a powerful visual tool for agitation at women's liberation conferences, trade union meetings and libraries, and was presented to welfare policymakers and at campaigns for nurseries.

The overwhelming cultural pressure on women to be the primary socialiser of their children is starkly encapsulated in an earlier work by Maureen Scott titled *Mother and Child at Breaking Point* 1970 (p.58). The stoic gaze of the woman in Scott's painting betrays the torment of the prerequisite of unconditional love as the basis for the child's development towards stability and happy integration into wider society. The conflict of competing needs, as a mother and artist, is compounded by the oppressive, claustrophobic domestic space.

Mary Kelly and Susan Hiller also used their own experiences of pregnancy and motherhood to reflect on the complexity of the mother–child relationship and various aspects of the process of the child's socialisation, as well as the impact of motherhood on the notion of self. Hiller's *Ten Months* 1977 (pp.104–5) is a presentation of ten framed pictures, each showing a grid of twenty-eight individual photographs of her growing abdomen, one for each day of the lunar month, over the course of her pregnancy. Stripped of sentimentality, the texts accompanying the pictures can be read as a probe into female subjectivity, as well as a wider critique of women's role in society.

Kelly's film *Ante Partum* 1973 features her abdomen at full term, captured in a single close-up shot on black and white film, in an almost abstracted manner, with minimal action but for her hand stroking the contours of her stomach as it manifests the foetal movements (p.103). Played on a loop it offers a durational, as-if 'real time', look at pregnancy. It is a precursor to her detailed and complex analysis and visualisation of the mother–child relationship in *Post-Partum Document* 1973–9. Made over the course of seven years, it focuses on her son's early infancy and consists of a configuration of objects and texts, presenting an analytical reading of the 'archaeology of everyday life'.[6] Both Kelly's and Hiller's work also points beyond the social-sexual division of labour, and furthermore suggests a connection between 'reproductive' and 'artistic' labour in being viewed as a 'vocation', as non-work, and as such being framed outside of social and economic working conditions.

The daily necessities of providing for a family on your own, as a single parent, are behind the title of *Bear it in Mind*, made by Su Richardson in 1976, two years after her son was born (p.63). This hanging textile sculpture is made from dungarees spliced on to the top part of a defunct pair of men's jeans. With the father figure absent, the mother figure has grown extra hands, but not enough to handle the various tools dangling from her many pockets. Too many

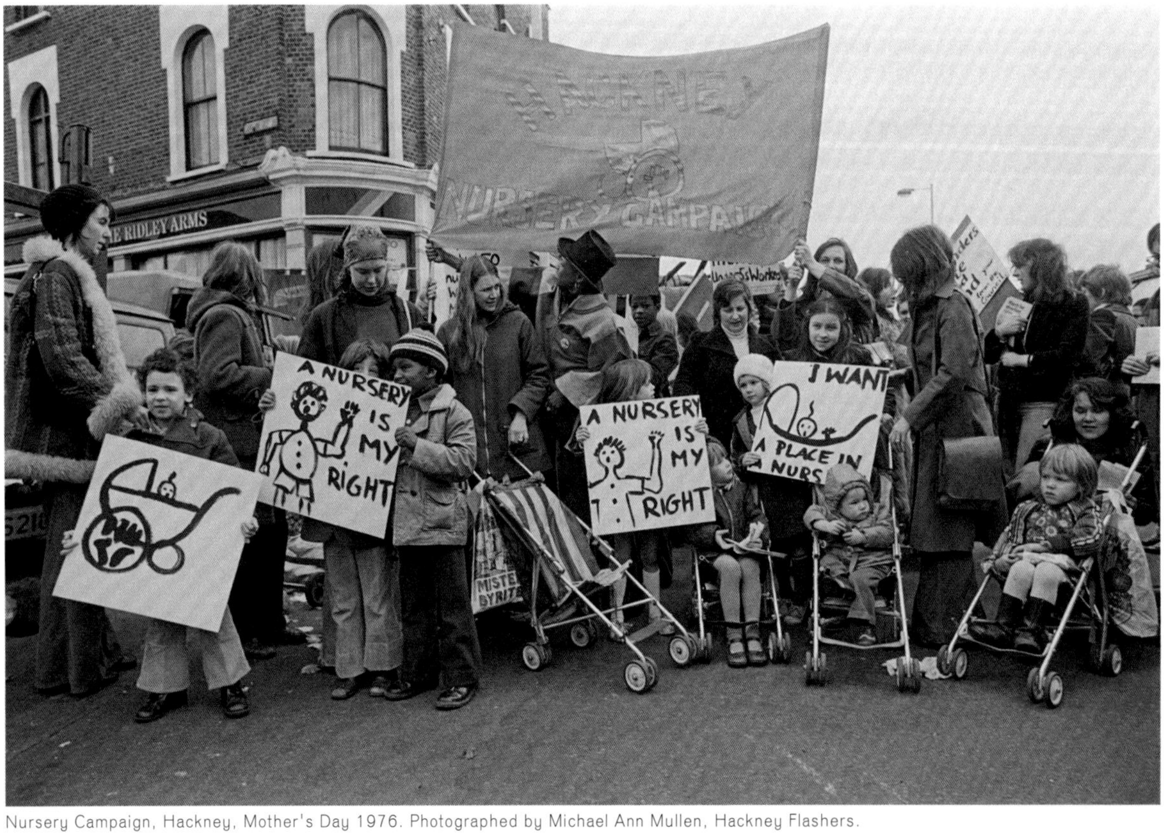

Nursery Campaign, Hackney, Mother's Day 1976. Photographed by Michael Ann Mullen, Hackney Flashers.

6 Mary Kelly, *Post-Partum Document*, London 1985, p.xvi.
7 Rozsika Parker and Griselda Pollock, *Framing Feminism: Art and the Women's Movement 1970–1985*, London and New York 1987, p.36.
8 See Steven McIntyre, 'A Whole New Attitude: The London Film Makers' Co-op in the Decade of Structural/Materialism', in Sue Clayton and Laura Mulvey (eds.), *Other Cinemas: Politics, Culture and Experimental Film in the 1970s*, London and New York 2017, p.165.
9 See 'Disrupting the Content – Feminism', in Catherine Elwes, *Video Art: A Guided Tour*, London 2004, pp.39–41.

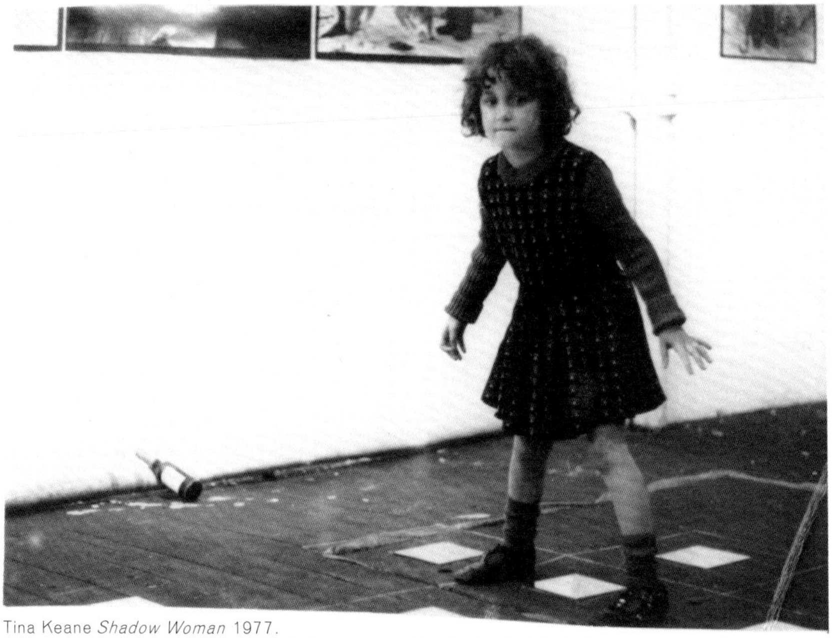

Tina Keane *Shadow Woman* 1977.
Documentation of a performance with Keane's daughter Emily, Artists for Democracy, London.

jobs to do and not enough time. Richardson's medium of choice was textile and crochet, which she continued to employ to irreverently subvert the traditional hierarchies between art and craft, home and workplace.

In the late 1970s and early 1980s a set of powerful expressions of maternal ambivalence came to the fore through performance, film and video practices by women artists. Not only do these works chart complex subjectivities, but they also constitute one of the most experimental tendencies of the period. The creative innovation was driven by resistance in the face of discrimination, and as an answer to not being taken seriously.

In the summer of 1978, members of the Women's Arts Alliance protested work that was degrading to women on display at Allen Jones's exhibition at the Institute of Contemporary Arts, London. They also criticised the institute for not giving women equivalent opportunities to show artwork, and proposed organising a show 'of women's attitudes towards men'. The response to the call for submissions to the exhibition, titled *Women's Images of Men*, was so intense that two exhibitions were planned instead. The first included painting, drawing, photography and sculpture, and the second, entitled *About Time*, showcased performance and video, both crucial mediums for feminist work.[7] Around the time of the show's preparation, in the spring of 1979, three women artist filmmakers, Annabel Nicolson, Tina Keane and Lis Rhodes, publicly walked out of the Hayward Gallery's exhibition *Film as Film: Formal Experiment in Film, 1910–1975*, protesting the show's marginalisation of women's practices.[8]

With their 'sphere of influence' often confined to the domestic space, feminist artists naturally sought to politicise the perception of their role in the family home. Reproductive rights and labour, motherhood and childbearing were top of the agenda. At the same time, the investigation of personal identity became a key concern, embarking on a redefinition of femininity itself at the level of representation.[9]

Tina Keane's young daughter, Emily, was the focus of her early works, as both the subject and protagonist of her performance, installation and video works, such as *Shadow Woman* 1977, *Playpen* 1979, *Clapping Songs* 1981 (p.108), and *Hopscotch* 1986. Keane acknowledged that a lot of her early work had her daughter in it as a natural consequence of them always being side by side. The time spent together surreptitiously becomes the material. In 1978 Keane was invited to participate in the Summer Show at the Serpentine Gallery. Having spent much time with Emily by their local park's swing set, Keane had the thought of transporting it into the gallery space. A playful yet powerful political gesture, it recalls the strategy of 'displacement', as enacted by the French artist Lea Lublin, who in 1968 transported herself and her son in a crib to the twenty-fourth Salon de Mai.[10] 'Displacing' moments of their life into an exhibition space points to a strong desire to cross the boundary, to enter a space where women and their resultant paraphernalia still, by and large, were not felt to belong. In their actions, they forcefully transition themselves and their concerns from the private to the public or, in other words, from the kitchen (due to lack of studio space) to the gallery.

Keane's next piece, *Playpen* 1979, in which she herself sits in a child's playpen, encompasses footage of eight women from different generations, underlining the narrative of life's continuity, from girlhood to womanhood. But *Playpen* also functions as an analogy for the entrapment of women in the web of social reproduction, and can be further read as a portrayal of the 'alienation of the artist from the resources, power and ability to represent through art'.[11]

Although Keane is predominantly known today as a film artist, the majority of her early work stemmed from performance, a foundational focus that she maintained in her transition to video art, and perhaps the distinguishing factor that has made her among the most instrumental figures of the first generation of British video artists. For many feminist artists, the choice of performance and video as the main vehicle for expression was not an accidental one. As a new medium, video was unburdened by a long patriarchal genealogy and was open to free artistic experimentation with the aesthetic form, language and content. With its ease of operation and a one-person crew, it also afforded optimal conditions for explorations of subjectivity and introspection.

There is a Myth
She can give Life
And she can take it away[12]

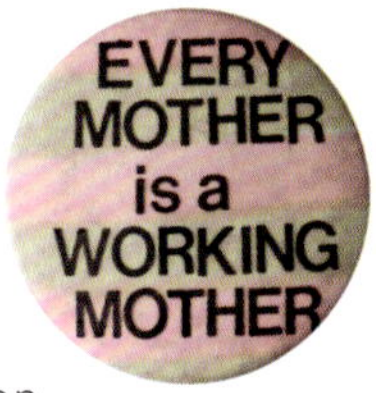

In her early video work, Catherine Elwes confronts the subject of maternal ambiguity head on. *There is a Myth* 1984 focuses on the (female) body and its functions, considered from a deeply personal as well as socio-cultural perspective. While breastfeeding her baby son, she zooms in on the free, lactating breast. This is 1984, and an engorged breast is still considered gross, a 'put it away' kind of thing. The focus on the breast as subject matter, rather than the child, is powerfully ambivalent. The nurturing substance of the milk sustains life – yet the breast having been rendered 'undesirable' challenges its patriarchal cultural subordination, no longer a seductive invitation to the male gaze. Here, the reproductive role of the breast is bared, just like that of menstruation, which Elwes dealt with in her earlier four-day performance piece *Menstruation 1* at the Slade School of Art in 1979 (p.100). But above all, seeing an infant sucking on the breast is bound to elicit a strong emotive response. A vulnerable child being nurtured by their mother is an image universally coded in anthropology to signify the continuation of life and 'humanity'. Despite the absence of the infant as a protagonist, his small hand clumsily fumbling at the breast will yield powerful emotions of empathy, and a sense of responsibility and liability.

Despite this universality, the lactating breast was so radical and threatening that at the time it was pronounced 'unbroadcastable' by a director at Channel 4. Only thirty-five years later, in November 2019, was a clip of the work broadcast on television as part of the documentary *Kill Your TV: Jim Moir's Weird World of Video Art* on BBC4. At the time of writing, although

10 Catherine Spencer, 'Acts of Displacement: Lea Lublin's *Mon fils*, May '68, and Feminist Psychosocial Revolt', *Oxford Art Journal*, vol.40, no.1, 2017, p.65.
11 Michael O'Pray, 'Tina Keane', *Performance*, no.53, April/May 1988.
12 Catherine Elwes *There is a Myth* 1984. Colour U-matic, 10 min.

breastfeeding in public is 'welcomed', should you want to do it comes down to your own confidence, need for privacy, levels of shyness, adventurousness and bravery. What I feel is missing is both a provision for sensitively designated spaces alongside an encouraging signage policy that would aim to normalise the simple fact of breastfeeding a child in public, when and where necessary and convenient for the parent.

> I am an artist. I am a woman. I am a wife. I am a mother (random order). I do a hell of a lot of washing, cleaning, cooking, renewing, supporting, preserving, etc. Also, (up to now and separately) I 'do' Art. Now, I will simply do these maintenance everyday things, and flush them up to consciousness, exhibit them, as Art.[13]

These words were written by the American artist Mierle Laderman Ukeles as part of her manifesto for what she called 'maintenance art' in 1969, a year after she gave birth to her first child. In a similar vein, in her 1988 performance *Drawing on a Mother's Experience*, British artist Bobby Baker tells her audience, 'I'm an experienced mother'. She then proceeds with an account that blends together the mundane activities and domestic routines of a homemaker. The disarmingly deadpan register of her delivery corresponds with the 'incommunicability of trying to sustain life', with all its demands and tasks that invite a feeling of failure.

Baker remarked that performing the various 'humiliations and inadequacies' has an effect that is akin to something therapeutic or cathartic.[14] Perhaps deciding to enact these moments is something only she can choose, something she wields power and control over, of how much she lets us in or not. And, despite the tragicomic undertones, the effects of the encounter have invariably been described by first-hand audiences as deeply moving and powerful in the way that they communicate 'excruciating vulnerability'.[15]

Marina Warner suggested that Baker could be described as a 'hunger artist', driven by her own urges and the human need for sustenance, but also for comfort and nourishment, which all go back to food.[16] In *Drawing on a Mother's Experience* Baker talks about her satisfaction and pride at being able to extract milk and send it to a baby unit. This is a decade after she had explored the dark fantasy of uprooting the order of dependency and sustenance provision in her work *An Edible Family in a Mobile Home* 1976 (see pp.114–15). In this 'cannibalistic' ensemble, the narratives of feeding and being fed are ambiguously subverted with humour.

In her Acme Housing Association prefab studio in Hackney, Baker papered the individual rooms of the 'household' with newsprint and inhabited them with a mother, father, son, daughter and baby. The family were made of cake, except the daughter, who was made of spindly wire and meringue, and the mother. The maternal figure was made from a dressmaker's dummy with a teapot for a head, and in place of her life-sustaining breasts she is fashioned with a drawer containing cakes and sandwiches to be continually replenished. But instead of being the homemaker, she invites the audience to cannibalise her family. She is the only one who survives.

These are but a few examples of the ways in which British women artists working at the time of the Women's Liberation Movement explored the tension between two drives, the maternal and the creative, and the maddening urge and desire to fulfil them and excel at both. But rather than being 'naturally' positioned at odds, it is instructive to be reminded that the challenge of reconciling these urges does not necessarily come from within. Rather, it is reinforced by the ungenerous policies and legislation, political structures and forces of economic reproduction that are wedded to the ideology of gender inequalities, based on the supposed grounds of men and women's divergent procreative roles.[17]

13 Mierle Laderman Ukeles, 'MANIFESTO, Maintenance Art – Proposal for an Exhibition', 1969, p.3.
14 Adrian Heathfield, 'Risk in Intimacy: An Interview with Bobby Baker', in Michèle Barrett and Bobby Baker (eds.), *Bobby Baker: Redeeming Features of Daily Life*, Abingdon 2007, p.83.
15 Ibid, p.84.
16 Marina Warner, 'The Rebel at the Heart of the Joker', in Barrett and Baker (eds.) 2007, p.100.
17 For an intersectional framework analysing the classed and racialised divisions in childcare, see Perrier 2022.

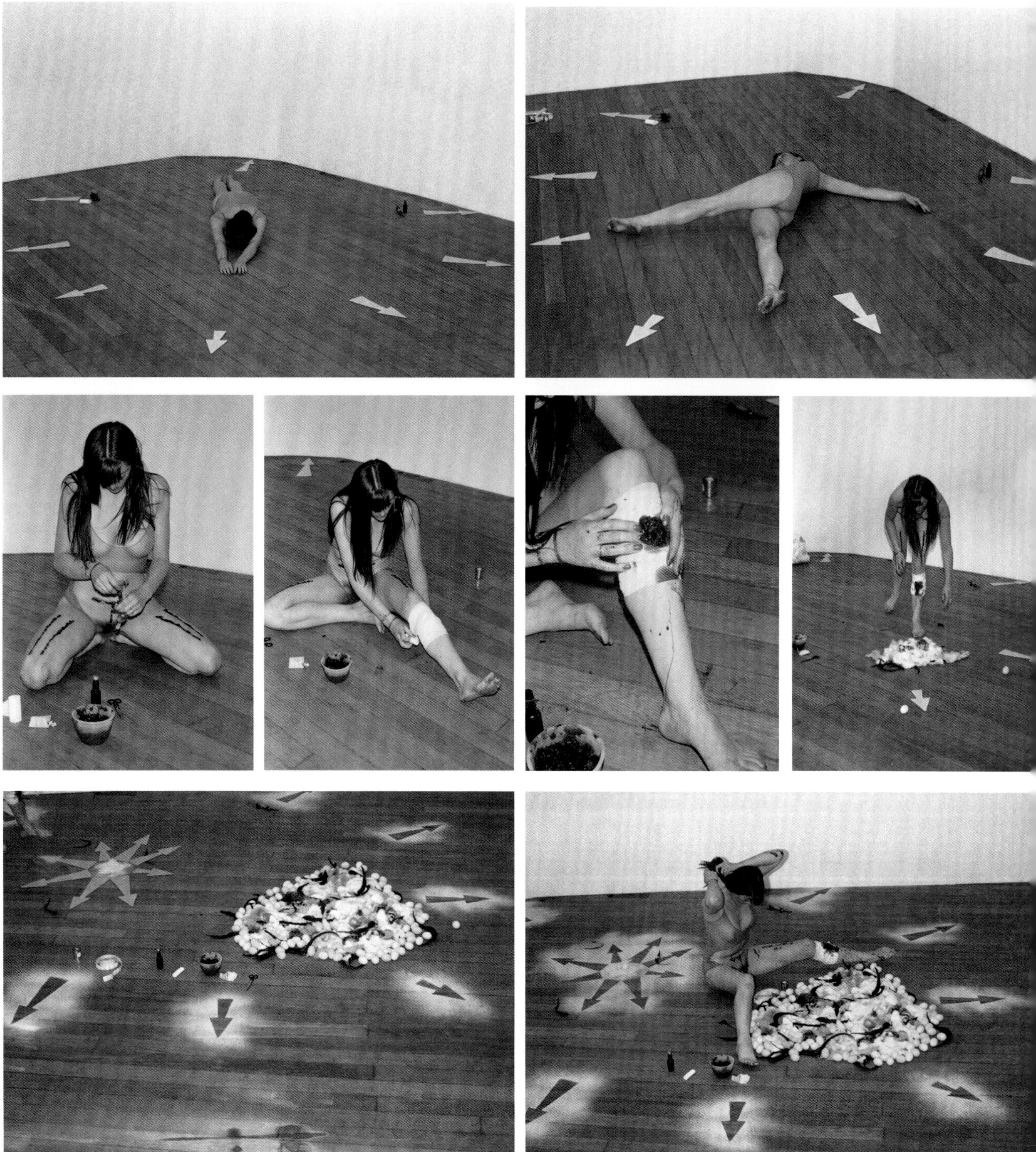

Woman's Roll 1978. 17 of 30 framed photographs; black-and-white silver bromide prints 21 × 29.7 (each)

Cosey Fanni Tutti was born in 1951 in Hull where she lived and worked until 1973. In 1969 she co-founded the music and performance art collective COUM Transmissions. Drawing inspiration from surrealism and underground music, the group sought to challenge aspects of conventional society. On moving to London in 1973 with members of COUM, Tutti continued to develop her solo performance practice with works such as *Woman's Roll*, performed at AIR Gallery, London in 1976, and through her investigation of self and sexuality in the context of the sex industry. Tutti's engagement with sex work was a highly sophisticated and knowing exploration of the transactional and commercial aspect of pornography. In her exhibition *Prostitution*, held at the ICA in 1976, Tutti displayed the pornographic magazines in which she featured, naming them 'magazine actions' and asserting them as her own artistic creations. The opening of *Prostitution* at the ICA was also on the night that COUM Transmissions became Throbbing Gristle, the industrial noise band in which Tutti would play until they disbanded in

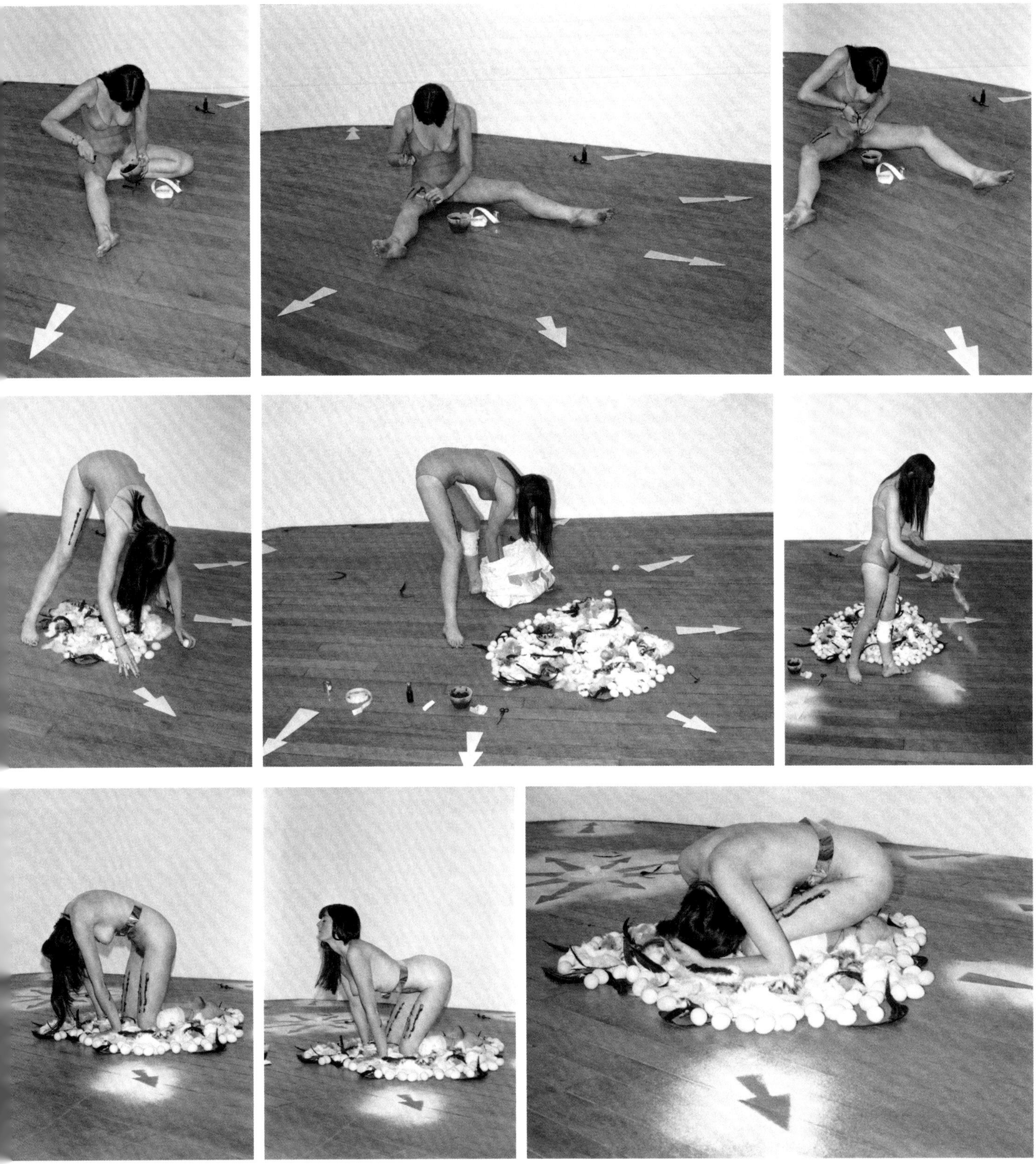

1981. Following the end of Throbbing Gristle, Tutti continued to produce and release music as 'Chris and Cosey' with her ex-Throbbing Gristle bandmate and partner Chris Carter.

Tutti, with Cabinet, co-curated the first COUM transmissions retrospective in Hull in 2017. Her autobiography, *Art Sex Music*, was published in 2017 and *Re-Sisters: The Lives and Recordings of Delia Derbyshire, Margery Kempe and Cosey Fanni Tutti* was published in 2022.

COSEY FANNI TUTTI

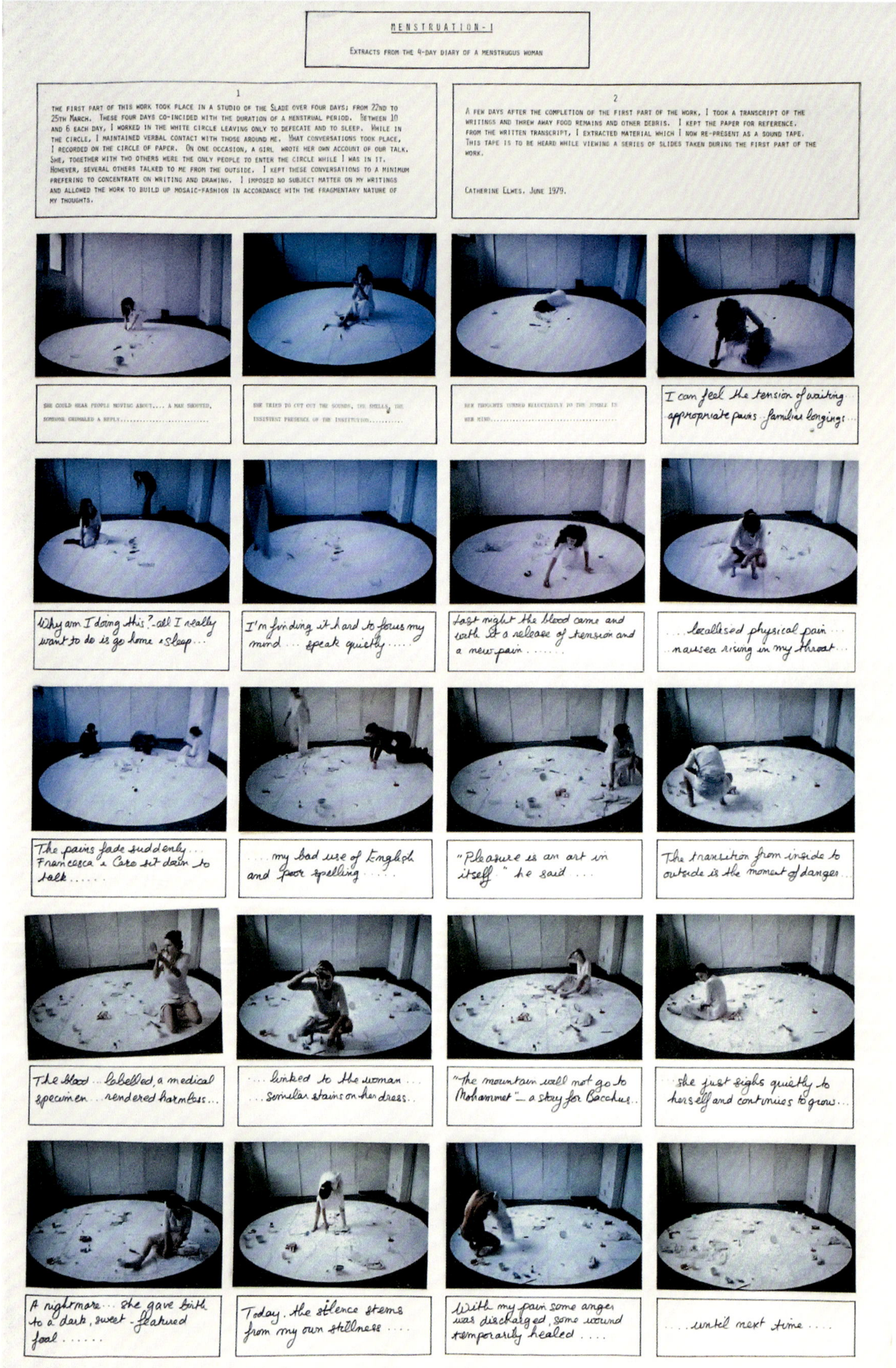

Menstruation 1 1979. Photographs and text on paper 85 × 60

Catherine Elwes was born in France in 1952, and studied in London at the Slade School of Fine Art and the Royal College of Art, graduating from the latter in 1982. She worked as a painter and explored performance before specialising in video and video installation, becoming an early pioneer of video art. In the late 1970s, Elwes was a member of the Women Artists' Collective and Women's Art Alliance. For her performances *Menstruation 1 and 2* (p.100), Elwes isolated herself on a circular paper platform and in a glass-fronted chamber in the Slade School of Fine Art and free bleed for the duration of her period, using the time to explore the creative potential of the physical and psychological experience of menstruation. In 1980, she co-curated two groundbreaking feminist art exhibitions in the UK, *Women's Images of Men* and *About Time*, both presented at the ICA, London. Elwes worked as Professor of Moving Image Art at Chelsea College of Art. She was founding editor of the *Moving Image Review & Art Journal* (MIRAJ) and is author of *Video Loupe* (2000), *Video Art, A Guided Tour* (2005), *Installation and the Moving Image* (2015) and *Landscape and the Moving Image* (2022).

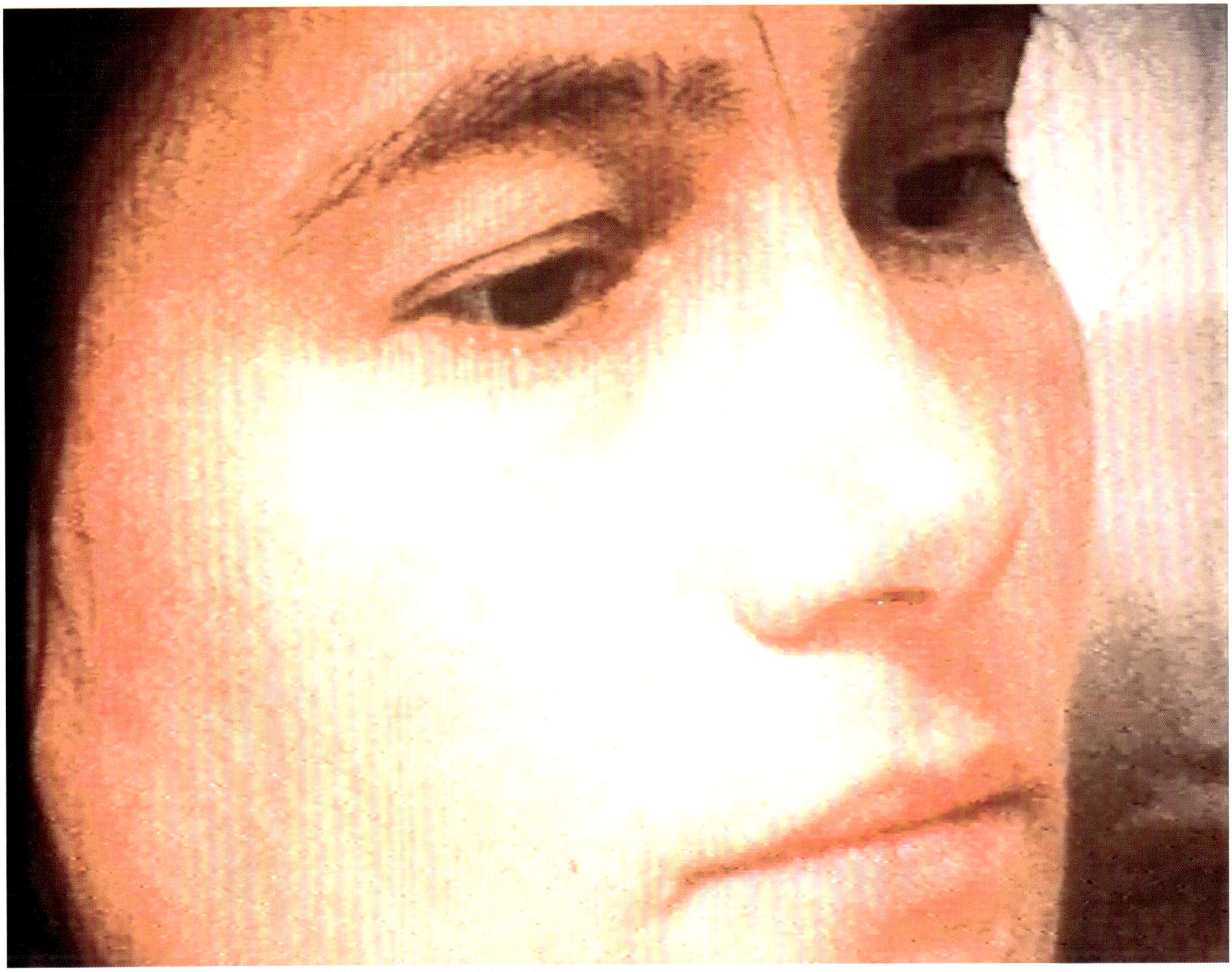

Birth Rites 1977. 16mm film shown as digital video; colour, sound. 53 min

Robina Rose was born in 1951 to German and Danish parents and grew up in Notting Hill, London. After leaving school, she became a Film Projectionist at the first Arts Lab on Drury Lane, Covent Garden. Rose graduated from the Royal College of Art in 1977, where she did camera work on Celestino Coronado's *Hamlet* starring Helen Mirren and Quentin Crisp. While at the RCA she worked at the Portobello Hotel and in 1981 made the film *Nightshift*, a record of the hotel as experienced by the receptionist. Rose was awarded a German Academic Exchange Service (DAAD) fellowship and moved to Berlin, where she was later invited to teach at the German Film and Television Academy (DFFB) and remained for the rest of the 1980s.On her return from Berlin she worked for the Community Programme Unit of the BBC, for which she made a film about pesticides in agriculture with an organic dairy farmer who plays the saxophone to his bull, and a film about prostitution in which the camera is the girl. She went on to become the London Chair of the Campaign to Protect Rural England, and ran for Parliament in the Royal Borough of Kensington and Chelsea for the Green Party at the 2015 general election.

Rose's graduation film *Birth Rites* 1977 portrays a woman (Julia Lauder) giving birth at home, an experience common to many but rarely depicted on film. The respectful depiction of this intimate process reflects on Rose's own questions about childbirth and motherhood, and the roles and choices women must adopt or make when considering it.

With special thanks to Emanuel, Cookie and Julia Lauder.

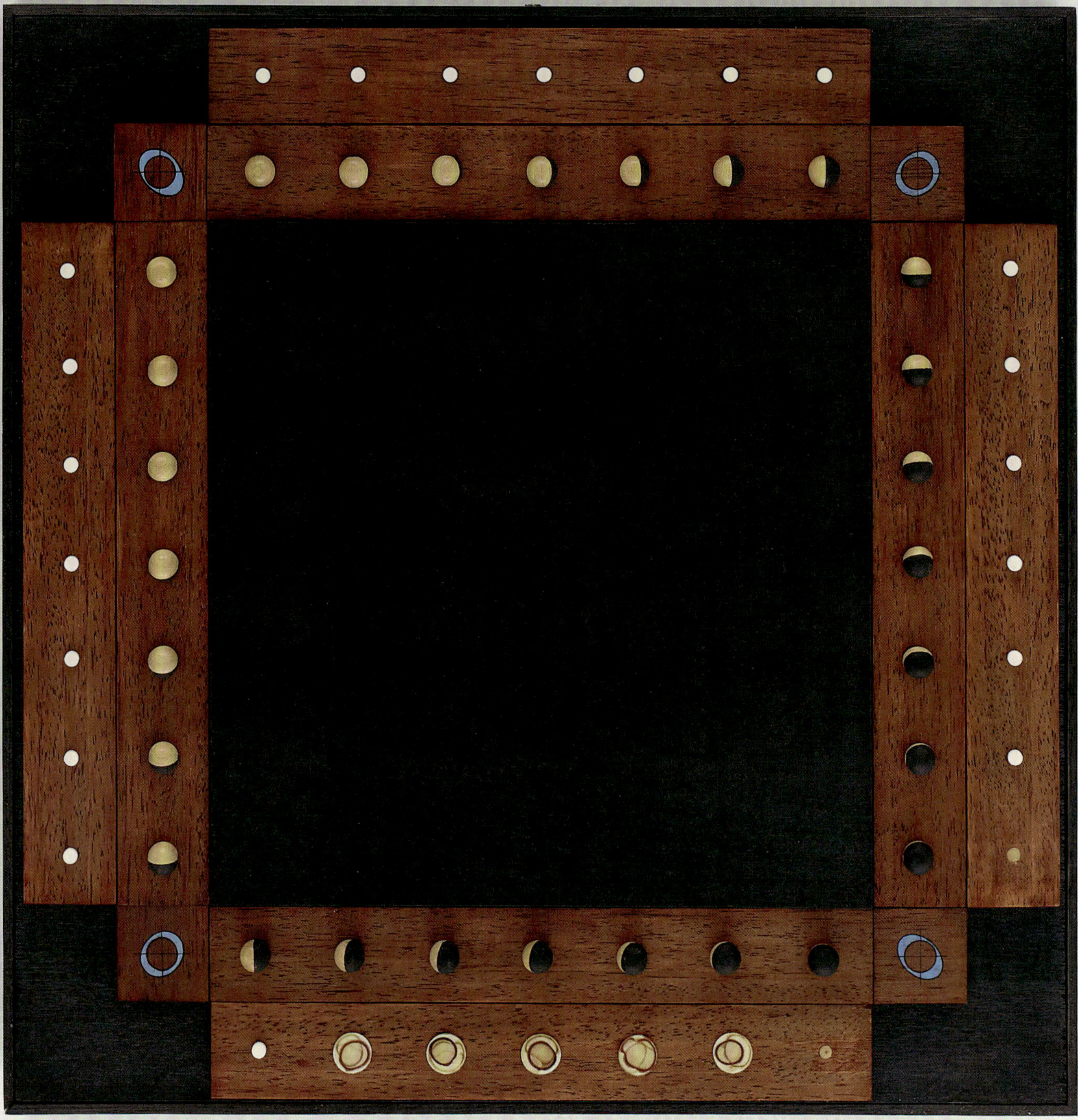

Cycle 1973. Wood, Perspex contraceptive pills, menstrual blood 68.7 × 67.6

JUDY CLARK

Judy Clark (b. 1949) studied fine art at Portsmouth Polytechnic and the Slade School of Art in London, graduating in 1973. Working across drawing, sculpture, painting, printing and photography, Clark was offered a solo exhibition at Garage Art in Covent Garden, London on the strength of her Slade degree show. The 1973 exhibition, titled *Issues*, used bodily detritus to explore issues of identity, especially in relation to women's bodies. The works were created from body hair, bodily fluids and menstrual blood, and were significant to the women's movement in the 1970s at a time when artists sought to reclaim portrayals of women's bodies from the tradition of the nude in Western art history. Clark's work influenced a generation of feminist artists, and contributed to women's fight to claim ownership of one's own body.

A solo exhibition of Clark's work was presented in 1998 at Pallant House Gallery, Chichester.

The artist lives and works in Wiltshire.

Born in Fort Dodge, Iowa, USA, in 1941, Mary Kelly studied painting in Florence, Italy, before moving to the UK for postgraduate study at Saint Martin's School of Art in London in 1968. There she became involved with the Women's Liberation Movement and worked on key art projects that spoke to the movement's concerns and demands, including *Women and Work* 1973–5 with Margaret Harrison and Kay Hunt (pp.82–3). Kelly is widely regarded as a prominent figure in feminist art history, with a profound impact on conceptual art and cultural politics. She was part of the Berwick Street Collective, contributing to the film *Nightcleaners* 1975, which sought to raise awareness of the lives of women who cleaned offices during night hours for minimal pay. In 1976 Kelly's work *Post-Partum Document* 1973–9 was presented in a solo exhibition at the ICA. It received notoriety in the tabloid press due to the inclusion of her son's soiled nappy liners. The work followed the film *Ante Partum* shown here, in which the artist's pregnant abdomen at full term is seen rising and falling with each breath, the movements of the baby at times visible under the skin.

Kelly lives and works in Los Angeles.

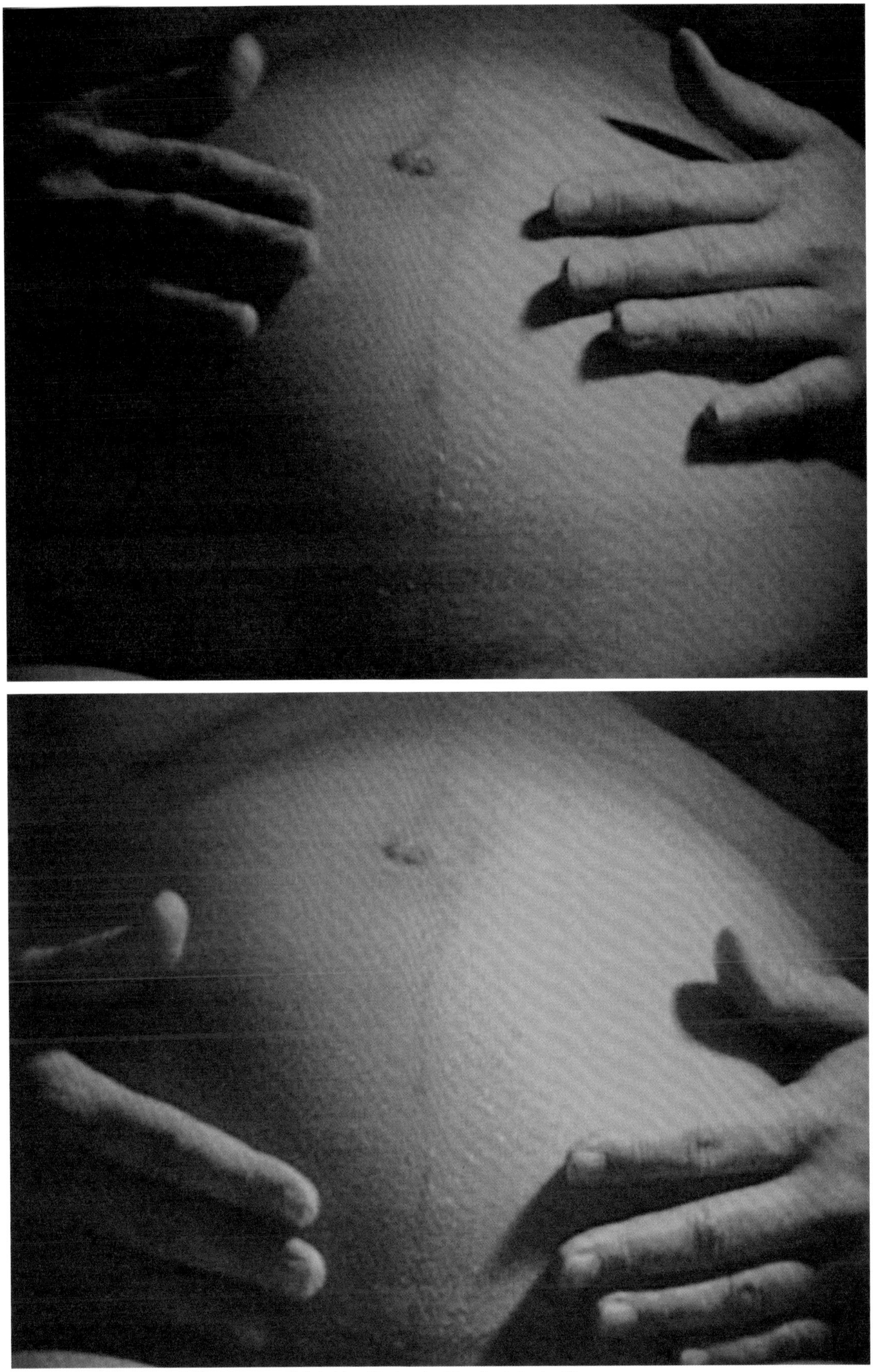

Ante Partum 1973. Super 8 film, shown as digital video; black and white, silent. 1 min, 30 sec

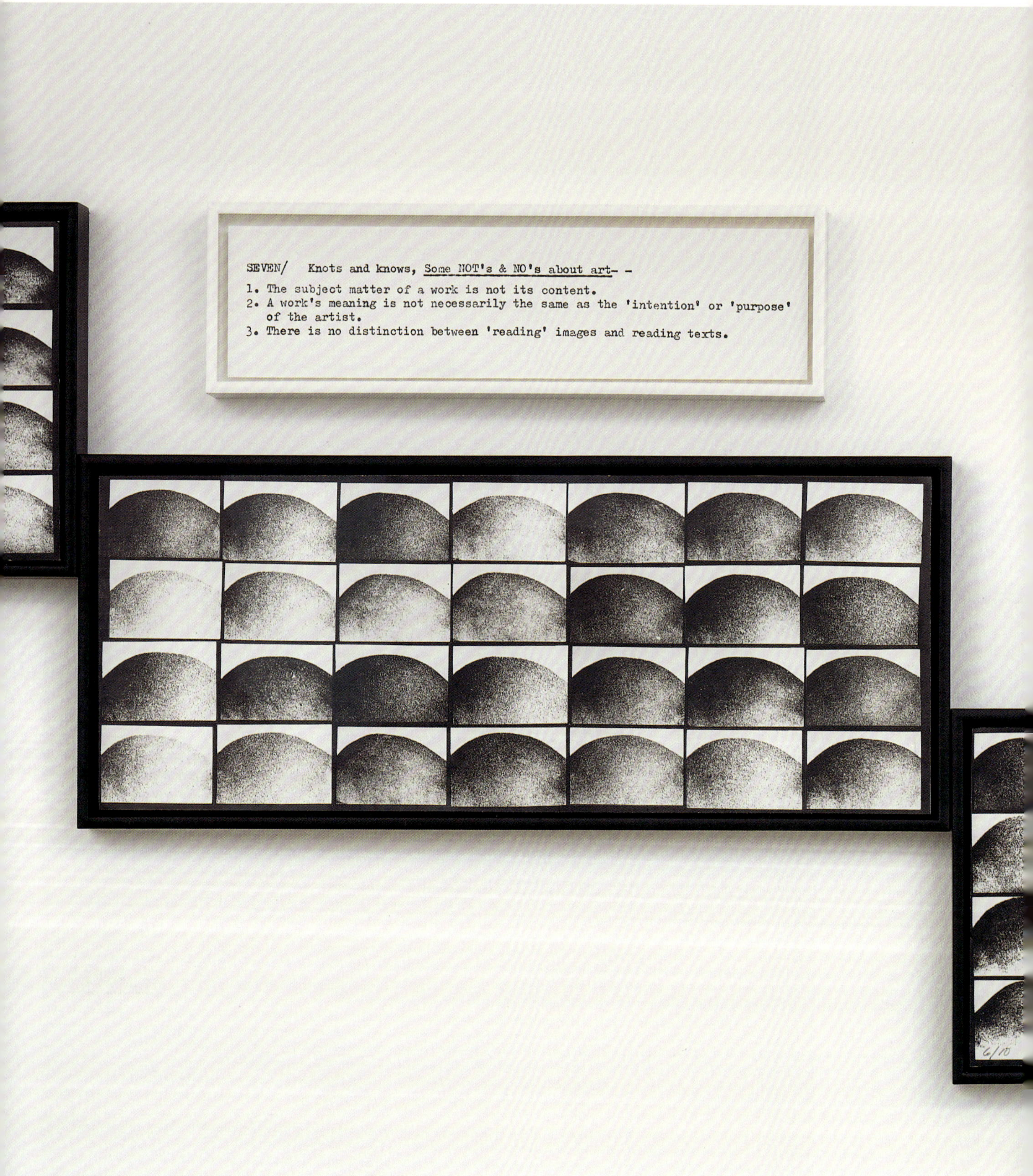
SEVEN/ Knots and knows, Some NOT's & NO's about art- -
1. The subject matter of a work is not its content.
2. A work's meaning is not necessarily the same as the 'intention' or 'purpose' of the artist.
3. There is no distinction between 'reading' images and reading texts.
6/10

Susan Hiller (1940–2019) was born in Tallahassee, Florida, USA, and raised in Cleveland, Ohio. In 1961 she received a bachelor's degree from Smith College, Massachusetts, before pursuing doctoral studies in anthropology. In the late 1960s Hiller moved to the UK, settling in London. Working across installation, video, photography, performance and writing, Hiller's practice considered our collective cultural experience, the subconscious and beliefs of what might be termed the paranormal or supernatural. Her influences included minimalism, surrealism and feminism. Beginning in the 1970s Hiller worked in a diverse range of media, with several pieces exploring notions of selfhood, subjectivity and her own experience as a woman. *Ten Months* 1977 consisted of ten frames containing twenty-eight individual photographs of her ever-growing abdomen during pregnancy. The accompanying texts challenge sentimental ideas around pregnancy and critically assess a woman's place within society. In the work Hiller crucially becomes the object of her own gaze.

A retrospective of Hiller's work was held at Tate Britain in 2011.

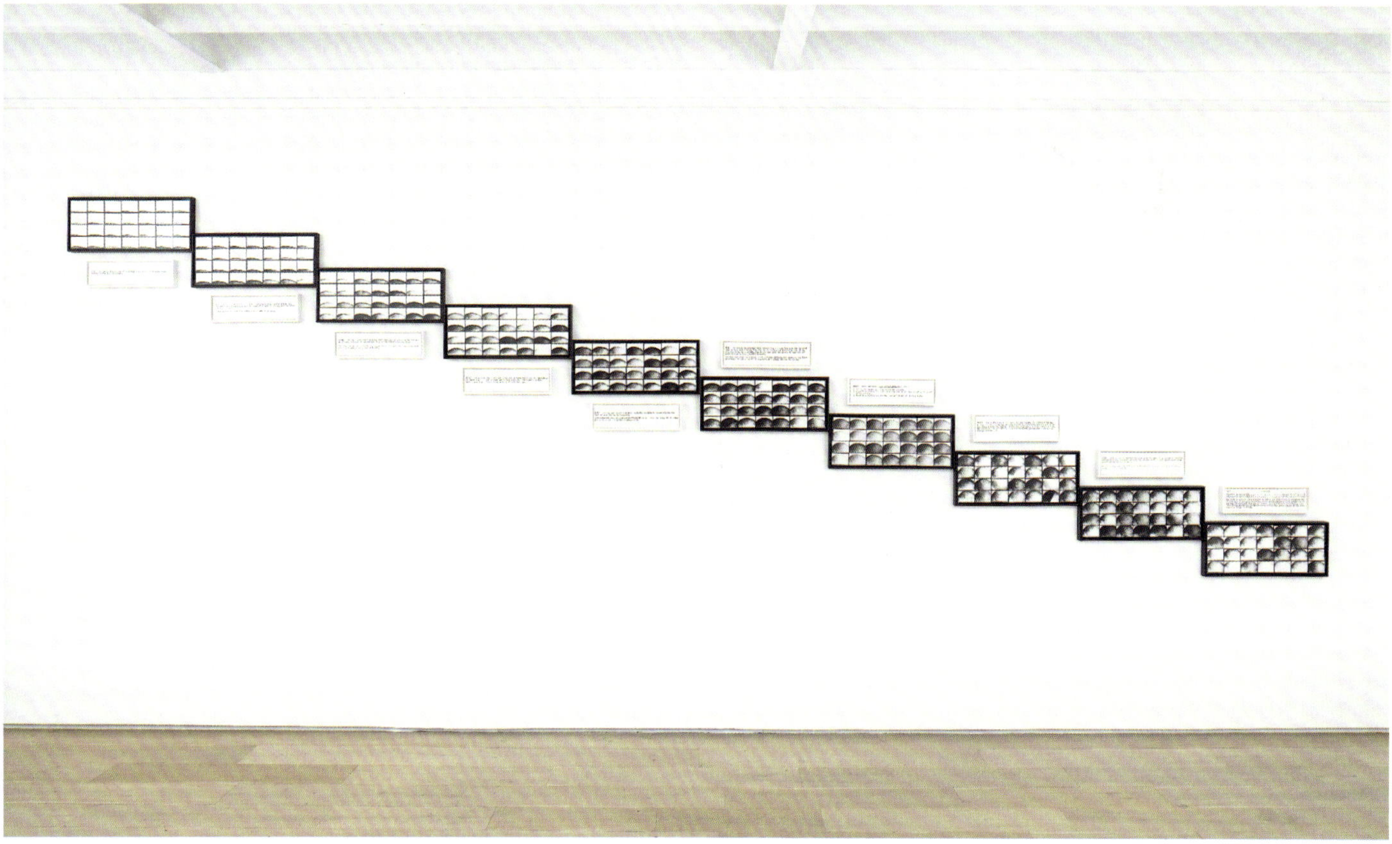

Ten Months 1977. 10 framed works; photographs and text. Photos: 24.3 × 57 (each). Text frames: 13.5 × 41.5 (each)

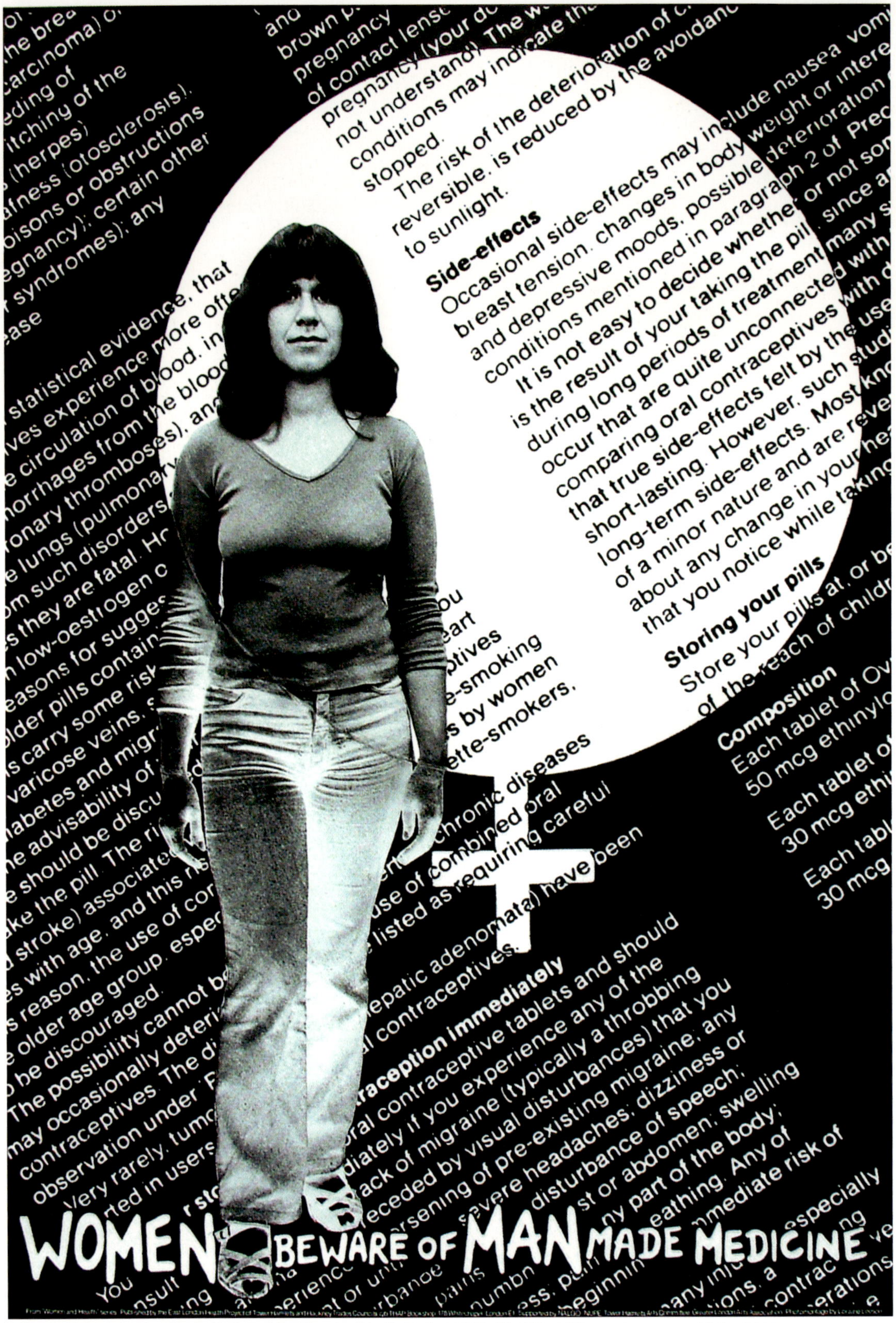

'Women Beware of Man Made Medicine' East London Health Project 1977–80. Offset lithograph on paper 62.3 × 44.2

Loraine Leeson (b.1951) grew up in Middlesex and studied art at Saint Martin's School of Art, the University of Reading and the Hochschule der Künste Berlin, Germany. She later received her PhD from the University of Ulster. Leeson's work focuses on how art can be used to support communities to bring about social and environmental change, an approach she first encountered at Reading through her involvement in Joseph Beuys' *Free International University*. As part of her subsequent work with artist Peter Dunn and health workers' unions on the East London Health Project she created a series of posters on women's health, including in 1980 *'Women Beware of Man Made Medicine'* and *'Things That Make You Sick'*. In 1981 Leeson and Dunn co-founded the Docklands Community Poster Project, involving other artists and designers over a decade in the creation of visual works that supported the campaigning communities of London's Docklands. They invented the format of the photo-mural, using sequences of these billboard-size images in several locations to make the case for a redevelopment of the area that would meet the needs of the local community.

A touring retrospective of Leeson's work travelled to Berlin, London, Toronto and Dublin in 2005–8. She lives and works in London.

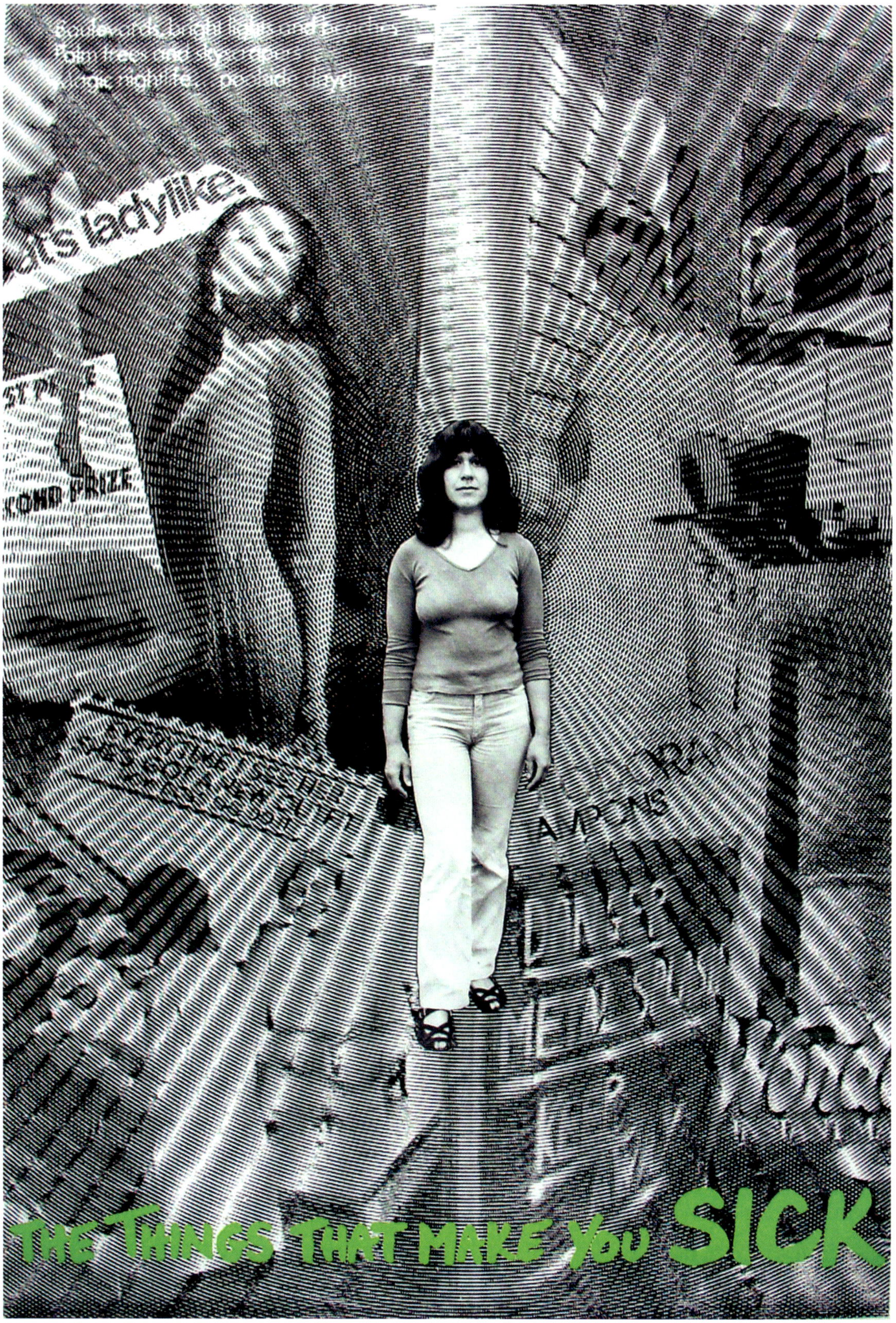

'Things That Make You Sick' East London Health Project 1980. Offset lithograph on paper 62.3 × 44.2

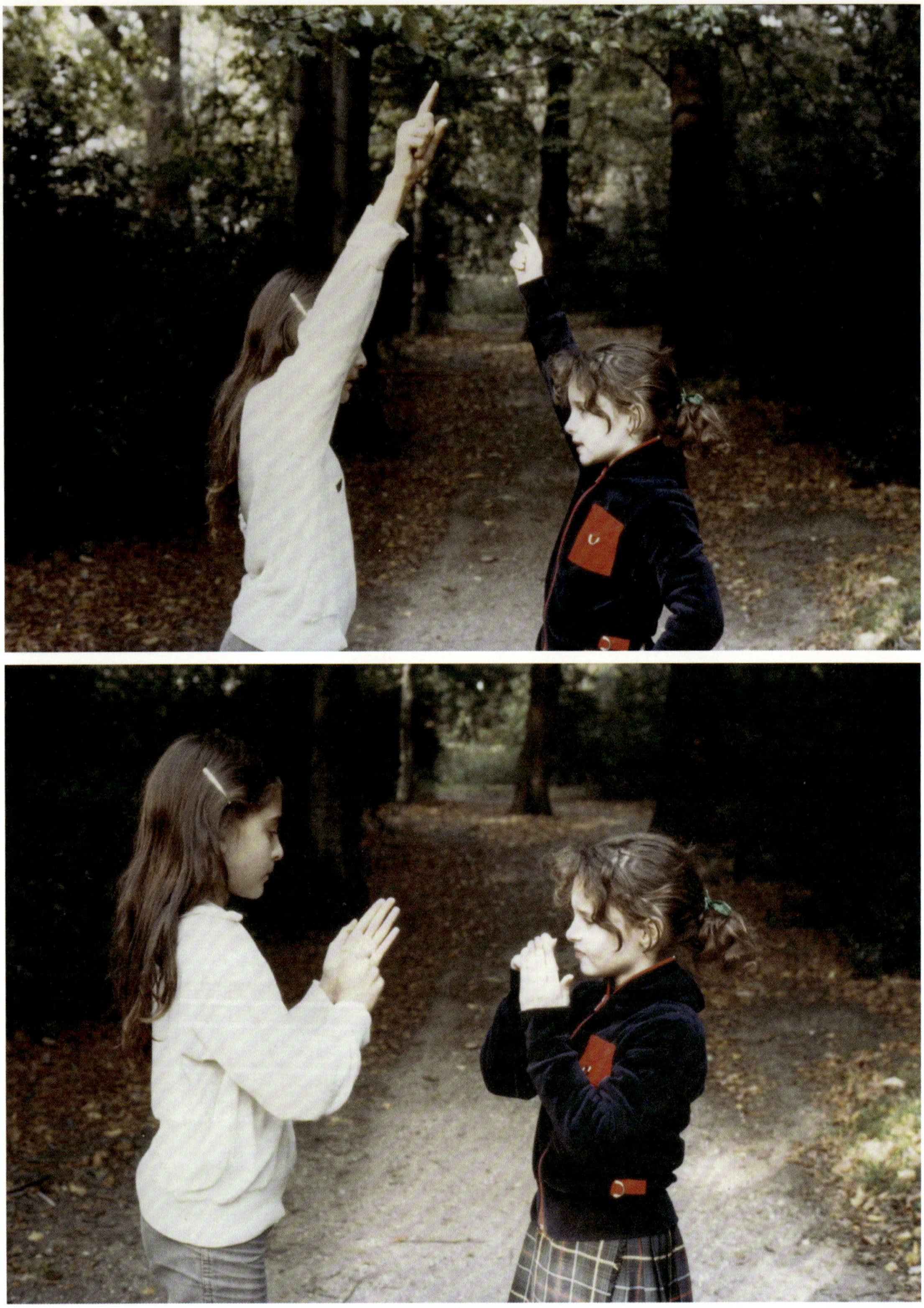

Clapping Songs 1981. Slide tape, transferred to video; shown digitally. 8 min

Tina Keane, a lecturer in film and video and later Research Fellow at Central Saint Martins until 2012, has exhibited both nationally and internationally. Born in London in 1940, Keane studied architecture and design at Hammersmith College of Art and the Sir John Cass School of Art, Architecture and Design, later receiving an MA in independent film and video from the London College of Printing in 1996. She is a pioneer of live performance art, multimedia and electronic art: she has worked with film, video, installation and neon sculpture. From painting to producing light shows in the late 1960s, she became a dynamic force in the rise of women's art in the 1970s and 1980s and contributed to the advancement of new perspectives and counter discourses made public at the time. Always innovative, she made use of the resources available to her and improvised and learnt new techniques to develop her practice. New and emerging technologies were also an opportunity to experiment with and discover new ways to realise her ideas. A proponent of digital art, she used computers and the internet to continue to explore and create new work in the 1990s and early 2000s.

Keane's early videos reference childhood play, from her on-screen performance in *The Swing* 1978 to the video and tape slide work *Clapping Songs* 1981, in which a playground clapping game reveals covert patriarchal messages.

Artist, writer and curator Janis Jefferies (b. 1952) initially trained as a painter and later moved into the field of textiles. With a long-standing engagement in how fibre intersects with feminist practice, Jefferies's work considers issues of gender and identity subjectivity and how they relate to art textiles. Her 1996 paper 'Text, Textile, Sex and Sexuality' deconstructs and critiques Freud's claim that weaving and plaiting are women's only contributions to civilisation. Jefferies's work *Double Labia* 1980 is a large-scale red-dyed woven construction depicting the inner and outer folds of a vulva, exploding notions of shame around women's body parts in Western psychology and philosophy. Her later research and practice expanded to encompass sonic art, digital art and haptic technology, considering how this relates to access for different audiences within museums.

Jefferies is Emeritus Professor of Visual Arts Goldsmiths, London and lives in St Leonards on Sea, East Sussex.

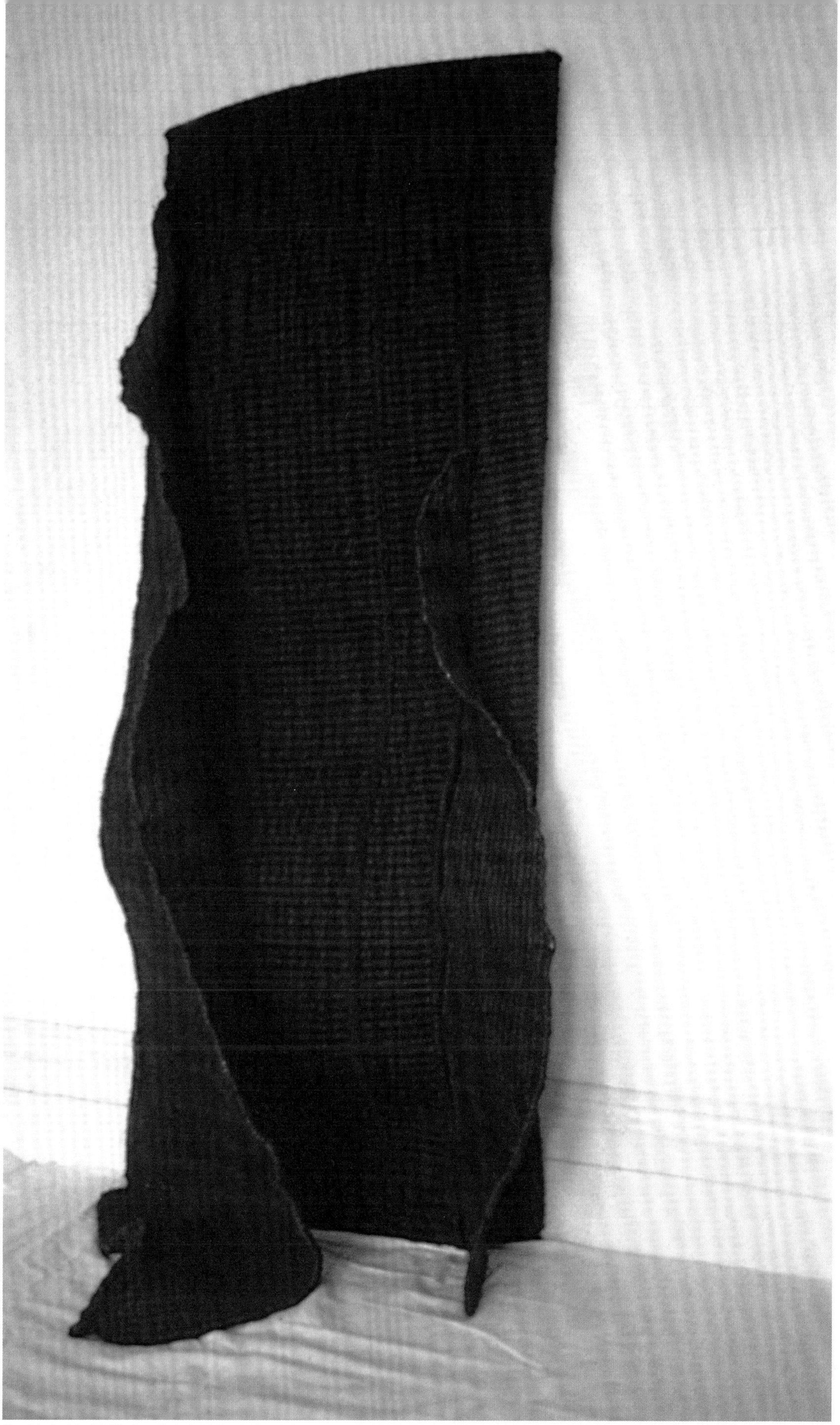

Double Labia 1980. Dyed sisal 220 × 101 × 94

JANIS JEFFERIES

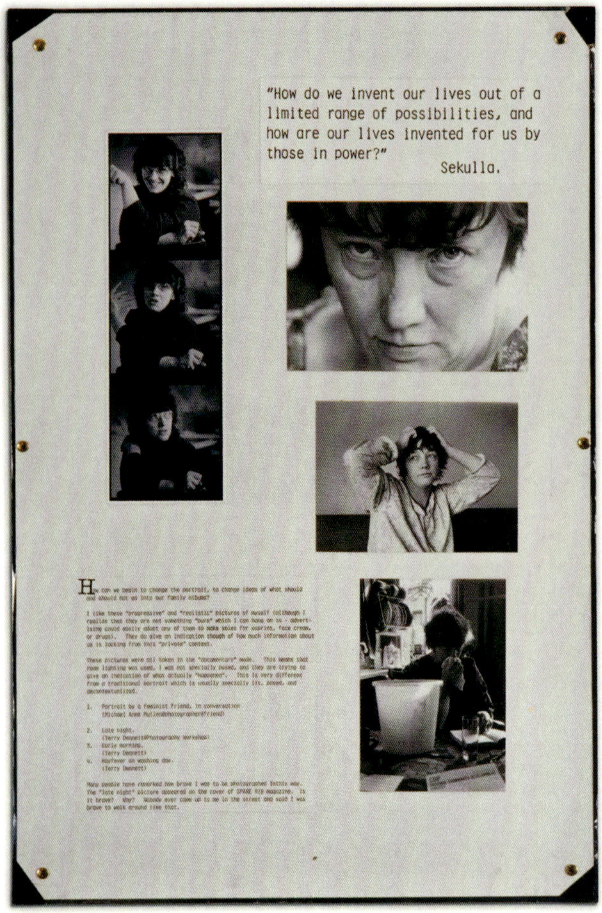

Born in London, Jo Spence (1934–92) began her career in 1967 as a photographer working in advertising and running a wedding photography studio. Spence came to reject these fields, feeling that she was contributing to 'an ideology which fixed and constructed people into particular class, race and gender positions'. Thereafter she practised photography through a more politically engaged, socialist lens. A founding member of the Hackney Flashers collective in 1974, Spence was a central figure in debates around the critique of representation in the 1970s and 80s, establishing the Photography Workshop in 1974, with Terry Dennett, and contributing to the important exhibitions *Women and Work* 1975 and *Who's Holding the Baby?* 1978. In *Beyond the Family Album* 1978–9, Spence includes traumatic events that are typically left out of family albums, believing that when we visually construct a narrative of family life, we do not represent the self. In 1982 Spence graduated with a first-class honours degree in the theory and practice of photography from the Polytechnic of Central London. A breast cancer diagnosis at the age of forty-six led to Spence making more autobiographical work, using photography as a means of therapy.

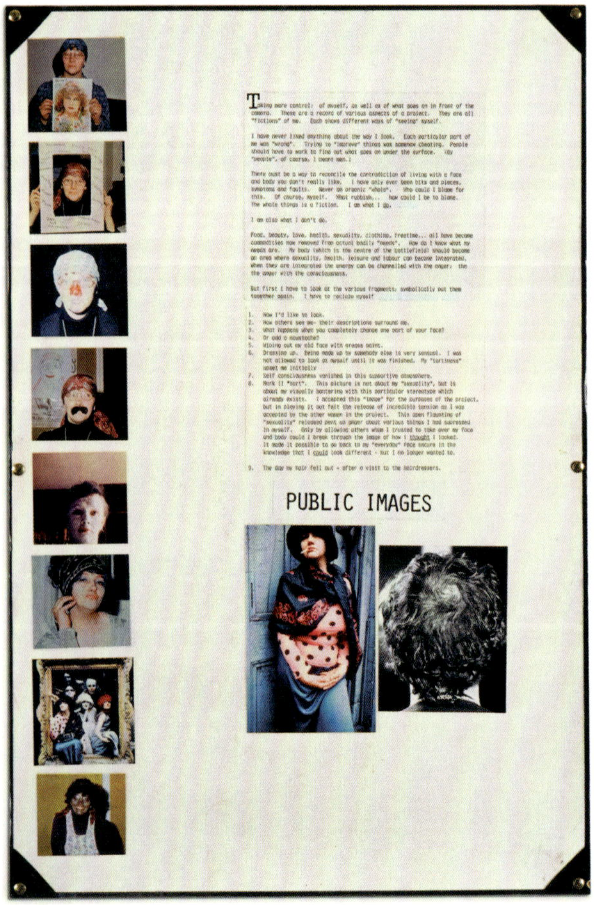

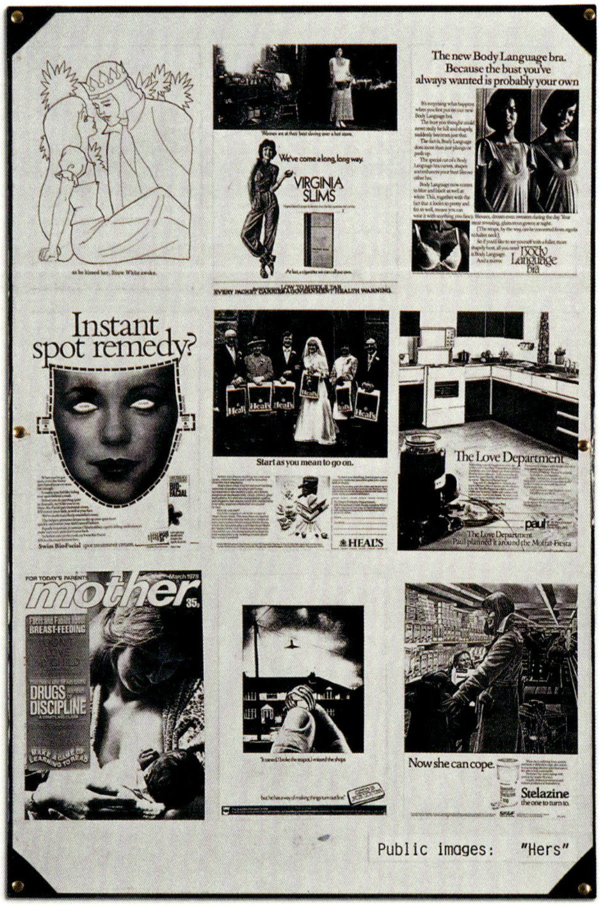

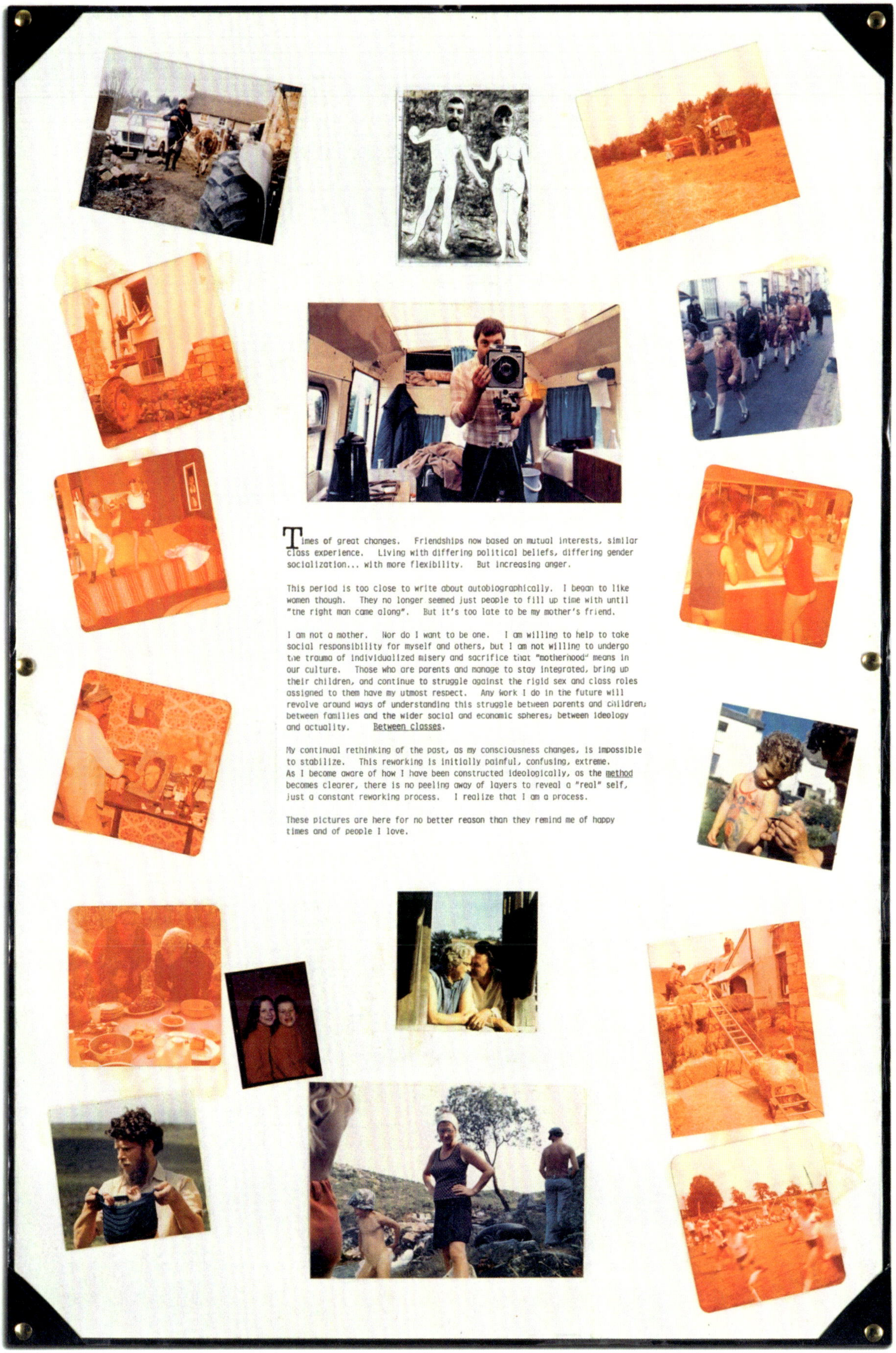

Beyond the Family Album 1978–9. Gelatin silver prints, C-prints and press cuttings 204 × 83 and 74 × 50 (each)

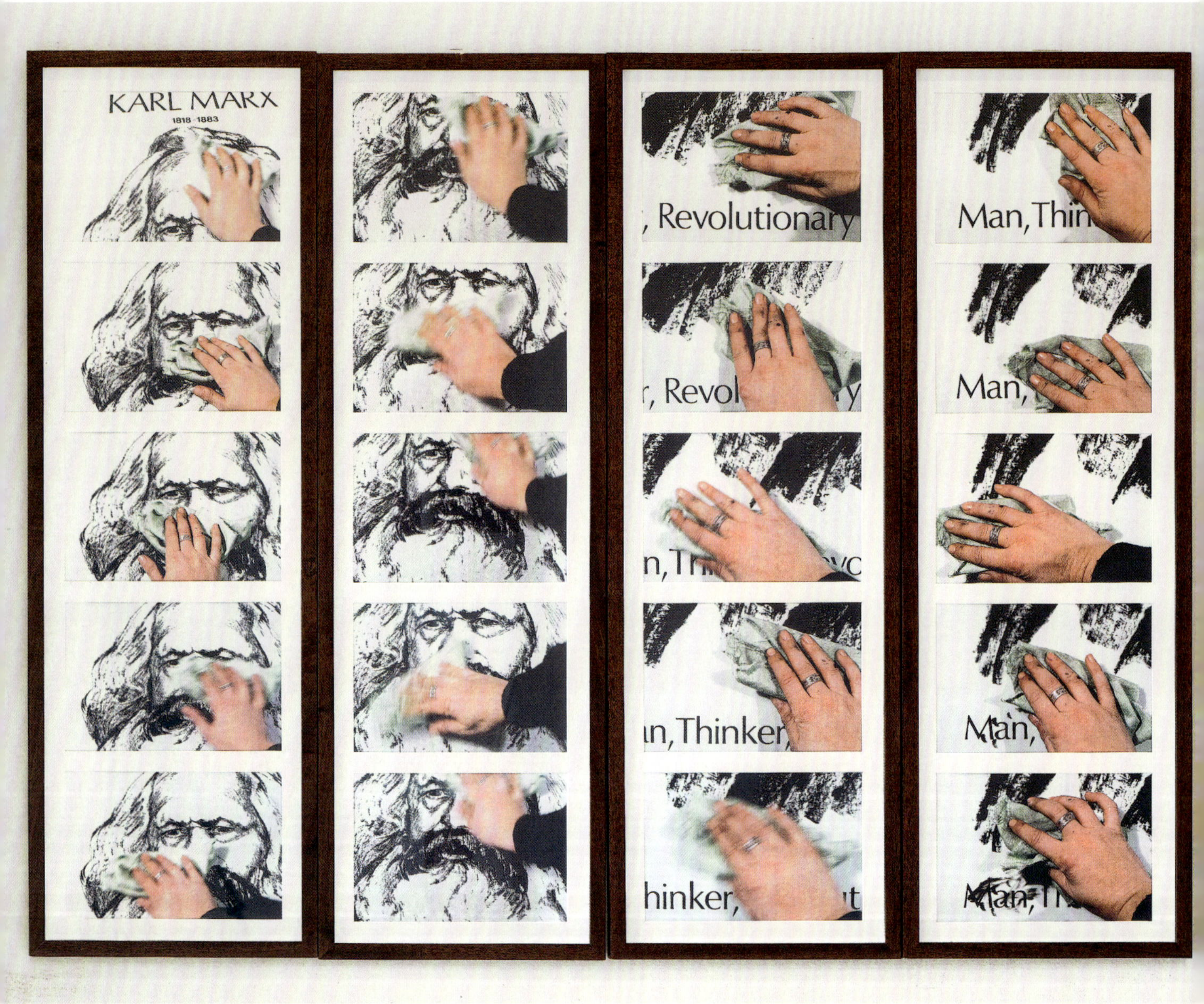

The Marxist's Wife (still does the housework) 1978/2005. 20 laser prints on archival paper, in 4 framed panels 109.5 × 36 (each panel)

ALEXIS HUNTER

Alexis Hunter (1948–2014) was born in Auckland, New Zealand, and studied at Elam School of Fine Arts. After a time living in a commune in Cairns, Australia, Hunter moved to London in 1972, working in film animation. A member of the Women's Workshop of the Artists' Union and the Women's Free Arts Alliance, Hunter worked across painting and photography, using art as a means of addressing and dismantling patriarchy and capitalism. She often sought to convey a narrative in her work using sequences of images. *The Marxist's Wife (still does the housework)* 1978 presents a sequence of images showing a hand cleaning the face of Karl Marx, the dirt getting thicker as it moves towards the word 'man'. The work critiques Marx's refusal to equate domestic labour with the work done beyond the home typically performed by men.

Hunter's work was included in the 2007–8 exhibition *WACK! Art and the Feminist Revolution*, and in 2018 a solo exhibition of her work was held at Goldsmiths Centre for Contemporary Art in London.

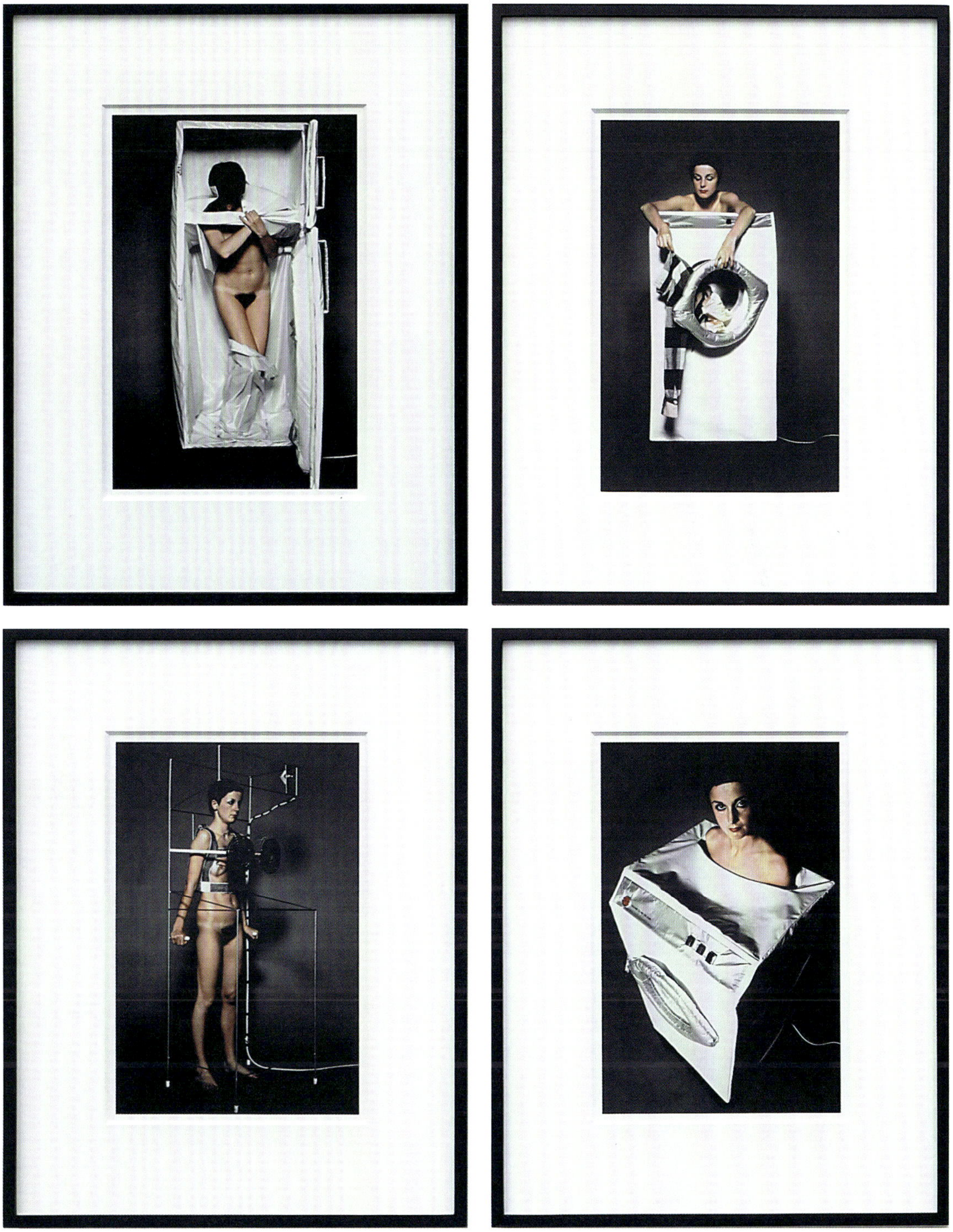

In the Kitchen 1977. 12 photographs; pigment prints 41 × 30.5 (each)

Helen Chadwick (1953–96) studied sculpture at Brighton Polytechnic, graduating in 1976, and went on to receive an MA in fine art from Chelsea College of Art in 1977. Her 1977 performance *In the Kitchen* was first staged with three other performers, and is recognised as a key moment in British feminist art practice. The four women wore costumes made by the artist representing kitchen appliances, each performing the role of an oven, fridge, sink or washing machine, satirically alluding to gendered tropes and the stereotypical role of a housewife. With a practice encompassing installation, photography and performance art, Chadwick is principally known for experimenting with unconventional materials to create complex installations and for challenging perceptions of the body, and an interest in binary oppositions, like in the sculpture series *Piss Flowers* 1991–2. With a breakthrough exhibition *Of Mutability* being held at the ICA in 1986, in 1987 Chadwick became one of the first women artists to be nominated for the Turner Prize.

HELEN CHADWICK

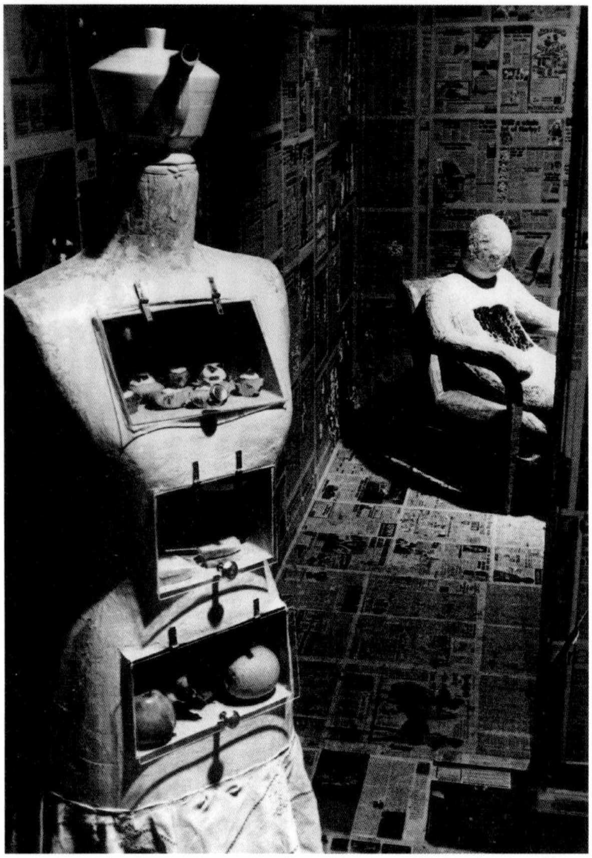

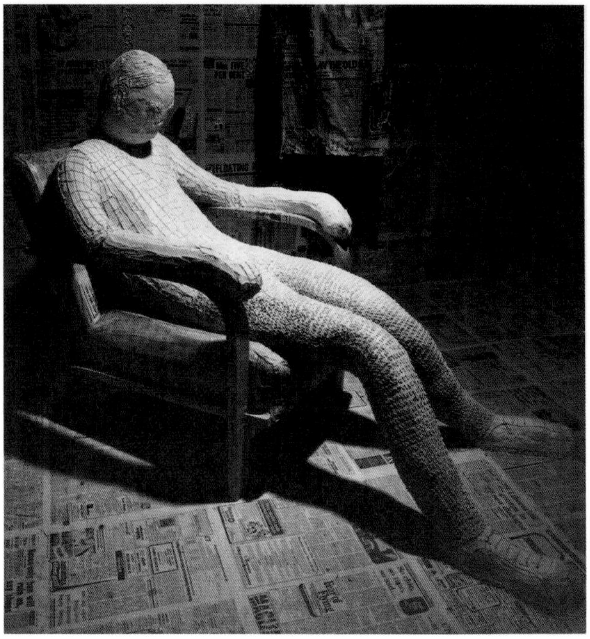

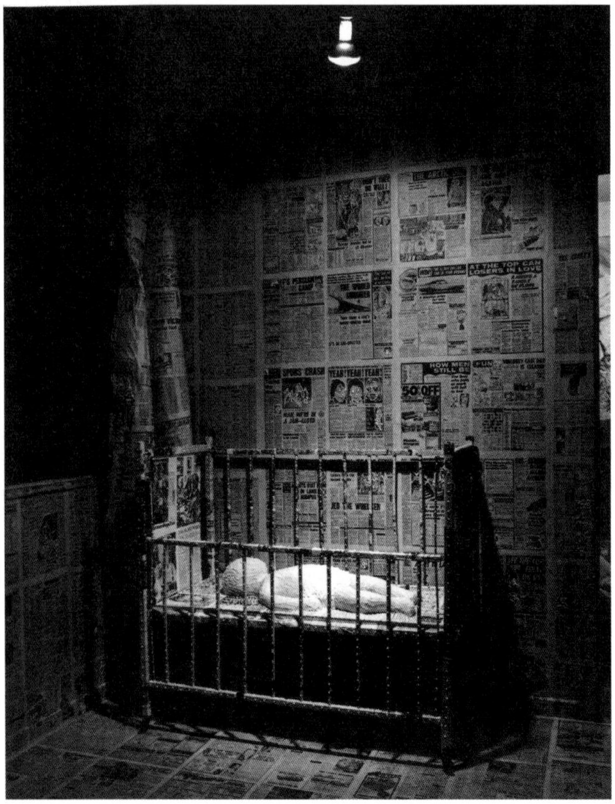

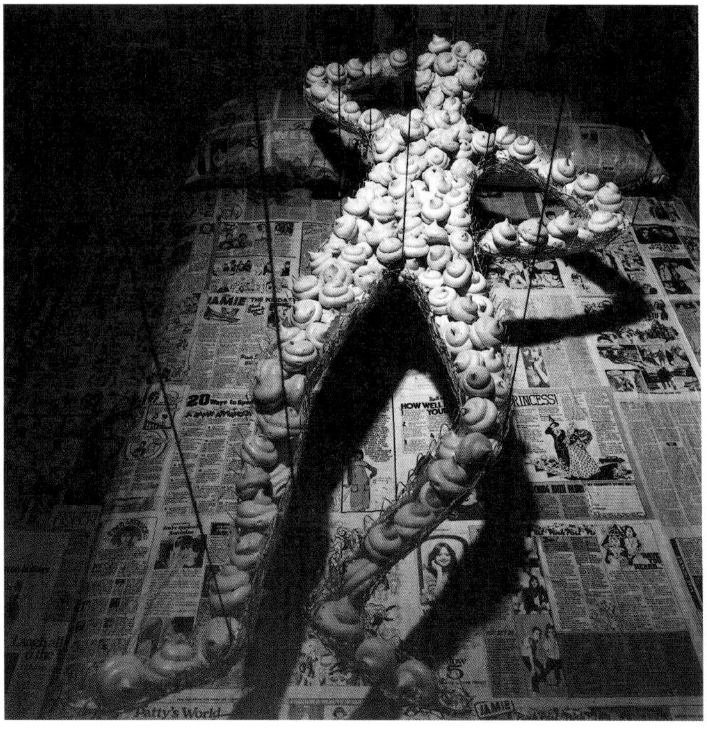

Documentation of An Edible Family in a Mobile Home 1976.
4 of 5 photographs

Born in Kent in 1950, Bobby Baker studied painting at Saint Martin's School of Art, London, graduating in 1972. In her practice, which spans performance, installation, film and drawing, Baker explores the relationship between art and everyday experience, drawing on her own family life and engaging critically with the various roles women are expected to fulfil in society, including that of a mother. The domestic space becomes a character in itself, with a particular focus on food. In the installation *An Edible Family in a Mobile Home* 1976, for example, the mother figure in the family is replenished with food daily that the audience is invited to eat. She is portrayed as a powerful, sustaining force who keeps society going, but who is ultimately stuck in the cycle of domestic labour. While the rest of the family is consumed by visitors, the mother continues to provide.

Baker lives in London, directing Daily Life Ltd, the arts organisation she founded in the 1990s to create work that engages with issues of feminism, daily life and social justice.

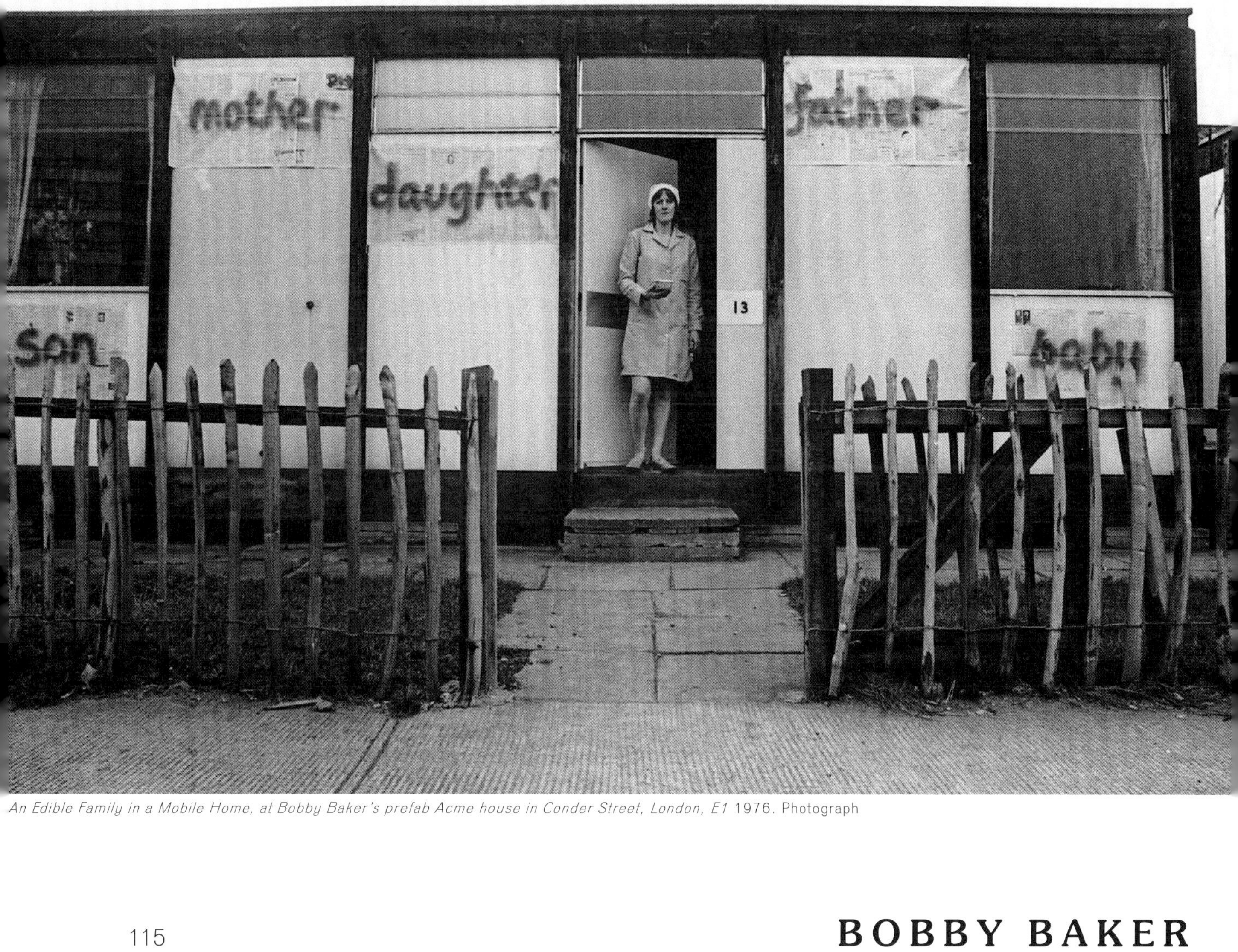

An Edible Family in a Mobile Home, at Bobby Baker's prefab Acme house in Conder Street, London, E1 1976. Photograph

BOBBY BAKER

Born in London in 1951, Christine Wilkinson completed an MA in printmaking at Chelsea School of Art in 1976 and after graduating went on to work in the University of Reading's Fine Art Department. Since the 1990s Wilkinson has exhibited nationally and internationally. Her artistic practice has always featured issue-based arts in community settings, focusing on work with women, particularly those engaged with the justice and care systems. She has devised and run Community Arts Training and specialised in supporting emerging women artists to work within communities. She has published and spoken regularly on these themes and describes her work as 'shaped by family history and women surviving and thriving'. The reclamation of stories of women from older generations and the use of modest or 'domestic' materials feature strongly in her work.

Wilkinson lives and works in Birmingham.

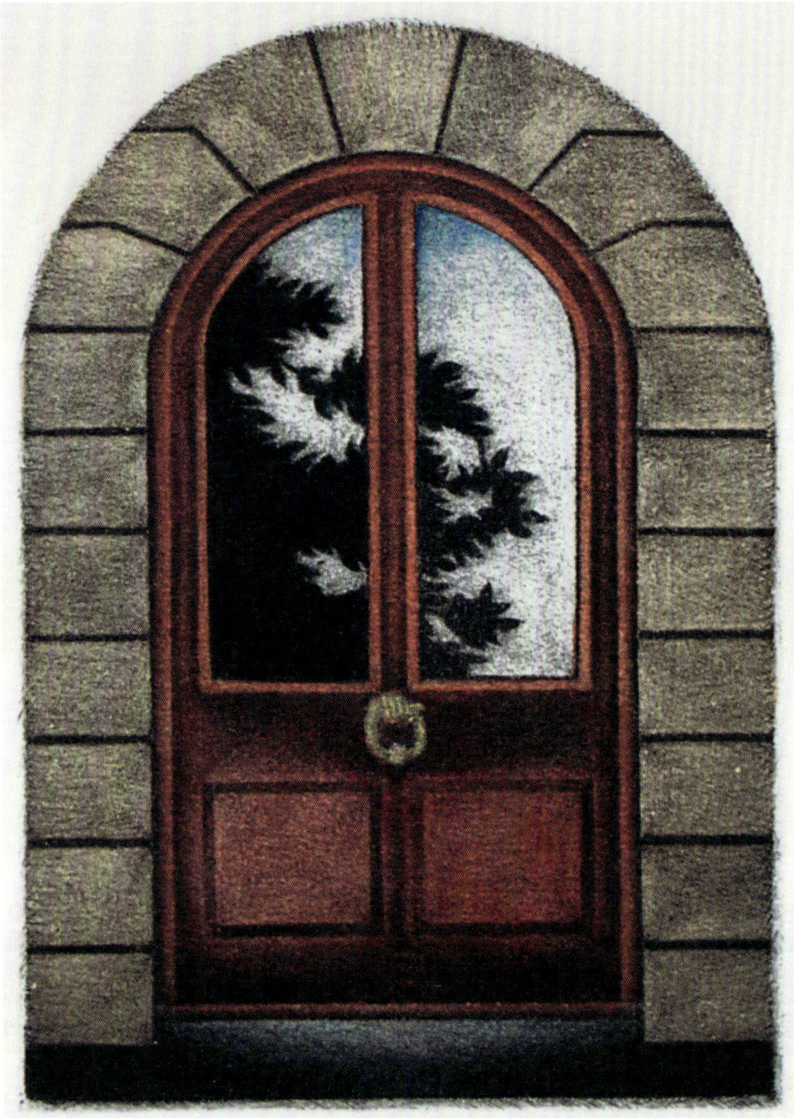

Reflections 1983. Hand-coloured mezzotint 8.2 × 11.7

CHRISTINE WILKINSON

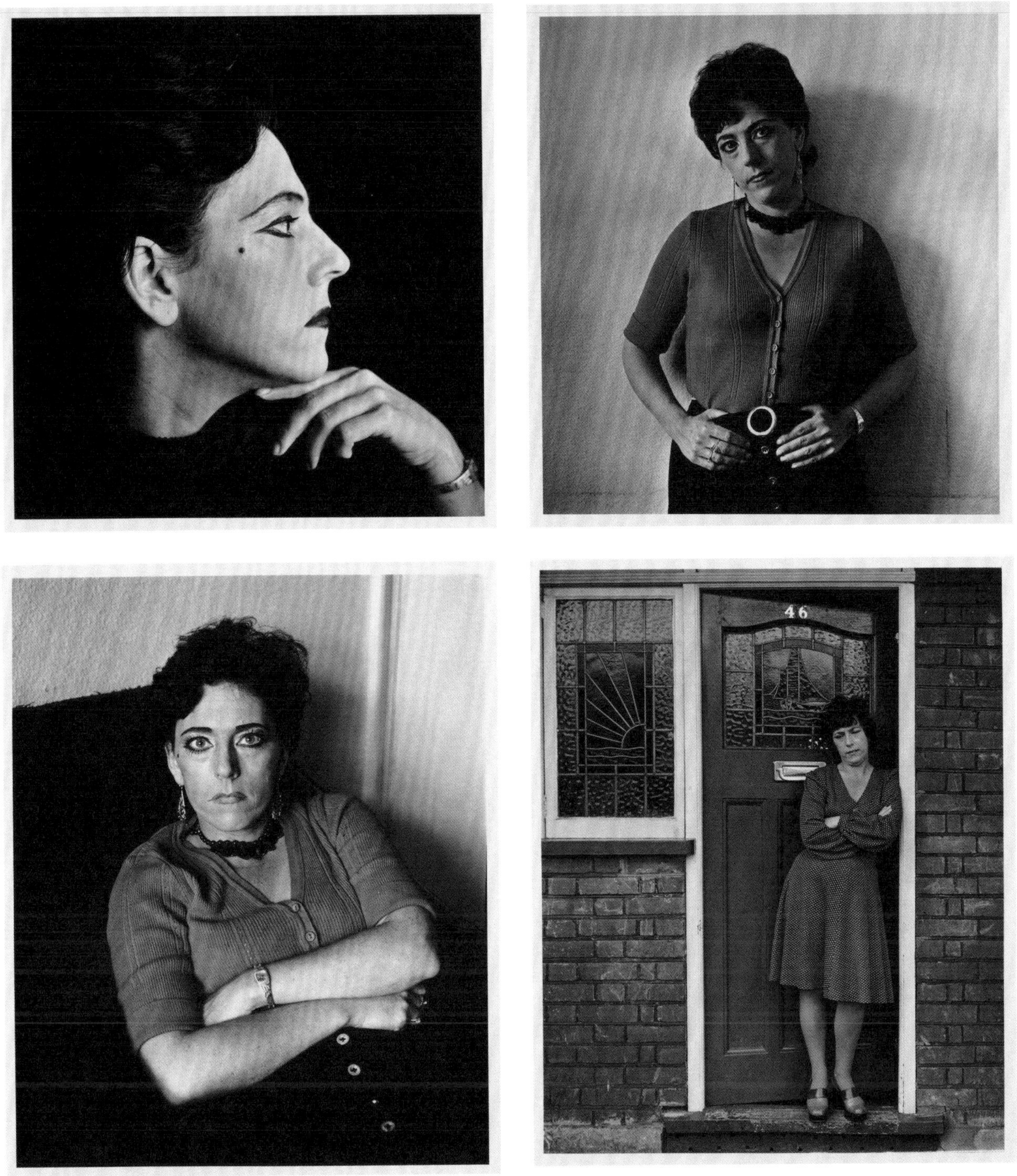

Moira 1–4 1975. Gelatin silver prints on paper
25.6 × 21; 22.9 × 27.4; 23.2 × 22.3; 25.6 × 21.1

Born in London in 1943, Aileen Ferriday studied for a BA in fine art and then an MA in photography at Manchester Polytechnic, graduating in 1975. She began her practice as a painter, focusing on portraits, before beginning to work as a photographer, using the camera to continue an exploration into portraiture. In 1979 Ferriday's portraits of her friends featured in one of the most important photography exhibitions of the decade, *Three Perspectives on Photography* at the Hayward Gallery. Curated by theme, Ferriday's series inspired by 1950s cinema was included in Angela Kelly's section on feminism and photography. In the exhibition catalogue Ferriday explained that all the women in her photographs were from working-class backgrounds and that her intention was to celebrate them within an aesthetic of nostalgia and glamour, reclaiming female beauty from the male gaze. The portrait series is held in the Arts Council Collection.

AILEEN FERRIDAY

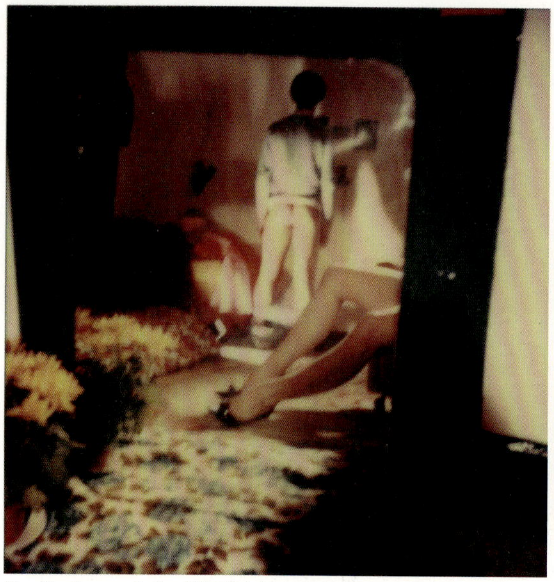

Romilly Crescent, Cardiff, Watching 1978. Polaroid photograph 10.5 × 8.5

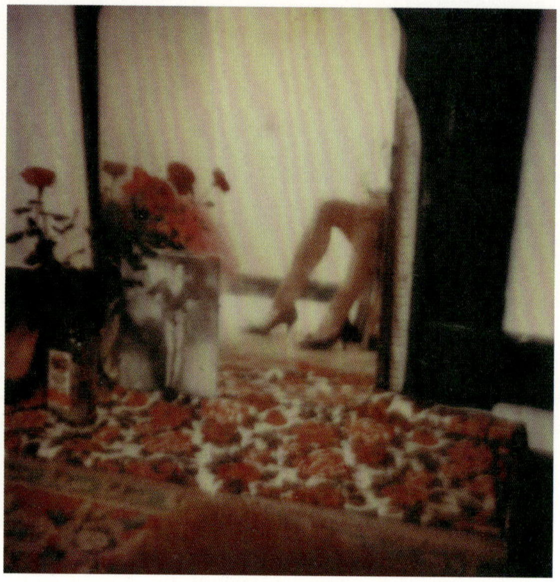

Romilly Crescent, Cardiff, Looking at Herbie 1978. Polaroid photograph 10.5 × 8.5

Alison Lloyd (1957–2024) was born in Witney, Oxfordshire. Her early artistic practice focused on photographing her lived experience. While studying at Cardiff in the late 1970s, Lloyd documented the experiences of the community of artists that worked in and around the shared house on Romilly Crescent. Often capturing highly-stylised fragments of bodies and movements, Lloyd's resulting stills and moving images sit between documentation and performance, communicating the atmosphere or mood of the time. She referred to her photographic series as 'events' which capture a range of speculative and choreographed happenings.

Lloyd's recent work has focused on women's artistic relationship to walking and to the land, exploring the distinct ways in which women might navigate or engage with remote spaces.

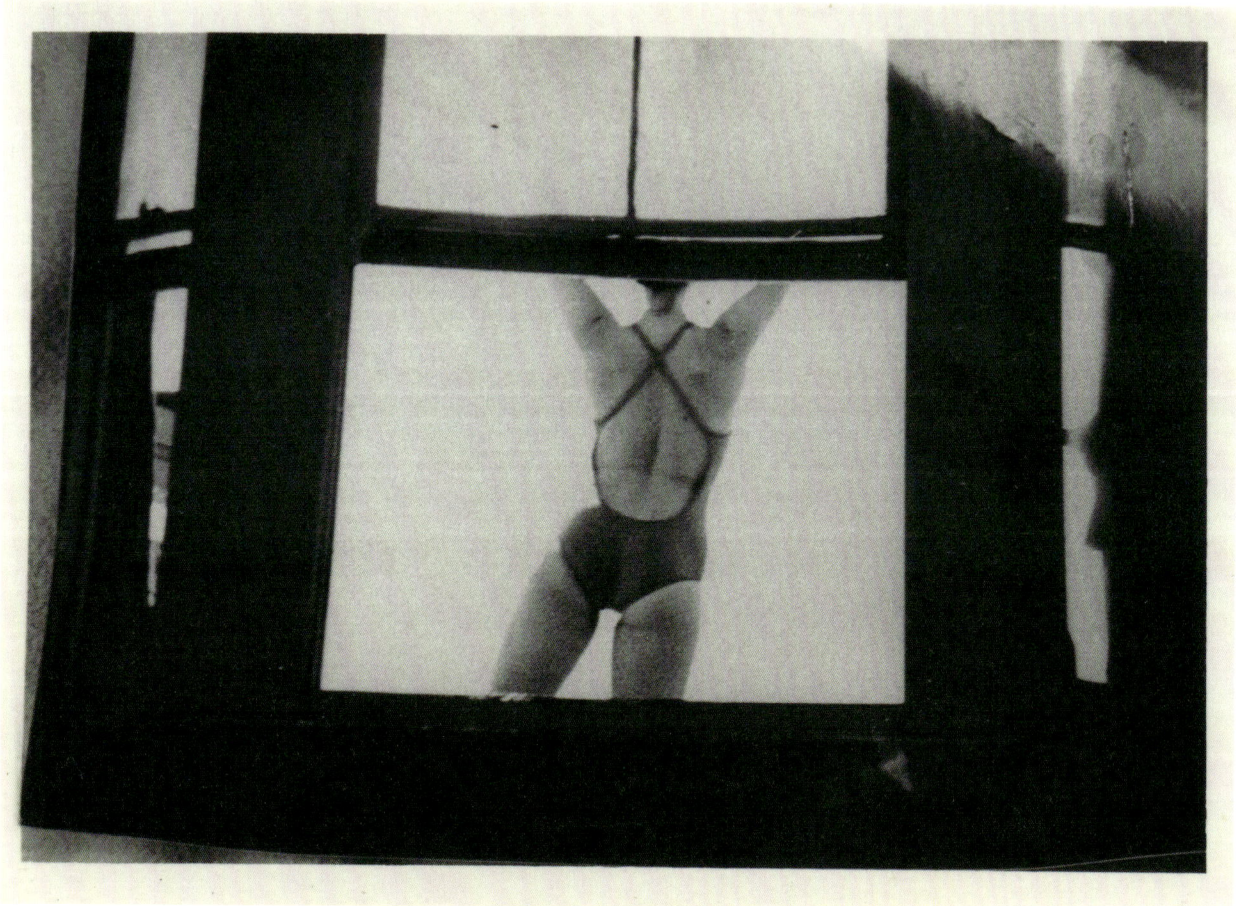

Romilly Crescent, Cardiff, at the window, Evening Performance 1978–9. Photograph 9 × 13

ALISON LLOYD

Elizabeth Radcliffe (b.1949) was brought up in Scotland, in Musselburgh and Edinburgh. After leaving school, she was employed as a screen-printer (working on tiles) at Dovecot Studios in Edinburgh and learned to weave tapestry at night classes. She then studied at Edinburgh College of Art in 1972–3, and again in 1975–8, having had two children in the meantime. Radcliffe's process incorporates a revision of the classical tradition of hand-weaving on a loom, adapting it in new and original ways. Rather than the conventional rectangular form of most tapestries, she weaves sculptural three-dimensional portraits with complex outlines. The work *Cool Bitch and Hot Dog* 1978 reflects the artist's desire to be a modern woman, defying many of the passive stereotypes of women as mothers, cleaners, caregivers or objects of sexual desire.

Radcliffe's work has been exhibited internationally throughout her career. She lives and works in Edinburgh.

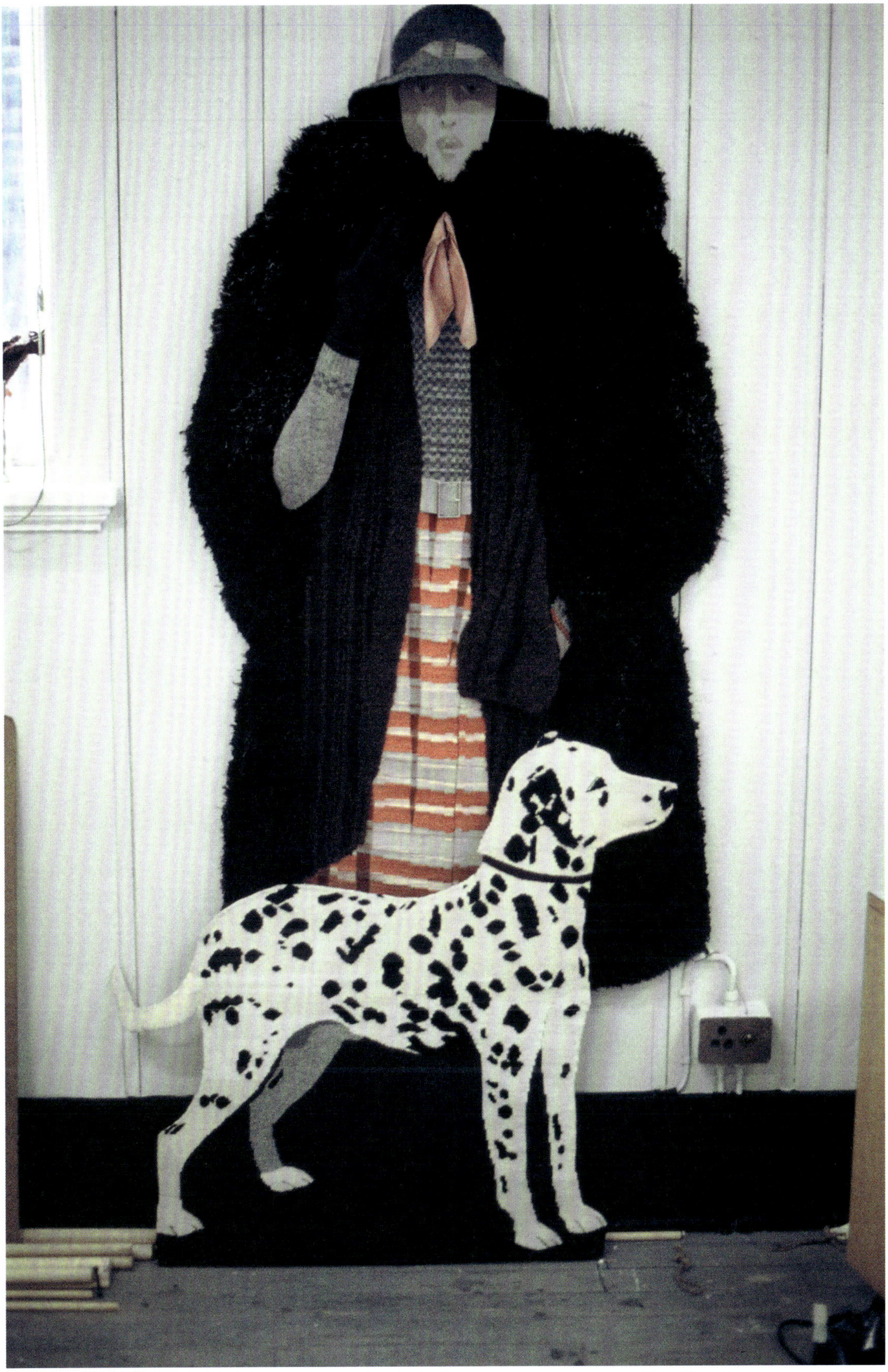

Cool Bitch and Hot Dog 1978. Wool, linen, papier mâché, metal buckle and nylon glove on plywood 180 × 83 × 50

ELIZABETH RADCLIFFE

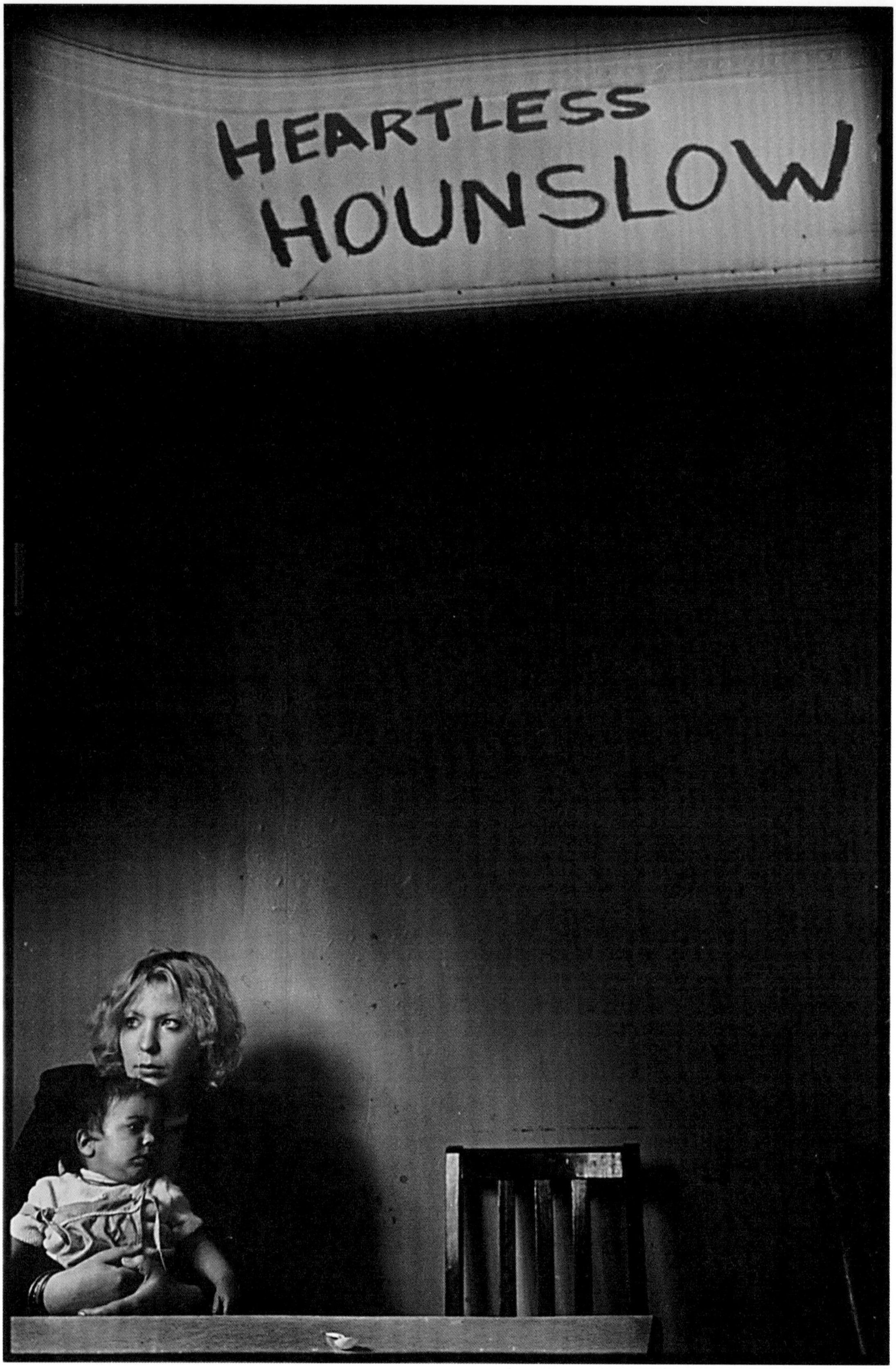

Untitled 1978. Gelatin silver print 29.7 × 20.1

Social documentary photographer Christine Voge (b. 1948) grew up in Iowa and Indianapolis, moving to the UK in 1976 to pursue her photography practice. In 1978 she visited Chiswick Women's Aid in London, the world's first women's refuge, for a press-related work assignment. Moved by the experience, Voge later returned to the refuge of her own accord and spent time with its founder, Erin Pizzey, and the residents to capture their daily lives. The images she made there depict both children and mothers, and were intended to demonstrate the refuge's significance to society, an act that had not been considered by other photographers at the time. The emotional trauma suffered is visibly evident in some images, particularly one that shows four women holding each other. Her work was included in the important exhibition *Three Perspectives on Photography: Recent British Photography* at the Hayward Gallery in 1979.

In 2013 Voge had a solo exhibition at the Royal Festival Hall in London as part of the Women of the World Festival. She lives and works in Hertfordshire.

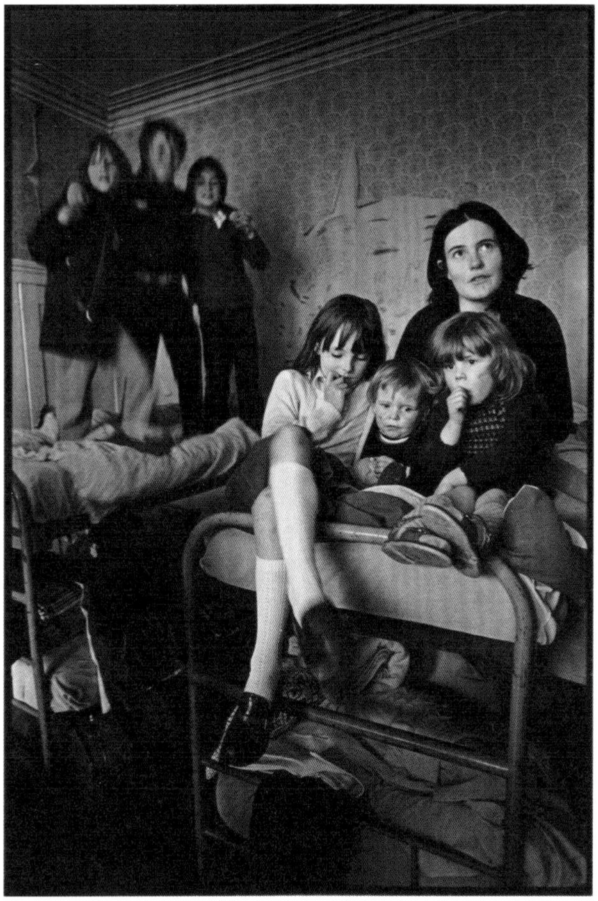

Untitled 1978. Gelatin silver print 29.3 × 20.3

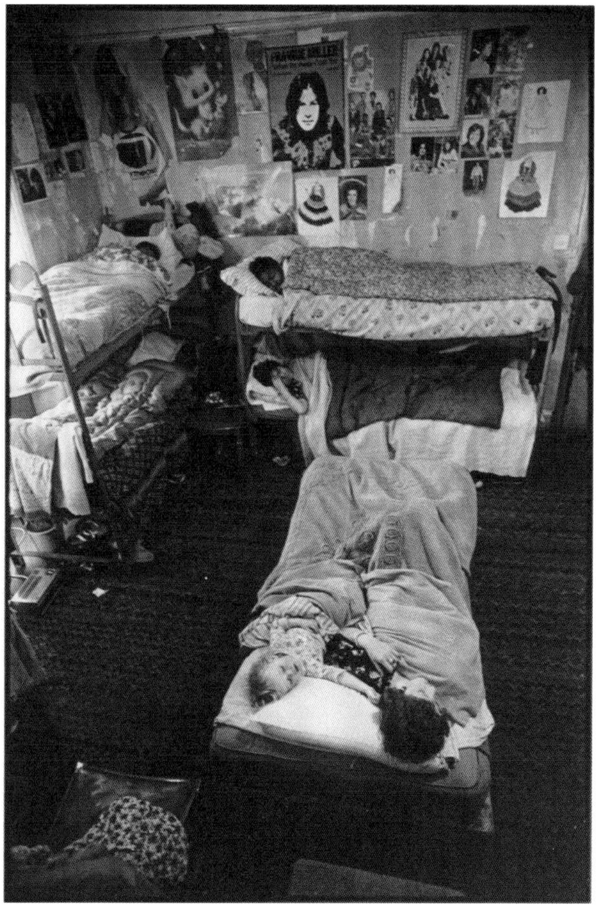

Untitled 1978. Gelatin silver print 29.3 × 20.1

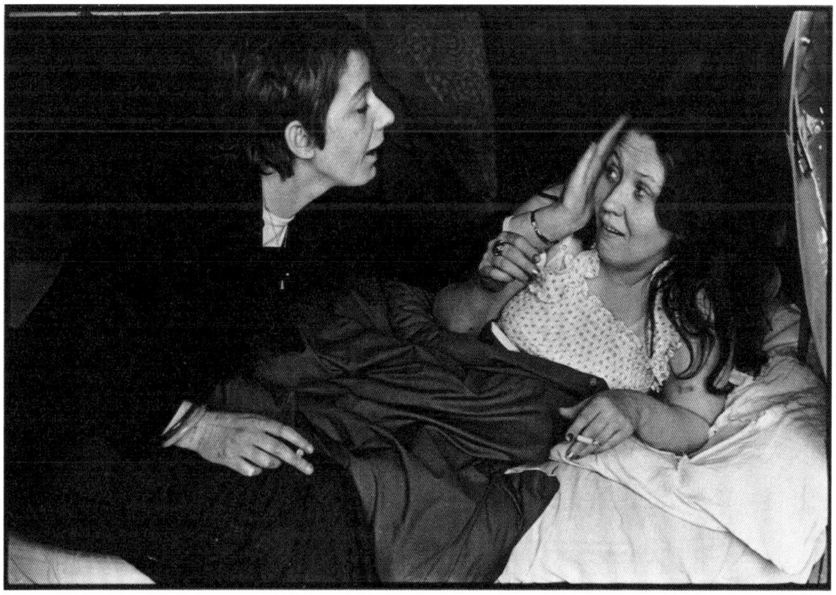

Untitled 1978. Gelatin silver print 19.9 × 29.3

Are there any choices?

"I was completely down, finished, and someone said 'there's a nursery opening up' - and from that day it changed my life completely".

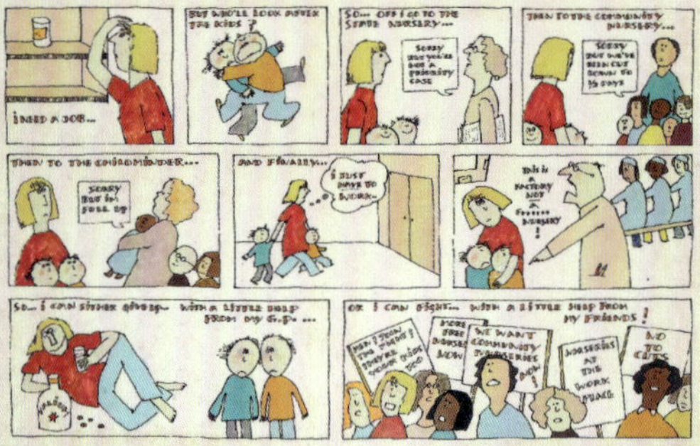

Looking for a solution

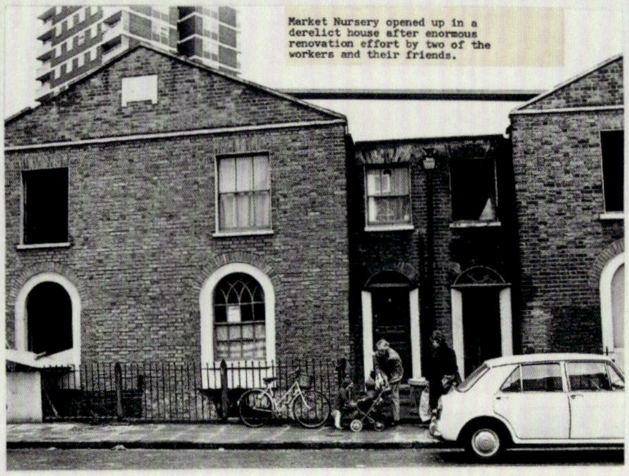

Market Nursery opened up in a derelict house after enormous renovation effort by two of the workers and their friends.

Market Nursery

Number of under-5's	- 20
Paid workers	- 3 women
Voluntary workers	- 2 men
Part-time secretary	- 1 woman
Building	- short-term loan by G.L.C.
Money	- from government and Hackney Council
Hours	- 9.30 - 3.30 p.m.
Cost	- £2. per week per child (to parents)
Meals	- included in fee
Management	- by committee and open meetings of parents. PARENTS' CONTROL.

"There were all kinds of things we hadn't known about. We had to wait for the Fire Officer, who wanted fire alarms on every floor, the Public Health Inspector, and registration from the Social Services. At first it seemed a miracle when we got through the day, there was always some problem. But to the kids it was paradise; they had a great range of toys and a lot of freedom compared to home, most of all a big garden, with a lot of equipment".

SUE, Market Nursery Worker.

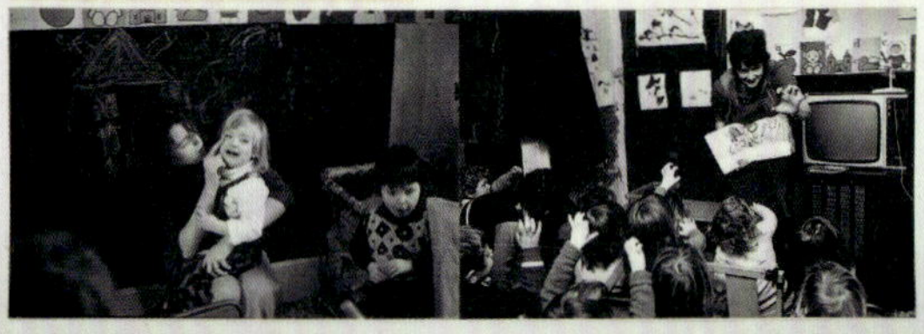

Who's holding the baby... and often alone

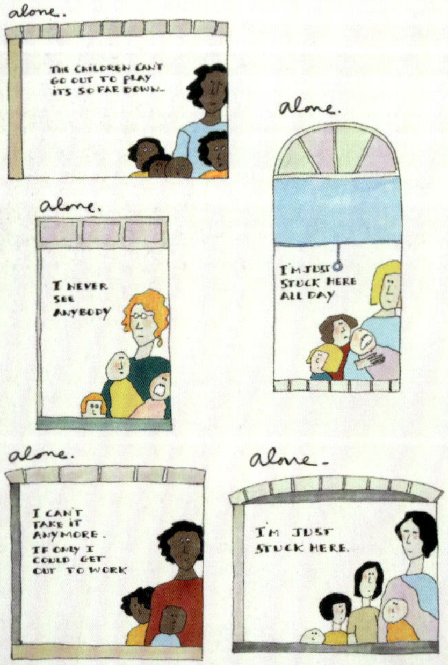

Private provision

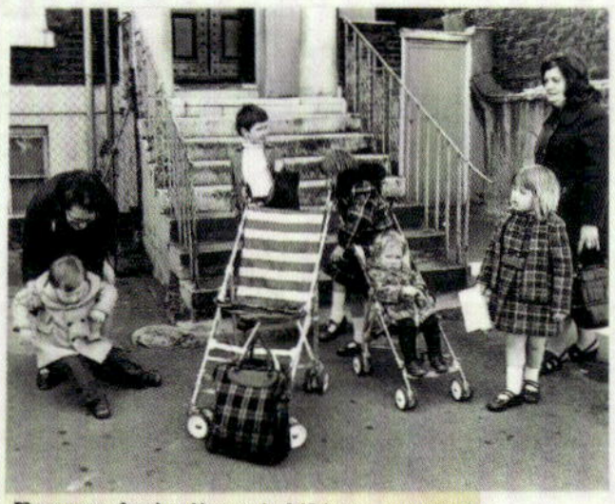

Playgroup for handicapped children, organised by parents

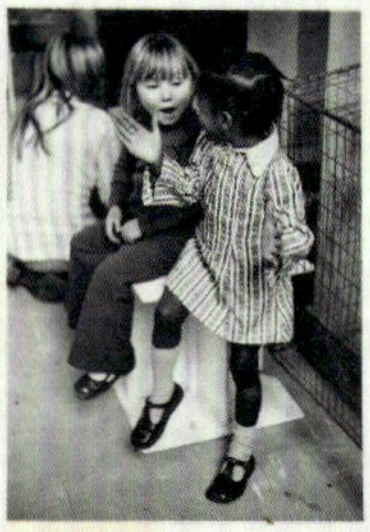

Playgroup

State provision for under-fives has to be supplemented. <u>Mothers at home</u> with small babies can go to One O'clock Clubs - approximately 2 hours. Mothers with toddlers can leave them at playgroups for 2 - 3 hours. <u>Mothers with jobs</u> have to leave their children with childminders for a full day.

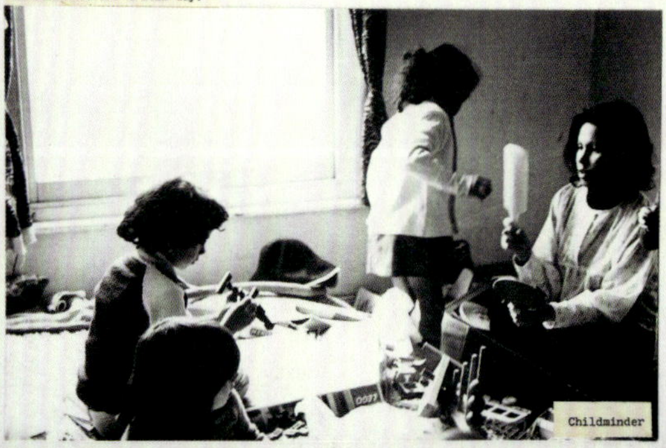

Childminder

Market Nursery, Hackney

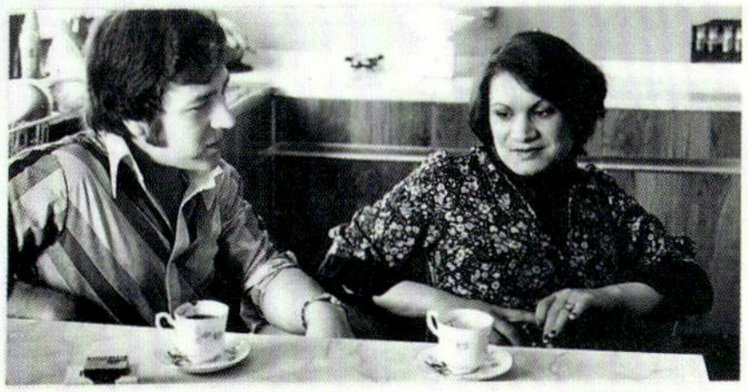

"Market Nursery was important for Johnny because when he went there he didn't speak a word of English and we wanted to get him ready for school. After two weeks he came home and wrote his name in English. Until he went to the nursery we spoke to him only in Greek because we wanted him to know our language. But he picked up English very quickly and now he speaks it better than Greek."

"Johnny loved the nursery, he always loved going. Sometimes he doesn't want to go to school".

STELLA ANGELIDES

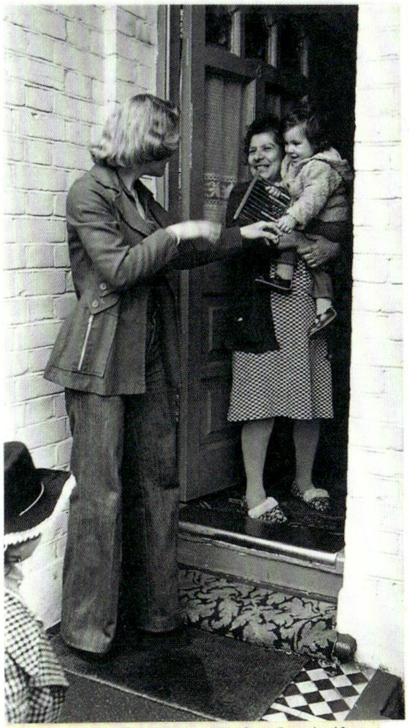

8.00 am Leaving Michael at the childminders.

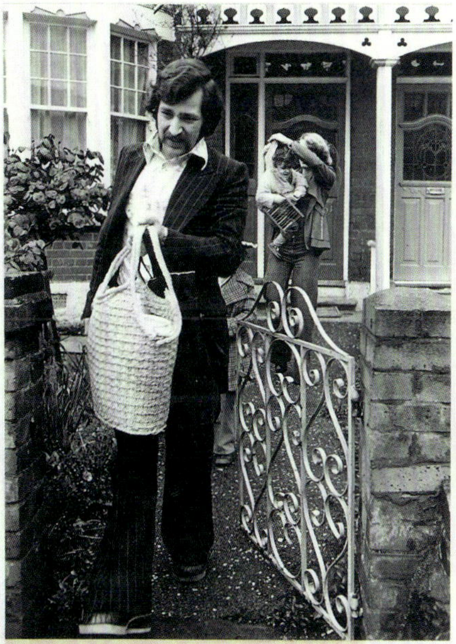

7.30 am Setting off from home.

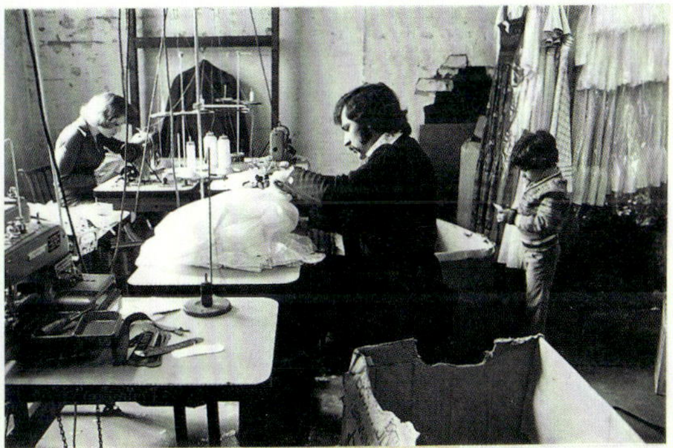

8.15 am Starting work at their dress-making factory before taking Johnny to Market Nursery.

Who's Holding the Baby? 1978, printed c.1980
5 of 23 panels; gelatin silver prints, ink, typed text, photomechanical prints and collage on paper and cardboard 77 × 51.5 (each)

1980, the socialist feminist women's agitprop collective Hackney Flashers focused their attention on the borough of Hackney in east London, home to some of the city's most severe poverty at the time. Their work was made for a purpose beyond the art gallery, intended to reach trade union events, women's liberation conferences and other forums dedicated to political activism and feminist action. The group members included An Dekker, Sally Greenhill, Gerda Jager, Liz Heron, Michael Ann Mullen, Maggie Murray, Christine Roche, Jo Spence and Julia Vellacott, but the work produced was always credited to the collective, without naming individuals.

Hackney Flashers produced two exhibitions, one of them travelling, *Women and Work* 1975 and *Who's Holding the Baby?* 1978. The latter addresses the importance of childcare, critiquing and highlighting the lack of government support, exploring the conflicting and impossible position of being both a mother and a worker in 1970s Britain. The collective stipulated that the installation could only be displayed at the Hayward Gallery if a public event about issues around childcare was laid on. In 2015 *Who's Holding the Baby?* was shown as a slide show in the Hayward Gallery exhibition, *History is Now*, curated by Hannah Starkey.

Gee Vaucher was born in Dagenham, Essex in 1945, and in the 1960s attended South-East Essex Technical College and School of Art, where she met her future long-time creative partner, Penny Rimbaud. With Rimbaud, Vaucher co-founded the anarcho-pacifist open house Dial House in Essex in 1967, a 'centre for radical creativity', where she lives and works to this day. Vaucher worked as a political illustrator in New York in the 1970s where she also founded and produced the first copy of her newspaper *International Anthem* (1978–82), 'a Nihilist Newspaper for the Living', so that she could explore ideas that were too radical for the mainstream press. Returning to the UK, Vaucher joined Crass, the English punk band that Rimbaud had formed with Steve Ignorant in 1977, which cited anarchism as its political ideology. In her art practice, Vaucher works across painting, drawing and collage, often adopting a surrealist approach. The covers and video collages she produced for Crass in the 1970s and 80s had a profound impact on anti-war and punk art at the time. Vaucher regards her art as a tool for social change, considering anarchist and feminist ideas, saying 'to me, art is politics, with a small p'.

A solo retrospective of Vaucher's fifty-year practice was held at Firstsite, Colchester, in 2016.

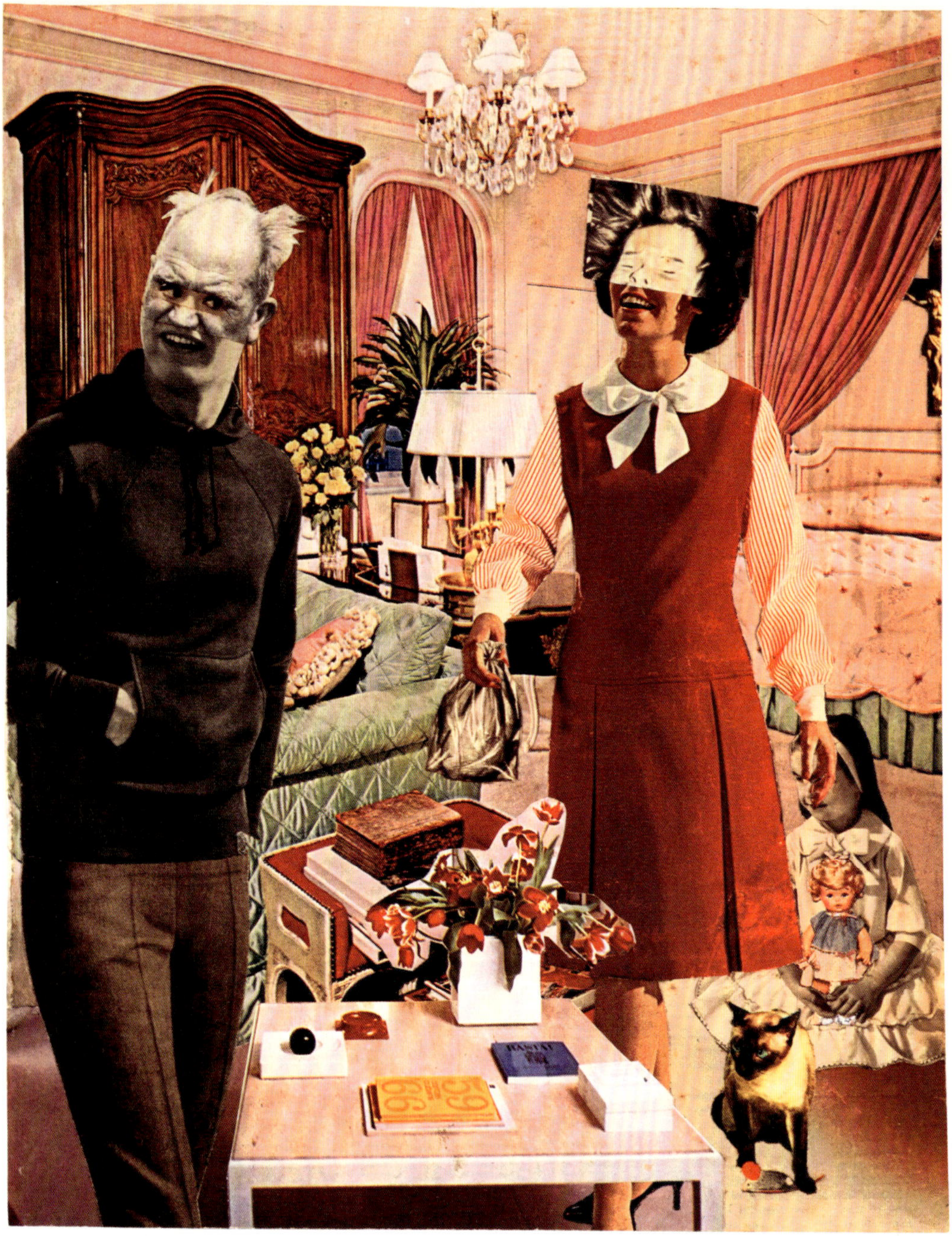

International Anthem No.2 Domestic Violence 1979. Printed magazine cuttings on card 34 × 27.5

Born in Glossop in 1953, Derbyshire, Eileen Cooper attended Goldsmiths College in London before going on to study painting at the Royal College of Art, graduating in 1977. Cooper's first solo exhibition was held at AIR Gallery, London in 1979, and in 1980 her painting *Two Figures on a Seesaw* was included in *Women's Images of Men*, one of three major exhibitions of women's art held at the ICA that year. Through metaphorical and allegorical paintings, Cooper's practice explores ideas around motherhood, sexuality, love and death, often with autobiographical allusions. *Woman Examining Her Shadow* 1988–9 sees the artist navigating her emotional and sexual life as a young woman. Representing herself in multiple forms in the painting, Cooper references the many roles women are expected to fulfil in society that restrict and forbid their own desires.

Cooper was elected a Royal Academician in 2001 and was awarded an OBE in 2016. From 2010 to 2017 she served as Keeper of the Royal Academy, the first woman to hold the position. She lives and works in London.

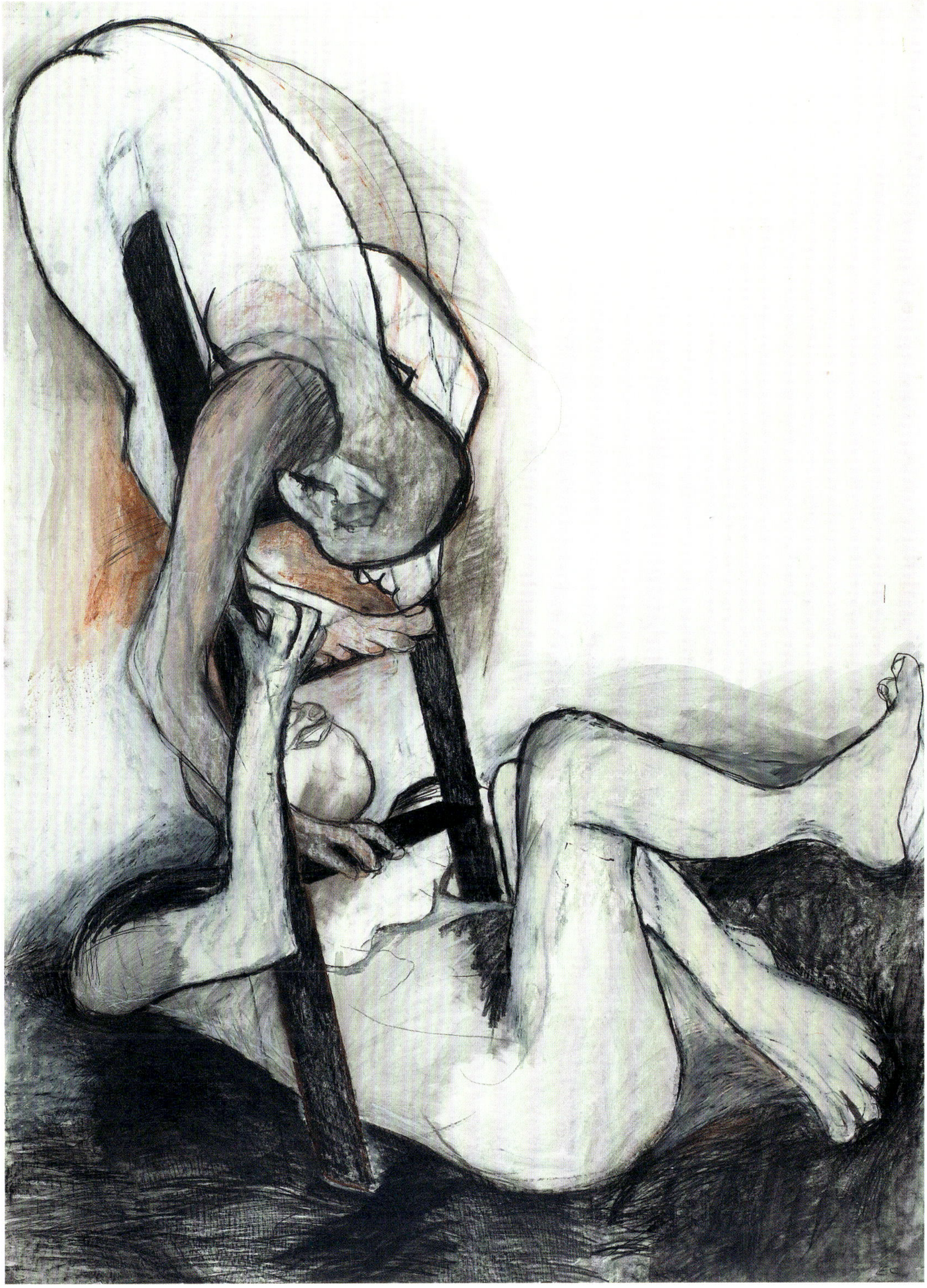

Figures on a Ladder 1979. Charcoal and pastel on paper 137 × 101.5

EILEEN COOPER

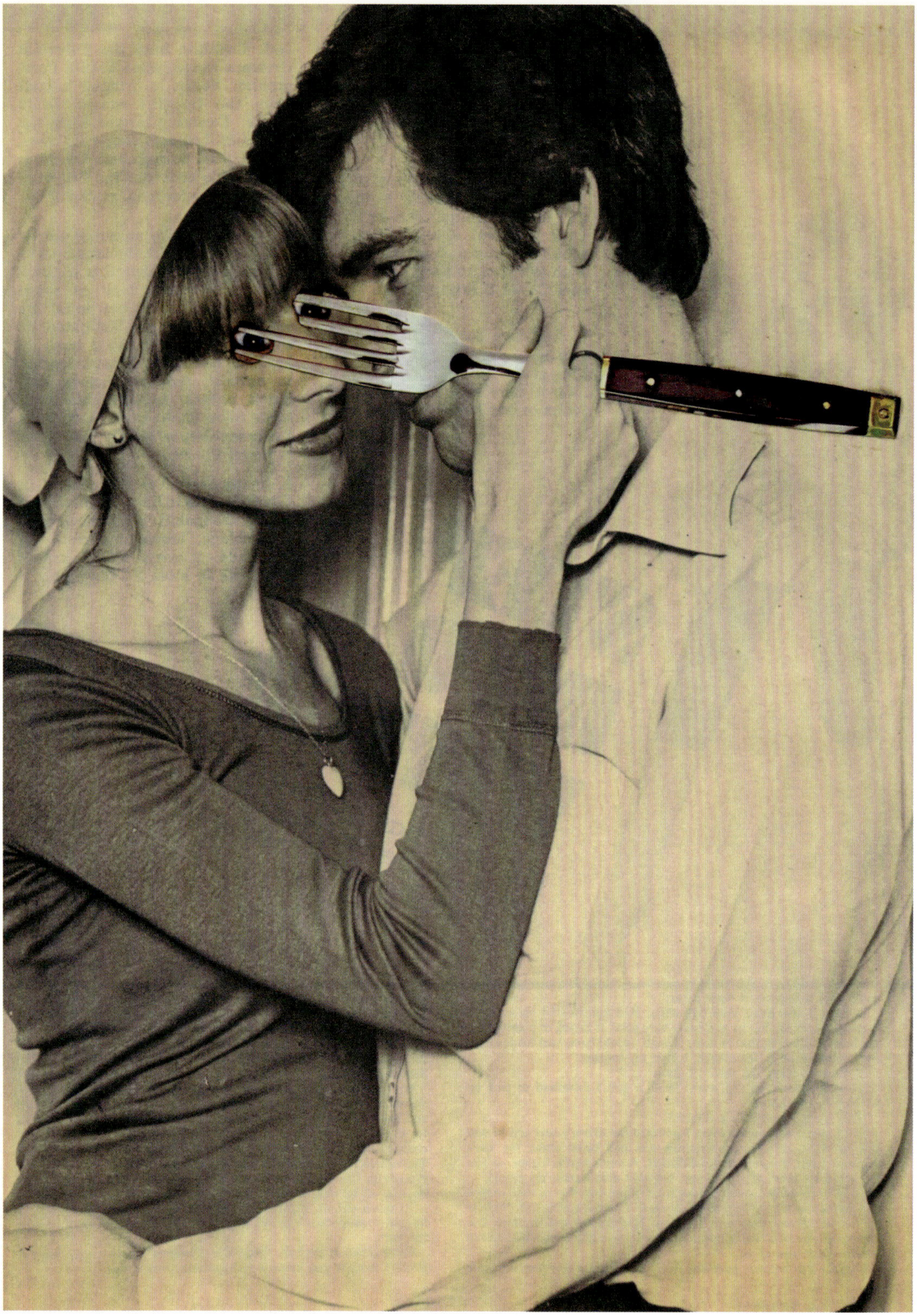

Untitled 1976. Printed papers on paper 27.9 × 19.6

Linder was born in Liverpool in 1954. She studied graphic design at Manchester Polytechnic, graduating in 1977. Linder works across photomontage, moving image and performance, citing artists such as Dadaist Hannah Höch as influences on her practice. Her work explores women's histories and feminism, and in particular the presentation and commodification of the female body.

In 1978 Linder founded the post-punk band Ludus, releasing two albums: *The Seduction* (1981) and *Danger Came Smiling* (1982). The lyrics sung by Linder included references to women's roles in society and menstruation. In 1982 she performed at the Haçienda in Manchester, wearing a dress decorated with meat and a sex toy in protest against the club's sale of meat products and its playing of pornography on monitors. In collaboration with Jon Savage, Linder published the fanzine-style publication *The Secret Public*, titled in reference to the fact that mainstream society paid little attention to the culture in which they were embedded.

The artist held solo exhibitions at Kettle's Yard in Cambridge (2020) and Nottingham Contemporary (2018), and has a retrospective at the Hayward Gallery in 2025. She lives and works in the north of England.

Rita McGurn (1940–2015) was born in Glasgow. Although she spent time at the Glasgow School of Art as a life model, she did not formally study there and her art practice was self-taught. McGurn worked in Glasgow as a film designer, and later had a successful career as an interior designer. Like many women artists working from the home during the 1970s and 80s, McGurn employed a range of found materials in her practice, making use of whatever was to hand. She typically worked in crochet, creating large life-sized people that she placed around the home. Her practice can thus be considered as sculpture and installation, while also spanning drawing and textiles. A solo exhibition of her work was held at Celine, Glasgow in 2017.

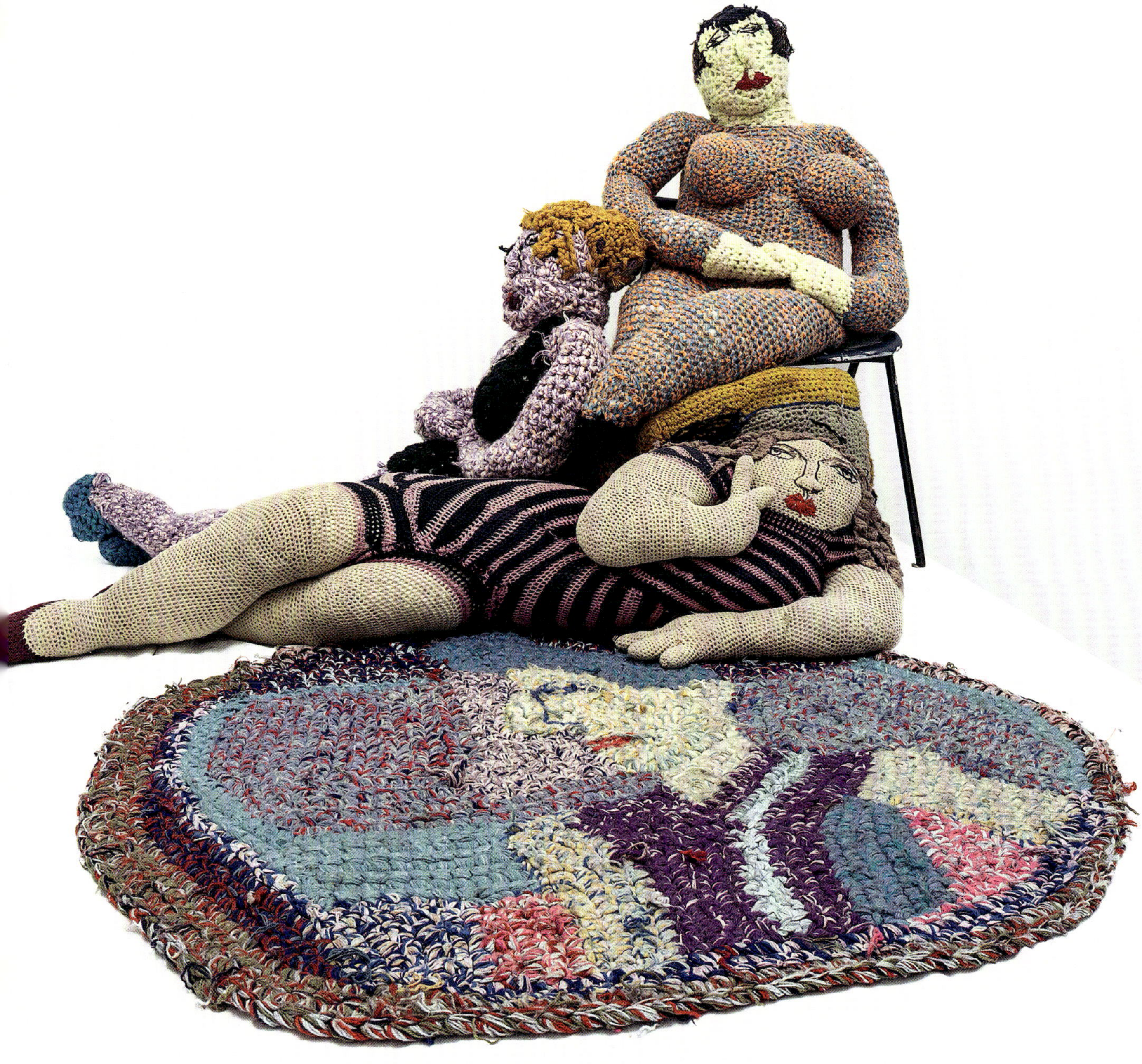

Untitled 1974–85. Acrylic, wool and cotton yarns, stuffed and other synthetic fibre. Carpet: 135 (diam.). Figures: various dimensions

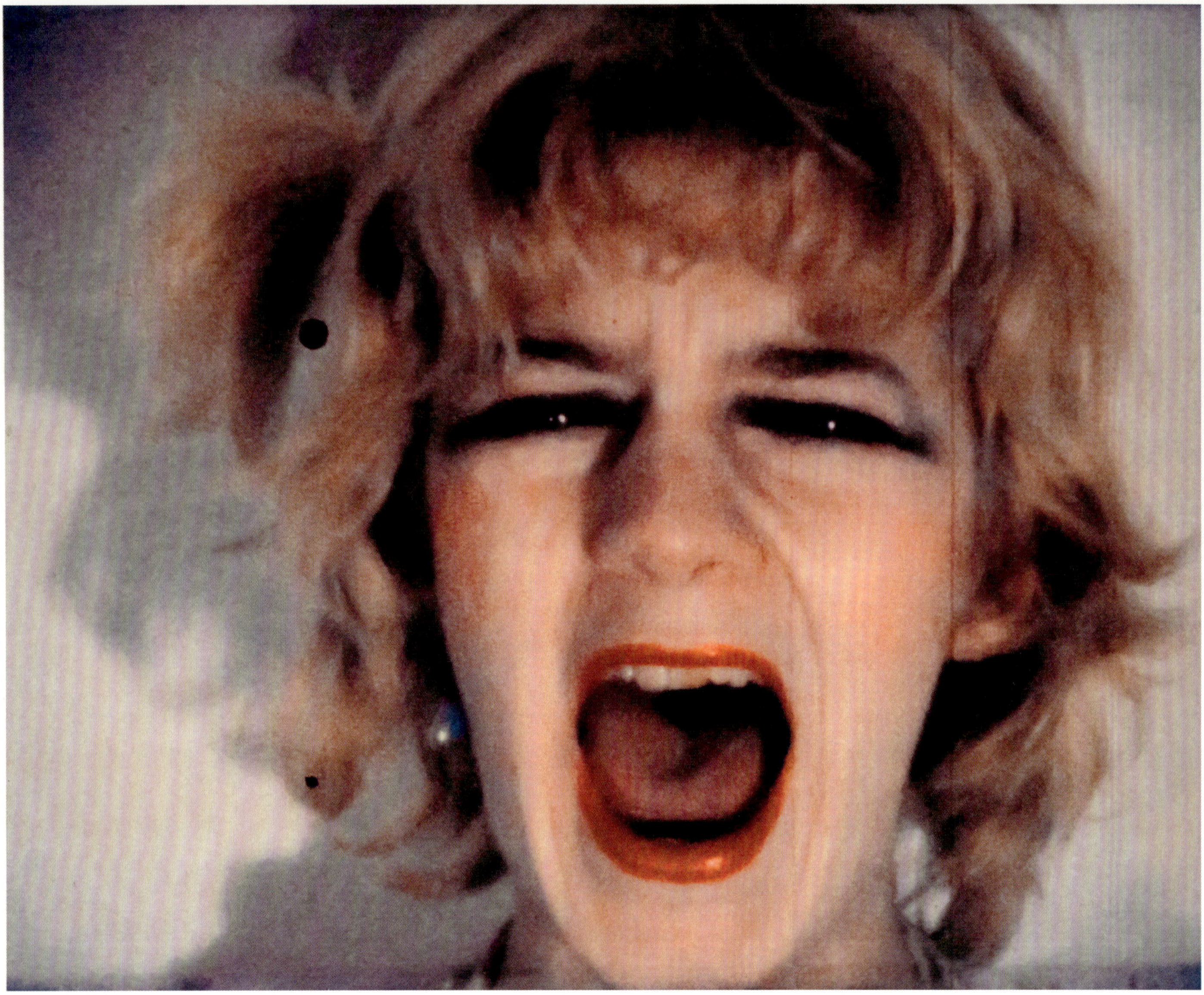

3 Minute Scream 1977. Super 8 film, shown as digital video; colour, sound. 2 min, 50 sec
Camera and sound by Nikki Bell

Born in Nottingham in 1955, Gina Birch attended Hornsey School of Art in London. There she met Ana da Silva, with whom she formed the experimental punk band The Raincoats in 1977. Taking inspiration from The Slits, The Raincoats defied expectations of how women were expected to look, sound and perform. Birch's challenging of patriarchal views is evident in her work as an artist and filmmaker. In the 1970s, she made Super 8 films inspired by Derek Jarman coming to show his work at her college. The 1980 Super 8 film *Joanna* presents a young woman negotiating various feelings on falling pregnant, liking the idea that something is growing inside her but acknowledging that she is not ready to be a parent. Sexism is ever-present as the doctors ask continuous questions about the woman's non-existent boyfriend. The film was groundbreaking in its candid approach to pregnancy in popular culture. In the 1977 film *3 Minute Scream*, Birch is seen screaming for the duration of a Super 8 cartridge – a powerful statement of defiance, which can be read as a comment on what so many young women were inarticulately feeling in the late 1970s.

In 2022 a solo exhibition of Birch's work was presented at Gallery 46 in London. In 2023, her solo album *I Play My Bass Loud* was released to great critical acclaim. The artist lives and works in London.

GINA BIRCH

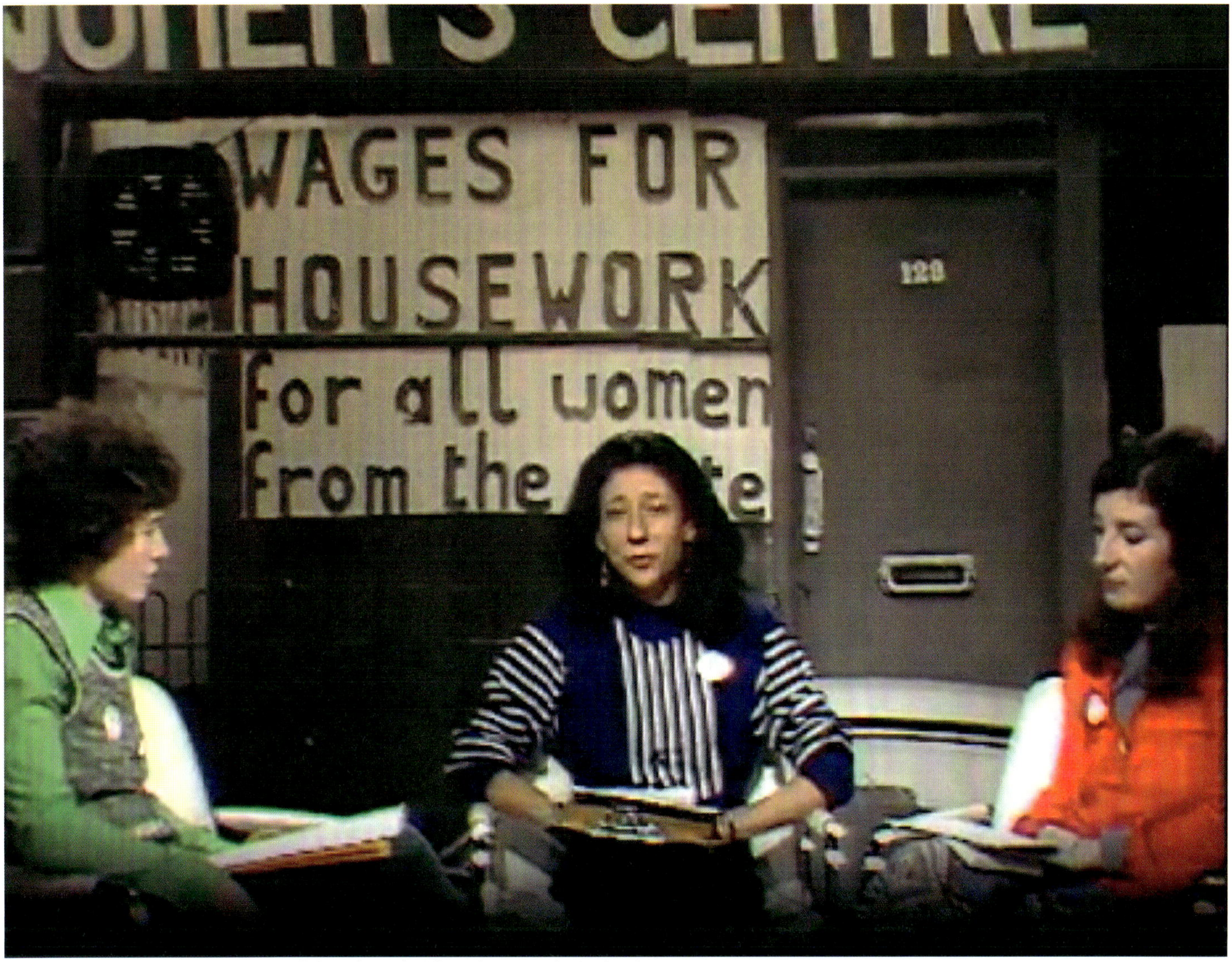

Still from *All Work and No Pay* 1975. Video, shown digitally; colour, sound. 13 min, 19 sec
(Directed by Wages for Housework Campaign for *Open Door*, 1975)

The video work *All Work and No Pay* was made in 1975 by the Wages for Housework Campaign (WFH), formerly the Power of Women Collective, and broadcast in February 1976 by the community access unit for the BBC, *Open Door*. The programme, which featured the prominent Wages for Housework founder Selma James interviewing women in the streets, as well as in the TV studio, provided much-needed airtime for the group's international demand for governments to pay women for the work they do in the home. The film shows women in different countries developing campaign strategies. It also features domestic violence survivors, a nurse and a lesbian waitress telling their stories; the Iceland women's Day Off of 1975, when women, from full-time housewives to farmers and waged workers, took to the streets and brought Iceland to a halt; women organising rent strikes across the religious divide in the North of Ireland; nurses in the UK coming together for higher pay; sex workers in London and factory workers in Ceylon; women's demonstrations; and original WFH songs in English and Italian. The multiracial women's centre featured in the film, now the Crossroads Women's Centre based in Kentish Town, London, continues to provide vital services for women in the community as well as internationally to this day. The Wages for Housework Campaign and the Global Women's Strike it co-ordinates are based there.

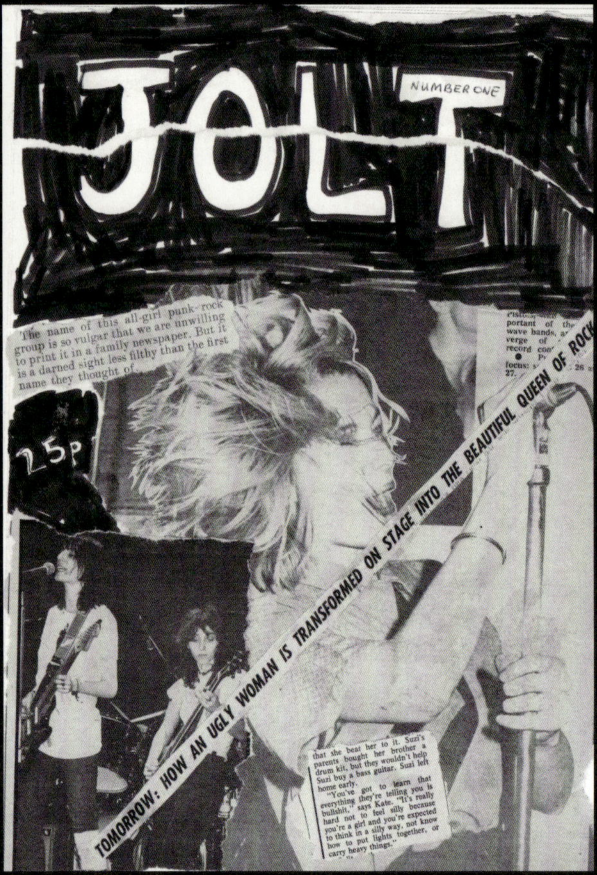

1

Oh Bondage! Up Yours!

In 1976 punk was born, a movement which included a large number of woman musicians and all-women bands, many of whom embraced the lifestyle and aesthetics of the movement to reject societal norms and form their own communities. Many punk women rejected any suggestion of direct engagement with feminist politics, but by simply choosing to dress and live as they did, outside of the strict confines of heteronormative society, they demonstrated a new way for women to live. Alongside its musical expression, punk came to define an entire subculture characterised by anti-establishment views, the pursuit of individual freedom and a commitment to low-cost, DIY ways of making and living. In this way punk, post-punk and alternative music more broadly offered young women new ways of engaging with society, from moving into squats, engaging with radical fashions, to exploring their sexuality.

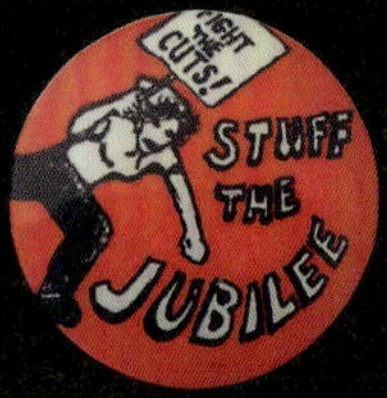

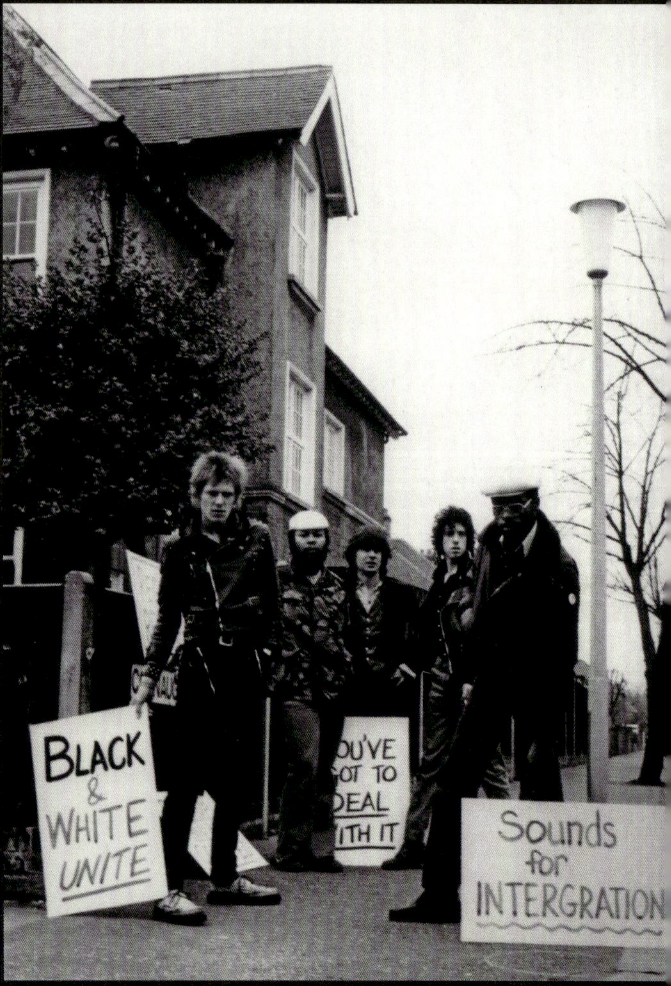

An anti-racism demonstration outside National Front leader Martin Webster's house 1977. From Right to Left: Mykaell Riley (Steel Pulse), Mick Jones (The Clash), Glen Matlock (The Sex Pistols), Andy Bowen (Steel Pulse) and Paul Simonon (The Clash). Photographed by Caroline Coon.

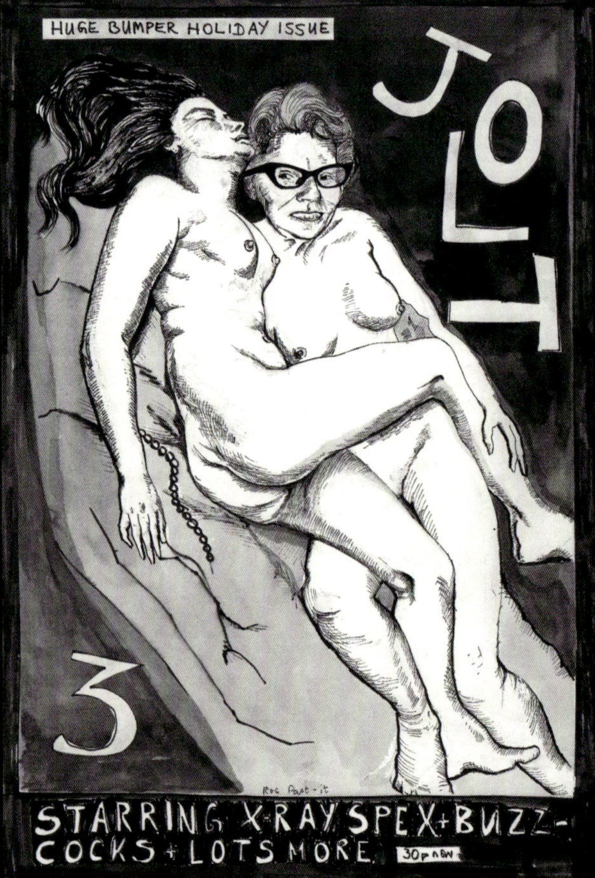

2

1 Lucy Whitman, artwork for *Jolt*, no.1, 1977. Newspaper and felt-tip pen on paper.
2 Lucy Whitman and Rosalind Whitman *Jolt*, no.3, featuring a drawing by Rosalind Whitman (after Courbet), August 1977, printed paper.
3 Vinyl Virgin (Sarah Shosubi) and Crystal Clear, *Moreon*, no.3, 1977.

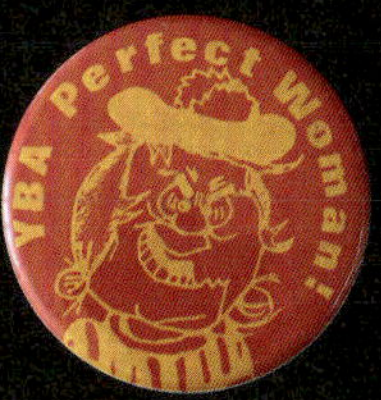

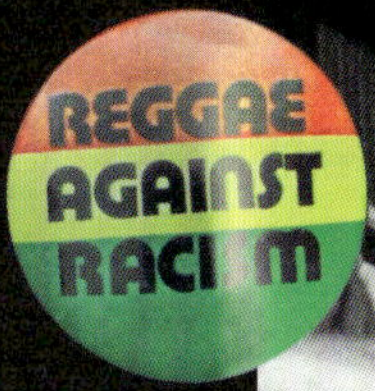

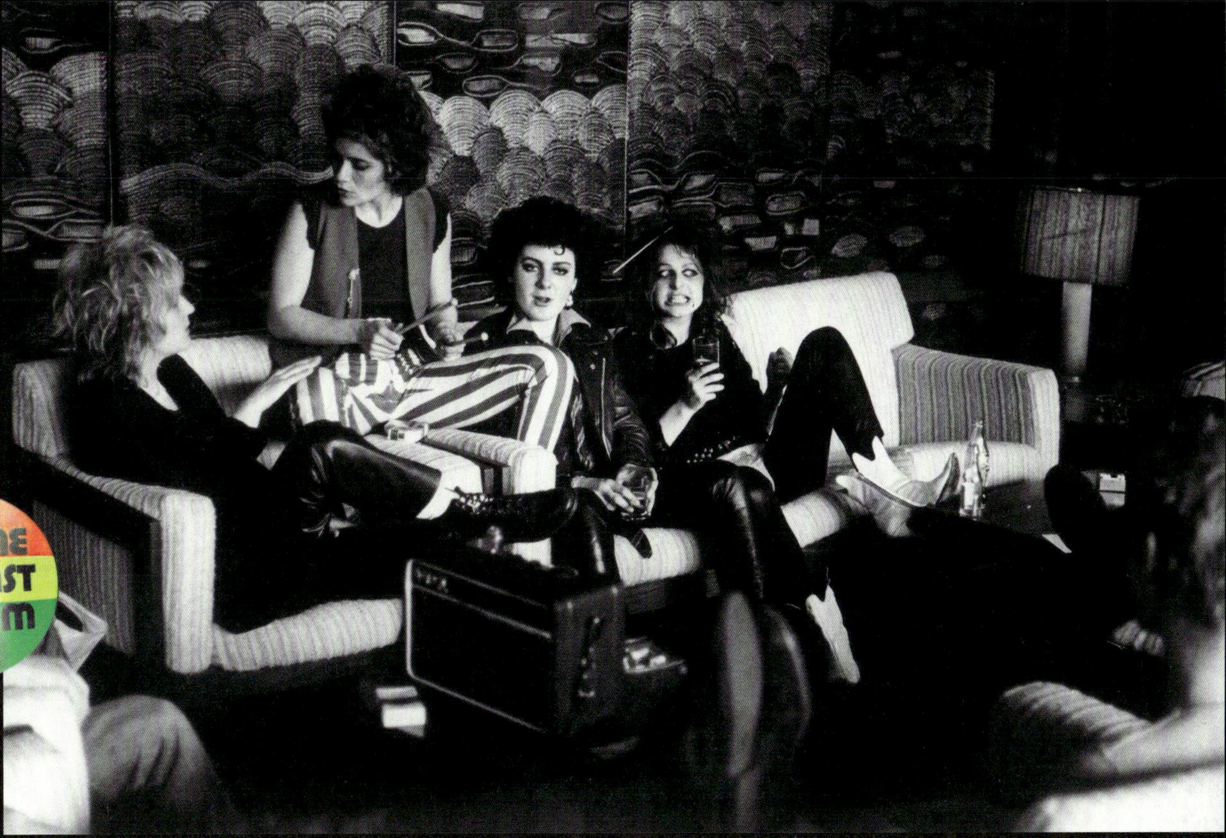

Post House hotel, Cardiff, June 1977. The Slits – Viv Albertine (guitar), Palmolive (drummer), Tessa Pollitt (bass) and Ari Up (lead singer) – in hotel reception waiting to be taken to the gig. Photographed by Caroline Coon.

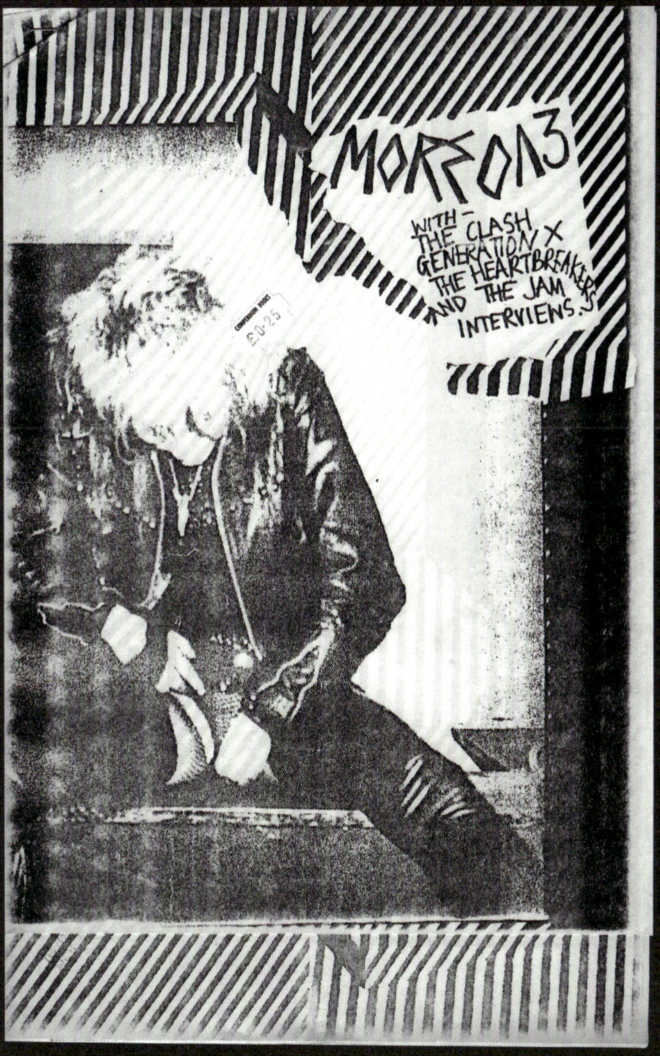

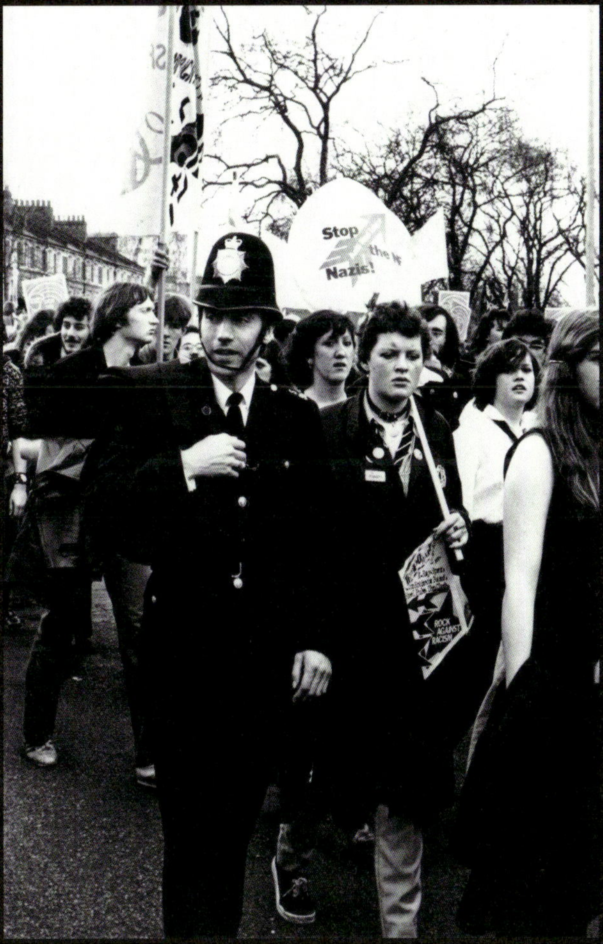

Punk fans on the first Rock Against Racism march, from Trafalgar Square to the concert in Victoria Park, Hackney in April 1978. The concert featured The Clash, Steel Pulse, Tom Robinson Band, X-Ray Spex, Jimmy Pursey (from Sham 69), and Patrik Fitzgerald. Photographed by Caroline Coon.

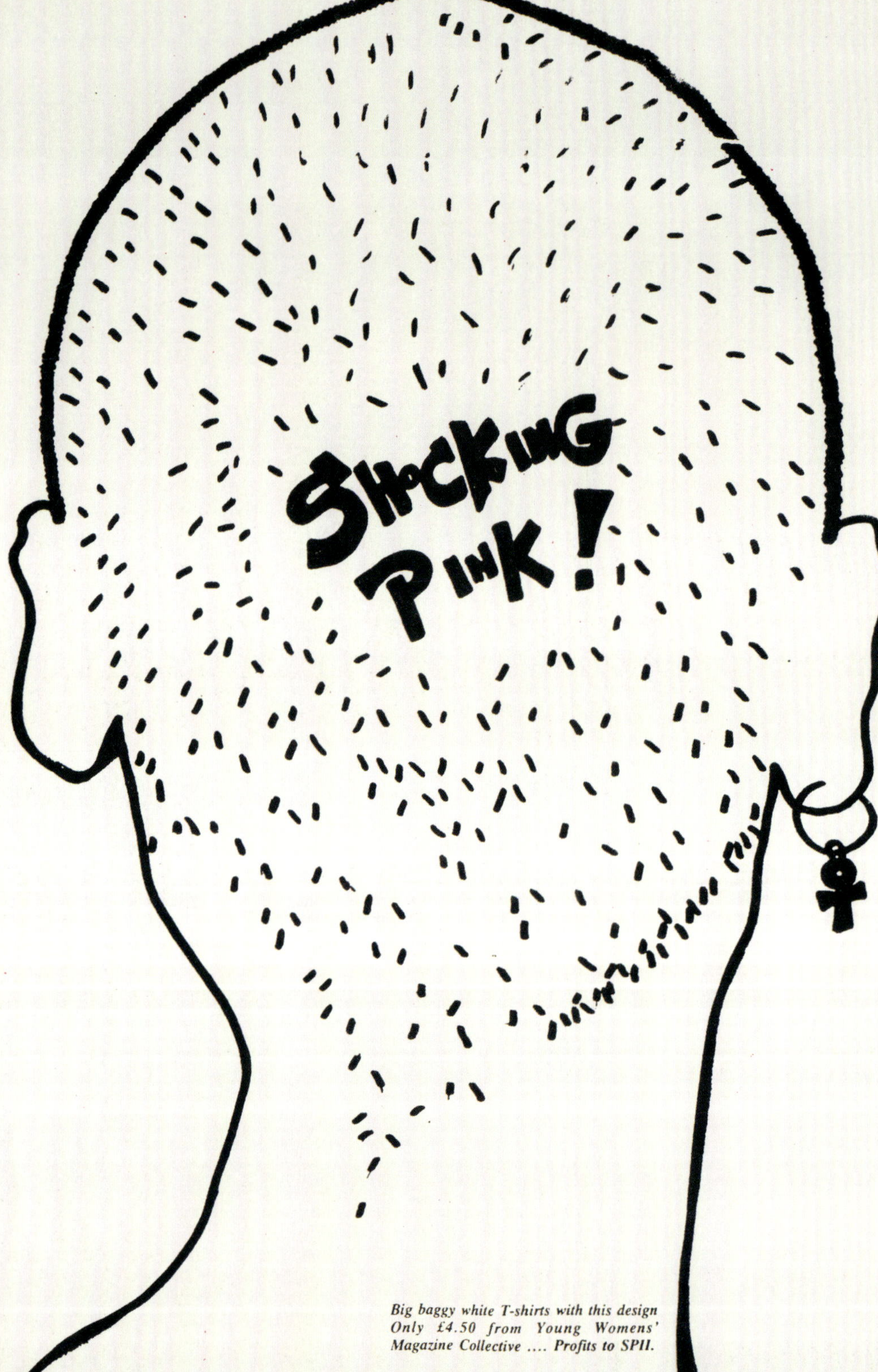

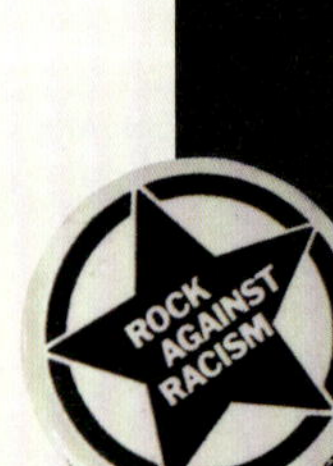

Big baggy white T-shirts with this design Only £4.50 from Young Womens' Magazine Collective .... Profits to SPII.

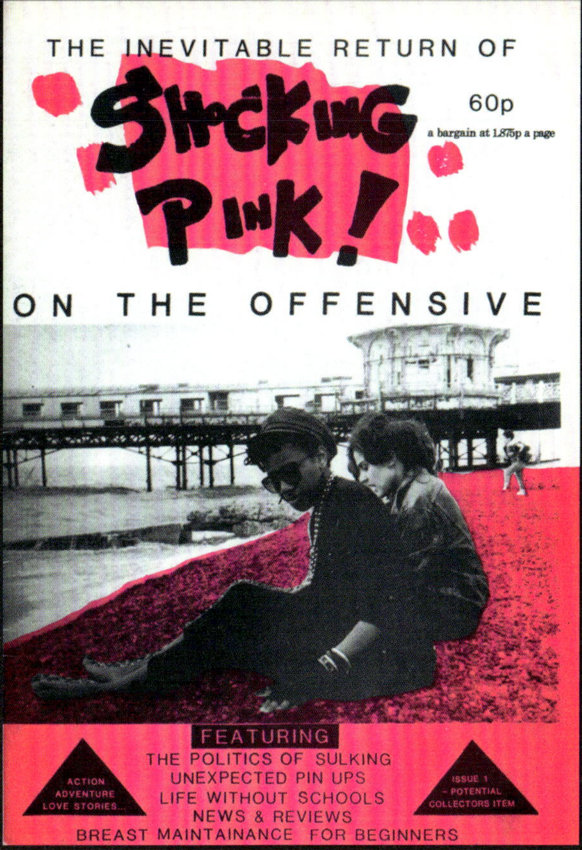

2

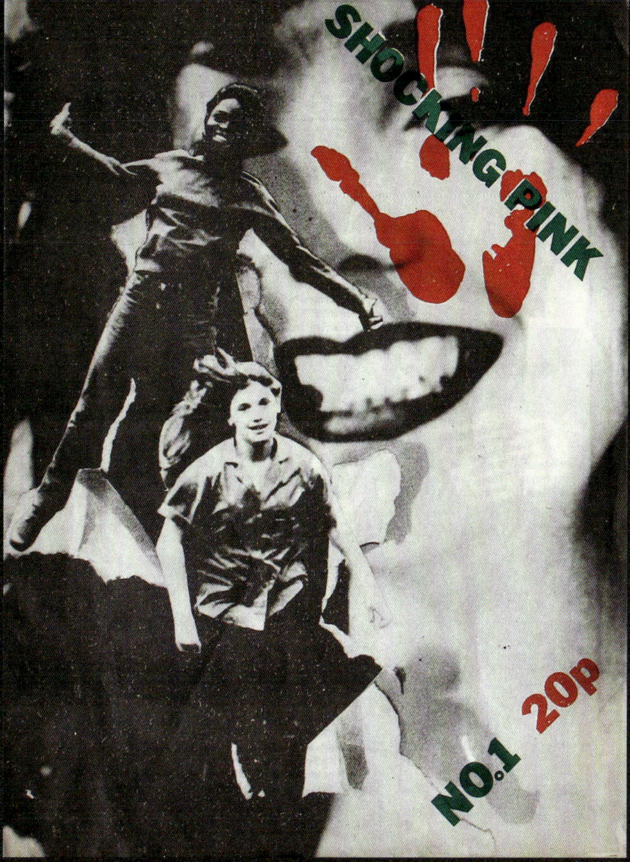

3

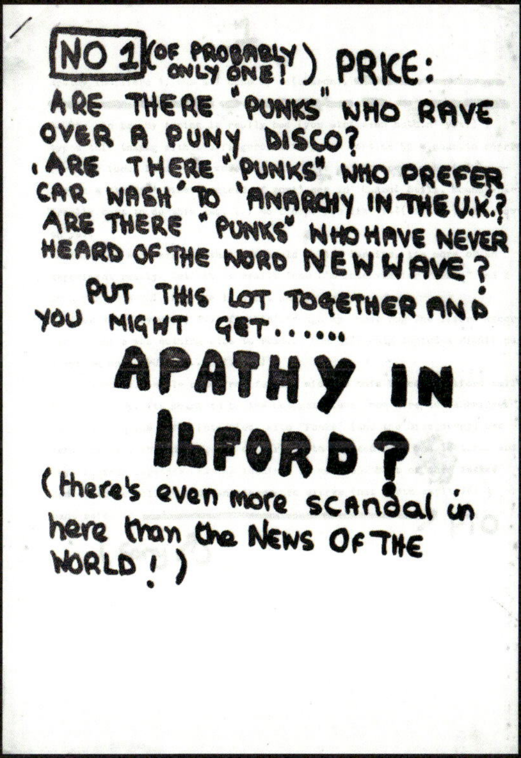

4

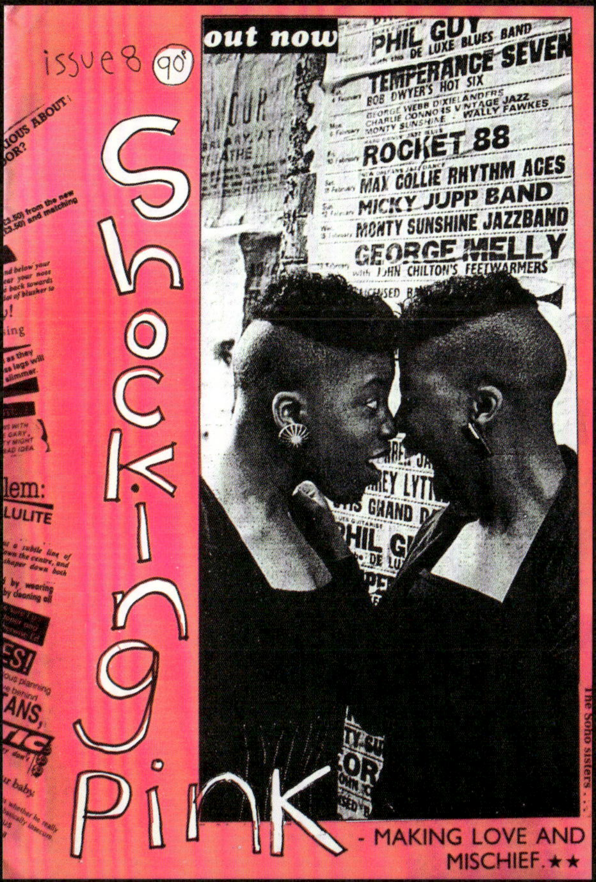

5

1 Back page of *Shocking Pink*, 1987 (issue number unknown). *Shocking Pink* was made by a collective of young women to look at 'issues that really affect us [women], like contraception, abortion, sexuality, periods, violence against women, racism, all aspects of women's rights, nuclear power and women's opportunities in education and at work'.
2 *Shocking Pink*, 1987 (issue number unknown).
3 *Shocking Pink*, no.1, 1981.
4 Sharon Spike (Sharon Dunham), *Apathy in Ilford*, no.1, 1977.
5 *Shocking Pink*, no.8, 1988.

UNEXPECTED PLEASURES: PUNK, FEMINISM AND ART

RACHEL GARFIELD

1 See Matthew Worley, 'Oi! Oi! Oi!: Class, Locality, and British Punk', *Twentieth Century British History*, vol.24, Dec. 2013, pp.606–36.
2 Roger Huddle and Red Saunders (eds.), *Reminiscences of RAR: Rocking Against Racism 1976–1982*, London 2016, pp.13–14.
3 Ibid., p.16.
4 Paul Gilroy, 'Rebel Souls: Dance-floor Justice and the Temporary Undoing of Britain's Babylon', in *Syd Shelton: Rock Against Racism*, London 2016, p.25.

Just as feminism and racial politics were bound together in the 1960s through an emancipatory outlook, so in the 1970s in the UK feminism, punk and intersectional struggles also were interlinked. Punk was at the heart of the Rock Against Racism (RAR) movement, and for many RAR was at the heart of punk. RAR gigs, which featured both punk and reggae bands, fostered allegiances between the overwhelmingly white followers of punk and Black and Asian people's struggles against racism; in short, in the fraught battle of the time between racists and anti-racists, RAR was instrumental in wresting fans of punk away from the possible lure of fascist politics and racist attitudes. This was at a time when there was a large increase in recruitment of young white people to fascist groups such as the National Front (NF), the British Movement (BM) and the British National Party (BNP), and when polls showed the NF battling with the Liberals for third place behind the Conservatives and Labour.[1]

Unlike the histories of Black activists fighting racism, which are only just beginning to receive wider attention, the story of RAR is relatively well documented. The apocryphal narrative is that Red Saunders, a documentary photographer, wrote a letter to the music press in protest at the racist and anti-immigration comments made by the guitarist and singer Eric Clapton at a concert in Birmingham in 1976. The letter asked for anyone wanting to join a rank-and-file protest to write in. Saunders reportedly received over three hundred letters, and subsequently organised several gigs, the first in a pub in Forest Gate, east London, and then at the Royal College of Art. The third was held after an anti-racist march in Victoria Park, east London, in 1978.[2] Their first open-air gig, it attracted a huge 80,000 people and defined a generation.[3] Punk and reggae had already been aligned for a couple of years, since the early days of the 100 Club on London's Oxford Street, where DJs would play reggae tracks between performances by punk bands, but the political purchase of this musical alignment was sealed through RAR. According to singer Billy Bragg, 'when punk came along, which was a bringing together of white culture punk and Black culture reggae, I was already primed for that so Rock Against Racism was the first activism I was ever involved in … going to see The Clash at the first Anti-Nazi League rally'.

So, for many white punks, RAR was part of a generational process of normalisation of a Black and Brown British presence through the alliance of music and politics. It had an impact on visual culture, particularly for those coming of age as filmmakers and artists in the 1980s. This in turn helped shape a new politics of representation. Through its influence on punk, RAR became part of a wider force for change beyond music. Without this alliance of punk and RAR, the prevailing mood could easily have been different: this was a period of economic recession, mass unemployment and a nihilistic disaffection among significant sections of the community. As it was, RAR, in what Paul Gilroy calls a unique 'radical populism', made anti-racism cool, and fascism deeply uncool, for a whole generation.[4]

Art schools saw the emergence of several punk bands, and many punks went to art school possibly because of the libertarian ethos that punk propagated and art education permitted at the time. Artists including Vivienne Dick,

Linder and Chila Kumari Singh Burman played in punk bands as well as making art. A long-standing relationship between art schools and music had existed both before the 1970s and has continued to since, but it is worth considering aspects of the precise relationship between punk, feminism and art. Much of the focus on punk – and on art school bands in general – has been on male musicians, yet for women punk was enabling in a different way. As a former punk, I can attest to its huge impact in giving women licence to re-evaluate not just who they were but how they inhabited their developing self. Punk's effect was to liberate a generation of women, and this in turn influenced the kind of art those who became artists would go on to produce, as can be seen in the work of Vivienne Dick, Linder and Cosey Fanni Tutti, among others – art that went against the prevalent feminist-infused paradigms of the time.

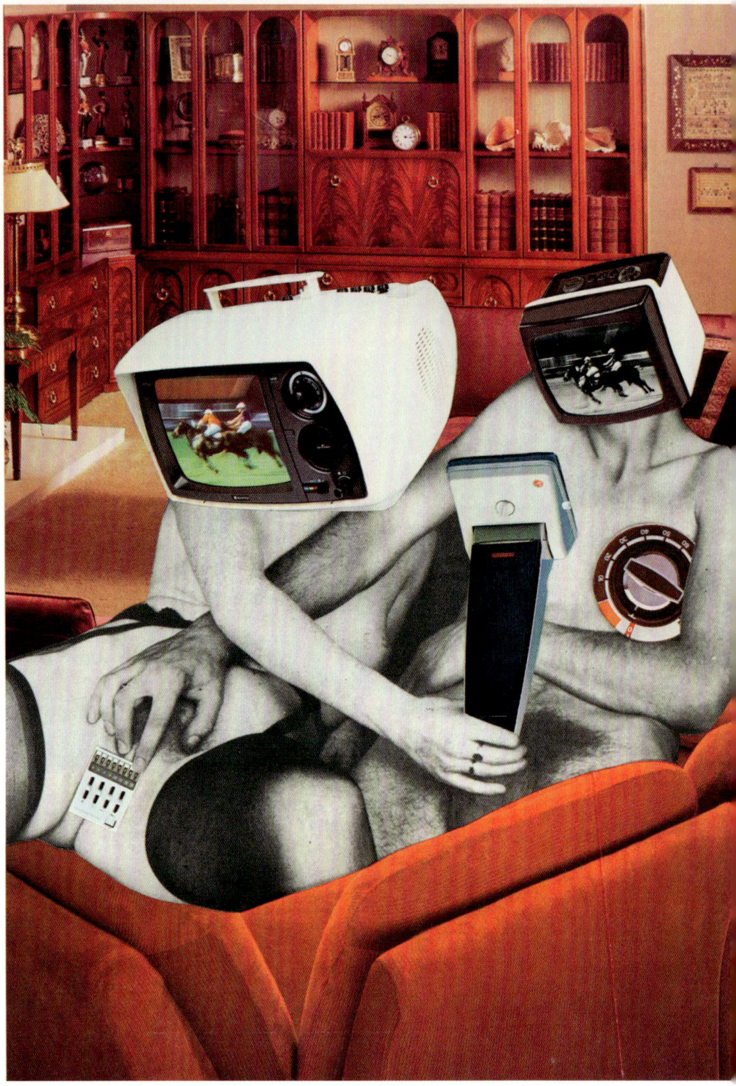

Linder *Untitled* 1976–7. Photomontage 29.5 × 20.8

Marsha Meskimmon has rightly argued that feminist art historians, perhaps unwittingly, have built a Eurocentric, linear history of art due to the predominant concentration on Anglo-American perspectives, producing 'an unmarked normative mainstream' with its focus on the anglophone Global North.[5] There have been some efforts to address this elision in recent years. However, to this I would also add other forms of marginality within the UK discourses and legacies of feminist art histories, which are finally being acknowledged in this expansive exhibition. This includes artists who explore various intersections of class, anglophone diasporic subjectivities and female desire and sexuality, such as Jo Spence, Chila Kumari Singh Burman, Joy Gregory, Cosey Fanni Tutti and Jill Westwood, to cite just a few of those who have been working, to varying degrees, in relative obscurity, championed only by a few art historians or critics, and even more rarely by the market until now.

These omissions can be seen within a paradigm of punk that in art terms, like Dada and Fluxus before it, meant throwing out the rule book and reinventing a visual language that was strident awkward, using DIY, lo-fi, collage-based approaches, often purposely ephemeral. While the lumpen persona of punk was real enough, the use of theoretical frameworks – like in Vivienne Dick's early film *Guerillère Talks* 1978, shot in New York and named after Monique Wittig's novel *Les Guérillères* – was turned to something that eschewed the appearance of erudition in the name of emancipation.

5 Marsha Meskimmon, 'Chronology through cartography: mapping 1970s feminist art globally', in Cornelia Butler and Lisa Gabrielle Mark (eds.), *WACK! Art and the Feminist Revolution*, Cambridge, MA, and London 2007, pp.322–35, p.327.

In a world where tattoos, multiple piercings and Dr. Martens boots are now merely a fashion choice, it is hard to imagine the bravery of the women who dared to dress as punks in the 1970s. X-Ray Spex frontwoman Poly Styrene was a defining exemplar for the ways in which punk represented emancipation for women. She went on stage with braces on her teeth, unconventionally clothed, shouting at the microphone, representing the very opposite of the slim, demure and well-groomed norms of sexual allure expected of women by patriarchy. Poly sang about disenfranchisement, ecological disaster and isolation – not romance and boys. The title of her early single 'Oh Bondage! Up Yours!' 1977 was purposefully, provocatively unfeminine. Her work created a space for women to stridently redefine themselves as defiant, independent and thinking for themselves, even if they were still trying to work out what that meant or might come to mean. For some women, part of that thinking was to dare themselves to be artists and to make art about their lived experience.

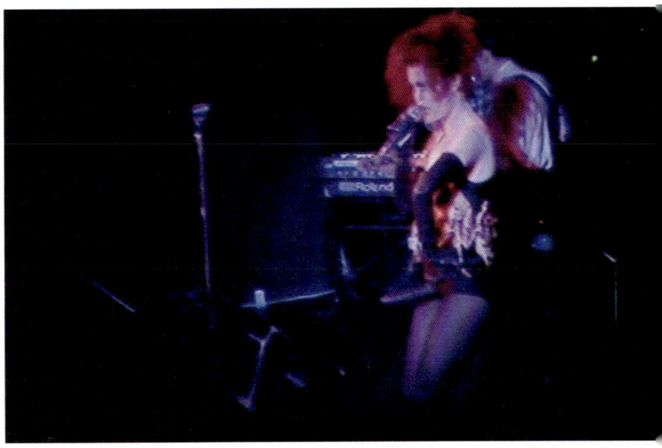

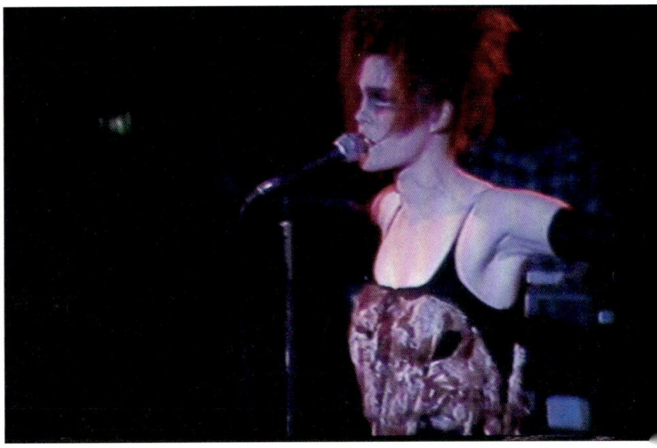

Linder *Ludus Concert with Meat Dress, Hacienda, Manchester* 1982.

The whole ethos of punk gave women licence to reject what had been constraining feminine mores of behaviour and to redefine themselves away from the man-pleasing norm; women often revelled in their ugliness. However, you didn't actually have to be a punk – the after-effects of punk itself opened up for women new ways of looking at the world, depicting a fragmented expressionism associated with libertarianism. Many punk women did not necessarily identify as feminists at the time, and much of this work was outside of the feminist art paradigm that was forming. These women were not averse to presenting a strident femininity, often incorporating shocking violent or sexual imagery as a fact of life rather than a political statement. Just as to be ugly was the new attractive, so art was redefined. In its methodology, it also demonstrated a defiant turning-away from previously held artistic imperatives of what was seen to be a mannered virtuosity of skill, form and theory within minimalism and conceptualism. This rejection came into play by way of radical gestures using clashing and often violent imagery or sexually-explicit material, instead of conforming to the usual expectations of taste, beauty or even critique.

Until very recently, the dominant feminist art historical legacy in the UK has been the focus on Brechtian and Lacanian theorisations, which tend to reject the depiction of the female figure. This has been, in some ways, a generational divide. Artists such as Mary Kelly or Susan Hiller – interestingly, both

Americans living in London – have been much celebrated, and deservedly so, but others such as Vivienne Dick or Anne Bean have not, and should be. This critical neglect can also be understood as the avant-garde versus the underground, exemplified in the differing approaches of these two generations to politics, and indeed the role of politics in art that can be traced through much older debates.

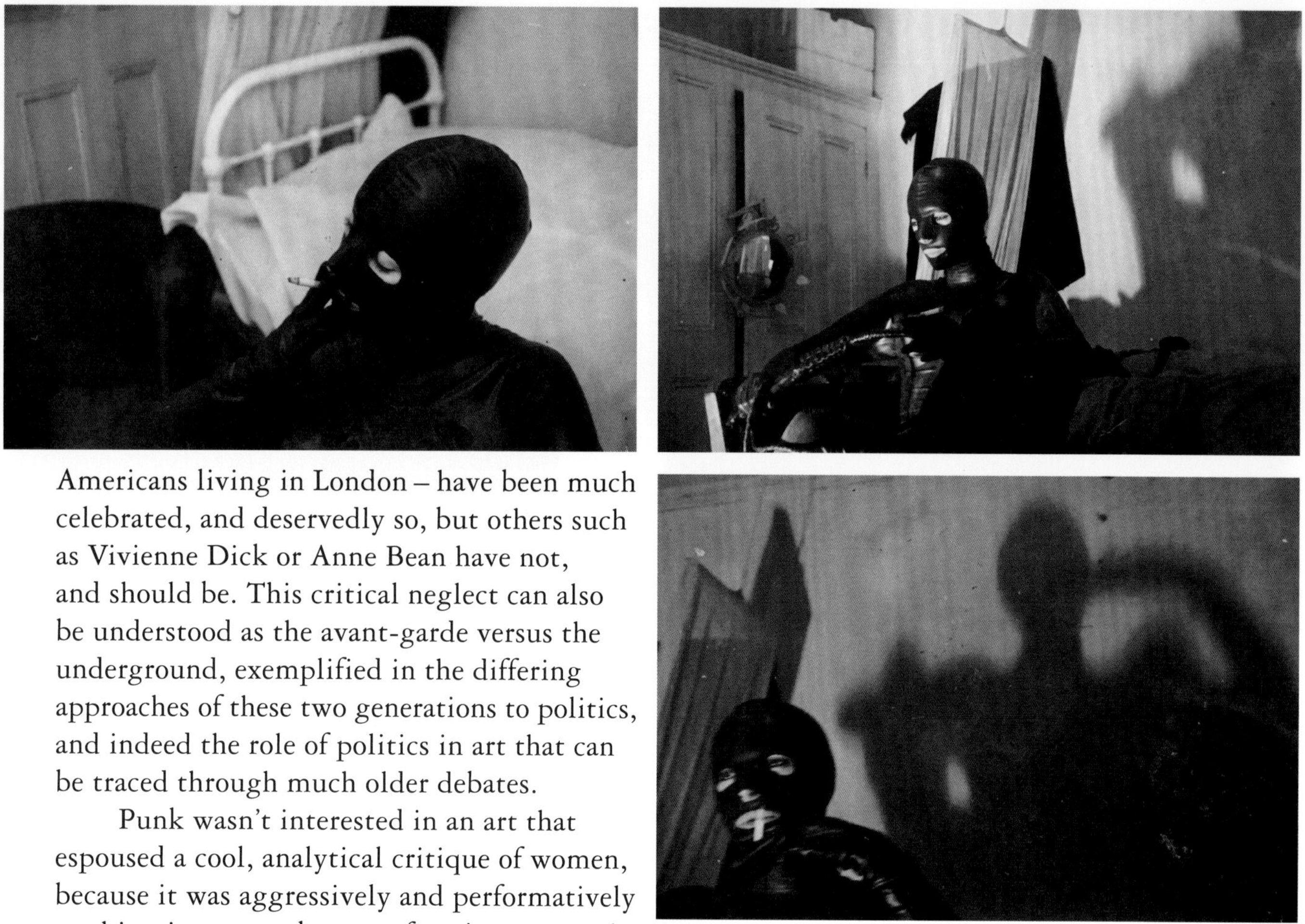

Jill Westwood *Alpha-Female Triptych* 1983. 3 photographs 8.5 × 12.5 (each)

Punk wasn't interested in an art that espoused a cool, analytical critique of women, because it was aggressively and performatively trashing its tenets, busy performing an outré and rather messy subjectivity that required an altogether different language of DIY iconoclasm. This manner of lumpen virtuosity focused on expressions, rather than theorisations, of lived experience. The spiky, individualistic nihilism of punk that burst forth at a time of economic hardship in the 1970s and Thatcherite austerity politics in the 1980s resulted in a different approach to art altogether. Nevertheless, like the performances of Poly Styrene or The Slits (as opposed to the more apparent skill of, say, Pink Floyd or Yes), this had a virtuosity of its own that can only now be recognised.

An important case in point is Linder, founding member and singer of the band Ludus and, as a visual artist, a key initiator of the punk aesthetic through her association with the band Buzzcocks. The iconic cover she designed for their 7-inch single 'Orgasm Addict' was for a long time the only work of hers that was widely known. But newspaper cut-outs and inky zine printing was not the only punk aesthetic, merely the main focus. Linder's ongoing sophisticated art practice – awkwardly witty collages that juxtapose porn magazine imagery with pictures from women's weeklies to expose the contradictions of women's lives in a shocking and absurdist manner – has only recently started to receive the attention it deserves.

Cosey Fanni Tutti went even further in merging the worlds of pornography and art by bringing her sex work into the gallery, while Jill Westwood made performative photographs of herself as a dominatrix, inhabiting a dowdy room

6 Peter Osborne, *Anywhere Or Not at All: Philosophy of Contemporary Art*, New York and London 2013.
7 Of course there were exceptions, such as the art of Carolee Schneemann or the crossover work of Margaret Harrison, but these were also under erasure and not the most visible.

in black leathers, her looming shadow behind her. Here, in the costuming, is where the grunge of punk and the glamour of the New Romantics merged in art, though not in life. Vivienne Dick, member of punk band Beirut Slump, defined a new language in Super 8 film by depicting the communities she inhabited in the wastelands of bankrupt 1970s Manhattan and the tower blocks and squats of 1980s London. Dick used the disjunction of jump cuts to interrupt the flow and narrative, presenting a drab mise-en-scène of the disenfranchised world she occupied with her friends. These pieces can be seen as a filmic analogy to the collages of Linder, both at odds with the post-conceptual moment that has dominated lens-based work over the last few decades.[6]

Both Linder and Dick, along with other artists such as Anne Robinson, Jill Posener, Suzan Swale and Caroline Coon, revelled in bringing together heterogeneous visions and a radical incompleteness. Their work portrayed a bleakness made redemptive through absurdist humour, typically explored via an expressive mode of address that drew not from the intellectual critique of the previous generation of anglophone feminists but from the Dada of Hannah Höch and the underground of queer New York filmmaker Jack Smith, respectively.[7] Desire was never far from the surface, but notably not to allure the viewer: not romance but sex work, not an embargo on porn but the use of it, from a position not of 'knowing' but instead being part of this complex version of womanhood that includes bad sex, sold sex and break-ups. This was a deflationary aesthetic that addressed the viewer through humility and humour as well as, at times, shock.

The artists of that generation embodied the libertarian spirit that gave voice to their anger in a different way to their predecessors such as Mary Kelly or Alexis Hunter. The punk approach was one of negation rather than transformation; however, in a typical dialectical twist, this work is often hopeful and full of humanity. In contrast to art that focused on problems, punk was about embracing life, with all its difficulties.

Just as Poly Styrene was redefining her femininity as a defiant act of negation, the adoption of the hypersexual was another way of pushing the boundaries of female acceptability as punks. The model Jordan (Pamela Rooke) wearing underwear as outerwear or Siouxsie Sioux dressing as a dominatrix are analogous to the work of Cosey Fanni Tutti, Jill Westwood and Jill Posener, who photographed explicit public lesbian sex acts, and different from the glamour that the New Romantics evoked slightly later as a parody of Hollywood desire. Reconfiguring the representation of women as overt and powerful 'in-your-face' sexual beings was integral to the punk aesthetic delineated here. But unlike artists such as Carolee Schneemann and Monica Sjöö, the punk expression of sexuality was not as earth-mother redemption but rather a gritty face-off with reality that was also a long way from the more prevalent and arguably prohibitive approach of groups like Women Against Pornography (WAP). For punk, both desexualisation and the parody of hypersexualisation were as important as each other for the rebuilding of the sense of self as emerging out of patriarchy to a new sexually powerful womanhood.

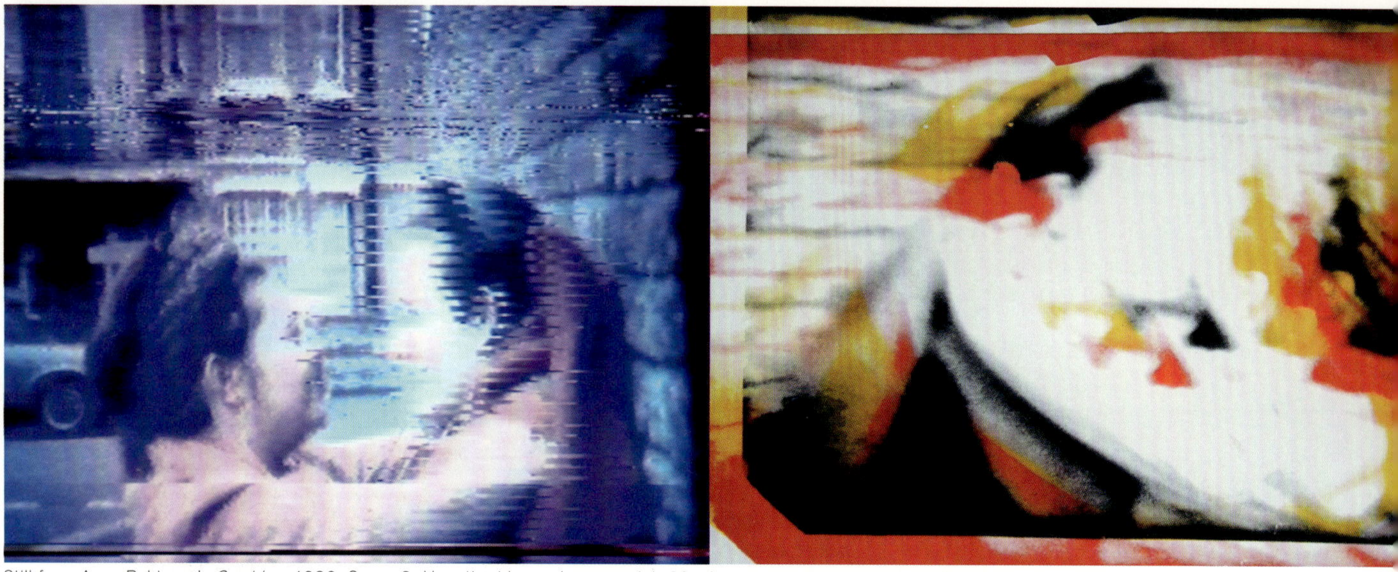

Still from Anne Robinson's *Corridors* 1986. Super-8, U-matic video and screenprint, 22 min

To this end, it wasn't so much the subject matter that counted but instead the means of production, which was immediate: not finessing artworks in the studio but making work on the kitchen table while the kids were in bed, or in a bedroom in a shared short-life house.[8] This matters, because women so often do not have the context to make perfect work amid other life demands. So the task in hand for making art is not to think about the museum, the audience or posterity, not even – for these artists – so much consciousness-raising, but merely getting on with it as best one can. Above all – and this is possibly the most important takeaway for our current moment – this ethos freed women from the necessity of being perfect, perfection in women being a requirement of patriarchy.[9] Through the tenets of punk, women were free as artists – for possibly the first time – not to have to be the best, the first or the most original, but to be able to work with the complexities and contradictions of life as their working practice, and to enjoy the possibility of failure as a means of defining a voice they had made for themselves.

8 Short-life housing was common in the UK in the 197 and 1980s, where housing cooperatives took on out-of-u buildings owned by the public sector (councils, or the Ministries of Defence or Transport) to be tenanted out cheaply and vacated when th were required again. Many artists lived and worked in th kinds of homes, helping to ma the lifestyle affordable. The property was often substand (hence why it was unused), a later refurbished for perman council tenants or road-buildi
9 Jack Halberstam, *The Queer Art of Failure*, Durham, NC, 2011.

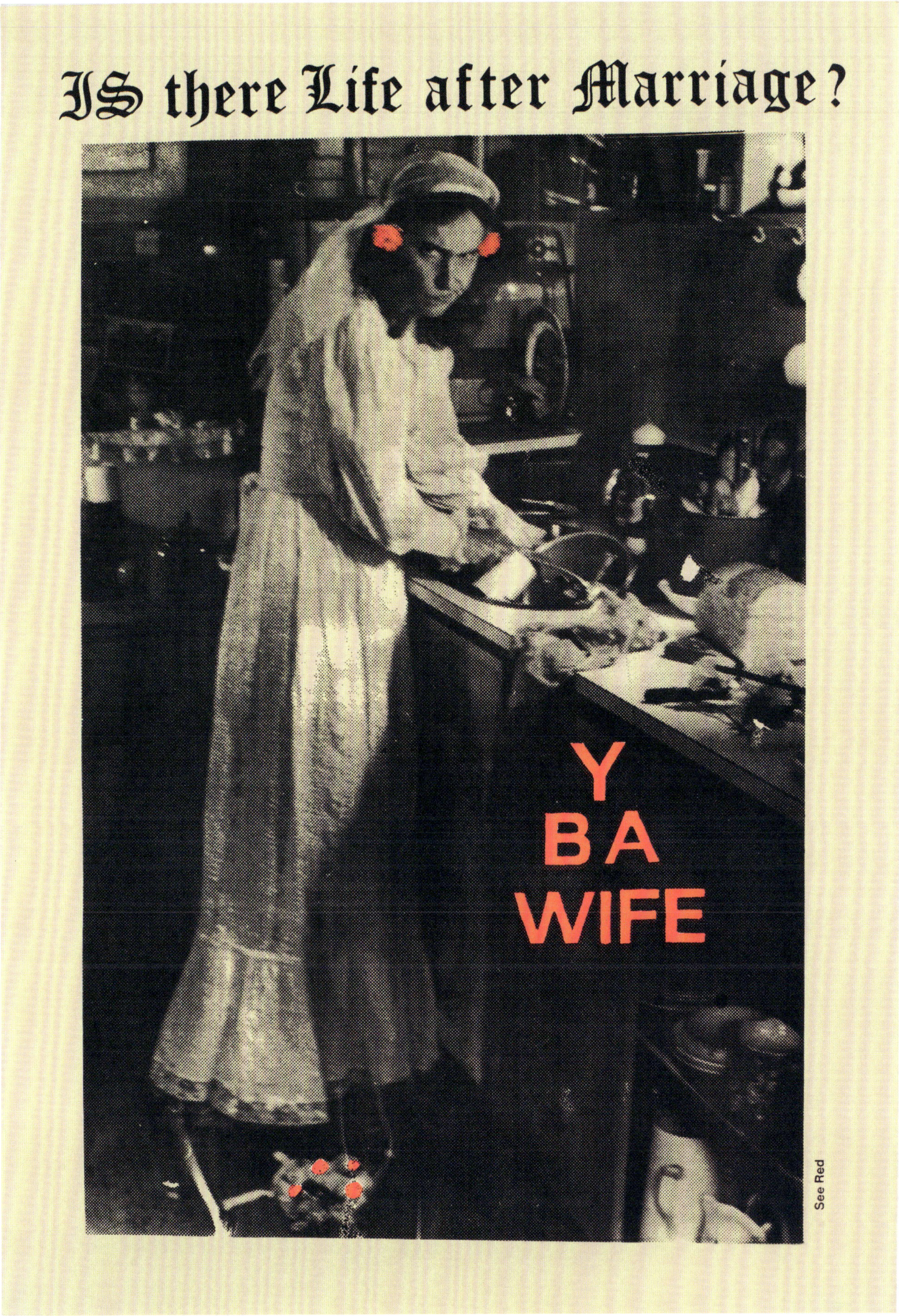

See Red Women's Workshop *YBA Wife – Is There Life After Marriage?* 1981. Screenprint on paper 61 × 43

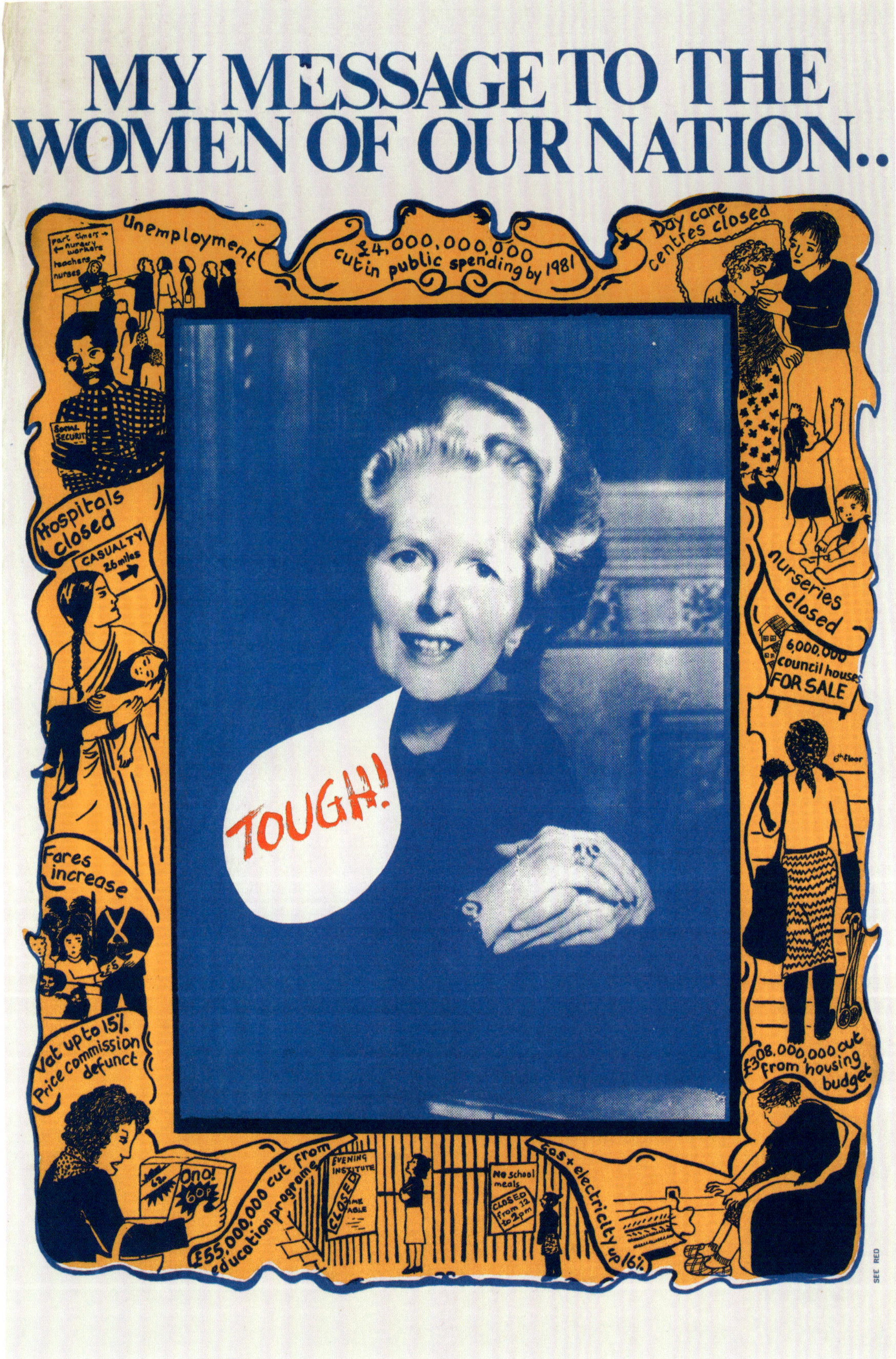

Tough! – My Message to the Women of Our Nation ... 1979. Photostencil, print on paper and plastic laminate 79 × 53

In 1974, upon seeing an advert in a radical women's liberation magazine asking for women interested in forming a group to explore and combat negative images of women in the media, three ex-art students formed the screenprinting collective See Red Women's Workshop. See Red (active 1974–90) set out to make posters that tackled sexist stereotypes and created positive and challenging alternatives, and spent the next sixteen years making some of the most powerful and instantly-recognisable protest posters of their time. See Red worked with over forty-five different women during this time, with four or five women in the workshop at any one time. Making posters that were accessible and affordable, all work was authored collectively with no hierarchy, and no one individual taking credit, and all tasks and skills were shared. Influenced by their members' respective interests, poster themes centred around childcare, housework, gender roles, identity, sexuality, class and race, and broadened out to include national and international themes supporting women's wider struggles for change. While mainly working on printing and selling their own posters, See Red also did service printing for the local community and LGBTQI+ groups to fund their work, focusing increasingly on this kind of work from 1984 to 1990.

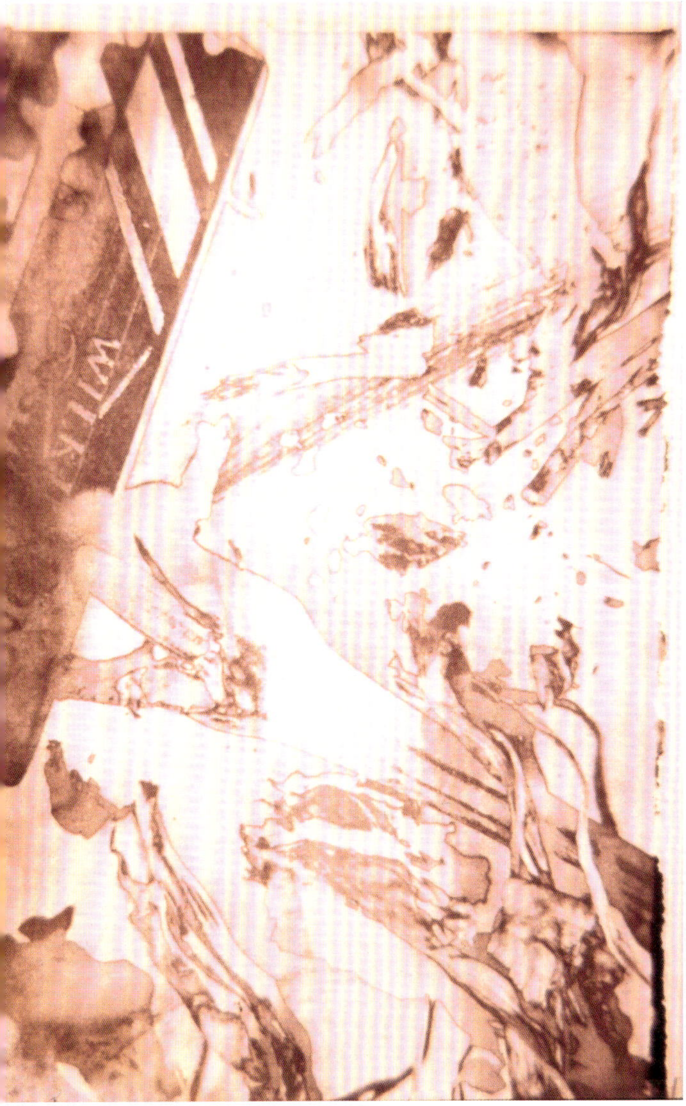

es and Razor Blades (solarised paper negative)* 1982. Photograph 25.4 × 20.3

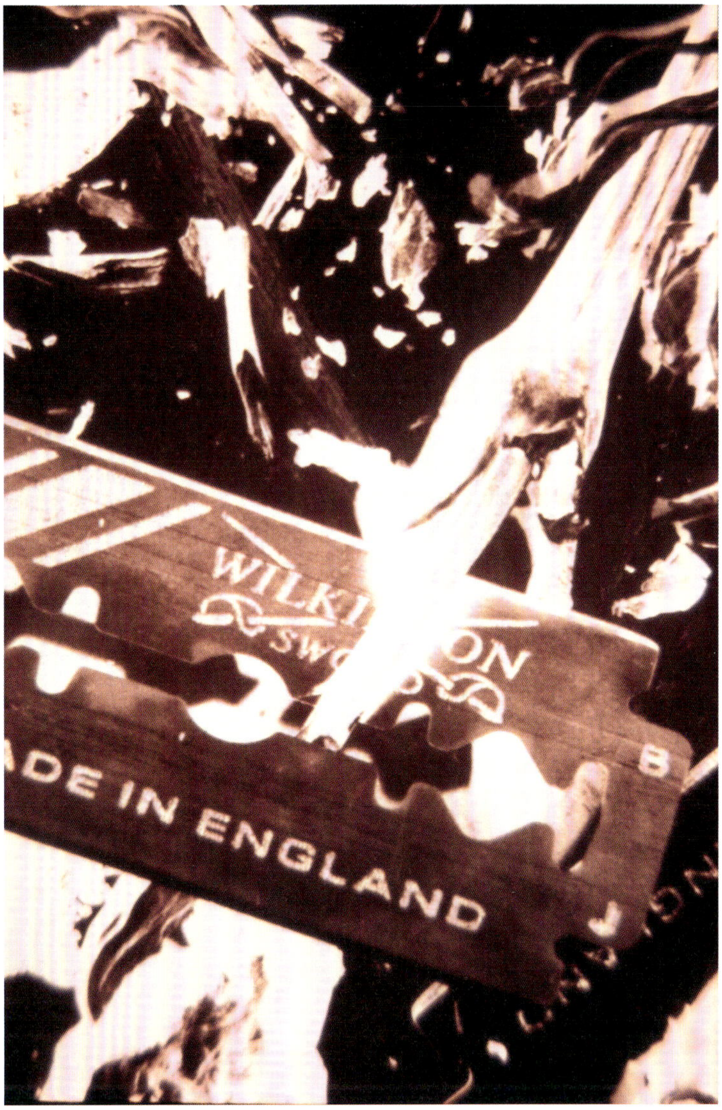

Roses and Razor Blades 1982. Photograph 30.5 × 25.4

oy Gregory was born in)xfordshire in 1959 to amaican parents. She tudied photography at Aanchester Polytechnic and he Royal College of Art, .ondon. In her practice, Gregory utilises film, ideo, analogue and digital photography and Victorian print processes. Her vork considers notions of difference in society, particularly in regard to ooth race and gender, and often challenges cultural and historical beauty standards. *Autoportraits* 1990, for example, comprises a series of self-portraits of the artist made in response to the lack of presentations of Black women's beauty. It was published at the time in *Ten.8*'s *Critical Decade: Black British Photography in the 80s* (vol.2, no.3), accompanied by Stuart Hall's essay on representation. Gregory is associated with the Black British photography movement, alongside artists such as Sunil Gupta and Roshini Kempadoo, who were also considering notions of cultural difference through their photography. Gregory has worked closely with Autograph, the Association of Black Photographers, with whom she continues to associate to this day. More recently, Gregory has exhibited in *A Tall Order*, at Rochdale Art Gallery, and undertook a commission at William Morris Gallery in 2022. Gregory is editor of the book *Shining Lights: Black Women Photographers in 1980s–90s Britain* (published 2024) in which her work also features.

JOY GREGORY

Cosey Fanni Tutti was born in 1951 in Hull where she lived and worked until 1973. In 1969 she co-founded the music and performance art collective COUM Transmissions. Drawing inspiration from surrealism and underground music, the group sought to challenge aspects of conventional society. On moving to London in 1973 with members of COUM, Tutti continued to develop her solo performance practice with works such as *Woman's Roll*, performed at AIR Gallery, London in 1976, and through her investigation of self and sexuality in the context of the sex industry. Tutti's engagement with sex work was a highly sophisticated and knowing exploration of the transactional and commercial aspect of pornography. In her exhibition *Prostitution*, held at the ICA in 1976, Tutti displayed the pornographic magazines in which she featured, naming them 'magazine actions' and asserting them as her own artistic creations. The opening of *Prostitution* at the ICA was also on the night that COUM Transmissions became Throbbing Gristle, the industrial noise band in which Tutti would play until they disbanded in 1981. Following the end of Throbbing Gristle, Tutti continued to produce and release music as 'Chris and Cosey' with her ex-Throbbing Gristle bandmate and partner Chris Carter.

Tutti, with Cabinet, co-curated the first COUM transmissions retrospective in Hull in 2017. Her autobiography, *Art Sex Music*, was also published in 2017 and *Re-Sisters: The Lives and Recordings of Delia Derbyshire, Margery Kempe and Cosey Fanni Tutti* was published in 2022.

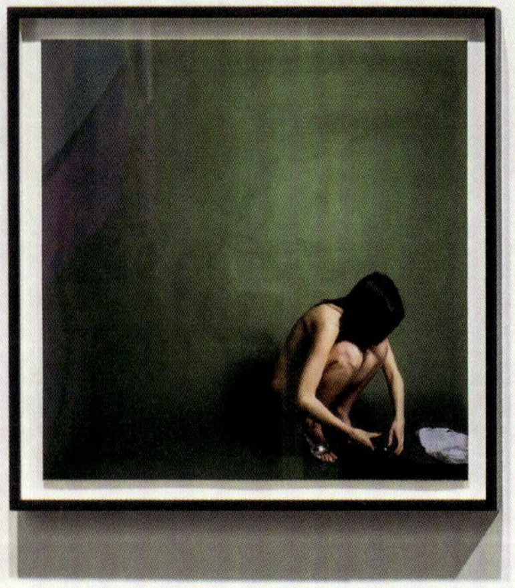

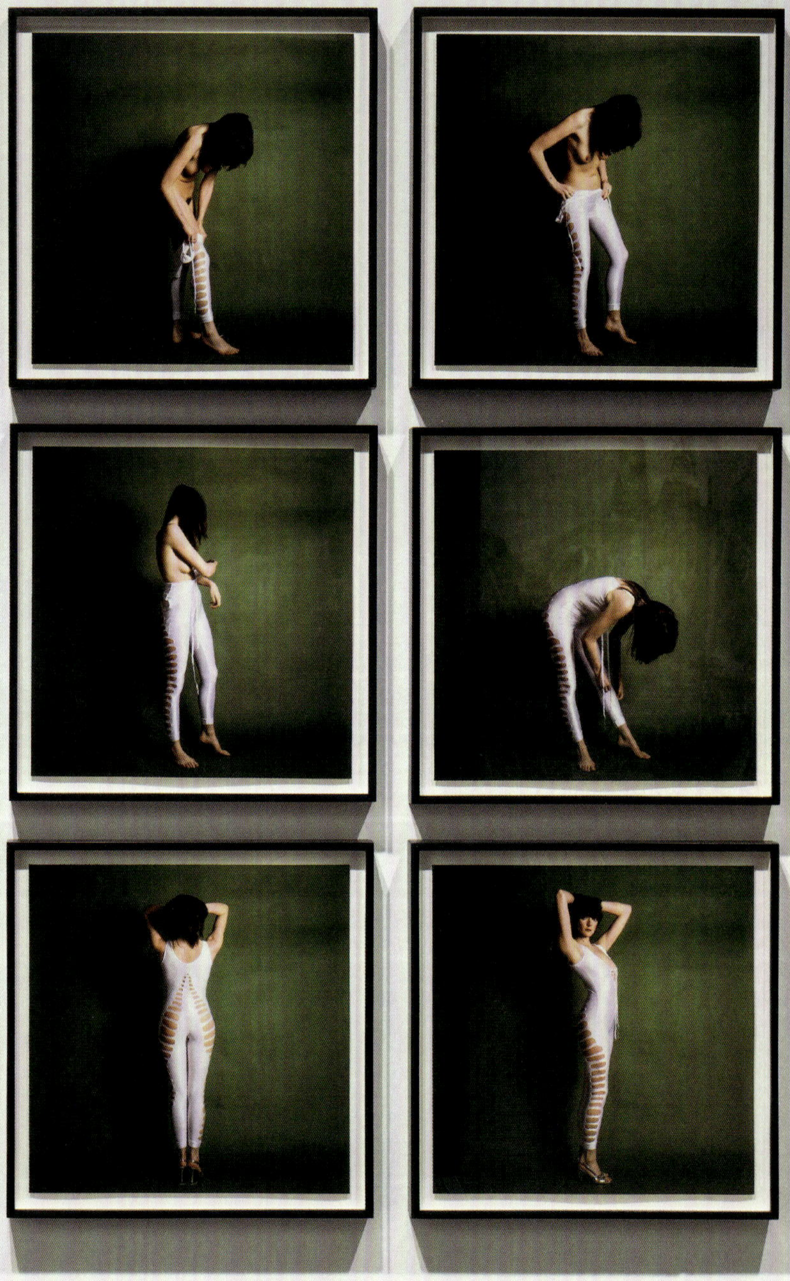

Incognito 1979–2021. 7 photographs; C-type prints 30.5 × 30.5 (each)

COSEY FANNI TUTTI

Caroline Coon was born in London in 1945 and studied fine art at Central Saint Martin's School of Art, between 1966 and 1967. There she carved out a distinctive style of hyper-realist figurative painting, made through a feminist socialist lens. Coon was heavily involved in the 1970s punk scene, managing The Clash and writing for the music magazine *Melody Maker*. She was a vocal critic of the misogyny that dominated the music scene at the time, confronting and challenging the problematic views towards women that she both witnessed and was subjected to. The artist's political activism is apparent across her fine art practice. During the 1960s and 70s Coon campaigned for the legalisation of sex work and drugs, founding the agency Release in 1967 with Rufus Harris, which sought to support young people who had been charged with possession. Her work *Between Parades* 1985 is from her *Brothel Series* of paintings which relate to her own experiences as a sex worker. Adapting the brothel scenes depicted by artists such as Picasso and Manet, Coon disrupts the traditional male gaze by being both the artist and the subject of the work and focusing attention on the friendships of sex workers.

Coon's first solo exhibition was held in 2018 at The Gallery, Liverpool. The artist lives and works in London.

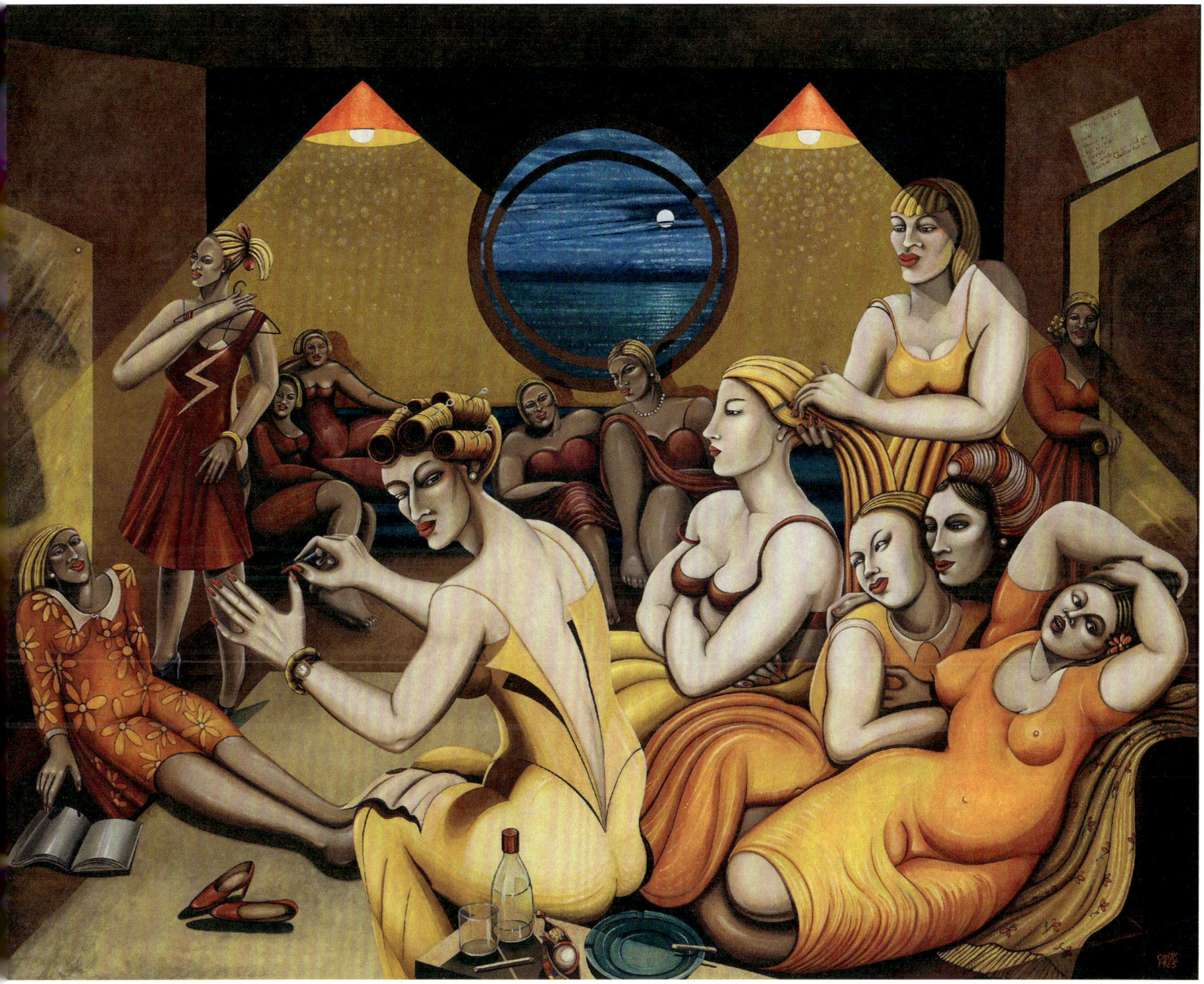

Between Parades 1985. Oil paint on canvas 122 × 152

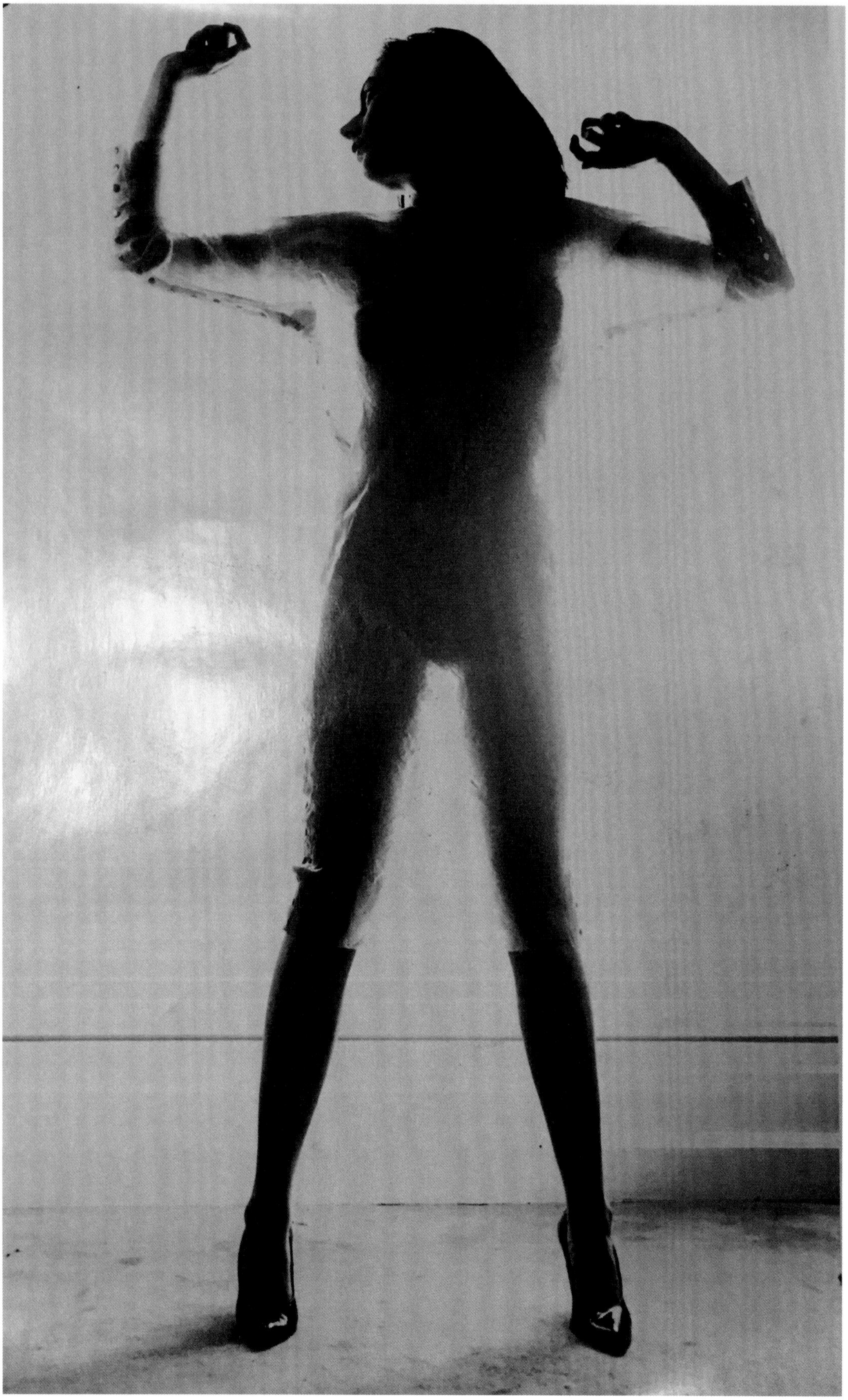

Potent-Female c.1983. Photograph 25 × 20

Jill Westwood (b.1960) is an artist and former lecturer and programme convenor for the celebrated Art Psychotherapy course at Goldsmiths, University of London. Westwood's work in the 1980s re-engineered and transformed ideas around pornographic and anti-censorship imagery, exploring aspects of sexuality. Her work challenged codes of male domination, by reconsidering power relations and reclaiming her own body and sexuality. This is particularly evident in works such as *Potent-Female* and *Hermetic-Female Triptych* where Westwood shares images of herself in fetish wear, clothing that she wore as part of her engagement with the performative practice of being a dominatrix. Embedded within artistic and musical subcultures, Westwood was in the industrial band FistFuck (1981–4), with Diana Rogerson and Antal Nemeth, peers of prominent industrial bands COIL and Nurse with Wound. FistFuck were one of very few women-led industrial bands and were particularly notable as they used the stage as a space in which to explore fetish and power dynamics. Recently, Westwood has been engaged in art as research around personal losses entangled with traumatic and historical political injustices and associated psychological effects. She lives and works between the Black Country and London.

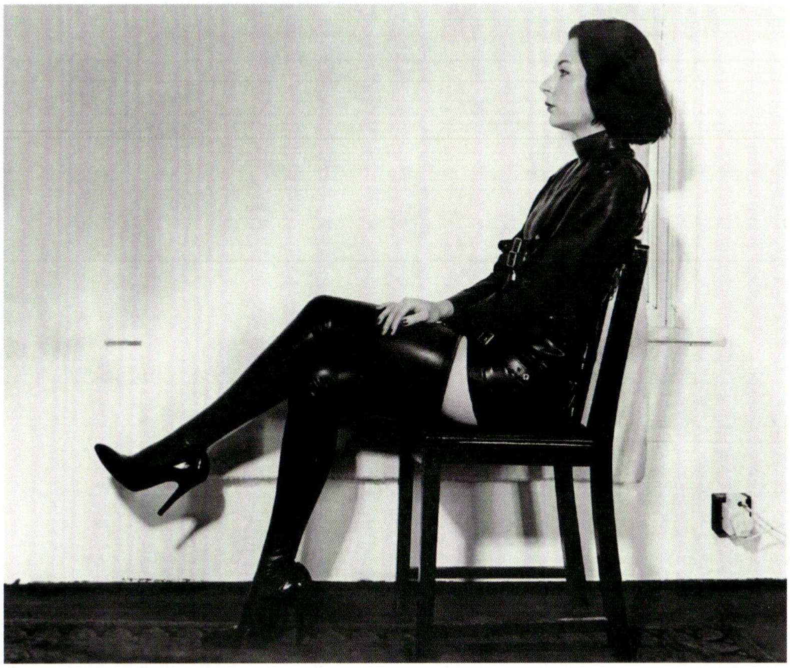

Transparent-Female c.1983. Photograph 30 × 40

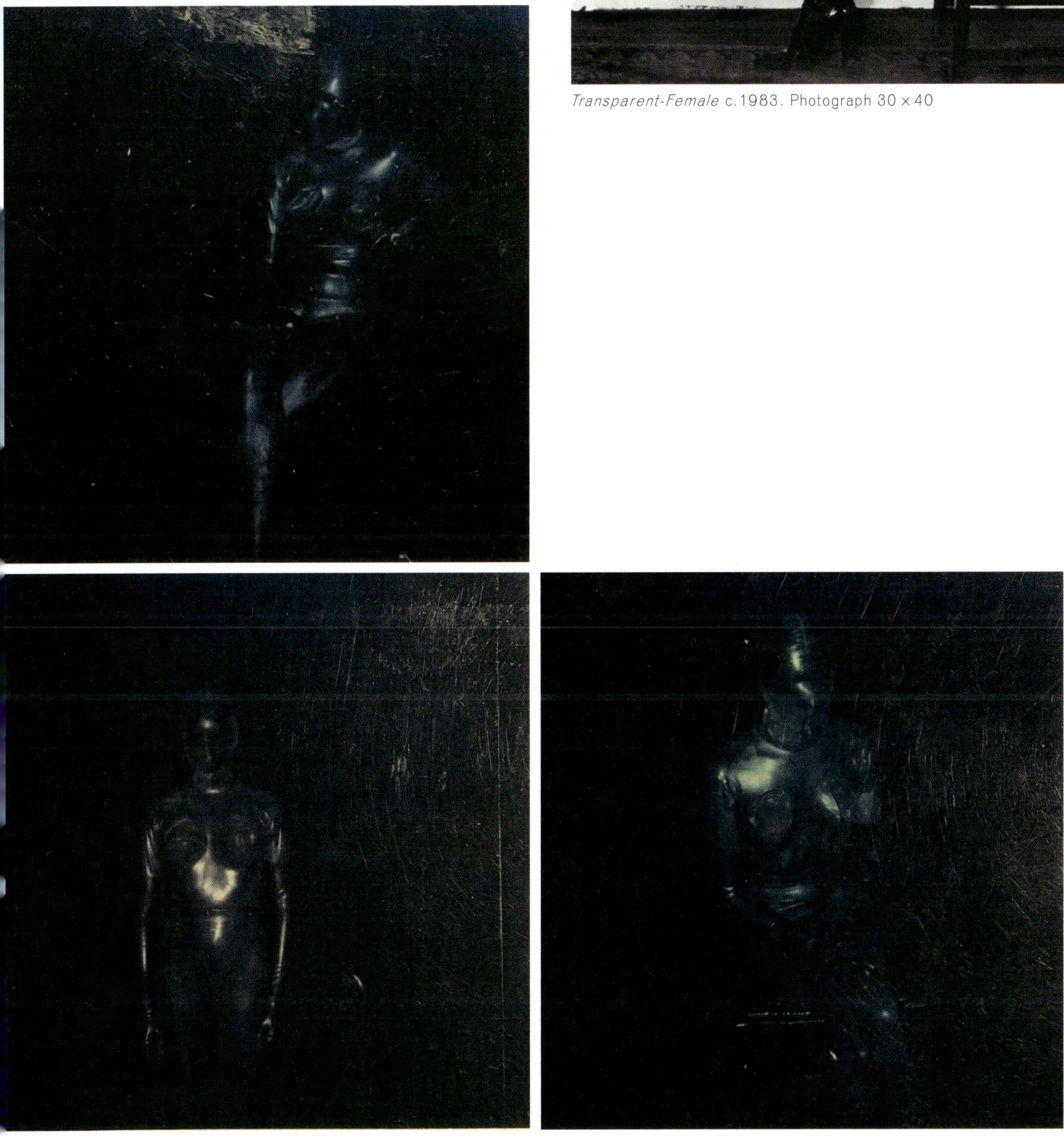

Hermetic-Female Triptych c.1982. 3 photographs; colour Polaroids 11.5 × 9 (each)

Marianne Elliott-Said, aka Poly Styrene (1957–2011), was born in Bromley, Kent and grew up in Brixton, London. Leaving school aged fifteen she became immersed in hippie culture as well as theatre, fashion, poetry and music. After seeing the Sex Pistols play in 1976, she placed an advert in the music magazine *Melody Maker* looking for 'Yung Punx' with whom to start a band. In the same year, she adopted the name Poly Styrene and formed the band X-Ray Spex, who would go on to become one of the most important and influential punk bands of the time, despite only releasing one album ('Germfree Adolescents') in 1978, months before they would split. Poly Styrene was the lead singer and frontwoman for the band, but also wrote their music and lyrics. She created artwork that was deeply political and explored topics including, feminism, racism, dystopian capitalist futures and environmental destruction. A person of dual heritage, Poly Styrene was one of very few women of colour to be visible in the UK's punk scene of the late 1970s. In 1983 Elliott-Said joined the Hare Krishna movement, which she remained committed to for the remainder of her life.

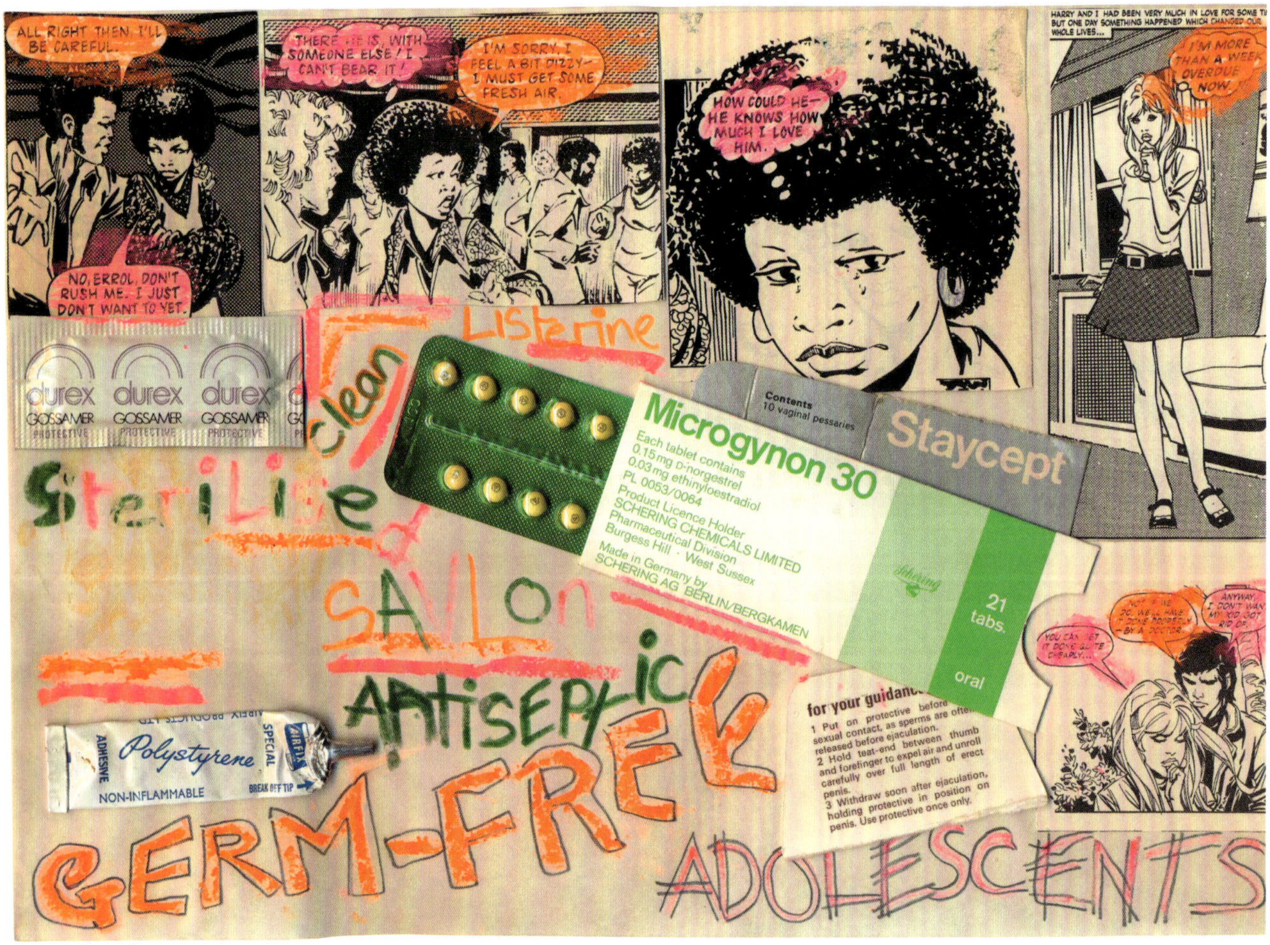

Germ-Free Adolescents 1977. Comic book cuttings, felt tip pen, pill packet and glue tube on paper 21 × 29

MARIANNE ELLIOTT-SAID (AKA POLY STYRENE)

Chila Kumari Singh Burman was born in 1957 in Bootle, near Liverpool, to Punjabi parents. She studied at Leeds Polytechnic and the Slade School of Fine Art in London, graduating in 1982. Working across a wide variety of mediums, Burman explores her experiences as a working class, South Asian woman in Britain. She was one of the first women artists of colour to exhibit overtly political work in the UK and was co-curator of the first Black women's art exhibition in the UK *Four Indian Women Artists* at the Indian Artists Gallery in 1981. She remains an integral figure among the British Black Arts Movement, and has exhibited in key shows, including *The Thin Black Line* (1985), *Jagrati: An Exhibition of Work by Asian Women Artists* (1986) and *Along the Lines of Resistance* (1987), all of which sought to highlight the work of Black and Asian artists and to challenge the white art establishment.

Burman's visceral work from the 1980s explores many of the urgent issues of the time, such as state violence, institutional racism, sexism and ecological concerns. Her groundbreaking essay 'There Have Always Been Great Blackwomen Artists', which responds to Linda Nochlin's equally influential 1971 essay 'Why Have There Been No Great Women Artists?', reflects on the inability of institutions to support or even to understand the work of women of colour, since they view it entirely from a white, Western position.

The artist presented her celebrated Winter Commission at Tate Britain in 2020–1, and had a solo exhibition at FACT in Liverpool in 2022–3. Burman lives and works in London.

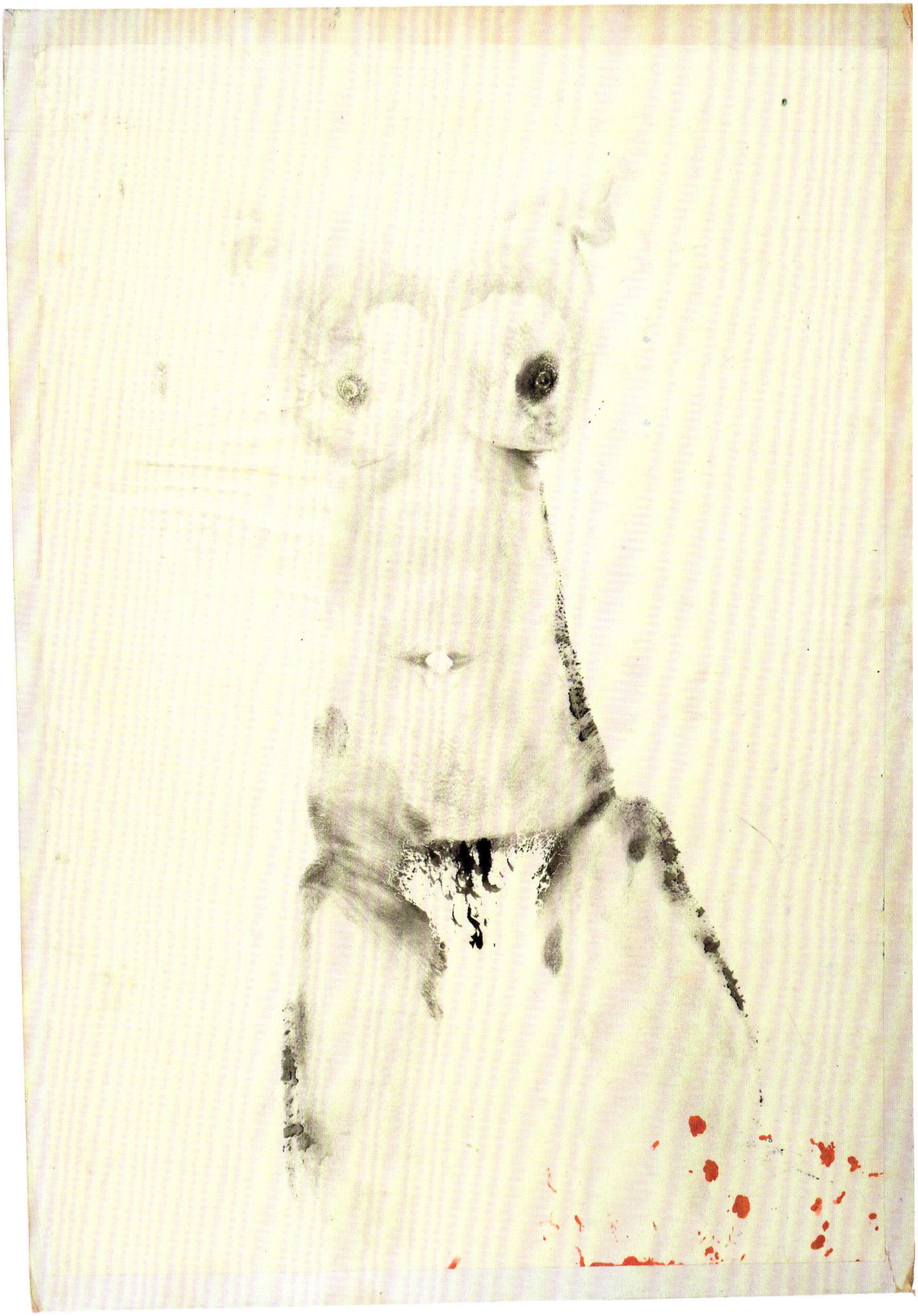

Splatter 1979. Poster paint on paper 88.6 × 63.2

CHILA KUMARI SINGH BURMAN

Born at RAF Halton, Buckinghamshire in 1954, Liz Rideal studied fine art and literature at Exeter University and Art College. In the mid 1980s Rideal began working almost exclusively with photo-booths, making large public and small-scale projects that saw her manipulate the ways in which the machine could be used and how the uncut photographic strips could be collaged. Other works saw her experimenting with the domestic environment, creating handmade papers out of unusual materials such as the contents of a vacuum-cleaner bag. In addition to exhibiting widely, her work is in both national and international collections. Rideal has received multiple awards and fellowships, including the Leverhulme Fellowship (2016–17) and the Wingate Scholarship at the British School in Rome. Since 1992 she has held the position of Professor of Fine Art at the Slade School of Fine Art, London.

Rideal lives and works in London.

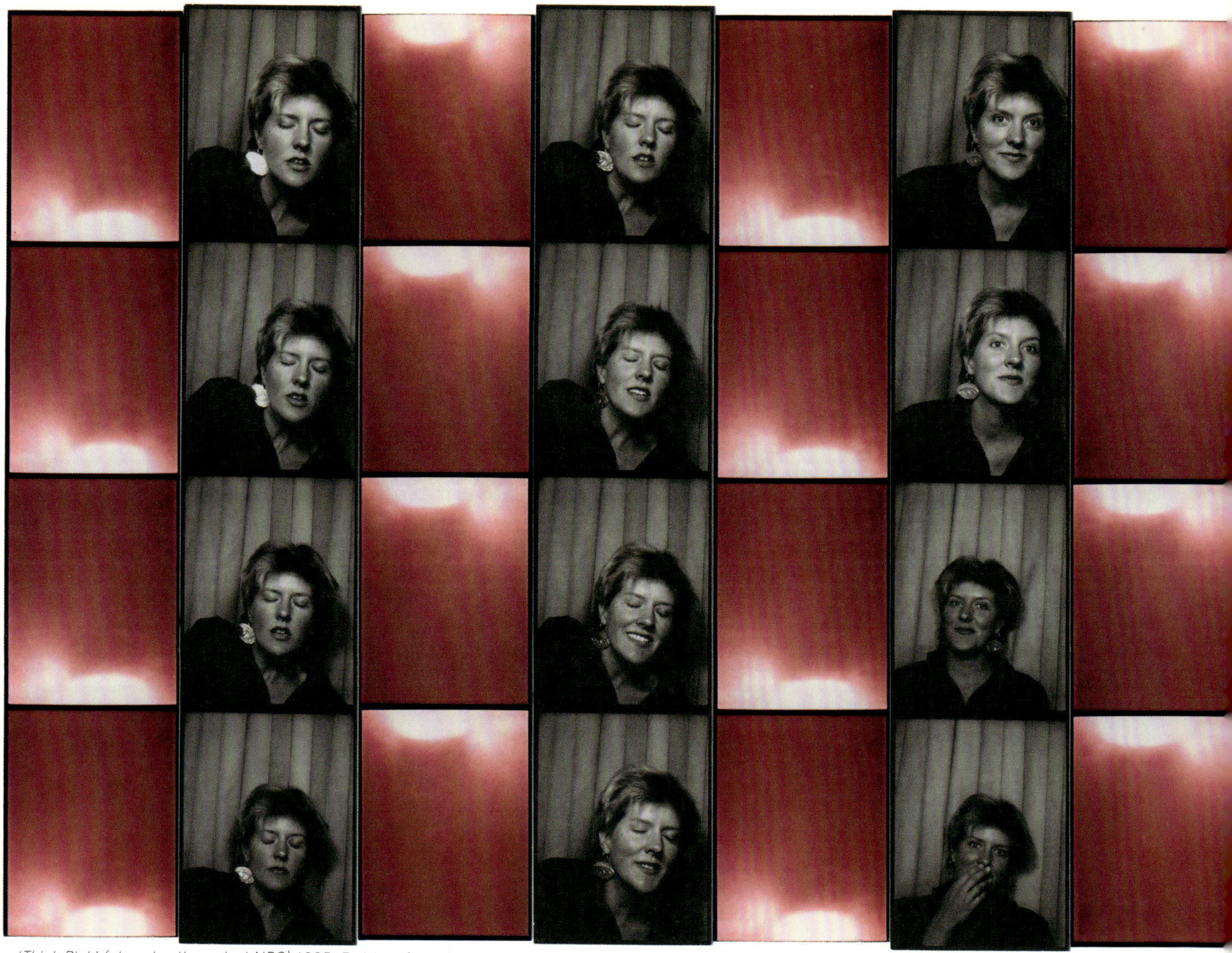

'Think Pink' (aka – booth wank at NPG) 1985. 7 strips of uncut, no negative photo-booth photos 20.5 × 28 (overall)

LIZ RIDEAL

Poulomi Desai was born in London in 1965. At the age of just thirteen she co-founded the Hounslow Arts Cooperative Theatre and on leaving school she became involved with anti-fascist groups and the anti-apartheid movement. A self-taught artist with a background in street theatre, Desai works with performance and photography. Research and learning are integral to her practice and she often works collaboratively. As a curator, Desai is responsible for two long-overdue exhibitions. In 2010 she organised the first retrospective by the influential artist Chila Burman. *Chila Burman's Royal Academy Summer Exhibition*, held at Usurp Art Gallery & Studios, London, featured works created over forty years, many of which had not been seen before. Then in 2017, she curated *We Are the Lions*, the first comprehensive exhibition about the 1976–8 Grunwick strike.

Desai has undertaken significant work as an activist, co-founding *Shakti*, the first South Asian LGBTQ+ campaigning organisation, in 1987, and the Naz Foundation International, the first HIV/AIDS charity in India. She lives in London and works internationally.

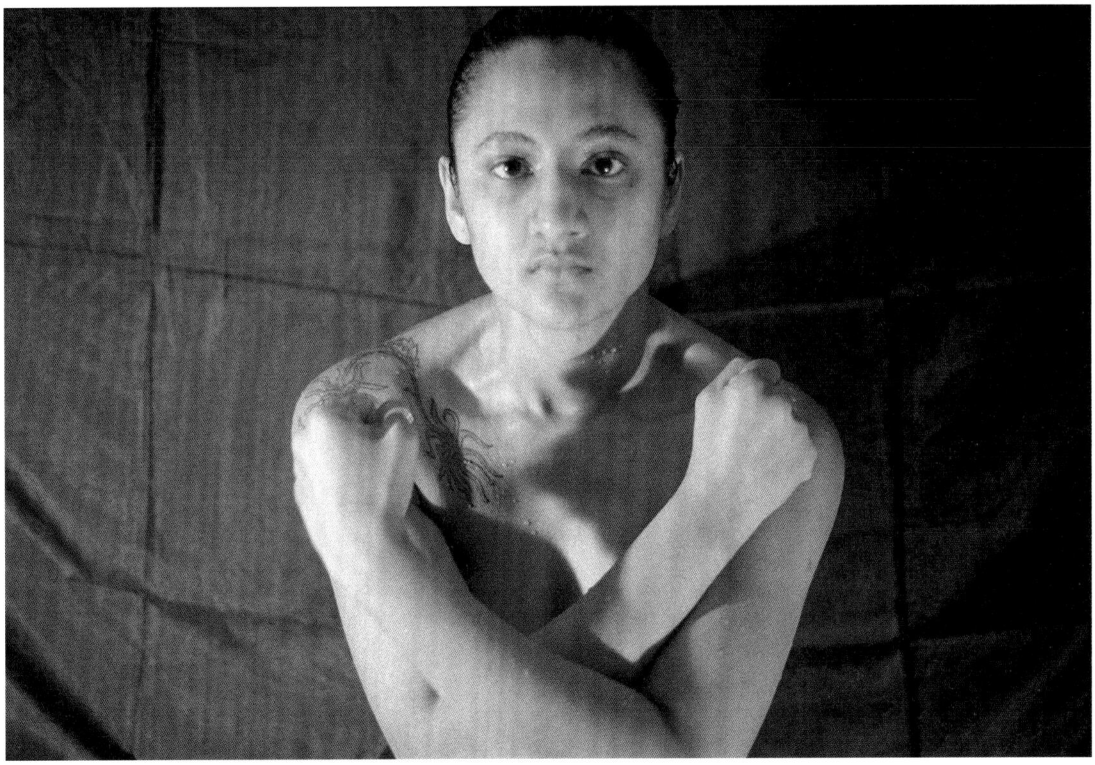

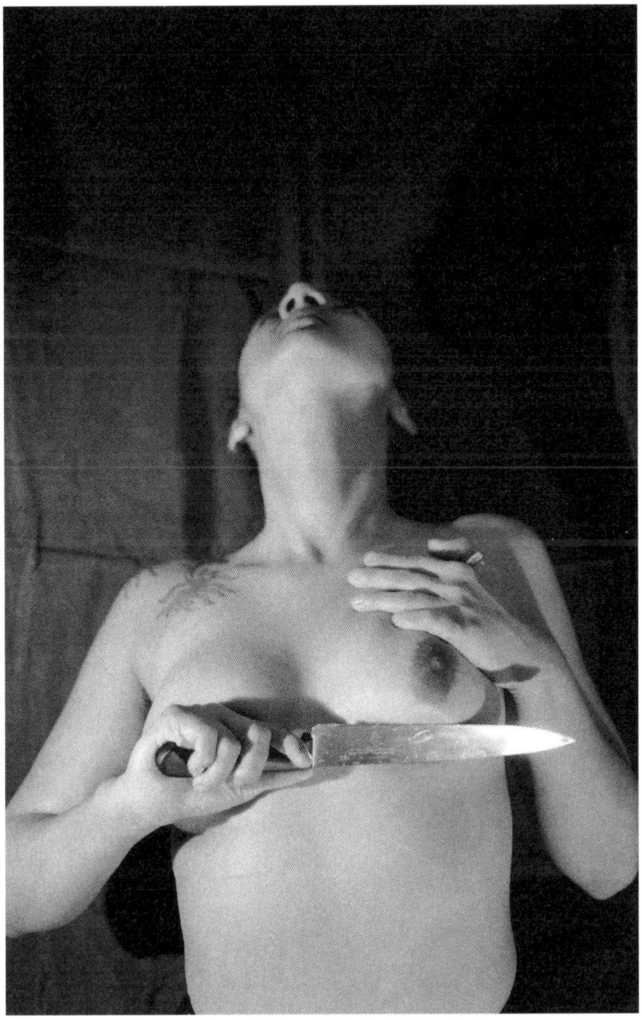

Nothing Between Denial and Acceptance 1983.
2 photographs 42 × 29.7 (each)

POULOMI DESAI

Linder was born in Liverpool in 1954. She studied graphic design at Manchester Polytechnic, graduating in 1977. She works across photomontage, moving image and performance citing artists such as Dadaist Hannah Höch as influences on her practice. Her work explores women's histories and feminism, and in particular the presentation and commodification of the female body.

In 1978 Linder founded the post-punk band Ludus, releasing two albums: *The Seduction* (1981) and *Danger Came Smiling* (1982). The lyrics sung by Linder included references to women's roles in society and menstruation. In 1982 she performed at the Haçienda in Manchester, wearing a dress decorated with meat and a sex toy in protest against the club's sale of meat products and its playing of pornography on monitors. In collaboration with Jon Savage, Linder published the fanzine-style publication *The Secret Public*, titled in reference to the fact that mainstream society paid little attention to the culture in which they were embedded.

The artist held solo exhibitions at Kettle's Yard in Cambridge (2020) and Nottingham Contemporary (2018), and has a retrospective at the Hayward Gallery in 2025. She lives and works in the north of England.

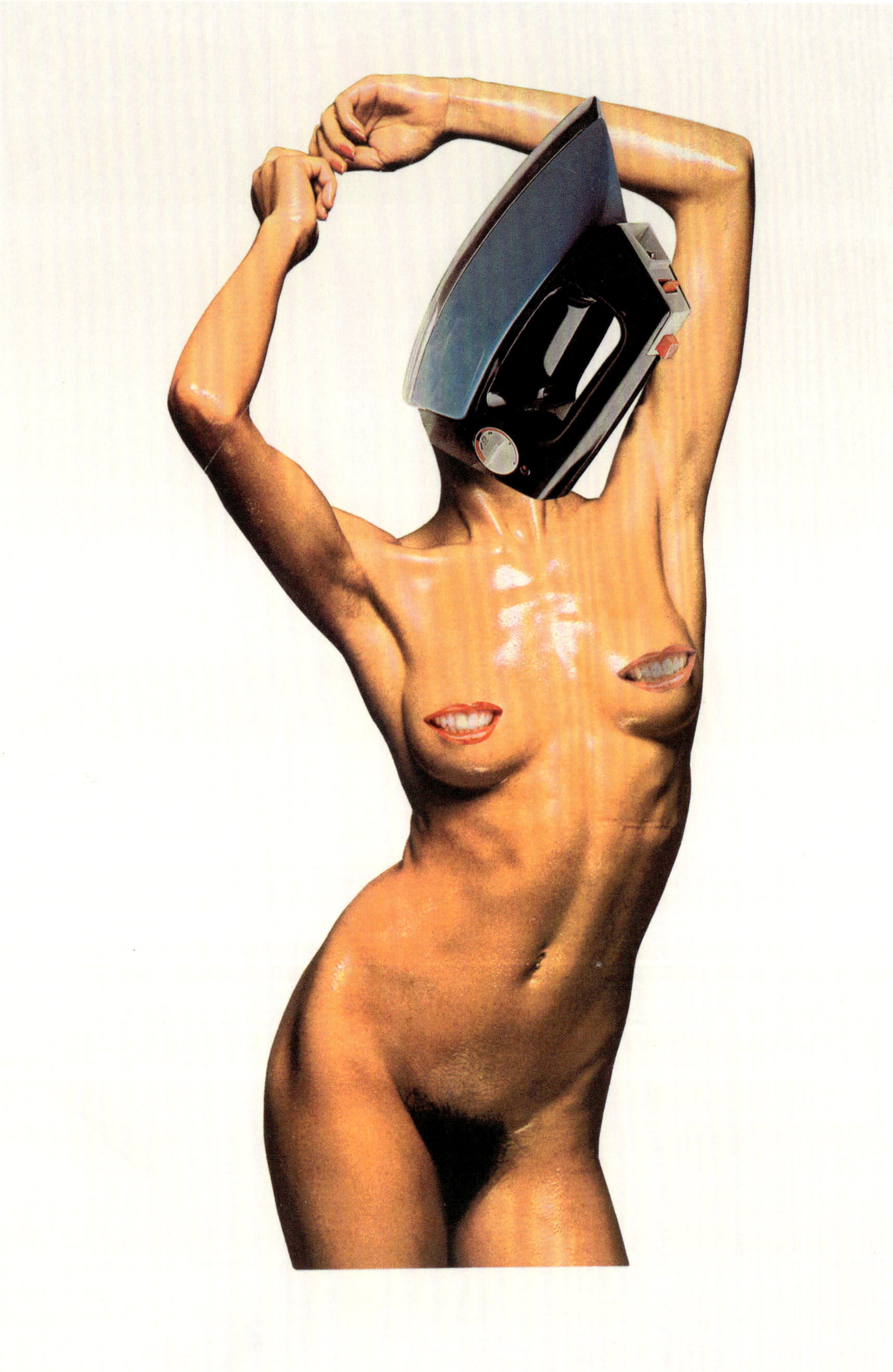

Untitled 1976. Printed papers on board 37 × 30

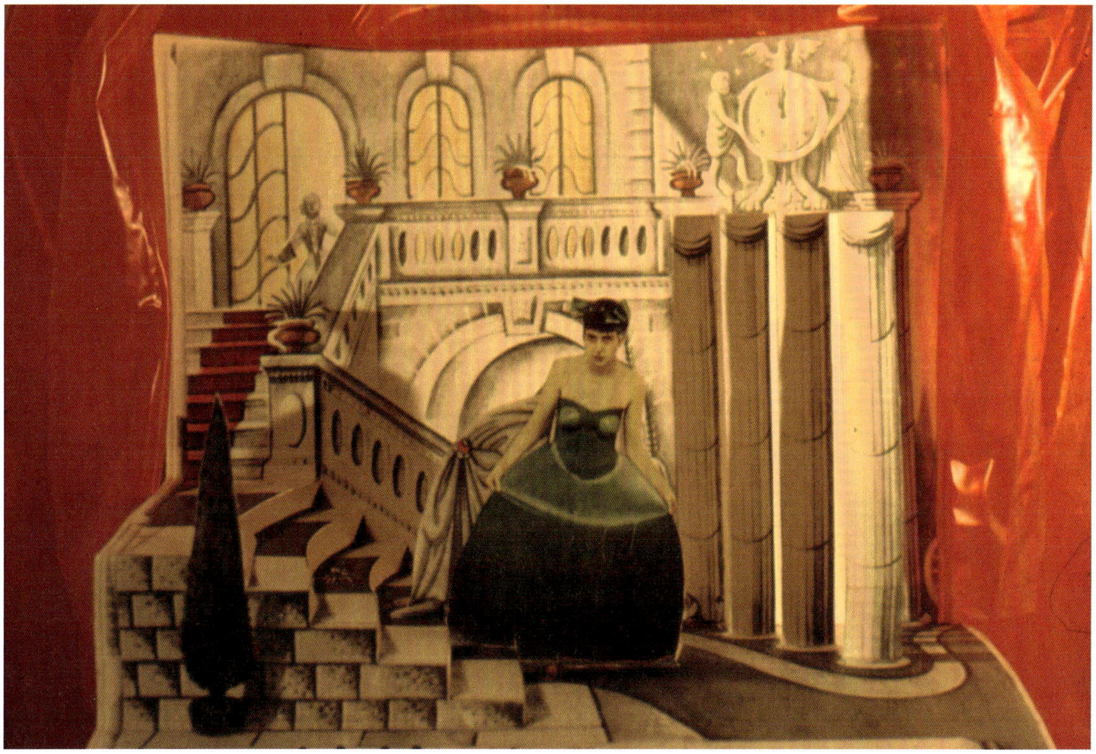

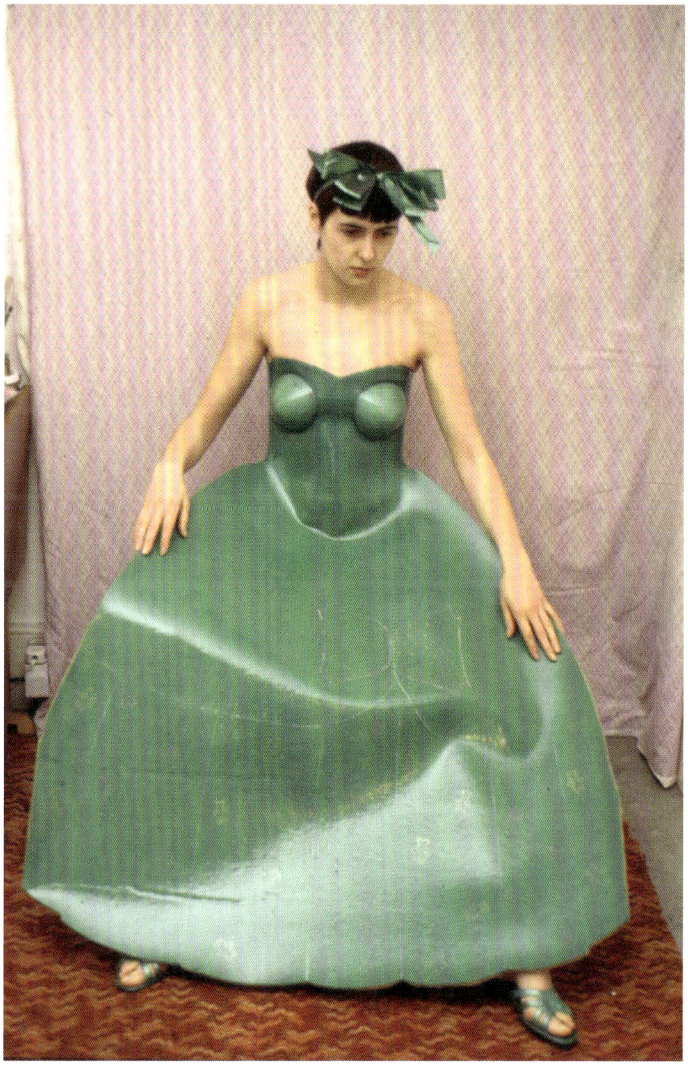

Faster Princess 1982.
Super 8 film, shown as digital video;
colour, sound. 10 min

Martine Thoquenne was born in northern France in 1956 where she studied for a fine art degree at L'Ecole des Beaux Arts de Cambrai. She moved to London in 1980 and continued her studies at Saint Martin's School of Art on the New Artist Film Course from 1982–6, followed by an MA in film at the Royal College of Art 1987–9. Thoquenne has worked across many media including music, photography and primarily experimental film. Her film practice reflects her French upbringing, her integration to the UK and its subcultures of the 1980s, and her commitment to a feminist discourse. Her award-winning short films have toured extensively at international film festivals, most recently at the Oberhausen Short Film Festival 2022, and were exhibited in key exhibitions of the 1980s and 1990s, such as: *Celluloid Bodies*, ICA, London (1987) and *The New Pluralism: British Film and Video 1980–1985*, Tate Britain, London (1985). Made in 1982, *Faster Princess* uses a mixture of live action, cut-outs and pop-up animation to tell the story of a young woman preparing herself for a ball.

Thoquenne lives and works in the Midlands.

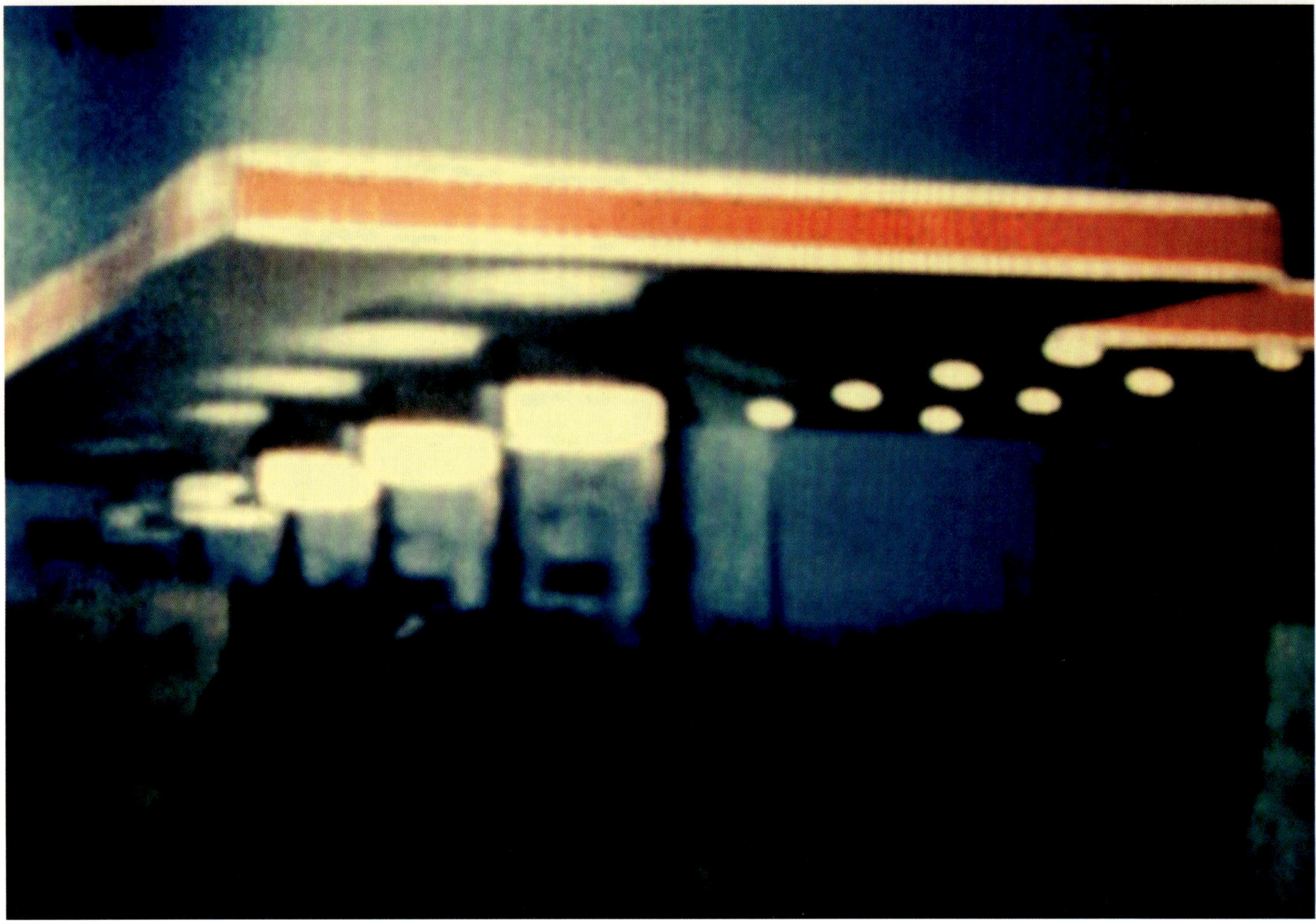

Tea Leaf 1986. 16mm film, shown as digital video; colour, sound. 8 min, 13 sec

RUTH NOVACZEK

Ruth Novaczek (b.1956) studied history of art at the Courtauld Institute of Art (1979–81), film and video at Saint Martin's School of Art (1983–6) and fine art at Central Saint Martins School of Art (1998–2000). She has since been making film, performance and installation work that explores diaspora, gender, humour, sexuality, cinematic language and philosophy. She has a practice-based PhD entitled '21st Century Avant-Garde: New Vernaculars and Feminine Ecriture' from the University of Westminster, London.

Made on Super 8 and transferred to 16mm film, Novaczek's first film *Tea Leaf* was completed in 1986 within the film department of the then Saint Martin's School of Art. *Tea Leaf* is a punk romance, set in bleak Thatcherite London, and shows a Black woman and a Jewish woman, dancing in the streets and wandering through the city. The narrator cites Violette Leduc's *La Batarde*, alongside her own memories of being sexually abused as a child. The super-imposition suggests a double-consciousness, a trauma, and moments of tenderness transform violent memories into a love story.

The artist lives and works in London.

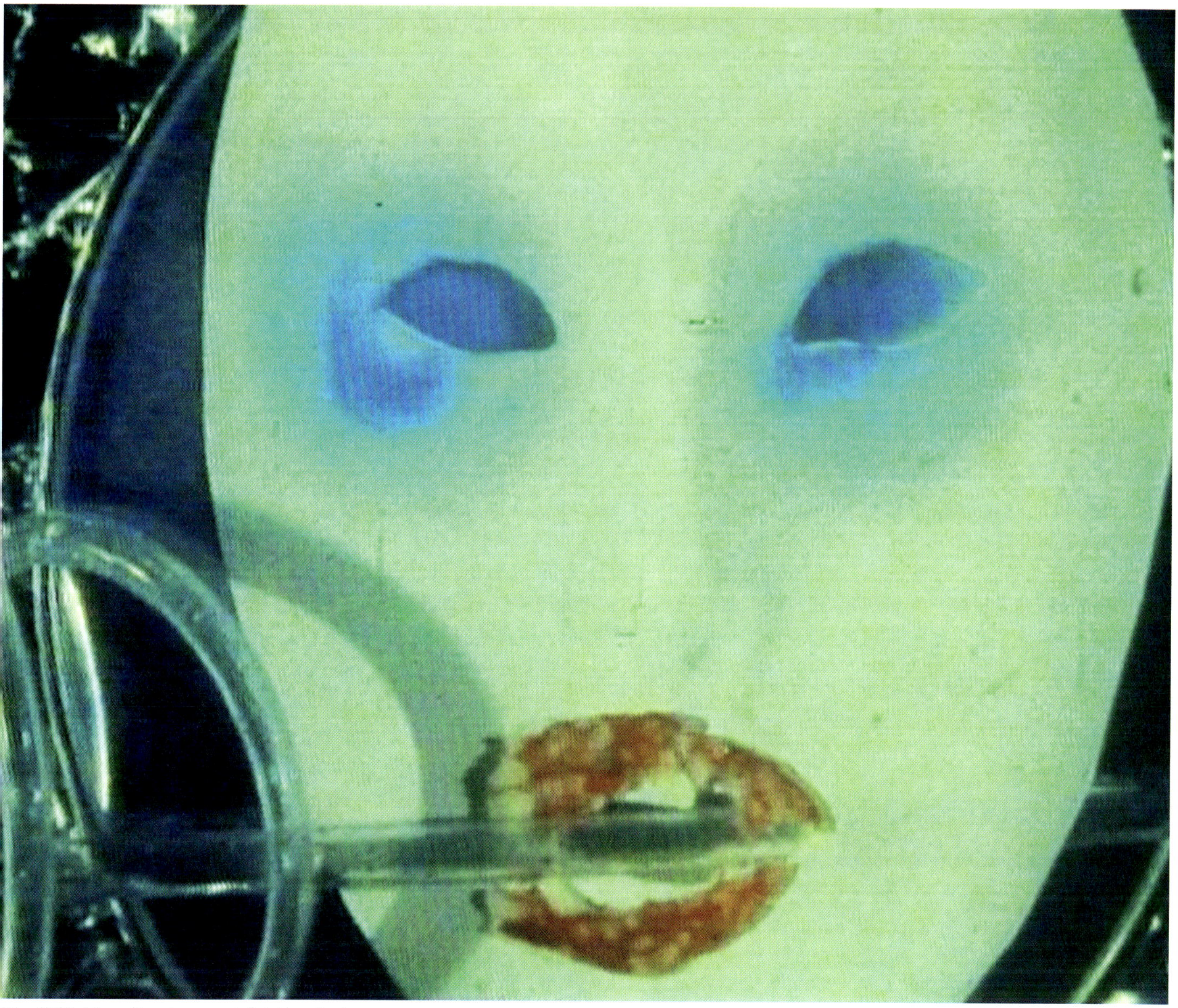

Edge 1986. 16mm film, shown as digital video. 8 min

Sandra Lahire (1950–2001) studied philosophy and English literature at the University of Newcastle before moving to London to study fine art film at Saint Martin's School of Art, and film and environmental media at the Royal College of Art. She was a galvanising figure in the feminist filmmaking community in London, working with the London Filmmakers' Co-operative and the women's film and video distribution collective Circles. The intricately layered sounds and images of her 16mm films fuse documentary testimony with staged and animated sequences to address resonant feminist questions of bodily fragilities and desire. Her films are marked by their intense political engagement with the politics of the 1980s and 1990s, including specifically environmental and nuclear concerns. The poems of Sylvia Plath were a potent point of identification for Lahire, and surface as fragments of poetry reading, audio recordings and images throughout her films. Her 1986 film *Edge* takes Plath's last poem as a starting point to address women's struggles under patriarchal oppression.

SANDRA LAHIRE

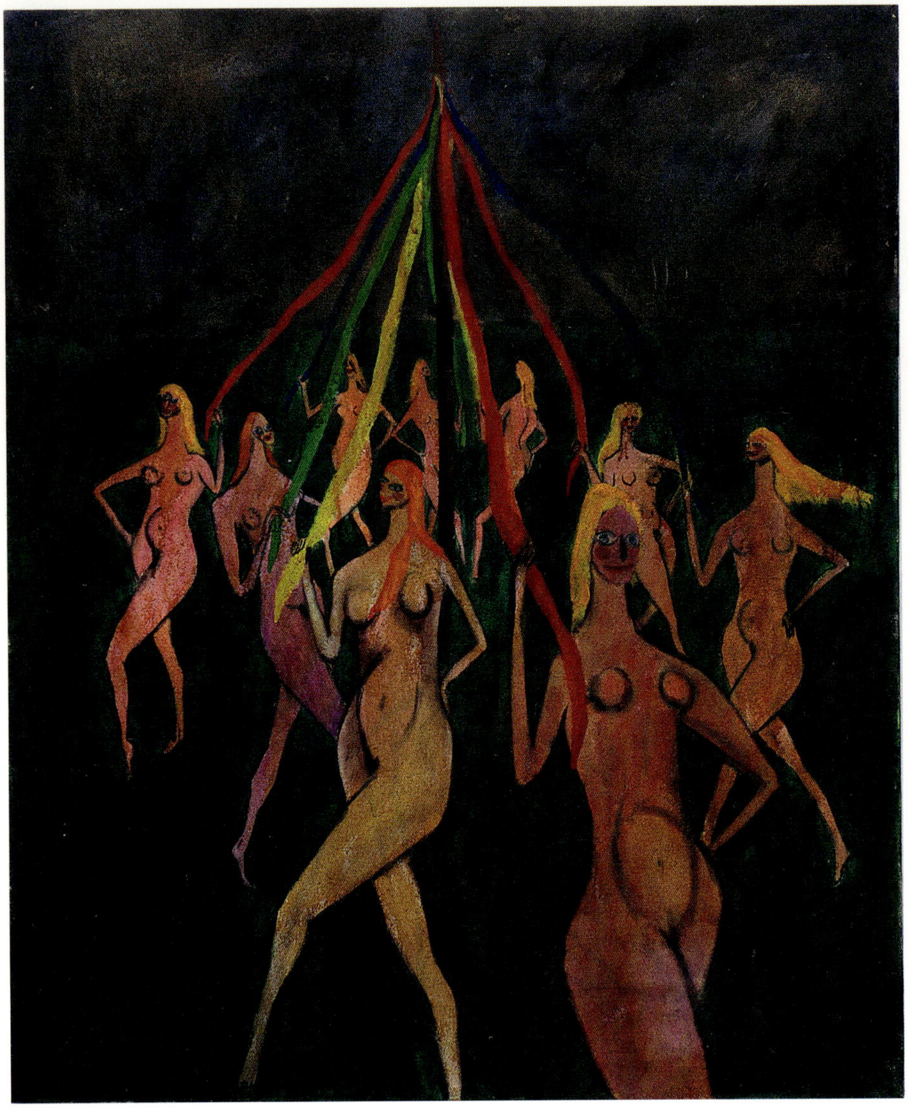

Wilma Johnson *The Maypole* 1982. Oil paint on canvas 96 × 82

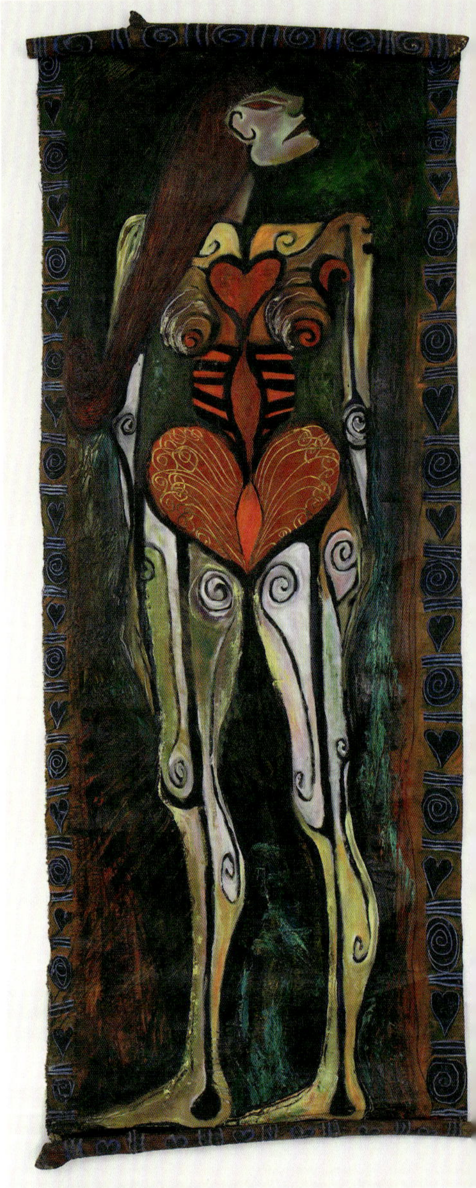

Jennifer Binnie *Woman* 1983. Oil paint on canvas with decorated branch 220 × 88 × 6

Pink Punk Performance, The Fridge, Brixton 1982. 3 of 4 photocopies 21.5 × 28 (each)

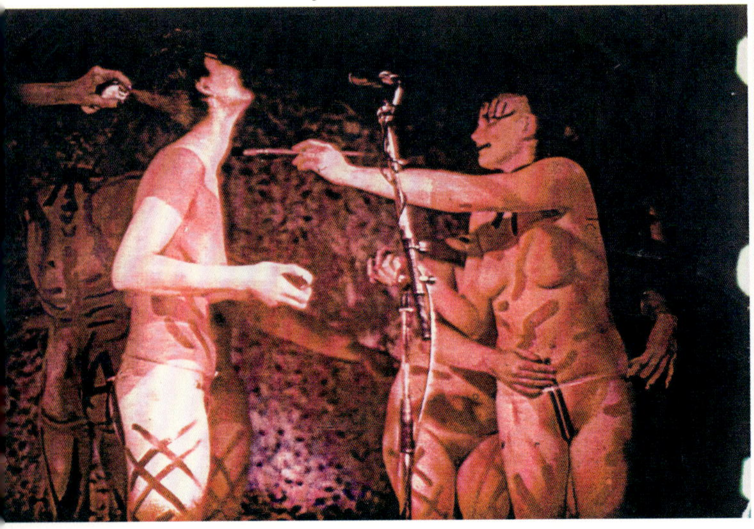

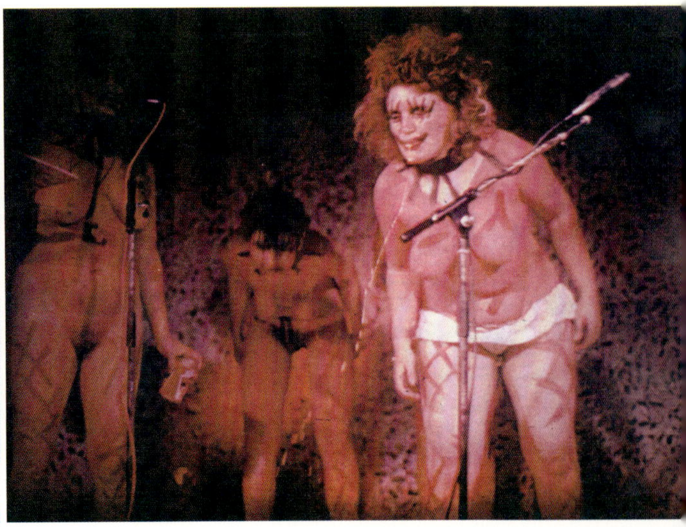

THE NEO NATURISTS

The performance art group The Neo Naturists was formed in 1980 by Christine Binnie (b.1955), Jennifer Binnie (b.1958) and Wilma Johnson (b.1960). The group was linked to various subcultures that formed counter to the social and political change marked by the rise of Thatcherism in the 1980s, including the later years of punk and the New Romantic club scene. Making performance-based work and paintings, they performed (with men as well as many other women) regularly in galleries and nightclubs, enabling a wide audience to experience their practice. The Neo Naturists' performances explored the commodification and objectification of women's bodies. By painting each other's naked bodies, the artists challenged beauty standards prevalent in advertising and other popular culture, presenting a body-positive stance in contrast to the male gaze, and in the process reclaiming their own bodies and agency.

In 2016 Studio Voltaire curated and hosted a retrospective of the Neo Naturists' 1980s performances, the first historical survey of their work in a public gallery.

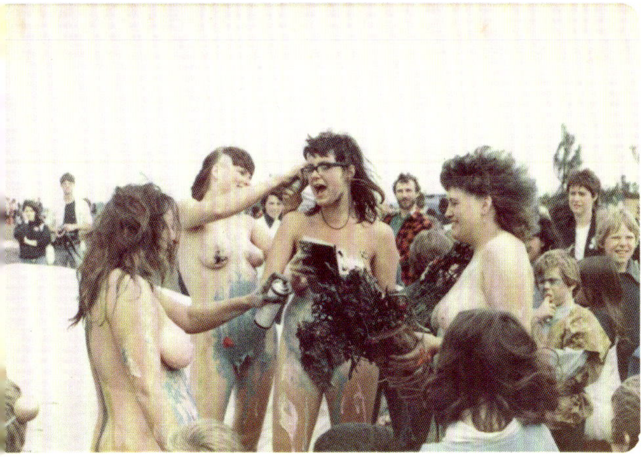

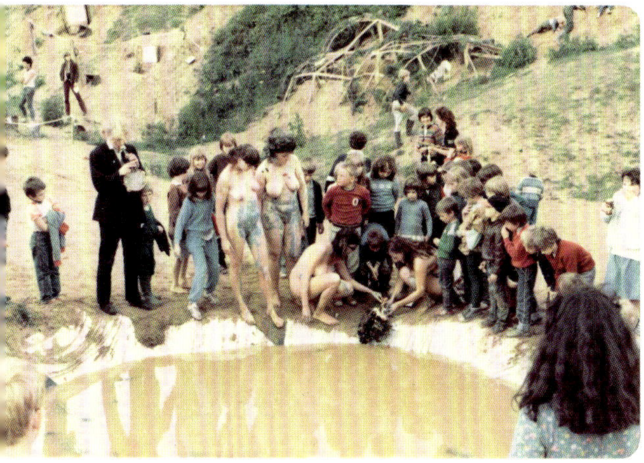

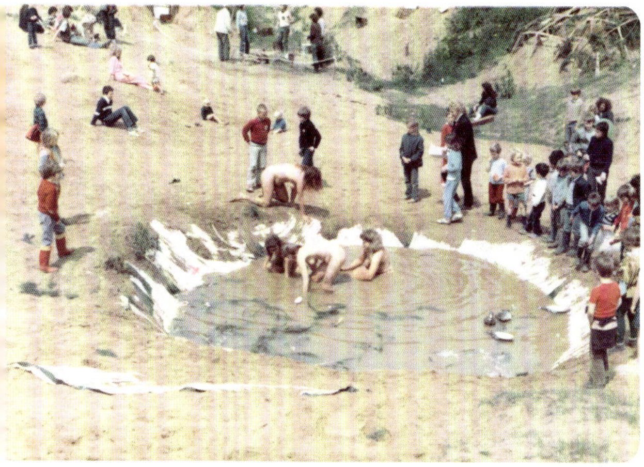

bove: *The Neo Naturist Sermon, Porridge and Black Roses at the Faerie Fair,* yng 1982. 3 of 11 photographs 13 × 9 (each)

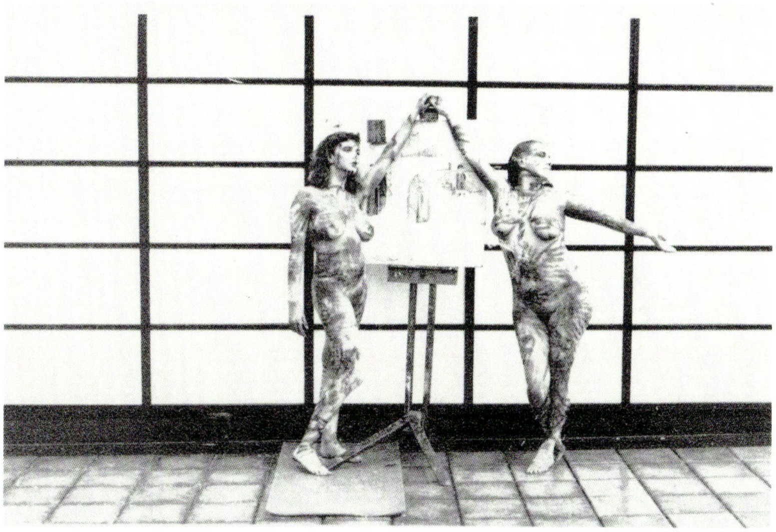

Art School Performance on the Roof of St. Martins 1981. Photograph 12.5 × 21.5

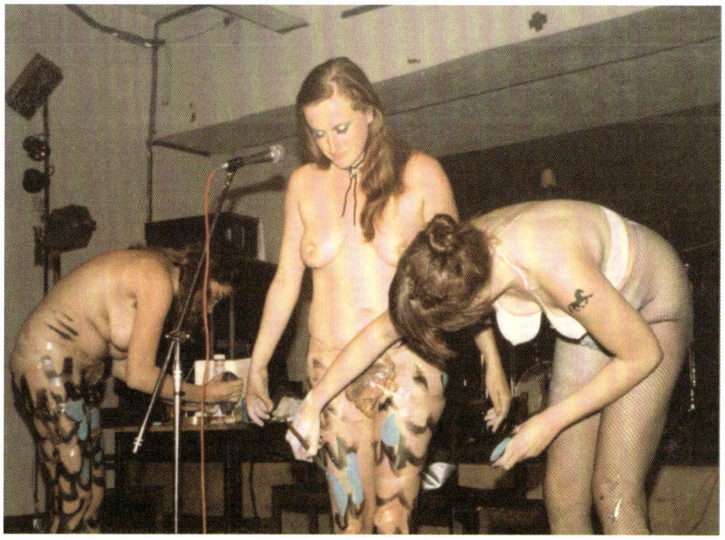

Sexist Crabs, The Zap Club, Brighton 1983. Photograph 10 × 15

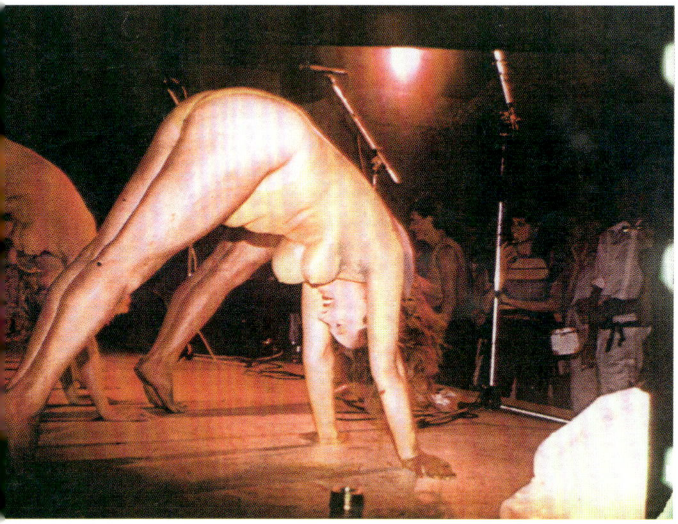

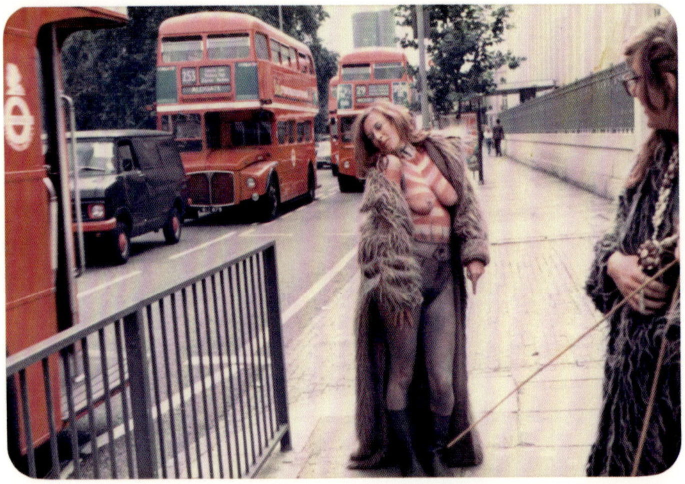

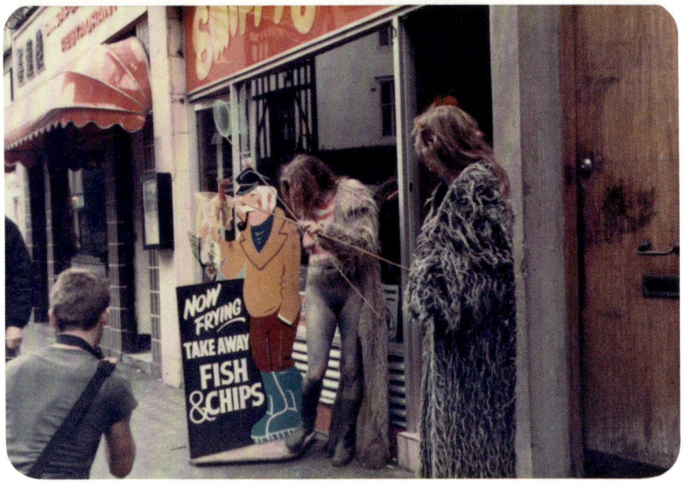

Centrepoint, Walking and Swimming Experiment 1984. Photographs 11 × 15 (each)

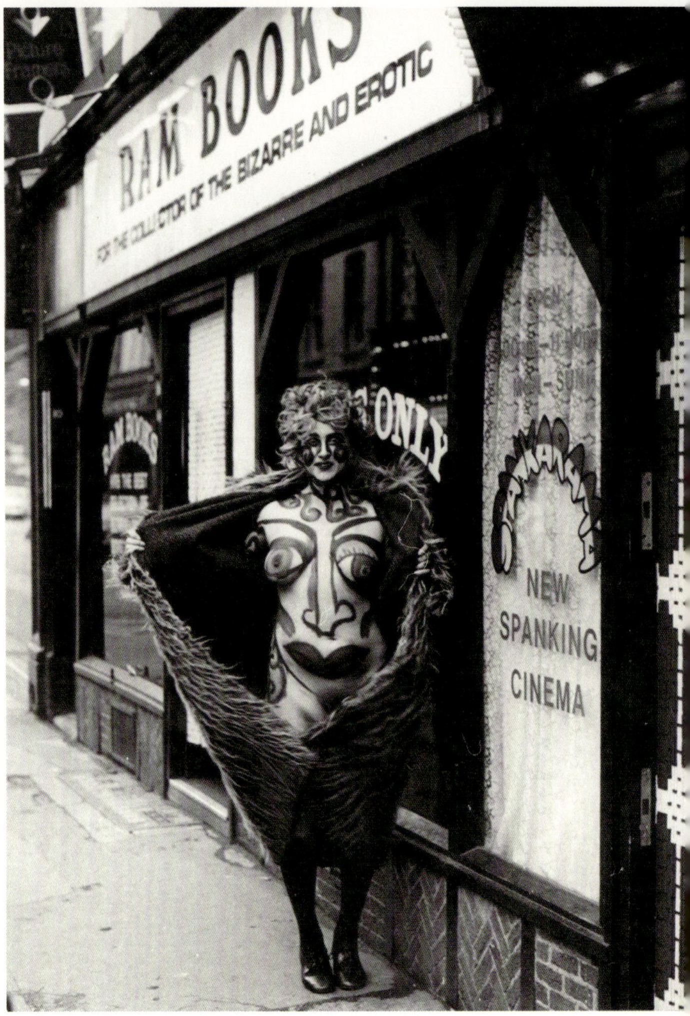

Christine Binnie Flashing in Soho 1982. Photograph 24.5 × 18

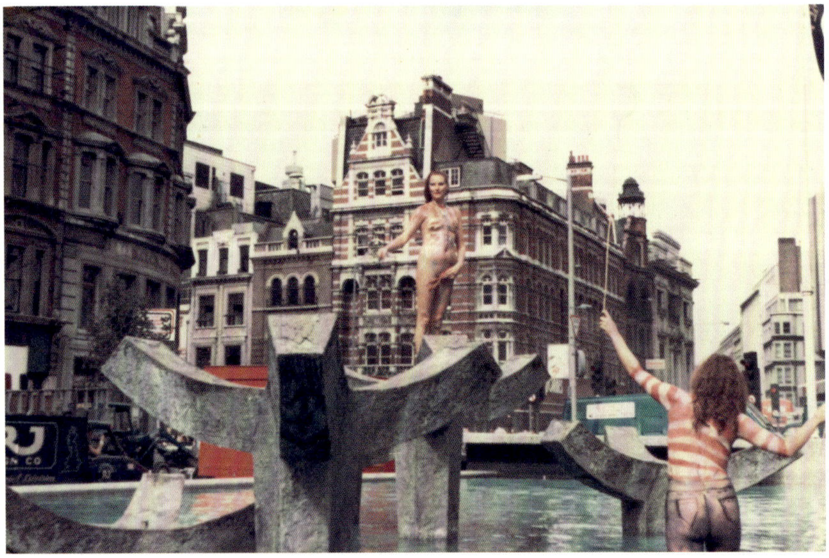

Centrepoint, Walking and Swimming Experiment 1984. Photograph 11 × 15

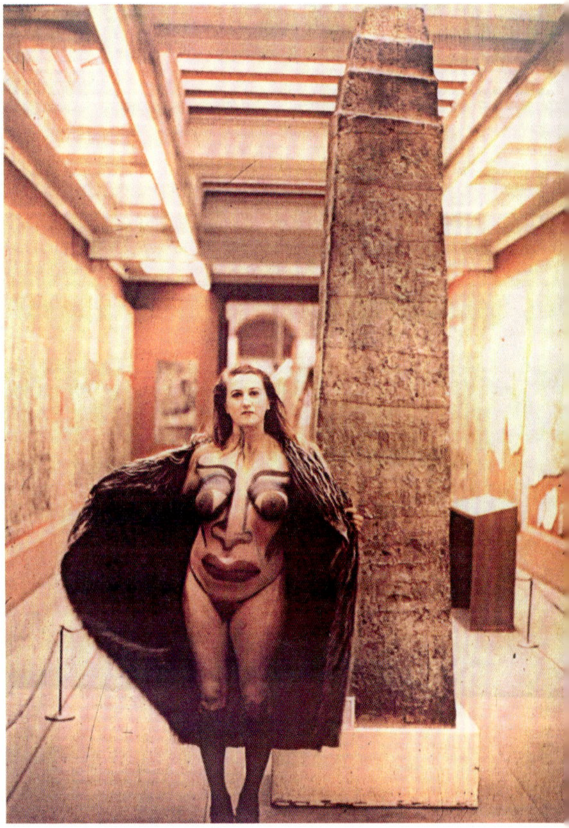

Flashing (British Museum) 1982. Photograph 28 × 21

THE NEO NATURISTS

Suzan Swale was born in Nottingham in 1946 and studied fine art at Bristol Polytechnic, graduating with a first-class honours degree in 1969. She went on to receive an MA in painting from the Royal College of Art in 1972. Swale's practice is led by painting, which she describes as the backbone of her work, but also encompasses performance, photography, printing, installation and mixed-media works. Her art, particularly from the 1980s, seeks to initiate a political dialogue with the viewer. In the mixed-media piece *Hegemony* 1982, for example, she takes the front pages from souvenir issues of British tabloid newspapers marking the royal wedding of Charles and Diana and distorts them with paint, encouraging her audience to challenge their content. Swale notes that she was a witness to the way in which the press in the 1980s played a huge role in perpetuating problematic ideas regarding women's roles and class in British society.

Swale lives and works in London and shows her work extensively in the UK and abroad. She is a member of The London Group.

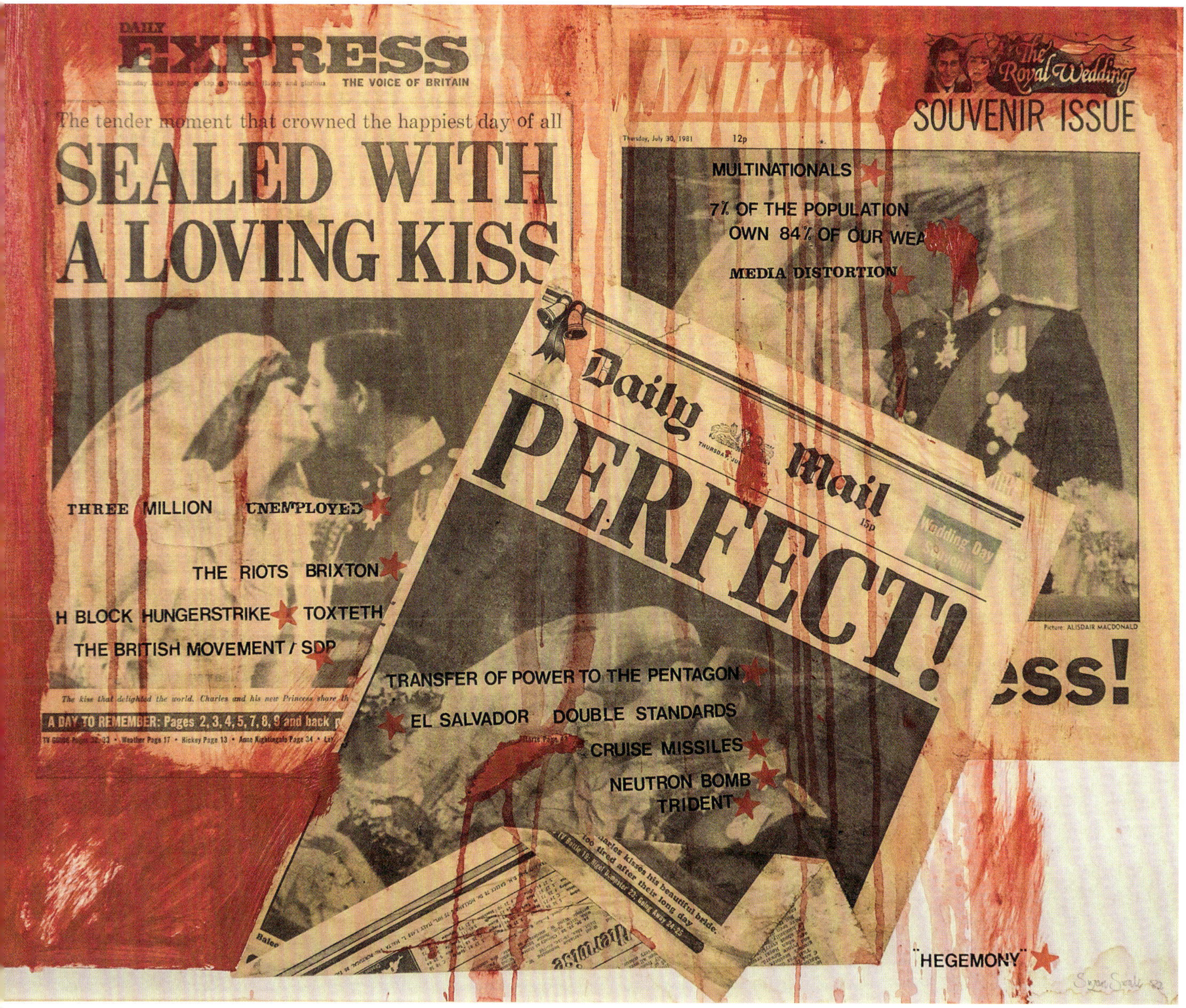

Hegemony 1982. Newspaper, acrylic paint and Letraset lettering on card 50.6 × 63.2

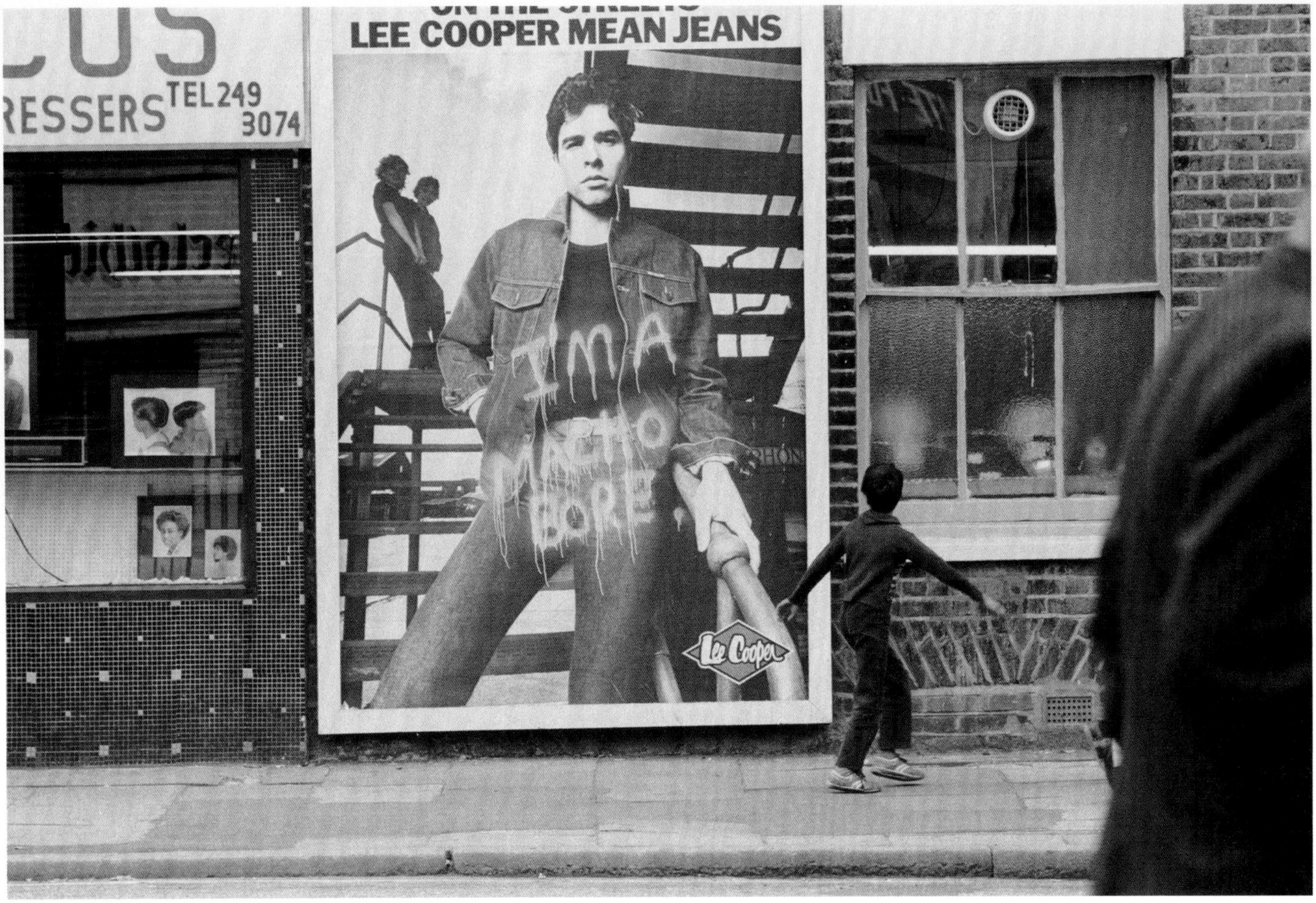
LEE COOPER MEAN JEANS
TEL 249
3074
I'M A
MACHO
BORE
Lee Cooper

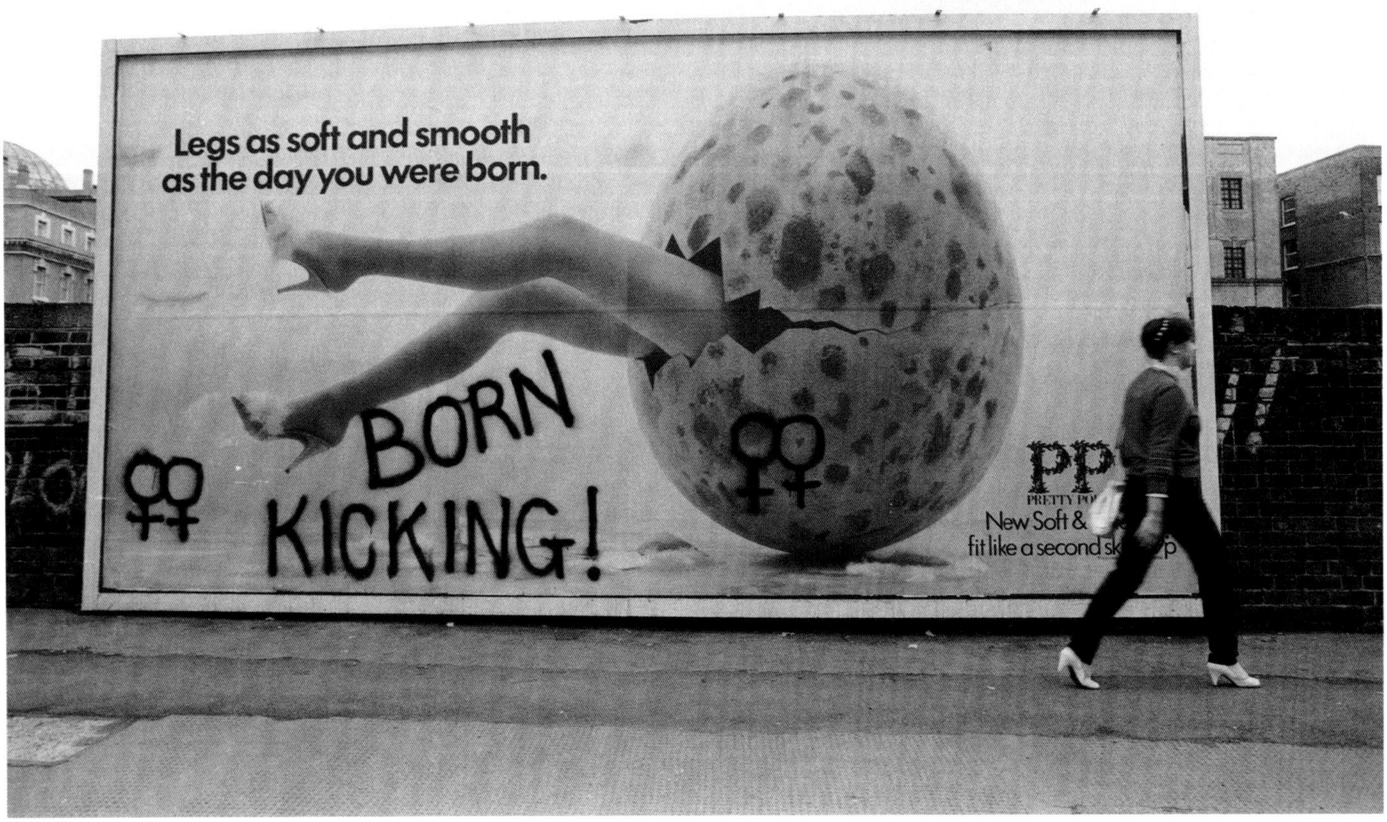
Legs as soft and smooth
as the day you were born.
BORN
KICKING!

JILL POSENER

Born in London in 1953, Jill Posener trained as a stage manager at the London Academy of Music and Dramatic Art, and in 1973, began working at the pioneering Kings Head Theatre in Islington, London. She bought her first SLR camera to document the productions there. With encouragement from American queer playwright Robert Patrick, she wrote *Any Woman Can*, a reflection on her own coming out, first produced in 1974. In 1976 she became the first woman to join the Gay Sweatshop, England's first professional gay theatre company. As Posener's interest in social commentary increased, she began focusing on photography, joining the National Union of Journalists (NUJ) in the late 1970s, and working as a freelancer in alternative and mainstream media. In 1982, *Spray It Loud*, her book of graffiti images, was published, followed by a second collection, *Louder Than Words* in 1986. In the late 1980s Posener moved to San Francisco where she met Susie Bright, the editor of the lesbian erotica magazine *On Our Backs*, known for its influence in shaping the aesthetic and narrative of US lesbian culture at the time. Posener became the photo editor at the magazine. In 1996 she collaborated with Bright on a landmark collection of lesbian erotic photography, *Nothing But the Girl: The Blatant Lesbian Image*.

Posener lives in California. In 2010, she founded a non-profit organisation providing free veterinary care for unhoused and low-income pet owners.

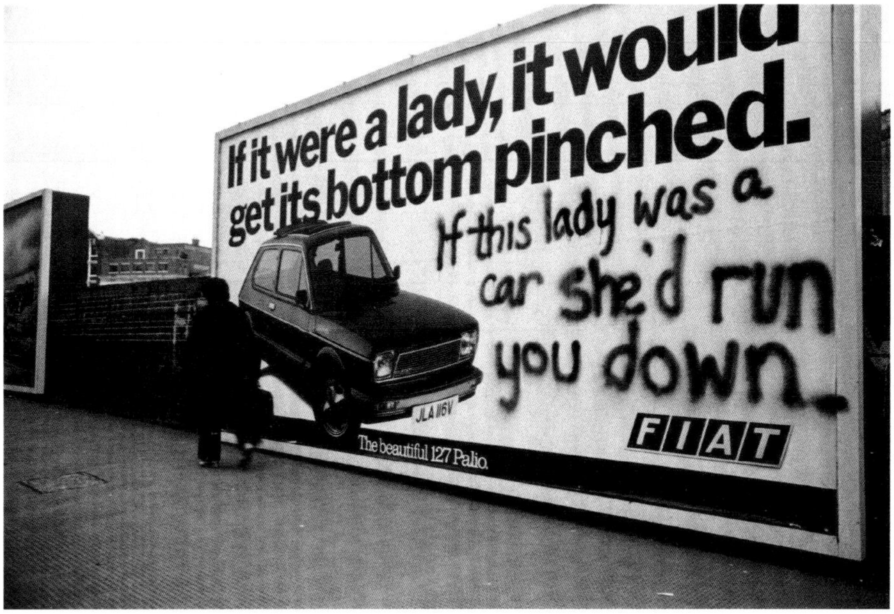

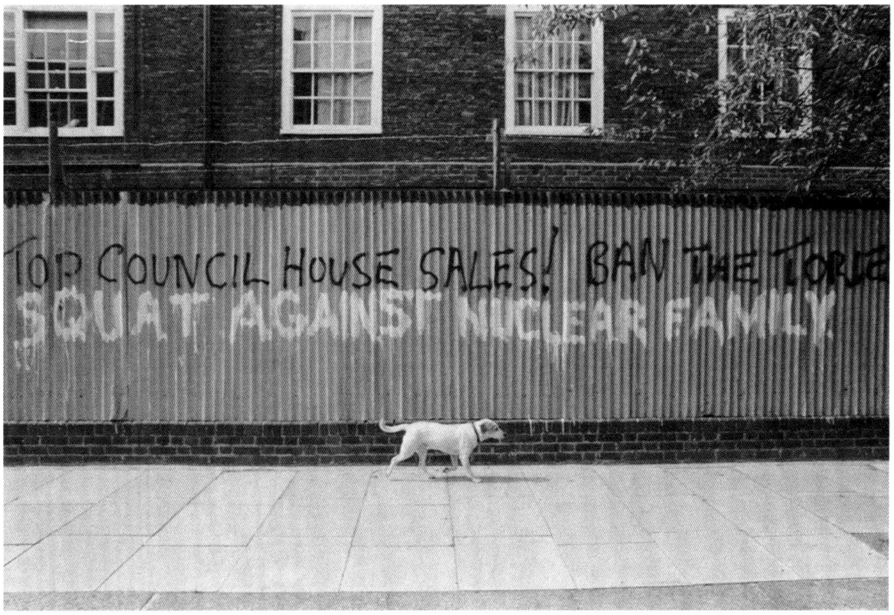

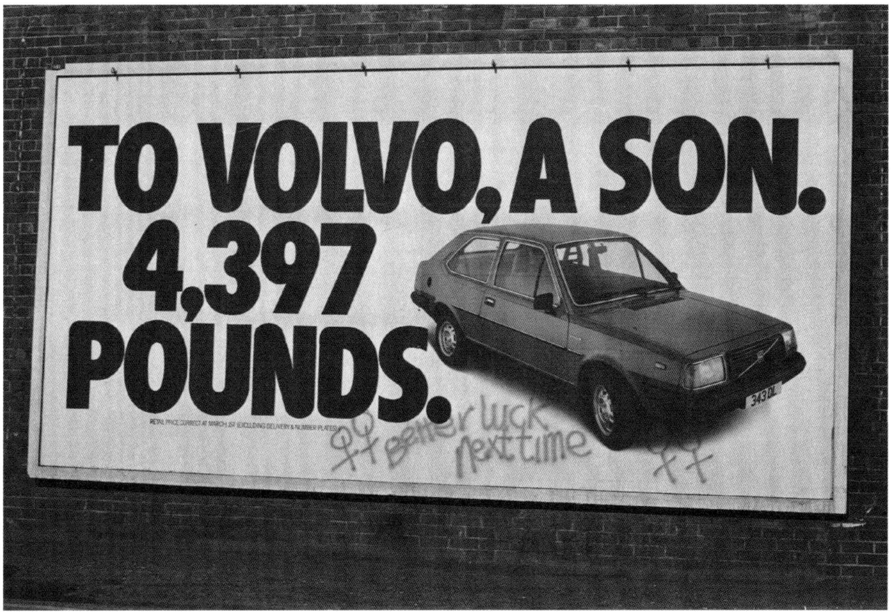

Macho Bore, London 1983
Born Kicking, London 1983
Fiat Ad, London 1979
Squat Against Nuclear Family 1982
To Volvo A Son, London 1982.
Photographs 40.6 × 50.8 (each)

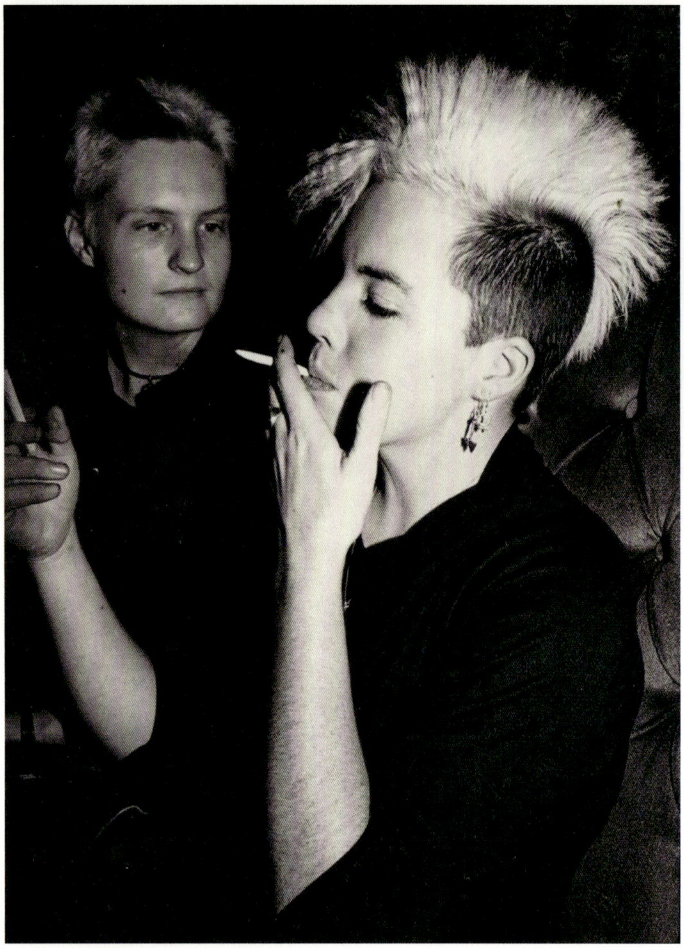

Untitled 1980s. Photograph 28 × 21

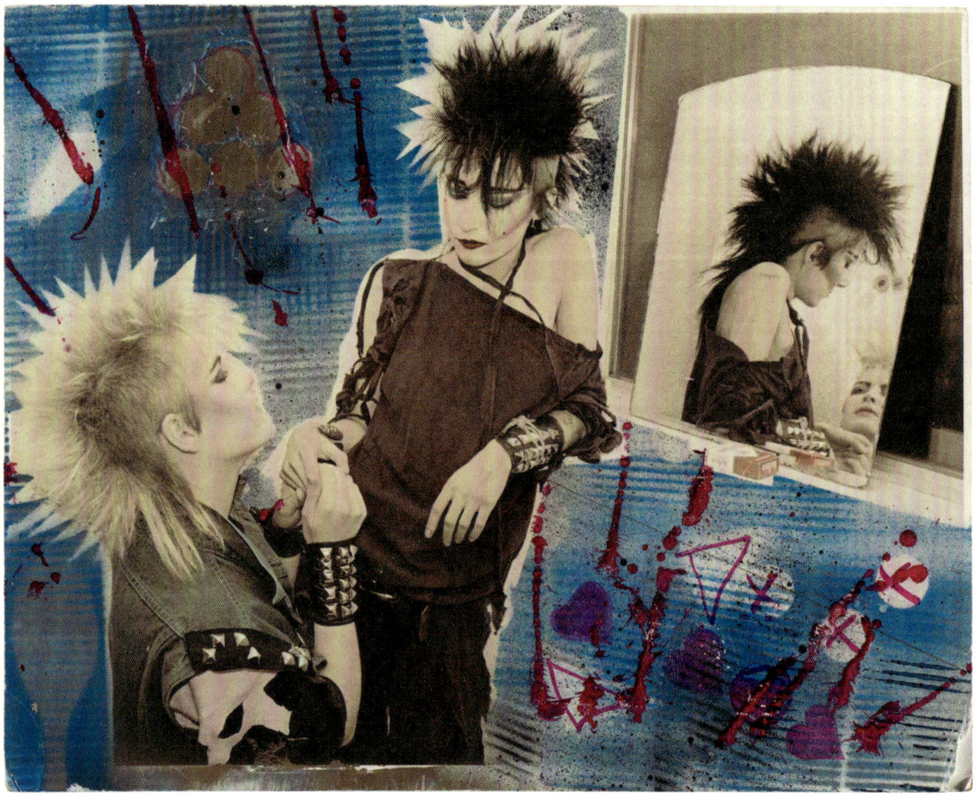

Snake and Linda, London 1983. Photograph 27.5 × 35

Del LaGrace Volcano, formerly Della Grace, is a photographer and activist whose forty-year career has been defined by a working practice informed by the core feminist principles that 'the personal is political' and that 'processes of production are as important as the final product.'

Born in California in 1957, Volcano studied at the San Francisco Art Institute from 1979–81 and obtained a Masters in photographic studies from the University of Derby in 1992. The four C's: Connection, Collaboration, Consent and Care form the scaffolding that intentionally subverts mainstream conventions and provides a visual voice to those who, like the artist, live without the cultural safety nets non-queers take for granted.

Their intention is to give a visual voice to those who have been vilified, neglected and erased. Works such as *Linda and Snake, London* 1983, are part of their strategy of resistance to challenge the homophobic heteronormative culture of the Thatcher era.

Celebratory images of queer subcultural movements have been a core part of the artist's practice throughout their career and are demonstrated in their portraits of members of the lesbian SM Sex & Performance sadomasochistic nightclub Chain Reaction, active in London in the late 1980s until the early 1990s. The photographs of queer women 'cruising' on Hampstead Heath present us with a tender display of solidarity with gay male subculture and give visibility to the 'Rebel Dykes' who insisted on reclaiming their sexuality from the patriarchal gaze.

Volcano has published a number of foundational photographic monographs on gender, sexuality and the queer body, including *Love Bites* (Gay Men's Press, 1991), *The Drag King Book* (Serpent's Tail, 1999), *Sublime Mutations* (Konkursbuchverlag, 2000) and *Femmes of Power: Exploding Queer Femininities* (Serpent's Tail, 2008), in collaboration with leading queer and trans-academics such as Jack Halberstam, Paul Preciado, Jay Prosser, Ulrika Dahl and Mojisola Adebayo.

Their work has widely published in art, academic and feminist art publications since the mid 1990s. In line with their queer feminist, anti-capitalist, anti-racist methodology they make a point of exhibiting in both alternative/queer community venues along with mainstream museums and art spaces.

Their most recent solo exhibition, *Bodies of Resistance*, was at the Tampere Art Museum in Finland in 2023. They now live and work in Sweden.

DEL LAGRACE VOLCANO

Penny Goring (b. 1962) studied fashion writing at the London College of Fashion between 1980 and 81 and graduated in 1994 from Kingston School of Art in London, having studied fine art and specialising in painting. The artist's practice spans painting, drawing, sculpture, poetry, video and internet art. The politics of the home, of gendered space, and particularly of the politics of property ownership and poverty in Conservative Britain are ongoing concerns for the artist, who through her work, explores her experiences of love and loss, of depression, living within the welfare state, alcohol dependency, ageing, sex and single motherhood. These concerns are rarely explicit in the objects that she produces and instead generate emotion. Goring has stated that, 'Everything I have ever done has been centred on feelings. It's easier to communicate emotions by inventing shapes that show how it feels'. She consciously works within her financial limits, using domestic materials, scraps of fabric and old clothes to make her soft sculptures, all of which are sewn by hand. She explains: 'I only want to make things I can do in my room with no help from anyone else'.

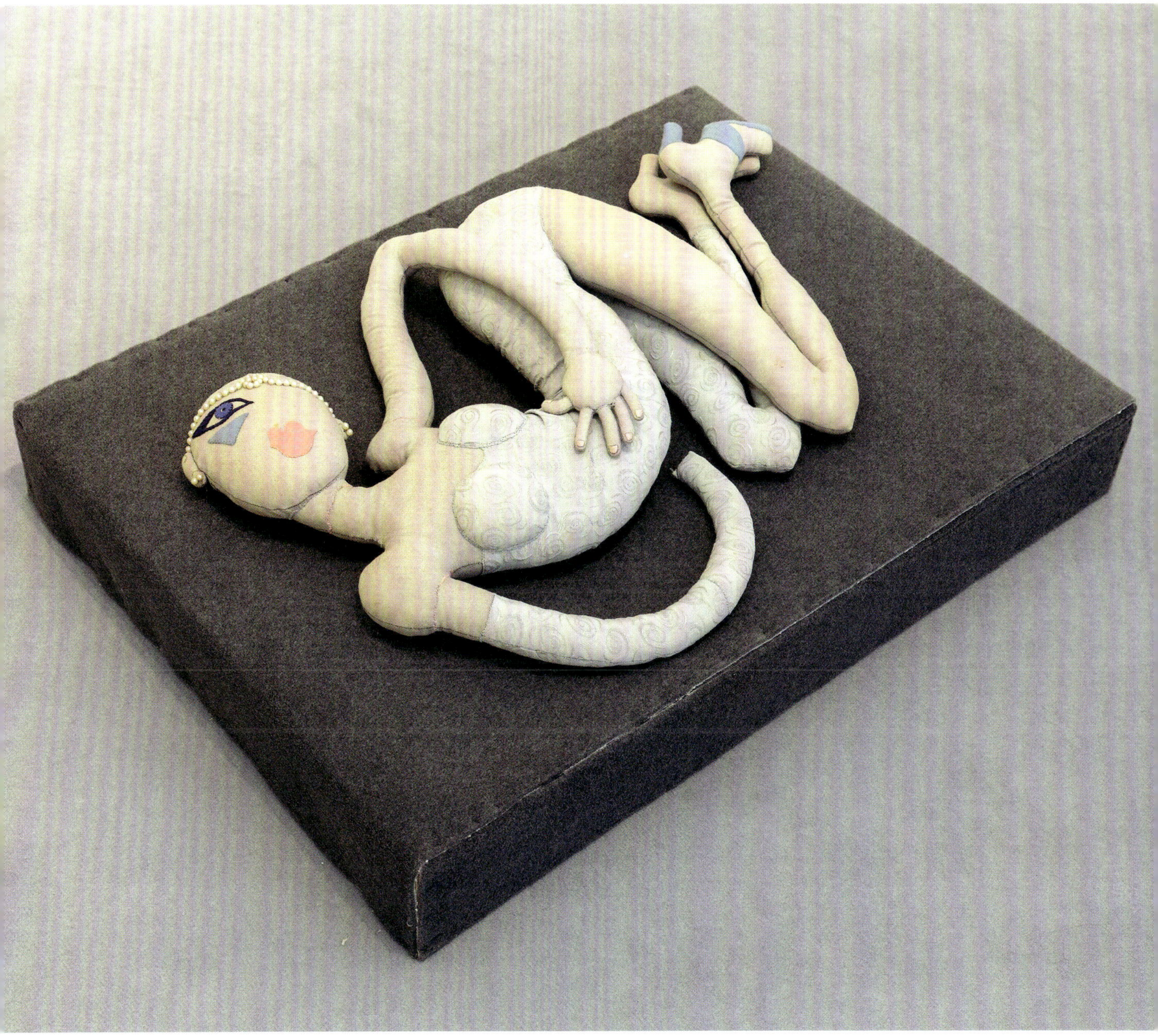

Shock-A-Lolly Dolly 1985. Fabric, stuffed textile ragdoll 14 × 43 × 76

DON'T DO IT FOR LOVE: FEMINIST FILM DISTRIBUTION IN 1980s BRITAIN

ASH REID

'HOW DO YOU IMAGE RELATIONS?'

How can the processes of group organising be made visible, and for what cause? Written halfway through a notebook of initial plans for *Reproductive Labour*, an exhibition on the feminist film and video distributor Cinenova at London's Showroom Gallery in 2011, the answer to this question is crucial when considering the wider histories of feminist film production in Britain. Kept inside a folder labelled simply '2009' in the organisation's paper archives, the notebook also marked the establishment of the Cinenova Working Group, a rotational assemblage of volunteer artists and writers who have sought to keep autonomous an international catalogue of feminist, queer and community film and video, a collection that spans the course of the twentieth century. Precariously reliant on the unpaid time and energy of its individual members, *Reproductive Labour* aimed not only to 'rehabilitate' the individual histories of the collection, but also to bear witness to the operational processes and time involved in 'reproducing' the organisation itself, its material conditions a reflection on the historical relation between the necessity of collective action within feminist film work and the wider systemic structures these in themselves document. Creating a space in which to examine the practices of feminist film and video in relation to present-day economic and political concerns, the exhibition echoed questions that have concerned those involved in their distribution from the beginning, a history that starts also in London in 1979. [1]

'LIST OF PEOPLE TOGETHER – DISCUSS THE PROCESSES WE'VE BEEN EXPERIENCING'

During this year, the filmmaker Lis Rhodes would find herself the only woman on the planning committee for *Film as Film* at the Hayward Gallery, an exhibition observing the history of formal filmmaking and the avant-garde. Rhodes was one of many women involved in the London Filmmakers Co-op, alongside fellow filmmaker and performer Annabel Nicolson and writer and organiser Felicity Sparrow, to whom she would also expand the Hayward invitation, joined later by Jane Clarke, Jeanette Iljon, Mary Pat Leece, Pat Murphy and Susan Stein. Research focused on the early women filmmaking pioneers Maya Deren, Germaine Dulac and Alice Guy, with a plan to incorporate and exhibit a changing display of responses by contemporary women filmmakers alongside. Moving away from what Rhodes described as 'a particular concept of feminine or feminist filmmaking', with work grouped together under the superficial categorisation of their gender, consideration would be given to the cultural and political climate in which they were made, an attempt to address not only the otherwise patriarchal inflections of the show, but historical depiction more generally.[2] Finding their ideas to be merely 'tolerated rather than considered seriously', as they would later write in a collective statement for the exhibition catalogue, and with no flexibility given to how they could be incorporated into the space overall, the group were left with no choice but to remove their research from the show, in protest against the apparent lack of value felt for these concerns.[3] 'Women appear,' wrote Rhodes, 'but on whose terms?'.[4]

1 See Mira Mattar, 'Out of the Past: An Interview with Cinenova', Text, *Mute* (Mute Publishing Limited, 28 June 2011), https://www.metamute.org/editorial/articles/out-past-interview-cinenova, accessed Jul. 2023.
2 Lis Rhodes, 'Whose History?', in Phillip Drummond (ed.), *Film as Film: Formal Experiment in Film, 1910–1975*, exh. cat., Hayward Gallery, London 1979, p.119.
3 Annabel Nicolson, Felicity Sparrow, Jane Clarke and others, 'Woman and the Formal Film', in Drummond 1979, p.118.
4 Rhodes 1979, p.119.

This is our statement:
The gesture of withholding our work and the presentation in its stead of a statement of opposition is the only form of intervention open to us. It was impossible to allow the Arts Council to present our work as if there had been no struggle, as if it had been nurtured in the spirit of public patronage.[5]

'HOW DO WE REPRESENT A FEMINIST POSITION?'

Desiring rather to set their own terms of circulation, shortly after, in 1980, the women involved in the Hayward action would go on to form the film and video distribution group Circles, becoming part of several strands of feminist production and action fighting back against the discriminatory legislation and workplace disputes of 1970s and 80s Britain. Fundamental to what art historian Griselda Pollock termed a 'series of tactical activities' deployed by women's art in this period, Circles's initial focus was on 're-presentation' of historical works, bringing them back into conversation with those of contemporary practitioners. Distributing film and video in relation to the myriad social, political and economic situations women in Britain found themselves in, the screening space specifically could act as a catalyst for a 'radically different order of knowledge',[6] with work that spoke directly to the experiences of the audience and invited analysis and discussion beyond the act of simple spectatorship, including the very category of 'woman' itself.[7]

'HOW TO ADDRESS THE MECHANISMS OF "DISTRIBUTION". HOW THINGS BECOME VISIBLE'

Operating out of Sparrow's flat in London and hosting screenings in Four Corners, a film and photography centre that had begun life as a squat in Tower Hamlets, Circles promoted not only film- and video-making but also performance and slide-tape work, seeing the crossover in practice for many of their artists. Every woman taken into distribution was also counted as a member of the group and given a say in organisational matters. Over the course of the decade, the emerging prominence and decreasing costs of video production saw the group able to distribute works not only via theatrical venues but also through schools, trade unions, women's centres, educational venues and more, allowing the group to acquire and produce curated programmes of works dealing with subjects from women's mental health to issues of representation for Black women in the UK. This ethos would also be echoed by another feminist distribution group in London at the time, Cinema of Women, which sought, through these routes of screening, to 'demystify' the ways in which films were produced and seen, encouraging more and more women to get involved in the process of making. Both groups would manage on local council funding that supported community arts practice until 1987, with the British Film Institute stepping in when rate-capping brought in by the Conservative government would limit spending in mostly Labour-led constituencies.

5 Nicolson et al 1979, p.118.
6 Griselda Pollock, 'Feminism and Modernism', in Rozsika Parker and Griselda Pollock (eds.), *Framing Feminism: Art and the Women's Movement 1970–85*, London 1987, p.81.
7 To write of the category of 'woman' is difficult; as Denise Riley says, it is a 'volatile collectivity', a surface-level grouping that tends to obscure the many social, racial and economic factors that differentiate the individual subjects within it. 'Woman' thus cannot be trusted as a category in and of itself, and, especially in the present, the idea of distribution networks based on its particular specifications is hardly without question. Its shorthanded volatility, however, is perhaps where it is also possible to find the power of networks of groups like Circles, whose actions coming together under this category allow for the exploration of these complex social relations in potentially different formations to those specified by capitalist forms of reproduction. What these distribution networks offer is not a fixed idea of what womanhood is told it is, but rather a changing encyclopedia of possible routes out of such stagnant identity roles. See Denise Riley, *'Am I That Name?': Feminism and the Category of 'Women' in History*, Basingstoke 1988.

CIRCLES

113 Roman Road London E2 0HU

CIRCLES and CINEMA OF WOMEN present:
a series of programmes on

WOMEN AND WORK

Thursday, 14th July, at 7.30 pm:

WHO NEEDS NURSERIES - WE DO! by Leeds Animation (GB 1977, 10 mins)
CLOTHESLINES by Roberta Cantow (USA 1982, 30 mins)
IT'S JUST A COMPLIMENT, LUV by Amanda King (video, Australia 1981, 27 mins)
HERE COMES THE BRIDE by Frances Bowyer (GB 1982, 30 mins)

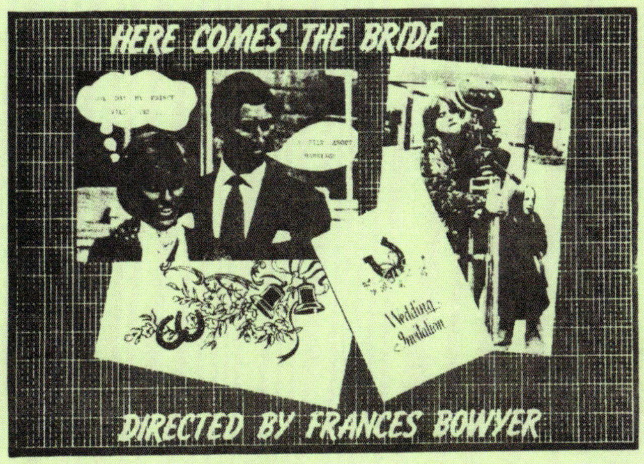

The programme looks at the conditions and expectations of women's work and how traditionally their labout - whether in the home or outside - has been geared to the servicing of men and the nuclear family. The same values placed by society on the "invisible" (unpaid) labour of domestic work are reinforced in other "visible" areas of work outside the home: from unequal opportunities to the sexual harassment often experienced by women at work.

Women-only screening with coffee and discussion

Admission £1.50 / 75p unwaged

Further details ring: 01-981 6828
Creche - but ring in advance

GLC funded

Women and Work: Programme detailing films in the Circles and Cinema of Women of Women screening c.1982

'WE SHOULD ALL GO THROUGH THE BUSINESS PLAN AND ADD PRACTICAL WORK IS IMPACTING ON THE DISCUSSIONS'

In this environment, arts funding would in many ways come to replace a lot of community support and care schemes previously provided by the welfare state. With 'integrative practice' a buzzword, the grassroots organising style of the independent film workshop movements from the previous few decades found itself formalised into funding streams such as the Workshop Declaration and the Enterprise Allowance Scheme,[8] financing filmmaking collectives to also act as community education hubs, with many run by – and thus focused directly on the politics of – women.[9] Taking place within the terms of the wider neoliberal project of the Thatcher government, however, meant such schemes would be financed on a fixed-term basis only, assuming an easy transition into a commercial market previously proven to be at odds with the working style and content of the collectives, a situation that had necessitated their funding in the first place. For similar reasons, groups such as Circles and Cinema of Women would also find themselves with less and less access to funding by the end of the decade, despite their importance to the continuing promotion, and thus commercial success, of this work. By 1991 the two would be forced to merge through a series of financial restrictions that would make both groups untenable on their own, working as they were with inherently non-commercial material.

8 Some examples of these groups include Sheffield Film Co-op, Vera Media in Leeds, Women's Independent Cinema House (W.I.T.C.H.) in Liverpool, and the Leeds Animation Workshop. Their videos continue to be distributed by Cinenova. More about these works can be found at cinenova.org.

9 In an interview with *Feminist Art News* in 1988, Vera Media's founder Al Garthwaite goes as far as to state that the group had specifically avoided becoming a workshop under the Declaration, its emphasis on integrative practice forcing filmmakers to perform 'cheap part-time' social work that stopped other collectives from actually being able to produce films, a weight that fell heavily on women at the time.

10 For a wider study of this scene, see B. Ruby Rich, *New Queer Cinema: The Director's Cut*, Durham, NC, 2013.

'DESIRE ⟷ MOBILISE → ARTIST RUN SPACES
VOLUNTEER RUN SPACES
PEOPLE FURTHER UP THE CHAIN
CIRCUITS OF DESIRE
CREDITS & ATTRIBUTION – VALUE SYSTEM – WHO BENEFITS, WHO DOES THE WORK
DO IT FOR LOVE, WHEN YOU HAVE ANOTHER SOURCE OF INCOME'

Cinenova would be the organisation to emerge from this merger, awarded funding on a 'mixed-economy' model that would finally manoeuvre the group towards a more mainstream theatrical market, in the process partially moving it away from the explicit feminist aims of the previous two groups. Indeed, there was a strange commercial viability to the queer work Cinenova came to distribute during this period. Former Cinenova employee Helen DeWitt saw this as the result of women's film and video becoming what she describes as 'more playful' over the 1990s, freed from its previous definitions, despite – or perhaps in the face of – increasing state-sanctioned homophobia and sexism which otherwise sought to divest from the very schemes it had set up the generation before to address such inequalities in the arts. With a growing international circuit of gay and lesbian film festivals in which to distribute, film and video moved beyond the agitprop of previous decades into work that reflected the everyday lives of the audiences who watched it.[10] Nevertheless, even with the popularity of this new genre, and a burgeoning market in which to promote it, the works remained within a wider social setting that shunned their existence, an effacement that would in turn cause Cinenova to remain reliant on public funding. By 2000, this situation would once again become unsustainable: with the creation of the UK Film Council and its focus on regionalisation and commercial sustainability leading Cinenova's core funder London Film and Video Development Agency to also alter its funding guidelines, the group would find itself without efficient financial backing, leaving its paid workers no choice but to cease its operations and wind up the business completely by 2002.

'HOW DO WE COMMUNICATE THE POLITICS OF 'WORKING TOGETHER'?

To work together from a feminist position is perhaps to enact what Griselda Pollock has termed a 'traumatic challenge' to hegemonic forms of history, its repeated emergence not only as a contestation to social order, but as a traumatic reassessment for those 'summoned by this movement in thought and action to a political and cultural collectivity', whose own subjectivity is undone as its repetition undoes the historical subject of feminism.[11] Pollock has called this the 'unthinkable event' of feminist memory, the 'colliding temporalities and coinhabited fantasies' of those who remember interrupting the chronological form of 'wave and generations' that currently structures the past.[12] Much like its predecessors, the present status of Cinenova raises ongoing questions of access and exploitation in the arts, not only in terms of gender but also along lines of class and race: who can afford – and who is expected – to work for free? With labour and identity becoming ever more marketable themes in the field of contemporary art, yet with even less possibility of renumeration for those involved in its production, another question from the notebook of 2009 feels pertinent to revisit: 'why', exactly, 'a separate distributor for women?'. As former working group member Marina Vishmidt has written, the collective actions at the heart of feminism bring up questions of what it means to identify exactly with a subject category you wish to also take apart, the threat of paradoxically being subsumed by it never far off.[13] Revisiting the collective struggles documented in the feminist film and video work of the 1970s and 80s, the current turn towards social reproduction observable once again in a myriad of arts organisations makes confronting the gendering logics of these modes of production more important than ever.

1 Griselda Pollock, s Feminism a Trauma, Bad Memory, or a Virtual uture?', *Differences* 27, o. 2 (1 Sept. 2016): 27, ttps://doi.org/10.1215/ 0407391-3621697.

2 Pollock, p.43.

3 'There is the truism that vhatever doesn't kill capital nly makes it stronger, and hat also goes for "excessive emands" such as Wages or Housework or the basic ncome which have been mplemented only to the egree that they enhance he surveillance capacities f the state on behalf of apital's ability to exploit he recipients of such enefits'.' Marina Vishmidt, Counter(Re-)Productive abour', in *We Have Our Own oncept of Time and Motion*, ondon 2011, p.10.

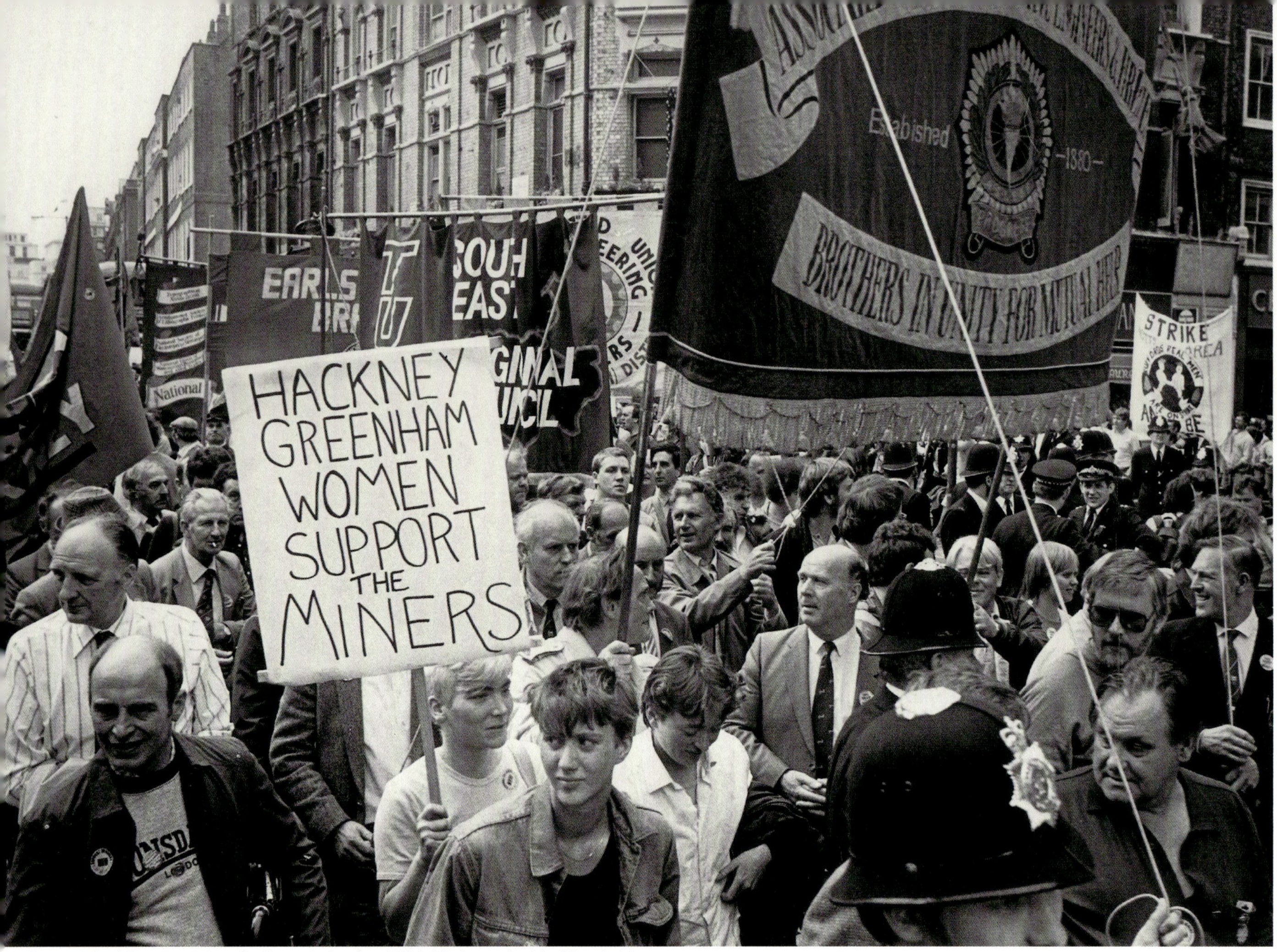

Support for Miners march on Parliament, London 1984. Photographed by Maggie Murray.

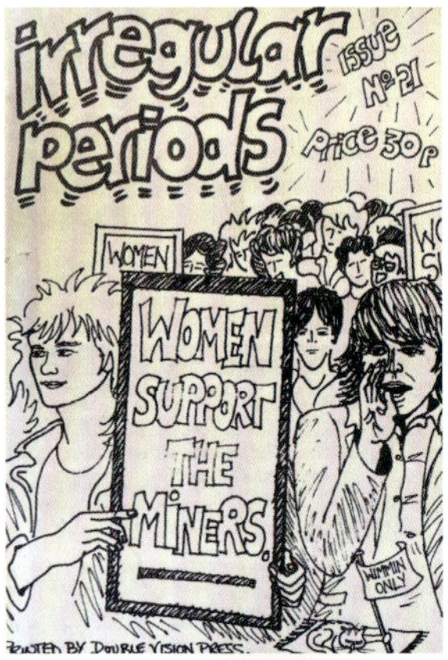

1

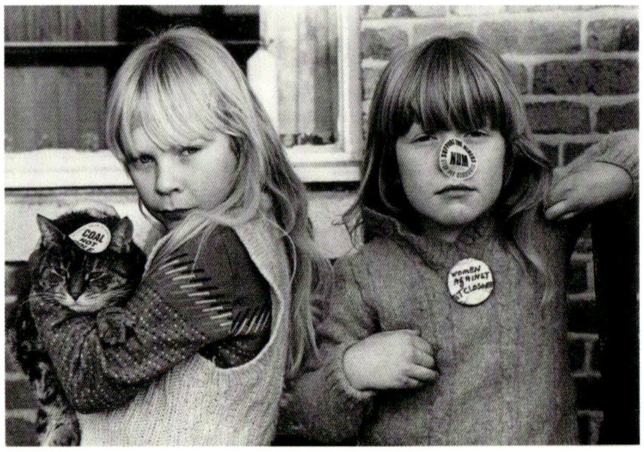

2

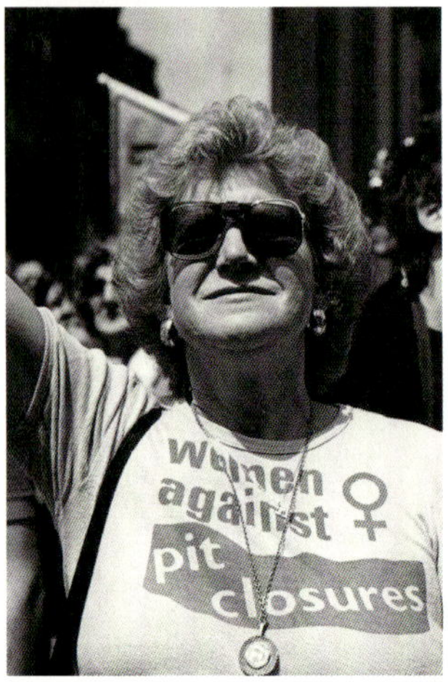

3

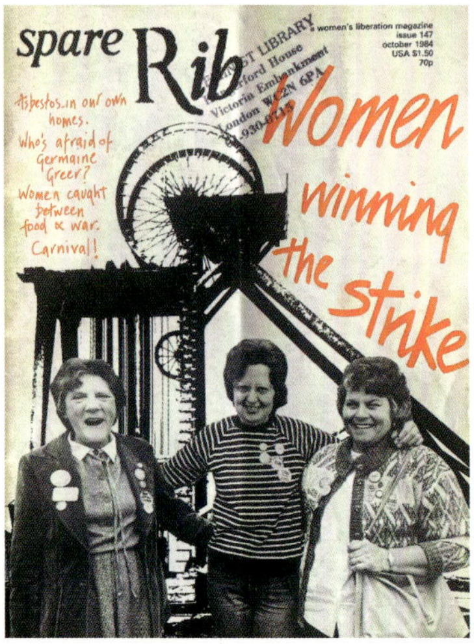

4

Coal not Dole

At its peak, following the First World War, there were one million miners in the UK. By the beginning of the 1980s, following years of decline in the coal industry, there were 200,000. In March 1984, after the National Coal Board announced plans for a wave of pit closures, miners under the leadership of Arthur Scargill began a series of financially and emotionally devastating year-long strikes. While all the miners were male, their female partners and family members acted as a powerful supporting force, setting up soup kitchens, campaigning and raising money. While mining communities were mostly located in remote areas, there was a groundswell of support throughout the country, with feminist, gay and lesbian activists joining in solidarity, aware that the governmental crack down on union activity and privatisation signalled a significant move to the right for British politics. Determined to break the miners' union, the Government bitterly fought against the miners, unleashing the media, the police and legislature to end their actions. On 3 March 1985, Scargill and the National Union of Miners voted to end the strike after 362 days. Thatcher's government had made not a single concession.

1 *Irregular Periods*, Bradford Women's Newsletter, no.21, 1984.
2 Mandy and Michelle Tomlinson, Ollerton Colliery, Nottinghamshire, 1980s. Photographed by Brenda Prince.
3 Women Against Pit Closures demonstration, London 1984. Photographed by Maggie Murray.
4 *Spare Rib* (a women's liberation magazine), no.147, October 1984.

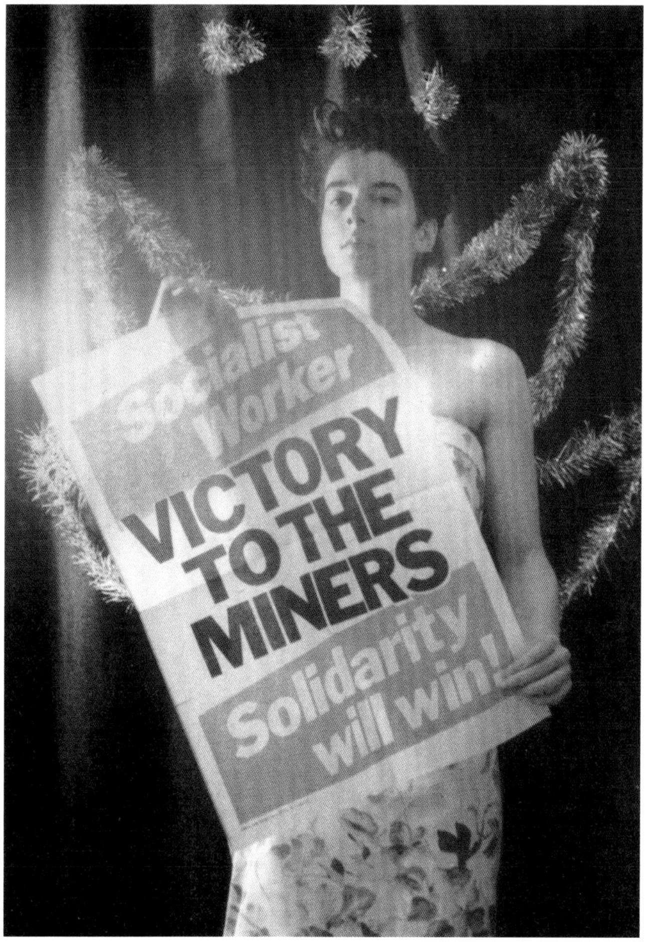

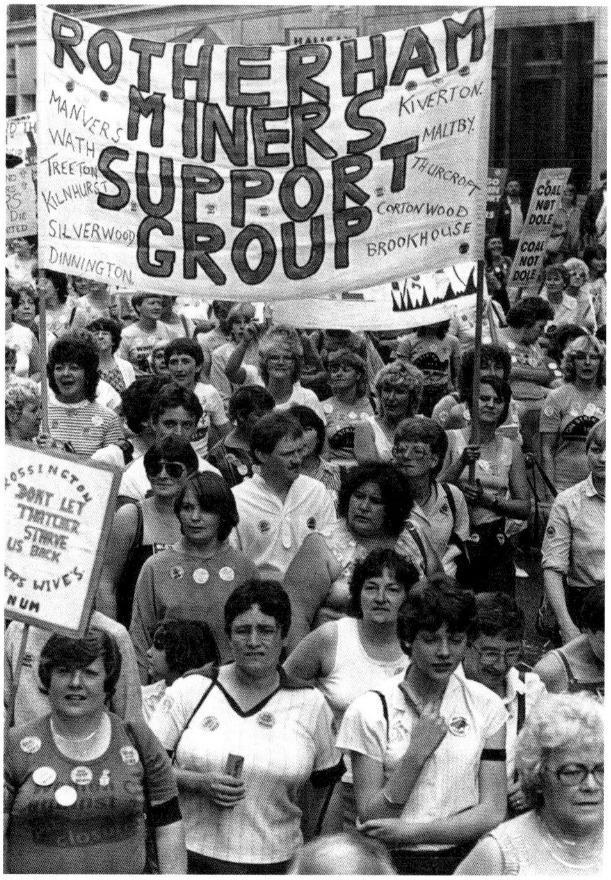

Above: Miners' Strike supporters, 1984 . Photographed by Jenny Matthews.

Above: Alison Lloyd, *SUPPORT THE MINERS, Solidarity will win!* 1984.

Below: Women's picket at Bevercotes Colliery, Nightshift, February 1985. Photographed by Brenda Prince.

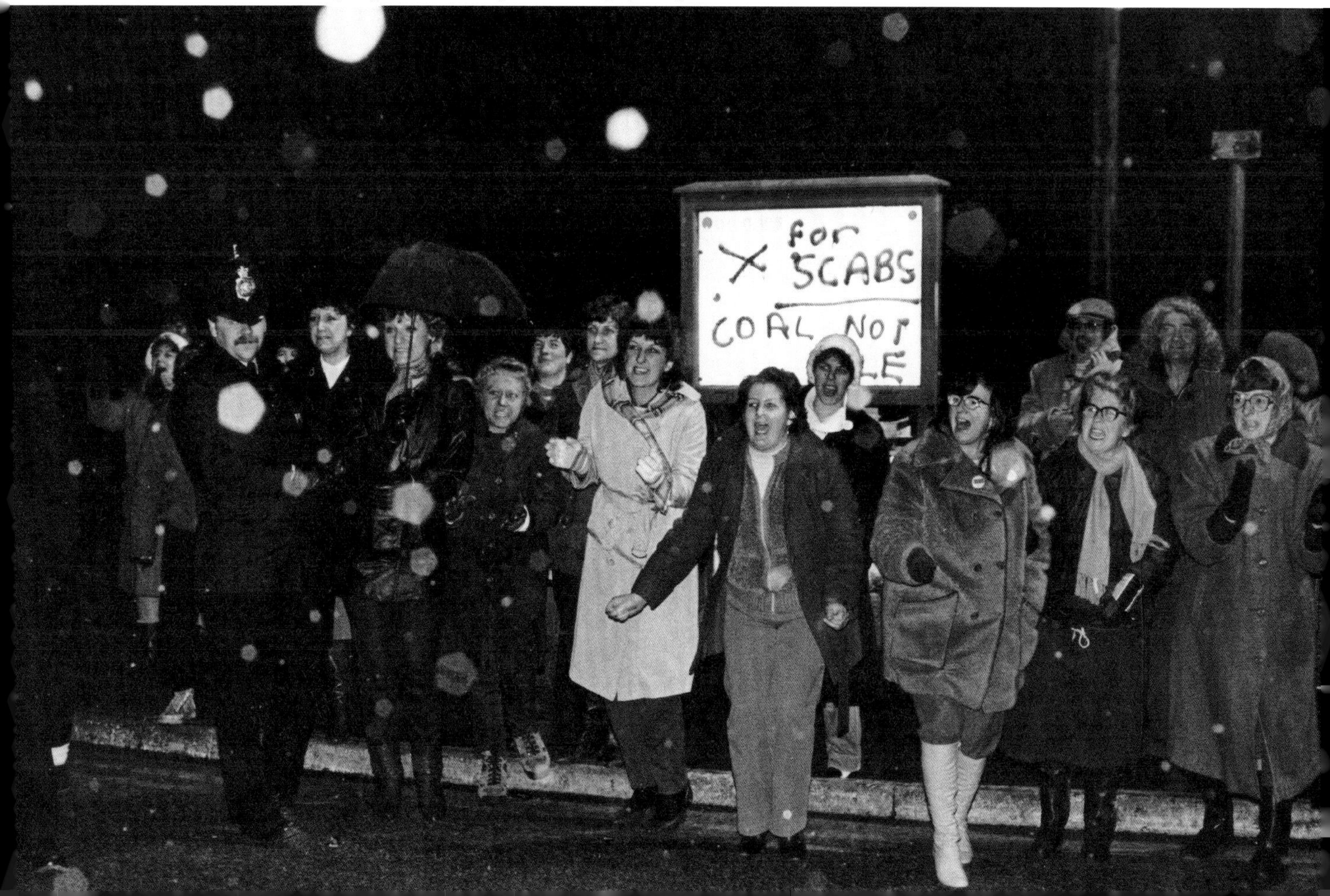

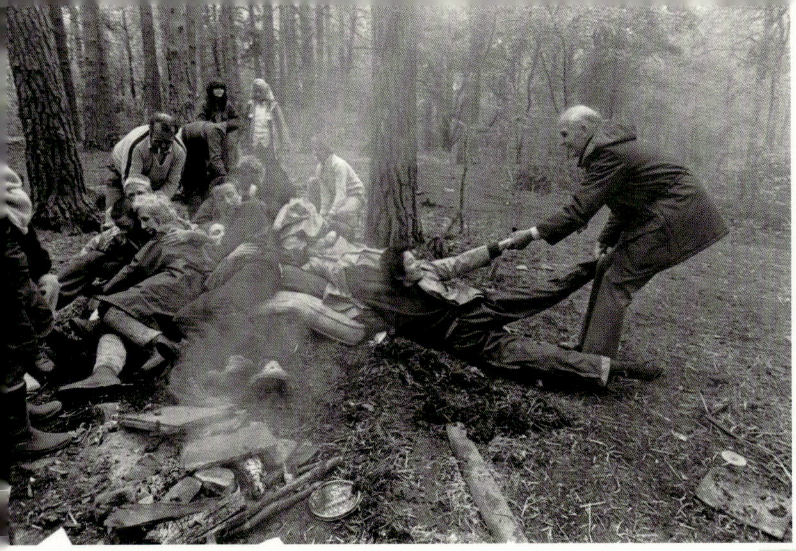

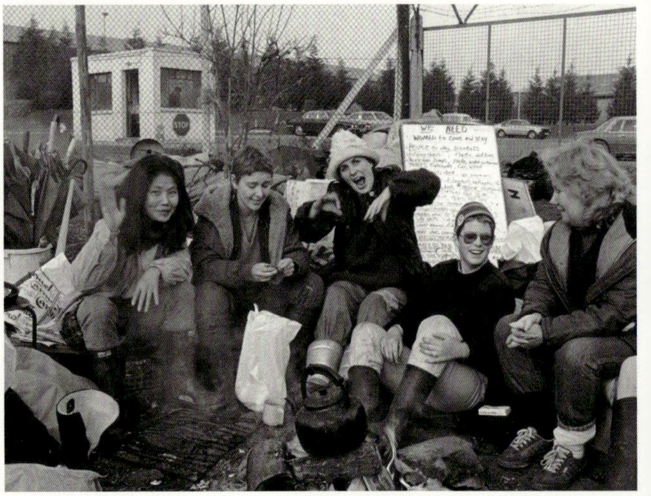

Greenham Common Women's Peace Camp, 1982. Photographed by Brenda Prin

Above: Bailiffs removing women at Greenham Women's Peace Camp, 1985. Photographed by Pam Isherwood.

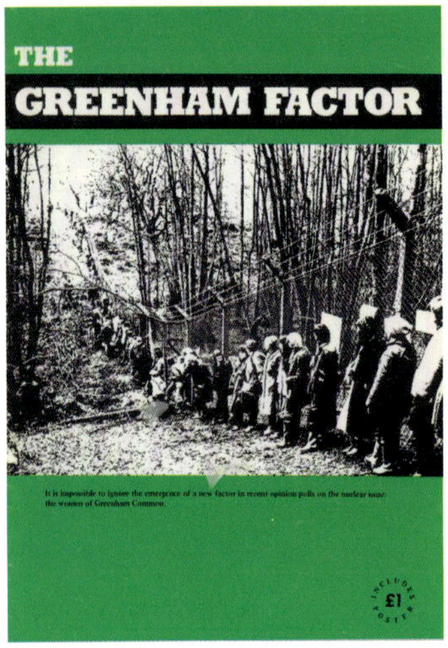

1

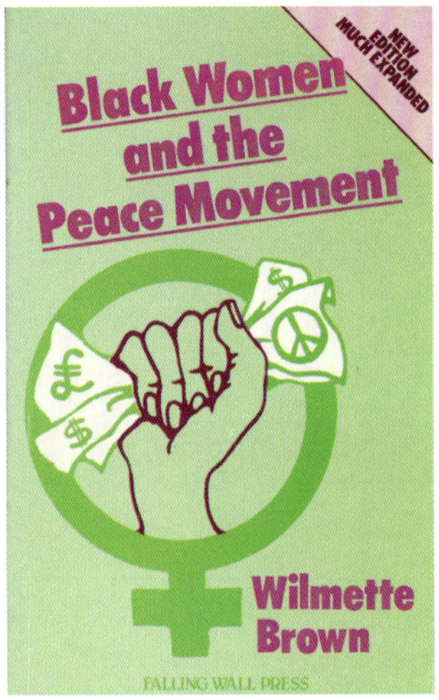

2

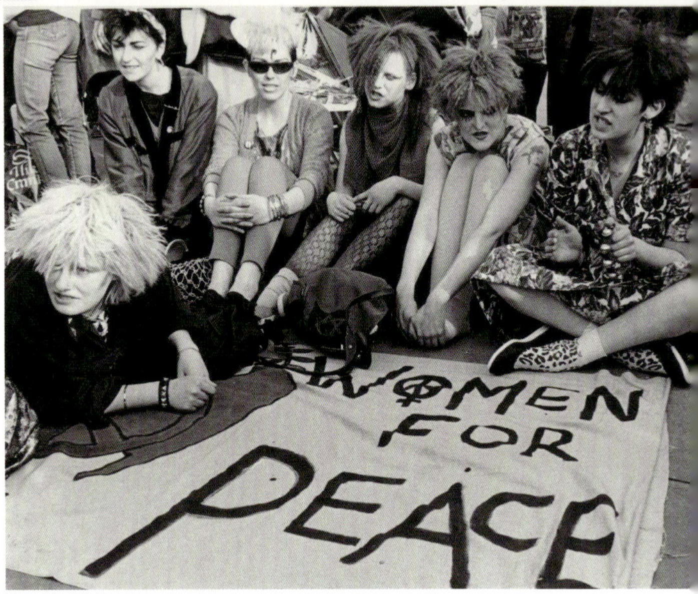

Group with 'Women for Peace' sign, 1983. Photographed by Jenny Matthews.

Women dancing on the silos at dawn after invading the base, New Year's Day 1983. Photographed by Raissa Page.

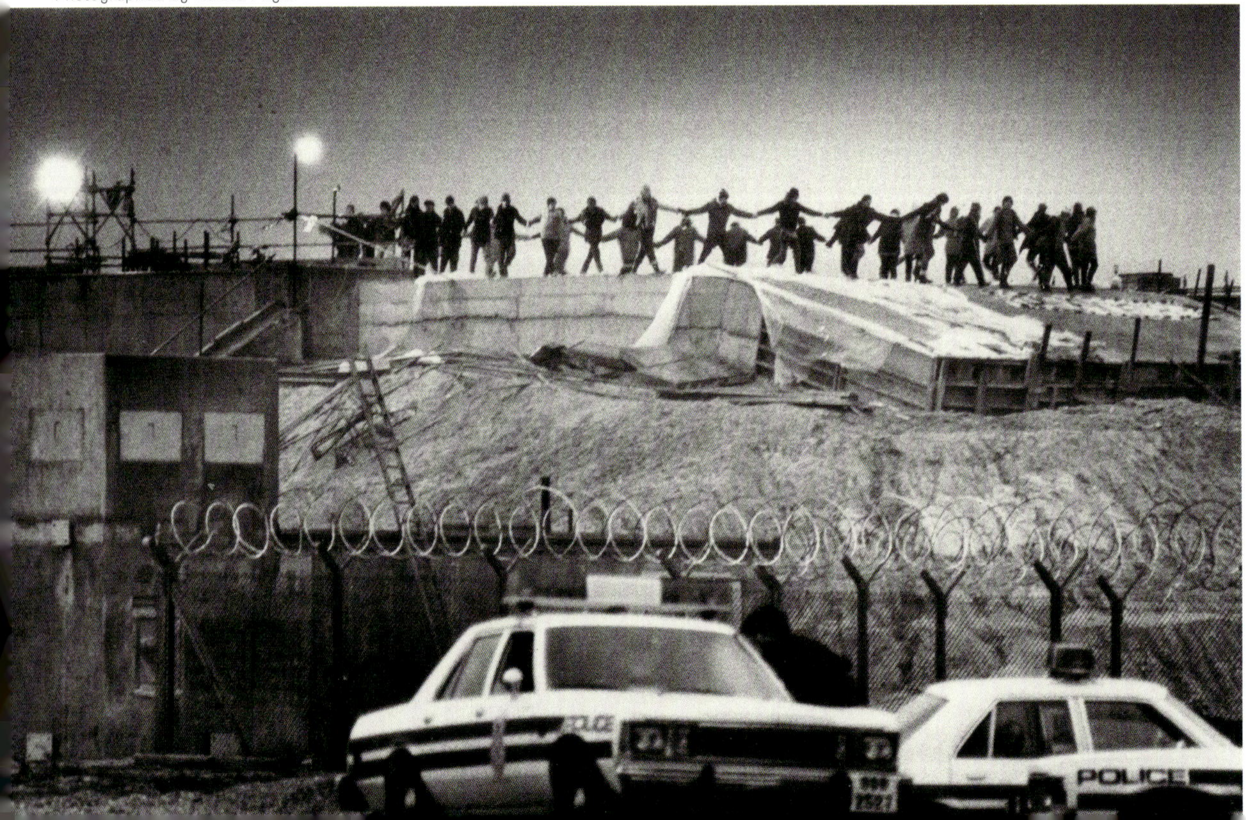

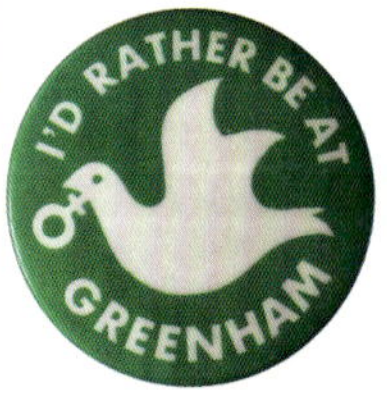

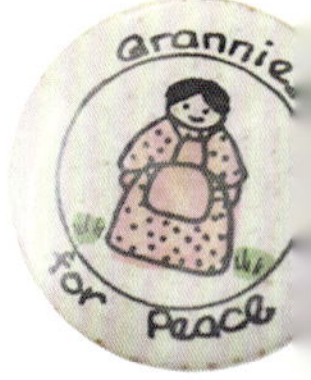

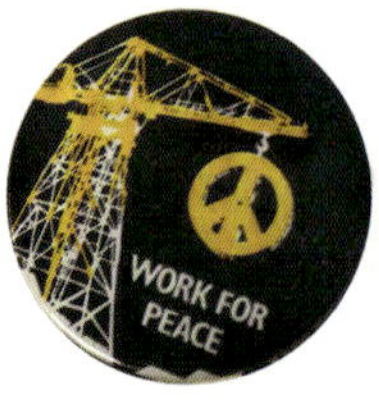

Greenham Women Are Everywhere

The Greenham Common Women's Peace Camp was established in September 1981 after a Welsh group, Women for Life on Earth, walked 120 miles from Cardiff to the Greenham Common military base in Newbury, Berkshire, to protest the decision of the UK government to store cruise missiles there. Many women chained themselves to the fence on arrival, while others established a peace camp outside the base which remained occupied from 1981 to 2000. Greenham Common was a meeting point for women from all walks of life and while some stayed for years, many dropped in and out as their personal circumstances allowed.

In 1982 over 30,000 women took part in the event 'Embrace the Base', gathering to link arms around the perimeter's barbed-wire fencing. They affixed a variety of personal objects to the fences – baby clothes, bottles, teething rings, family photographs and stuffed animals – to demonstrate the human toll of nuclear catastrophe. In Scotland, Faslane Peace Camp, near Helensburgh in Argyll and Bute, has been continuously occupied since 12 June 1982. It was set up in protest of the location of Trident missile warheads at the Faslane military base. Peace camps were often seen as particularly white, middle-class places as women needed a degree of privilege to be able to join them. Many Black women were thus ambivalent about the actions taking place, citing that decolonial narratives and the ecological destruction of non-Western countries remained of little interest to the majority of white feminist groups.

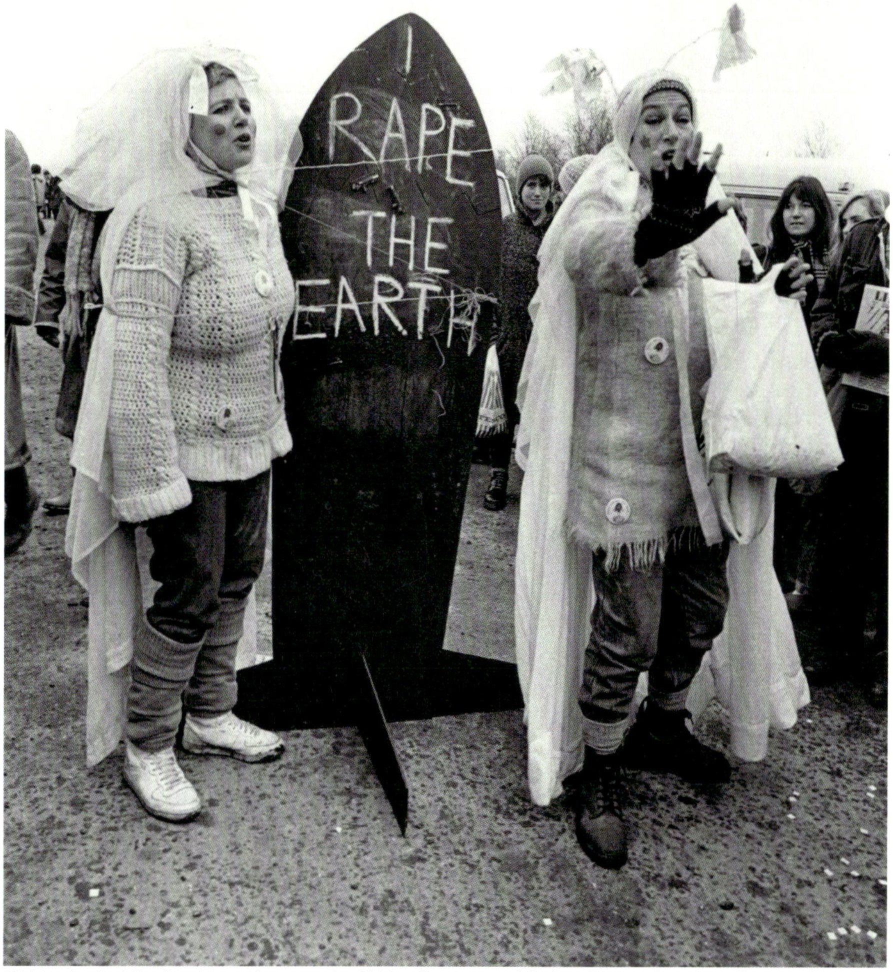

'Brides Against the Bomb': performance by Shirley Cameron and Evelyn Silver at Greenham Common Women's Peace Camp, 1983. Photographed by Pam Isherwood.

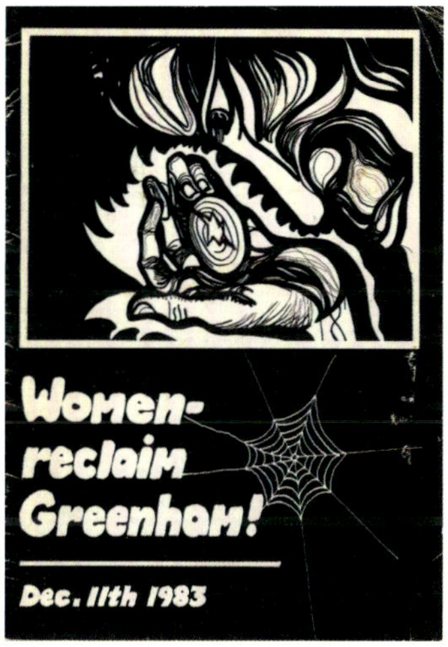

3

Map of Greenham Common

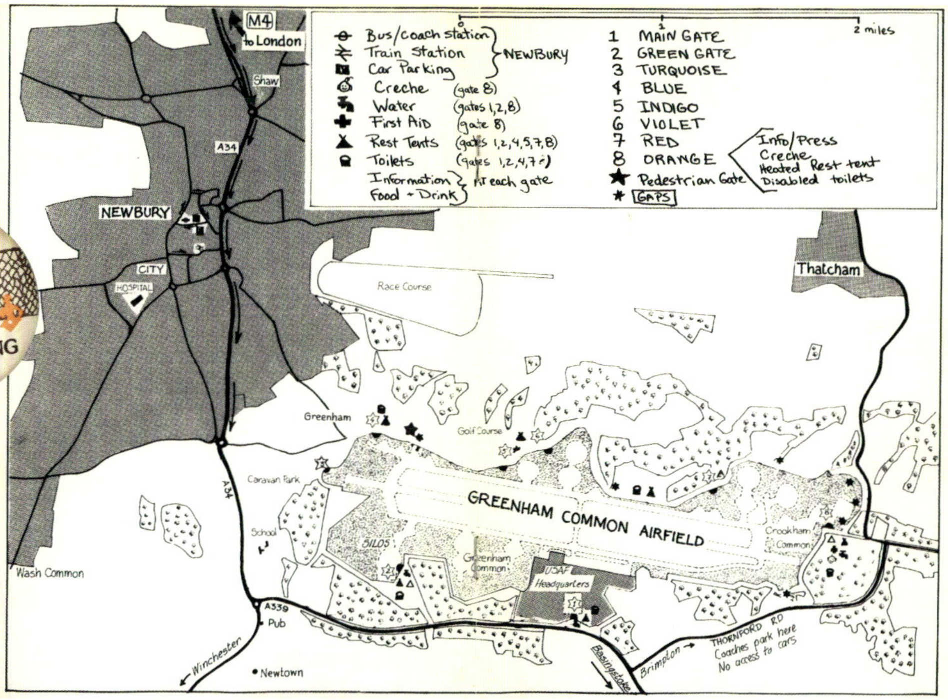

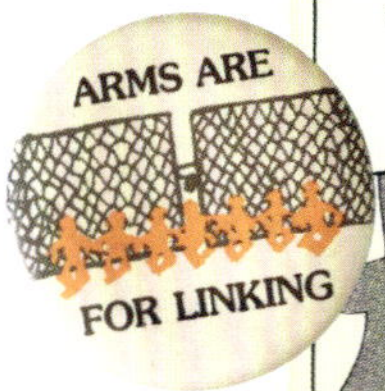

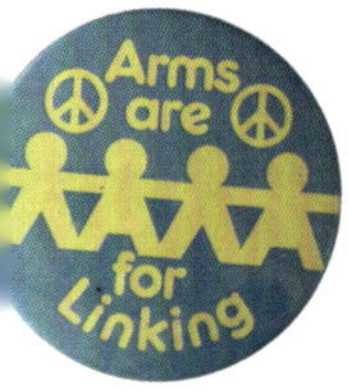

1 *The Greenham Factor*, published by Greenham Print Prop, London 1984.
2 *Black Women and the Peace Movement* by Wilmette Brown, Falling Wall Press, 1984 .
3 *Women Reclaim Greenham* pamphlet from the day of action on the 11 December 1983, when an estimated 50,000 women gathered at Greenham Common and encircled the military base.

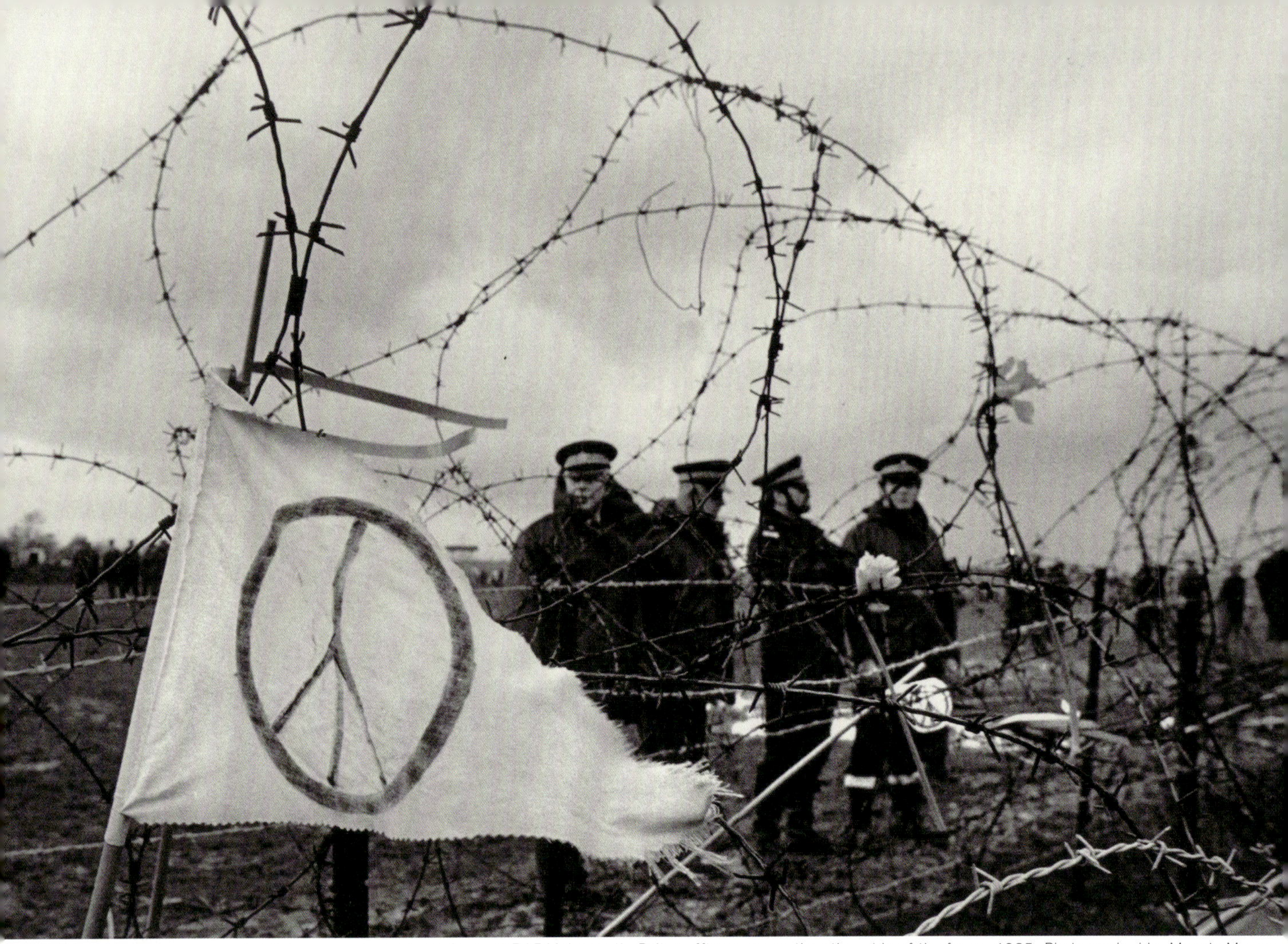

Flag featuring the peace symbol flying near a barbed wire fence at RAF Molesworth. Police officers are on the other side of the fence, 1985. Photographed by Maggie Murray.

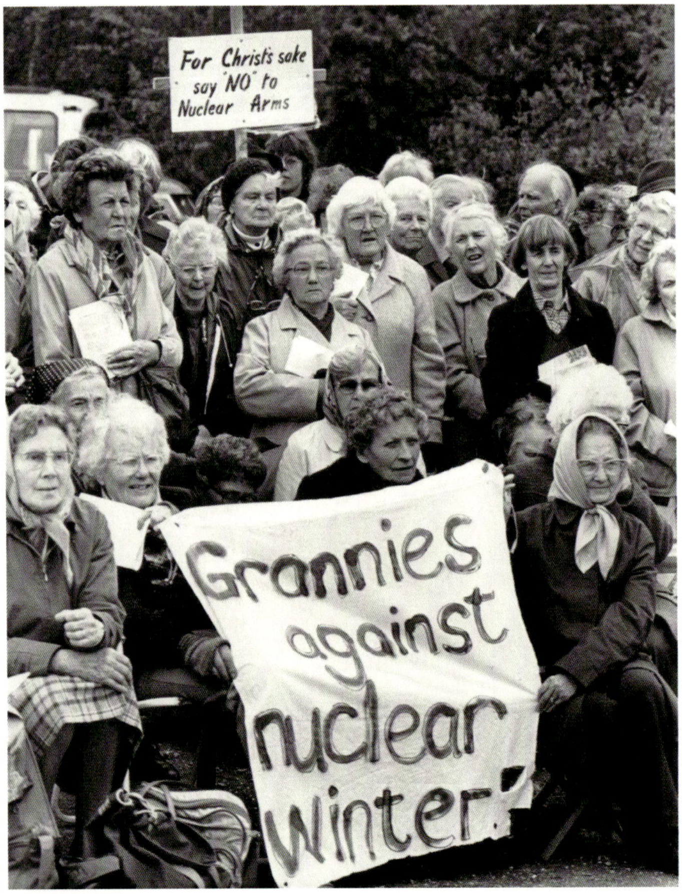

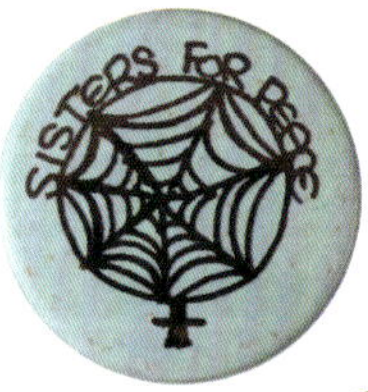

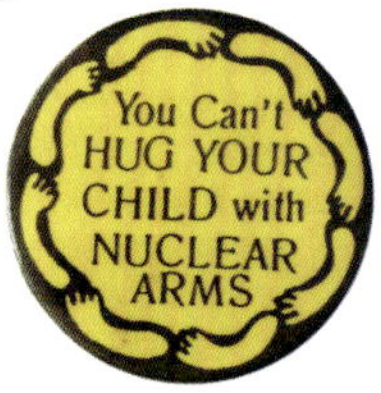

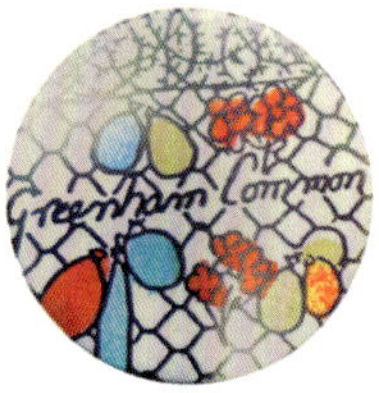

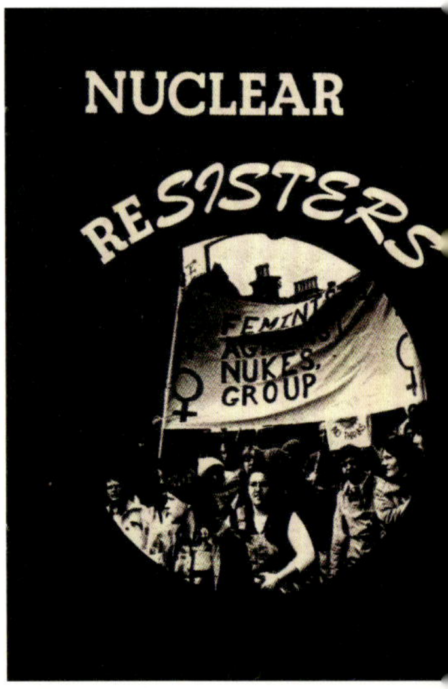

Nuclear Re-Sisters, published by Onlywomen Press, a 'women's liberation publishing and printing group, producing work by and for women as part of creating a feminist communication network and, ultimately, a feminist revolution'.

Pensioners at Greenham Common's Orange Gate, 1984, with elderly women to the front of the photograph holding a 'Grannies against nuclear winter' banner. Nearly 1,000 pensioners visited Greenham Common on the day of the photograph to express concern about a nuclear winter and the survival of the younger generation. After singing peace songs around a camp fire they held a silent vigil. Photographed by Melanie Friend.

n 1974, upon seeing an advert in a radical women's iberation magazine asking or women interested in orming a group to explore and combat negative images of women in the media, hree ex-art students ormed the screenprinting collective See Red Women's Workshop. See Red (active 1974–90) set out to make posters that tackled sexist stereotypes and created positive and challenging alternatives, and spent the next sixteen years making some of the most powerful and instantly-recognisable protest posters of their ime. See Red worked with over forty-five different women during this time, with four or five women n the workshop at any one time. Making posters hat were accessible and affordable, all work was authored collectively with no hierarchy, and no one ndividual taking credit, and all tasks and skills were shared. Influenced by heir members' respective nterests, poster themes centred around childcare, housework, gender roles, dentity, sexuality, class and race, and broadened out to include national and nternational themes supporting women's wider struggles for change. While mainly working on printing and selling their own posters, See Red also did service printing for he local community and LGBTQI+ groups to fund heir work, focusing ncreasingly on this kind of work from 1984 to 1990.

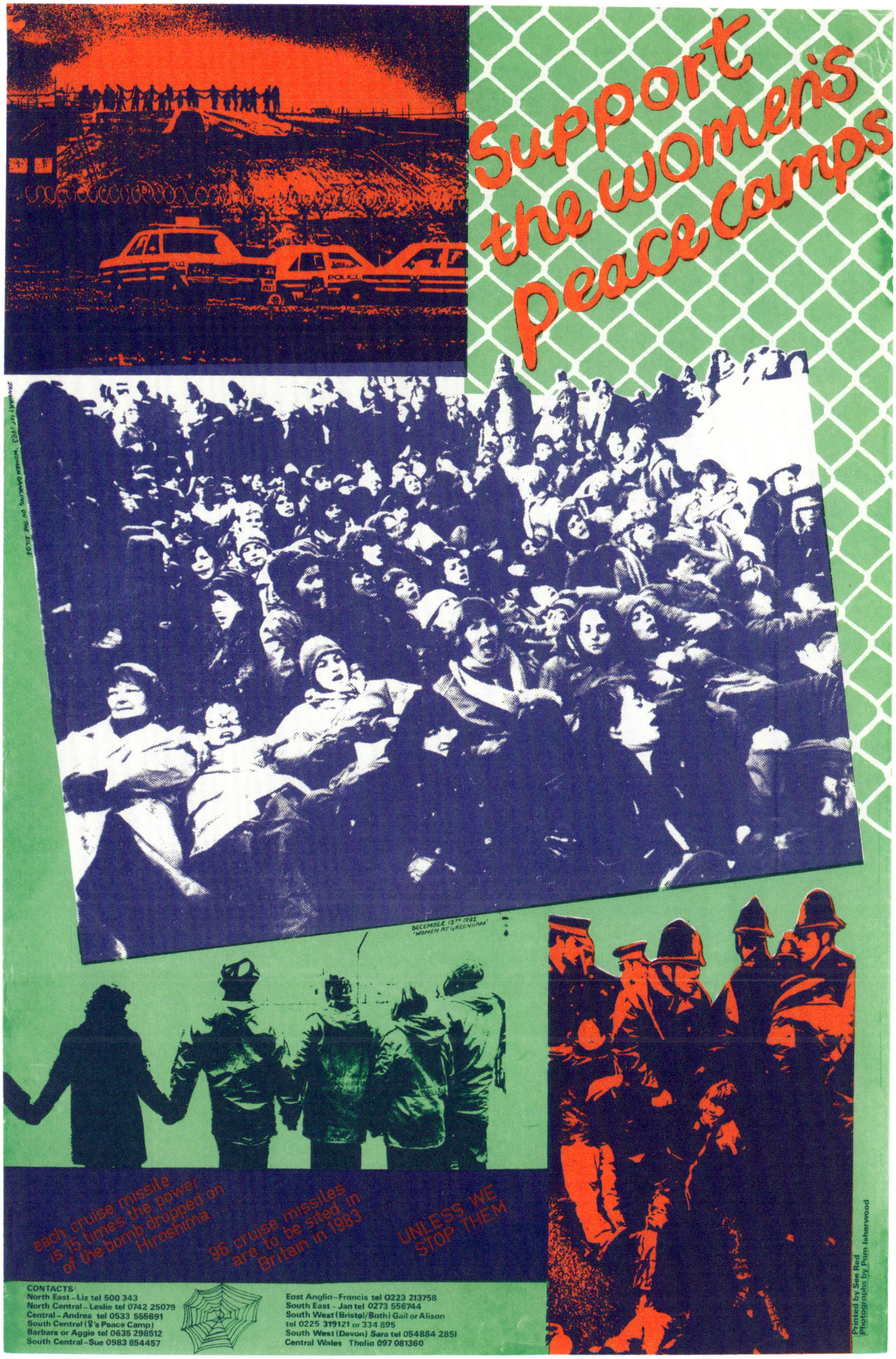

Support the Women's Peace Camps 1983. Screenprint on paper 74 × 50.5

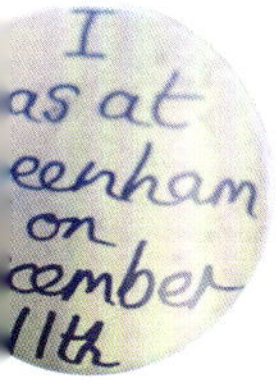

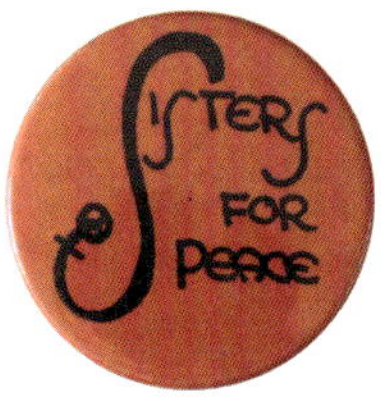

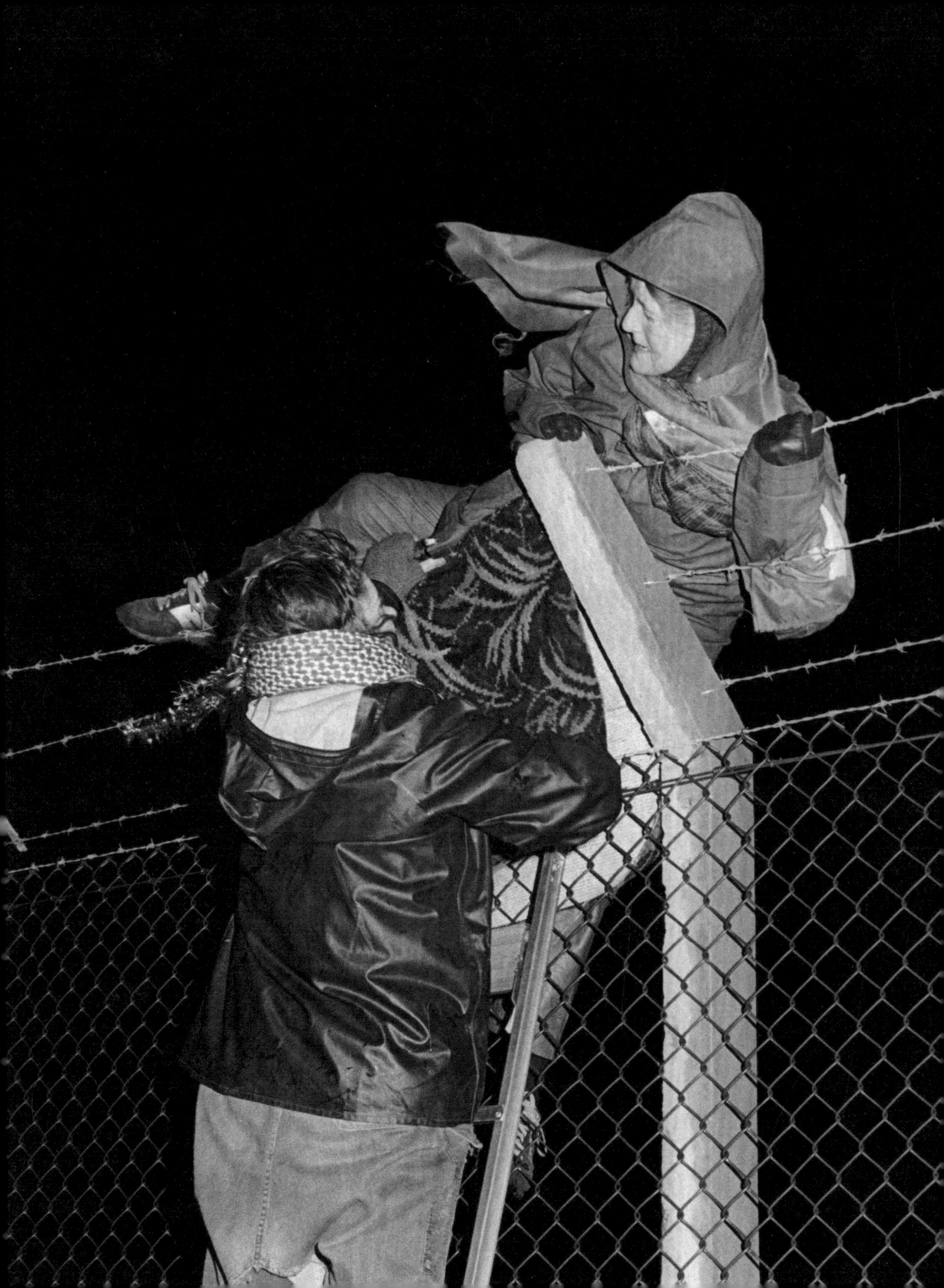

Format Photographers was founded in 1983 as a collective run by women photographers for women photographers. It offered members a route into the professional world, some control over how their work was used and support in developing their skills and creativity. The woman-only agency chose to focus on the representation of issues and individuals otherwise receiving little attention in the mainstream press of the day – such as anti-nuclear protests, LGBTQ+ campaigns, women's involvement in the miners' strike, anti-racism.
The agency was established by Maggie Murray, Val Wilmer, Joanne O'Brien, Jenny Matthews, Pam Isherwood, Sheila Gray, Anita Corbin and Raissa Page. Other prominent members included Brenda Prince, Melanie Friend, Judy Harrison, Roshini Kempadoo, Jacky Chapman and Mo Wilson. Format's photographs have been used across *Women in Revolt!* to ensure that the socio-political gaze of the exhibition is from a women's perspective. The agency disbanded in 2003 and their archive is now at the Bishopsgate Institute in London.

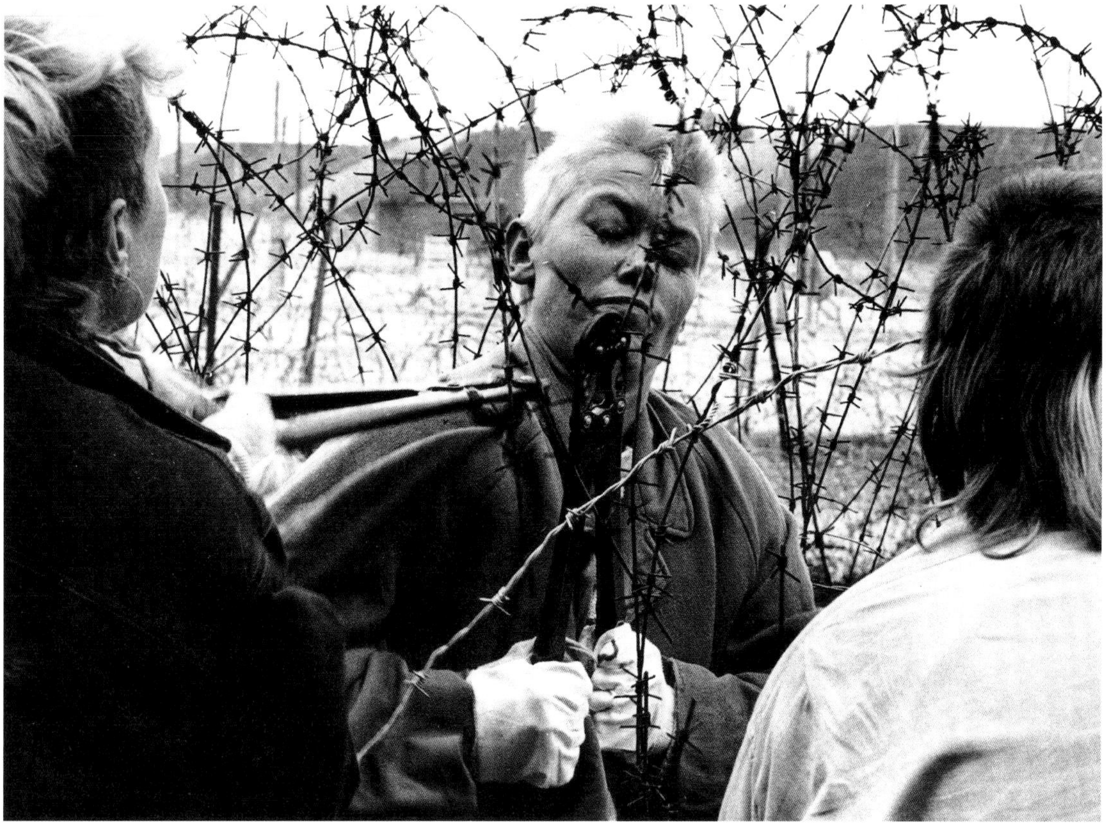

Joanne O'Brien *Greenham Common, Peace Camp Activist* 1983. Photograph 30.5 × 40.6

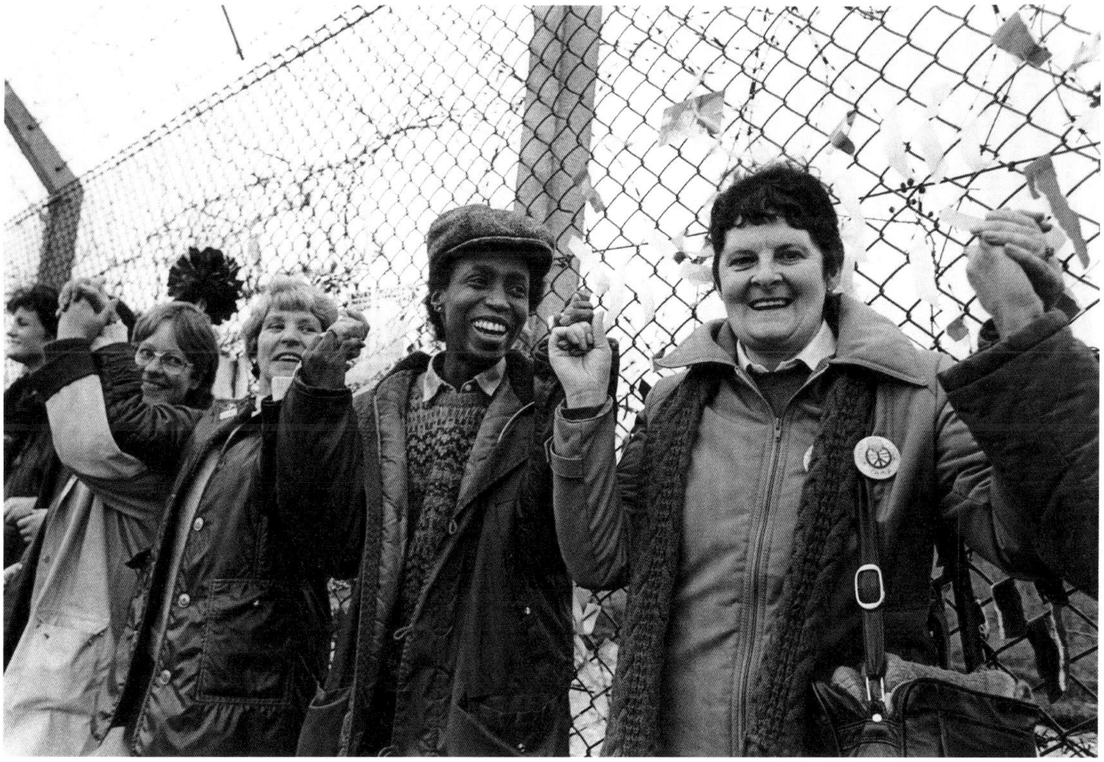

Melanie Friend *Greenham Common* 1985. Photograph 30.5 × 40.6

Maggie Murray *Women of Greenham Common Peace Camp invade the base to dance on the nuclear missile silos at dawn on New Year's Day* 1983. Photograph on paper 40.6 × 30.5

FORMAT PHOTOGRAPHERS

Born in Khemis Miliana, Algeria, in 1948, Houria Niati grew up during the French occupation and the Algerian Revolution. She emigrated to the UK in 1977 and went on to receive a diploma in fine art from Croydon College of Art and later an MA in fine arts from Middlesex University. Niati's practice is deeply rooted in her upbringing and heritage. She was vocal in the 1980s about the institutional racism she observed and experienced, discussing the pressure she felt at art school to become an 'ethnic artist'. Niati understood the lack of acknowledgement of contemporary African art in Western discourse as a continuation of the prejudice that stemmed from colonial depictions of African people and landscapes by European artists, and reflected these concerns in the oil paintings and pastel drawings that formed her practice. *No to Torture* counters the exoticisation and exploitation of Algerian women's bodies by Eugène Delacroix in *Women of Algiers* 1834, made during French colonial rule. In 1986 it was shown at the Whitechapel Gallery and then the Fruitmarket in Edinburgh, and at the Cartwright Hall Art Gallery in Bradford in 1989.

Niati's work was included in the important show *Five Black Women* at the Africa Centre in 1983, and the artist presented her first solo exhibition, *Delirium*, there in 1984–5.

Niati lives and works in London.

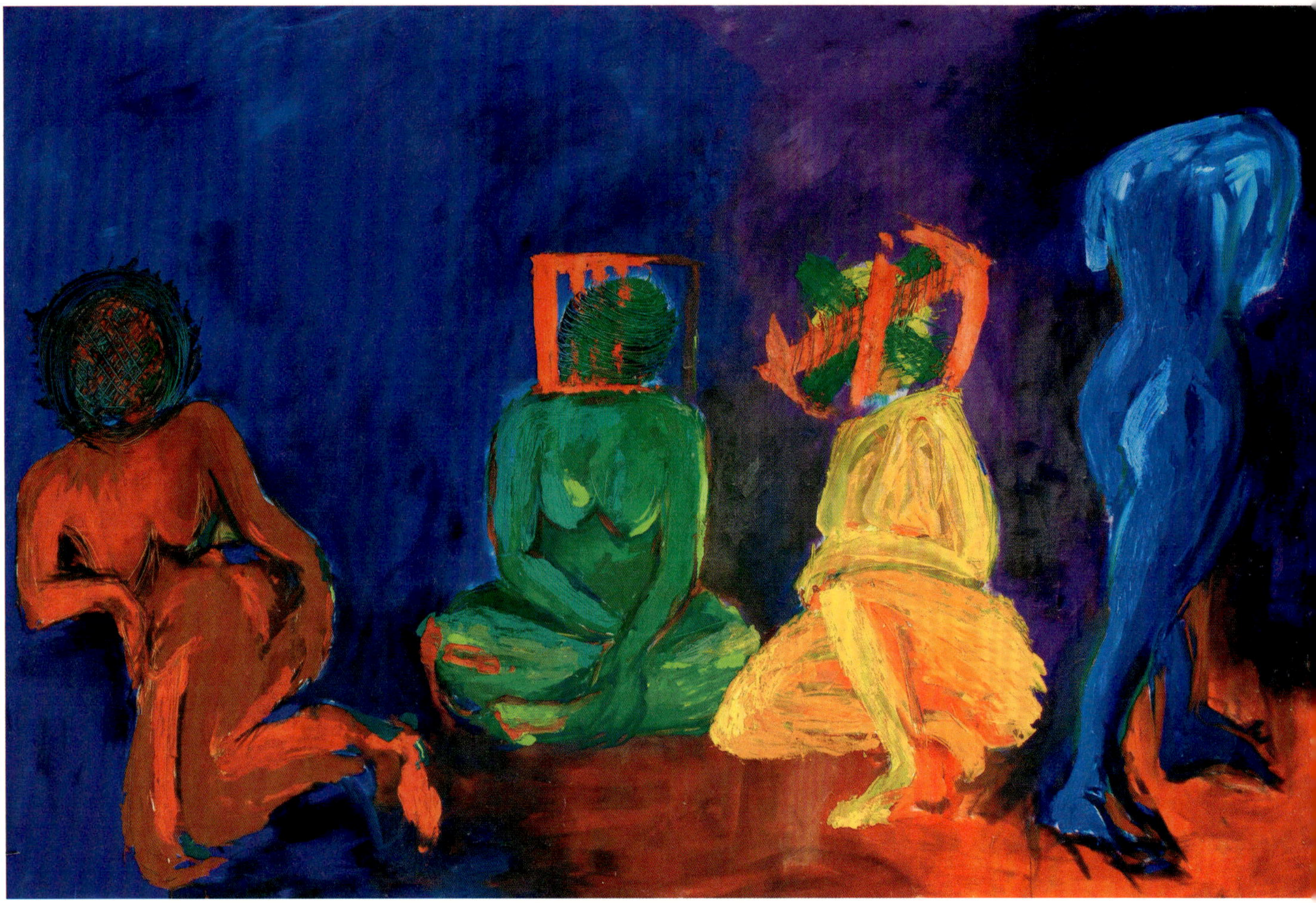

No to Torture (After Delacroix 'Women of Algiers') 1982–3. Oil paint on canvas 83 × 273.5

HOURIA NIATI

Born in North Shields in 1950, Sam Ainsley studied painting at Newcastle Polytechnic, graduating in 1977, and in 1978, went on to receive a Post Graduate Diploma in art from Edinburgh College of Art. Ainsley's radical approach to figurative painting, ambitious in both scale and concept, expresses feminist concerns, challenging the patriarchy by addressing the aggression and competitiveness of men while asserting the power of women. At the 1987 exhibition *Why I Choose Red* at the Third Eye Centre in Glasgow (now CCA), her sixty-foot-high *Woman in Red confronts her own reflection* towered over the gallery, making a powerful statement about a woman's right to take up space and be visible. An active and vocal participant in feminist discourse and activism during the 1980s and since, Ainsley also produced banners for the Greenham Common peace camp. Alongside her artistic practice, Ainsley has had a long career as a teacher, tutoring for over twenty-five years at the Glasgow School of Art, where she co-founded the MFA programme. In 2017, Ainsley was inducted into the Saltire Society's 'Outstanding Women of Scotland', and in 2018, she was awarded an Honorary Degree from Glasgow School of Art for her contribution to art and teaching. She lives and works in Glasgow.

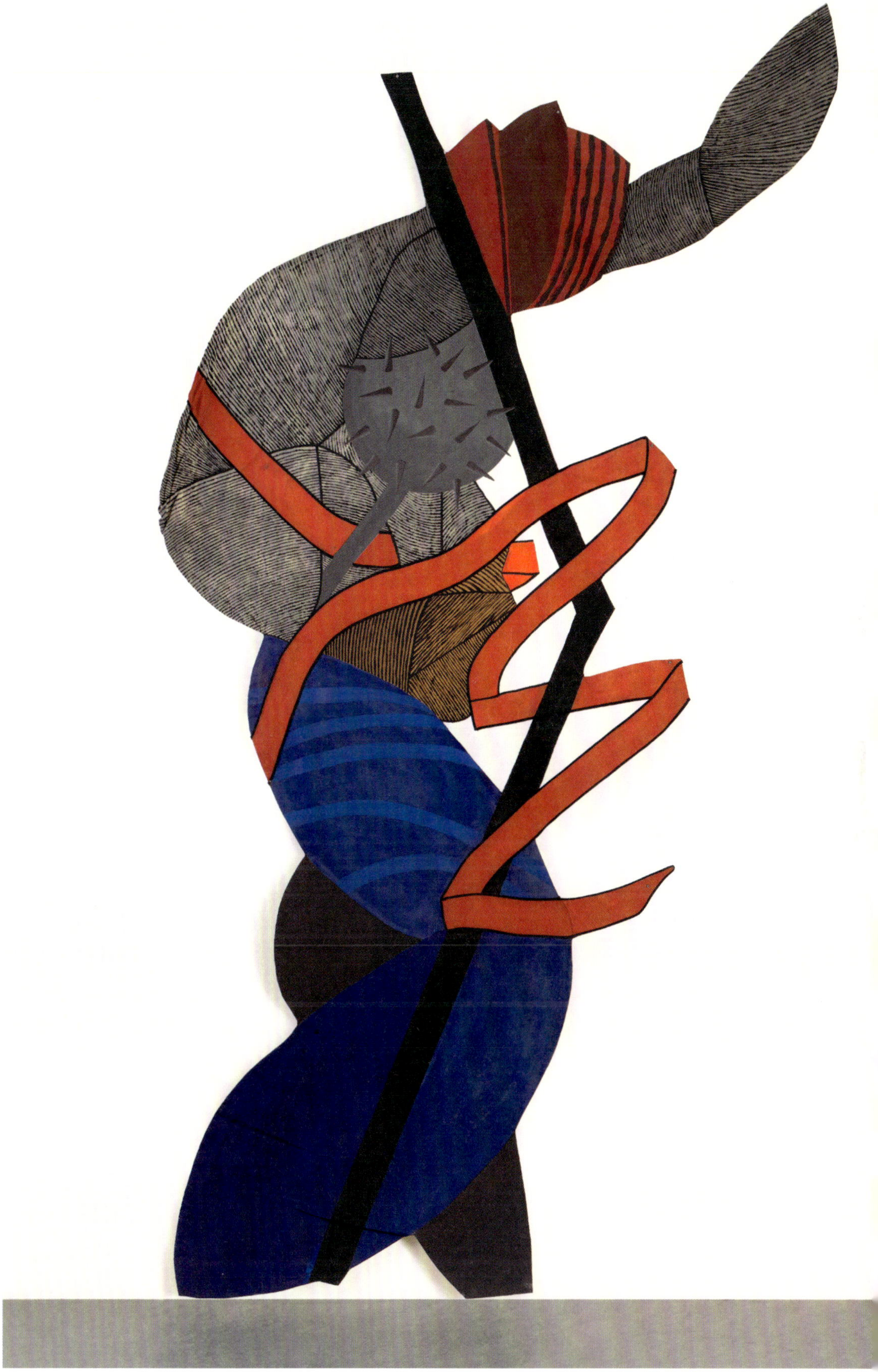

Warrior Woman V: The Artist 1986. Acrylic paint on canvas with cotton binding 346.5 × 217.5

SAM AINSLEY

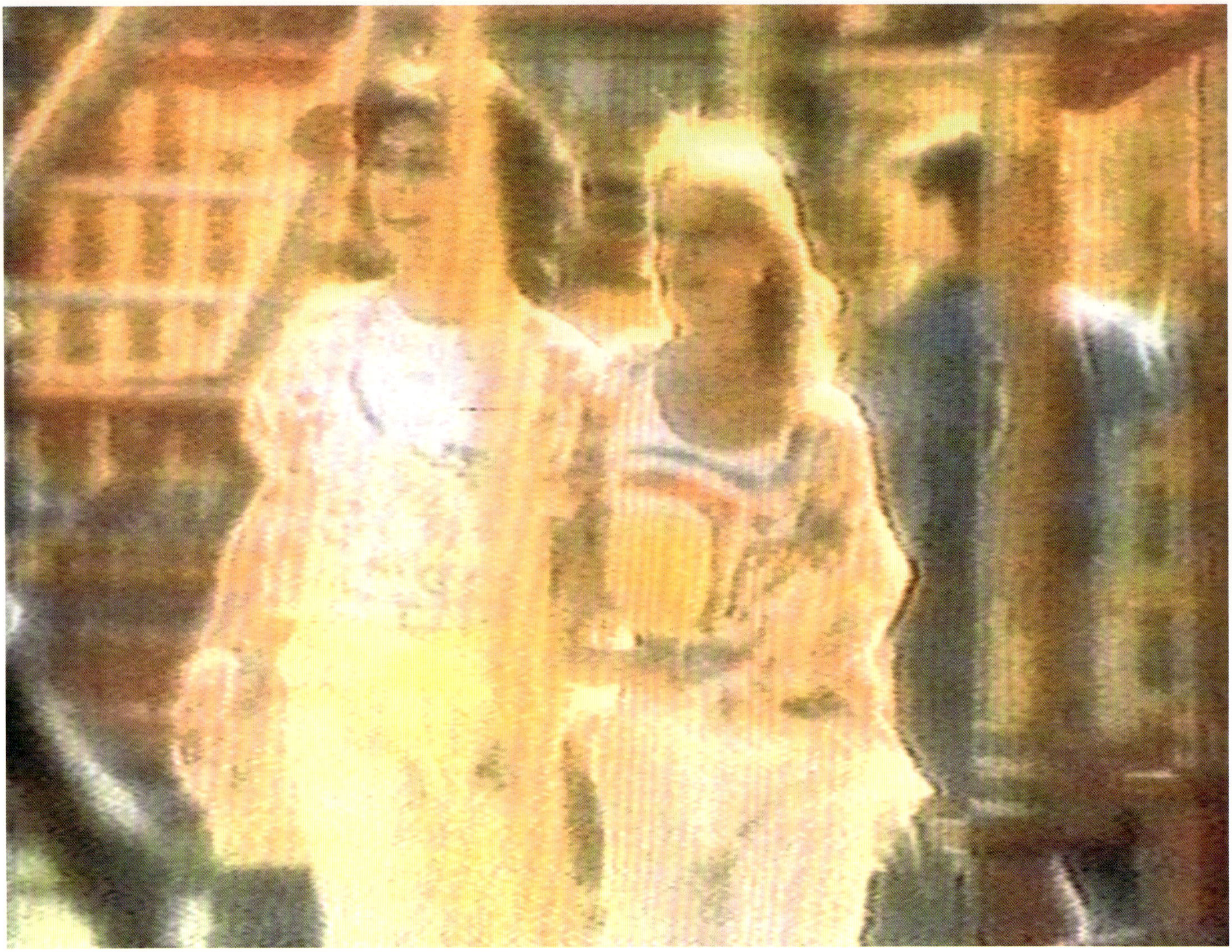

Impulse 1987. Video, shown digitally; colour, sound. 1 min

Ramona Metcalfe (b.1962) grew up in London. Following her studies in independent film at Central Saint Martins in the 1980s, she became immersed in community activism, as part of the Despite TV Co-operative, making 'scratch' videos for community magazine tapes, and with Dogray Productions, making experimental pop promos for the indie music scene.

Metcalfe continued using independent media for community mobilisation, advocacy and campaigning, with charities such as Age Concern and Refugee Action. Her commitment to equality can be seen throughout her subsequent work with deprived communities, in which she uses creative approaches informed more widely by feminist theory.

Metcalfe also went on to work in live performance: acting, clowning and physical theatre, collaborating with companies such as Commedia Works and Words Out Loud. Her own devised and scripted performances include reworkings of fairy tales, news articles and satirical comment on themes of gender, class and disintegration.

Speaking of making *Impulse*, Metcalfe reflected, 'Through simple juxtaposition of popular imagery, the "scratch" video form can be used to make powerful comments that audiences can easily recognise and understand. I hope to achieve that in all my work.'

Along with *Impulse*, Metcalfe also distributed a short abstract animation *Reggae Piece* 1987 through Cinenova, an organisation dedicated to distributing film and and videos made by women.

RAMONA METCALFE

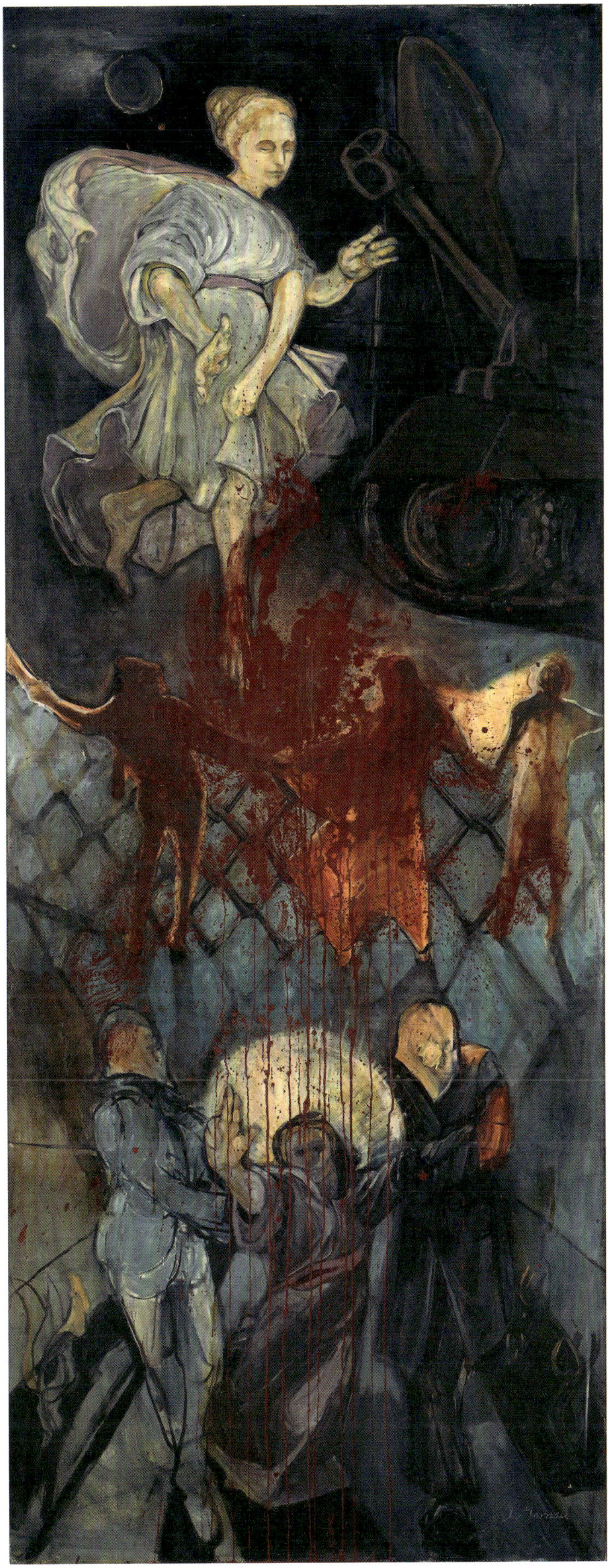

If Mary Came to Greenham 1983.
Oil paint on board 202 × 81

Born in Wisconsin, USA, Jacqueline Morreau (1929–2016) relocated with her family to Los Angeles in her teens. She studied art at the Jepson Art Institute and spent time living in France and New York before returning to California in 1951, where she trained in medical illustration. In 1971 Morreau moved to London with her husband and children and began to paint again, gaining recognition for her work and becoming an important figure in the British women's art movement. Her practice consisted of mostly figurative paintings and drawings that sought to address feminist concerns, often referencing Greek myths, like in her painting *She Who Spins* 1983. Morreau campaigned for the representation of women artists and understood the difficulties they faced in juggling the conflicting demands of motherhood, marriage and art-making, while dealing with wider gender oppression in society. With Joyce Agee, Catherine Elwes and Pat Whiteread, she spent two years in the late 1970s seeking out women artists working in figuration, resulting in the pioneering touring exhibitions *Women's Images of Men* and *About Time* which opened at the ICA in 1980.

JACQUELINE MORREAU

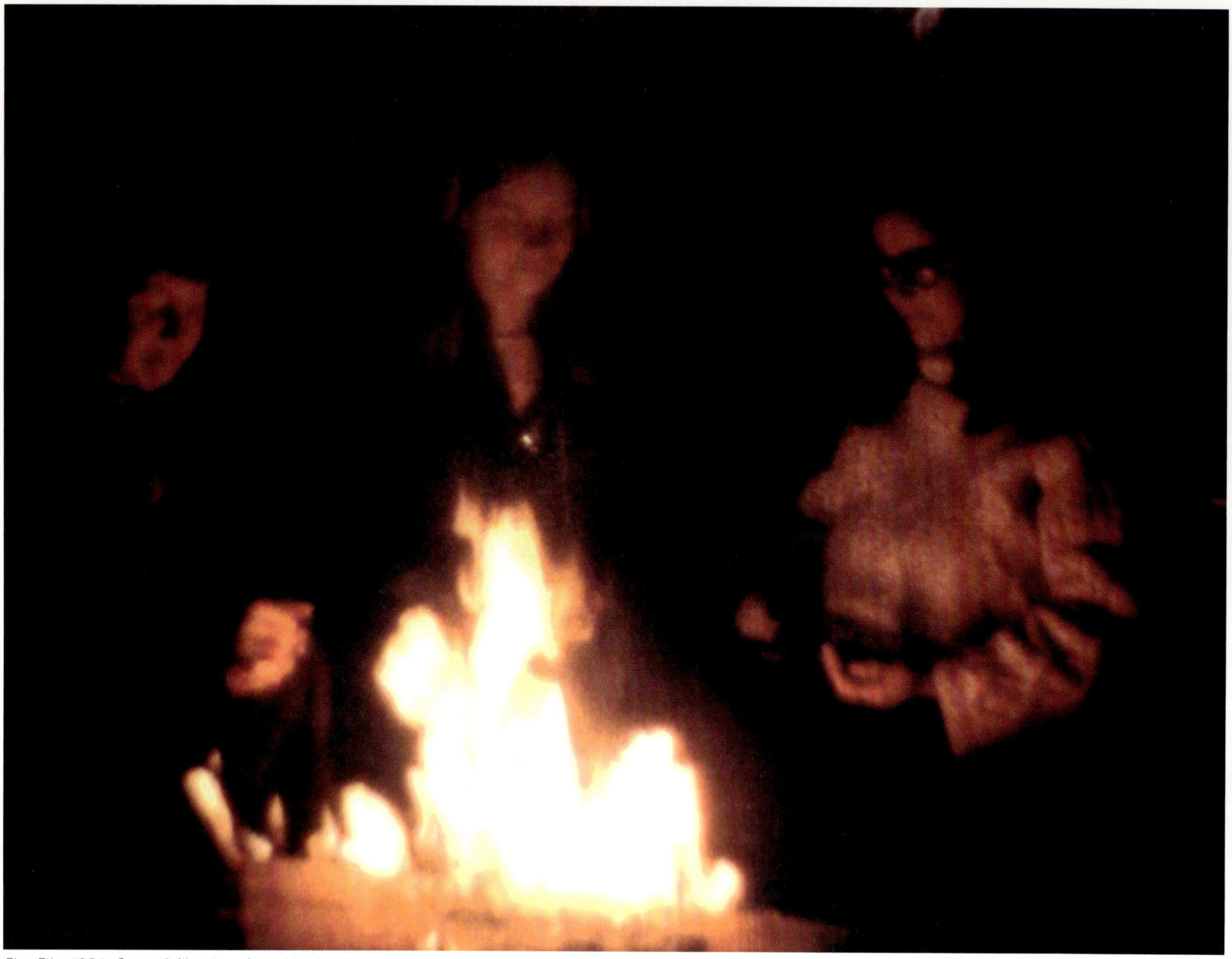

Fire Film 1981. Super 8 film, transferred to digital; colour, sound. 10 min

ANNABEL NICOLSON

Artist and filmmaker Annabel Nicolson was born in 1946 and studied at Edinburgh School of Art and Saint Martin's School of Art in London, graduating in 1971. As a central figure of the London Filmmakers' Co-operative during the 1970s, she was instrumental in the development of its distinctive medium-specific aesthetic, particularly through her film actions, which reimagined the scope for film projection as a live event. Film performances such as *Reel Time* 1973, where she threaded a film strip between a 16mm film projector and sewing machine, explored film's potential in new and experimental ways. Nicolson was a founding member of the women's film and video distribution collective Circles, and her engagement with the Women's Movement through the late 1970s and 80s is reflected in the sound works, artist's book and performances that she created at this time.

Nicolson's *Fire Film* 1981 was made in the earliest days of the Greenham Common Peace Camp when the first few women, who had just walked from Wales, sat around a small campfire discussing their hopes and aspirations for the camp in the context of the wider women's protest movement. As one of the guest editors of *Feminist Art News*, Nicolson used text, drawings and collage to evoke Greenham on the page. She included images from *Concerning Ourselves*, the group exhibition at Norwich School of Art at the end of her year long residency from 1980–1. The main focus of the exhibition was the collaborative work *Menstrual Hut* 1981, a tent-like structure made of reeds and rushes which created a communal women's space.

Nicolson lives and works between London and northwest Scotland.

Joanna Davis (b.1945) and Lis Rhodes (b.1942) are founding members of the women's film and video distribution collective Circles and collaborated on *Hang on a Minute*, a series of thirteen one-minute films in 1983. Originally commissioned by Channel 4 as films to be inserted between advertisements, *Hang on a Minute* was based on short poems by Rhodes, which address subjects ranging from domestic violence and poverty to nuclear weapons, and were accompanied by music composed by Lindsay Cooper and sung by Dagmar Krause. *Ironing to Greenham*, *Goose and Green* and *No. 8 Bus* address the issues of nuclear proliferation through the all-women anti-nuclear protests at Greenham Common. Only six of the films were transmitted after the legal department intervened.

Joanna Davis was co-founder in 1973 of Four Corners Films in London's East End, which continues to this day to provide workshops, screenings and facilities for filmmaking in the community. Films such as *Often During the Day* 1979 and *Born and Bred*, made in collaboration with Mary Pat Leece, reflect feminist concerns and identities.

Lis Rhodes' installations, performances, sound-works and writings engage with pressing political and social conditions and oppressions. Her films have been screened and exhibited widely, and her book of collected writings *Telling Invents Told*, was published by the Visible Press in 2019.

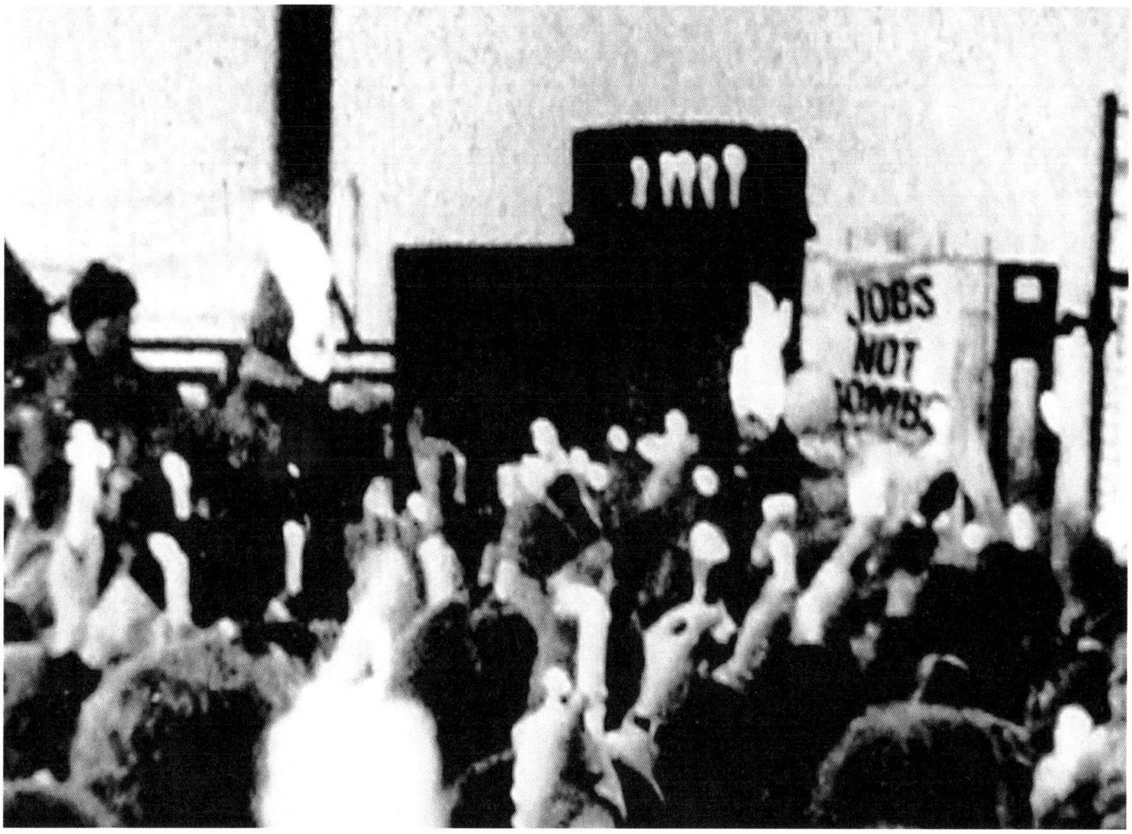

ironing to Greenham

the more she respected other opinions
the less she listened
the less she learnt

so then - she said
i put in my teeth

the more she respected her own experience
the more she heard
the more she knew

the angrier she became
the calmer she was

the more outraged she seems
the surer she is
that her words will emerge
when the iron is hot

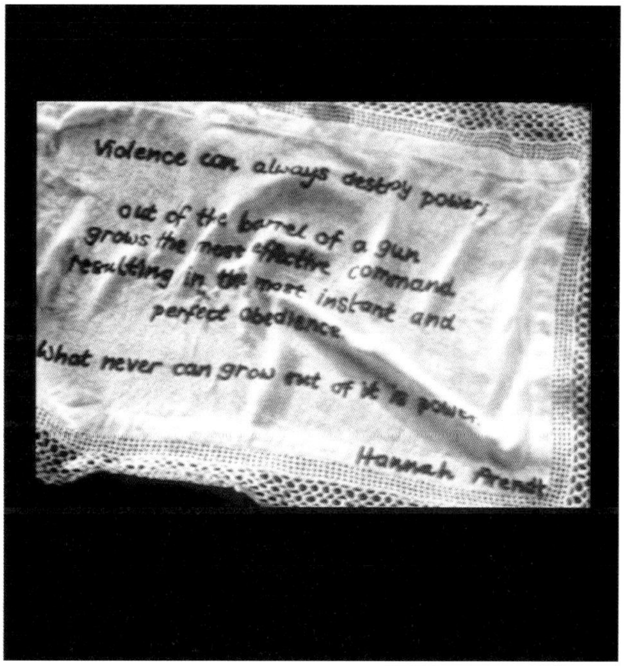

Ironing to Greenham 1983. 16mm film, shown as digital video; colour, sound. 1 min

JOANNA DAVIS LIS RHODES

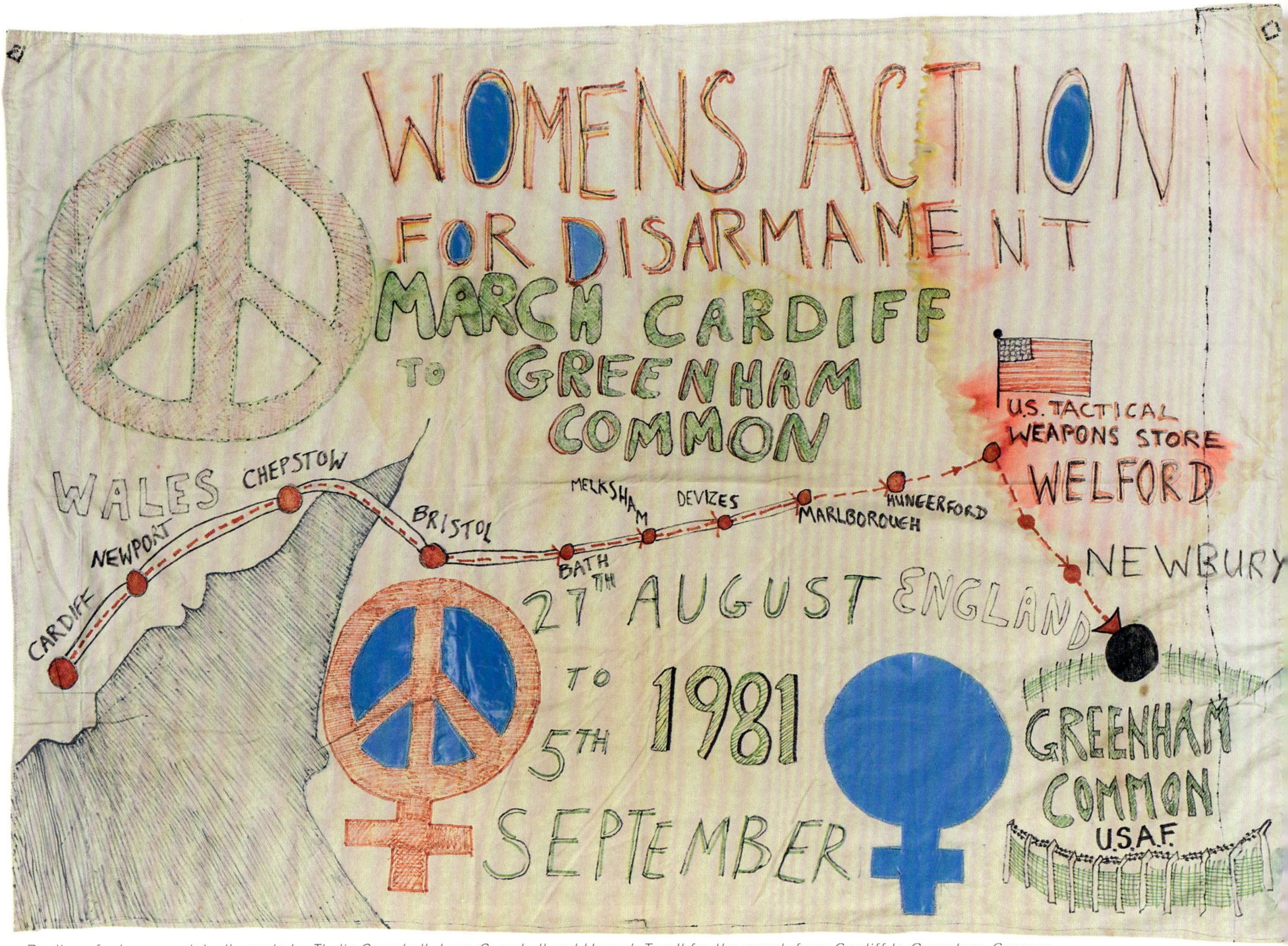

Replica of a banner originally made by Thalia Campbell, Lucy Campbell and Hannah Tyrell for the march from Cardiff to Greenham Common, 27 August to 5 September 1981 c.1981. Cotton, nylon and coloured marker pen 156 × 205

Born in Torquay in 1937, Thalia Campbell studied art in Aberystwyth, Wales, receiving a bachelor's degree. She engaged with feminist discourse from a young age, growing up with a grandmother who had spent time with the suffragettes and witnessed their experiences. In 1981 Campbell was one of the founders of the Greenham Common women's peace camp. There she made a series of banners to display on the camp's fences. These were beautifully crafted using a ground fabric of woven cotton and silk inscribed with slogans and imagery such as peace signs, maps and the woman symbol. Campbell has described the banners as 'art, politics and sewing all wrapped up in one beautiful parcel', and she used them to challenge the misogynistic press coverage of the women and the camps at the time. One banner, *Women for Life on Earth* 1981, was made by Campbell with artists Lucy Campbell and Hannah Tyrrell for a march from Cardiff to Greenham Common and was a visual illustration of the route taken. The original banner was destroyed by the authorities, but Campbell has created a replica for exhibition purposes, which is illustrated here.

Campbell now lives in the Midlands.

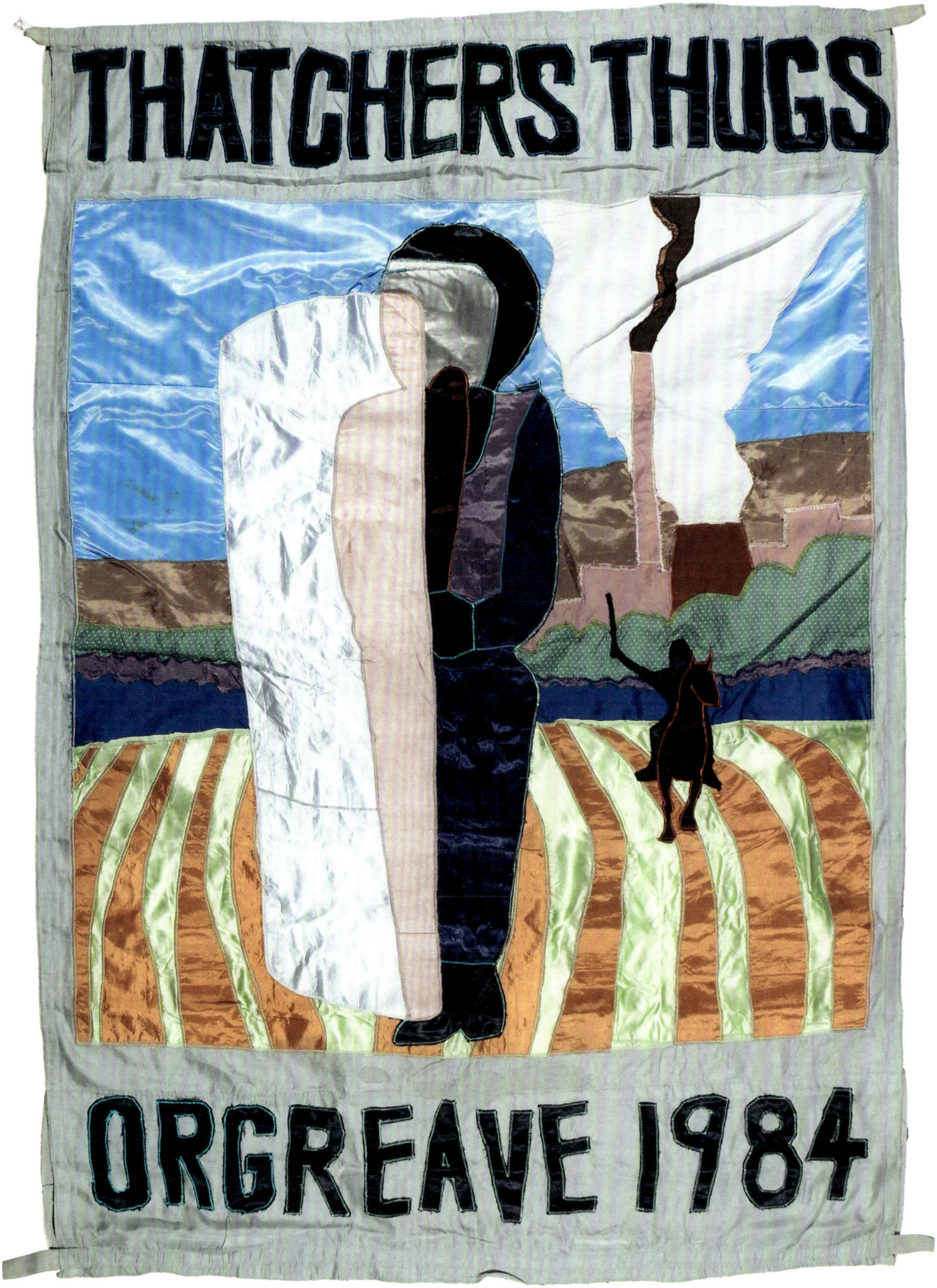

Thatcher's Thugs 1984. Mixed fabrics 177 × 119

THALIA CAMPBELL

Margaret Harrison was born in Wakefield in 1940 and studied at Carlisle College of Art, the Royal Academy Schools and the Accademia di Belli Arti di Perugia in Italy. Working across drawing, installation, collage and textiles, Harrison was a key figure in the feminist art scene of the 1970s and one of the founders of the London Women's Liberation Art Group and a member of the Women's Workshop of the Artists' Union. A 1971 solo exhibition by Harrison at Motif Editions in London displayed a series of drawings that sought to challenge the portrayal of women in popular culture. Some works depicted women with large pieces of food, suggestive of pornographic imagery and society's reduction of women to objects of consumption. Harrison intended the series to reclaim the depiction of women's bodies, describing it as 'anti-pornographic'. The exhibition was closed by the police on grounds of indecency. In 1973–5 Harrison collaborated with artists Kay Hunt and Mary Kelly to conduct a study of women's experiences working in a factory in Bermondsey, London. This resulted in the installation *Women and Work: A Document on the Division of Labour in Industry*, which used the women's accounts to consider their working environment and the recent Equal Pay Act (pp.82–3). Harrison lives and works in Carlisle.

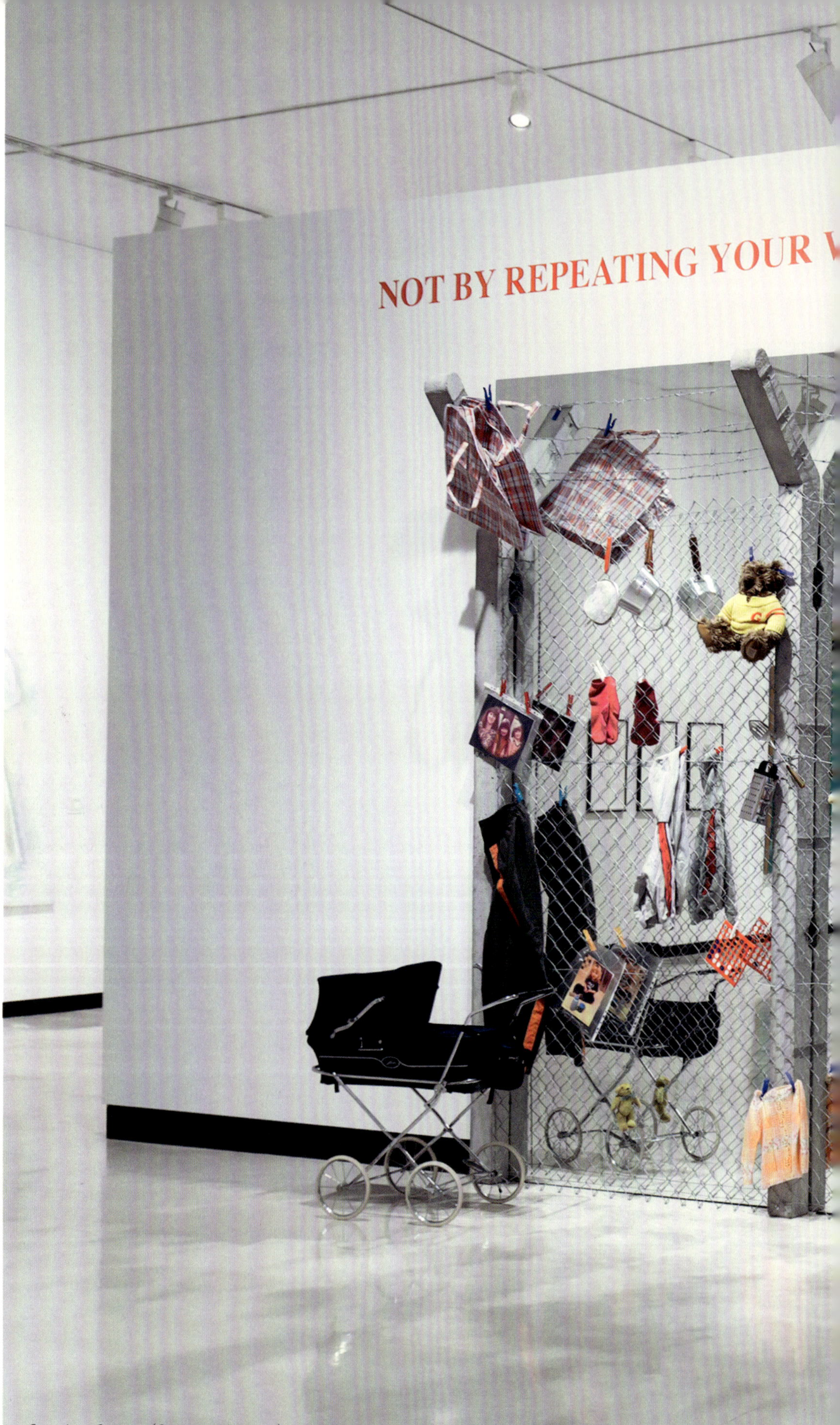

Greenham Common (Common reflections) 1989–2013. Installation of concrete, mirrors, clothes, children's boots, pram, soft toys, photographs, plastic bags, wire netting and barbed wire 282 × 440 (overall)

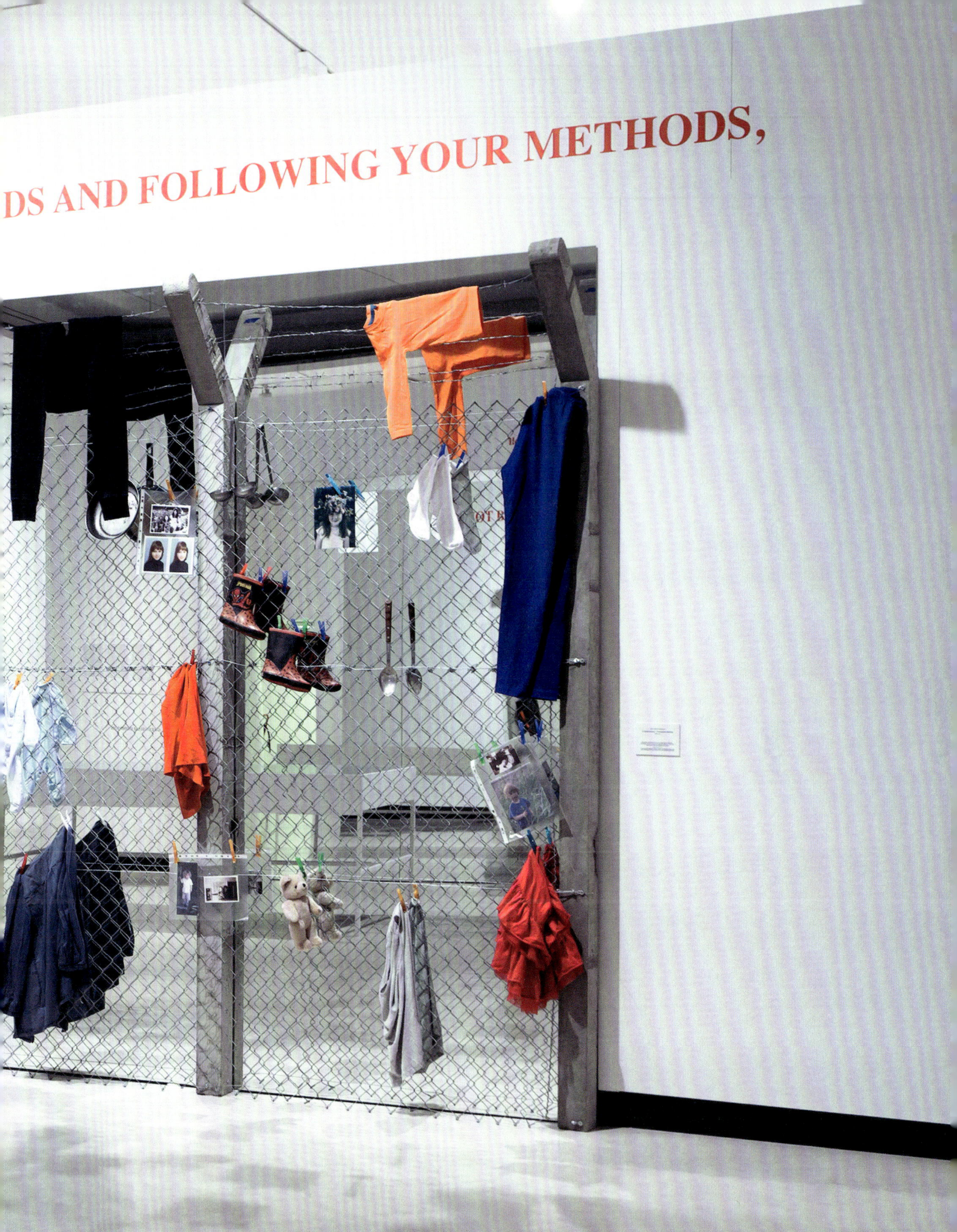
DS AND FOLLOWING YOUR METHODS,

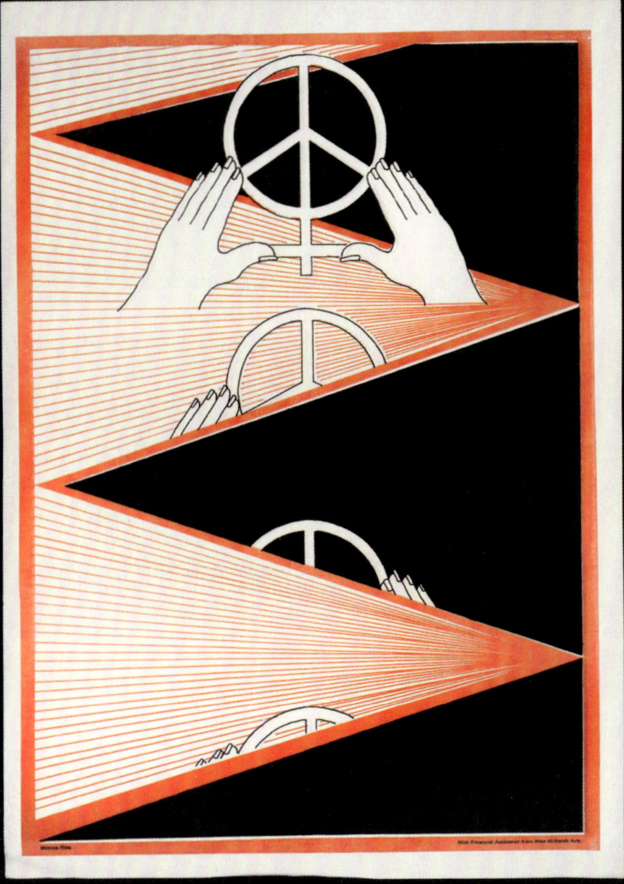

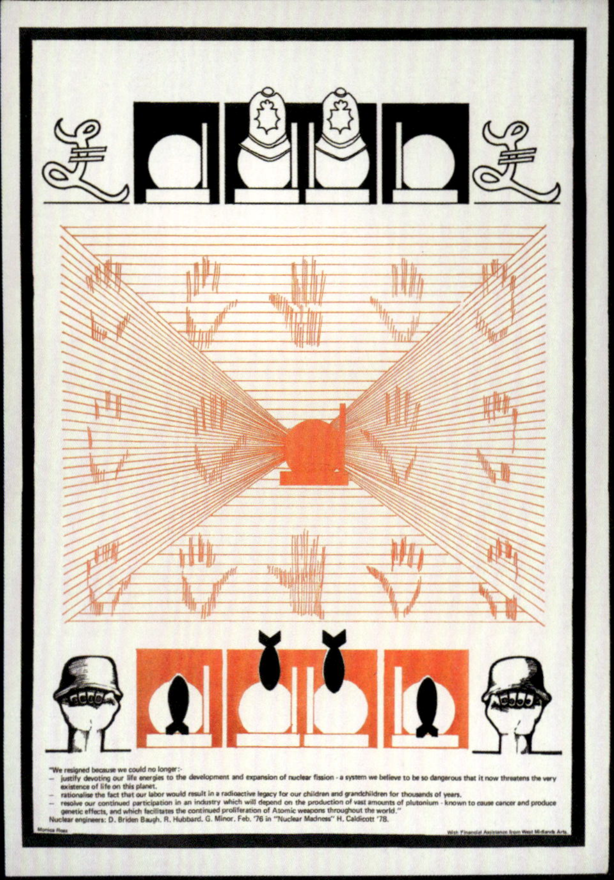

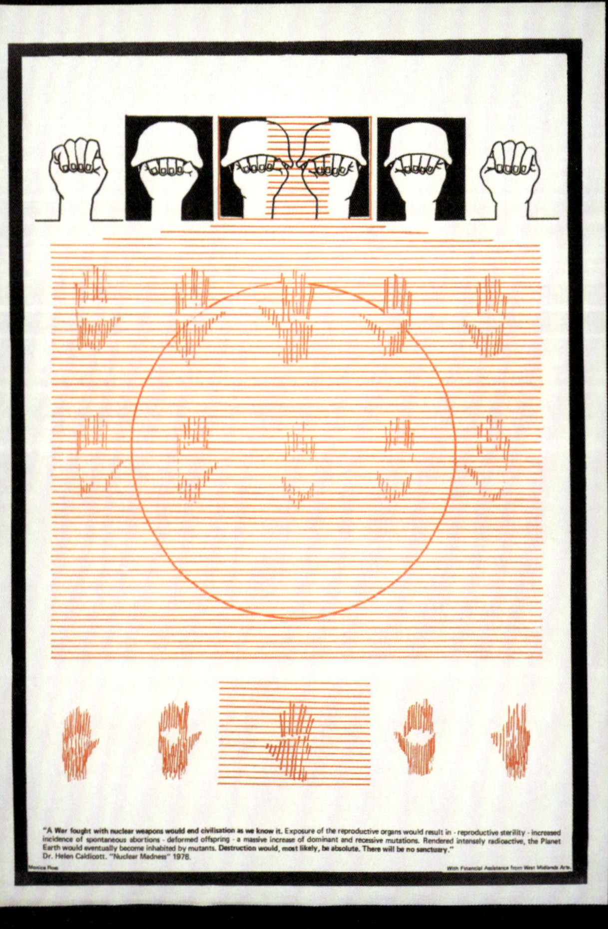

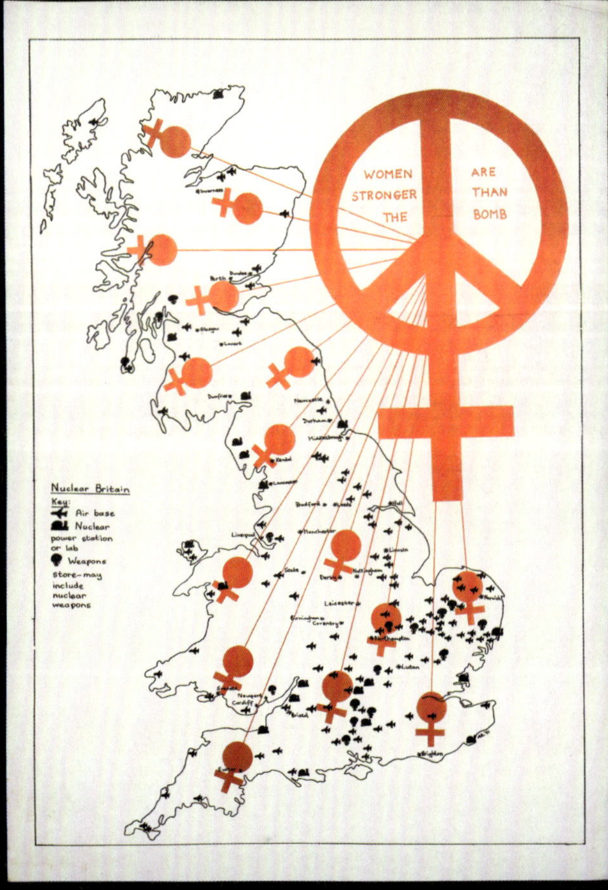

Here and p.190: Sister Seven touring show posters 1981.
Printed paper, laminated 45.7 × 33

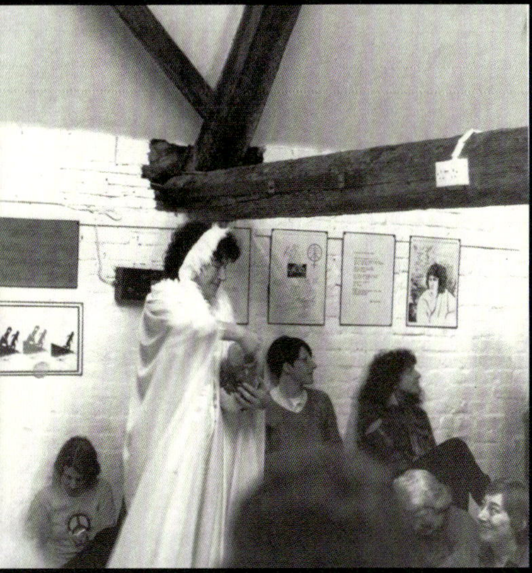

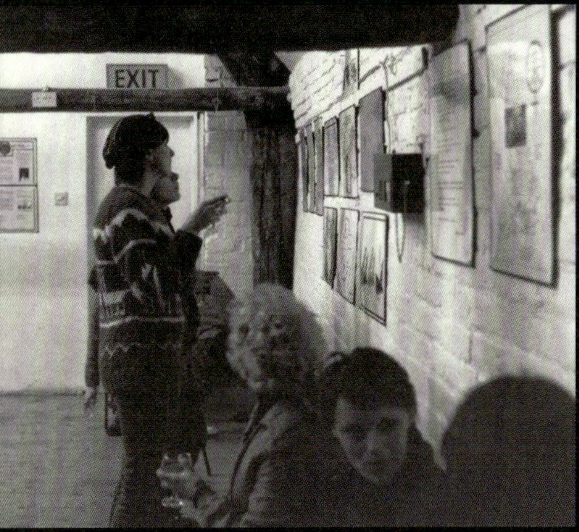

Installation views of Sister Seven touring exhibition.

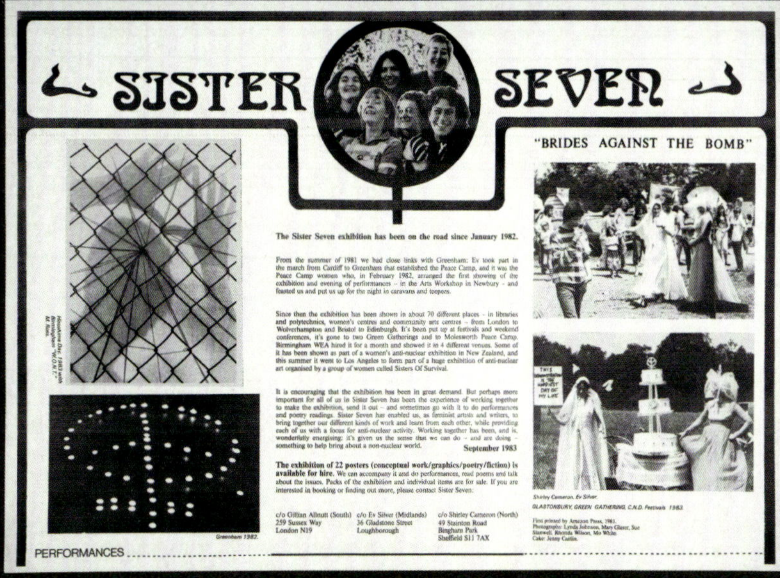

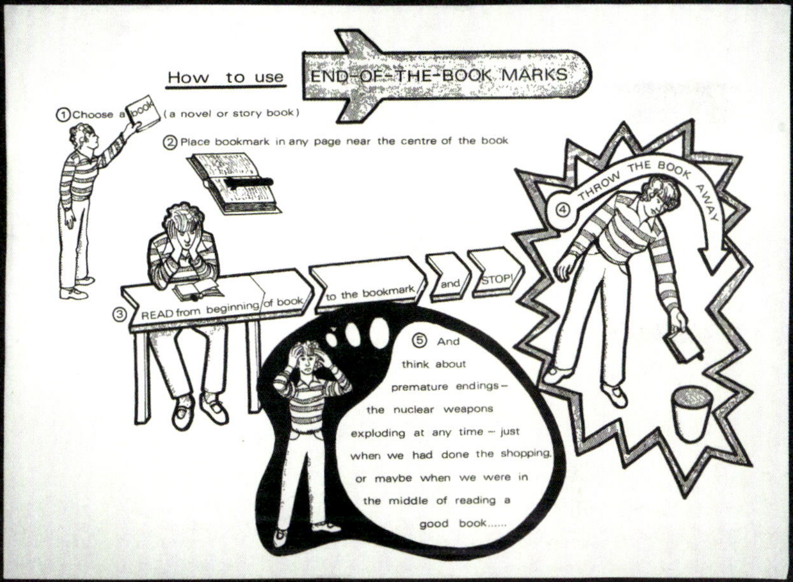

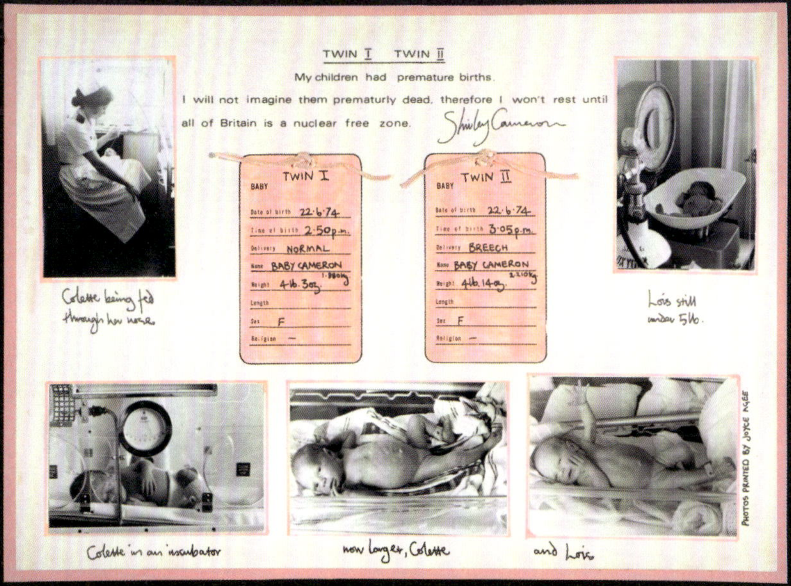

Sister Seven (active 1981–4) was a collaborative group formed of visual artists Monica Ross, Shirley Cameron and Evelyn Silver and poets Mary Michaels and Gillian Allnutt, all of whom had close links to Greenham Peace Camp. Evelyn Silver was one of the founders of the camp. They produced an exhibition of anti-nuclear images and poems, which were then hired out to colleges, church groups, libraries, conferences, art galleries, peace festivals and camps, and displayed as laminated posters. The first exhibition was shown along with performances and poetry readings at Newbury Arts Centre near to Greenham Common. The exhibition was greatly received, and went on tour to over seventy venues, including one in New Zealand, where it featured in a large-scale anti-nuclear exhibition organised by the collective Sisters of Survival, who were based in Los Angeles.

Ross, Cameron and Silver continued to work together, performing *Monument to Working Women* and *Britannia Waives the Rules* (both 1985), under the moniker 'Triple Transformations'. Ross and Allnutt went on to collaborate on the installation *Sea Change* as part of *Seadrifts* 1986, at the Laing Art Gallery, Newcastle upon Tyne and commissioned by Projects UK.

Cameron and Silver, among their many collaborative performance artworks and installations, went on to produce *United Matrons* 1987 at Glastonbury Festival and Nottingham Women's Festival.

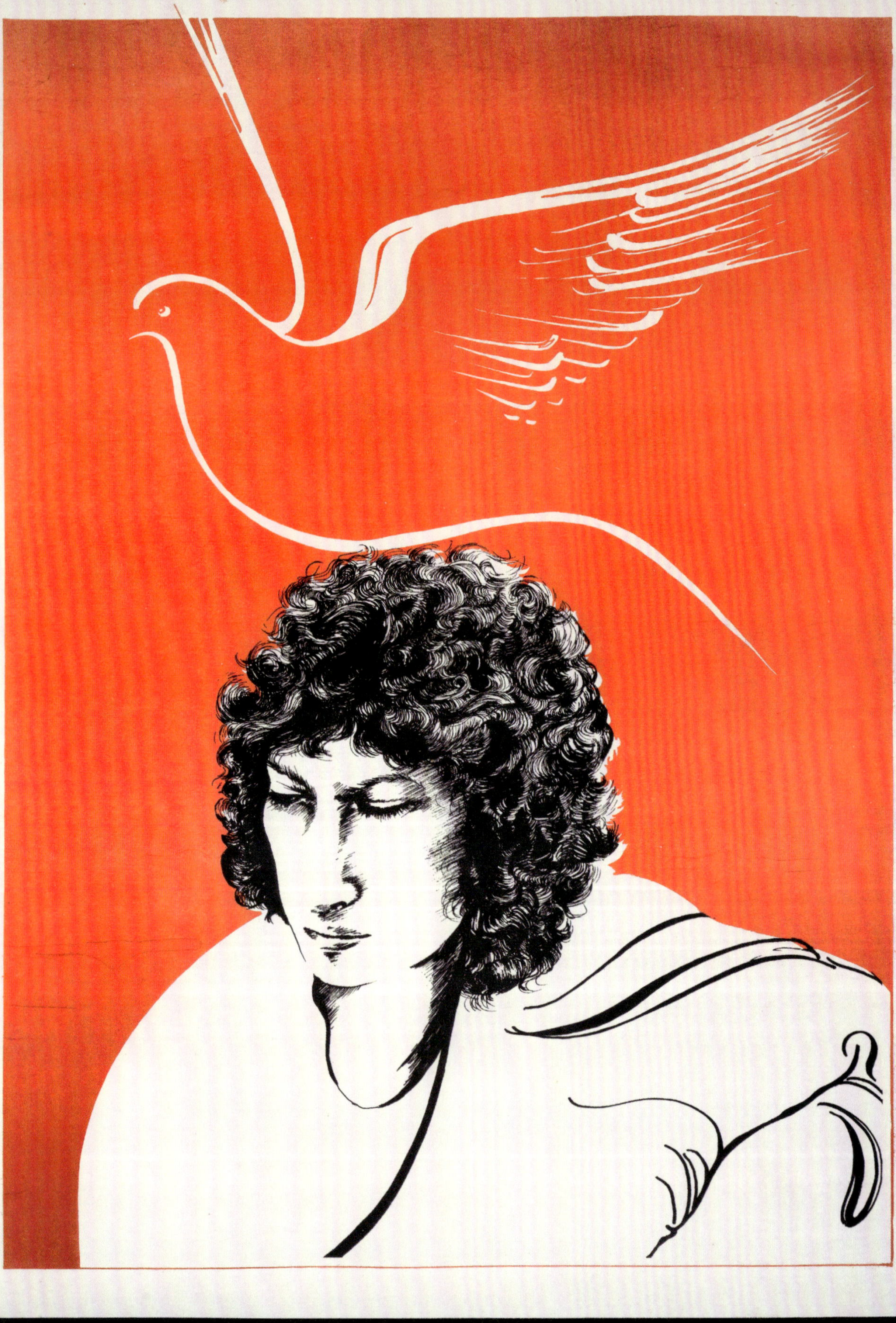

Sister Seven touring show poster 1981. Printed paper, laminated 45.7 × 33

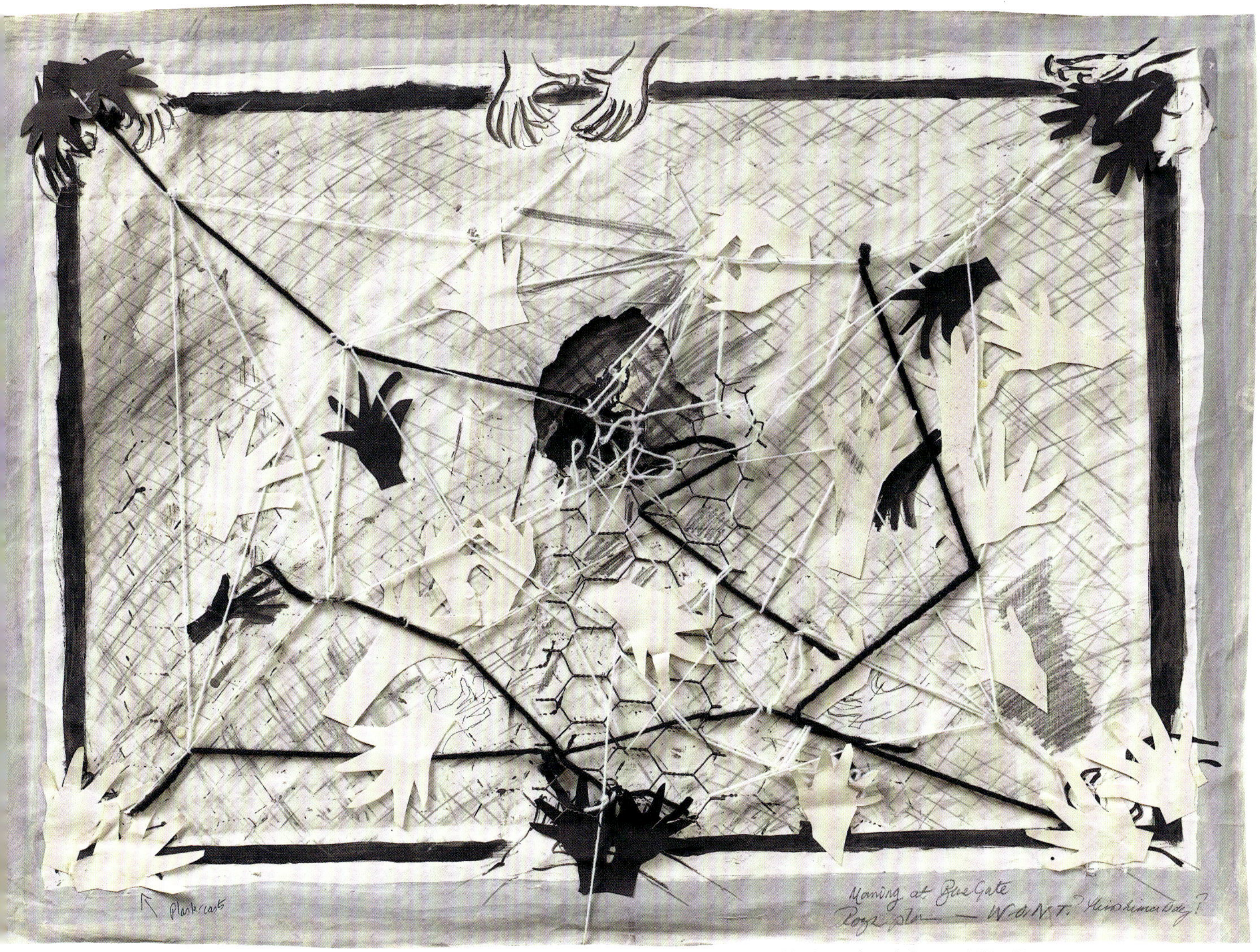

Morning at Blue Gate 1983. Graphite, grey and black paint, cut-outs made of paper, cotton and wool strings, black metal mesh fragment 55 × 71

MONICA ROSS

Monica Ross (1950–2013) was born in Lancashire and studied at the University of Reading. Working across multimedia, text and performance, her practice was underpinned by feminism and other movements for social, cultural and political change. Ross' work critiques patriarchal industrial capitalism and the social and political constraints imposed on working-class women through experimental and often collaborative art practice. It addresses how we experience events in the present and the cultural transitions which transform them, or not, into memory and history.

Ross played a significant role as a feminist organiser, co-founding the Women's Postal Art Event and Fenix with artists Su Richardson, Suzy Varty and Kate Walker (see pp.64–6), and later the women's art group Sister Seven (pp.188–90). Her work with Fenix was included in the important feminist exhibition *Issue: Social Strategies by Women Artists* at the ICA in 1980.

Alongside her art practice, Ross had a long career as an influential educator, teaching at Central Saint Martins from 1985 to 1998, and later at the University of Brighton and University of the Arts, Berlin. Following the artist's death in 2013, the Monica Ross Action Group was set up to enable new audiences to benefit from her legacy.

A RADICAL DECADE: BLACK WOMEN ARTISTS IN 1980s BRITAIN

DOROTHY PRICE

1 Claudette Johnson, 'A Statement from the Artist' in *Pushing Back the Boundaries*, exh. cat. Rochdale Art Gallery 1990, p.2. The exhibition ran from 13 October to 17 November 1990.
2 Sulter established Urban Fox Press in 1989 with the aim of fostering networks for Black women's creativity, having already co-founded the Blackwomen's Creativity Project with Ingrid Pollard in 1982. As Sulter noted on the back page of her edited collection *Passion: Discourses on Blackwomen's Creativity*, also published by Urban Fox Press in the same year as *Pushing Back the Boundaries* and illustrated with photographs by Pollard: 'Urban Fox Press was established in 1989. Committed to publishing only the most exciting and dynamic works of fine art and literature. UFP is particularly passionate about Blackwomen's creativity across continents.' See Maud Sulter (ed.), *Passion: Discourses on Blackwomen's Creativity*, Hebden Bridge 1990, p.256.
3 Indeed, as Johnson herself has since indicated, 'to suggest there was a movement implies more cohesiveness than there was at the time'. See E. Ifekoya, C. Johnson, R. Kabir, R. Rage and R. Zaman, 'Processes of Identification' in Nick Aikens and Elizabeth Robles (eds.), *The Place is Here: The Work of Black Artists in 1980s Britain*, Berlin 2019, p.397. For other information on the British Black Arts Movement see 'Blk Art Group Research', https://issuu.com/blkres (accessed 11 Aug. 2023) and Bluecoat Library's 'British Black Arts Movement', https://www.thebluecoat.org.uk/library/british-black-arts-movement (accessed 11 Aug. 2023).
4 See essays, interviews and contributions by Emma Ridgway, Ella Mills, Gilane Tawadros and Courtney J. Martin in Emma Ridgway (ed.), *Claudette Johnson: I Came to Dance*, Oxford 2019. Wolverhampton Polytechnic was granted University status in 1991 and is known today as the University of Wolverhampton; for more about its institutional history see 'University of Wolverhampton: Our History', https://www.wlv.ac.uk/about-us/our-history (accessed 12 Aug. 2023).
5 Another iteration of the group, whose membership remained fluid and also included the artist Donald Rodney, was the Pan-Afrikan Connection. Between 1981 and 1983, the group created exhibitions at the Herbert Gallery, Coventry; Ikon Gallery, Birmingham; and the Africa Centre in Covent Garden, London: see for example, *The Pan-Afrikan Connection*, exh. cat., Herbert Gallery & Museum, Coventry 1983, https://issuu.com/blkres/docs/herbert_art_gallery (accessed 12 August 2023). Eddie Chambers has explained of the Blk Art Group's name that it 'directly copied Black Power activists like LeRoi Jones who had taken to writing "Black" as "Blk" in part to infuse the word with a new, defiant resonance that set it apart from and above what Jones saw as its debased, oppressive and depoliticized usage.' Furthermore, Chambers commented that the decision to spell Pan-Afrikan with a 'k' 'is part of the process of reclaiming our languages and developing a political frame of reference which is centred on Afrikan principles and values'. See Eddie Chambers, *The Emergence and Development of Black Visual Arts Activity in England Between 1981 and 1986: Press and Public Responses*, unpublished PhD thesis, Goldsmiths University 1998, p.351.
6 Claudette Johnson in conversation with the author, 20 July 2023.
7 This was a country characterised, during the 1980s especially, by growing right-wing nationalism, mass unemployment, police harassment of young Black men through so-called 'sus' laws. Multiple incidents of racially motivated violent civic unrest had taken place during the summer of 1981 across many inner-city areas including Handsworth in Birmingham, Brixton in London, Toxteth in Liverpool and St Pauls in Bristol. For more on the Midlands in particular see Kieran Connell, *Black Handsworth: Race in 1980s Britain*, Oakland, CA 2019.

> I am a Blackwoman and my work is concerned with making images of Blackwomen. Sounds simple enough – but I'm not interested in portraiture or its tradition. I'm interested in giving space to Blackwomen's presence. A presence which has been distorted, hidden and denied. I'm interested in our humanity, our feelings and our politics; some things which have been neglected …
>
> Claudette Johnson[1]

Claudette Johnson wrote these words as part of a longer statement published in an exhibition catalogue for a solo show at Rochdale Art Gallery in 1990. The exhibition was curated by fellow artist Lubaina Himid and the catalogue was produced by poet, artist and activist Maud Sulter through Sulter's publishing imprint, Urban Fox Press.[2] The collaborative efforts of three creative Black women to enable the Rochdale exhibition and its catalogue to exist – in a period when the visibility of Black women in the art world was still negligible even after a decade of art activism – exemplifies an important strategy for women artists of colour during the early decades of what has since become known, somewhat loosely, as the British Black Arts Movement.[3]

Johnson's by now well-documented journey to become one of the pioneering Black feminist artists of her generation began in the early 1980s, while she was an art student at what was then Wolverhampton Polytechnic.[4] In the final year of her undergraduate fine art degree, she met fellow artist Eddie Chambers. He was giving a talk at the polytechnic to coincide with the group exhibition *Black Art an' Done* at Wolverhampton Art Gallery in summer 1981, which also included work by then art students Keith Piper, Andrew Hazel, Dominic Dawes and Ian Palmer. After the talk, Johnson and Chambers started chatting about their art practice, and Chambers invited Johnson to join the Wolverhampton Young Black Artists group (WYBAs), a precursor to the Blk Art Group.[5] WYBA members included Marlene Smith, Wenda Leslie, Donald Rodney and Janet Vernon as well as Johnson, Piper and Chambers, all of whom were Black art students based in the Midlands.

It was at meetings of the WYBAs that the idea to hold the First National Black Art Convention was conceived. This pivotal moment in contemporary art history was the first manifestation of the collaborative work that became a hallmark of Johnson's and Himid's early visibility as artists. As Johnson recalls:

> We were all aware that some of us was the only black student in our year and sometimes the only black student on the whole Fine Art course. We found each other, so there must be more. Where were they? What were they experiencing? And most importantly, what were they making? So the Convention came about.[6]

Held at Wolverhampton Polytechnic on Thursday 28 October 1982, the First National Black Art Convention – 'to discuss the form, functioning and future of Black art' – attracted over 100 art students of colour from across the UK, as well as already established artists such as Frank Bowling and Rasheed Araeen. It clearly met a need in a climate when there was no other provision for the otherwise isolated practitioners of colour within the white majority art world of Thatcher's Britain.[7]

As part of the programme for the day it had been agreed in advance that Johnson, the only Black woman on the schedule, would speak about her practice in a talk titled 'Images of Black Women in Art':

> I presented a slide lecture about the black female figure in my work, and I used examples from Velázquez and Manet, to show the difference in how women were positioned in their works, as opposed to how I was positioning them. One of the men in the audience said he didn't see a difference between what I was doing and what they [Velázquez and Manet] were doing. I think he may have interrupted me to say that. At that point there was uproar.[8]

As Ella Spencer-Mills has commented of this turbulent punctum in arts histories of the era, 'the honesty of black female subjectivity, sexuality and creativity' that the twenty-three year-old Johnson 'so bravely articulated was spoken over, shut down and physically removed by her black male contemporaries.'[9] Amid the noise, it was agreed that anyone who wanted to continue the discussion around Johnson's work should join her in a different room. As she recalls, 'it became apparent that it was mostly women who were interested in hearing more.'[10] Those who joined her to continue the conversation included fellow artists and art students from across London and the Midlands, Marlene Smith, Lubaina Himid, Ingrid Pollard and Sonia Boyce – all key members of what was to become the British Black Arts movement.

At that time, Lubaina Himid was studying for her MA in cultural history at the Royal College of Art. In 1982, during her first term at the RCA, and within a month of the First National Black Art Convention, she advertised in *Art Monthly* for questionnaire participants:

> I am at present doing research at the Royal College of Art in London, into the extent to which young black people are being visually creative in Britain today. If you are between 20 and 40, living in London (provinces soon to be approached), and are black and an artist, in your studio, at an art school, at home or with your community, please can you send me a stamped self-addressed envelope for a questionnaire and further details.[11]

Everyone who responded received a questionnaire, the individual results of which Himid eventually collated as part of the research process for her Master's thesis (she would graduate in 1984). Her dissertation, *On Being a Young Black Artist in Britain Today: A Political Response to a Personal Experience*, made for a sober read, in which Black women's experiences at art school and after were shown to be those of isolation, alienation and lack of opportunities. In the face of these experiences, shared by so many individual artists of colour from the era, Himid was nonetheless able to bring about collective action, organising exhibitions and creating important networks, spaces and outlets for Black women's creativity to flourish despite the conditions of neglect for artists of colour in the white-centric art world.

Having met fellow artists of colour in person in Johnson's studio during the First National Black Art Convention, the following year Himid invited Johnson and Boyce to participate in two exhibitions – *Five Black Women* at the

8 Claudette Johnson and Emma Ridgway in Ridgway 2019.
9 Ella Spencer-Mills, 'Doing the Discourse: Spaces of Black Feminist Subjectivity in British Art History' in Ridgway 2019, p.74.
10 Claudette Johnson and Emma Ridgway in Ridgway 2019, p.23.
11 Lubaina Himid, 'Attention Young Black Artists', *Art Monthly*, no.61, Nov. 1982, p.18.

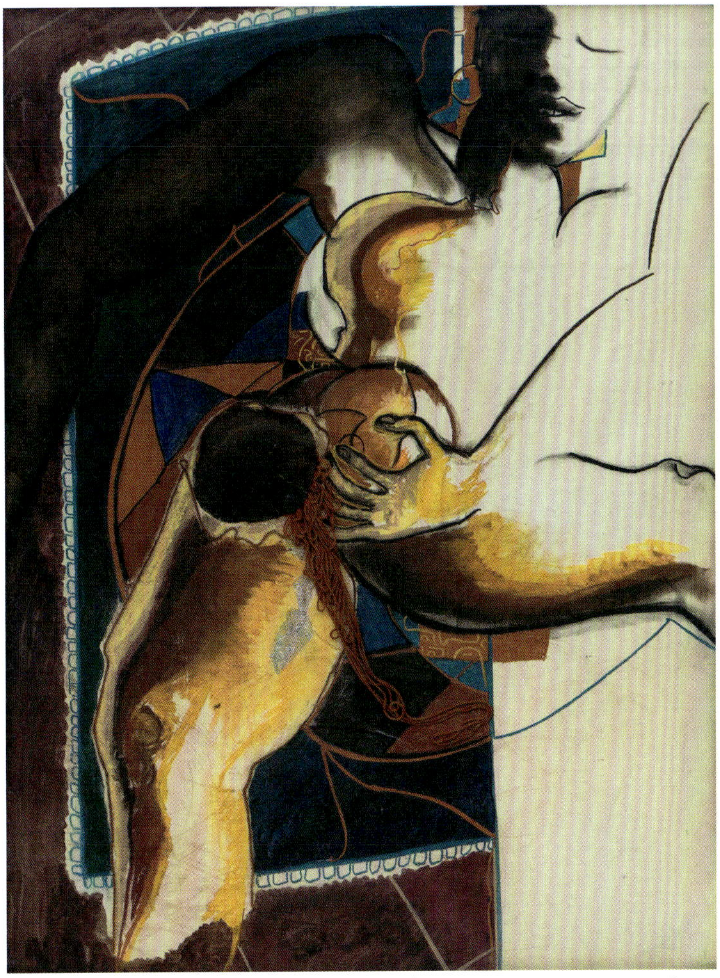

Claudette Johnson *Untitled (with wool and leather)* 1982. Pastel, gouache paint, silver paper, leather and wool 76 × 45

Africa Centre in Covent Garden alongside herself, Houria Niati and Veronica Ryan, and *Black Woman Time Now*, held at Battersea Arts Centre as part of a larger fifteen-woman exhibition of works by the same five artists with the addition of Chila Kumari Singh Burman, Ingrid Pollard, Brenda Agard, Mumtaz Karimjee, Cherry Lawrence, Margaret Cooper, Leslee Wills, Andrea Telman, Elizabeth Eugene and Jean Campbell. And so began a five decade-long set of personal and professional friendship networks that pivoted around these early encounters between Black women artists of the 1980s and that continues among many of them today.[12] For Himid and others, meeting Johnson and listening to her discuss her work at the Wolverhampton conference was an important moment in the birth of Black feminist art practices in the UK. As Himid subsequently recalled, 'in visual terms [Johnson] said things about black women's bodies, experiences, and aspirations that changed lives. She introduced the idea of collaboration.'[13]

A further association to emerge indirectly as a result of the First National Black Art Convention was that between Ingrid Pollard and Maud Sulter, both artists with an overriding interest in photography and photographic practices. Pollard had been one of the artists in attendance at the break-out discussion of women artists in Johnson's studio. She worked at the community screenprinting project Lenthall Road Workshop in Hackney, where Johnson also worked for seven years after graduating from Wolverhampton. Recalling the birth of her *Blackwomen's Creativity Project* in an overview essay published in *Passion* in 1990, Sulter commented:

> A short report back on a Black Arts Convention in Wolverhampton written by Ingrid Pollard and published in *Outwrite* led me to calling the author, alerting her to my idea and arranging to meet and discuss. Ingrid shared with me the information she had and also invited me to *Black Woman Time Now* at Battersea Arts Centre in 1983. That exhibition had been curated by Lubaina Himid. Together, Ingrid Pollard and I began to work – she took pictures, I wrote words. Some of these collaborations appeared in publications such as *Artrage, Spare Rib* and *FAN (Feminist Art News)*.[14]

Outwrite newspaper, produced by a collective of women throughout the 1980s, was dedicated to publishing news by women, for women. Defining itself as an 'internationalist feminist' publication, the paper focused on 'the development

12 Courtney Martin, 'Curating Another Artist: Lubaina Himid and Claudette Johnson' in Ridgway 2019, pp.82–4.
13 Lubaina Himid, 'Inside the Invisible: For/Getting Strategy', in David A. Bailey, Ian Baucom and Sonia Boyce (eds.), *Shades of Black: Assembling Black Arts in 1980s Britain*, Durham, NC 2005, p.43.
14 Maud Sulter, 'Blackwomen's Creativity Project: an Overview' in Sulter 1990, p.15.

of feminism worldwide' and an examination of women's oppressions 'in the context of imperialism, racism and class divisions.'[15] Like *Outwrite*, the Lenthall Road Workshop, where both Pollard and Johnson worked, was a feminist collective, founded in 1975 by three women – Chia Moan, Viv Mullett and Jenny Smith – who, according to an entry on the V&A collections database, took over an existing screen printing shop and turned it into a community printing workshop, focusing predominantly on engaging with local feminist, anti-racist and LGBTQ+ rights groups. Their ethos was 'once you start seeing yourself as a person who can do things then you're in a position to take control of your life'. Running various courses, in particular for women of colour and queer communities, their premises at 81 Lenthall Road was a valued creative hub which lasted for approximately fifteen years.[16]

The role of photography and printmaking in radical Black feminist praxis during this era was centrally allied to the political activism that informed the motivations of many women artists of colour as they sought a place for themselves in a hostile political climate under Thatcher's right-wing government.

The artist Rita Keegan, who had arrived in London from the USA in the late 1970s, not only helped to establish the Brixton Art Gallery in 1983 and curated the first exhibition of the Black Women Artists collective there, but also co-founded the Community CopyArt Resource Centre in 1983. In 1985 Keegan also established the 'Women of Colour Index' at the Women's Artist Slide Library – another example of the ways in which Black women's invisibility could be challenged through documentation within female-created networks. The 'CopyArt' project was a radical way of visual messaging that combined photography, collage and print with photocopying technology to enable the construction of new visual narratives centralising the concerns of radical Black women – indeed, the activist politics of printmaking in all its forms among women of colour during the 1980s was an extremely significant feature of radical feminist art practice of the era. Initially funded by a grant from the Greater London Council, Community CopyArt was based at 41 Battle Bridge Road, Kings Cross. As Kadish Morris has noted, the centre 'ran workshops for activist and community groups and helped to produce print materials for events such as the 1986 anti-apartheid demonstration'.[17]

In October 1988, CopyArt staged *Through Our Black Eyes: A Photocopy Based Exhibition*, a show explicitly addressed to Black women. A flyer advertising CopyArt workshops in advance of the exhibition is worth quoting in full for the picture it provides of the democratic aims of the CopyArt collective in giving space to Black female creative practitioners:

> Community Copyart, an arts collective based in Kings Cross, is organising a photocopy based exhibition on the theme of Black Womens experiences of living in Britain. The exhibition is to be held at Copyart in October and is part of the Spectrum Womens Photography Festival. The aim of the exhibition is for Black Women to document their lives and experiences working from photographs as a base material and extending these images to the medium of photocopying.

15 The full run of *Outwrite: Women's Newspaper*, published in London by the Feminist Newspaper Group between 1982 and 1988, is available from the British Library, Dewey 305.4205.

16 Ingrid Pollard's *Black Lesbian* poster, made in 1984 at Lenthall Road Workshop, is now held by the V&A, accession number E.525-2013. See https://collections.vam.ac.uk/item/O1275026/black-lesbian-poster-ingrid-pollard, accessed 12 Aug. 2023.

17 Kadish Morris, 'Rita Keegan: The Return of Black British Art's Forgotten Pioneer', *Observer*, 11 Sept. 2021, https://www.theguardian.com/artanddesign/2021/sep/11/rita-keegan-the-return-of-black-british-arts-forgotten-pioneer, accessed 12 Aug. 2023.

18 All typographical quirks of the original flyer are as printed. The flyer is reproduced in Adya Jalan, 'Not just a Photocopier: Exploring CopyArt Through Rita Keegan's Practice', (2021), https://sites.gold.ac.uk/library-blog/not-just-a-photocopier-exploring-copyart-through-rita-keegans-practice, accessed 12 Aug. 2023. The exhibition *Through Our Black Eyes: A Photocopy Based Exhibition* took place from 18 October to 2 November 1988.

19 For more on The Elbow Room see Sulter 1990, and Eddie Chambers's Diaspora Artists website, www.diaspora-artists.net, accessed 12 Aug. 2023.

Photocopying is a very effective and accessible medium in creating images which extend beyond photography, in terms of size, colour and shape.

A series of workshops have been organised on 24th & 25th September and the 1st & 2nd October with Rita Keegan and Marlene Smith to show the photocopying techniques that are possible.

Anyone can participate in the workshops & exhibition no art experience is necessary.[18]

In March 1989 Maud Sulter published a statement to coincide with an exhibition she curated at Elbow Room, *Passion: Blackwomen's Creativity of the African Diaspora*, in which Angèle Etoundi Essamba, Lubaina Himid, Ingrid Pollard, Rita Keegan, Dionne Sparks and Michelle Parkerson all participated. (Elbow Room, located in Vine Yard, London SE1, had been established by Lubaina Himid in 1986 as a temporary venue for her *Unrecorded Truths* exhibition which featured works by Brenda Agard, Simone Alexander, David A. Bailey, Sutapa Biswas, Sonia Boyce, Allan deSouza, Keith Piper, Donald Rodney and Marlene Smith.)[19] In Sulter's 1989 statement, published as a flyer to accompany the exhibition of the same name, she defines and elaborates her choice of terms: 'Passion', 'Beauty', 'Sex', 'Lust' and 'Love'. In 'Passion', she writes:

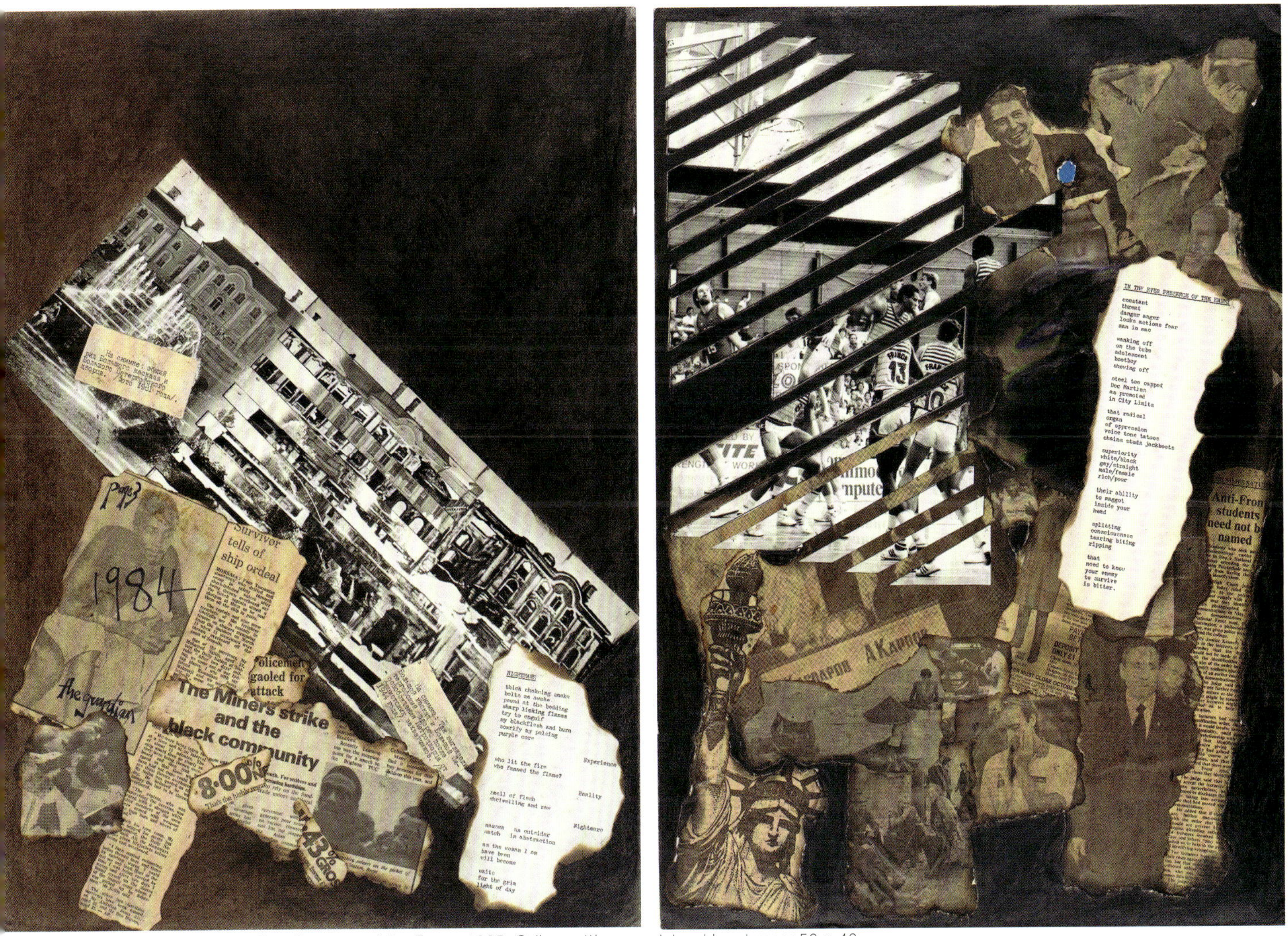

Maud Sulter *Nightmare* and *In the Ever Presence of the Enemy* 1985. Collage with newsprint and burnt paper 59 × 42

> PASSION is a provocative theme for the first International exhibition of contemporary Blackwomen's creativity of the African diaspora. Not because it enters the dangerous terrain of pleasure and danger. No, its provocation lies in the authority of these artists to engage on their own terms in the creation of art around an area blanketed in a patriarchal necrophiliac shroud.

And in 'Lust', she makes an important point about the lineage of her exhibition in relation to a continuum of exhibitions centring on Black female creativity:

> LUST in the guise of a genuine on-going need is paramount in the continuity of not only the staging of Blackwomen's exhibitions but also the more individual and often private process of the production of the work. This exhibition is one of a continuum. 5 BLACK WOMEN AT THE AFRICA CENTRE, BLACK WOMEN TIME NOW, THE THIN BLACK LINE, TESTIMONY, are sister exhibitions to PASSION. Without each groundbreaking step no Blackwoman would have *both* recognition *and* the opportunity to name herself in the myriad facets of her being a *Black Woman Artist*.[20]

Sulter's statement was reproduced one year later in her archival book project *Passion: Discourses on Blackwomen's Creativity* (1990), published by her own imprint, Urban Fox Press. Lubaina Himid's contribution to the book was an essay entitled 'Mapping: A Decade of Black Women Artists 1980–1990', in which she looked back on the achievements of the past decade in a characteristically incisive critique on visibility and invisibility, 'funding, education, galleries, art history and audiences'.

> Being the first has its triumphs, keeping going is where the hard work begins. If we really believed we were the first black women to call ourselves artists, we would have an excuse to give up, we were not, we are the continuum. We are part of an enormous international movement which stretches far back in time.[21]

The plethora of radical Black women's networks of creative practice in the 1980s is a major testament to the strength of purpose to which all of the women discussed in this essay and many more besides were committed. The power of collective action in the face of a hostile and unwelcoming political climate has never been more evident than in the energy, drive and commitment shown by creative women of colour during this fiercely embattled decade.

20 Maud Sulter 'PASSION: Blackwomen's Creativity of the African Diaspora Statement 1989', flyer reproduced in Sulter 1990, p.232.
21 Lubaina Himid, 'Mapping: A Decade of Black Women Artists 1980–1990', in Sulter 1990, pp.63–4.

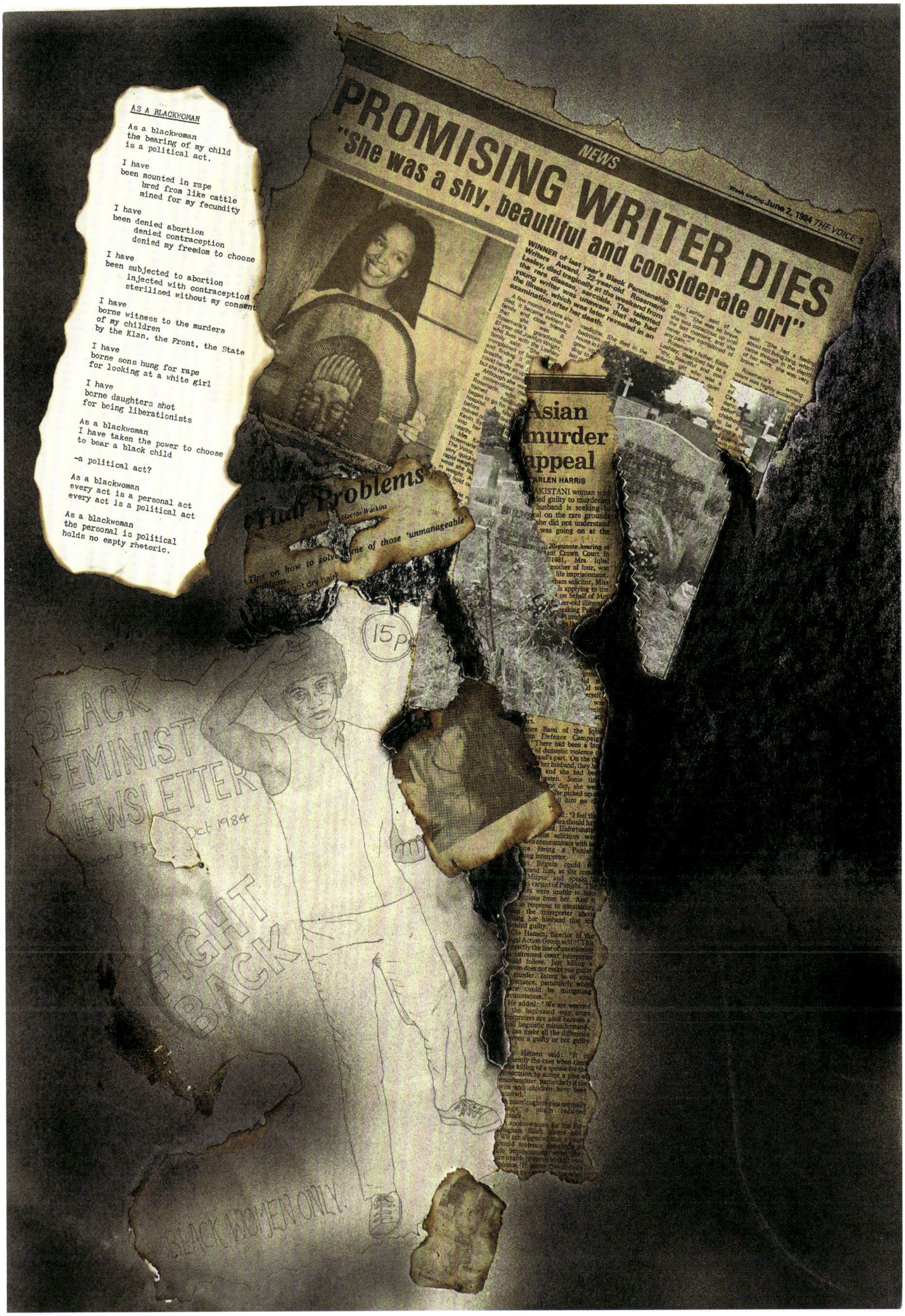

Maud Sulter *As a Blackwoman* 1985. Collage with newsprint and burnt paper 59 × 42

REPRESENTING SOUTH ASIAN WOMEN IN BRITAIN

ALICE CORREIA

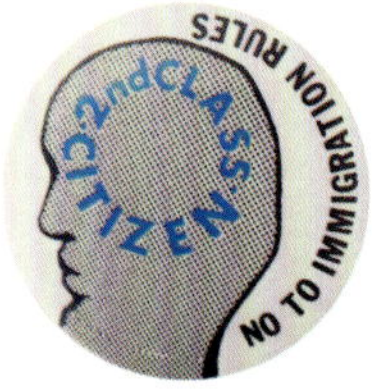

Conjure up a picture of an Asian woman ...
Have the words "passive, submissive", been part of your portrayal? [1]

During the late 1970s and early 1980s, a generation of women artists of South Asian heritage graduated from art colleges across the UK. Utilising a range of fine art, lens-based and craft media, their work was driven by personal and political desires to challenge hegemonic visual discourses in Britain that, as filmmaker Pratibha Parmar observed, stereotyped South Asian women as 'meek and passive victims'.[2]

Although nominally used to describe people originating from India, Pakistan, Bangladesh and Sri Lanka, the term 'South Asian' also includes those born in Uganda, Kenya, Tanzania, Mozambique and elsewhere, and encompasses people from different social classes, religions and castes.[3] As such, within the categorisation of 'South Asian women' are people with different regional cultures, languages, belief systems and socio-economic and political agency. Yet, during the 1970s and 80s, in Britain these differences were largely ignored, and women of South Asian heritage found that they were expected to conform to prejudiced stereotypes. As artist Sutapa Biswas observed in 1986, 'The only way in which we now assess Asian culture is to say, "Oh aren't they oppressed, what d'you think about arranged marriages?"'.[4] By creating new images of South Asian women, during the 1980s artists including Biswas, Zarina Bhimji, Chila Kumari Singh Burman, Nina Edge, Bhajan Hunjan, Mumtaz Karimjee, Symrath Patti, Pratibha Parmar, Samena Rana, Gurminder Sikand and Shanti Thomas challenged British audiences to reconsider long-standing colonial assumptions regarding South Asian womanhood. These artists sought to make work that expressed their particular experiences of being British *and* South Asian, and their art, in its various forms, offered a space for the articulation of both personal and cultural reflection and reconstruction, for social commentary and critique.

Discussing the presence and absence of South Asian women within British colonial narratives of India, Gayatri Chakravorty Spivak observed, 'The most detailed record of women's names in early colonial India is in the context of widow self-immolation', and yet she notes that even in these instances their names are poorly or incorrectly translated and incomplete.[5] Spivak gives the example of the 'Rani of Sirmur', noting that, 'A title and a vaguely sketched first name will suffice for the King of Sirmur's wife because of the specific purpose she is made to serve'.[6] Here, the noblewoman is noteworthy only in terms of her position within a patriarchal society: her subservience to, and potential self-sacrifice in honour of, her husband. Such constructions of South Asian womanhood as dutiful, passive and accepting of a subservient role were applied to women regardless of their status within society, and were further reinforced in contemporaneous portraits, such as Joshua Reynolds's painting of Tysoe Saul Hancock and his family with Indian servant Clarinda (above).

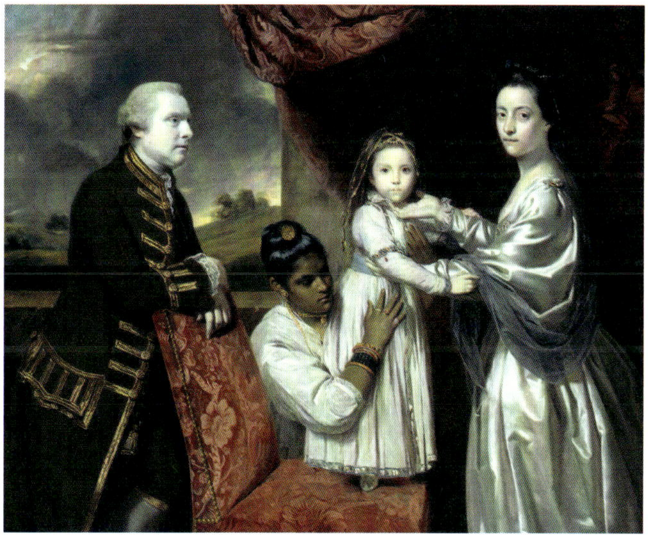

Joshua Reynolds *Tysoe Saul Hancock and his wife Philadelphia (née Austen) with their daughter Elizabeth and Indian servant Clarinda* 1765–7. Oil paint on canvas 140.8 × 173.7

1 Parita Trivedi, '"To Deny Our Fullness": Asian Women in the Making of History', *Feminist Review: Many Voices, One Chant, Black Feminist Perspectives*, no.17, Autumn 1984, pp.37–50, p.38.
2 Pratibha Parmar, 'Black Feminism: The Politics of Articulation', in Jonathan Rutherford (ed.), *Identity: Community, Culture, Difference*, London 1991, pp.101–26, p.116.
3 Avtar Brah, *Cartographies of Diaspora: Contesting Identities*, London 1996, pp.67–83.
4 Sutapa Biswas cited in Yasmin Kureishi, 'Reworking Myths', *Spare Rib*, no.173, Dec. 1986, pp.14–17, p.15.
5 Gayatri Chakravorty Spivak, 'The Rani of Sirmur: An Essay in Reading the Archives', *History and Theory*, vol.24, no.3, Oct. 1985, pp.247–72, p.266.
6 Ibid., p.267.

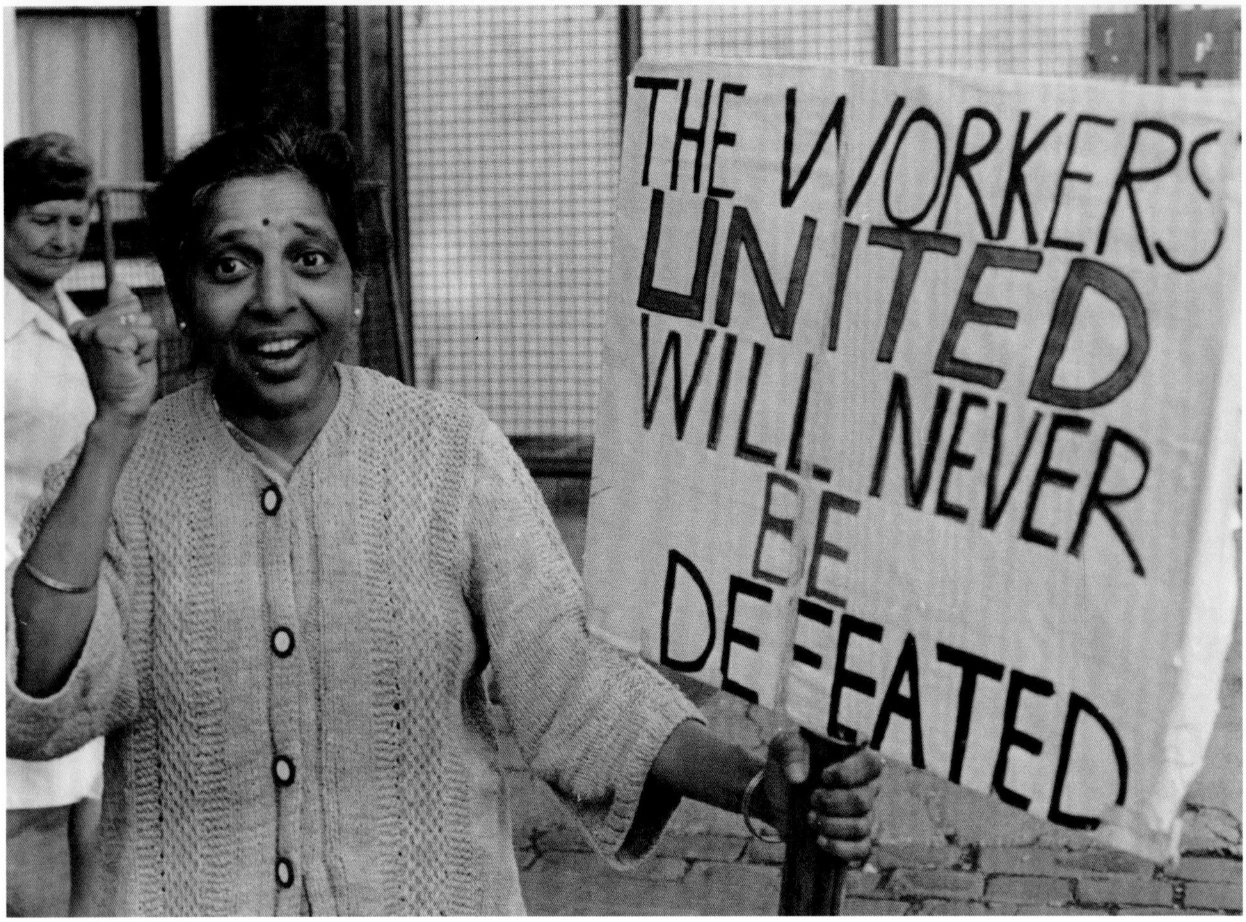

Jayaben Desai, leader of the strike at Grunwick photo processing lab, Willesden 1976, photographed by Sheila Gray, Format Photographers.

By the early twentieth century South Asian women in Britain were broadly characterised as either 'ayahs' (nursemaids) or members of the aristocracy.[7] While Princess Sophia Duleep Singh, goddaughter of Queen Victoria, was active in the women's suffrage movement,[8] generations of women had been transported to Britain to work in the service of wealthy families, often caring for children.[9] After the Second World War, the majority of female South Asian migrants came to Britain to join husbands and fathers who were already working in the country; these women were usually regarded by the Home Office as 'dependants' and were rarely granted British citizenship in their own right.[10] This characterisation of South Asian women as dependent wives and mothers worked together with colonial stereotypes of subservience to silence South Asian women within mainstream British culture. And, as Parmar noted, even broadly sympathetic sociological studies examining the lived experiences of South Asian women in Britain undertaken in the late 1960s and 70s had the tendency to deny women their individual agency.[11]

Yet by the later 1970s, groups of vocal and fearless women broke into public consciousness. Despite constituting a relatively small proportion of the national workforce, South Asian women became involved in organised, and increasingly militant, industrial action. In August 1976 South Asian workers walked out on strike from the Grunwick film processing plant in north-west London. The strike

7 See Rozina Visram, *Ayahs, Lascars and Princes: Indians in Britain, 1700–1947*, London 1986.
8 See Anita Anand, *Sophia: Princess, Suffragette, Revolutionary*, London 2015.
9 Trivedi, 1984, p.40.
10 See Pratibha Parmar, 'Gender, Race and Class: Asian Women in Resistance', in *The Empire Strikes Back: Race and Racism in 70s Britain*, ed. CCCS, London 1982, p.241.
11 See ibid., p.250, and Parmar's discussion of Zaynab Dahya's essay 'Pakistani Wives in Britain', *Race & Class*, vol.6, April 1965, pp.311–21.

12 For a useful introduction to the Grunwick strike, see 'The Grunwick Dispute', https://www.striking-women.org/module/striking-out/grunwick-dispute, accessed 10 Jan. 2023
13 See Radha Kumar, 'From Chipko to Sati: The Contemporary Indian Women's Movement', in Amrita Basu, *The Challenges of Local Feminisms: Women's Movements in Global Perspective*, Boulder, Co., 1995, pp.58–86.
14 See Tobe Levin, 'Introducing Manushi: An Indian Feminist Journal', *Women Studies Newsletter*, vol.8, no.1, Winter 1980, pp.30–1.
15 See Tania Guha, 'Transition of Riches', *Third Text*, vol.7, no.25, 1993, pp.81–6, p.82.
16 See Amrit Wilson, 'Racism and sexism – how they are linked under the Immigration Act', *Spare Rib*, no.25, July 1974, p.174.
17 See Donna Chambers and Rob Worrall, 'The Frontiers of Sisterhood: Representations of Black Feminism in *Spare Rib* (1972–1979)', in Angela Smith (ed.), *Re-reading Spare Rib*, Cham 2017, pp.159–78.
18 Amrit Wilson, *Finding a Voice: Asian Women in Britain*, Wakefield, Québec 2018, new and expanded edn, p.xiv.
19 Julia Sudbury, *'Other Kinds of Dreams': Black Women's Organisations and the Politics of Transformation*, London 1998, p.8.
20 See Brixton Black Women's Group, 'Black Women Organizing', *Feminist Review*, no.17, Autumn 1984, pp.84–9.

was led by Jayaben Desai (left) and undertaken by the mainly female workforce, unwilling to accept poor pay and degrading treatment by the managers and owners.[12] The dispute lasted for fourteen months, and the striking women were subjected to particular forms of racial and sexual provocation as factory management sought to use their preconceived understanding of familial and social structures as a mode of control, arguing that those on the picket line brought shame on their families. What such racist and sexist strategies failed to recognise, however, was the context of feminist activism found in South Asia that Desai and her co-workers were acting within. During this time in India, women's groups were organising collective protests against rape and violence against women, and the exploitation of the environment; and were agitating for better health education and workers' rights, amongst other things.[13] From 1979, the pioneering Delhi-based journal *Manushi: A Journal about Women and Society* brought accounts of women's action to an international audience.[14] Meanwhile in Britain, the roles of Kalpana Dutta and Sarojini Naidu in the independence movement were written out of Richard Attenborough's 1982 film *Gandhi*.[15]

In her early prints such as *Militant Women* 1981 (pp.216–17) and *Jhansi Ki Rani and Public Enemy* 1982, Chila Kumari Singh Burman drew on a matrilineal history of anti-colonial struggle in India and contemporary international protests to challenge hierarchies of power and oppression. A few years later, Gurminder Sikand's watercolour paintings drew on the non-violent protests of women in the Chipko movement in order to address the devastating consequences of the exploitation of natural resources in the Global South (p.238). Since the nineteenth century, women active in the Chipko movement in northern India had embraced trees to prevent deforestation by colonial landlords, and then multinational corporations. While using different visual media and stylistic forms, works by Burman and Sikand recall the histories of protesting South Asian women that those at Grunwick, and elsewhere, were party to.

In 1978 Amrit Wilson's landmark book, *Finding a Voice: Asian Women in Britain*, further dispelled regurgitated notions of docile passivity among South Asian women. First-person accounts of the experience of migration, of trade union protests against exploitative working conditions, and of teenage dreaming of leaving home and escaping generational conflict (as well as other memories and aspirations) provided hitherto unrecorded stories of the diverse and complex realities of South Asian women. Wilson had written the book from the position of a feminist activist who as an independent journalist had written articles about racist legislation, including the 1971 Immigration Act.[16] Although she was a regular contributor to the feminist magazine *Spare Rib* throughout the 1970s, and the magazine did include articles about Desai and the Grunwick strike,[17] Wilson was also alert to the prejudices and fragility of some white feminists. On her encounters with white middle-class women after the publication of *Finding a Voice*, she recalled, 'Confronted with the reality of racism in South Asian women's lives or told that white women too could be racist, they would cry or be openly hostile'.[18]

The reluctance of white feminists within the Women's Liberation Movement (WLM) 'to face racism either as an internal problem or as part of an agenda for political action'[19] during the 1970s and early 1980s was an urgent concern for women of colour. By the late 1970s women of Asian, Caribbean and African heritage joined forces in solidarity against their shared experiences of racism.[20] For Heidi Safia Mirza, the evolution of Black British feminism in the late 1970s was political and polyvocal: 'In naming the shared space of marginalization as "black", postcolonial migrants of different languages, religions, cultures and classes consciously constructed a political identity shaped by the shared experience of racialization and its consequences.'[21]

In 1984 the journal *Feminist Review* published a special issue titled 'Many Voices, One Chant: Black Feminist Perspectives'. In the opening essay, 'Challenging Imperial Feminism', Valerie Amos and Pratibha Parmar discussed the legacies of colonial stereotypes, paternalistic and reductive attitudes to 'Third World Women', and the seeming inability of the WLM to include British women of colour within its conception of universal sisterhood.[22] In reaction to what Amos and Parmar describe as the 'racial chauvinism' found within white feminist groups,[23] coalitions were forged by women of colour who sought to challenge racialised misogyny and dismantle discriminatory social and political structures.[24] The Organisation of Women of African and Asian Descent (OWAAD) and Southall Black Sisters, both established in 1978, offered practical support to women in their communities, and focused on challenging racist practices within housing and social welfare provision, and achieving justice for victims of domestic abuse and forced marriage.[25] Both groups demonstrated against the so-called 'virginity testing' of South Asian women at Heathrow Airport in 1979,[26] while in June that year, Awaz, 'the first organisation of feminist Asian women activists in the UK', joined forces with Brixton Black Women's Group and the Indian Workers' Association GB to co-organise a large-scale 'national demonstration against police brutality'.[27]

It was against this backdrop that artists and writers of South Asian heritage regularly expressed their agency as 'Black' women. The exhibition *Four Indian Women Artists* at the Indian Artists UK (IAUK) gallery, London, staged in 1981, was identified by Rozsika Parker and Griselda Pollock as the first exhibition of Black women artists in the UK.[28] It was organised by Bhajan Hunjan and Chila Kumari Singh Burman, who exhibited their own work alongside that of Naomi Iny and Vinodini Ebdon. On display were intricately patterned ceramics by Ebdon, soft fabric and carved wooden figurative sculptures by Iny, and textured abstract paintings by Hunjan. Burman exhibited recent politicised works including *Bloody Cages* 1980 and *Ban the Bomb* 1981; examples of her body prints referenced Yves Klein's use of the female body as paintbrush and feminist concerns about pornography, while simultaneously challenging white feminist calls for the removal of the female body from artistic representation.[29]

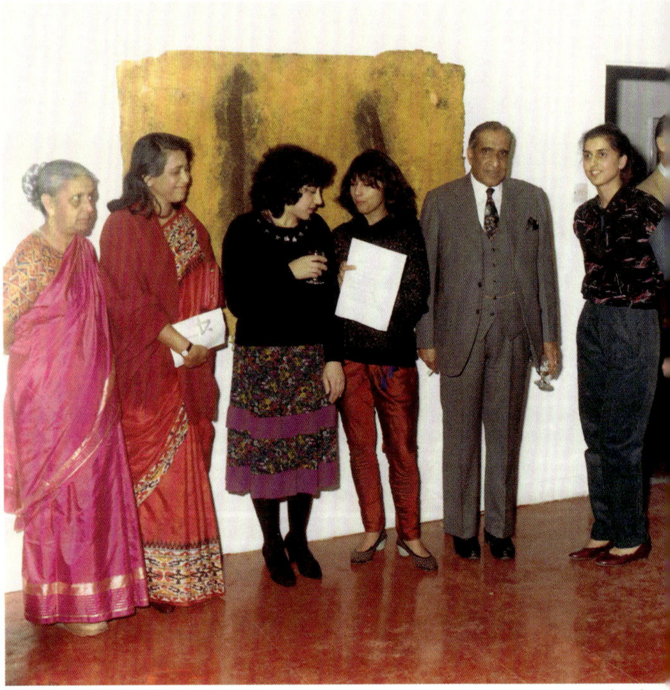

Photograph of the private view of *Four Indian Women Artists*, Indian Artists (UK) Gallery, 1981–2. From left to right: Vinodini Ebdon, Sara Muhammad, Naomi Iny, Chila Kumari Singh Burman, the Indian High Commissioner Dr V.A. Seyid Muhammad and Bhajan Hunjan.

As the 1980s progressed, South Asian artists regularly featured in exhibitions of 'Black art'. In 1985 Zarina Bhimji and Chila Kumari Singh Burman exhibited in *Mirror Reflecting Darkly: Black Women Artists*, curated by Rita Keegan at Brixton Art Gallery, and in that same year Sutapa Biswas's painting *Housewives with Steak Knives* 1985 (p.224) was included in Lubaina Himid's landmark exhibition *The Thin Black Line* at the Institute of Contemporary Arts (ICA), London. Originally part of Biswas's degree show at the University of Leeds, where it was exhibited alongside her film

21 Heidi Safia Mirza, 'Introduction: Mapping a Genealogy of Black British Feminism', in Heidi Safia Mirza (ed.), *Black British Feminism: A Reader*, London 1997, pp.1–28, p.3.
22 Valerie Amos and Pratibha Parmar, 'Challenging Imperial Feminism', *Feminist Review*, no.17, Autumn 1984, pp.3–19.
23 Ibid., p.6.
24 See Mirza 1997, p.4.
25 See Southall Black Sisters, https://southallblacksisters.org.uk, accessed 10 Jan. 2023.
26 See Wilson 2018, p.xix, and Hannana Siddiqui, 'Black Women's Activism: Coming of Age?', *Feminist Review*, no.64, Spring 2000, pp.83–96. For more on 'virginity testing', see Evan Smith and Marinella Marmo, 'Uncovering the "Virginity Testing" Controversy in the National Archives: The Intersectionality of Discrimination in British Immigration History', *Gender & History*, vol.23, no.1, 2011, pp.147–65.

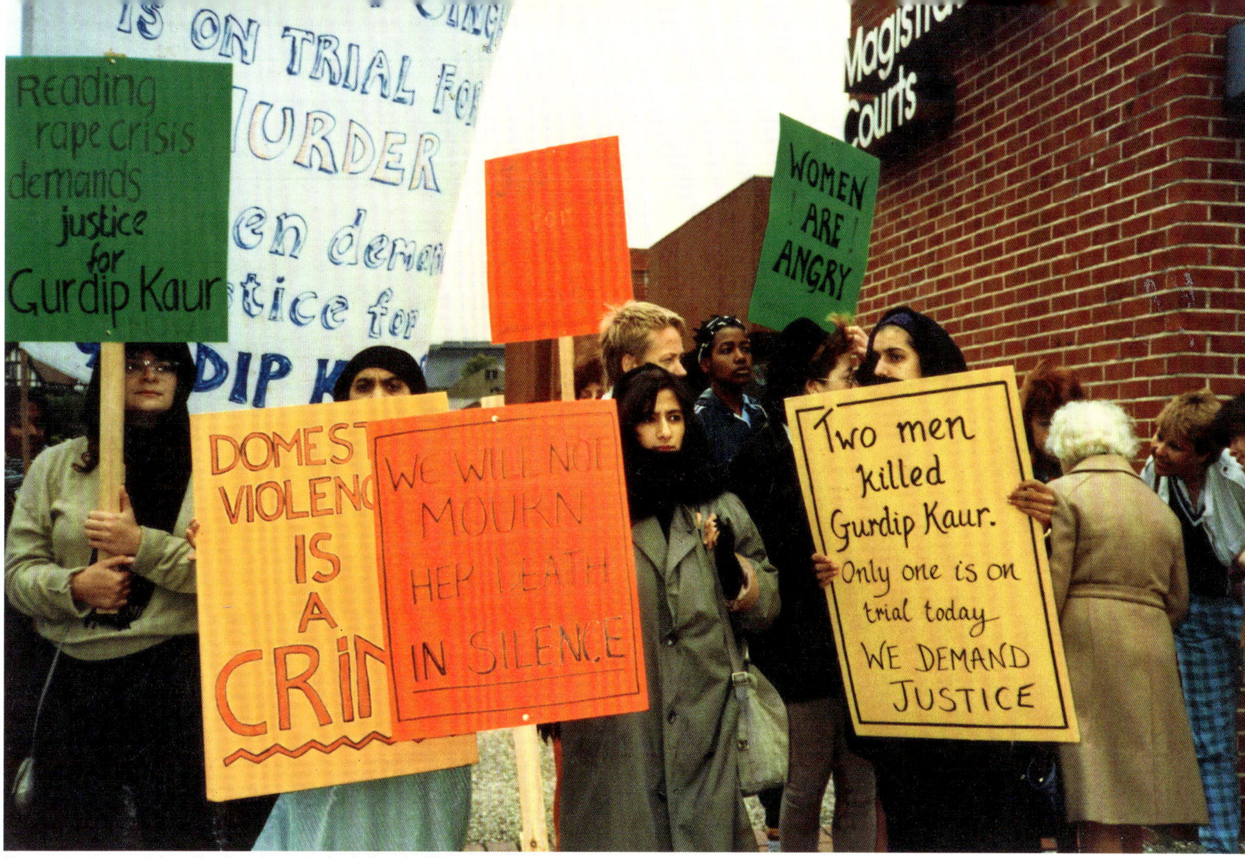

Demonstrators outside Reading Magistrates' Court, 1986.

Kali 1983–5 (p.225), the painting depicts a multi-armed woman staring out at the viewer, brandishing a machete above her head. Described via the nominally derogatory term 'housewife' she is transformed into Kali, a Hindu goddess of war, who is shown as heroic and defiant in the face of both misogynistic patriarchy and exclusionary white feminisms. For curator Gilane Tawadros, *Housewives with Steak Knives* offered the 'clearest enunciation of ... black femininity as a form of creative resistance'.[30]

Chila Kumari Singh Burman also exhibited in *The Thin Black Line*, and in 1986 she gave a talk entitled 'There Have Always Been Great Black Women Artists' at the Black Visual Arts Forum, held at the ICA. Her presentation drew on interviews with other Black women artists, as well as her personal experiences of art college, to describe the barriers and exclusions that women of colour faced individually and collectively when attempting to forge their artistic careers. Burman adapted and extended the arguments made by feminist art historian Linda Nochlin in her celebrated 1971 essay 'Why Have There Been No Great Women Artists?', which identified and discussed the obstacles to female artistic success. However, Burman argued that white feminists and feminist art historians had been complicit in the oppression of Black women artists, stating that they had failed to engage with either the specific challenges faced by Black women artists or the nuances of their work.[31] In light of such pervasive neglect, Burman argued that Black women needed to work collectively – for example in Black women-only exhibitions – to carve a space for themselves, on their own terms. Arguably, the type of collective endeavour promoted by Burman was exemplified in the 1987 journal *Polareyes: A Journal by and about Black Women Working in Photography*, which included an interview with Ingrid Pollard and a visual-poem by Zarina Bhimji alongside Samena Rana's searing essay 'Disability and Photography'.[32] In her text Rana vividly recounts the challenges and resistance that she encountered as a wheel-chair user when attempting to access and work in photographic darkrooms.

27 Wilson 2018, pp.xviii–xix.
28 Rozsika Parker and Griselda Pollock (eds.), *Framing Feminism: Art and the Women's Movement 1970–85*, London 1987, p.64.
29 See Amelia Jones, *Body Art: Performing the Subject*, Minneapolis 1998, p.24.
30 Gilane Tawadros, 'Beyond the Boundary: The Work of Three Black Women Artists in Britain', *Third Text*, vol.3, no.8, 1989, pp.121–50, p.145. For more on Biswas' work see, Sutapa Biswas, *Lumen*, London 2021.
31 Chila Kumari Singh Burman, 'There Have Always Been Great Black Women Artists', paper presented at the Black Visual Arts Forum at the Institute of Contemporary Arts, London, 25–26 Oct. 1986, reprinted in *Women Artists Slide Library Journal*, no.15, Feb. 1987, pp.9–12.
32 *Polareyes: A Journal by and about Black Women Working in Photography*, London 1987. Samena Rana's essay is reproduced in Alice Correia (ed.), *What is Black Art? Writings on African, Caribbean and Asian Artists in Britain, 1981–1989*, London 2022, pp.152–4.

While artists and writers of African, Asian and Caribbean heritage were working together under the banner of 'Blackness', there were also instances where South Asian artists came together to address the specificities of their experience as South Asian women. In 1986 Bhajan Hunjan organised *Numaish: An Exhibition of 5 Asian Women's Work* at the People's Gallery, London, and that same year Mumtaz Karimjee and Amina Patel, with Manjula Mukherjee and Vibha Osbon, organised *Aurat Shakti* at the Cockpit Gallery, London.[33] Also in 1986, artist Symrath Patti organised *Jagrati – an exhibition by 13 Asian Women Artists* at the Greenwich Citizens Gallery in Woolwich, south-east London. The exhibition included the work of Dushka Ahmed, Zarina Bhimji, Sutapa Biswas, Chila Kumari Singh Burman, Nina Edge, Bhajan Hunjan, Naomi Iny, Mumtaz Karimjee, Shamina Khanour, Symrath Patti, Sukhwinder Saund, Ranjan Shadra and Shanti Thomas, and aimed to connect 'the work of these artists to the experience of the Asian community; enabling the artist to develop a dialogue within the community to raise issues of artistic and political relevance'.[34]

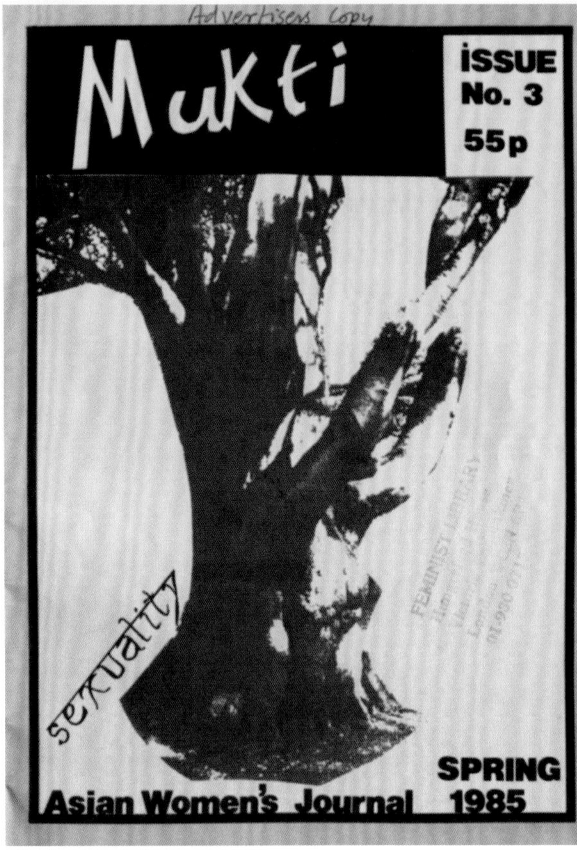

Mukti, issue no.3 on sexuality, Spring 1985.

Jagrati, which means 'awakening' in Hindi, had originally been conceived as a thematic show concentrating on the issue of domestic violence, but during the planning stages Patti expanded the exhibition's remit to include a broader consideration of the lived-experiences of South Asian women. As a student at Leeds Polytechnic, Patti had endured persistent racist misogyny from her tutors, and her decision to champion South Asian women artists may be regarded as a proactive strategy to establish a support network for artists who were often working in isolation. The show presented various forms of feminist resistance, from Shanti Thomas's depiction of a chic London office worker in *City Tempo* 1985, to Sutapa Biswas' *Que Sera Sera* 1985–6 which presents a woman carving a face into a potato while sitting in an armchair watching the news on television. On the screen is Conservative MP Leon Brittan, then Secretary of State for Trade and Industry, and Biswas addresses the jobs women undertake within the home, and the extent to which the value of that work is recognised. Zarina Bhimji exhibited her photo-text work *In Response to the F-Stops Exhibition (For the White Feminists)*, which positioned quotations by feminist authors including Hazel Carby, bell hooks and Audre Lorde alongside enigmatic still-life images of domestic objects (p.239).[35] For critic Jyll Bradley, Bhimji's work 'seemed to address the unacknowledged absence of black women in white feminist discourses which encouraged women to re-see, re-read and re-invent lives and histories. Bhimji was using the "new" language of sight to discuss that which was silenced.'[36]

Bhajan Hunjan's contribution to *Jagrati*, *Tribute to Late Balwant Kaur and Gurdip Kaur – Victims of Domestic Violence* 1986 (p.228), was a response to the killings of Blawant Kaur, murdered by her husband at the Brent Asian Women's Refuge in 1985, and Gurdip Kaur, murdered in Reading by her husband and brother-in-law in 1986. At the time Hunjan's approach to art-making was informed by her experiences of working at Sahara Asian Women's Refuge in Reading, where she was confronted

33 For more on *Numaish*, see Alice Correia, 'Researching Exhibitions of South Asian Women Artists in Britain in the 1980s', *British Art Studies*, no.13, Sept. 2019, https://doi.org/10.17658/issn.2058-5462/issue-13/acorreia, accessed 6 Feb. 2023. For more on *Aurat Shakti*, see Mumtaz Karimjee and Amina Patel, 'Aurat Shakti', *Ten:8 The Critical Decade*, vol.2, no.3, Spring 1992, pp.146–7.

34 Fay Rodrigues, *Jagrati – an exhibition by 13 Asian Women Artists*, exh. pamphlet, Greenwich Citizens Gallery, London 1986, p.1. Panchayat Special Collection, Tate Archive.

with the hardship and violence that many women faced. Together with others from Sahara, Southall Black Sisters, Berkshire Women's Aid, Reading, and Reading Rape Crisis, she demonstrated outside Reading Magistrates' Court to demand justice for Gurdip Kaur (p.205). In her work Hunjan approached the traumas experienced by women with a quiet sensitivity and compassion, and her painted tribute may be regarded as an extension of her activism.

Mumtaz Karimjee also exhibited in *Jagrati*, and was a member of the editorial group for *Polareyes*. For Karimjee, working in solidarity with other Black photographers as well as participating in shows dedicated to South Asian artists, was not a contradictory decision:

> There are differences between the different groups which make up the Black community in Britain, and I believe it is only possible to become a positive force in the community as a whole if first of all I accept and claim for myself my own specific identity. To do this is not to deny or negate my place in the Black community, but rather to say, I, a British woman of Indian origin, am part of the Black struggle and join in that struggle with all the strength and creative force that comes out of being who I am.[37]

Karimjee's essay on the simultaneity of being Black and Asian was published in the grassroots feminist magazine *Mukti* in 1987. *Mukti* was produced by a collective coalition of South Asian women based in London; it ran for seven issues from 1983 to 1987. The collective's aim was to foster a sense of kinship and provide a safe space where discussions could be voiced and experiences shared in non-judgemental ways. From the outset the magazine aspired to be accessible and open to all, and was initially produced in six languages – English, Hindi, Gujarati, Bengali, Urdu and Punjabi. Articles, poems and short stories addressed such topics as violent confrontations between National Front members and young local South Asians in Southall, and the arrest of the Newham 8 in 1981; the 1984 Bhopal disaster; deportations and citizenship rights; and female sexual fulfilment. Regular news features addressed contemporaneous feminist activism in South Asia; issue no.1 reported on women's protests in India based on articles published in *Manushi* and *Eve's Weekly (India)*, while issue no.2 included a report on Nirmala Nithyanandan, a renowned feminist and revolutionary freedom fighter who became the first woman to be arrested – on 20 November 1982 – under Sri Lanka's Prevention of Terrorism Act.

Mukti issue no.3, published in Spring 1985 (left), was dedicated to the theme of sexuality, and the collectively written first article opened with the line, 'We Asian women are denied the space, choice, time and right to talk or even think about our own sexuality and about sex, on OUR terms'.[38] A photograph by Karimjee of a tree was placed on the front cover of the issue, and anticipated her groundbreaking work *In Search of an Image* 1987 (pp.262–3). In this multi-part photographic work, Karimjee constructed a self-portrait that reckoned with the multiple and intersectional aspects of her identity, openly addressing her own sexuality through an engagement with both colonial British and contemporary Indian attitudes towards lesbianism. The central panel depicts the artist crouching under the branches of an ancient oak, echoing the tree featured on the cover of *Mukti*. Reflecting on *In Search of an Image*, artist Sunil Gupta later noted, 'Karimjee's work is a brave attempt to reclaim a space for herself, caught as we are in a climate of blame and the instant threat of excommunication from the culture/race. As the first published piece of "out" lesbian work by a Muslim woman in this country it is historic.'[39]

35 For further discussion of this work see Allison K. Young, 'Lady of Silences: The Enigmatic Photo-Text Work of Zarina Bhimji', *British Art Studies*, no.20, July 2021, https://doi.org/10.17658/issn.2058-5462/issue-20/ayoung, accessed 6 Feb. 2023.
36 Jyll Bradley, 'An Audience unto Herself: Zarina Bhimji profiled by Jyll Bradley', *Women's Art Magazine*, no.51, March–April 1993, p.23.
37 Mumtaz Karimjee, 'Black and Asian: Definitions and Redefinitions', *Mukti*, no.6, Spring 1987, p.8.
38 Mukti collective, 'Self-Fulfilment', *Mukti*, no.3, Spring 1985, pp.4–6, p.4.
39 Sunil Gupta, 'Culture Wars: Race and Queer Art', in Peter Horne and Reina Lewis (eds.), *Outlooks: Lesbian and Gay Sexualities and Visual Cultures*, London 2002, pp.170–7, p.174.

Like Karimjee's written and photographic work, Pratibha Parmar also offered layered and nuanced accounts of female agency from a lesbian perspective. In her film *Sari Red* 1988, montaged archival and staged images overlap and repeat, time is slowed (p.235); the colour and word 'red' are used explicitly to denote blood and bloodshed, but also symbolically to convey 'sensuality and intimacy between Asian women'.[40] Parmar identified the film as a memorial to the young Indian woman Kalbinder Kaur Hayre, who was killed in a racially motivated attack in Dartford, Kent, in 1985. Moving between public and private spaces, the film poignantly addresses the everyday fear of violence held by young women, while also offering glimpses of tenderness and care. Multiple voices tell the story of Kalbinder Kaur Hayre, while the refrain, 'for her dignity and pride, she shouted back', is repeated. These repetitions serve as a reminder: although *Sari Red* may be understood as a work of mourning, it is also an assertion of resistance, a refusal to be confined.

In 1988 Sutapa Biswas co-curated the touring exhibition *Along the Lines of Resistance*, with Sarah Edge of Rochdale Art Gallery and Claire Slattery of the Cooper Gallery, Barnsley. The exhibition recognised and sought to address the exclusion of women of colour from previous white feminist exhibitions and art histories and showcased the work of twenty young women artists, providing space for a plurality of voices.[41] The curators asserted the need to confront the violence experienced by women, whether in the form of racist language, as in Lesley Sanderson's *Self-Portrait as a Chinky* 1984 or because of civil war, as in Leslie Hakim-Dowek's *Chaque Matin On se Lève à un Monde moins Fertile (Each Morning We Awake to a Less Fertile World)* 1986. Nina Edge exhibited *Snakes and Ladders* 1985, a multi-part batik and ceramic work that challenged colonial orthodoxies (p.249). Through graffiti-like text, the central, sari-clad female figure is called upon to embody a submissive yet alluring exotic eroticism, while she is simultaneously regarded as a potential threat to the national – white – status-quo. Her life takes place within a dangerous game of snakes and ladders, where one false move could see her tumble. However, in making reference to the infamous nineteenth century 'Indian Rope Trick', riffing on, and subverting the stereotype of Eastern, or Asian people as cunning and not to be trusted, Edge and her agile woman refuse to submit to racist expectations.

Writing on the significance of *Along the Lines of Resistance* in its catalogue, Pratibha Parmar noted that, 'it is heartening to see that the challenges made in the early part of this decade by black women to an exclusionary and imperial definition of feminism have been taken up and acted upon'.[42] For Parmar and the other women artists of South Asian heritage discussed here, Black British feminism provided 'a space and a framework' for discussion and debate that not only engaged with the complexities of their ethnicity, class, and sexuality, but also for challenging white chauvinistic feminism and endemic racism, in solidarity with other women artists of colour.[43] While this generation each conveyed their politics differently, and worked in a range of artistic media and stylistic approaches, they also collaborated to create their own spaces and forums in which to exhibit and debate their work. While Parmar acknowledged that at times those spaces 'had to be fought for and negotiated',[44] artists nonetheless confidently and unapologetically articulated their personal and collective experiences of being a South Asian woman in Britain. Their art may be regarded as assertive acts of resistance, reclamation and empowerment.

40 Pratibha Parmar, *Sari Red*, film outline dated 6 June 1990, Rochdale Art Gallery Archives, Touchstones, Rochdale.
41 See Biswas, Edge and Slattery 1988, and Jane Beckett, 'Resistance, Continuity, Struggle: The Organisers of *Along the Lines of Resistance* Talk to Jane Beckett', *Feminist Art News*, vol.2, no.9, 1988, pp.4–7.
42 Pratibha Parmar in Sutapa Biswas, Sarah Edge and Claire Slattery (eds.), *Along the Lines of Resistance: An Exhibition of Contemporary Feminist Art*, exh. cat., Cooper Gallery, Barnsley 1988, pp.5–7, p.5.
43 Parmar 1988, p.7.
44 Parmar 1991, p.106.

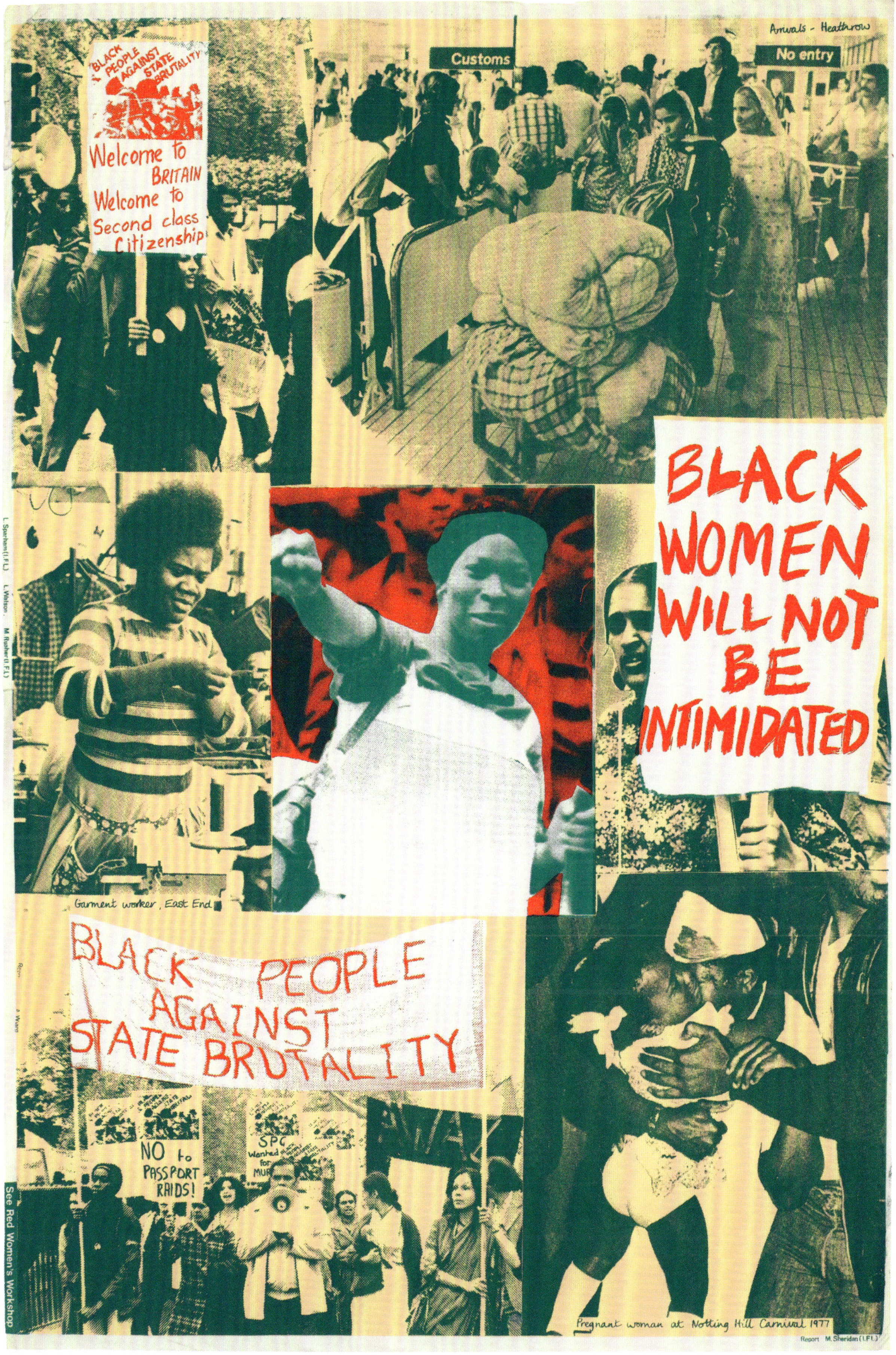

See Red Women's Workshop *Black Women Will Not be Intimidated* 1980–1. Screenprint on paper 79 × 53

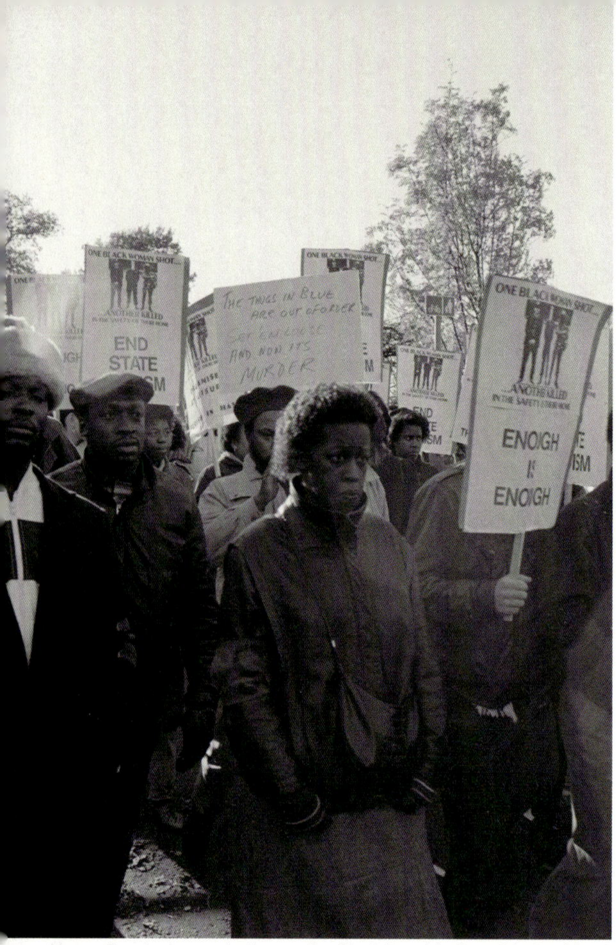

Above: People demonstrating on the Black People's Day of Action March in 1981, which took place following the New Cross Fire. Photographed by Mumtaz Karimjee.

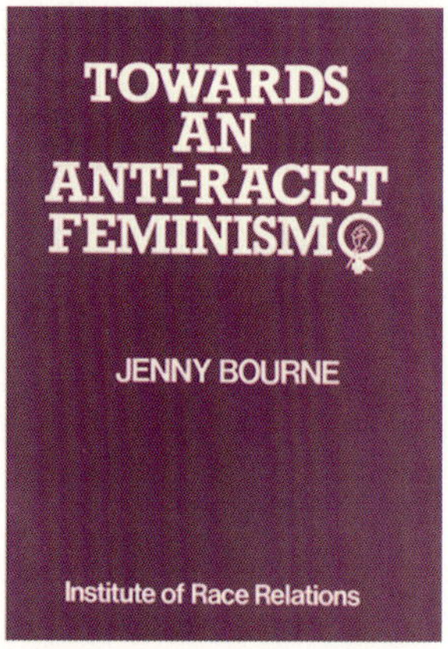

1

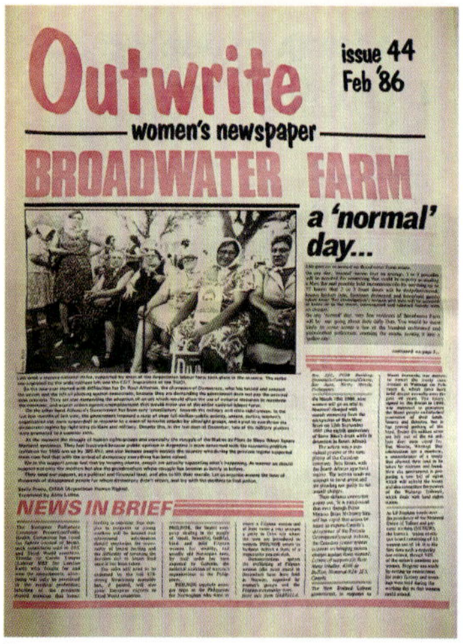

2

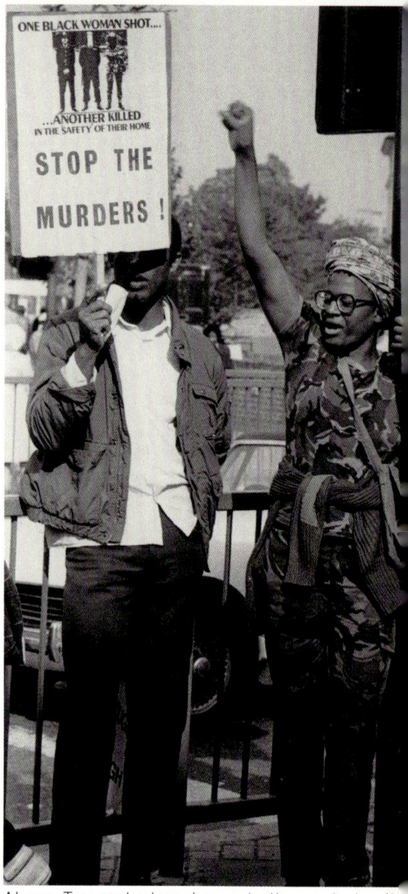

Above: Two protesters demonstrating against polic brutality outside Brixton Police Station, 1980s. Th protester on the left is holding a 'Stop The Murde placard. Photographed by Joanne O'Brien.

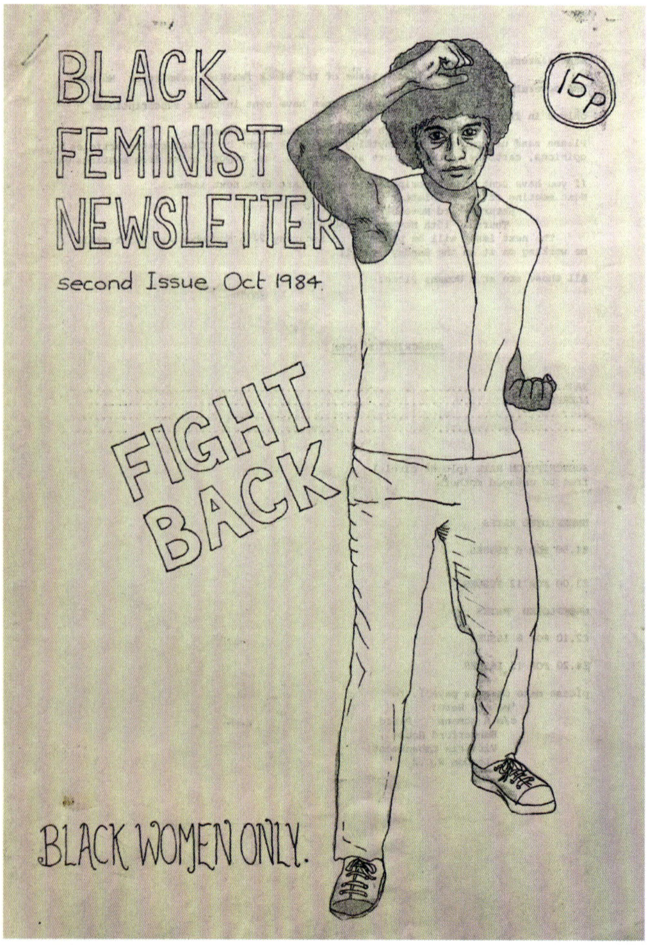

3

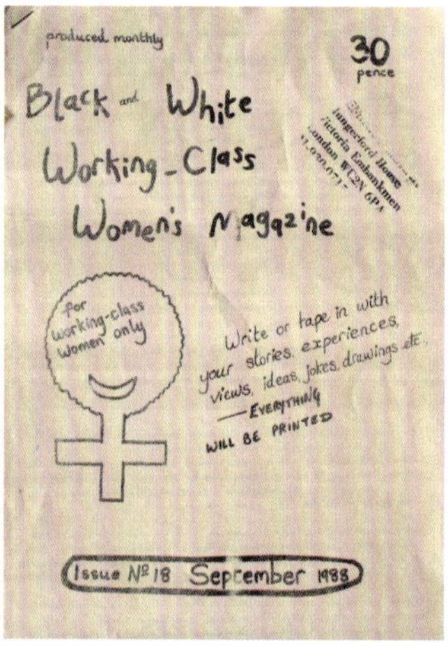

4

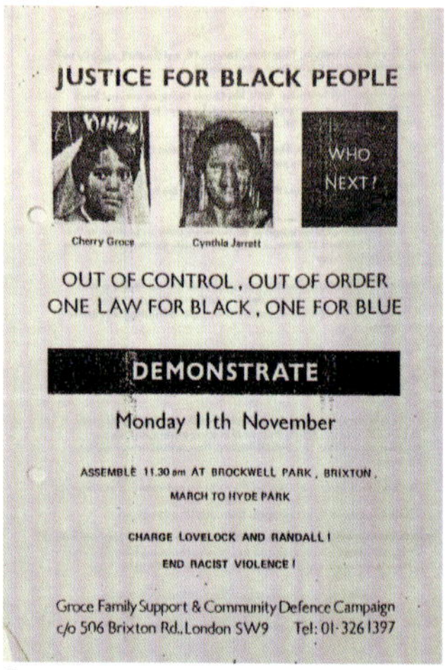

5

Below: Police officers with riot shields during a demonstration on the Black People's Day of Action, 1981. Photographed by Joanne O'Brien.

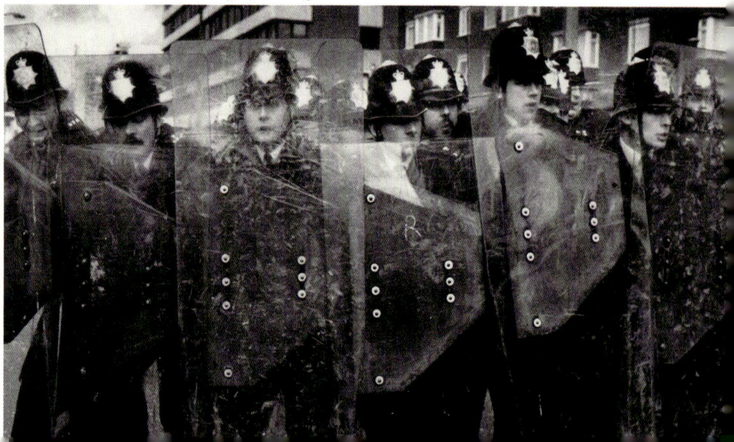

We Are Here

Although the term 'Political Blackness', referring to all people who experience discrimination based on skin colour, is often contested today, during the late 1970s, many Asian women joined forces with Black women from the African and Caribbean diaspora 'in an expression of solidarity against the shared experience of anti-black racism'.[1] Groups such as the Southall Black Sisters and the Sari Squad were at the forefront of activism seeking to achieve justice for unfair labour practices, immigration cases and victims of domestic violence and honour-based violence, and to protest state violence, such as the much-publicised practice of 'Virginity Testing' that took place at Heathrow Airport in the 1970s. Publications such as *We Are Here: Black Feminist Newsletter*, *In Print: Newsletter of Peckham Black Women's Group* and *FOWAAD!* appealed to an audience of both Black and Asian women. *Mukti*, the journal published by the Mukti Collective, founded in 1983, was produced by and for South Asian women. It was printed in six languages and covered a range of diverse and pertinent topics including sexuality, immigration and self-defence.

[1] 'Black Women Organizing', *Feminist Review: Many Voices, One Chant, Black Feminist Perspectives*, no.17, Autumn 1984, pp.84–9.

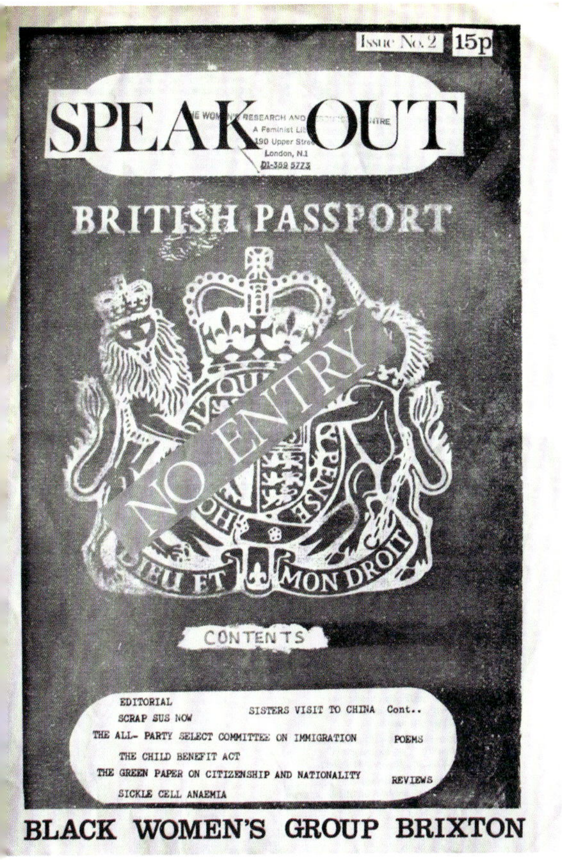

Issue No.2 15p

SPEAK OUT

BRITISH PASSPORT

NO ENTRY

DIEU ET MON DROIT

CONTENTS

EDITORIAL
SCRAP SUS NOW
SISTERS VISIT TO CHINA Cont..
THE ALL- PARTY SELECT COMMITTEE ON IMMIGRATION
POEMS
THE CHILD BENEFIT ACT
THE GREEN PAPER ON CITIZENSHIP AND NATIONALITY
REVIEWS
SICKLE CELL ANAEMIA

BLACK WOMEN'S GROUP BRIXTON

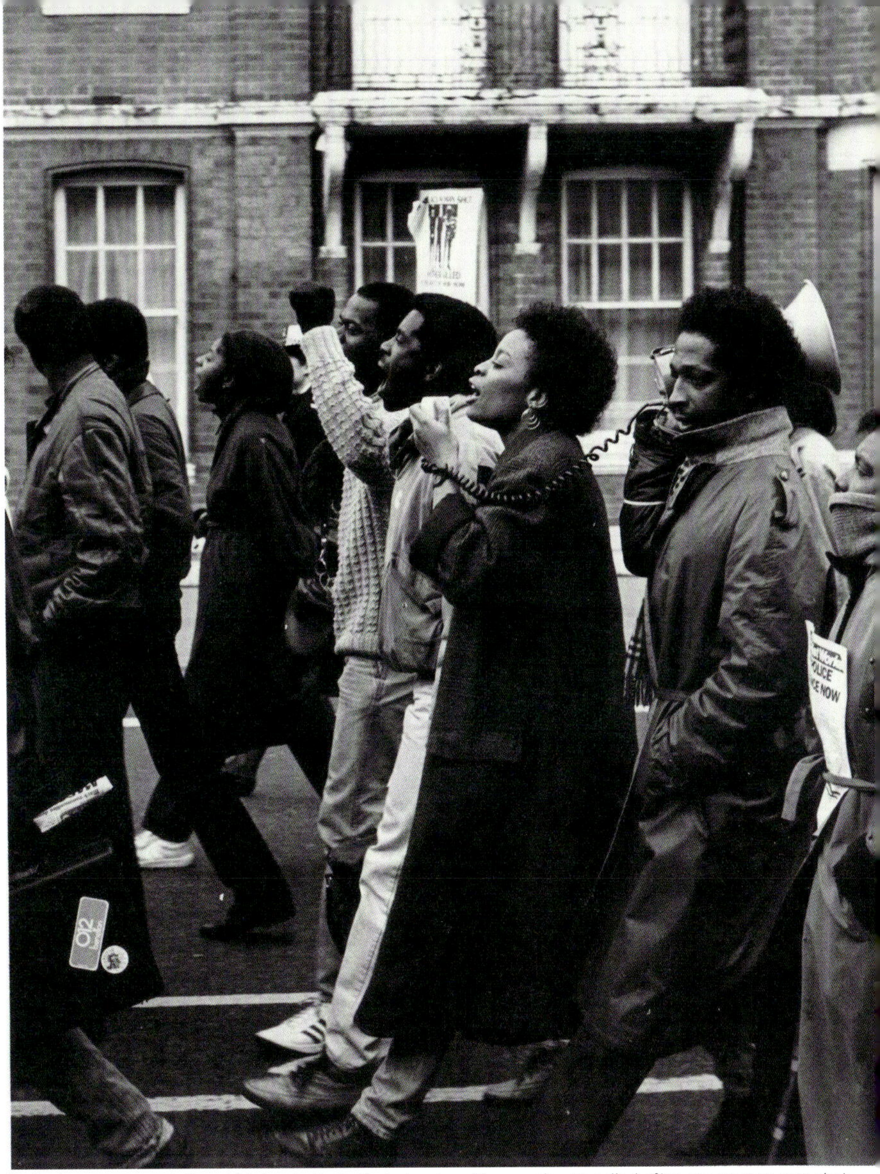

Protesters on a march from Brixton to Hyde Park, London. The march was called after one woman was shot and another died during police raids on their house, c.1980s. Photographed by Suzanne Roden.

Campaigners protesting for justice for Black people, November 1985. Photographed by Brenda Prince.

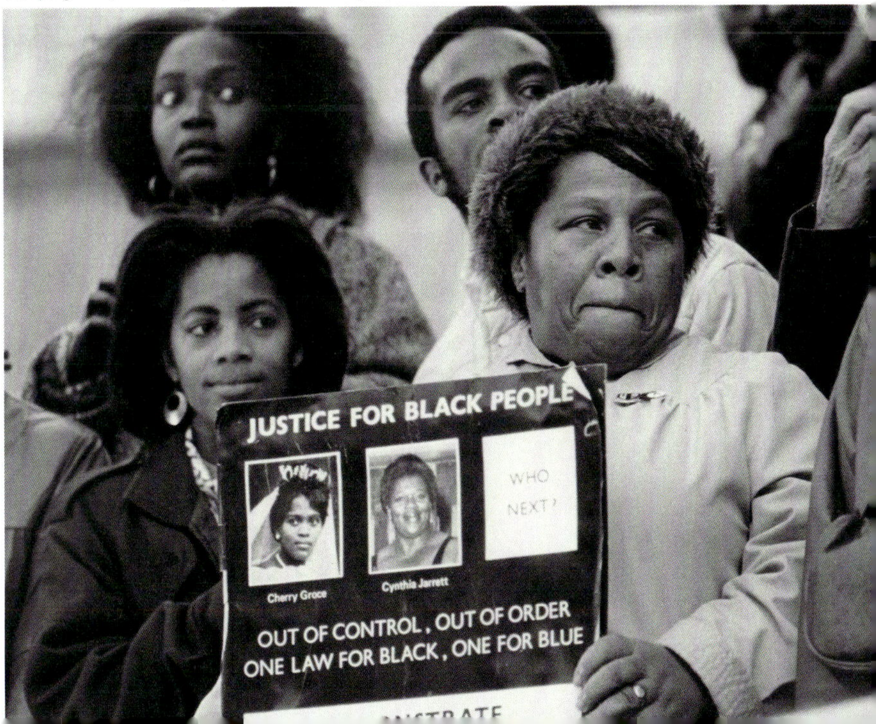

- Jenny Bourne, *Towards an Anti-Racist Feminism*, London 1984.
- *Outwrite Women's Newspaper*, no.44, February 1986.
- *Fight Back: Black Feminist Newsletter*, no.2, October 1984.
- *Black and White Working-Class Women's Magazine*, no.18, September 1988.
- Justice for Black People: leaflet for demonstration march from Brixton to Hyde Park, London on 11 November 1985. The march was to protest against racist violence in response to the police shooting of Cherry Groce.
- *Speak Out*, no.2, c.1979. *Speak Out* was the publication of the Black Women's Group, Brixton.

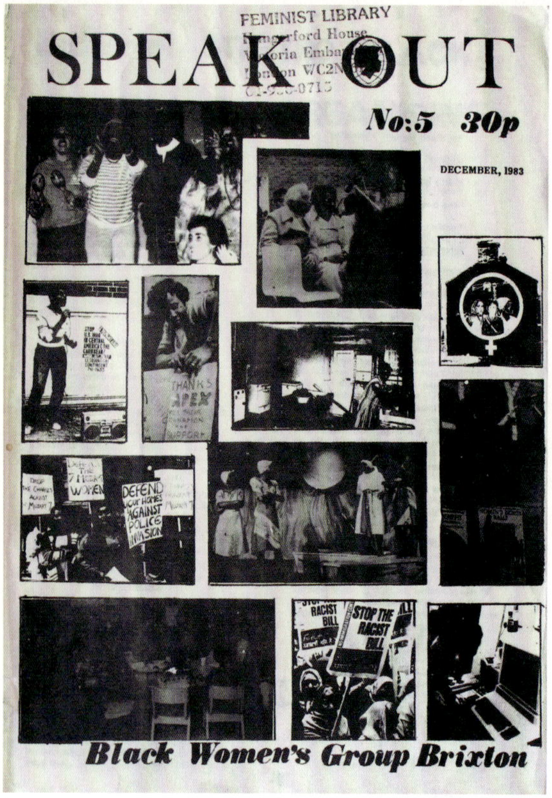

1

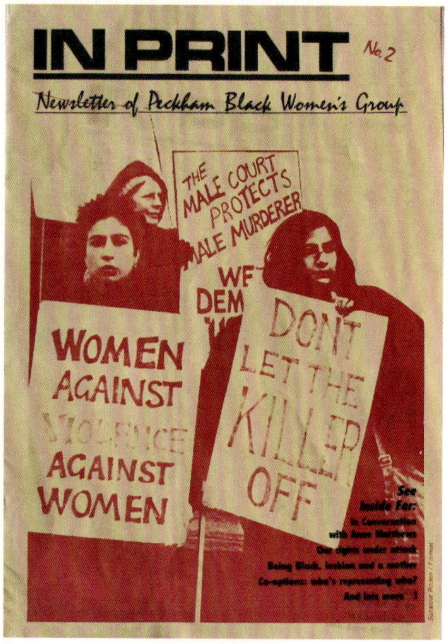

2

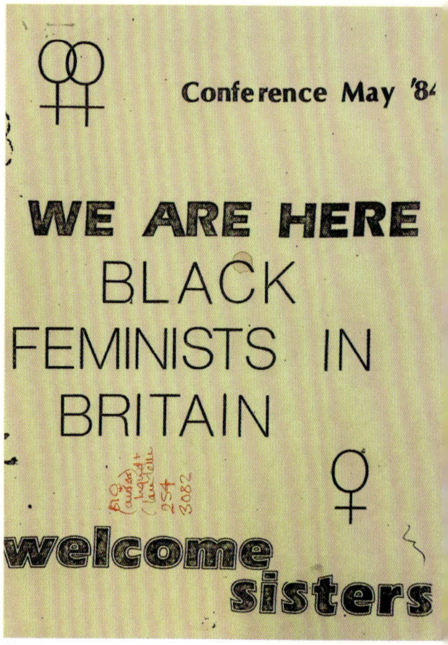

3

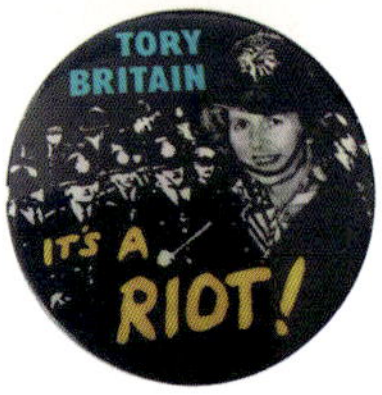

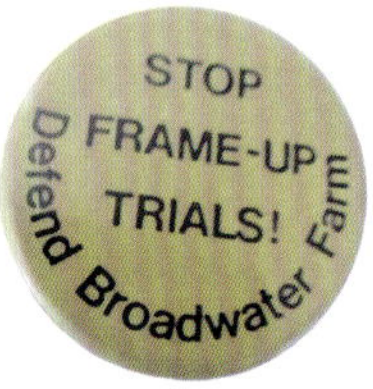

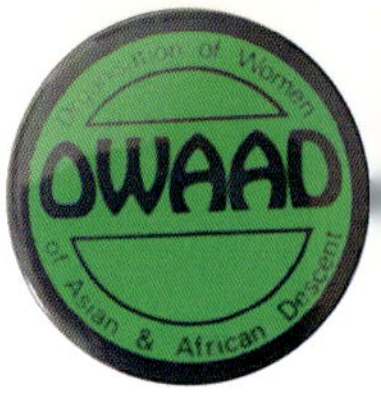

Campaigners against the government immigration bill, 1981. Photographed by Val Wilmer.

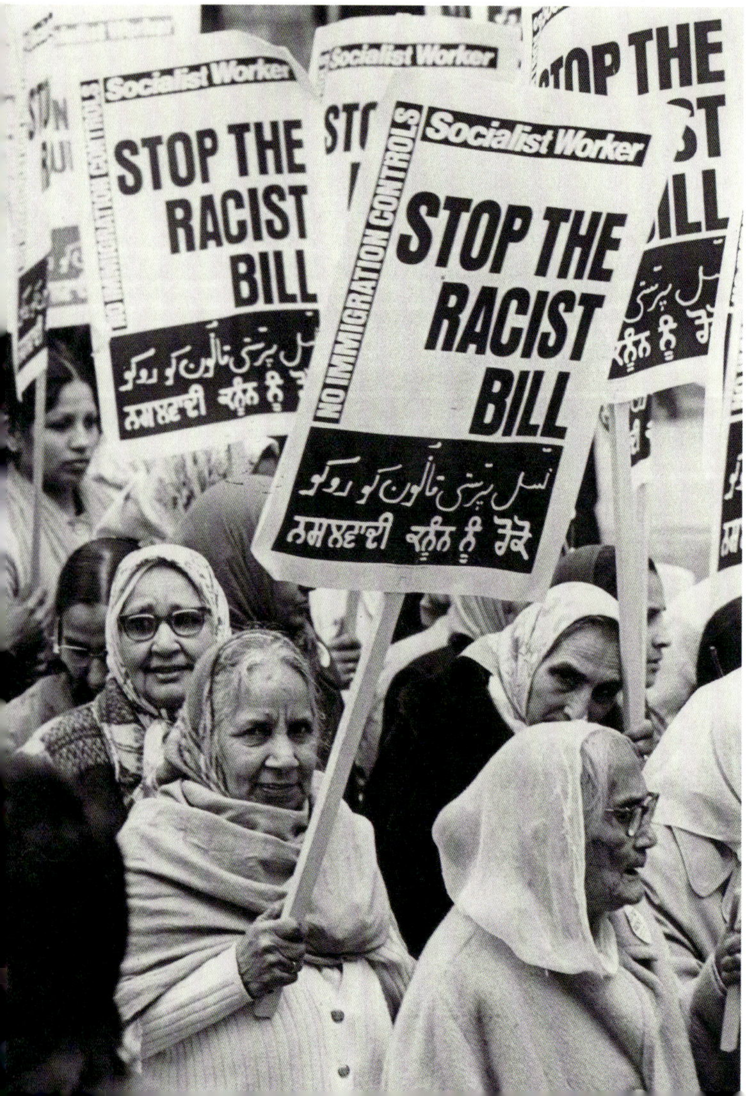

8

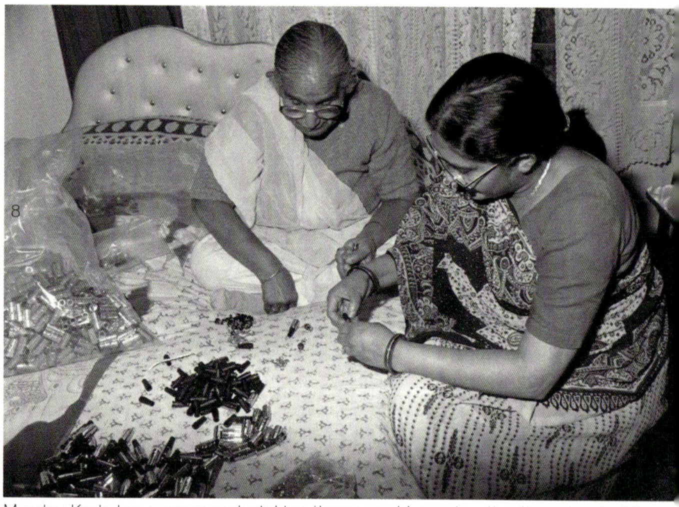

Mumtaz Karimjee, women undertaking 'home work' constructing lipsticks, 1988.

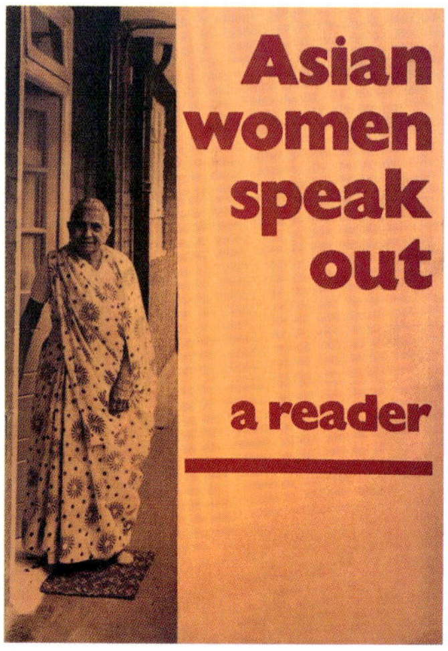

4

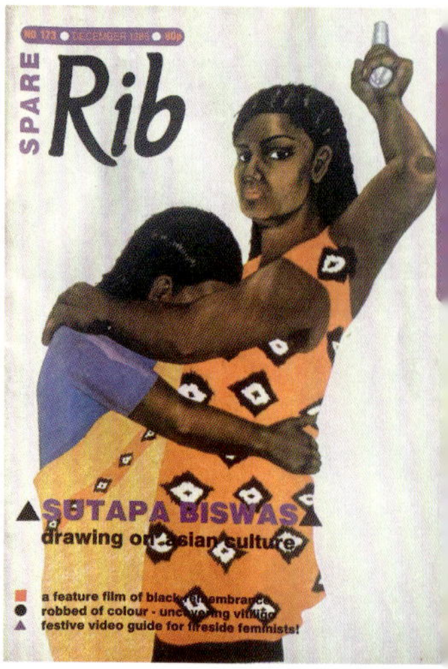

5

Black Women Time Now

In the early 1980s racial tension in the UK was at fever pitch. On the 18 January 1981 at a house party in New Cross, London, thirteen Black teenagers died in what is suspected to have been a racially-motivated arson attack. In response, an action committee was set up and the Black People's Day of Action that followed on 2 March 1981 saw some 20,000 people march through London. At the same time, an increased use of police powers to stop and search Black people was triggering public outrage at the inequality, institutional racism and police brutality experienced by Black communities. These tensions culminated in the Brixton, Toxteth, Moss Side and Handsworth Uprisings of 1981. The Scarman Report commissioned by the UK government following the uprisings was published in November 1981. While it did not concede to institutional racism, it directly criticised the police and stated that 'racial disadvantage is a current fact of British life', and advised that 'urgent action is needed if it is not to become an endemic, ineradicable disease, threatening the very survival of our society.'

On the 28 September 1985, police officers raided Cherry Groce's house in Brixton, where she was shot and paralysed as a result. Groce suffered the complications of the attack until her death in 2011, aged 63. On the 5 October 1985, Cynthia Jarrett suffered a fatal heart attack during a police raid on her home by officers who were looking for her son who they incorrectly believed had stolen a car. These two instances in close succession fuelled further uprisings in Brixton, Peckham, Tottenham and Toxteth at the end of 1985.

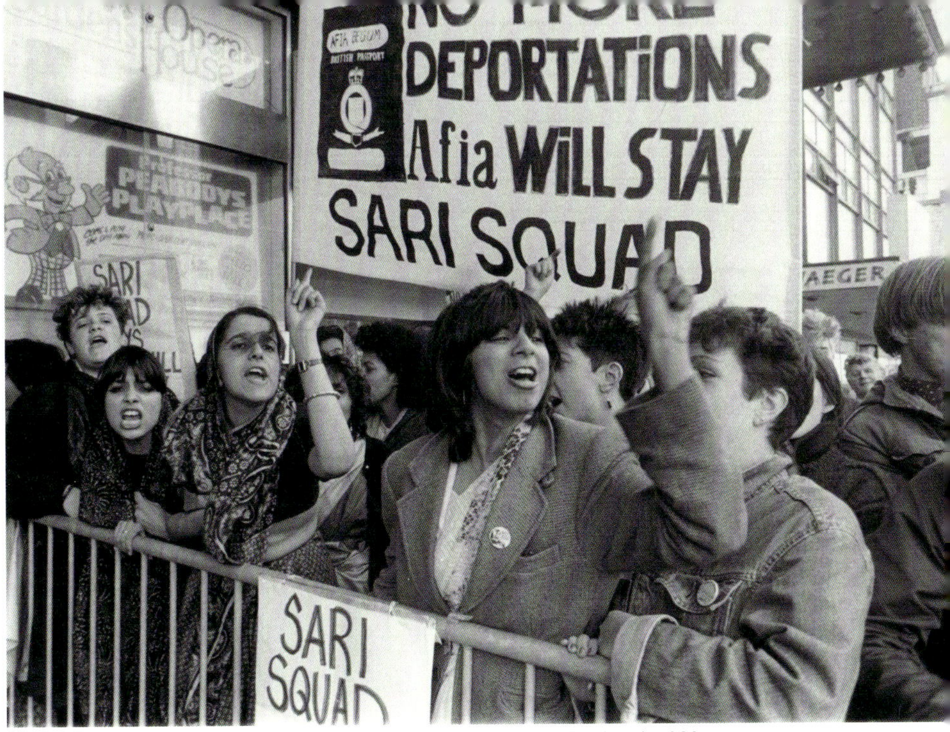

The Sari Squad protesting outside the Conservative Party Conference, Blackpool, 1983. Photographed by Sheila Gray.

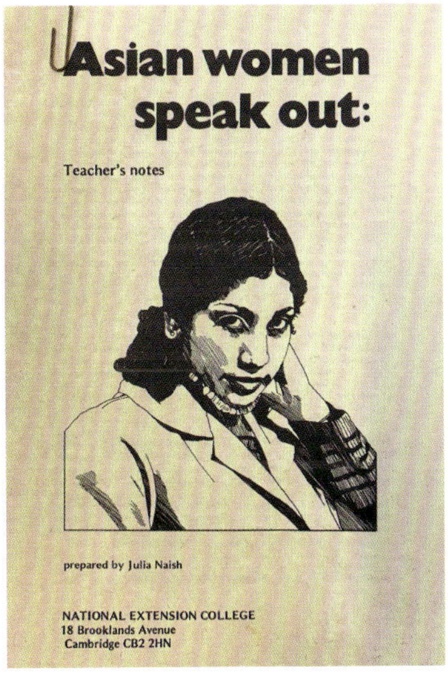

6

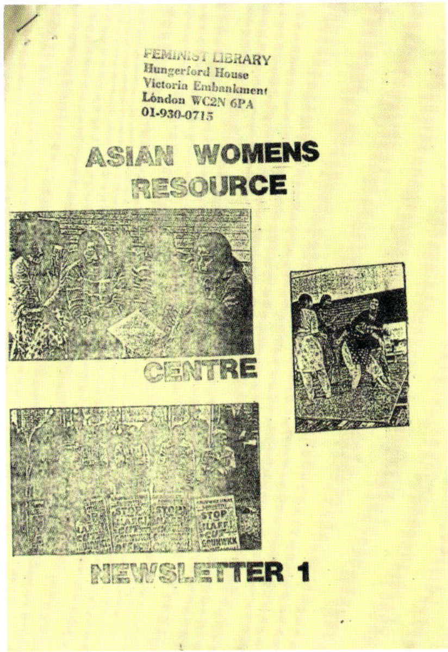

7

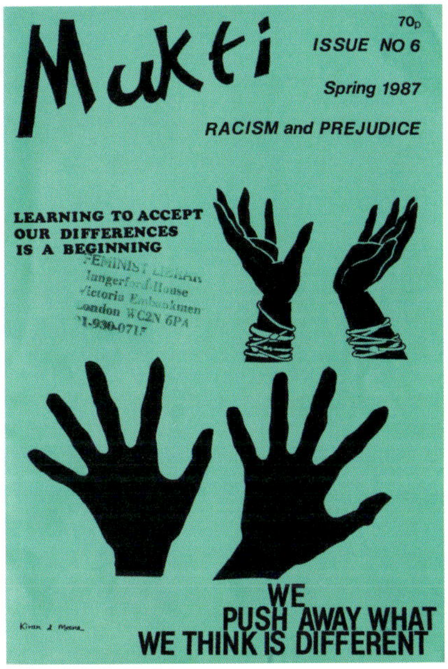

8

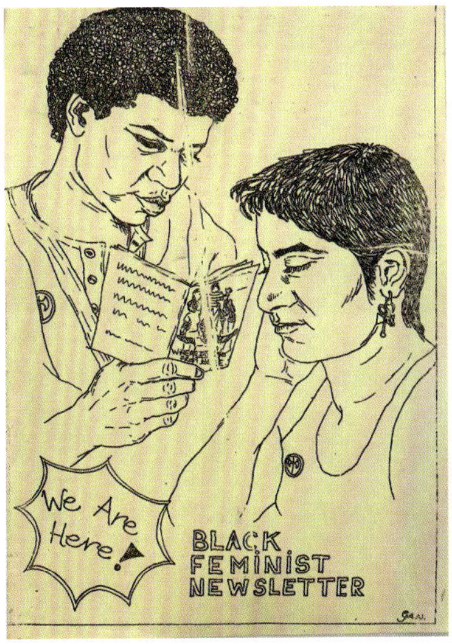

9

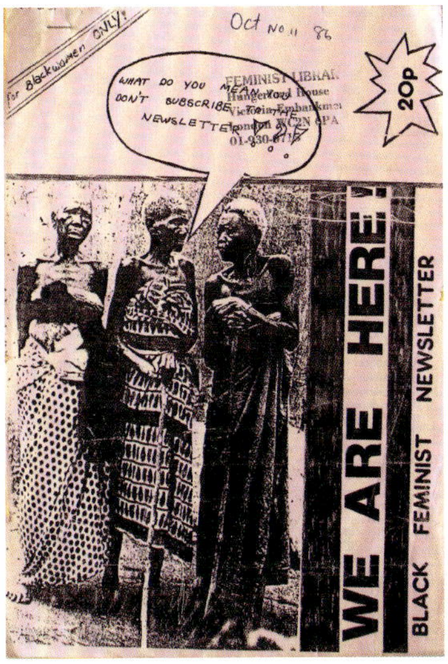

10

1 *Speak Out*, publication of Black Women's Group Brixton, no.5, December 1982.
2 *In Print, Newsletter of Peckham Black Women's Group*, no.2, c.1988.
3 *We are Here: Black Feminists in Britain*, conference pamphlet, May 1984.
4 *Asian Women Speak Out: A Reader*, Cambridge 1979.
5 *Spare Rib*, no.*173*, December 1986.
6 *Asian Women Speak Out: Teacher's Notes*, Cambridge, 1979.
7 *Asian Women's Resource Centre: Newsletter 1*, date unknown.
8 *Mukti*, no.6, Spring 1987. Established in 1983 by Mukti Collective, the magazine was published in six languages and focused on the South Asian feminist community.
9 *We Are Here: Black Feminist Newsletter*, late 1980s. Cover drawing by Glynis Neslen.
10 *We Are Here: Black Feminist Newsletter*, October 1986.

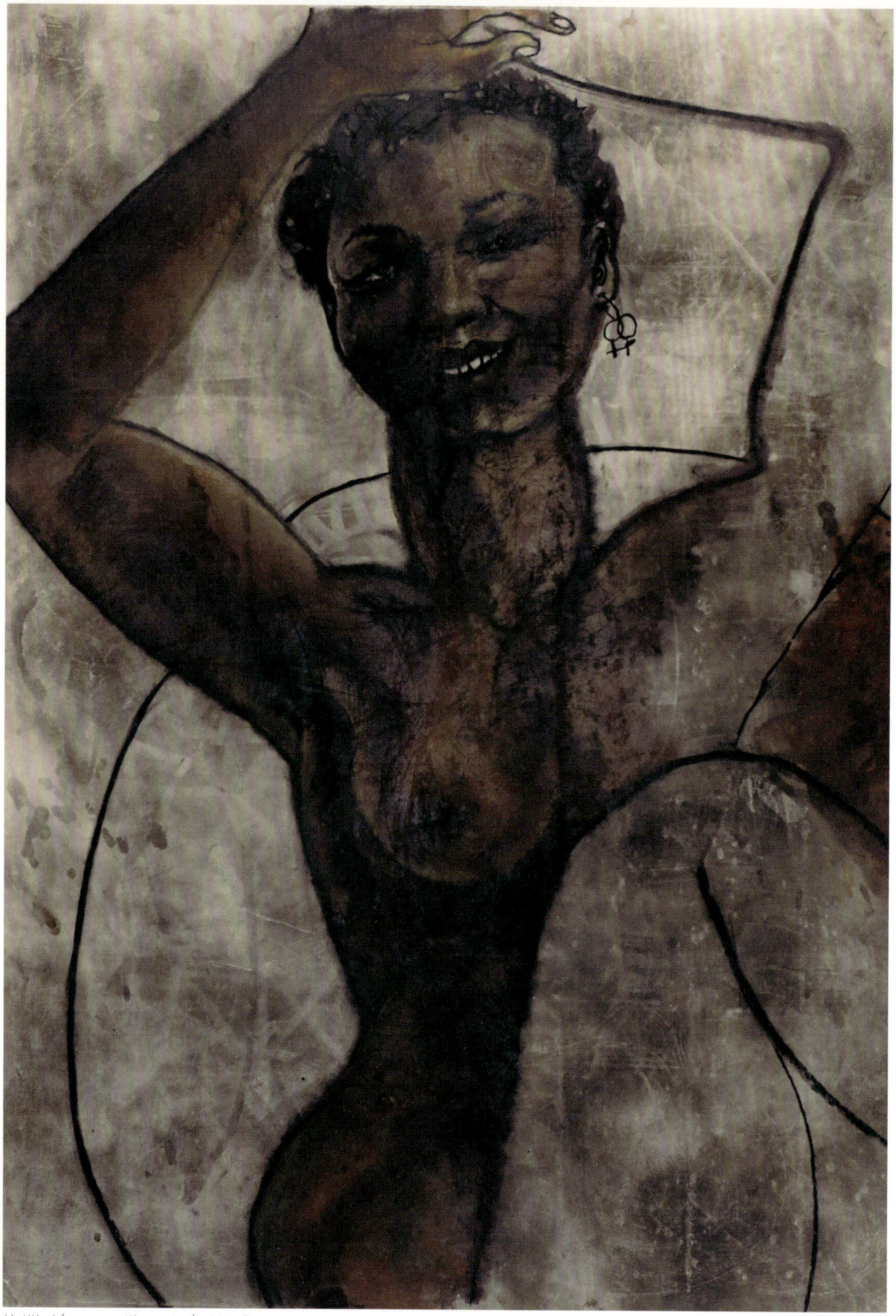

Untitled (woman with earring) 1982. Pastel and wax carbon on paper 76 × 45

Claudette Johnson was born in Manchester in 1959 and studied fine art at Wolverhampton Polytechnic. A key figure in the Black Arts Movement, particularly in mobilising women, she joined the Blk Art Group (formerly WYBA – Wolverhampton Young Black Artists) in 1981 and continued to exhibit with the group after leaving in 1982. Johnson co-organised the first National Black Arts Conference in 1982, and her presentation at the conference marked a formative shift in Black feminist art. She took part in some of the most important exhibitions of Black art in the 1980s, including *The Pan-Afrikan Connection* (Africa Centre, 1982 and Herbert Art Gallery and Museum, Coventry, 1983); *Five Black Women* (Africa Centre, 1983), *Black Woman Time Now* (Battersea Arts Centre, 1983), *Into The Open* (Mappin Art Gallery, Sheffield, 1984) and *The Thin Black Line* (ICA, 1985). Her work has consistently mounted a challenge to the invisibility of Black women in the artistic canon, and in British history and society more widely. Johnson's practice is characterised by portraits created in paint, pencil and charcoal. Large in scale, these typically depict Black women who appear to push beyond the frame, claiming their space and negating and challenging their historic relegation.

Johnson held a solo exhibition at Modern Art Oxford in 2019. She was awarded an MBE in 2022, and in 2023–4, the Courtauld Gallery in London presented a major solo exhibition of her work. She lives and works in London.

Born in Glasgow to a Scottish mother and a Ghanaian father, Maud Sulter (1960–2008) was an important voice in feminist discourse and a significant figure in the Black Arts Movement in the 1980s, exhibiting in Lubaina Himid's *The Thin Black Line* at the ICA in 1985. Sulter gained a MA in photography from the University of Derby in 1990. In her practice she sought to challenge white supremacism and rewrite history through a personal lens as a Black woman, writing that, for her, the personal was political. This is demonstrated for example, in *The Alabama Branch of My Family Tree* 1988, which is comprised of an image of the artist as a baby and type-written text affixed to black card which has been purposefully burnt. Alongside her artistic practice, Sulter was a writer and publisher, setting up Urban Fox Press with Himid. In 1990 they published the landmark book *Passion: Discourses on Blackwomen's Creativity*, edited by Sulter with photography by Ingrid Pollard. With Pollard Sulter also established the Blackwomen's Creativity Project, which led to both women travelling the UK to find the work of Black women artists. She won the Vera Bell Prize for Poetry in 1985, and with *Zabat* 1989, the British Telecom New Contemporaries Award for 1989/90.

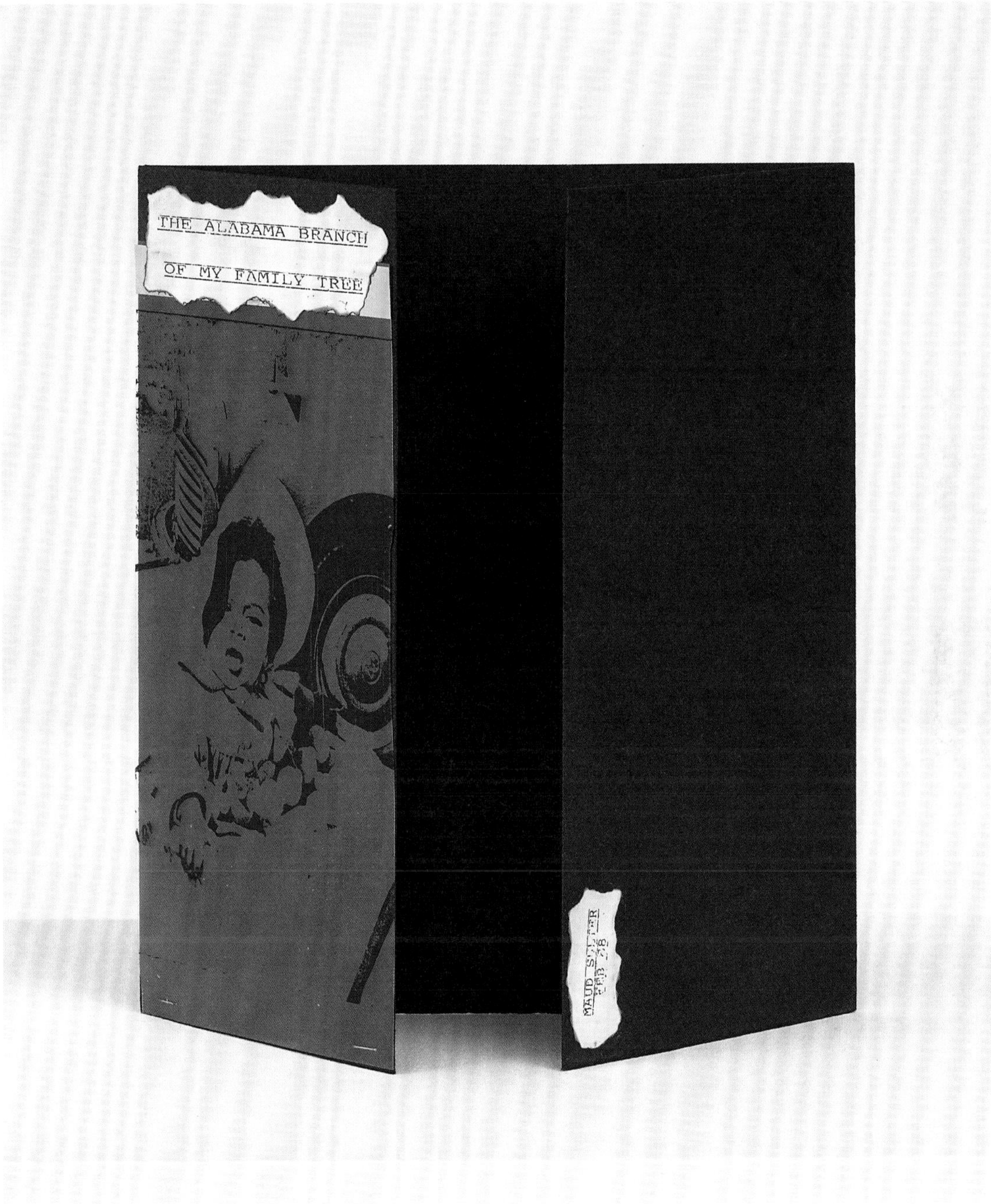

The Alabama Branch of My Family Tree 1988. Mixed media, card and burnt paper 29.7 × 42.2

MAUD SULTER

Chila Kumari Singh Burman was born in 1957 in Bootle, near Liverpool, to Punjabi parents. She studied at Leeds Polytechnic and the Slade School of Fine Art in London, graduating in 1982. Working across a wide variety of mediums, Burman explores her experiences as a working class, South Asian woman in Britain. She was one of the first women artists of colour to exhibit overtly political work in the UK and was co-curator of the first Black women's art exhibition in the UK *Four Indian Women Artists* at the Indian Artists Gallery in 1981. She remains an integral figure among the British Black Arts Movement, and has exhibited in key shows, including *The Thin Black Line* (1985), *Jagrati: An Exhibition of Work by Asian Women Artists* (1986) and *Along the Lines of Resistance* (1987), all of which sought to highlight the work of Black and Asian artists and to challenge the white art establishment.

Burman's visceral work from the 1980s explores many of the urgent issues of the time, such as state violence, institutional racism, sexism and ecological concerns. Her groundbreaking essay 'There Have Always Been Great Blackwomen Artists', which responds to Linda Nochlin's equally influential 1971 essay 'Why Have There Been No Great Women Artists?', reflects on the inability of institutions to support or even to understand the work of women of colour, since they view it entirely from a white, Western position.

The artist presented her celebrated Winter Commission at Tate Britain in 2020–1, and had a solo exhibition at FACT in Liverpool in 2022–3. Burman lives and works in London.

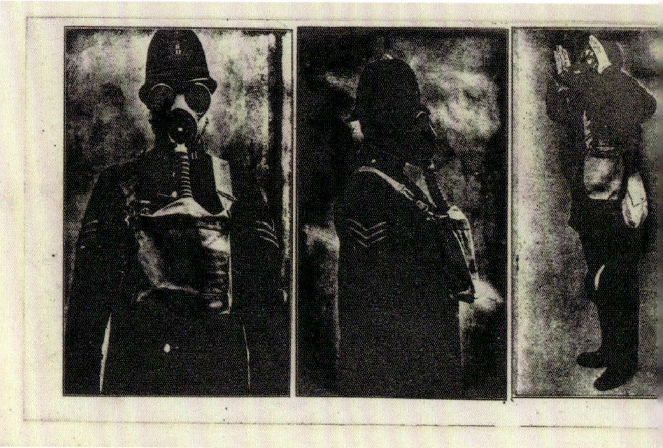

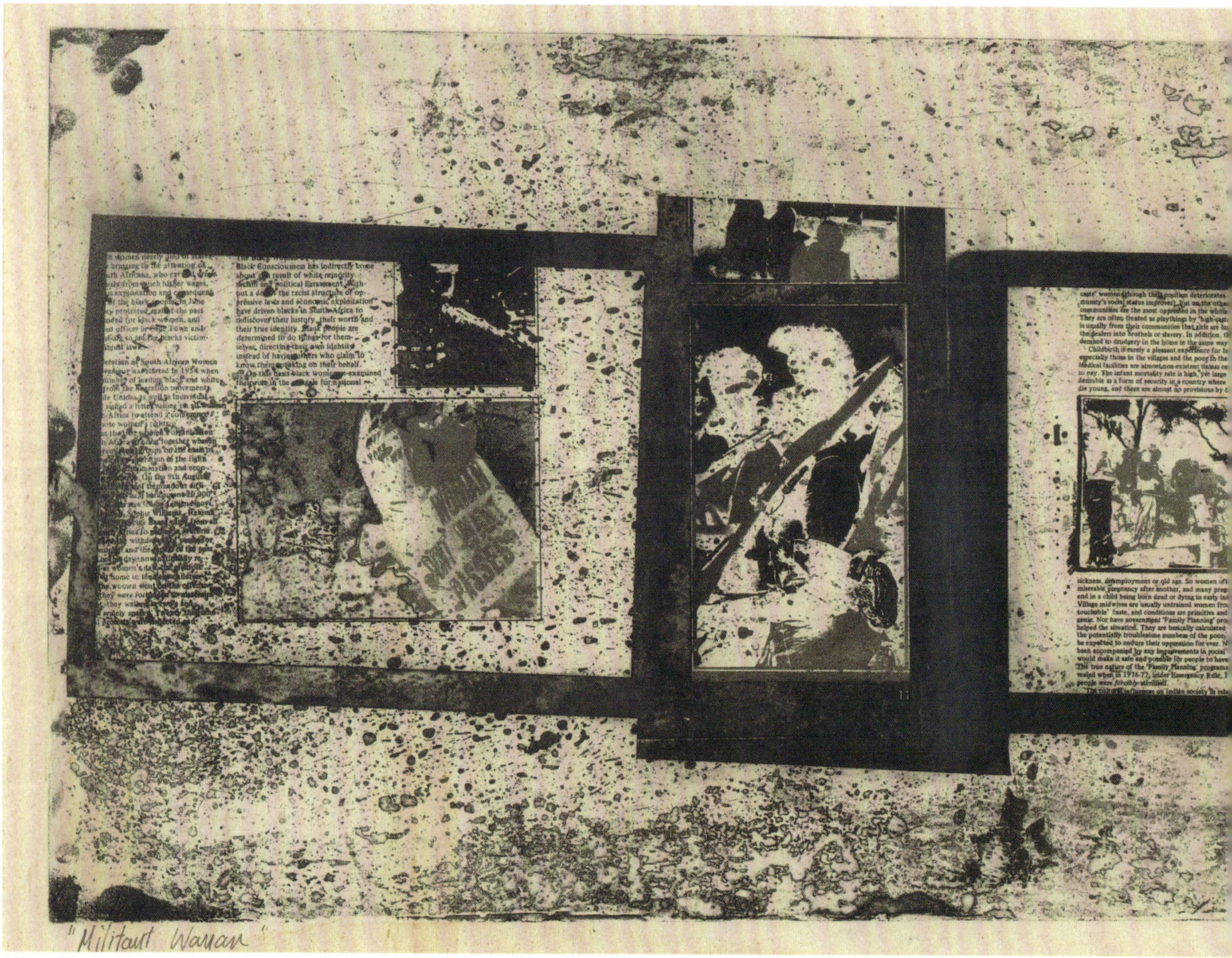

Militant Women 1982. Photo-etching and aquatint on paper 40.6 × 99.5

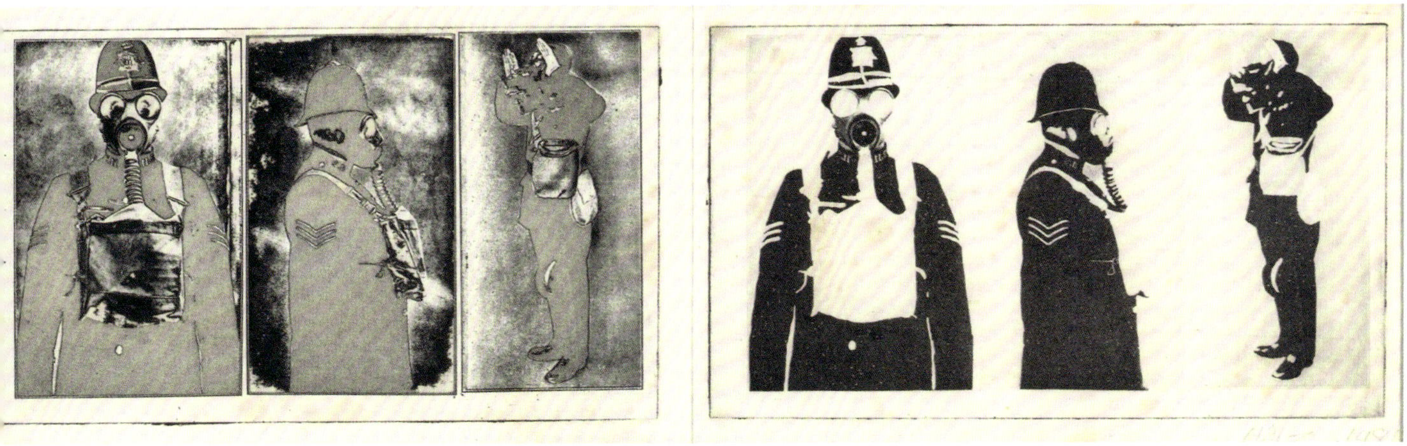

Three Mugshots in a Row 1982. Photo-etching and aquatint on paper 16.8 × 81.5

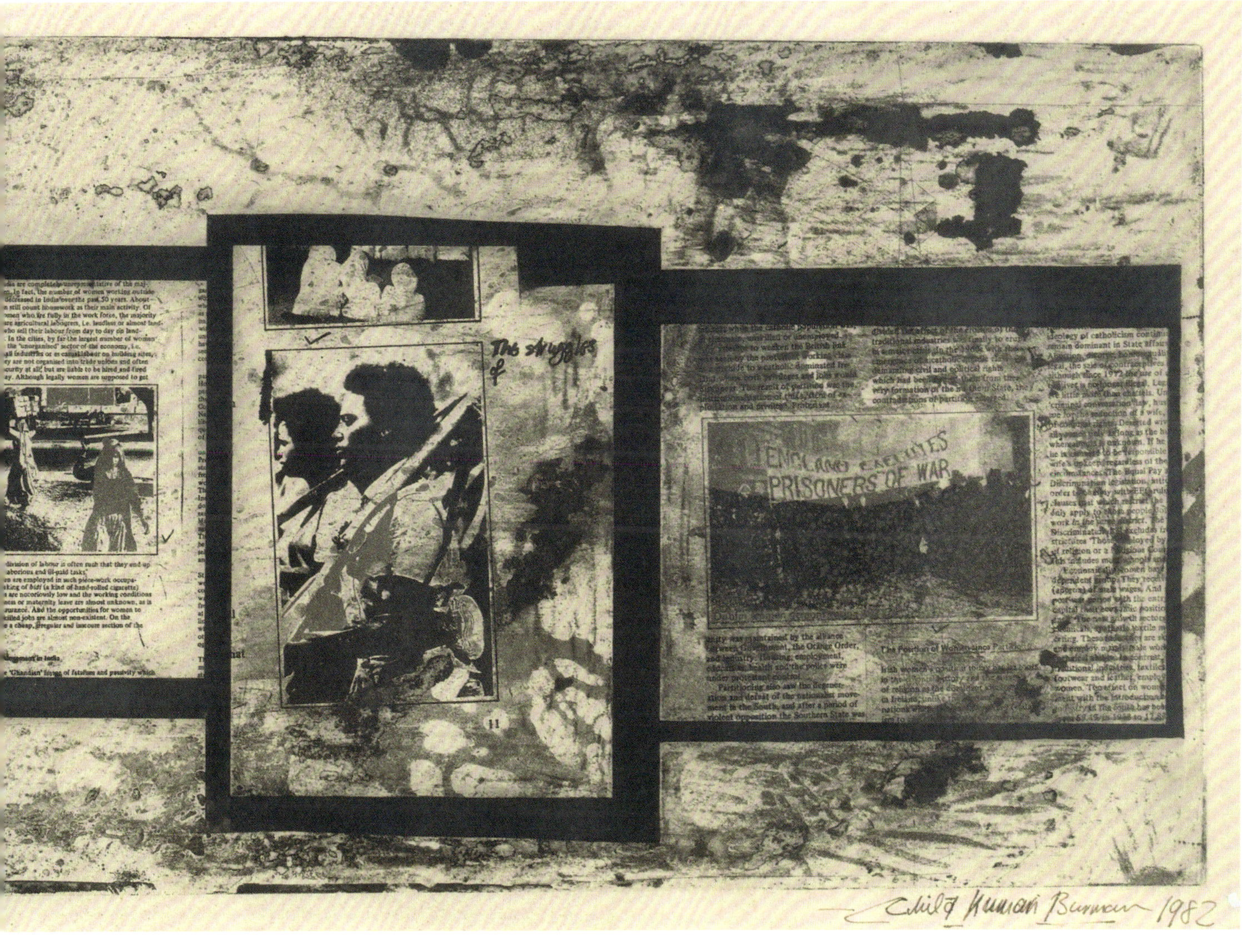

CHILA KUMARI SINGH BURMAN

Born in Birmingham in 1964, Marlene Smith studied art and design at Bradford College. In 1982 she joined the Blk Art Group, and with them played an important role in organising the first National Black Art Convention at Wolverhampton Polytechnic in 1982 and the Radical Black Art Working Convention in 1984. Working across media including clay, fabric and photography, Smith's research and writing underpins her practice, which assesses the lack of visibility of Black history and confronts racist structures in society. Her mixed-media work *Good Housekeeping I* 1985, created in response to the doorstep shooting of Cherry Groce by police that year, was included in Lubaina Himid's exhibition *The Thin Black Line* (ICA, 1985). Alongside her art practice, Smith also has a significant career as a curator, holding a curatorship at the Black Art Gallery in Finsbury Park, London, and in 1987 she co-organised with Keith Piper the exhibition *The Image Employed* at the Cornerhouse, Manchester.

Smith lives and works in Birmingham. In 2019 her work featured in the exhibition *Get Up, Stand Up Now* at Somerset House in London, and she will have a solo exhibition at Cubitt Gallery in 2024.

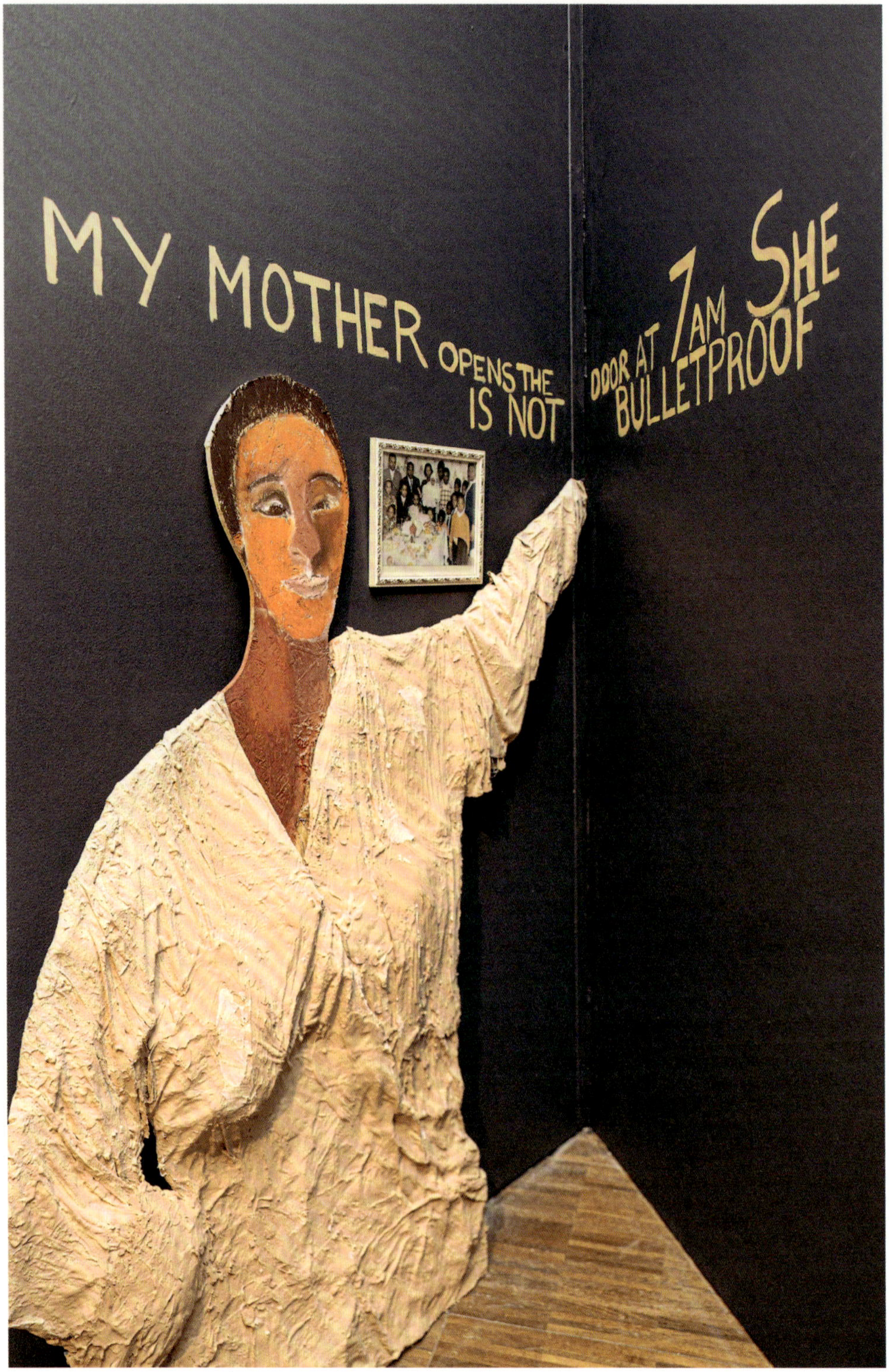

Good Housekeeping III 2023 (remake after original work in 1985). Chipboard, plaster, wire mesh, J-cloths and gouache 213.4 × 304.8

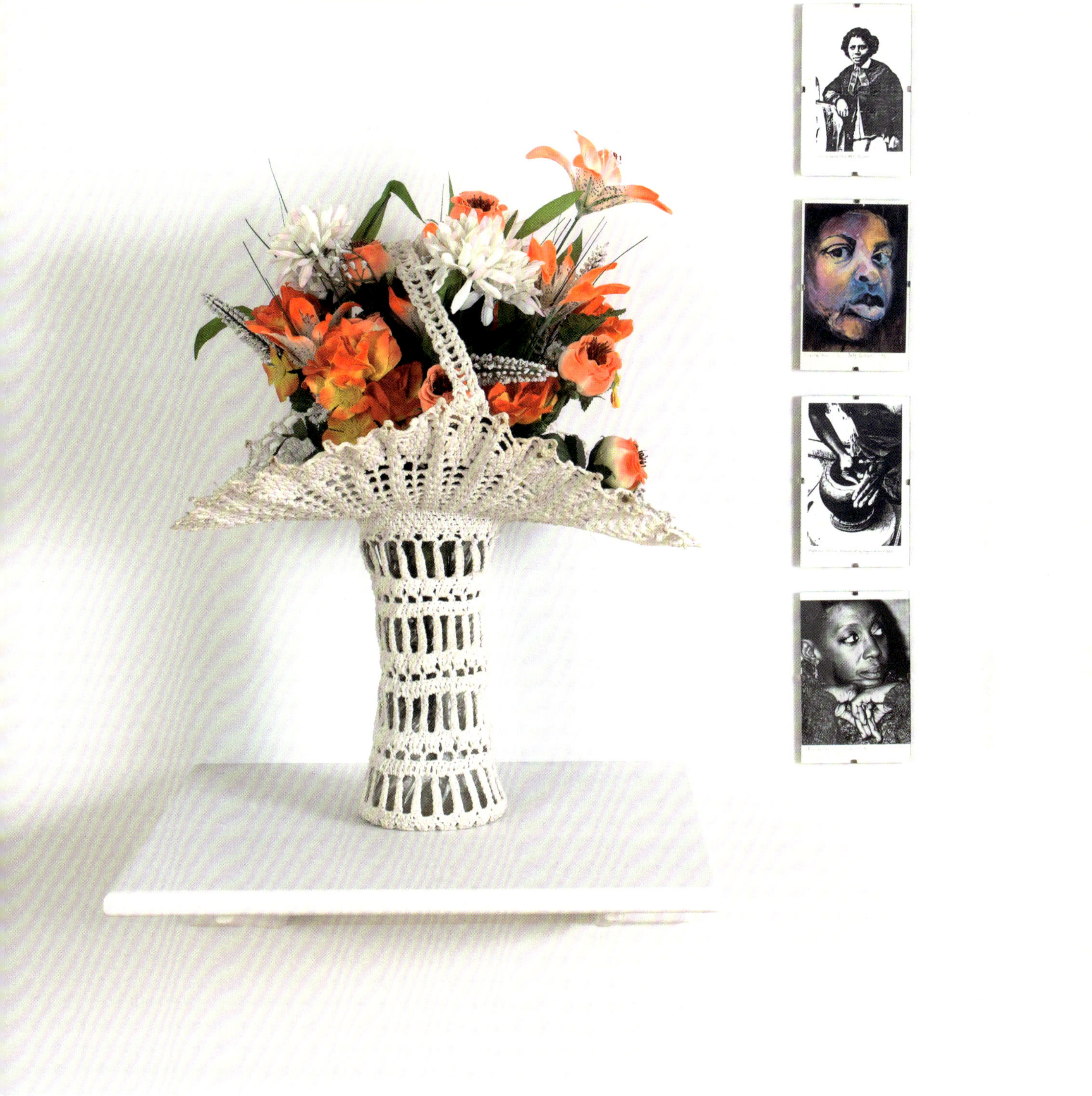

Art History 1987. Plastic flowers, vase and framed images 80.7 × 72 (overall)

Jennifer Comrie was born in Leeds in 1960. An important figure in the Black Arts Movement in the 1980s, her practice focuses on drawing and painting, typically using self-portraiture as a means to critique a racist British society through her own lived experience. Comrie's work was included in *Mirror Reflecting Darkly* (Brixton Art Gallery, 1985) and *The Thin Black Line* (ICA, 1985), an important exhibition curated by Lubaina Himid that, as artist Eddie Chambers notes, contributed to the creation of a community of Black artists and a crucial exchange of ideas about art. She was also part of *The Devil's Feast* (Chelsea School of Art, 1987), a show that was particularly significant for Comrie in allowing her to work with like-minded artists who shared a similar goal in dismantling white ideologies that restricted the work of Black artists.

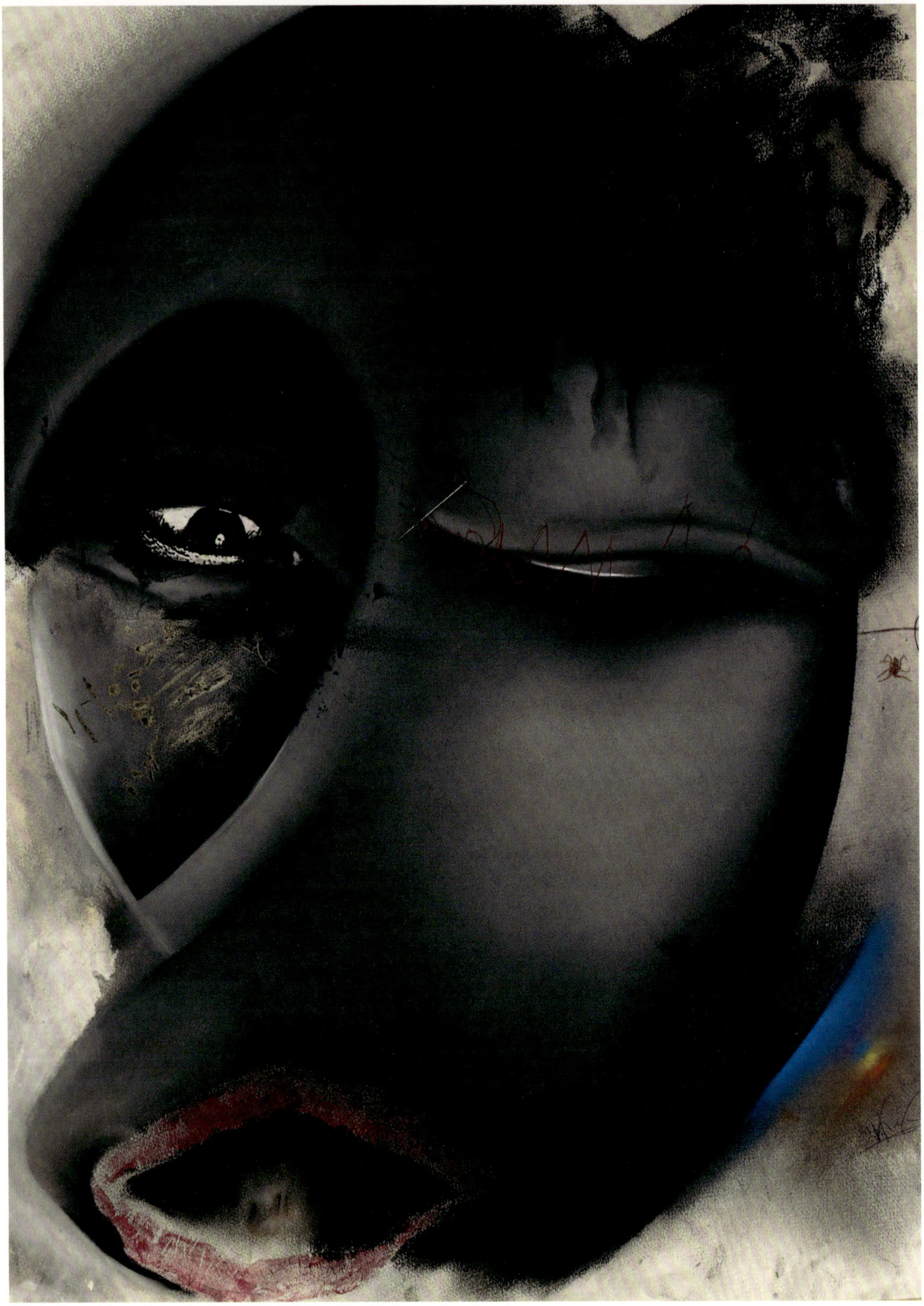

By your fruits you shall know them!

Conflict 1985. Photocopy, pastels, graphite, metal, needle and cotton thread on paper 73.5 × 54

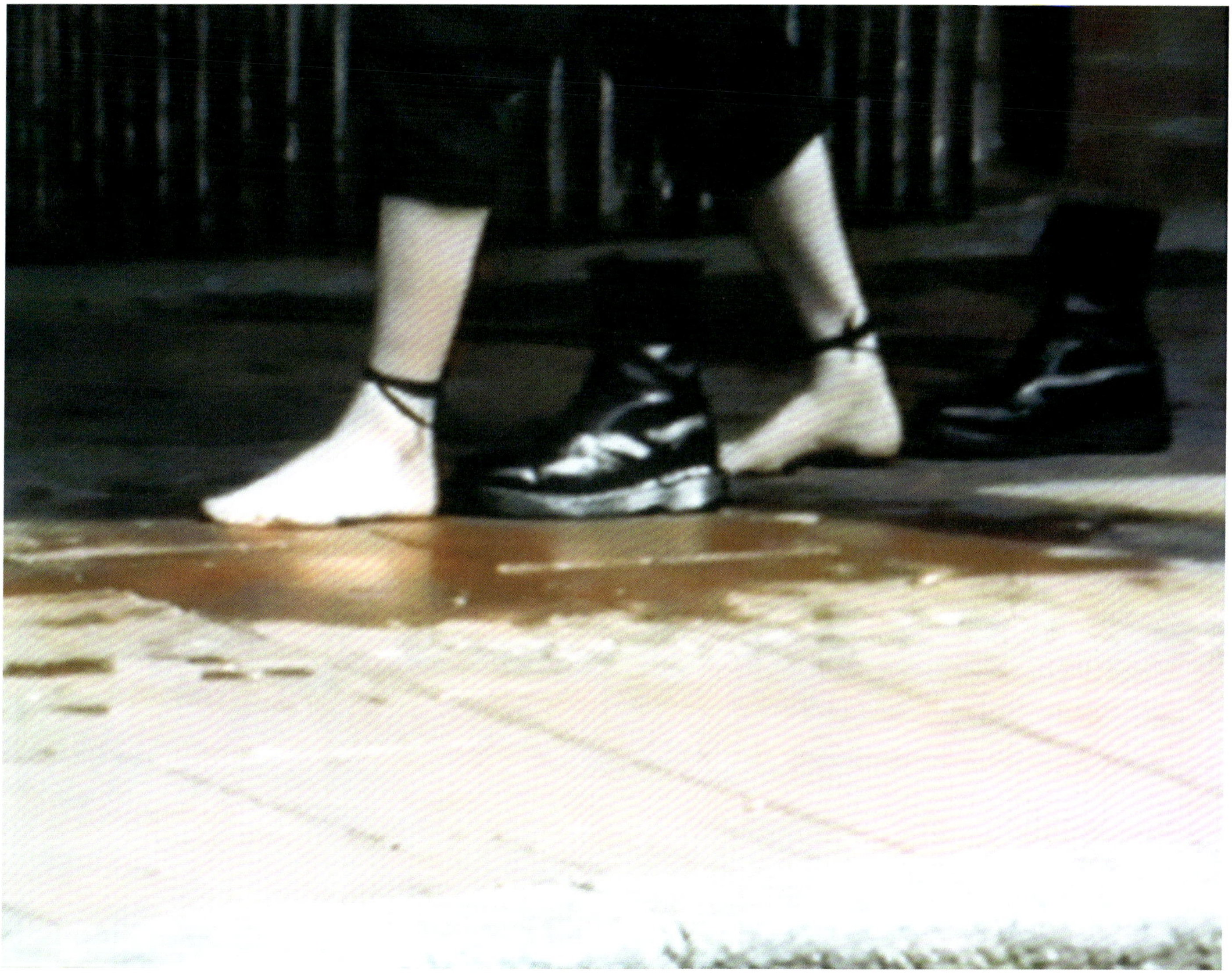

Roadworks 1985. Documentation of performance, Brixton, London. Video with sound, 6 min, 45 sec

Mona Hatoum was born in Beirut, Lebanon, to a Palestinian family in 1952. During a short visit to London in 1975, civil war broke out in Lebanon preventing her from returning home. Stranded in London, she decided to study art, first at the Byam Shaw School of Art and then the Slade School of Fine Art until 1981. Hatoum's experience of being stranded in the UK significantly shaped her practice, which deals with issues of living in exile, displacement, containment and the notion of home. She works across installation, sculpture, video, photography, performance and works on paper.

Roadworks is a six-minute colour video of an hour-long performance undertaken by the artist for Brixton Art Gallery, London in 1985, during which she walked around barefoot with Doc Martin boots tied to her ankles. The work responded to the socio-political context of Brixton, which at the time was plagued by police violence towards people of colour, which had fuelled the uprisings of 1981 and 1985.

Major solo exhibitions of Hatoum's work have been held across the globe throughout her career, including at Tate Modern in 2016. Hatoum lives and works in London.

MONA HATOUM

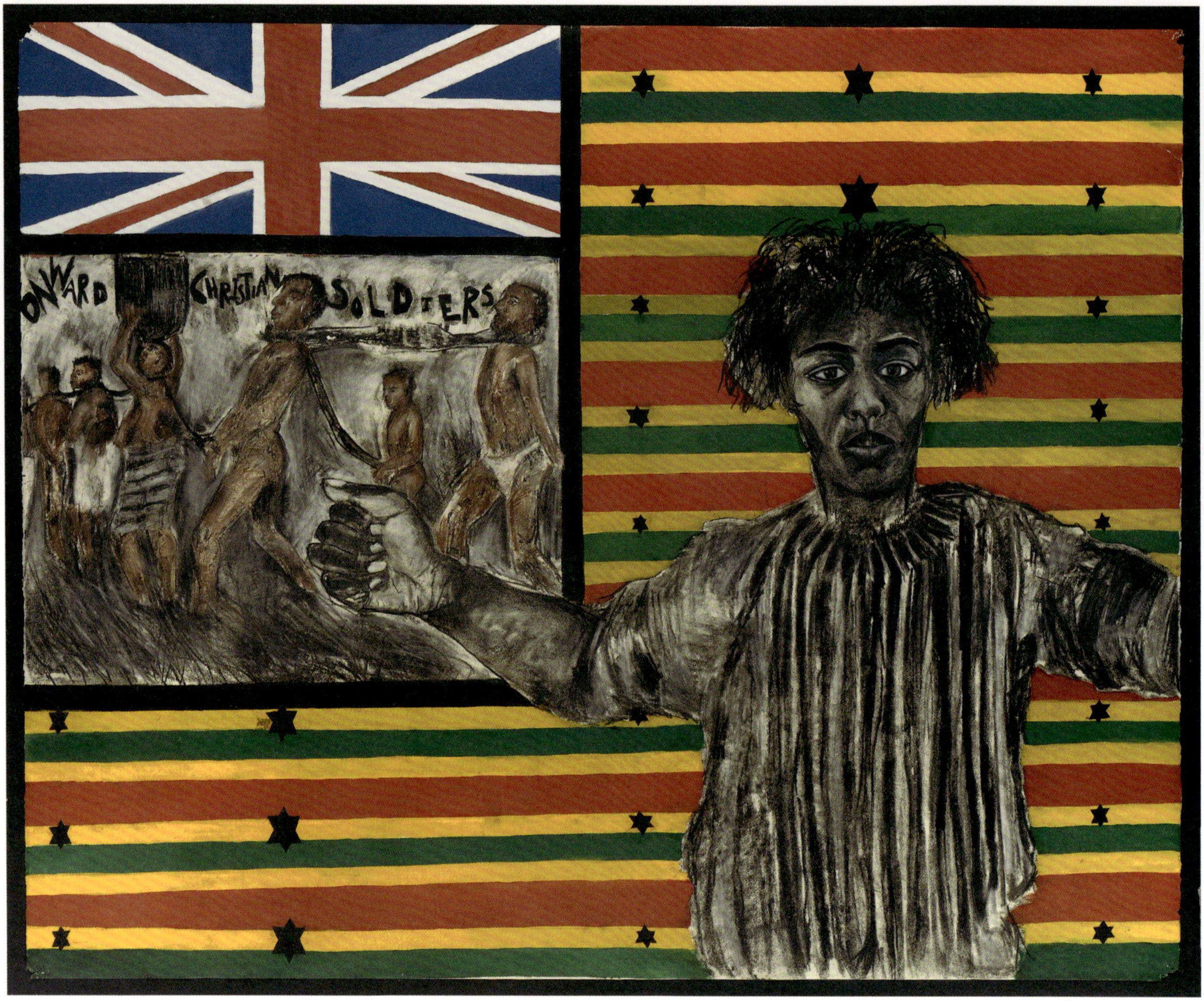

Onward Christian Soldiers 1987. Acrylic paint on paper 152 × 182

MOWBRAY ODONKOR

Mowbray Odonkor was born in London to Ghanaian parents in 1962, and graduated from Wimbledon College of Art in 1987 with a degree in art. A key presence in the Black Arts Movement in the late 1980s, she exhibited alongside artists such as Sonia Boyce and Amanda Holiday, fighting for acknowledgement, space and better representation for Black artists. Through painting and drawing, Odonkor's work in the 1980s focused on Black women from the diaspora, often using self-portraiture to explore the subject. Her art addressed the legacies of slavery and the lived experience of Black women and expressed a sense of empathy and solidarity with them, centring herself within the struggle. An example of the artist's political engagement is her painting *Onward Christian Soldiers* 1987, held in the Arts Council Collection, in which she juxtaposes the British flag with a drawing of slaves, directly implicating Britain in the trans-atlantic slave trade. Odonkor's work was included in the exhibition *The Image Employed* at the Cornerhouse in Manchester in 1987, curated by Keith Piper and Marlene Smith.

Born in Zanzibar, Tanzania in 1954, Lubaina Himid moved to London as a child. She studied theatre design at Wimbledon College of Arts and went on to graduate from the Royal College of Art in 1984. Himid's practice encompasses painting, printing, drawing and poetry and interrogates histories of colonialism and imperialism, the European art canon and the art world's exclusion of Black women. Himid has always sought to highlight the work of Black and Asian women artists working in the UK and in the early 1980s she began curating and publishing. *Five Black Women* (Africa Centre, 1983), *Black Woman Time Now* (Battersea Arts Centre, 1983) and *The Thin Black Line* (ICA, 1985) were key exhibitions in the Black Arts Movement that have had a profound and lasting impact on British art. The fight for recognition is mirrored in Himid's art, which often depicts Black women together, occupying the very spaces from which they have historically been excluded.

In 2017, Himid won the Turner Prize, and in 2018 she was both elected a Royal Academician and awarded a CBE. A solo exhibition of her work was held at Tate Modern in 2021–2. She lives and works in Preston.

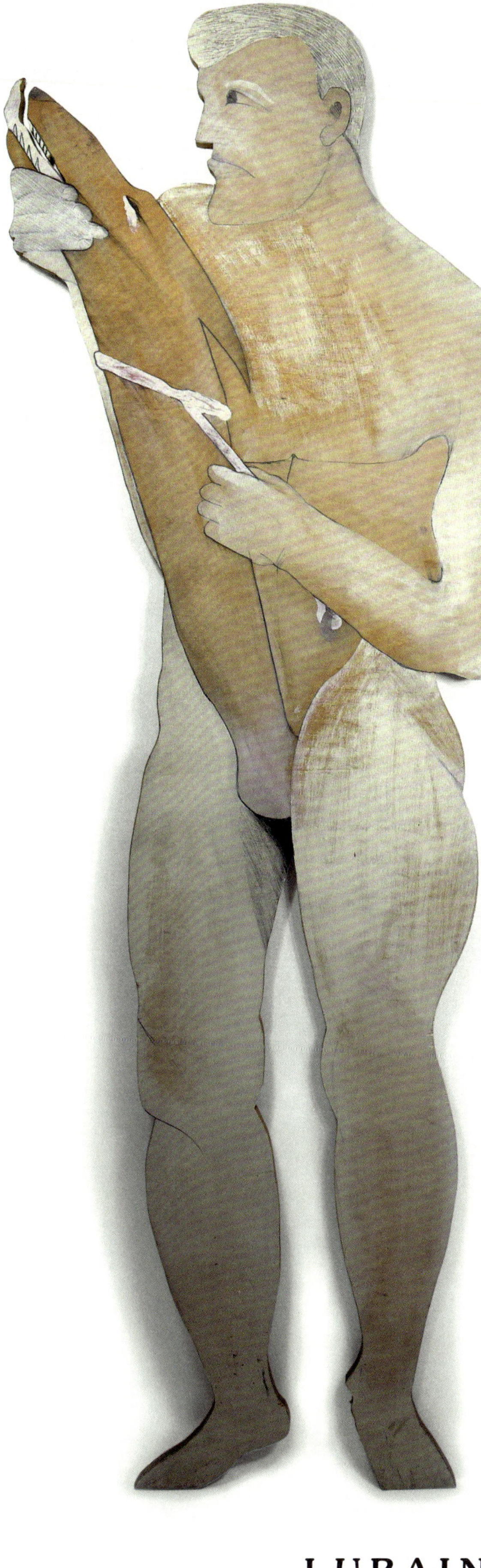

Dog Years 1981–3.
Acrylic paint on wood 170 × 66 × 1.5

LUBAINA HIMID

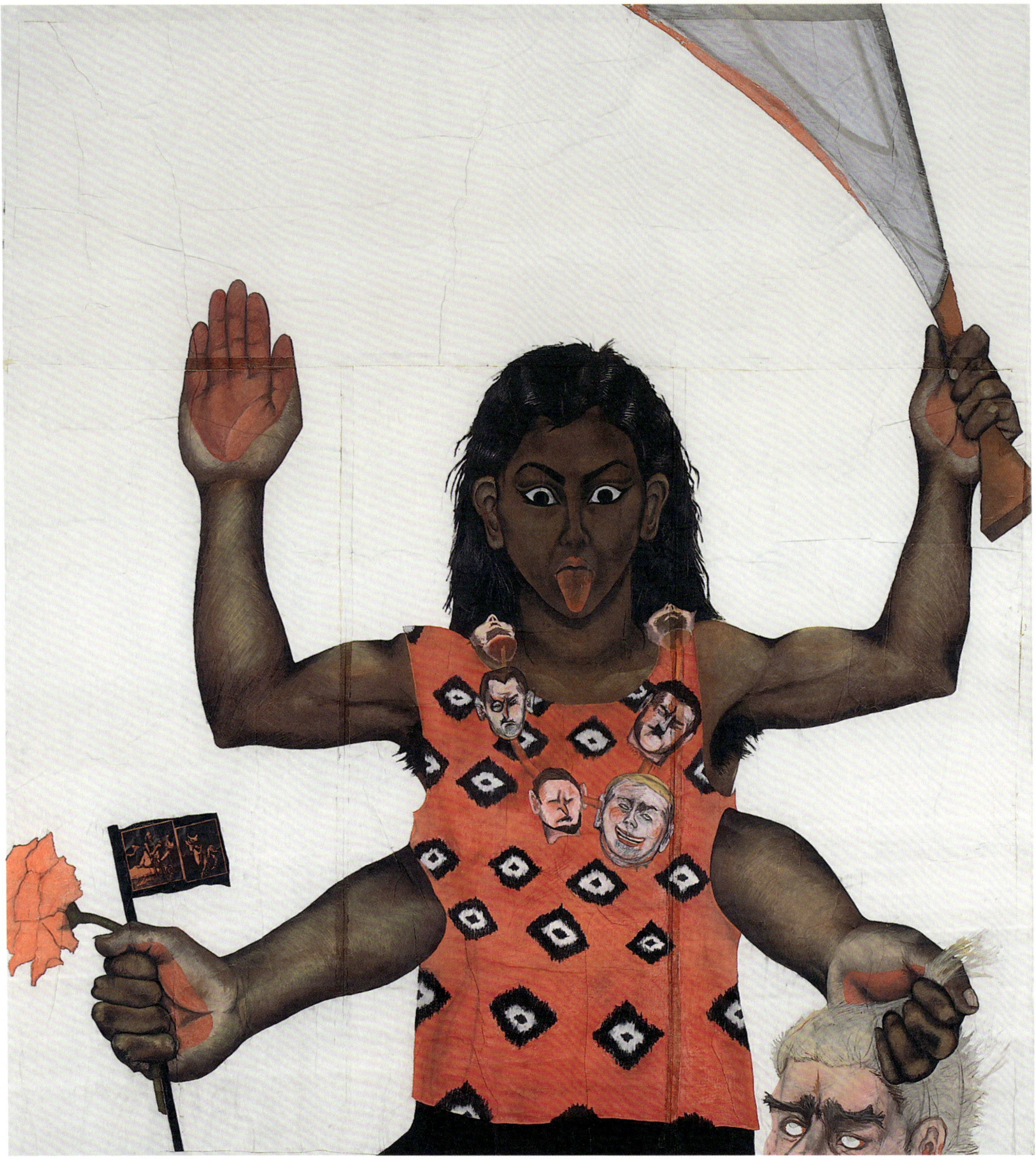

Housewives with Steak Knives 1985. Oil paint, acrylic paint and pastel on paper, mounted on canvas 246 × 222 × 2.5

Sutapa Biswas was born in Santiniketan, India, in 1962 and moved to London at the age of four. Between 1981 and 1985 she studied fine art, art history, and history and philosophy of science at the University of Leeds. Completing her postgraduate diploma at the Slade School of Fine Art (1988–90), she then went on to be a research student at the Royal College of Art between 1995 and 1998. Conceptually underpinned, Biswas's practice incorporates painting, drawing, film and time-based media. Her often stark but poetic works explore history's grand narratives, including colonialism and imperialism, and how these collide with everyday narratives. While at the University of Leeds, Biswas performed *Kali* 1983–85 (Tate Collection, accessioned 2017), in which she dressed as the black mythical Hindu deity Kali, created to rid the world of evil. Biswas's performance included her tutor, art historian Griselda Pollock, who stands in for the Western imperialist canon. Pollock has noted that Biswas's presence on the course had a profound impact, leading the school in a process of decolonisation in its art historical curriculum. An important figure within the 1980s British Black Arts Movement, Biswas featured in key exhibitions, including *The Thin Black Line* (ICA, 1985).

In 2019, Biswas was made a Fellow of Yale University, and in 2021–2 she held major solo exhibitions at Kettle's Yard, University of Cambridge, and at the BALTIC Centre for Contemporary Art, Gateshead. She lives and works in London.

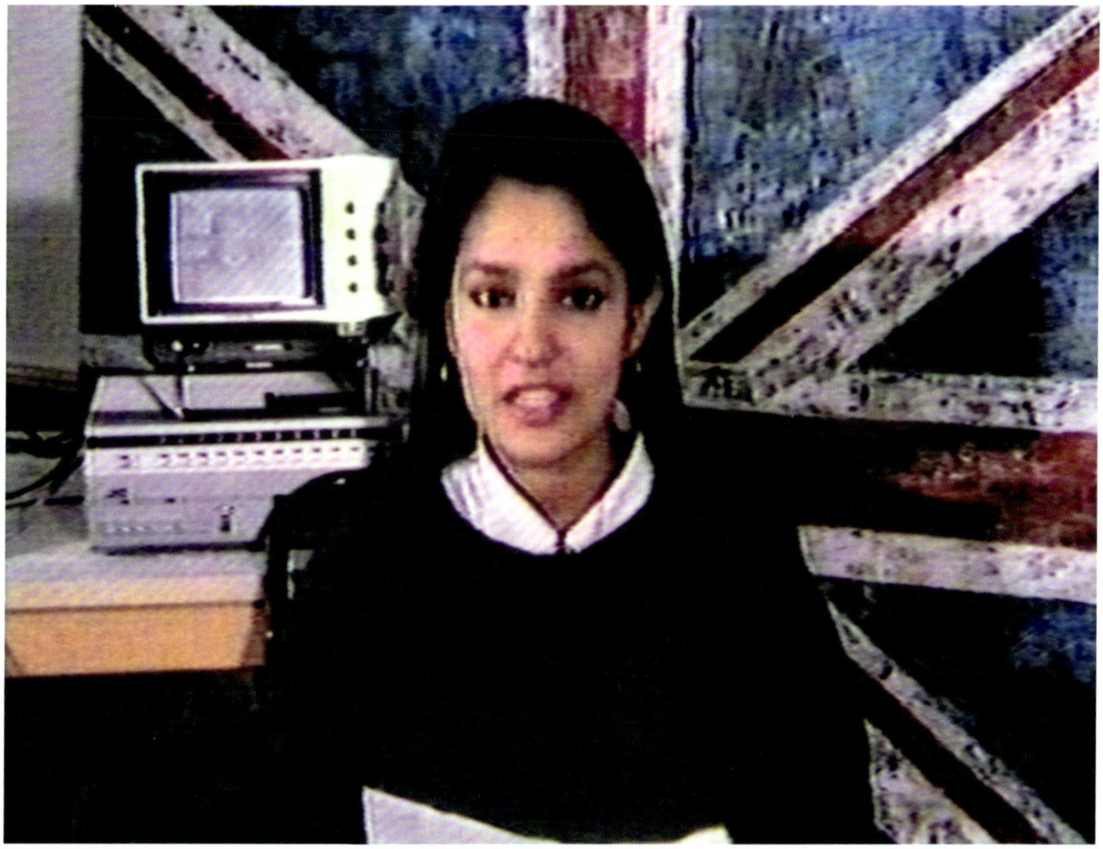

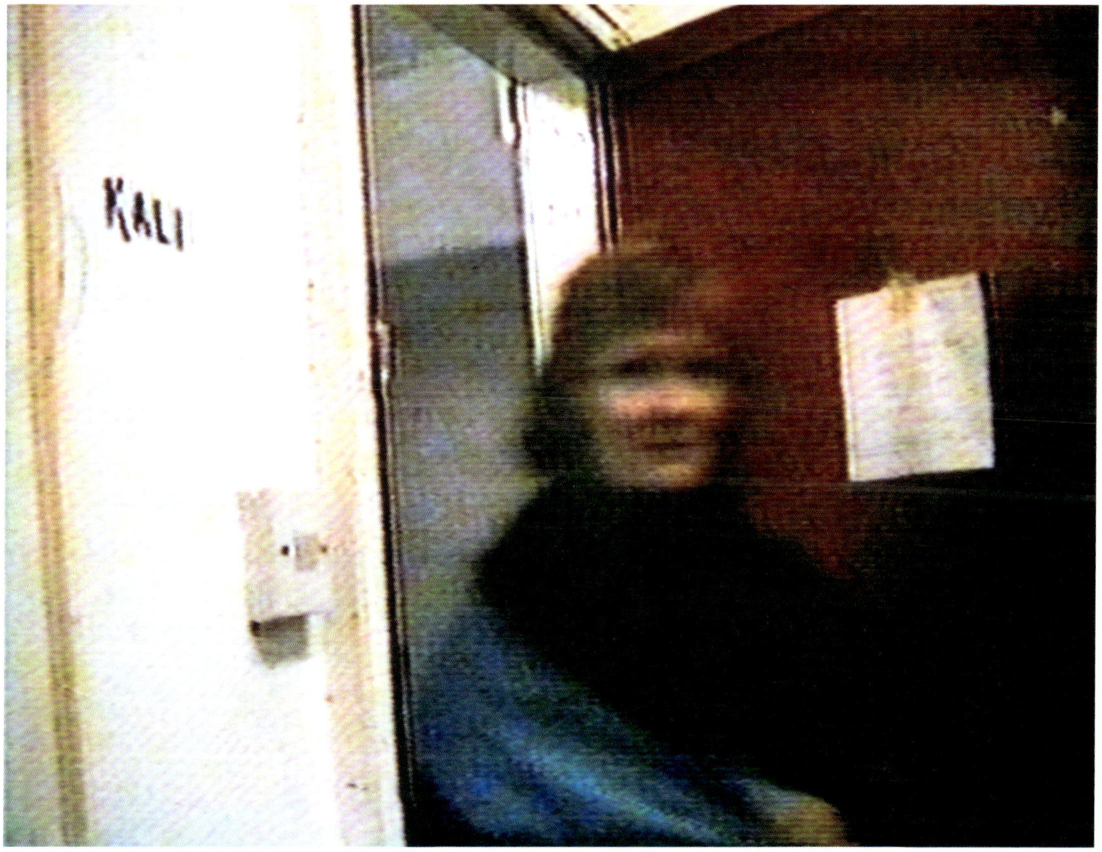

Kali 1983–5. Video; colour and sound (stereo). 23 min, 24 sec

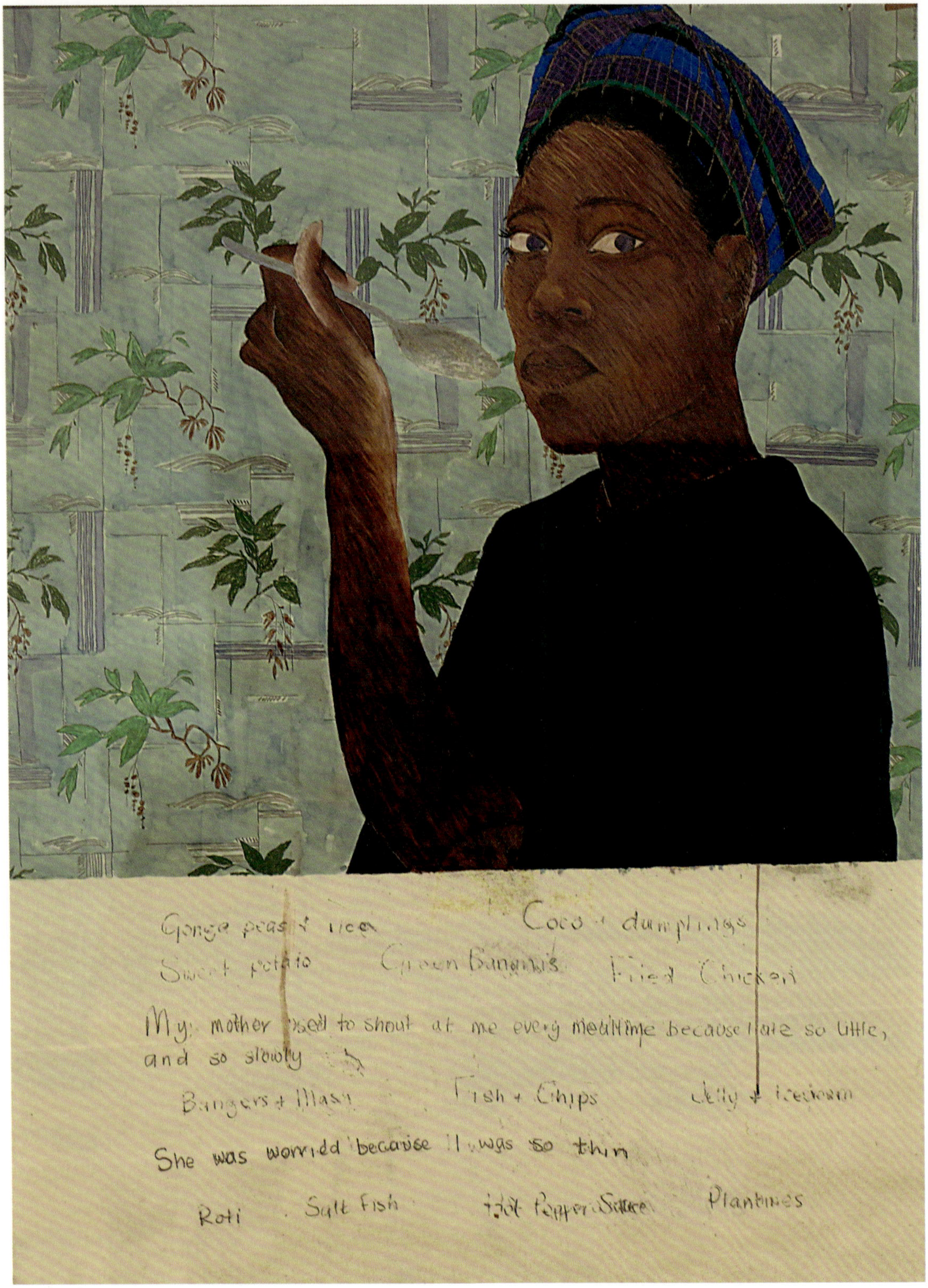

Rice n Peas 1982. Pastel on paper 137 × 102

Sonia Boyce was born in London in 1962 and graduated with a degree in fine art from Stourbridge College in 1983. With an interdisciplinary practice working across film, photography, print, sound and installation, Boyce's early work was dominated by autobiographical observations in pastel and pencil, creating drawings that considered her own experience as a young Black woman, often with references to other women artists – most notably Frida Kahlo. In 1982 Boyce attended a conference for Black artists in Wolverhampton, a moment she cites as significant in being the first time she was surrounded by so many other artists of colour. Her work featured in some of the most notable exhibitions of Black art in the 1980s, including *Five Black Women* (Africa Centre, 1983), *Black Woman Time Now* (Battersea Arts Centre, 1983) and *The Thin Black Line* (ICA, 1985).

Boyce's recent work explores themes of memory, space and sound, often inviting engagement with the viewer. She was elected a Royal Academician in 2016 and was awarded an OBE in 2019. In 2022 she represented Britain at the Venice Biennale for which she was awarded the prestigious Golden Lion. Boyce lives and works in London.

W.I.T.C.H. (Black Women's Media Project) was established as part of the Liverpool women's film collective Women's Independent Cinema House (W.I.T.C.H.). Initially founded in 1980 by Judy Mazonowicz, Sally Evans and Steph Bunn and based at the Open Eye Gallery, W.I.T.C.H. was an enabling space for women to access training in the scripting, editing and distribution and screening of films by and for women during the 1980s and 90s. In response to the lack of attention and visibility given to Black women's issues, W.I.T.C.H. members Barbara Phillips and Ann Carney ran workshops, and made videos and films specifically engaged with amplifying the voices and concerns of Black communities in Liverpool. Their video *A Tribute to Black Women (They don't get a chance)* 1986 was made with the group Liverpool Black Sisters and the Community and Unemployed Resource Centre (CRC), and was aimed at improving awareness of Black history and the achievement of Black students in schools and universities. The video's use of interviews and vox pops in the streets of Liverpool, alongside discussion of key figures, such as Mary Seacole and Harriet Tubman, starts to redress the balance.

W.I.T.C.H.(Black Women's Media Project) continued to enable access to media production and make films with Black communities in Liverpool into the 2000s.

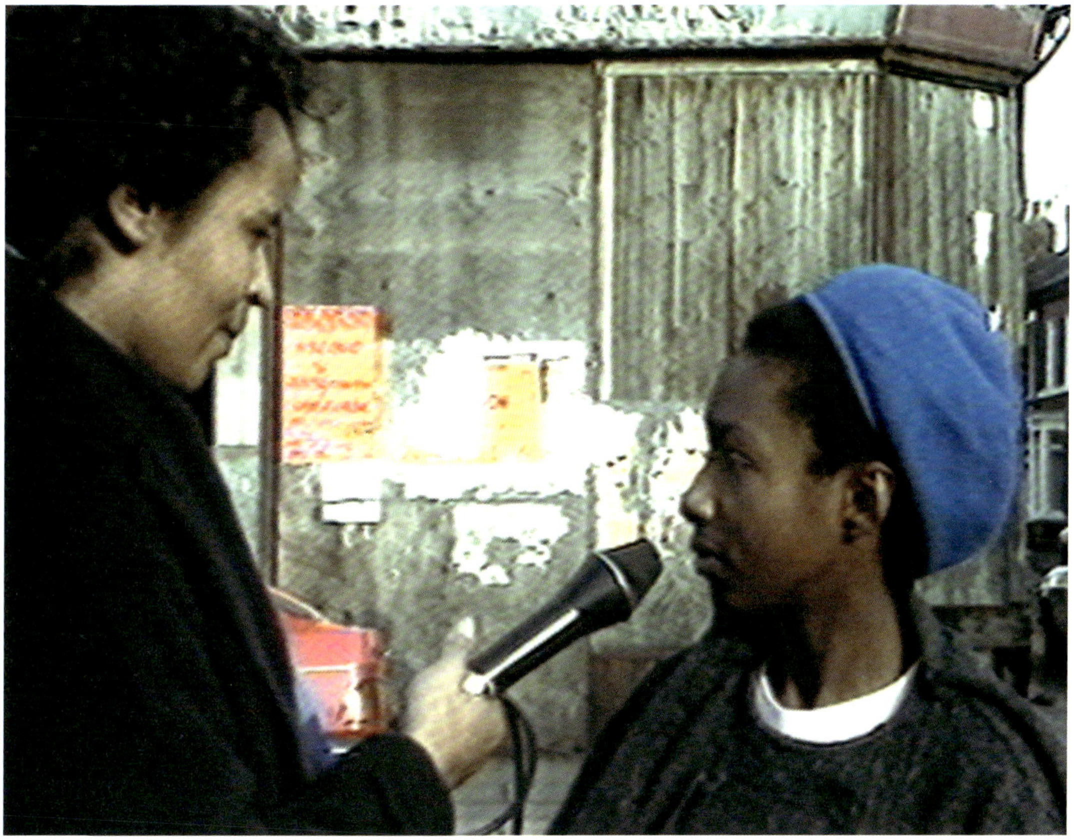

A Tribute to Black Women (They don't get a chance) 1986. Video, shown digitally; colour, sound. 22 min

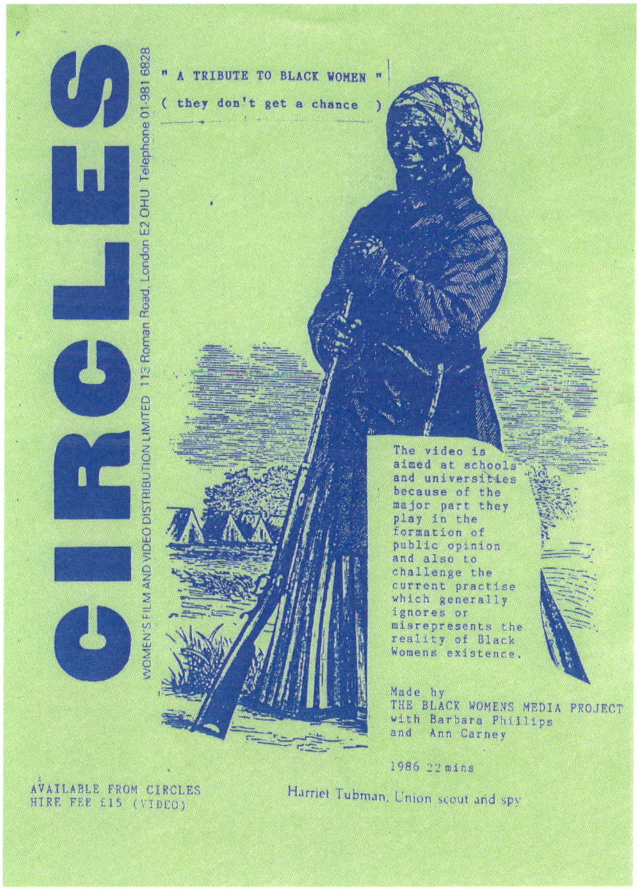

The original distribution leaflet for the film.

W.I.T.C.H. (BLACK WOMEN'S MEDIA PROJECT)

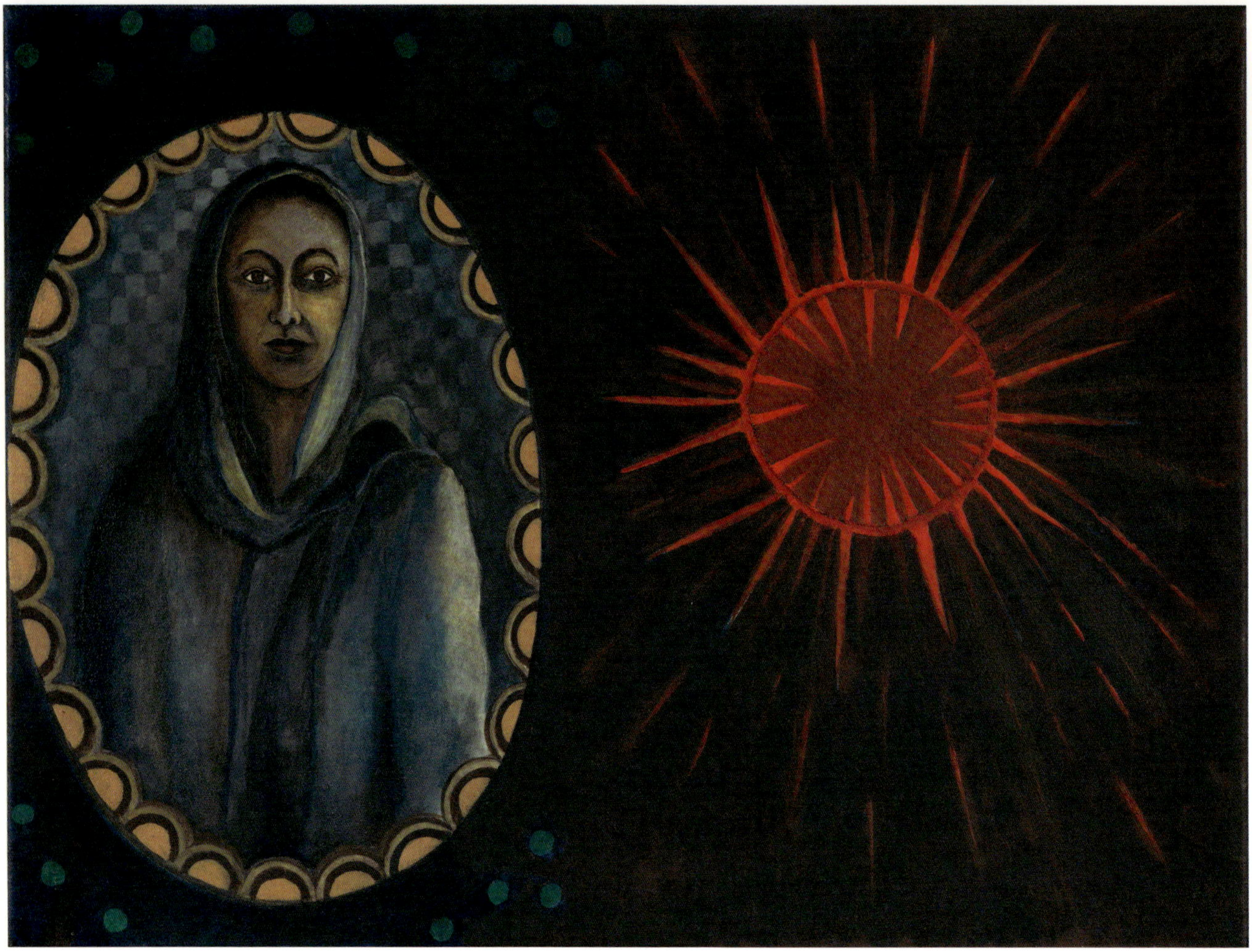

Tribute to Late Balwant Kaur and Gurdip Kaur – Victims of Domestic Violence 1986. Acrylic paint and paper on canvas 56 × 76 × 2

Born in Nanyuki, Kenya in 1956, Bhajan Hunjan moved to the UK in 1975 to study fine art at the University of Reading. She went on to gain a postgraduate degree from the Slade School of Fine Art in London, graduating in 1981, while also enrolling on a part-time ceramics course at Central School of Art and Design. While studying, Hunjan began to reflect on her own identity and sense of belonging, resulting in an increasing awareness of feminist politics. In Reading she volunteered at a South Asian women's refuge, which exposed her to the struggles many women faced, particularly South Asian women, and shaped her work. In the 1980s Hunjan began to explore her experiences and those of other women through figurative painting. An active figure in the Black Arts Movement, in 1981 Hunjan curated *Four Indian Women Artists* with Chila Burman at the Indian Artists (UK) Gallery, acknowledged by Griselda Pollock and Rozsika Parker as the first exhibition of Black women artists in the UK. She was also involved in the formation of the Panchayat Collection, a reference library relating to cultural activities and activism from the 1980s to 2003. In 2023 Hunjan was short-listed for the Max Mara prize. She lives and works between Reading and London.

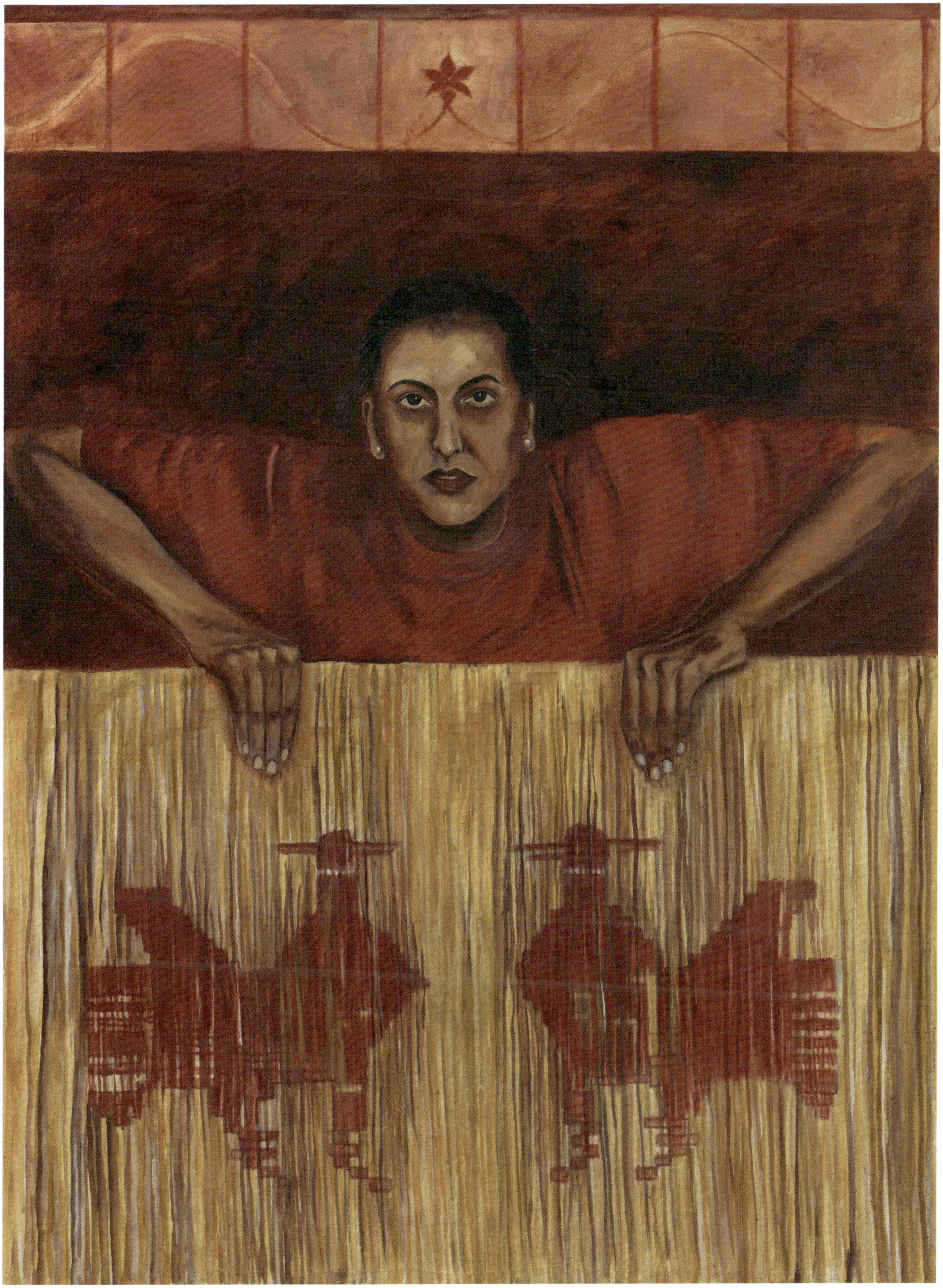

The Affair 1987–8. Acrylic paint on canvas 122 × 91.5

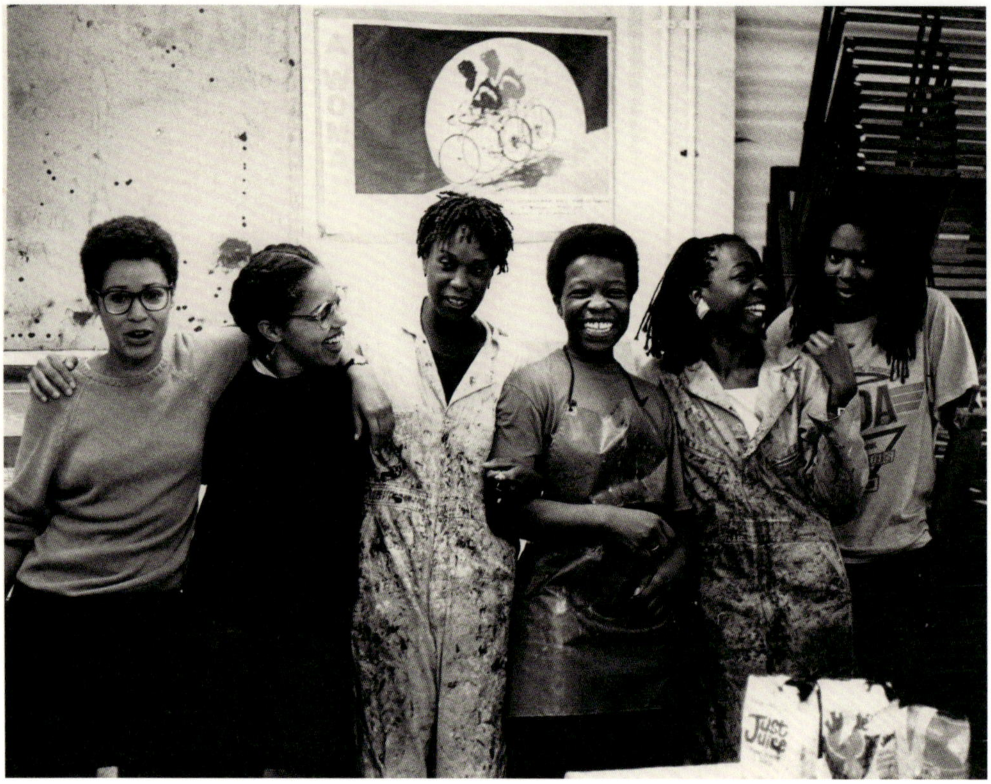

Women's printing group at Lenthall Road Workshop, 1980s. From left to right: Joy Kahumbu, Amanda Kahumbu, Mo Ross, Sonia Johnson, Donna Keane and Louisa Jean-Baptiste.

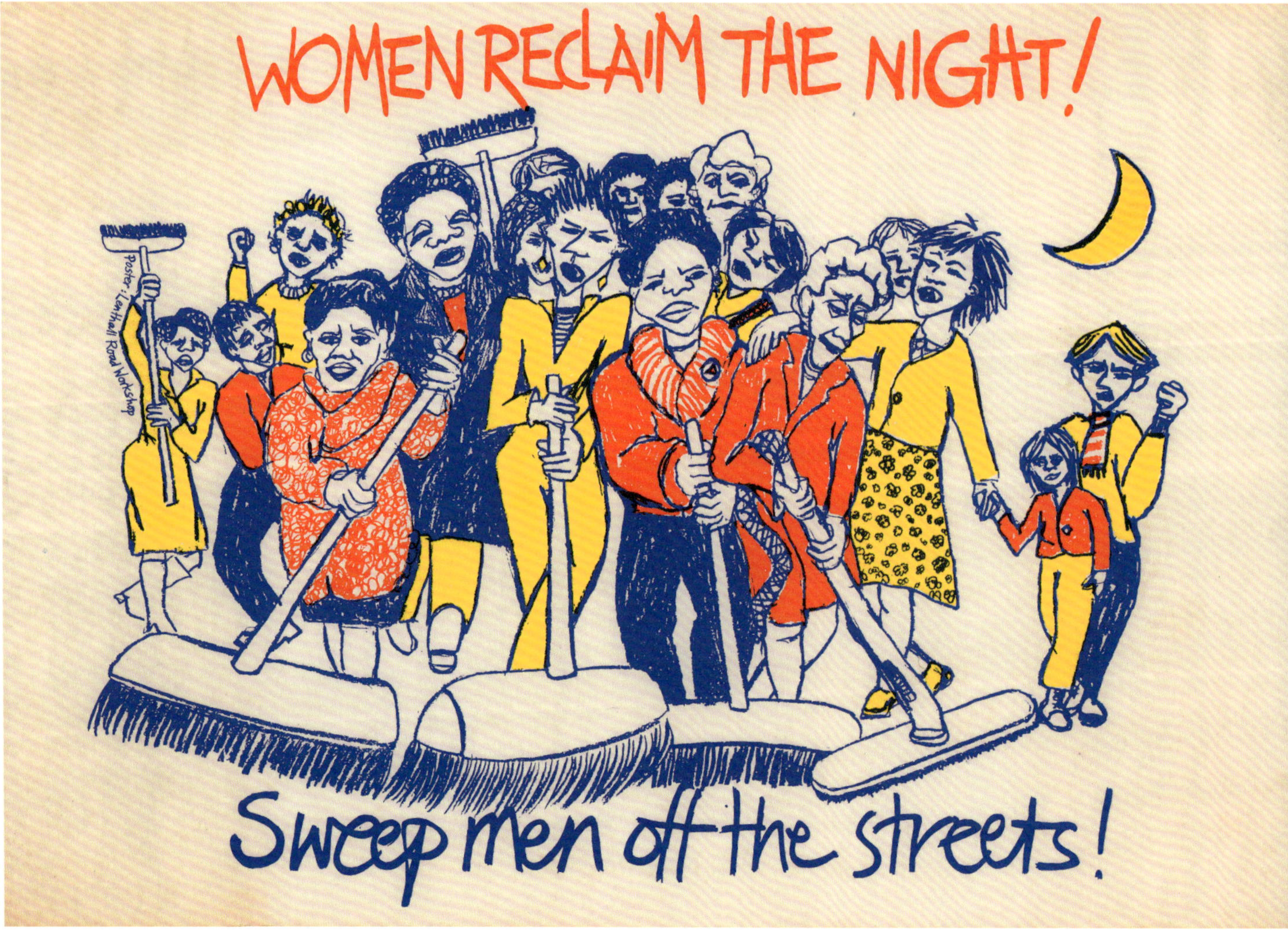

Women Reclaim the Night c.1980. Print on paper 50 × 74

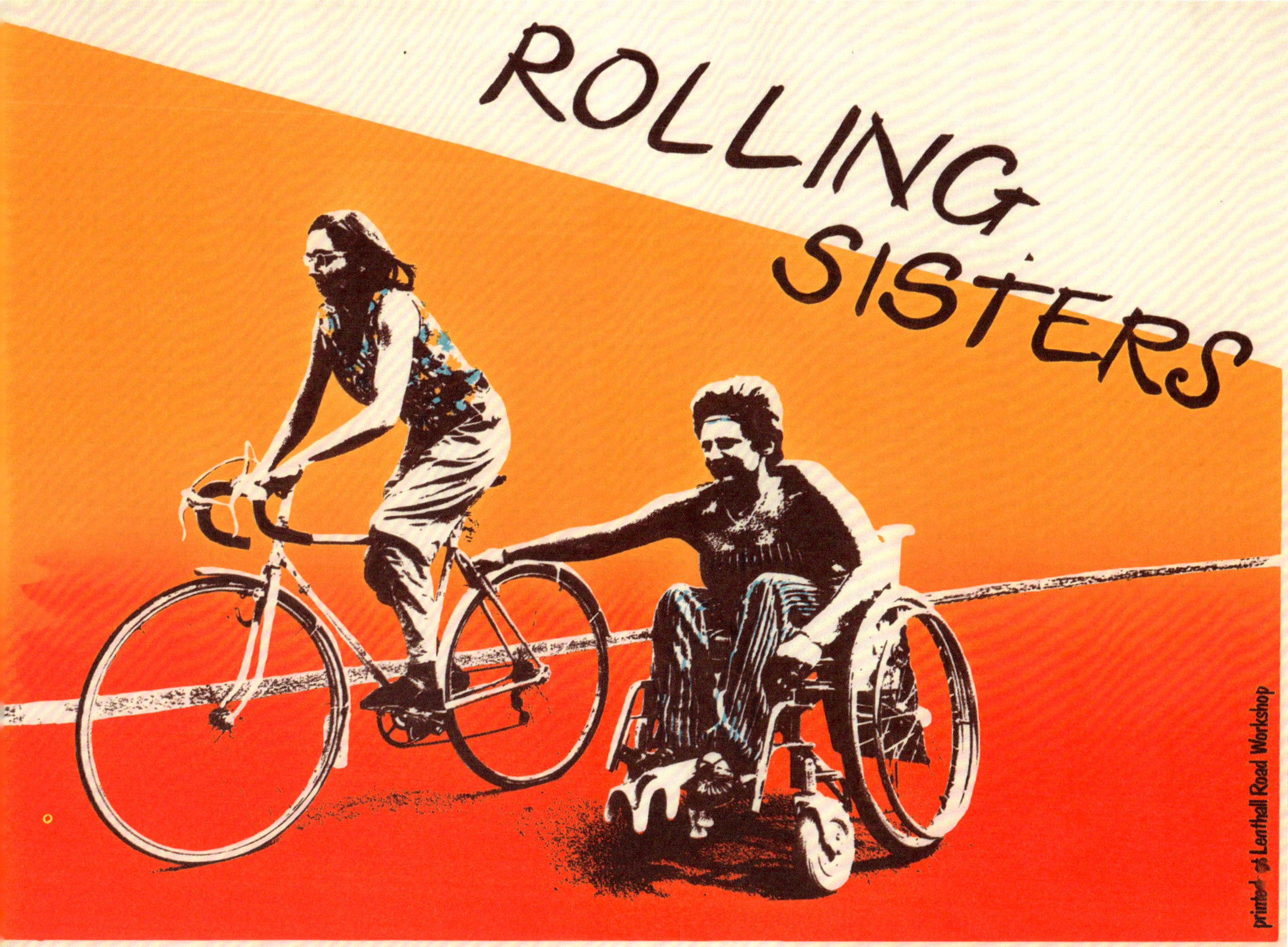

Rolling Sisters c.1983, featuring Nina Nissen (on the left) and Daniela von Raffay (on the right). Print on paper 45 × 65. Original photograph by Jill Posener

Lenthall Road Workshop opened in Hackney, East London in 1975 when Chia Moan, Viv Mullett and Jenny Smith took over a commercial screen-printing business and turned it into an all-women community printing workshop. Run on the feminist principles of equality and sharing, the workshop collaborated on community arts projects, and provided training and affordable access to printing and photographic equipment. Members of the workshop created and distributed posters, T-shirts, books and postcards that supported feminist, disability activist, anti-racist and LGBTQ+ campaigns which sought to disrupt the dominant patriarchal narratives of the time. Active until 1990, the workshop supported hundreds of individuals and groups during its lifetime. In addition to its founders, members included: Barbara Bennett, Claudette Johnson, Ingrid Pollard, Suzy Stiles, Nicole Superville, Harriet Tod and Rebecca Wilson.

LENTHALL ROAD WORKSHOP

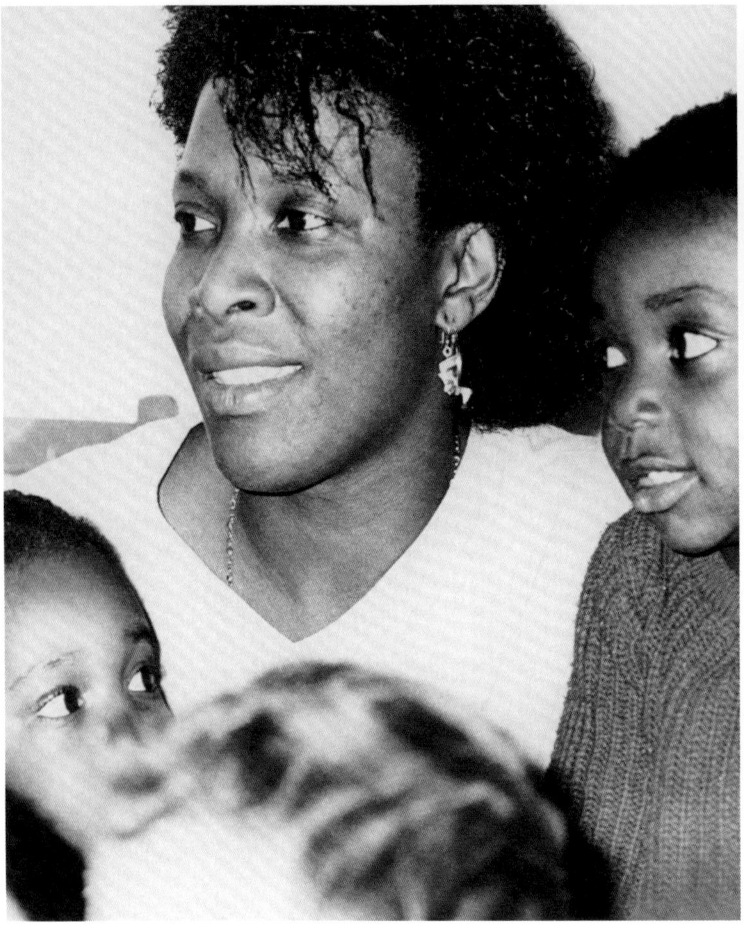
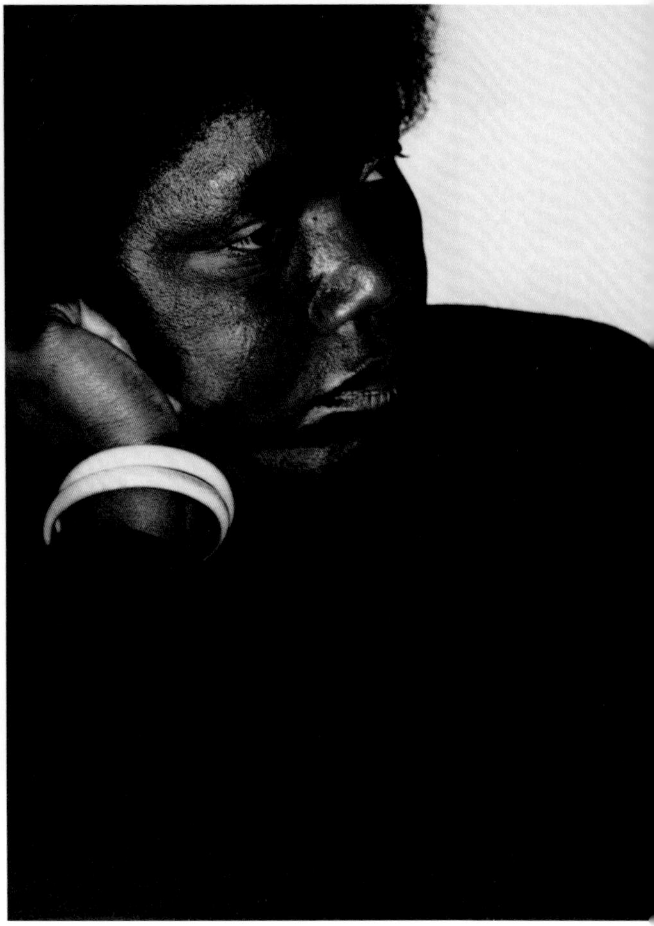

Untitled, from the series *Portrait of Black Women* 1985. Photographs 40.5 × 30.5 (each)

BRENDA AGARD

Brenda Agard (1961–2012), a photographer, artist, poet and script writer, was born in London. After studying Politics and English at A-Level, she gained an MA in Film and Television at Westminster University and a BSC in Psychology at East London University. Agard was a member of the Black Photographers Group, associated with the Blk Art Group, and her work featured in some of the most important group exhibitions connected to the British Black Arts Movement in the 1980s – including *Black Woman Time Now* (Battersea Arts Centre, 1983), *The Thin Black Line* (ICA, 1985), *Some of Us Are Brave, All of Us Are Strong: An Exhibition by and about Black Women* (The Black-Art Gallery, London, 1986), *UnRecorded Truths* (The Elbow Room, London, 1986) and *Influences* (South London Gallery, 1988). Agard used her lens to convey the strength and resilience of Black communities, and especially Black women, often photographing individuals speaking at political conferences, and translating that into powerful work; namely *We Will Rock You* and her photograph *Portrait of Our Time*, in the collection of Museums Sheffield. Agard was also a founding member of *Polareyes: A Journal by and about Black Women Working in Photography*.

Simone Alexander was born in London in 1964 and studied fine art at Camberwell School of Arts and Crafts and Byam Shaw School of Art, from where she graduated in 1986. In 1990, she completed her postgraduate degree at the Slade School of Fine Art. Alexander's practice explores the nuances of her lived experience with the aim of driving discussions at the cross-section of race, gender, sexuality and class. Her work is informed by the literature of Toni Morrison and Ntozake Shange, among others.

The 1987 work *Beyond the Nursery Door* portrays two little girls clutching hands in a domestic setting, populated by characters from fairy tales. This painting is from a collection of work which investigates the childhood spaces where literature and play hide the constructed narrative of the dominating normative bias.

In the 1980s, Alexander was involved in the British Black Arts Movement, featuring in important exhibitions, including *The Image Employed: The Use of the Narrative in Black Art* (Cornerhouse, Manchester, 1987); *Caribbean Expression in Britain* (Leicestershire Museum and Art Gallery, 1988); *Dislocations* (Kettles Yard, Cambridge, 1988) and *Influences* (South London Gallery, 1988).

Alexander lives and works in London.

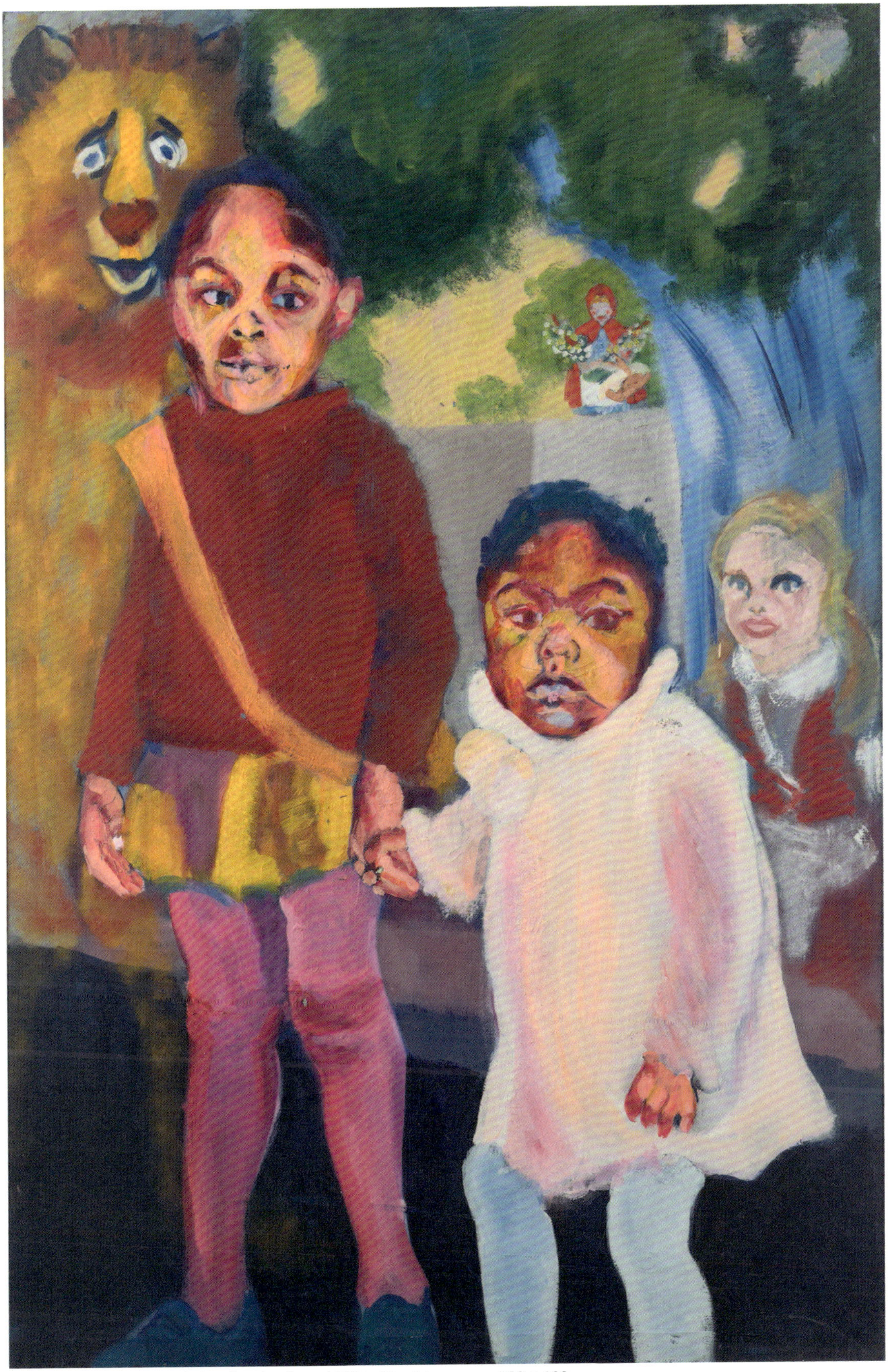

Beyond the Nursery Door (When You Are Queen) 1987. Oil paint on canvas 180 × 120

SIMONE ALEXANDER

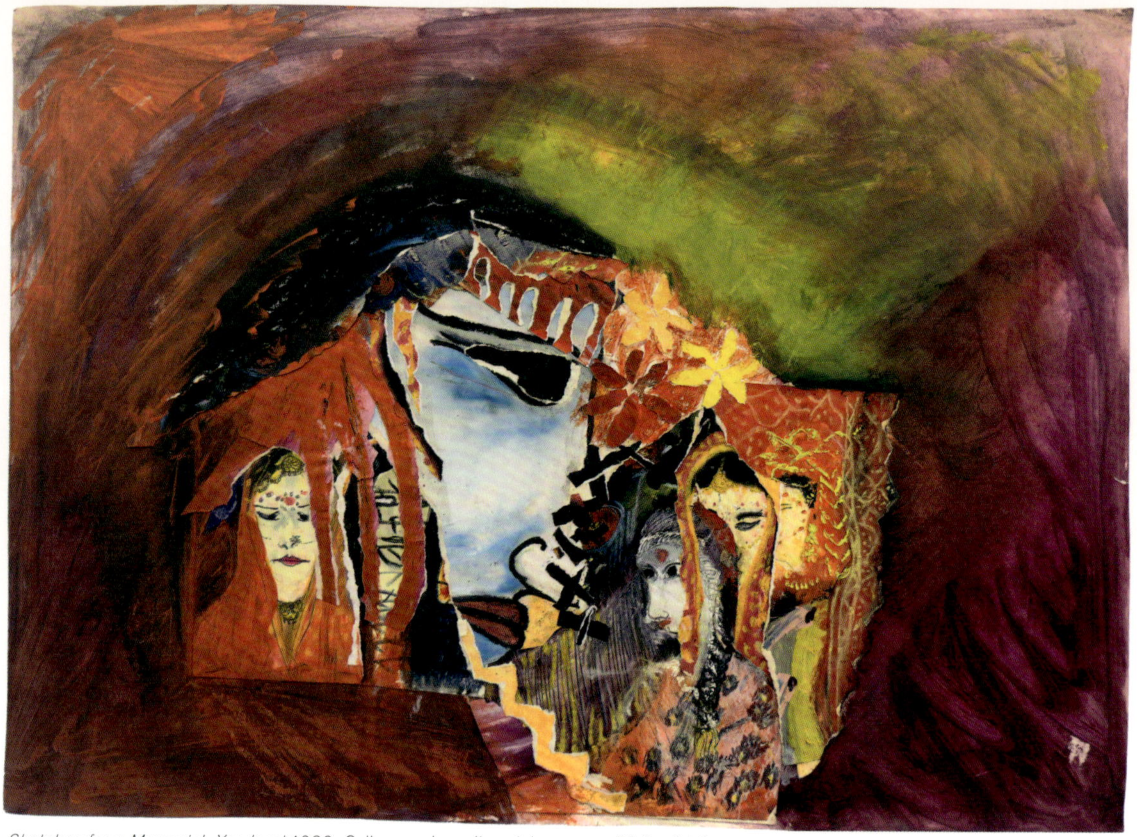

Sketches for a Memorial–Yaadgari 1986. Collage and acrylic paint on paper 59.5 × 84.2

Born in Nakuru, Kenya in 1961, Symrath Patti moved to London as a child with her family. She graduated from Leeds Polytechnic in 1984, where she worked across photography, performance, painting and moving image. Returning to London, Patti continued her artistic practice while working in arts administration to support herself and getting involved in community engagement. Patti's work in the 1980s considered the political climate around her, addressing racism and expressing concern for the experiences of South Asian women, such as honour killings, domestic abuse, sexual violence and arranged marriages. In *Sketches for a Memorial – Yaadgari* 1986, the god of love Krishna is at the centre of a collage, viewing the situation of the women who surround him. Patti was a founding member of Panchayat, a South Asian arts collective focused on inclusion, visibility and representation, and conducted several studio visits to South Asian women artists working in London to bring them together. In 1986 she curated *Jagrati* at Greenwich Citizens Gallery, still the largest exhibition of work by South Asian women artists in Britain.

A solo exhibition of Patti's work was held at Muse Gallery, London, in 2023. She lives and works in London.

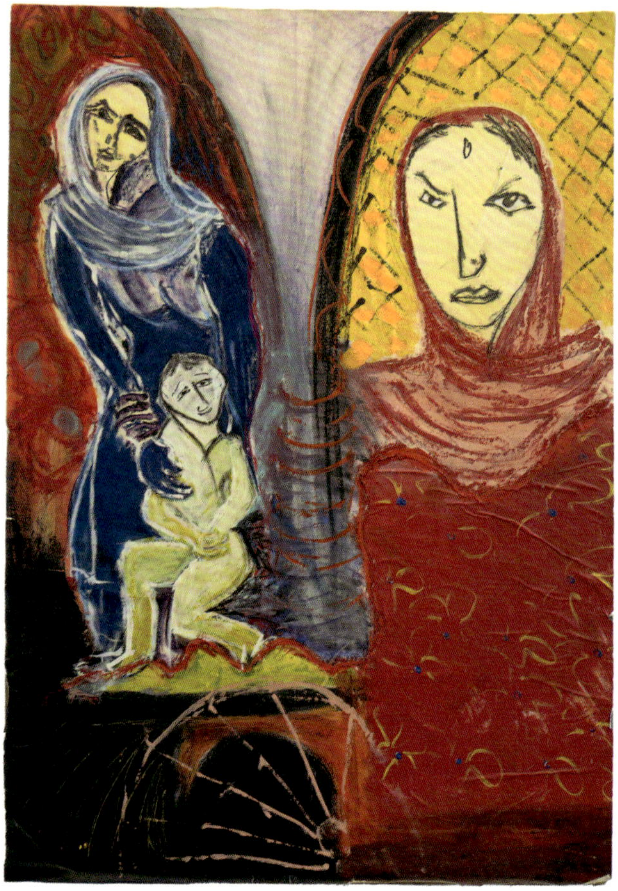

Woman in Red 1986. Acrylic paint and pastel on paper 113.5 × 81

SYMRATH PATTI

Born in Nairobi, Kenya, to Indian parents in 1955, Pratibha Parmar moved to England with her family at the age of twelve. She received a BA from Bradford University and a postgraduate degree from Birmingham University. Parmar's practice is fuelled by the desire to portray the stories of those who have been relegated to the margins of mainstream culture, looking at the intersection of art and social justice, with feminism at the core. In both her films and her writing, Parmar pinpoints the contradicting stereotypes of Asian women in society as both sexually exotic creatures, full of promise, and as mute, dominated and oppressed by men. *Sari Red* 1988 was made in memory of Kalbinder Kaur Hayre, a young Indian woman killed in a racist attack in 1985. The film sensitively examines the threat of violence faced by South Asian women in the United Kingdom, in both public and private spaces. The colour red is symbolically deployed throughout, referencing intimacy, blood and the colour of a sari.

Parmar divides her time between Berkeley, California, and London.

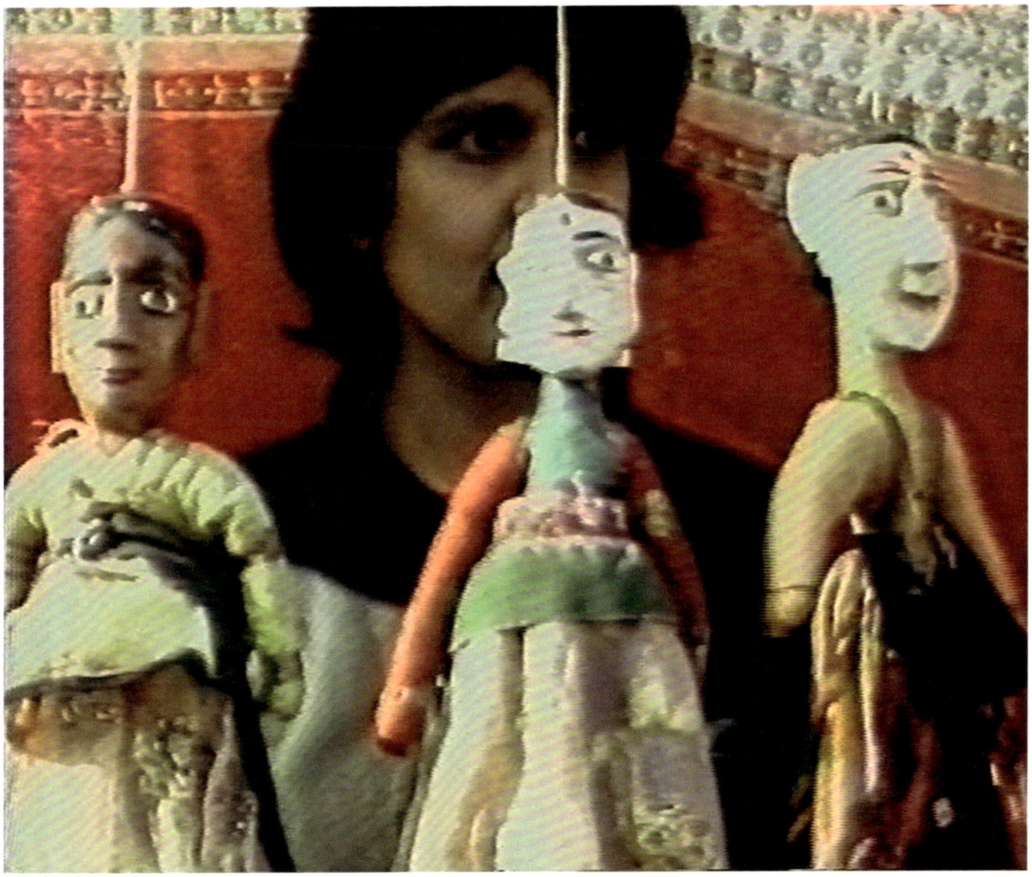

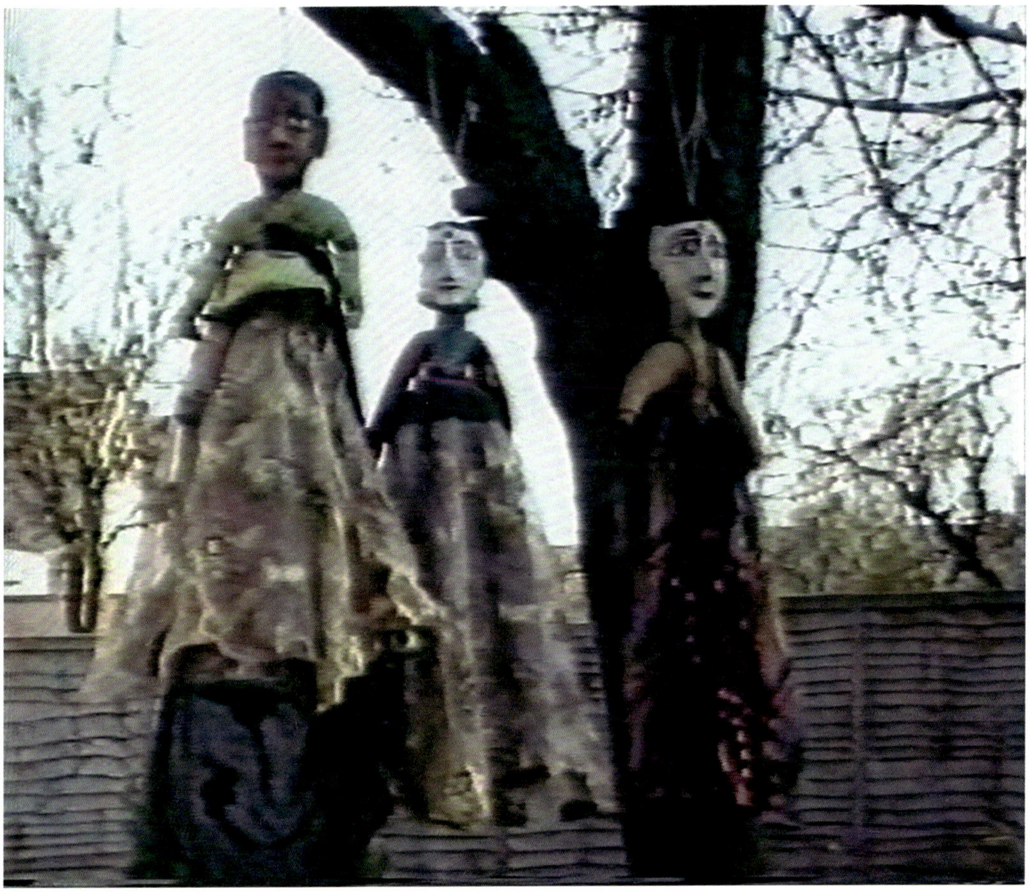

Sari Red 1988. Video, shown digitally; colour, sound. 13 min, 26 sec

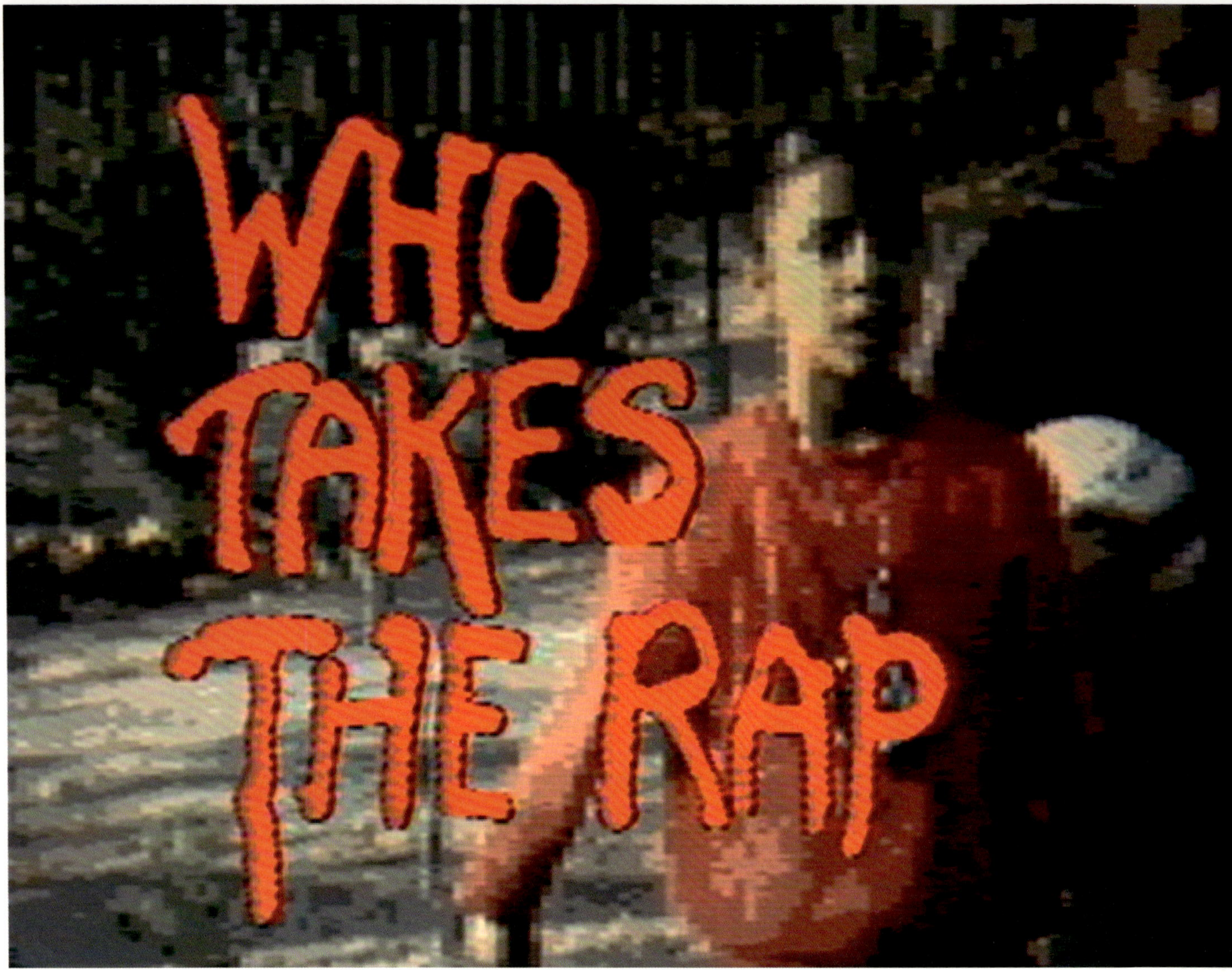

Who Takes the Rap – Immigration 1986. Video, shown digitally; colour, sound. 38 min

Lai Ngan Walsh (b.1949) has worked in film and television production as a director, script consultant and sound recordist. Her short film *One Man's Meat* 1989 was shown at film festivals in London, Edinburgh, Montreal and Cherbourg-en-Cotentin, and was nominated for a Gold Hugo at the Chicago International Film Festival. In 1990–1 she wrote a FourPlay for Channel 4. In addition to her work in film, she also works as a photo stylist and writer, printmaker and painter. Her prints have been exhibited and collected in England, France, Malaysia and Bali.

Who Takes the Rap 1986 was made with the Women and the Law Collective. The film addresses how earlier histories of legal discrimination have continued to affect the status and opportunities of different immigrants to the UK. It includes footage of strikes where workers fought back against racism, alongside interviews with those affected by the UK's restrictive and racist law-making practices. In writing the film's commentary, the challenge was how to express the anger at this institutional cruelty, and at the same time, encapsulate the history of the laws in an accessible way. Rap was fairly new in the UK at that time and a rap poem seemed the perfect vehicle. The rap was performed passionately by Lorna Gee.

LAI NGAN WALSH

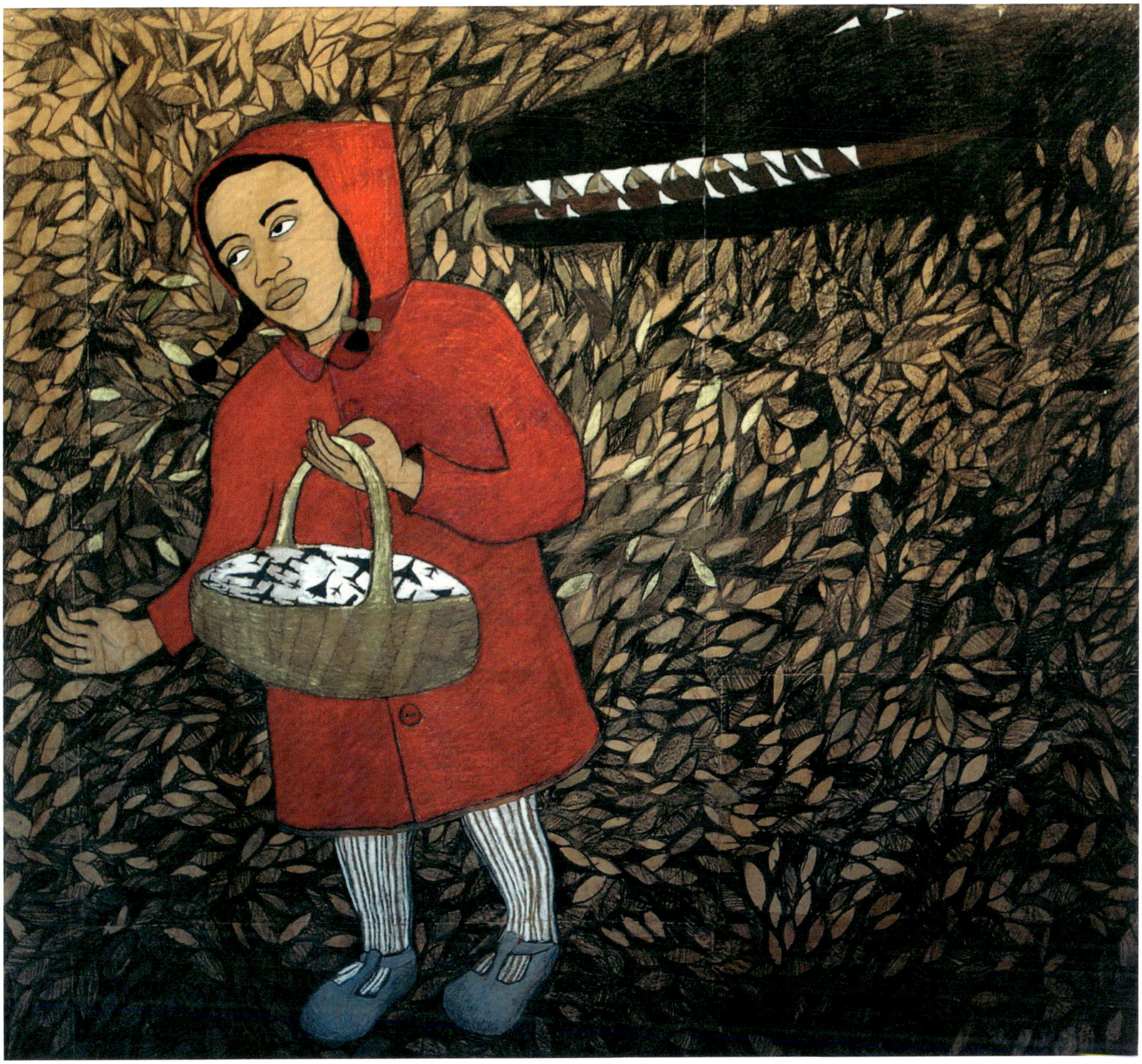

Red Riding Hood 1987. Pastel on paper 189 × 214

Amanda Holiday (b. 1964) is a Sierra Leonean-British artist, filmmaker and poet. Holiday grew up in Wigan after emigrating with her family to the UK at the age of five. She received a degree in fine art from Wimbledon School of Arts in 1987 and during her study was involved in the British Black Arts Movement, setting up a Black art student group. She featured in major exhibitions in the 1980s, such as, *Some of Us are Brave, All of Us are Strong: An Exhibition by and about Black Women* (Black-Art Gallery, London, 1986), *Black Perspectives* (South London Art Gallery, 1987) and *Black Art: Plotting the Course* (Oldham Art Gallery, 1988). Her art practice is characterised by large-scale figurative mixed-media works which consider the experiences of Black women. Her work *Red Riding Hood* 1987 powerfully portrays the fairy tale character as a young Black woman; in her basket she carries small aeroplanes – imagery taken from an advertisement of the time – and behind her is a large wolf.

More recently, Holiday founded Black Sunflowers, a poetry press focused on the work of women and Black poets. She lives and works in London.

AMANDA HOLIDAY

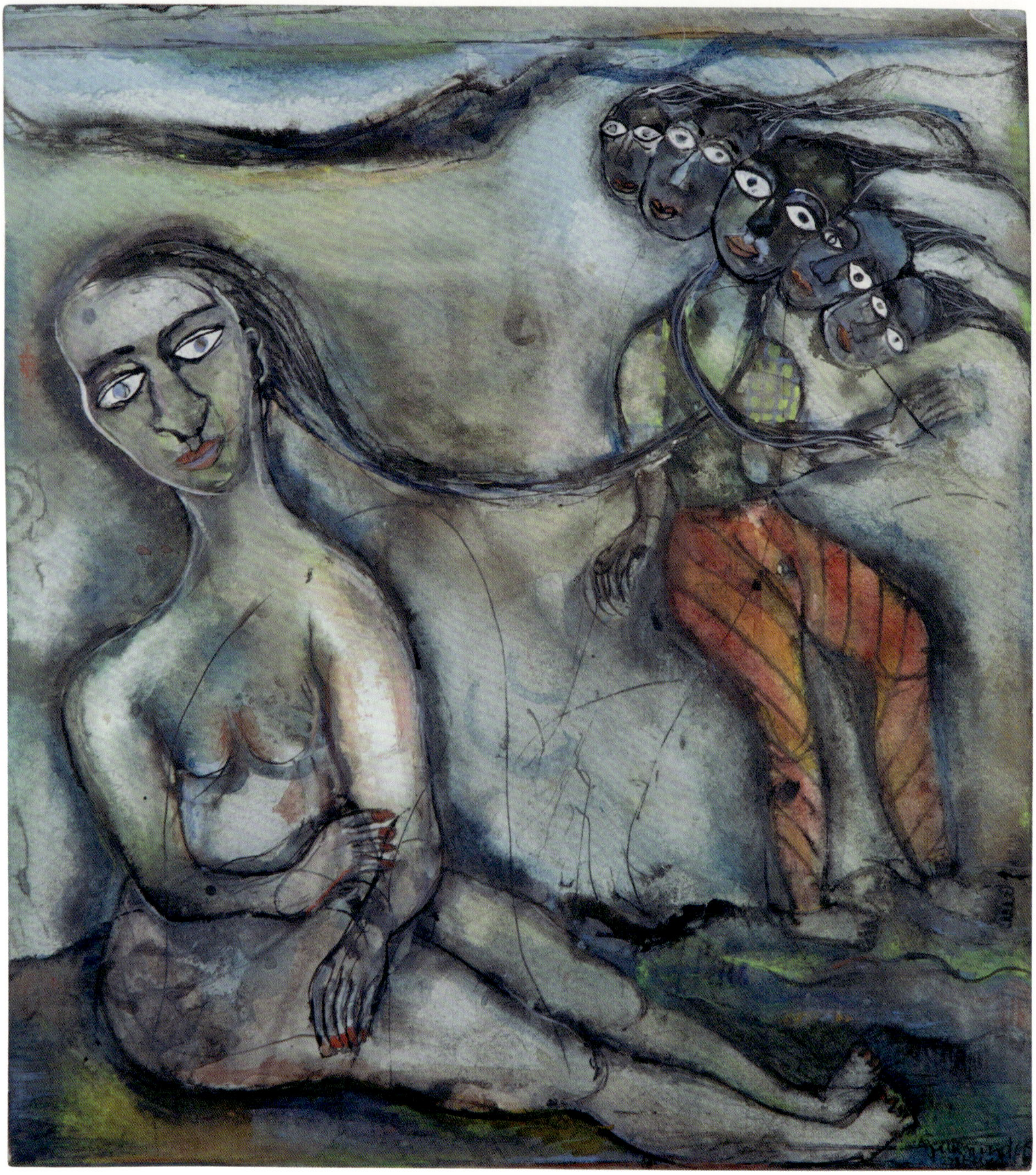

Woman Strangling a Demon / 1990. Watercolour, ink, gouache and wax crayon on paper 35.5 × 32.1

GURMINDER SIKAND

Born in the Punjab region of north-western India, Gurminder Sikand (1960–2021) moved to the UK with her family at the age of ten, settling in South Wales after spells in the north of England and North Wales. She studied fine art at the City of Birmingham Polytechnic, graduating in 1983, before moving to Nottingham, where she lived for the rest of her life. Working across painting and latterly drawing, Sikand often referenced Indian folklore and cultural symbolism in her art, with an emphasis on depicting strong female figures, as seen in the watercolour *Woman Strangling a Demon* / 1990. A notable figure in Black and Asian art circles in the 1980s and 90s, Sikand co-founded the Nottingham Asian Artists' Group in 1985. Throughout her career, she focused on the situation of women, particularly in relation to nature. Many of her works were influenced by the Chipko movement in India.

Sikand's final solo exhibition was at TG in Nottingham in 2021. The drawings shown there were produced over three years. Her portraits of muscular women standing outside buildings reflect her view of social structures as constricting for women.

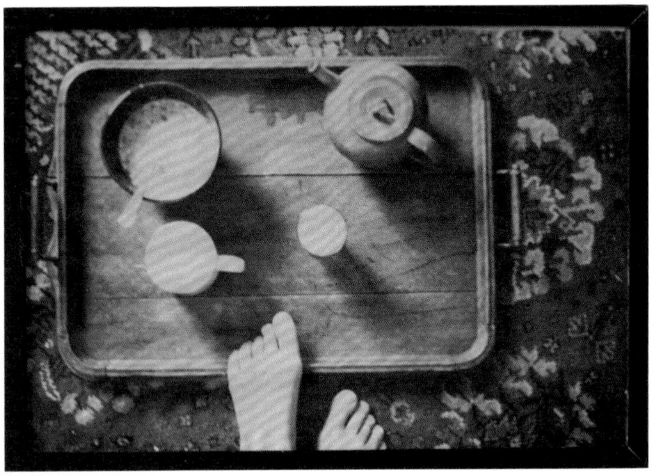

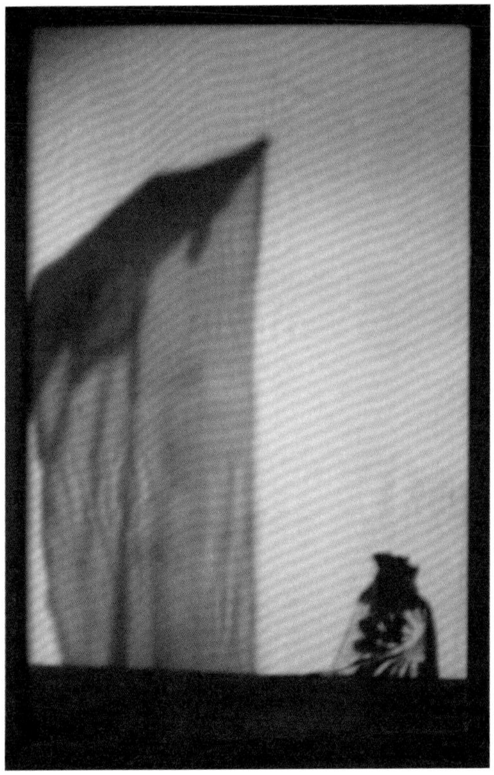

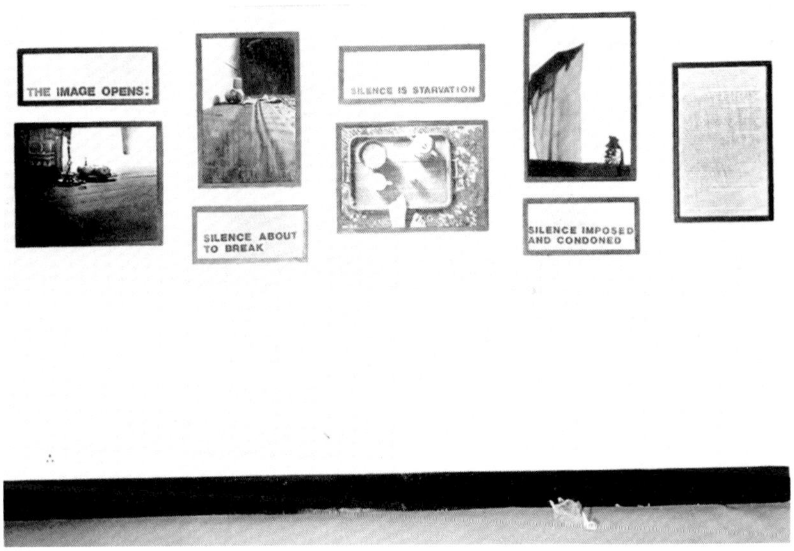

In Response to the F-Stops Exhibition (For the White Feminists) 1986.
9 copper-toned photographs and printed texts. Dimensions variable

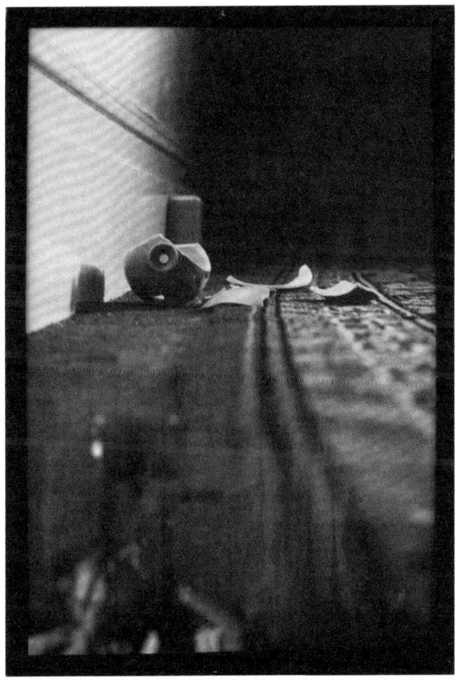

ZARINA BHIMJI

Zarina Bhimji was born in Mbarara, Uganda in 1963. She graduated from Goldsmiths College in London with a BA in fine art in 1986, going on to receive an MA in fine art from the Slade School of Art. She rose to prominence as an active figure within the British Black Arts Movement. Working across photography, film and installation, Bhimji's work engages with questions of institutional power and vulnerability, universality and intimacy.

Solo exhibitions of Bhimji's work have been presented at the Whitechapel Gallery in London (2012), Tate Britain (2018) and at the Fruitmarket Gallery in Edinburgh (2023), and her work is in many museum and private collections. The artist has received the Smithsonian Artist Research Fellowship (2023); Rauschenberg Residency Award (2014) and the Paul Hamlyn Foundation Award (1999), and she was a DAAD Artist-in-Residence in 2002. She was also nominated for the Turner Prize in 2007. She lives and works in London.

Rita Keegan (née Morrison) was born in 1949 in the Bronx, New York, USA, to a Dominican mother and a Canadian father. Having graduated with a fine arts degree from the San Francisco Art Institute in 1972, she moved to the UK in 1980, settling in London. There she co-founded the Brixton Art Gallery and became an important figure in the Black Arts Movement. Keegan works across print, photography, film, sound and installation. Her work considers the representation of Black communities historically and acts of self-fashioning in relation to the experience of Black women, often through self-portraiture. In *Love, Sex and Romance* 1984, Keegan created a series of self-portraits using photocopying, placing herself at the centre. In 1984 Keegan co-founded Community CopyArt, a resource centre set up to facilitate activist workshops and produce print materials, and in 1985 she established the Women Artists of Colour Index, to catalogue, document and remember the work of Black women artists.

An exhibition of Keegan's work was held at the South London Gallery in 2021. Recent group exhibitions include those at La Trobe Art Institute, Melbourne and The Royal Academy, London, with talks and film in collaboration with The Caribbean Cultural Center African Diaspora Institute, New York and Government Art Collection, UK, among others. In 2023 Keegan founded the Rita Keegan Heritage Project, which is currently awaiting charitable status.

She lives and works in London.

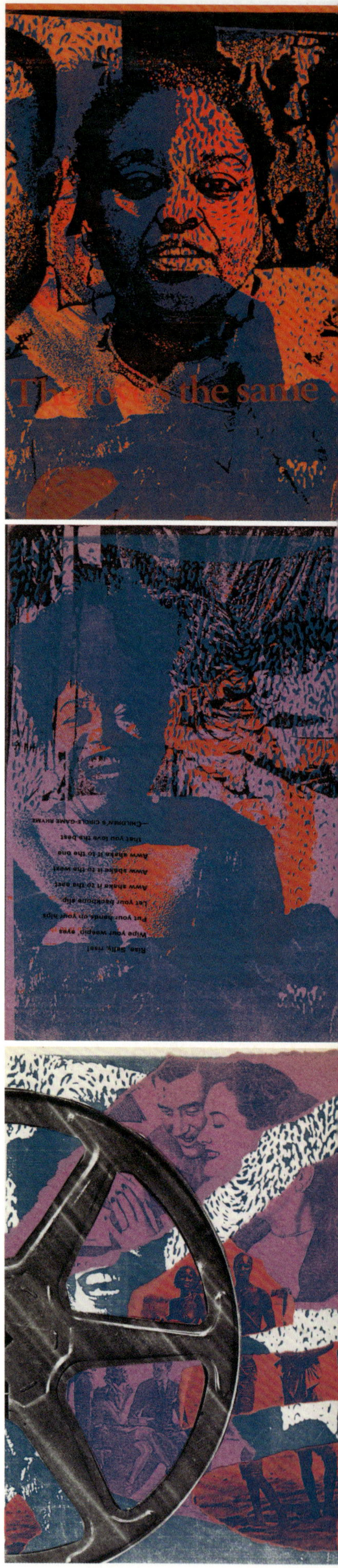

Love, Sex and Romance 1984.
12 photocopies and screenprints on paper 28.9 × 20.1 (each)

RITA KEEGAN

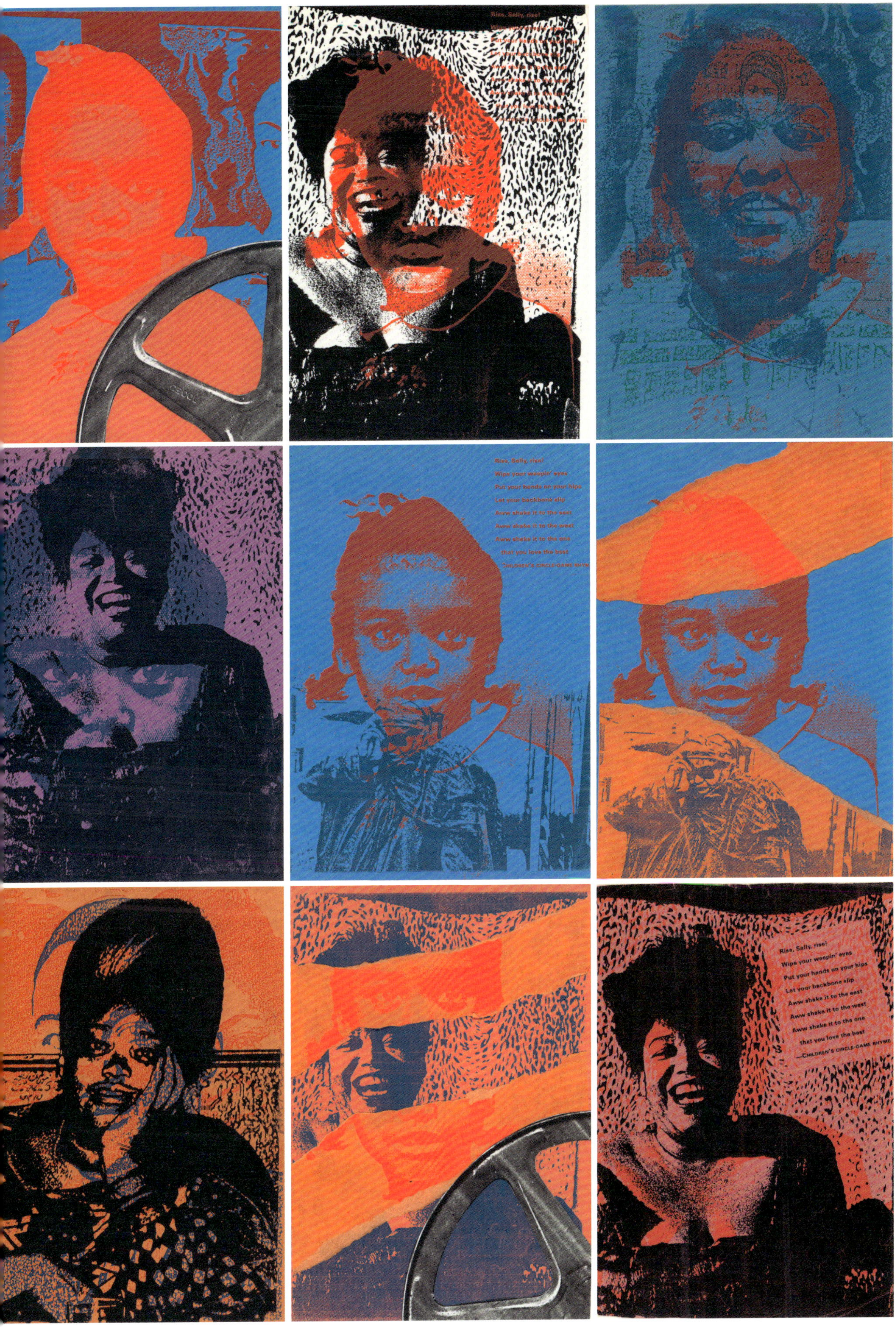
Rise, Sally, rise!
Wipe your weepin' eyes
Put your hands on your hips
Let your backbone slip
Aww shake it to the east
Aww shake it to the west
Aww shake it to the one
that you love the best
—CHILDREN'S CIRCLE-GAME RHYME

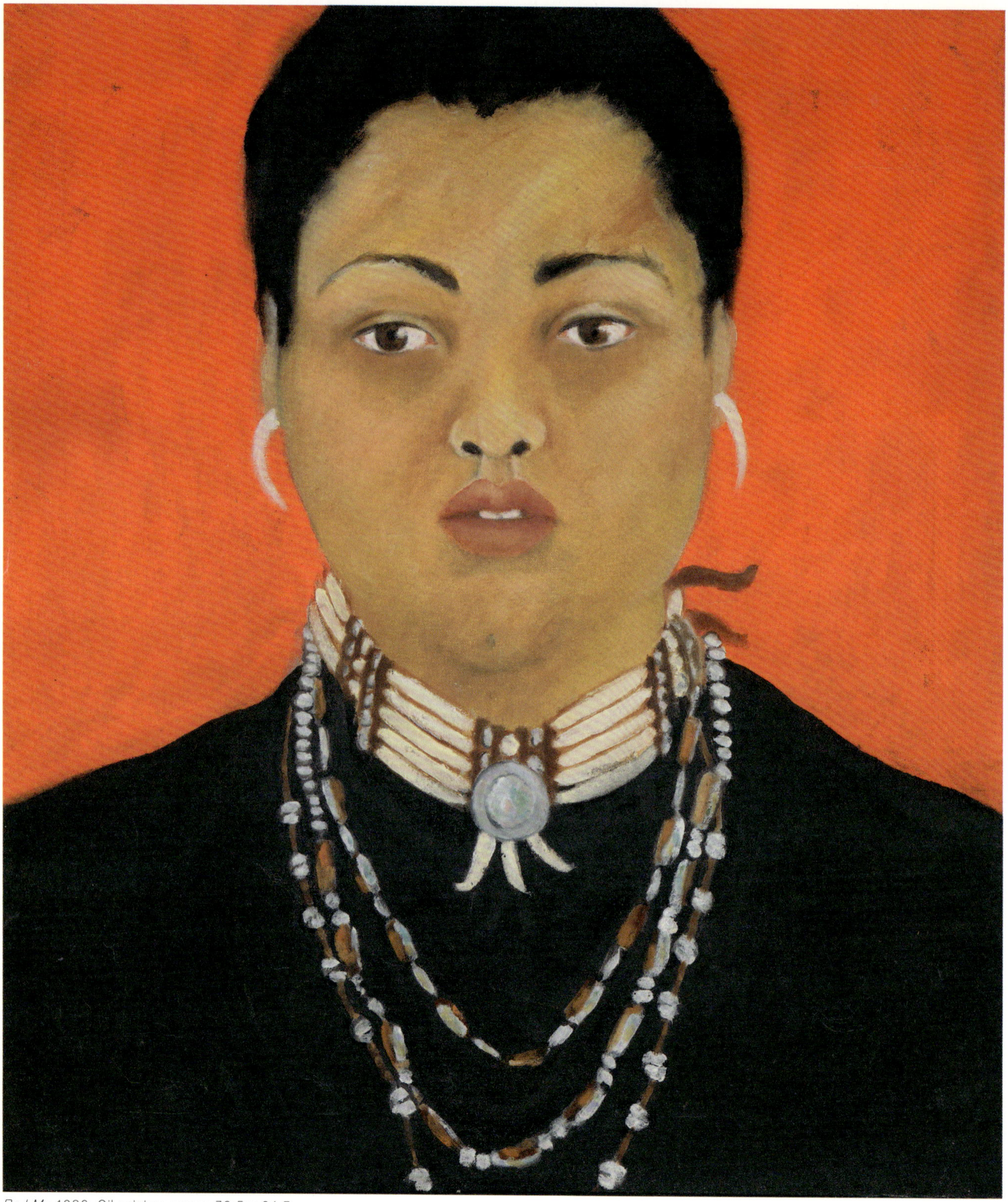

Red Me 1986. Oil paint on canvas 72.5 × 64.7

RITA KEEGAN

London-born writer, historian, activist and artist Stella Dadzie (b.1952) is a pioneering figure in British Black feminist politics. Together with Olive Morris (1952–79), Gail Lewis (b.1951) and others, she was a founder member of the Organisation of Women of African and Asian Descent, or OWAAD (1978–83), which fought for equality for Black and Brown women through its activism, national conferences and publications. In addition to co-organising OWAAD activity, Dadzie painted OWAAD's banner and contributed illustrations to the organisation's newsletter *FOWAAD!*.

In 1985, with co-authors Beverley Bryan and Suzanne Scafe, Dadzie published *The Heart of the Race: Black Women's Lives in Britain*, a foundational feminist text that explores the lives of Black women in the UK and the extraordinary challenges and burdens that are placed on them by a society that consistently demonstrates institutional racism and sexual inequality. Dadzie's painting *Motherland* c.1984 was reproduced on the cover (p.49). *The Heart of the Race* was republished as a feminist classic in 2018 and has become a touchstone for a new generation of women.

Dadzie lives and works in London.

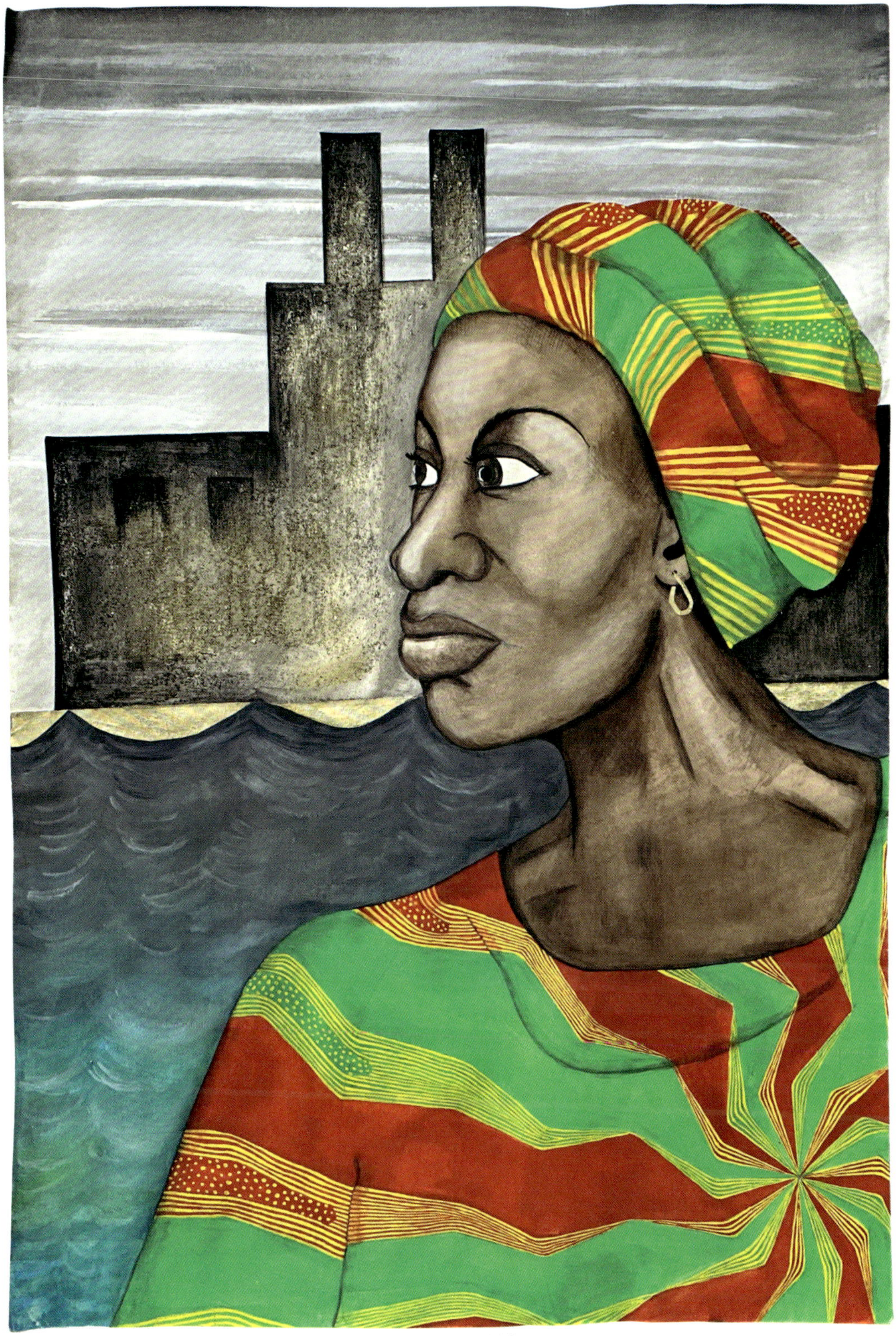

Motherland c.1984. Watercolour, gold foil and sand on card 60.5 × 41.5

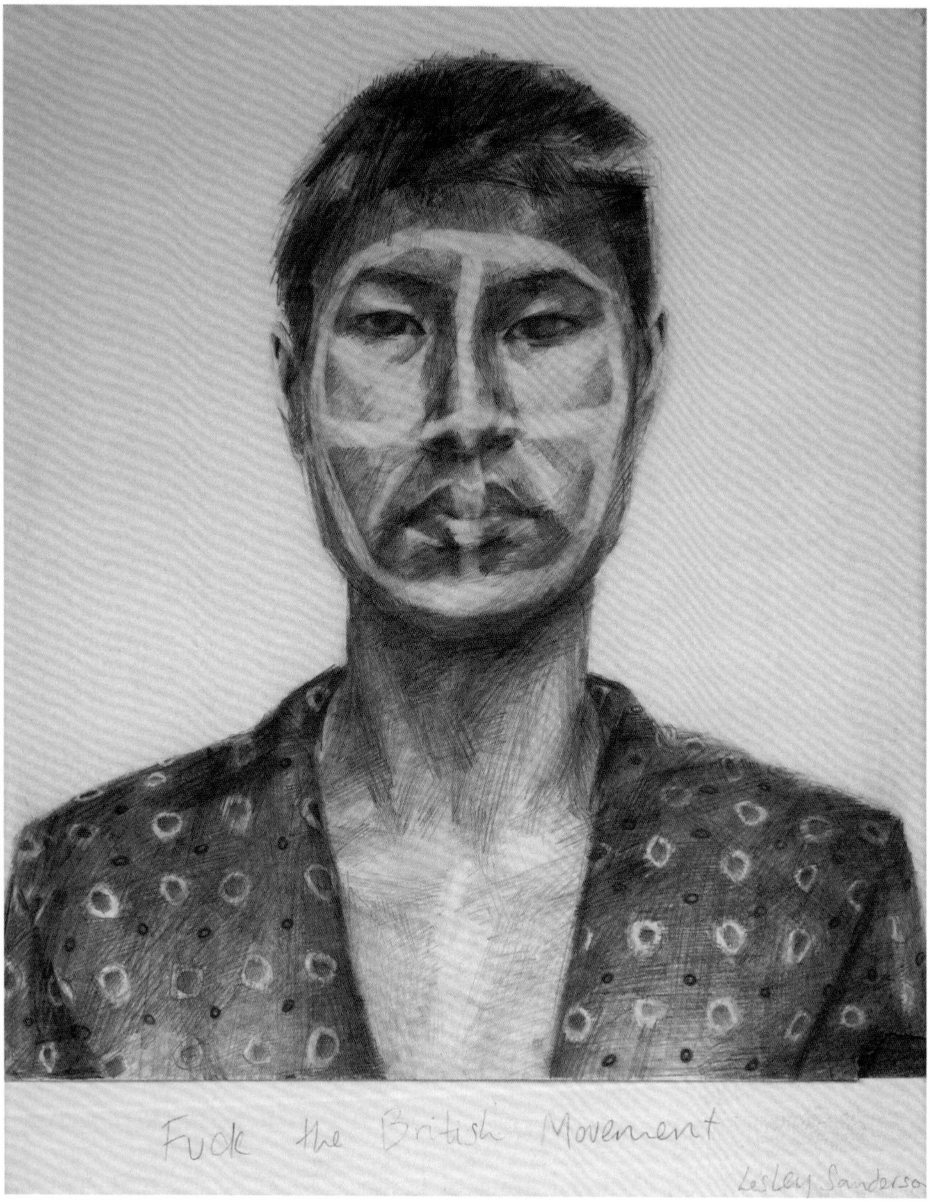

Fuck the British Movement 1984. Graphite on paper 67.5 × 54

Lesley Sanderson was born in Malaysia to a Chinese-Malaysian mother and a British father in 1962. She graduated from Sheffield Polytechnic in 1984 with a degree in fine art. Working across drawing and painting, Sanderson's work from the 1980s often used self-portraiture to explore the artist's dual Chinese-Malaysian and British identity. Regarding portrayals of non-white women in art history as problematic, positioned as submissive, exotic and readily available for the male gaze, she felt that people's perceptions of her were dominated by her identity and in her practice she challenged the stereotypes of women whose ethnic origins led to their exoticisation by society. Sanderson's highly political works such as *Fuck the British Movement* 1984, which offers a critique of racism towards women of colour in Britain, counter these perceptions and stereotypes. In her later work, Sanderson began to focus on other parts of her body (skin, hands, feet) or portraits of family, and to work with materials such as fabric and glass that lend themselves to being fragmented, exploring further ideas around how identity is constructed by society.

Since 1998, she has worked collaboratively with the artist Neil Conroy as Conroy/Sanderson. She lives and works in Sheffield.

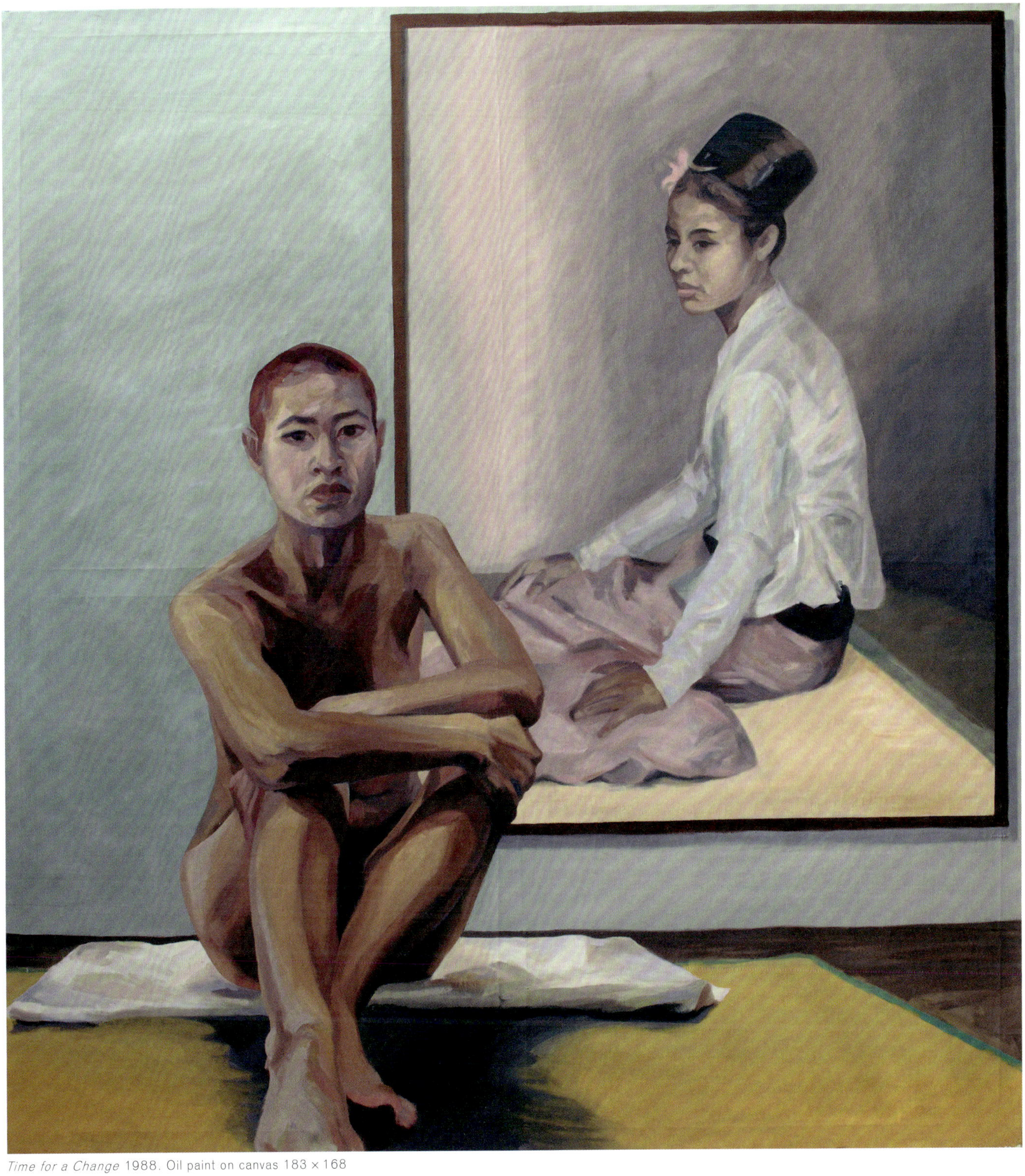

Time for a Change 1988. Oil paint on canvas 183 × 168

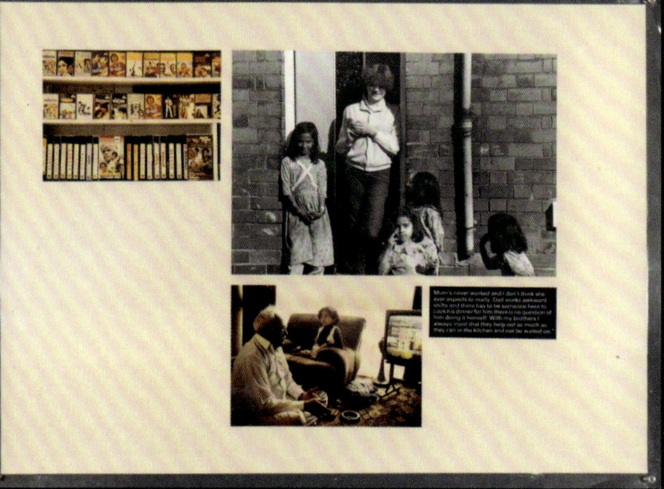

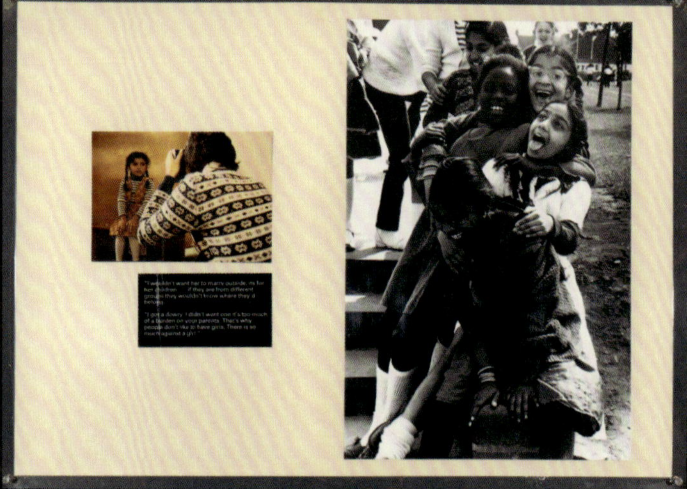

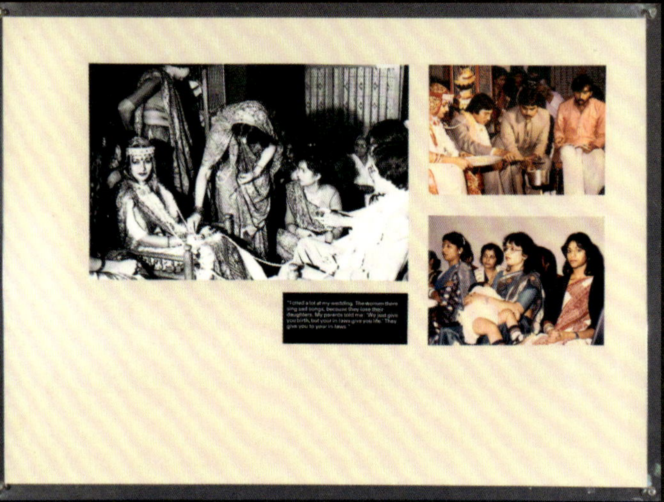

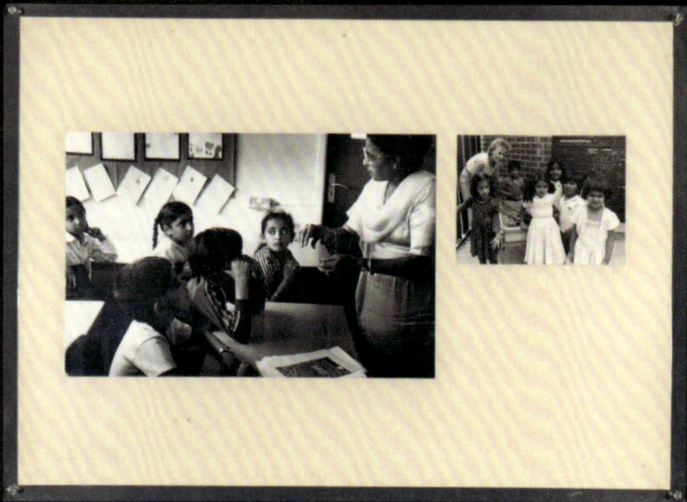

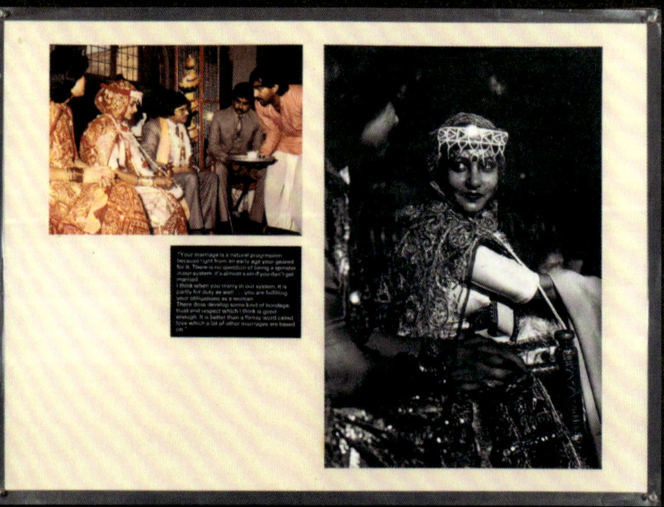

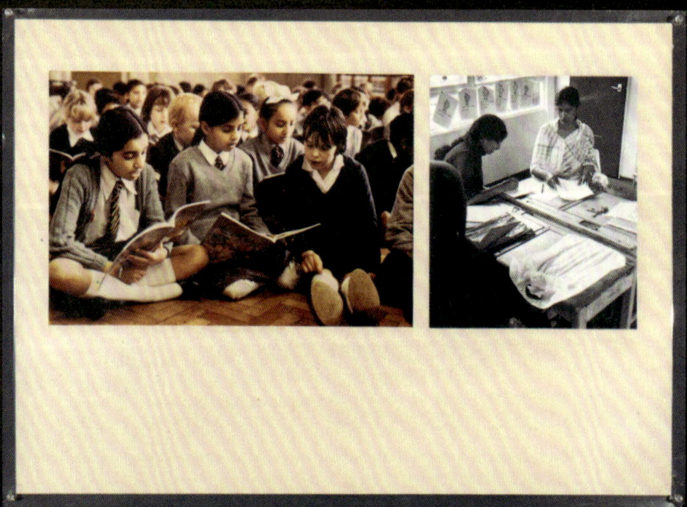

Roshini Kempadoo was born in Sussex in 1959 but spent her formative years in Guyana and other Caribbean countries. In England, she completed an MA in photographic studies at the University of Derby and a PhD at Goldsmiths College. Kempadoo describes herself as a photographer, media artist and scholar and is active in all fields, making and exhibiting art and working as a professor at the University of Westminster School of Arts, London. She characterises her artworks as 'factual and fictional re-imaginings of everyday experiences, histories and memories by Caribbean persons and its diaspora'.

Between 1983 and 2003 Kempadoo was part of Format Photographers Agency where she specialised in documenting Black communities, women's groups and trade union activity. In the late 1980s she was instrumental in founding the Association of Black Photographers (now Autograph ABP) and was actively involved in developing the photography magazine *Ten.8*. More recently, she has exhibited in *Life Between Islands: Caribbean-British Art 1950s–Now* (Tate Britain, 2021–2), and *Thirteen Ways of Looking* (Herbert Art Gallery, Coventry, 2020). She published the monograph *Creole in the Archive: Imagery, Presence and Location of the Caribbean Figure* in 2016.

Kempadoo lives and works in London.

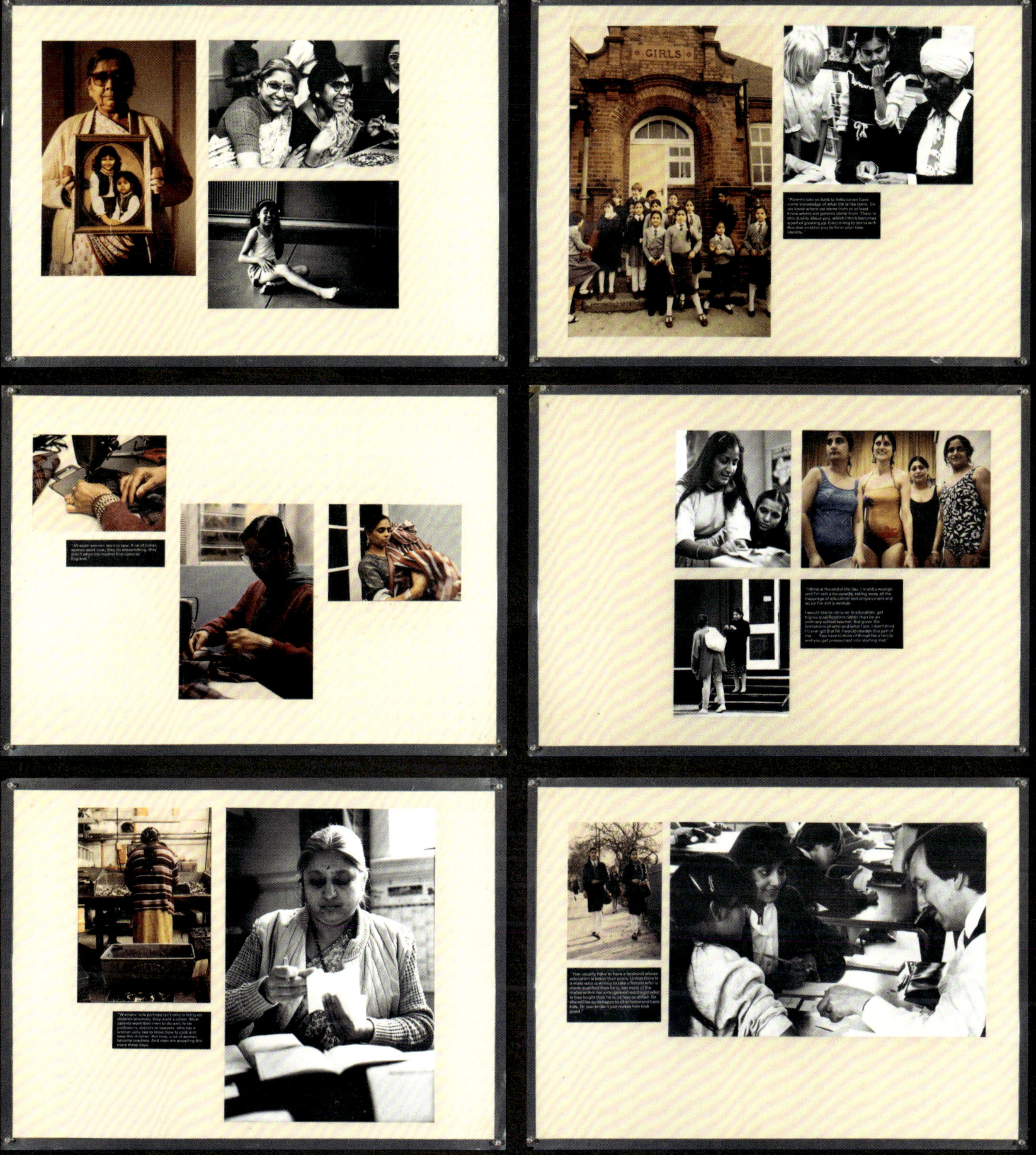

My Daughter's Mind 1984–5. 12 parts; photographs and prints on paper 47.5 × 67 (each)

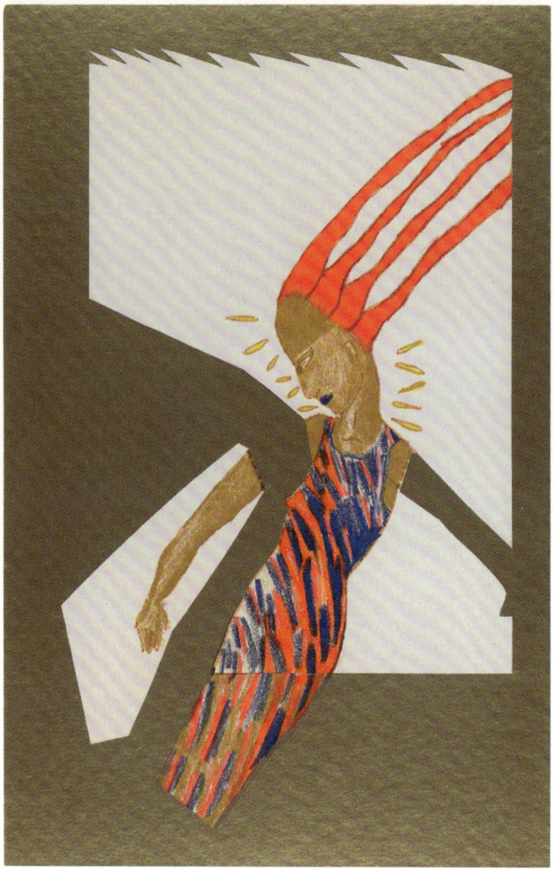

Chips on Her Shoulders, Her Arms Fell Off 1986. Permanent marker and oil crayon on paper on gold board 40.2 × 26.7

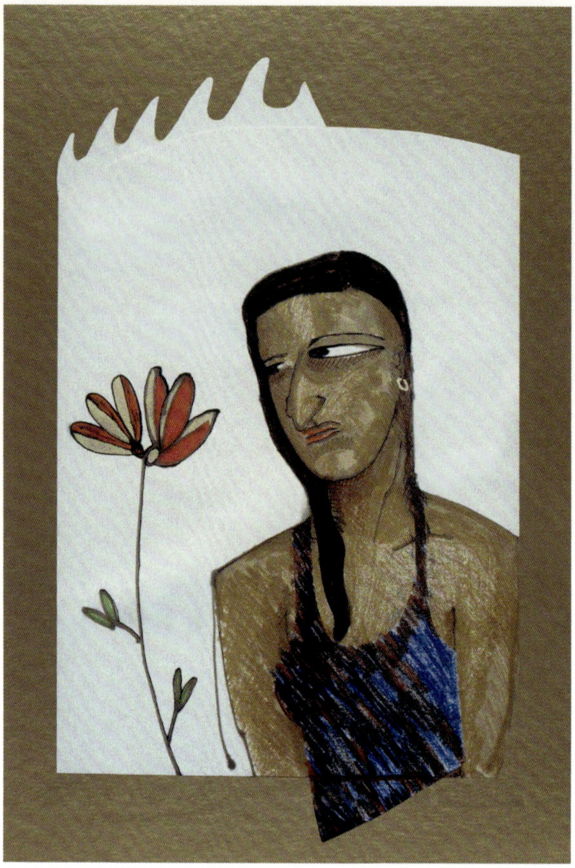

Searching for Flowers in the Tandoori Garden 1986. Permanent marker and oil crayon on paper on gold board 40.5 × 26.5

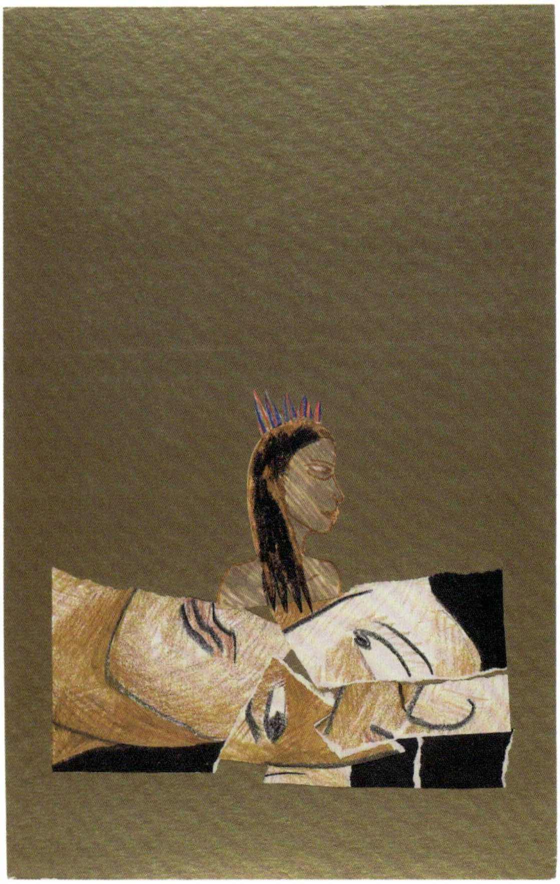

Trying Not to Offend My Parents 1986. Permanent marker and oil crayon on paper on gold board 40.5 × 26.5

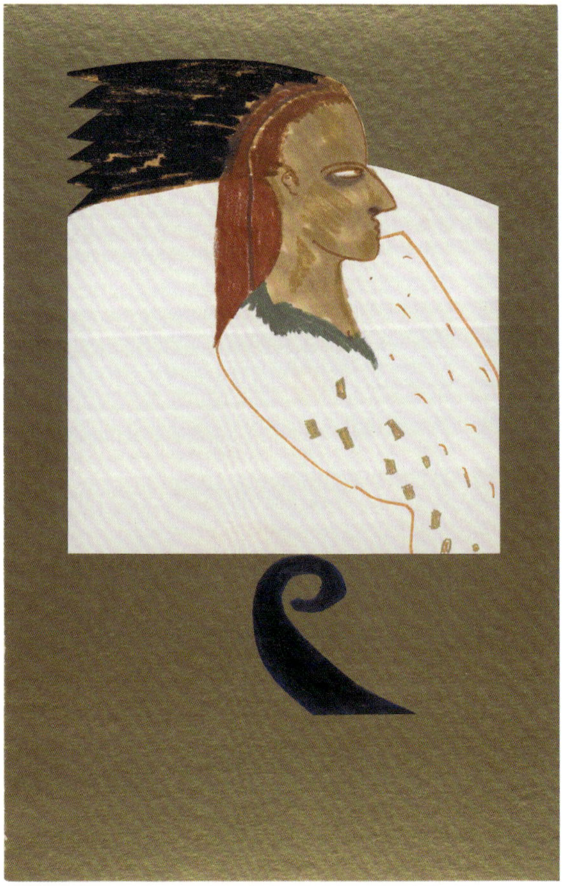

Paki Ride Home on a Piece of Spit 1986. Permanent marker and oil crayon on paper on gold board 40.2 × 26.7

NINA EDGE

Of Ugandan Asian and English heritage, Nina Edge (b.1962) grew up in Gloucestershire. Having trained in Cardiff as a ceramicist, she established a practice working across drawing, printing, ceramics, sculpture and performance. Edge's work featured in several key exhibitions of South Asian women artists in the 1980s, including *Jagrati* (Greenwich Citizens Gallery, 1986), *Numaish* (People's Gallery, 1986) and the 1988 touring exhibition *Along the Lines of Resistance*. Her powerful, confrontational art challenged the portrayal of South Asian women in British society and expressed her own lived experience, using non-Western craft techniques, such as batik and shisha embroidery, alongside English traditions, such as slip trailing.

In the mixed-media work *Snakes and Ladders* 1985, Edge depicts a South Asian woman of great stature, physically above the viewer's eye level, reclaiming her own gaze and disrupting notions of herself as 'exotic'. Edge also created an important series of collaged drawings in the 1980s that address her experience of racial abuse in England and Wales, highlighting the treatment that South Asian women were subjected to at that time.

Edge lives and works in Liverpool as an artist and urban design activist.

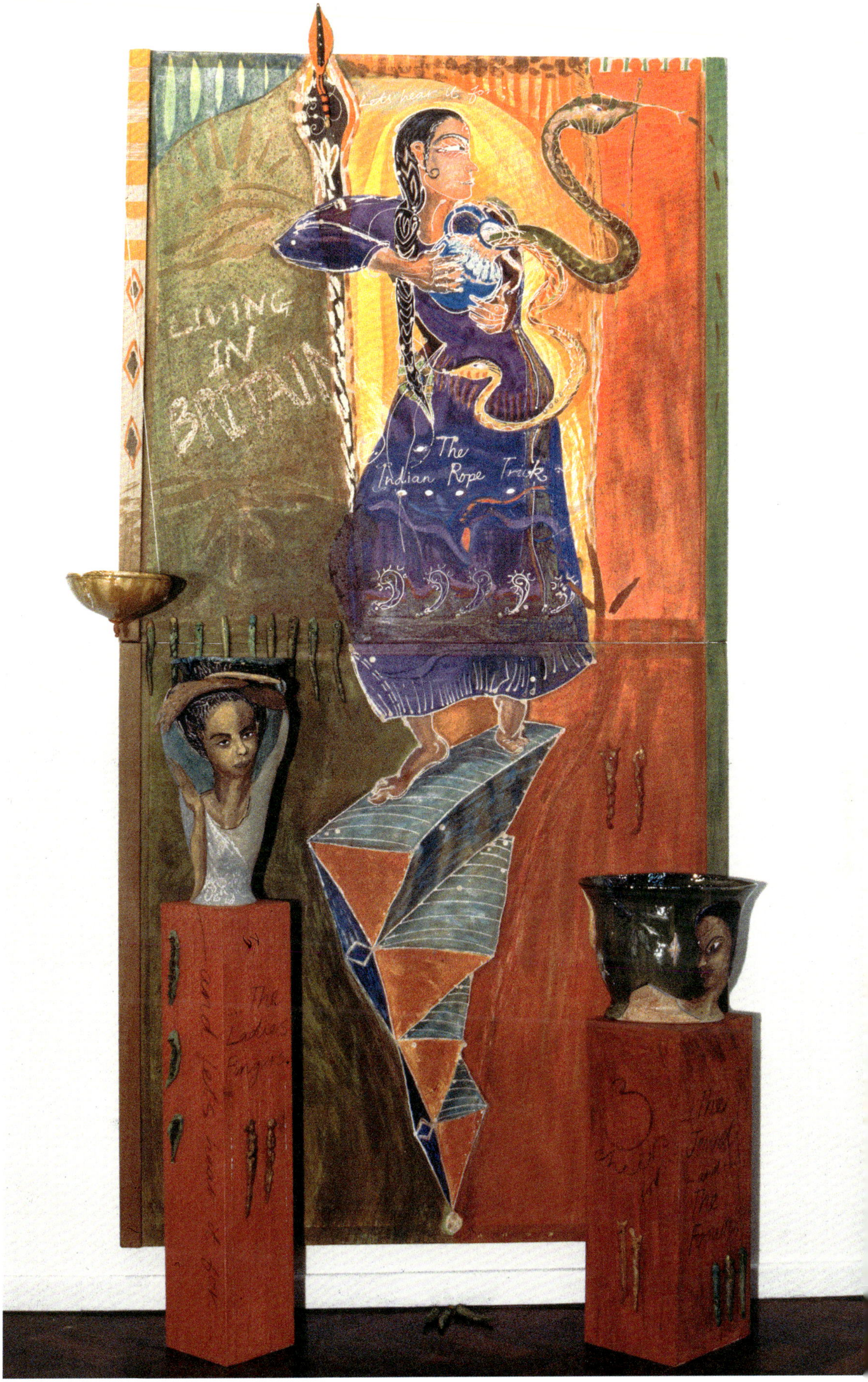

Snakes and Ladders 1985.
Batik on paper mounted on board, ceramics, string, wooden plinths and handwritten text on paper
250 × 177 × 65

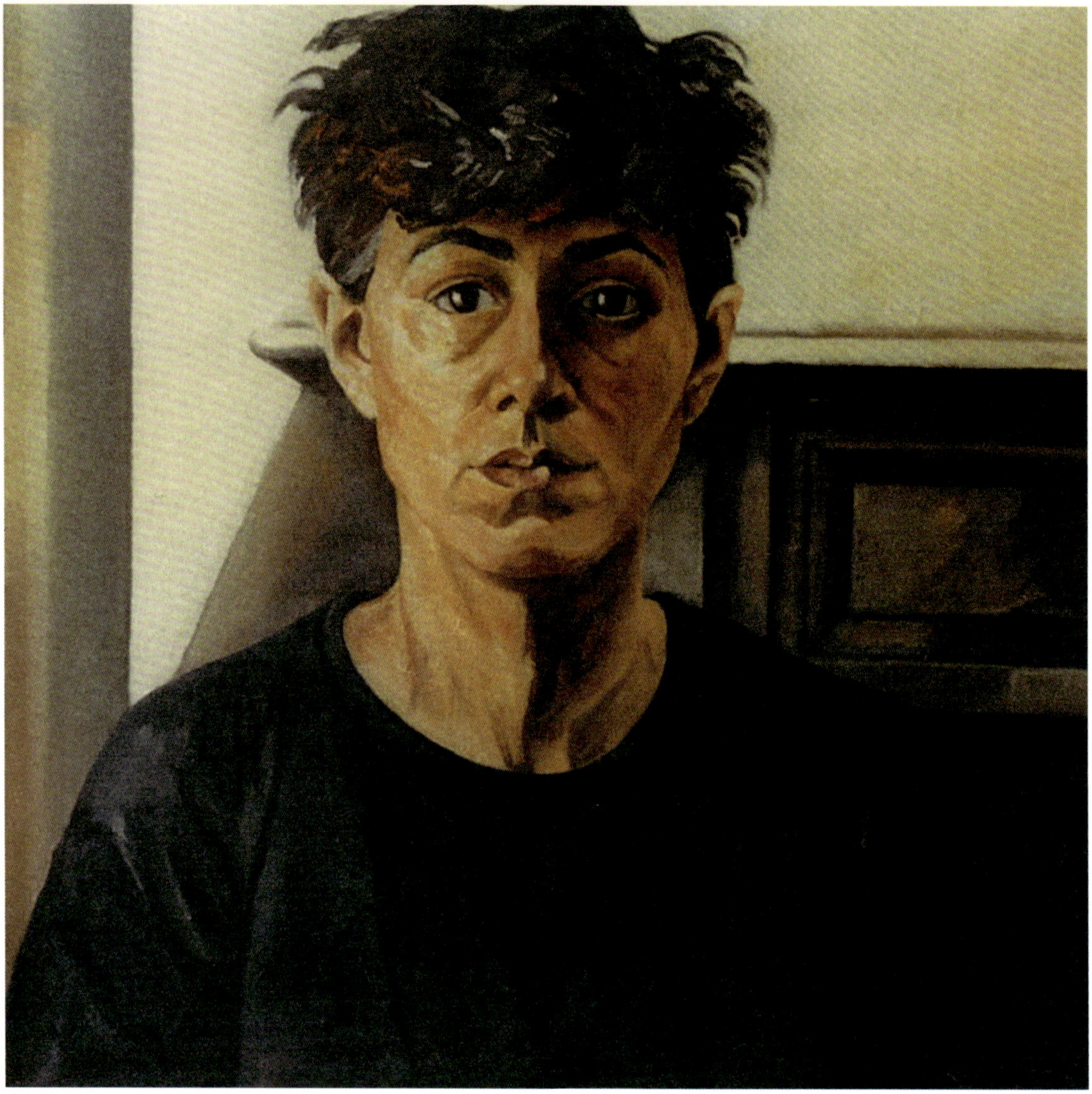

Self-Portrait 1984. Oil paint on canvas 60 × 60

Shanti Thomas was born in London in 1949, and as a child, frequently visited Florence, Italy. She studied at the Academy of Fine Arts in Florence and then at Camberwell School of Arts and Crafts in London, before travelling to India, which proved to be an influential experience. Considerations of displacement, migration and alienation, drawn from her own experiences, are at the core of her practice, which typically encompasses figurative paintings and drawings. In an essay for the periodical *Feminist Art News*, Thomas addressed the feeling of being 'rootless', a term reflected in her work of the 1980s. Active in the Black Arts Movement, she also critiqued the lack of equality and recognition of the work of Black women artists by the art world, and was involved with Creation for Liberation, a Black artists cultural organisation based in Brixton, London, which held exhibitions at Brixton Art Gallery. Thomas was a co-founder of the Panchayat Collection, a reference library relating to cultural activities and activism from the 1980s to 2003. Her work was included in Eddie Chambers's important 1989 touring exhibition *Black Art: Plotting the Course*, and in 1993 she undertook a three-month residency at Gatwick Airport, to record passengers' arrivals and departures.

Previously London-based, Thomas now lives in Farnborough, Hampshire.

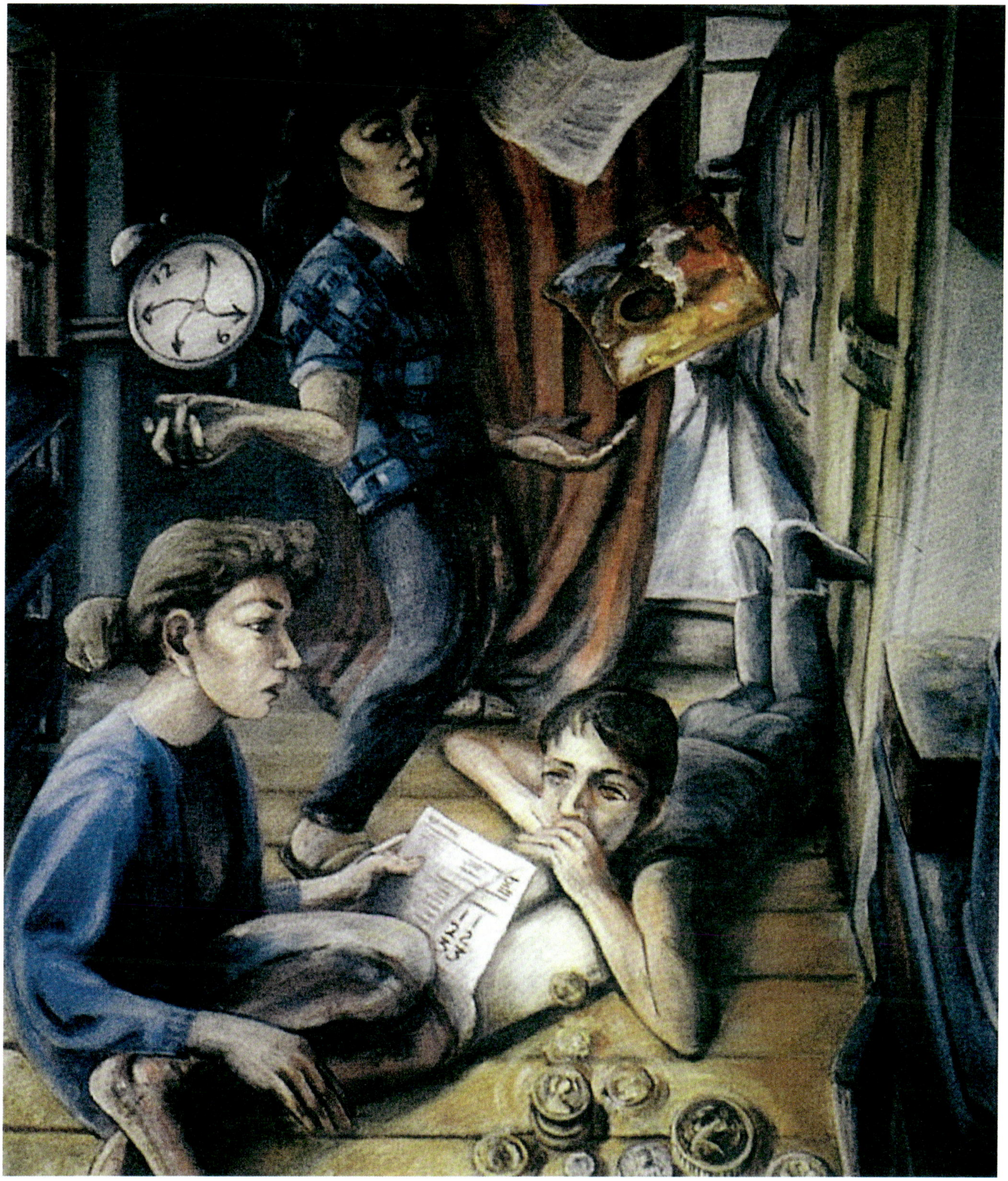

Juggling c.1987. Oil paint on canvas 89 × 89

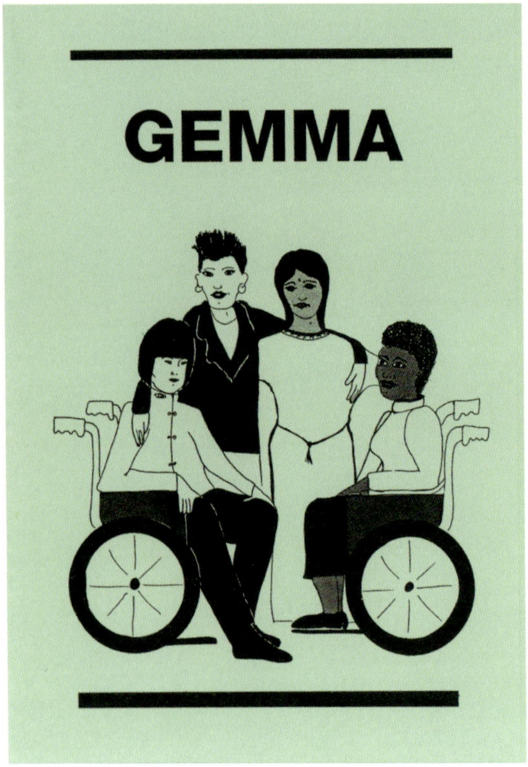

1

Disability Arts

In 1976 partners Elsa Beckett and Kathryn Bell formed the pioneering support group GEMMA, 'a national self help group of lesbians with and without disabilities, formed to lessen the isolation of other disabled lesbians.' In the late 1970s, the Disability Arts Movement (DAM) was initiated in the UK and saw artists and activists coming together to creatively campaign for the civil rights and visibility of disabled people. While the majority of DAM activity happened between the early and mid 1990s, some early women pioneers were engaged with this work from the mid 1980s. On the 25 October 1985, Samena Rana spoke on disability and photography as part of Black Arts Forum Weekend at the ICA, London, and in 1988 Nancy Willis was joint organiser of the Disabled Women Artists Conference at the Women Artists' Slide Library in London.

Protests against Thatcher's government, 1980s. Photographed by Brenda Prince

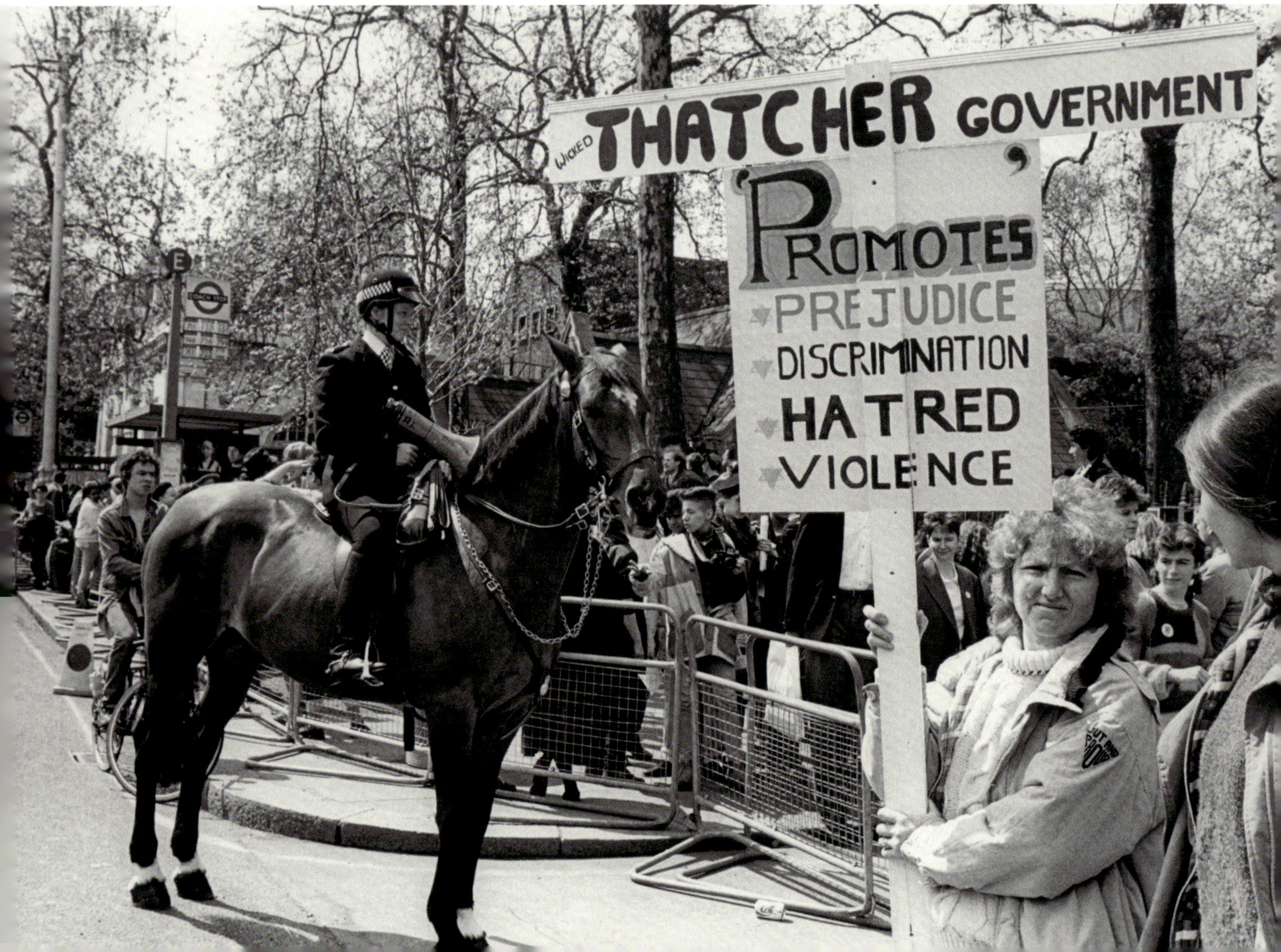

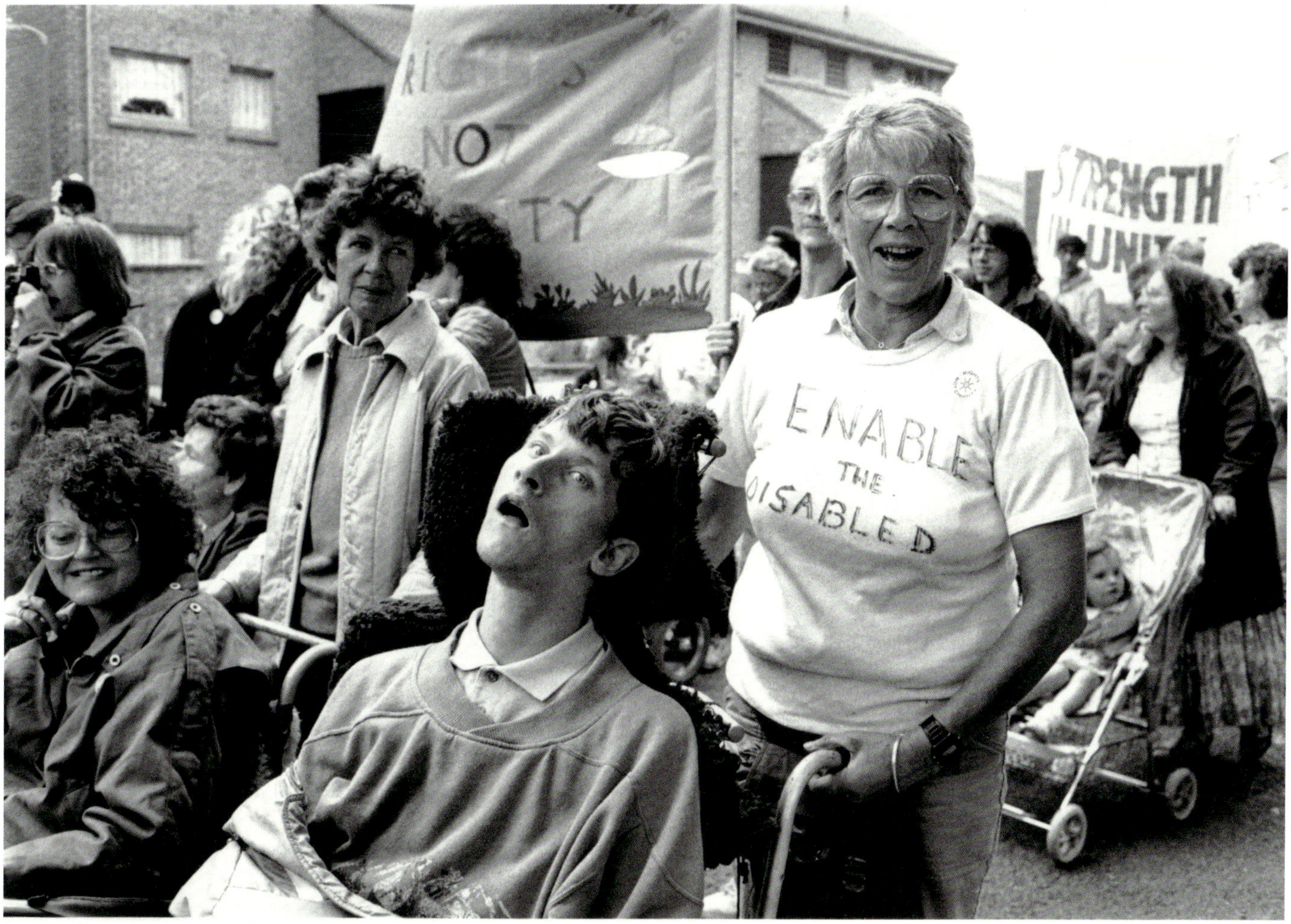

Disability Rights March, 1980s. Photographed by Pam Isherwood.

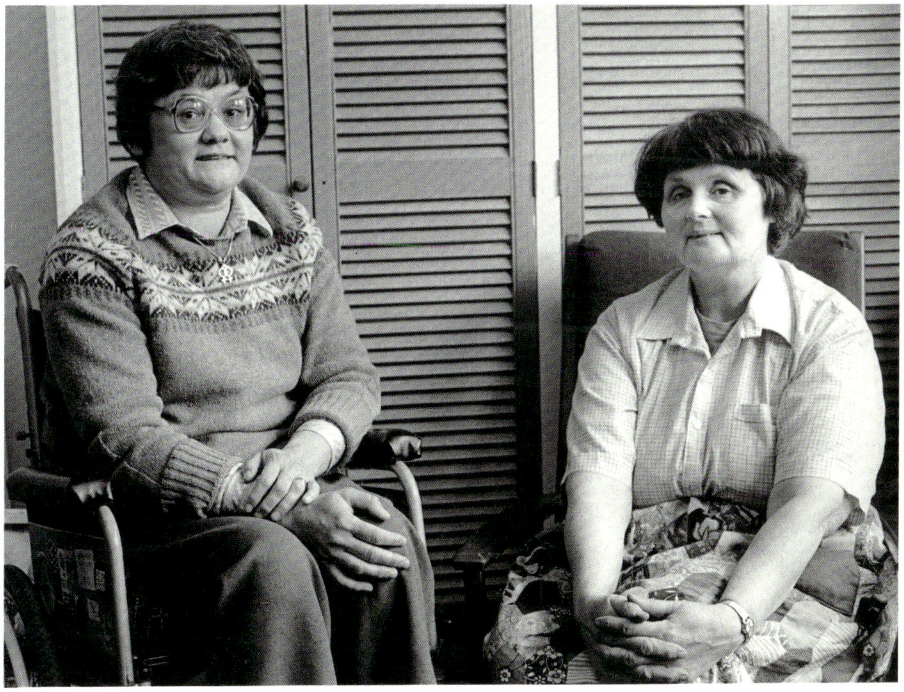

Elsa Beckett and Kathryn Bell, founder members of the GEMMA support group and magazine. Photographed by Brenda Prince.

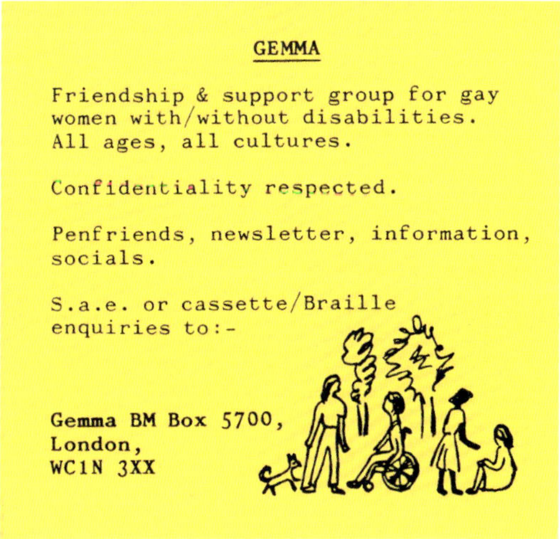

GEMMA

Friendship & support group for gay women with/without disabilities. All ages, all cultures.

Confidentiality respected.

Penfriends, newsletter, information, socials.

S.a.e. or cassette/Braille enquiries to:-

Gemma BM Box 5700, London, WC1N 3XX

2

1 Pamphlet for the organisation, GEMMA, a national self-help group of lesbians with and without disabilities, formed in 1976 to lessen the isolation of other disabled lesbians. Date unknown.
2 GEMMA business card, date unknown.

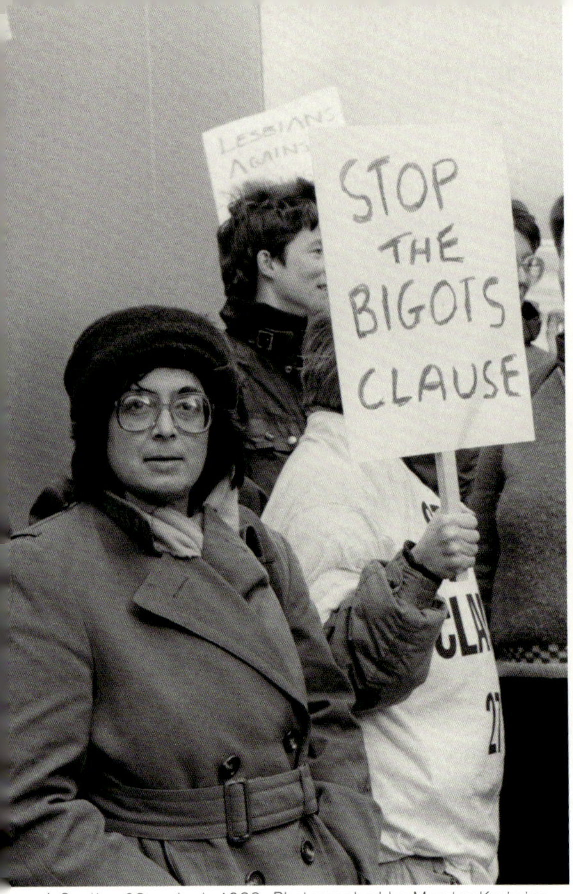

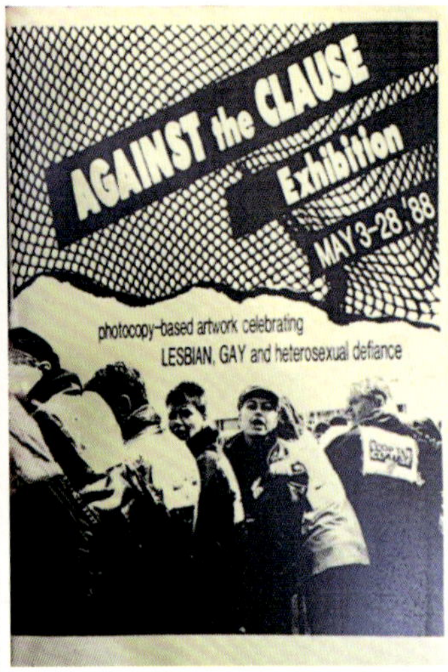

1

The AIDS Epidemic

In 1982 thirty-seven-year-old Terrence Higgins became one of the first people in the UK to die of an AIDS-related illness and a year later a trust in his name was founded to support people living with HIV / AIDS. During the 1980s it was largely left to organisations such as the Terrence Higgins Trust and communities to research the virus and support each other as the government showed a lack of understanding and willingness to engage with a situation that largely affected Lesbian and Gay people. Throughout the UK people with HIV or AIDS struggled to access proper treatment and were often treated as outcasts when receiving medical care, leaving much of the responsibility to often very young groups of friends. Lesbian women played a crucial role in the fight against the virus. In 1985 London Lesbian Line was set up with a campaign to encourage lesbians to donate blood, in the hope that transfusions would prolong the lives of their male friends, and to represent the openly gay men who had recently been banned from giving blood for life.

A Section 28 protest, 1988. Photographed by Mumtaz Karimjee.

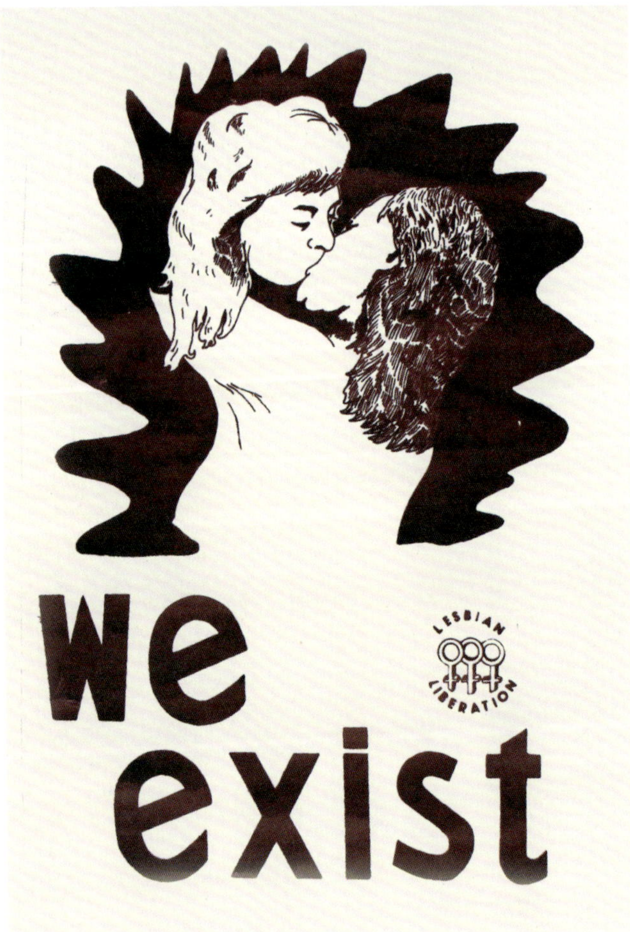

2

Protest to stop Clause 27, 1987. Photographed by Brenda Prince.

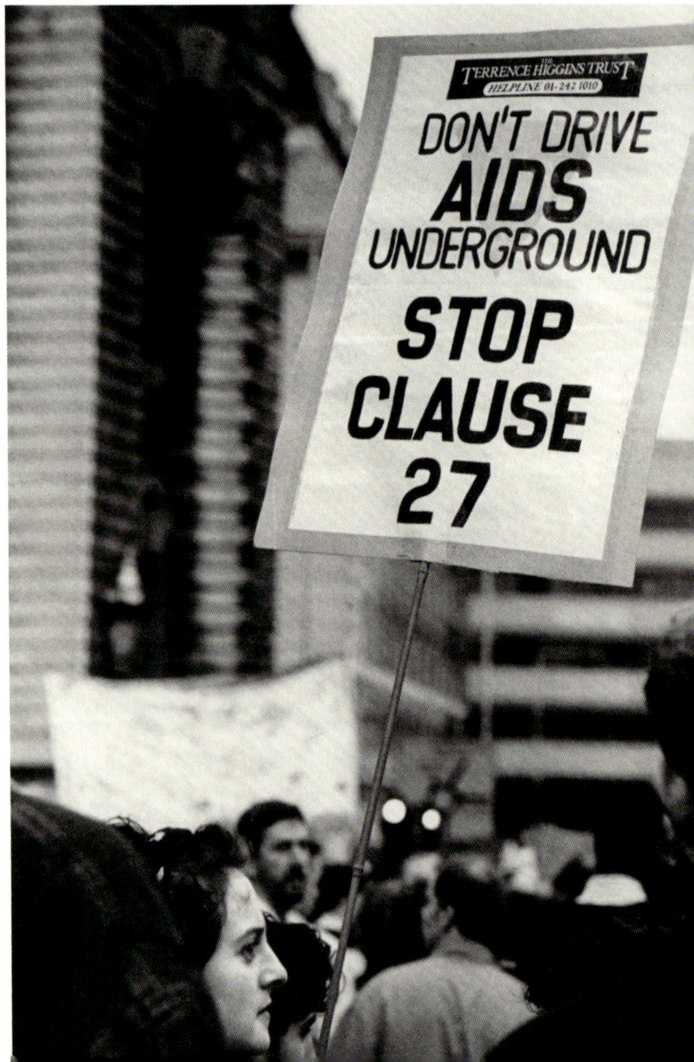

Section 28

Clause 28, which would later become Section 28 once passed into law, was legislation introduced by the Conservative government under Margaret Thatcher. The law, which was in effect between 1988 and 2000 in Scotland and 1988 and 2003 in England and Wales, stated that a local authority 'shall not intentionally promote homosexuality or publish material with the intention of promoting homosexuality' or 'promote the teaching in any maintained school of the acceptability of homosexuality as a pretended family relationship'. The law was an attack on communities and the practical implications of these changes was that many LGBTQ+ people were no longer able to access education and the support – be it emotional or physical – that they needed. That this legislation was promoted and celebrated during a public health emergency made it particularly callous.

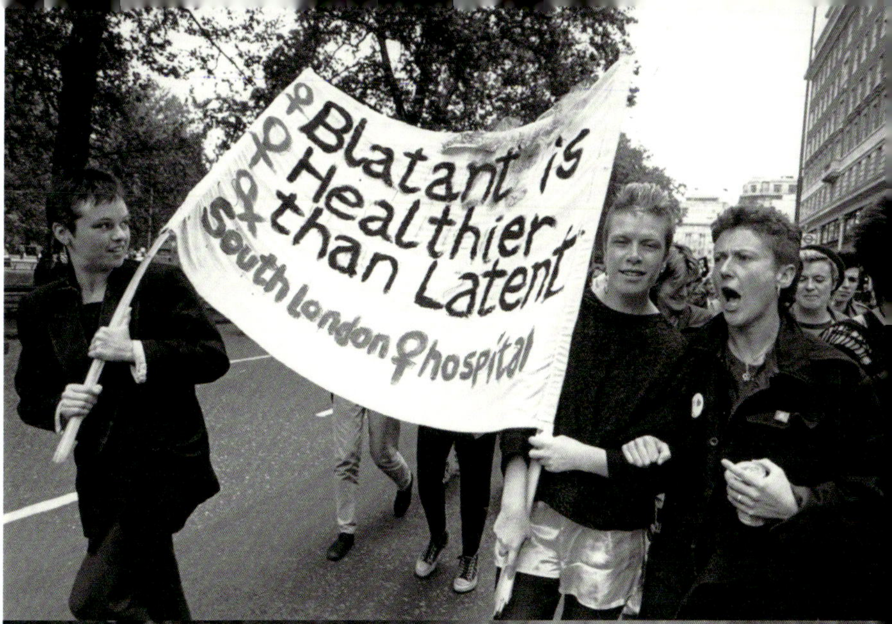

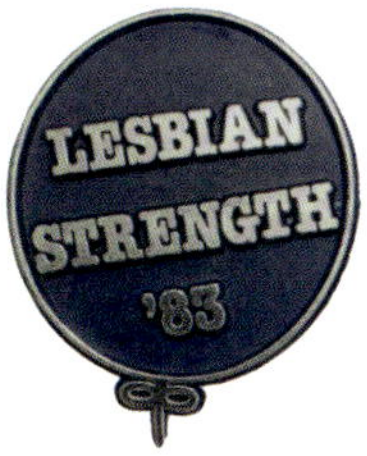

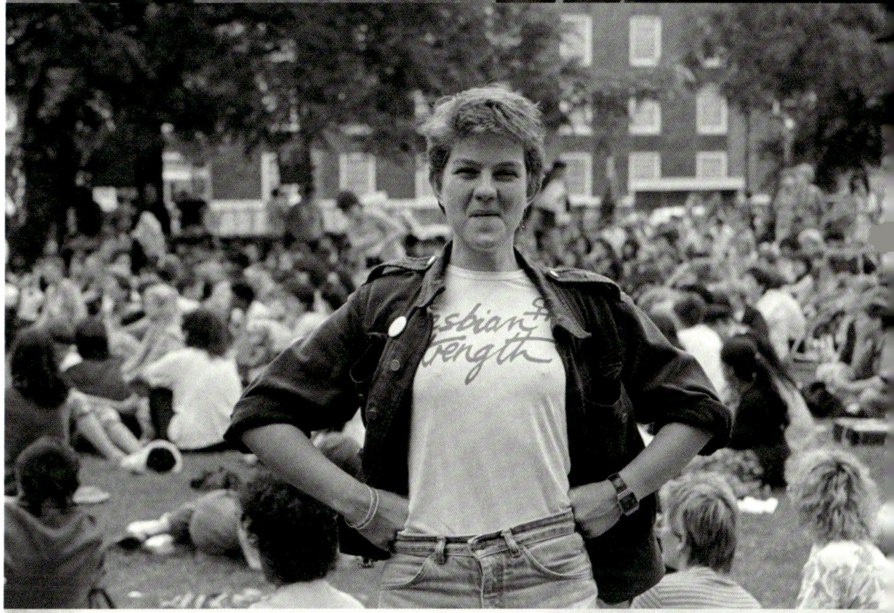

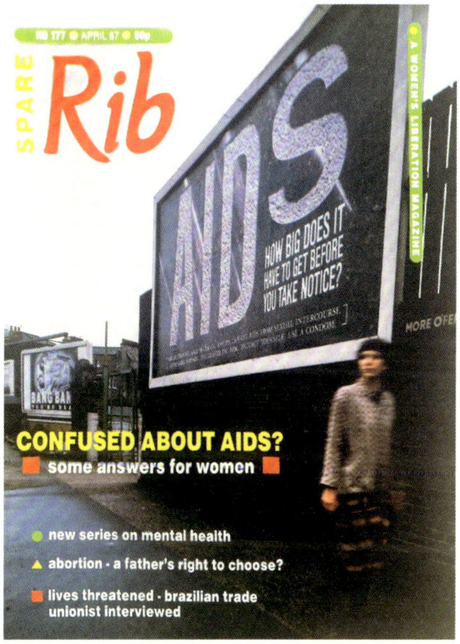

3

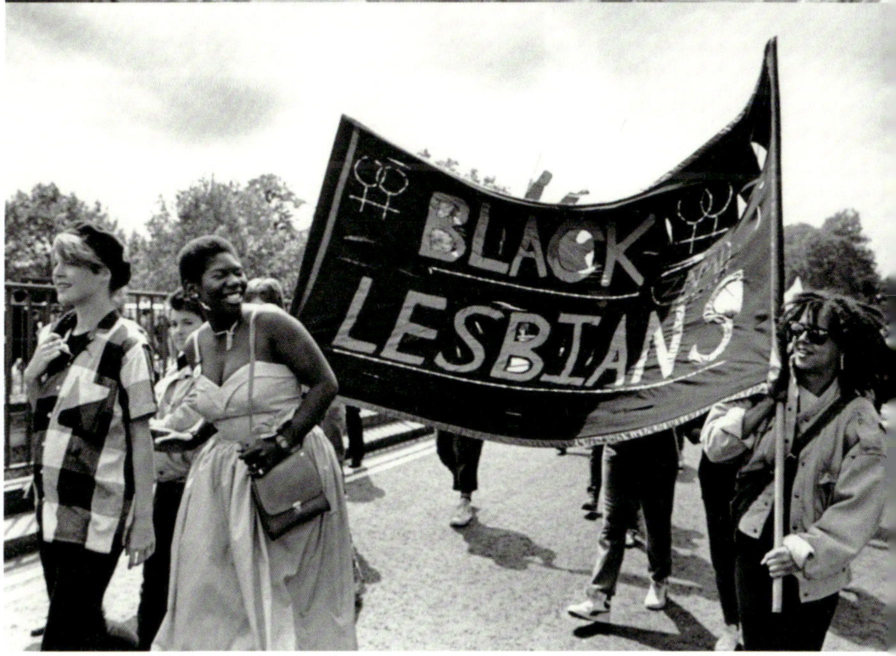

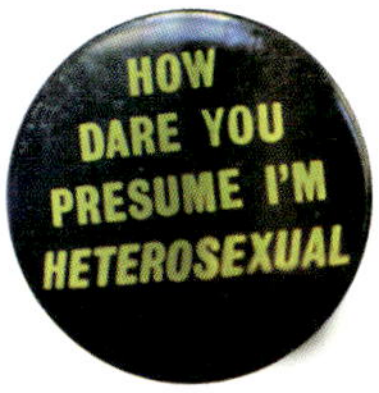

1 *Against the Clause* exhibition pamphlet cover, 1988.
2 *We Exist*, Lesbian Liberation poster, c.1970s.
3 *Spare Rib*, no.177, April 1987.

Pride March, 1980s. Photographed by Pam Isherwood.
Woman wearing a 'Lesbian Strength' T-shirt, 1988. Photographed by Mumtaz Karimjee.
Lesbian Strength March, London, June 1985. Photographed by Pam Isherwood.

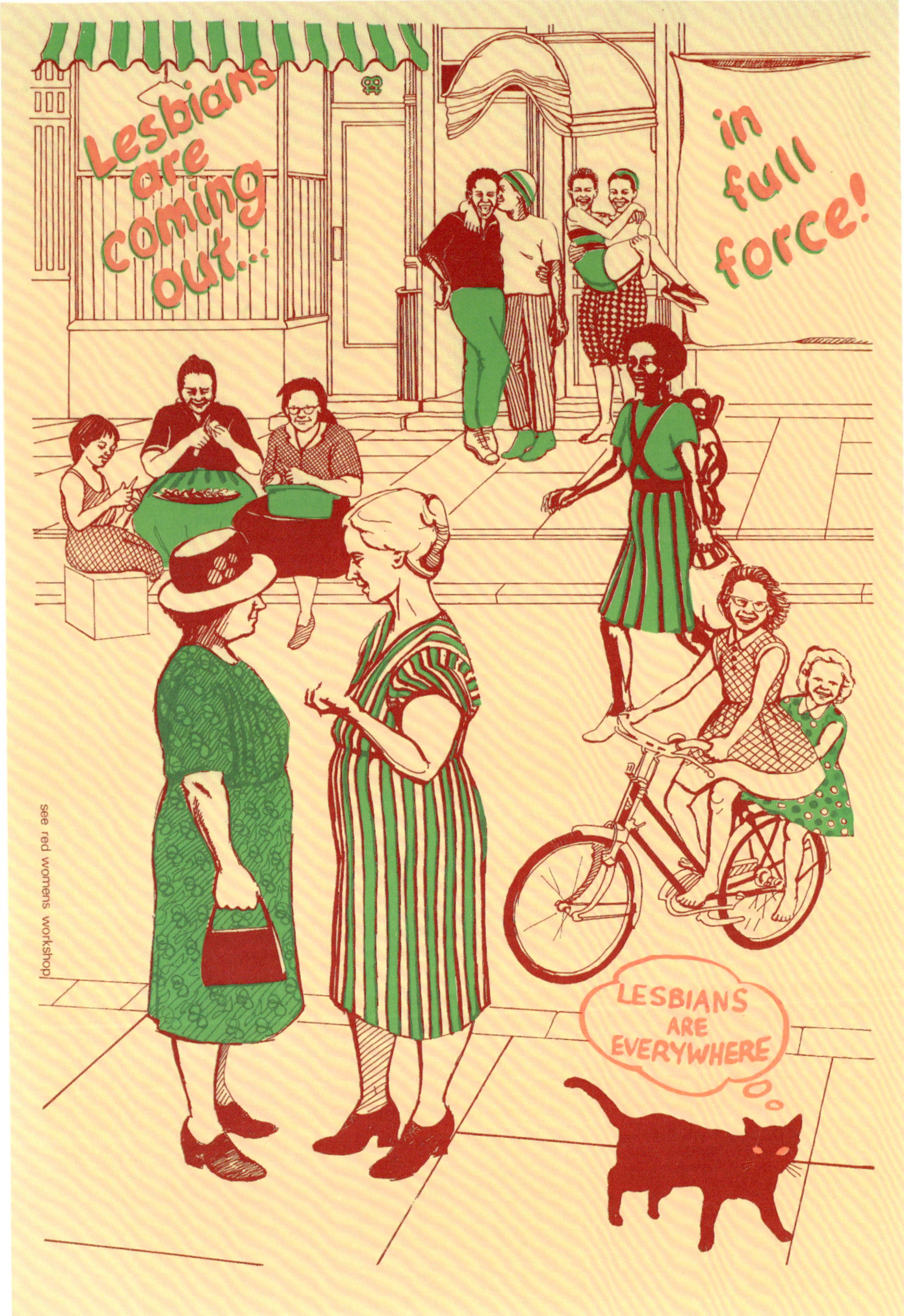

Lesbians Are Coming Out 1982. Screenprint on paper 64 × 46

In 1974, upon seeing an advert in a radical women's liberation magazine asking for women interested in forming a group to explore and combat negative images of women in the media, three ex-art students formed the screenprinting collective See Red Women's Workshop. See Red (active 1974–90) set out to make posters that tackled sexist stereotypes and created positive and challenging alternatives, and spent the next sixteen years making some of the most powerful and instantly-recognisable protest posters of their time. See Red worked with over forty-five different women during this time, with four or five women in the workshop at any one time. Making posters that were accessible and affordable, all work was authored collectively with no hierarchy, and no one individual taking credit, and all tasks and skills were shared. Influenced by their members' respective interests, poster themes centred around childcare, housework, gender roles, identity, sexuality, class and race, and broadened out to include national and international themes supporting women's wider struggles for change. While mainly working on printing and selling their own posters, See Red also did service printing for the local community and LGBTQI+ groups to fund their work, focusing increasingly on this kind of work from 1984 to 1990.

British artist Ingrid Pollard was born in Georgetown, Guyana in 1953. She studied film and video at the London College of Printing (now Communication) and went on to receive an MA in photographic studies from the University of Derby in 1995. In 2016 she received her PhD doctorate from the University of Westminster.

Pollard was engaged with the work of the British Black Arts Movement and featured in many of the associated well-known exhibitions in the 1990s. She was also a founding member of the Association of Black Photographers (now Autograph ABP). In the 1980s, Pollard was a member of the Lenthall Road Workshop, a women's print workshop which worked with the community to educate in printmaking techniques and produce printed materials for campaigns and protests.

Pollard was part of Maud Sulter's Blackwomen's Creativity Project, which saw them travel the UK to research work being made by Black women. The project culminated in an exhibition at Rochdale Gallery and the publication of Maud Sulter's *Passion* in 1990.

Pollard has participated in recent group exhibitions including *Deep Down Body Thirst*, with curatorial collective Radclyffe Hall (2018), and also had a solo show *No Cover Up* (2021) at Glasgow Women's Library – both were shown as part of Glasgow International. She also participated in *Hot Moment*, at Auto Italia, London (2020). In 2022, Pollard was nominated for the Turner Prize for her solo exhibition at MK Gallery, Milton Keynes.

The artist lives and works in the north of England.

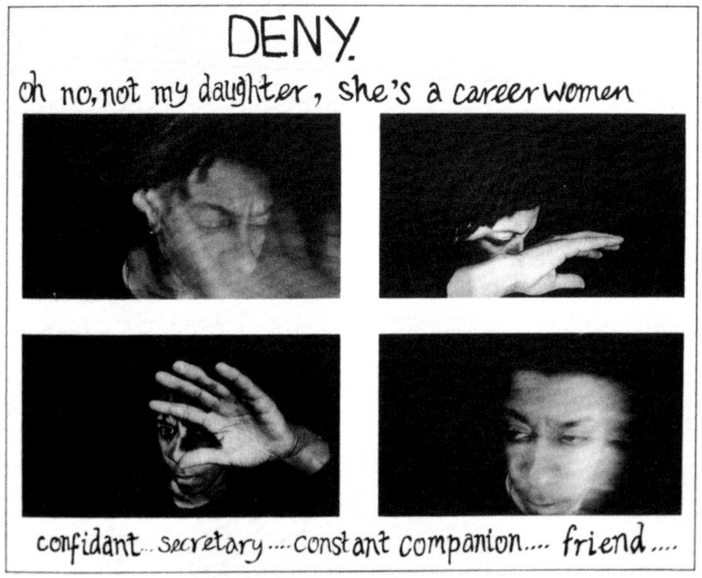

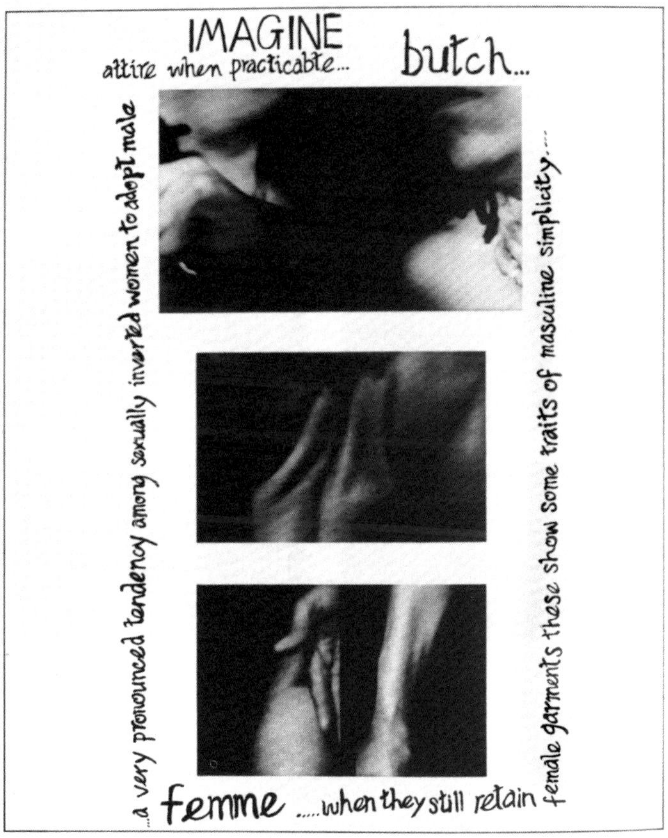

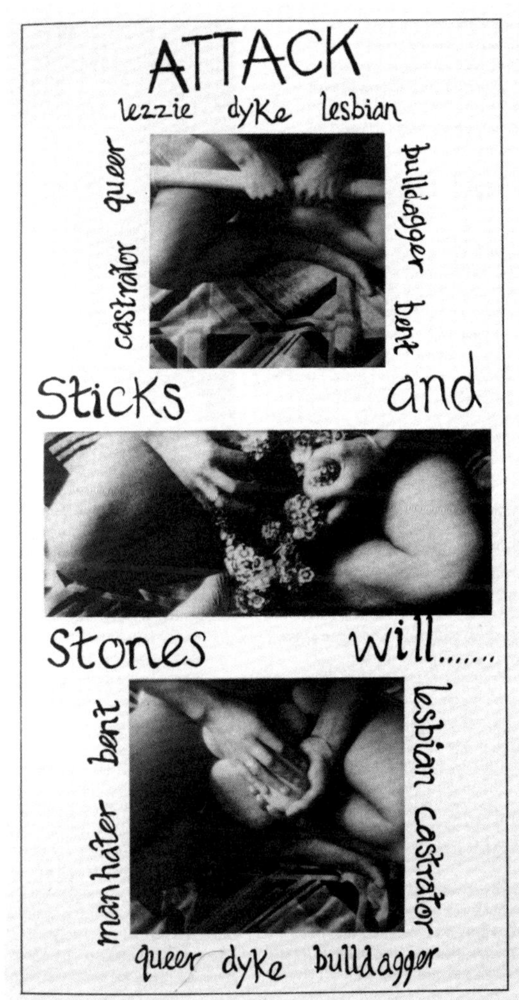

Deny: Imagine: Attack: Silence 1991.
3 of 4 sets of framed gelatin silver photographic prints, Xerox prints and hand-painted mount card
61 × 56; 85 × 47; 76 × 40

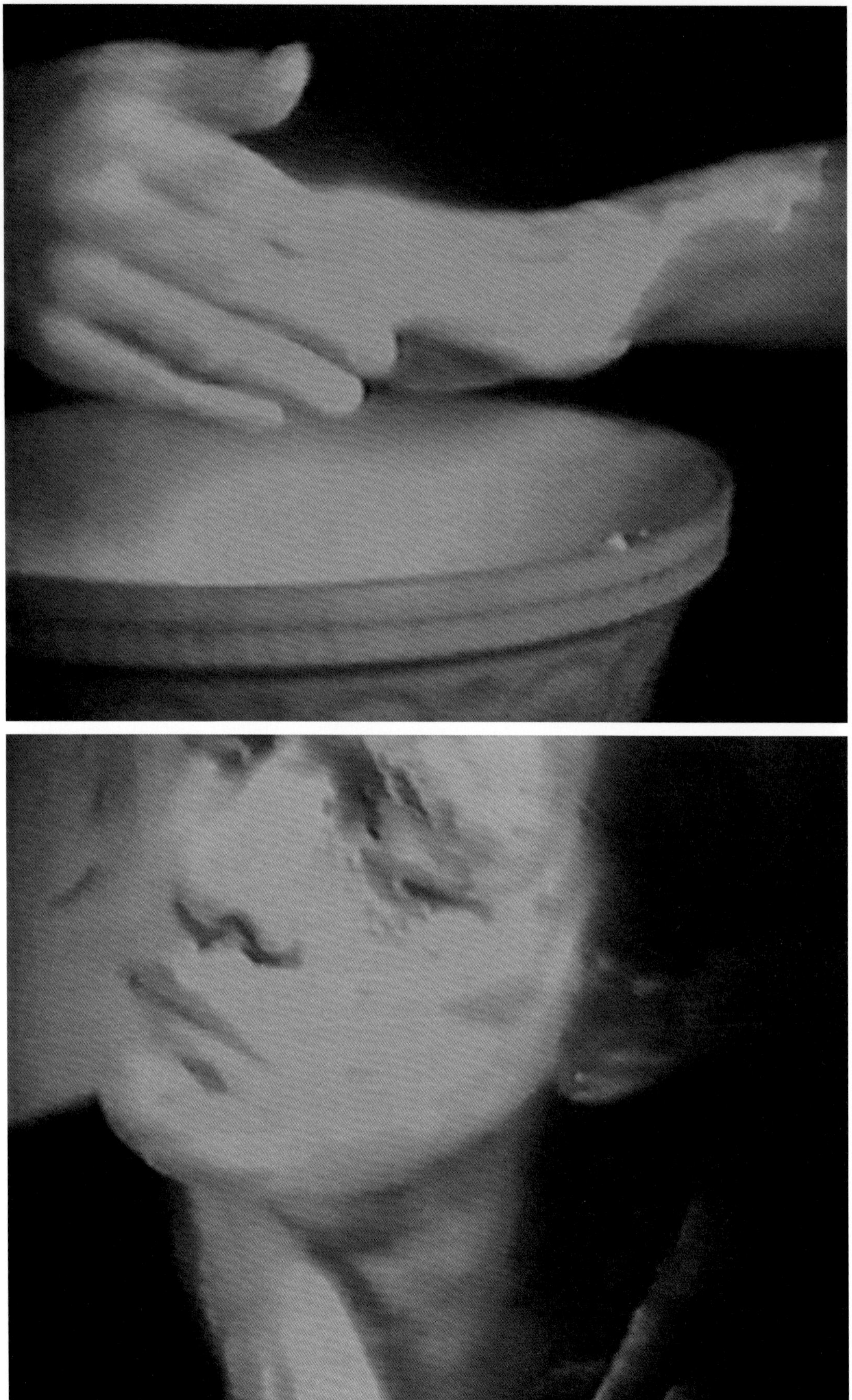

Forbidden Heroines 1987. Video, shown digitally; black and white, silent. 7 min, 56 sec

Anne Tallentire was born in 1949 in County Armagh, Northern Ireland. She studied printmaking at The School of Visual Arts, New York in 1983 and was a Postgraduate in fine art media at the Slade School of Art between 1986 and 1988. She has lived and worked in London since 1984. She is Professor Emerita at Central Saint Martins College of Art and Design, where she taught in the fine art department from the 1990s to 2014. Tallentire works across a wide range of media including film, installation, performance, photography, sound and video. Concerned with the politics of location, her visual and textual interrogation of everyday materials and structures has continuously addressed the shifting geographies, demographics and working practices of the displaced. Since 1993 she has also worked in collaboration with artist John Seth, as part of work-seth/tallentire.

Taking a cue from everyday activities, she stages and records her own actions and those of others, actions that are both improvised and derived through the structure of given tasks. Her 1987 video *Forbidden Heroines* consists of a re-enactment of Tallentire's actions that originally formed part of a live performance with Alanna O'Kelly at The London Film Makers Co-op for the event 'Channel 6', curated by Tina Keane.

ANNE TALLENTIRE

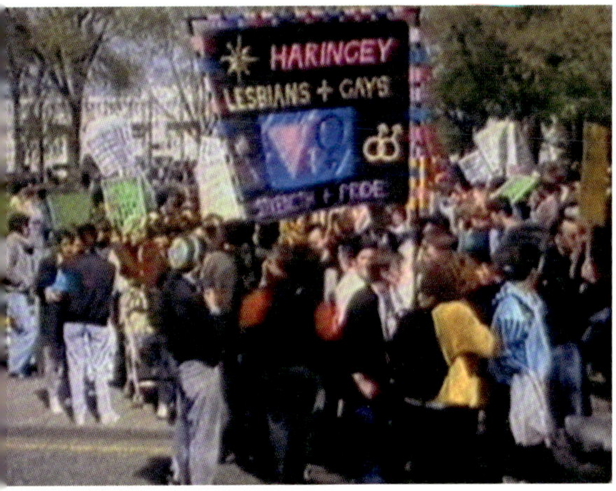

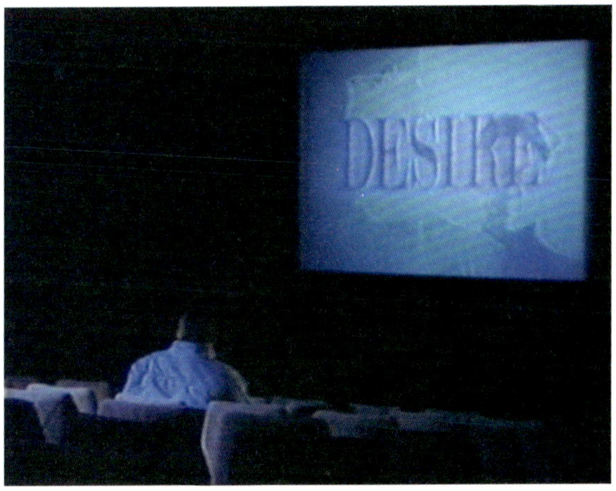

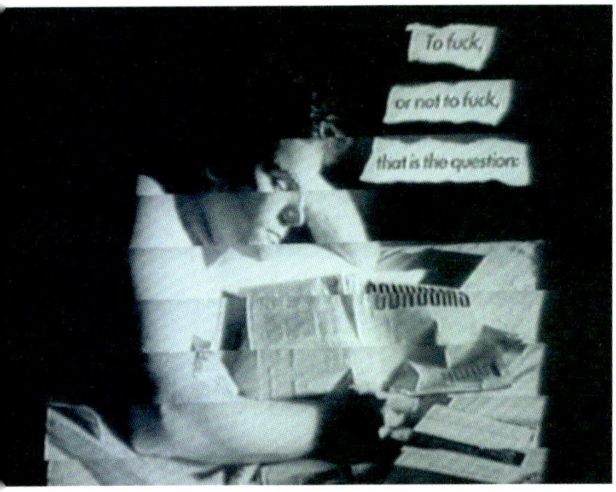

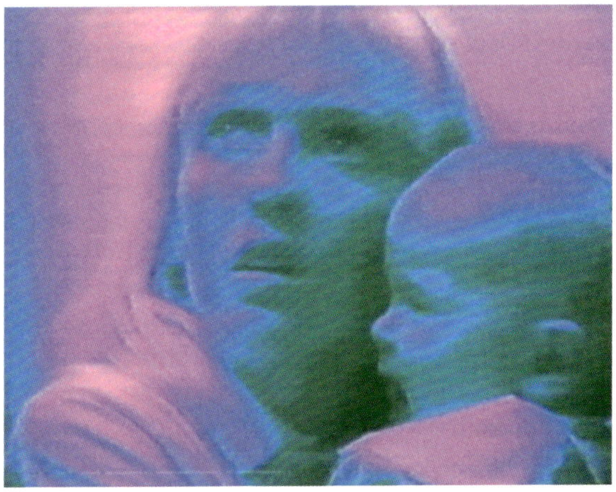

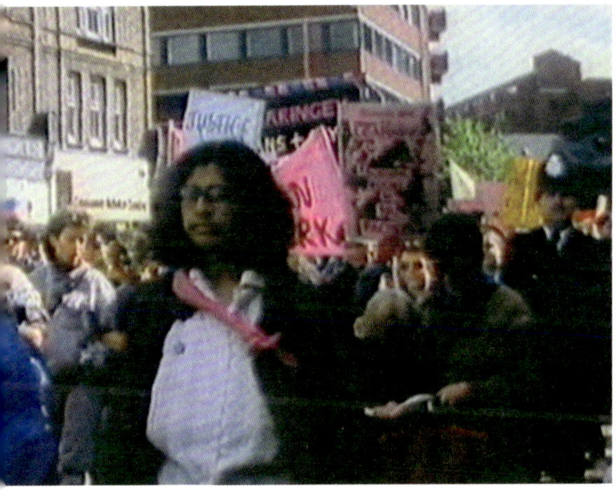

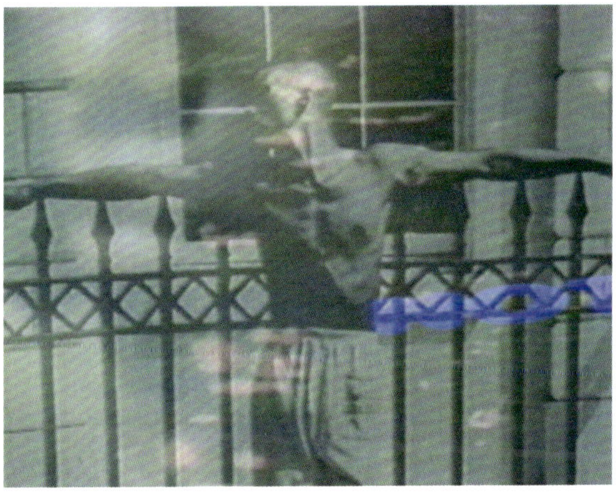

Reframing AIDS 1987. Video, shown digitally; colour, sound. 35 min, 59 sec

Born in Nairobi, Kenya, to Indian parents in 1955, Pratibha Parmar moved to England with her family at the age of twelve. She received a BA from Bradford University and a postgraduate degree from Birmingham University. Parmar's practice is fuelled by the desire to portray the stories of those who have been relegated to the margins of mainstream culture, looking at the intersection of art and social justice, with feminism at the core. In both her films and her writing, Parmar pinpoints the contradicting stereotypes of Asian women in society as both sexually exotic creatures, full of promise, and as mute, dominated and oppressed by men. *Sari Red* 1988 was made in memory of Kalbinder Kaur Hayre, a young Indian woman killed in a racist attack in 1985. The film sensitively examines the threat of violence faced by South Asian women in the United Kingdom, in both public and private spaces. The colour red is symbolically deployed throughout, referencing intimacy, blood and the colour of a sari.

Parmar divides her time between Berkeley, California, and London.

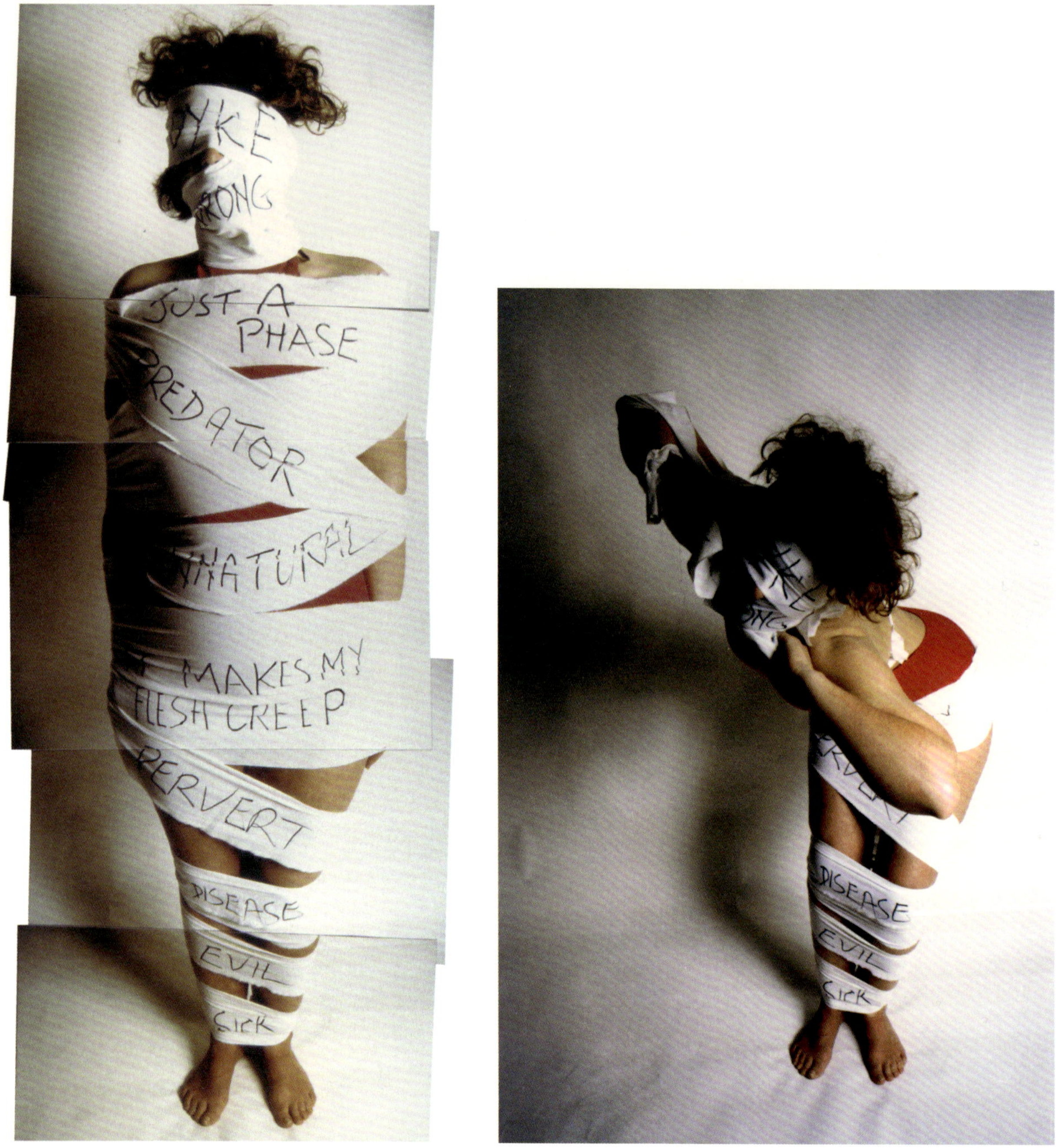

Unwind the Lies That Bind 1988. 2 of 7 photographic prints, mounted on aluminium 170 × 60 and 80 × 57

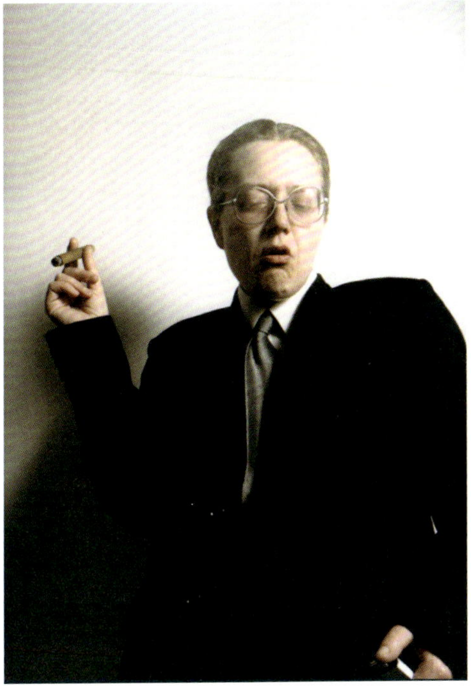
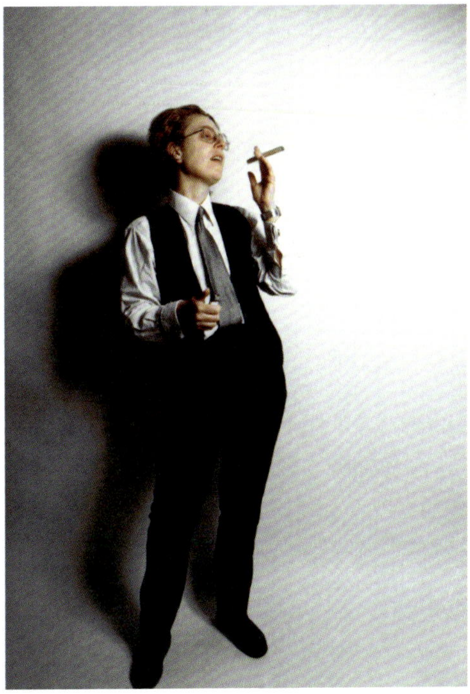
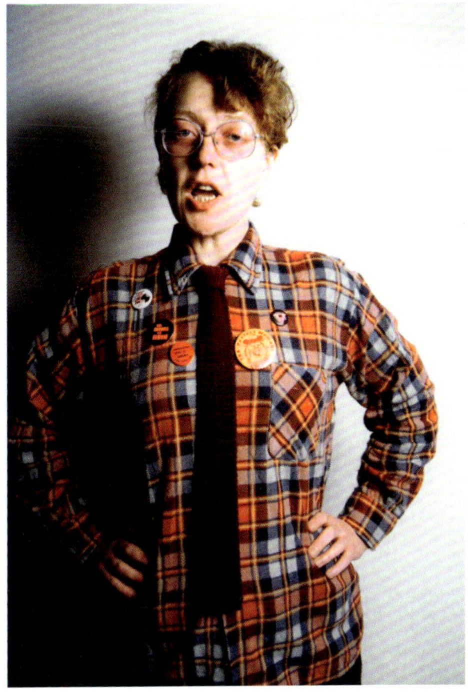
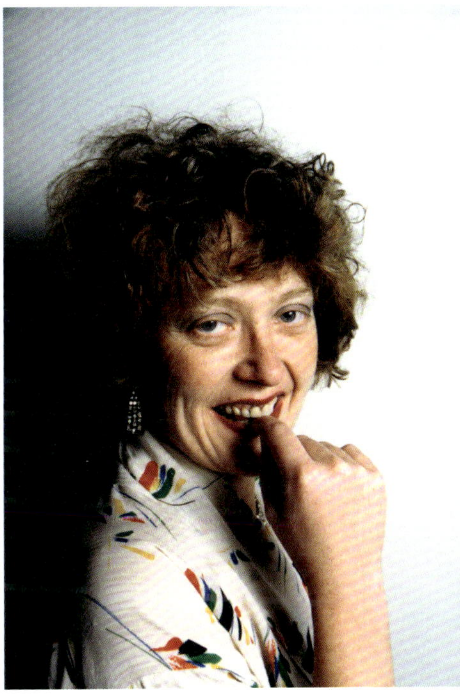
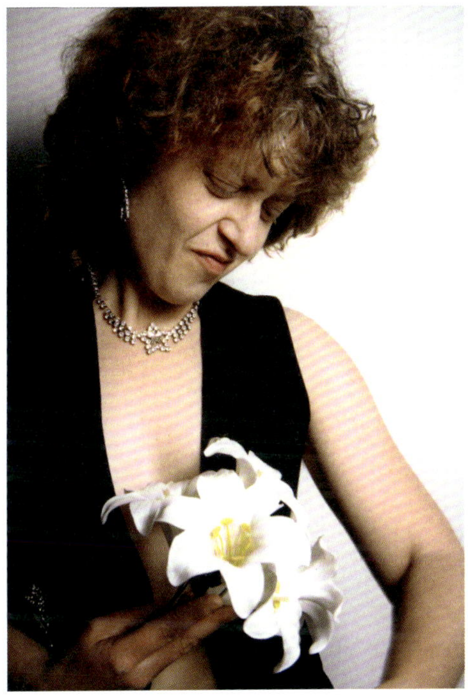

Transforming the suit: what does a lesbian look like? 1987
Part I: The Patriarch The Capitalist The Boss
Part II: What do Lesbians Look Like?
Part III: An Alter Ego
Part IV: Mother of Three
Part V: The Madonna
Photographs and text mounted on card 76.2 × 60.8 (each)

Born in London in 1946, Rosy Martin graduated from University College London in 1967 with a degree in chemistry. She then studied art and design gaining three postgraduate degrees or diplomas in industrial design, design for disability, and also in counselling and therapy. Martin's practice, which encompasses photography, digital imaging, video and therapy, explores the relationships between photography, identities and memory. In 1983 she began working with photographer Jo Spence, and together they created 'phototherapy', a method of photographing collaboratively that relies on empathy, performativity, and re-enactment to interrogate the notion of the self as something that can be constructed and deconstructed. Martin's work, *Transforming the suit: what do lesbians look like?* 1987, sought to challenge stereotypical ideas of lesbian identity perpetuated in society. Martin's photographic project *Unwind the Lies That Bind* from the following year was one of few works by a woman artist to address Clause 28 and its damaging impact on the lesbian and gay community. Martin has published widely and exhibited internationally since 1985.

She lives and works in London.

ROSY MARTIN

The moslem harem is a great school for this 'Lesbian' (which I call Attossan) love; these tribades* are mostly known by peculiarities of form and features, hairy cheeks and upper lips, gruff voices, hircine** odour and the large projecting clitoris with erectile powers.

Burton, *Thousand Nights*, vol.ii, p.234, as quoted by Rana Kabbani, *Europe's Myths of Orient*, Kitchener,ON 1986, p.53.

* A woman who practises unnatural vice with other women – *The Shorter Oxford English Dictionary.*

** of, belonging to, or resembling a goat; having a goatish smell – *The Shorter Oxford English Dictionary.*

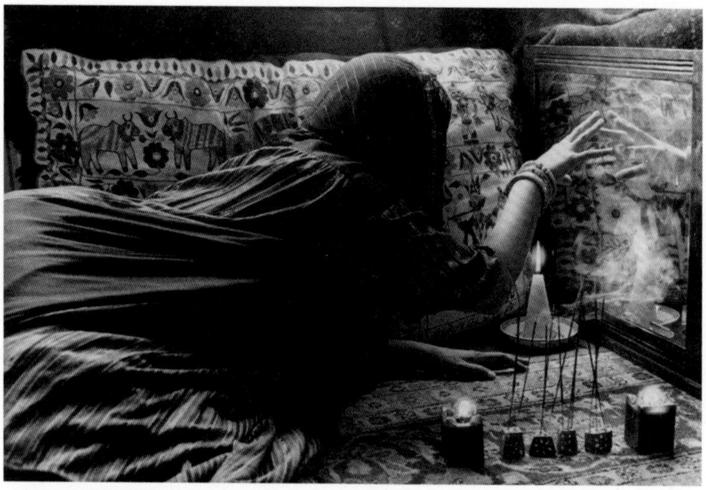

'... indignant at Miss Cumming (who was half Indian) for having made such an accusation in the first place.

The judges suggested that Miss Cumming, having been raised in the lascivious East, had no idea of the horror such an accusation would stir in Britain.

Lord Meadowbank explained ... that he had been to India, and he would venture to guess that Miss Cumming had developed her curiosity about sexual matters from her lewd Indian nurses, who were, in contrast to British women, entirely capable of obscene chatter on such subjects.

Lord Boyle, on the other hand, did not believe tribadism impossible among savages, but certainly Improbable in civilised Britain.'

Rana Kabbani, *Europe's Myths of the Orient*, Kitchener, ON 1986, p.53.

Lillian Faderman, *Surpassing the Love of Men*, New York 1981, pp.148–50.

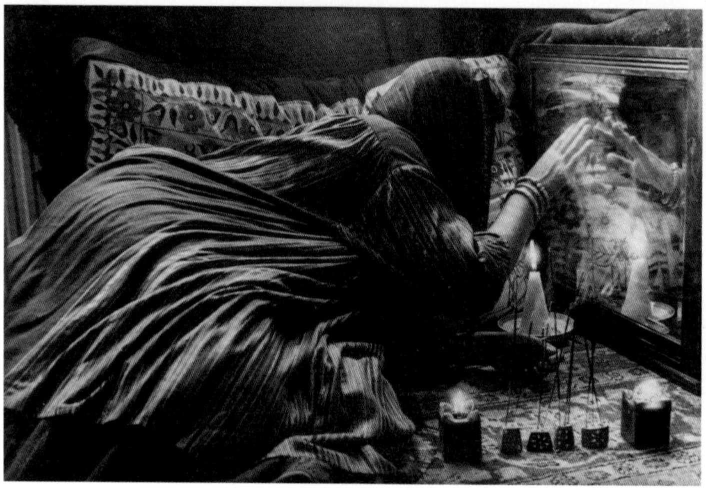

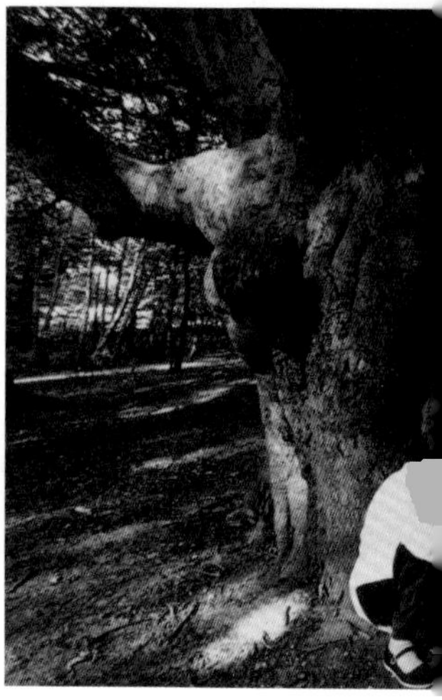

The Eastern Disease?

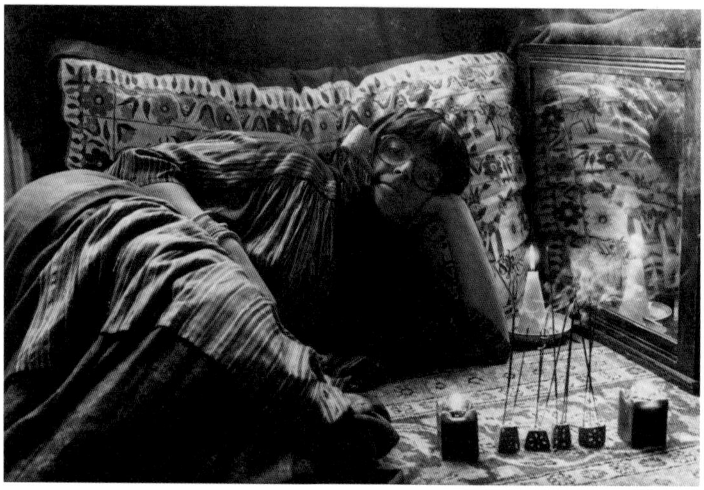

In Search of an Image 1987. 7 of 13 framed photographs and printed text 111.1 × 111.1 (overall)

Mumtaz Karimjee was born in Mumbai (then Bombay), India in 1950. She attended the Polytechnic of Central London, graduating in 1982, with periods spent studying in China at Beijing University and Nanjing University. While in China Karimjee photographed extensively, producing an important body of work in which she documented women in contemporary Chinese society. The series set the tone for her later photographic practice, which considered feminist, post-colonial and queer issues. Karimjee was a member of the group Black Women and Photography, which produced the journal *Polareyes*, and a member of the Mukti collective which produced the periodical

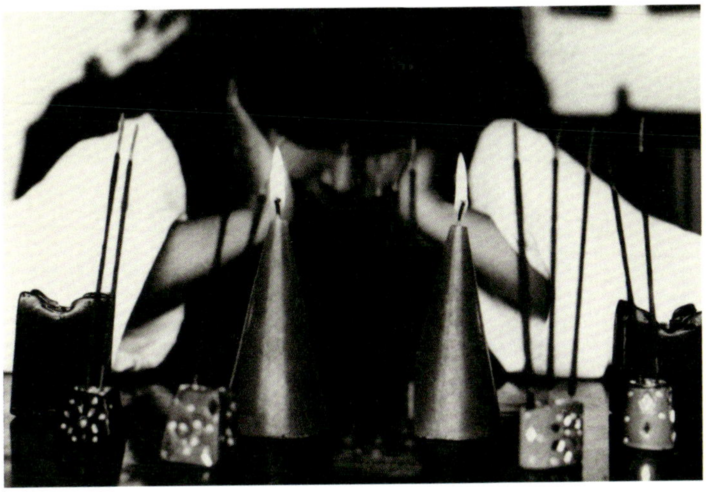

Burdened with carrying the weight of the honour of the patriarchal society and injured in the name of protecting that honour.

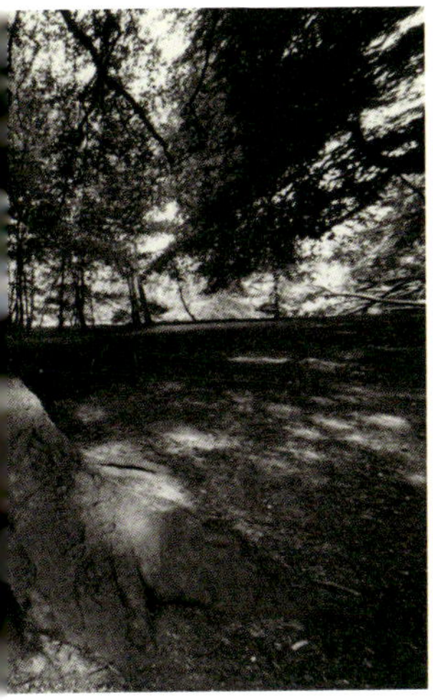

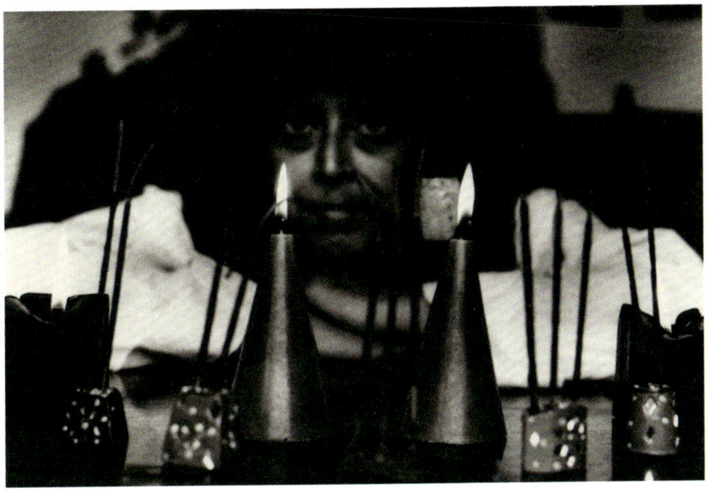

So, don't give me your tenets and your laws. Don't give me your lukewarm gods. What I want is an accounting with all three cultures – white, Moslem*, Indian. I want to staunch the bleeding with ashes, to fashion my own Gods out of my entrails. And if going home is denied me, then I will have to stand and claim my space, making a new culture – *una cultura mestiza* – with my own lumber, my own bricks and mortar and my own feminist architecture.

Gloria Anzaldúa, *Borderlands/La Frontera: The New Mestiza*, San Francisco 1987, p.22.

* In putting together this piece of work, I have changed 'Mexican' for 'Moslem.'
– Mumtaz Karimjee

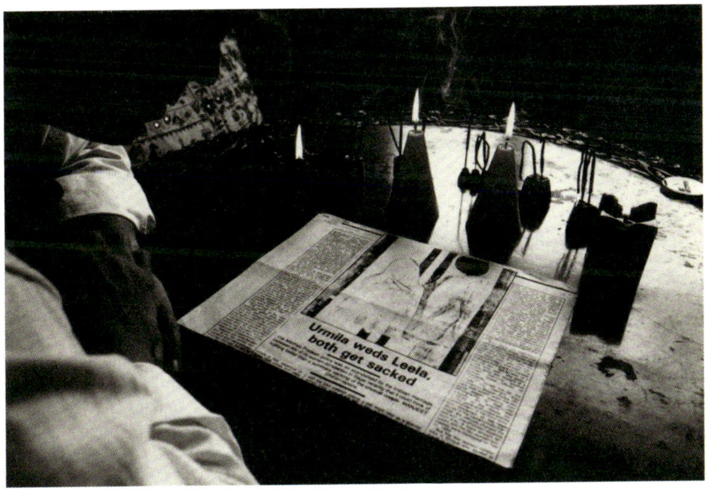

The Western Disease?

Mukti. Her work was included in the important exhibitions *Black Woman Time Now* (Battersea Arts Centre, 1983) and *Jagrati* (Greenwich Citizens Gallery, 1986), and she curated the show *Four Indian Women Photographers* (Horizon Gallery, 1988).

The work *In Search of an Image* 1987, which featured in the groundbreaking book *Stolen Glances: Lesbians Take Photographs* (1991), is described by the artist as 'the beginning of anexploration of the racism, sexism and homophobia of the white dominant society in which I live and the sexism and homophobia of the society into which I was born'.

Karimjee now lives and works in Liverpool.

MUMTAZ KARIMJEE

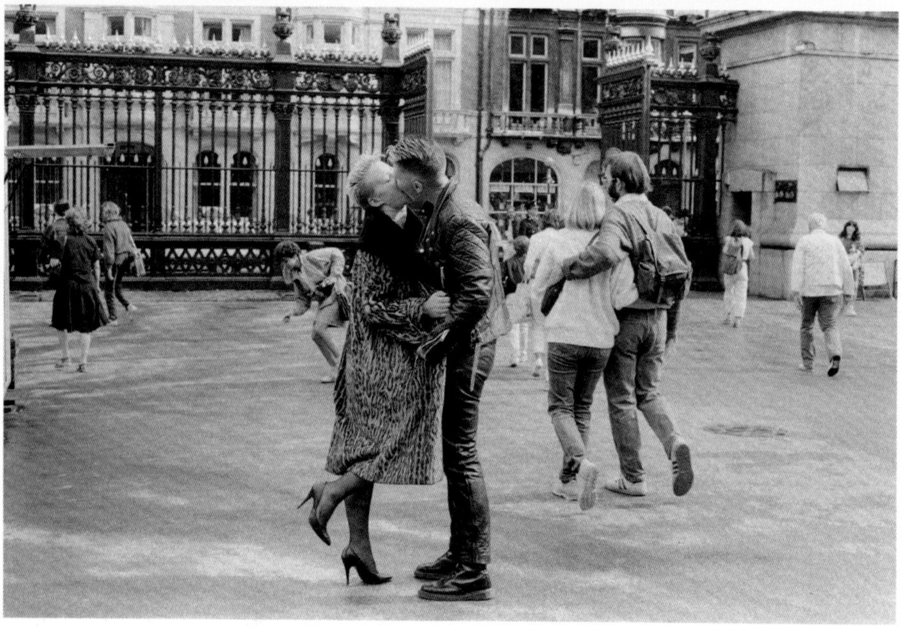

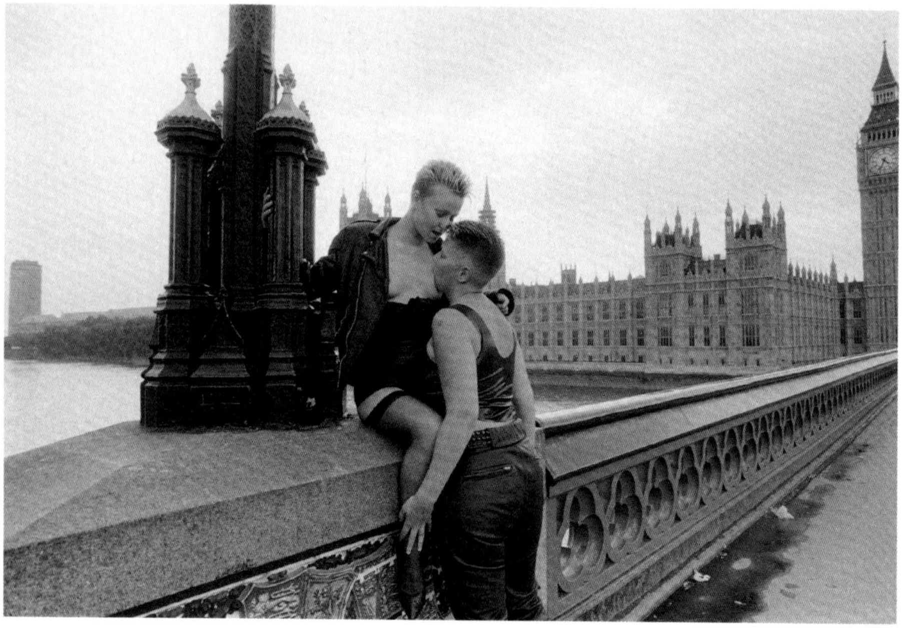

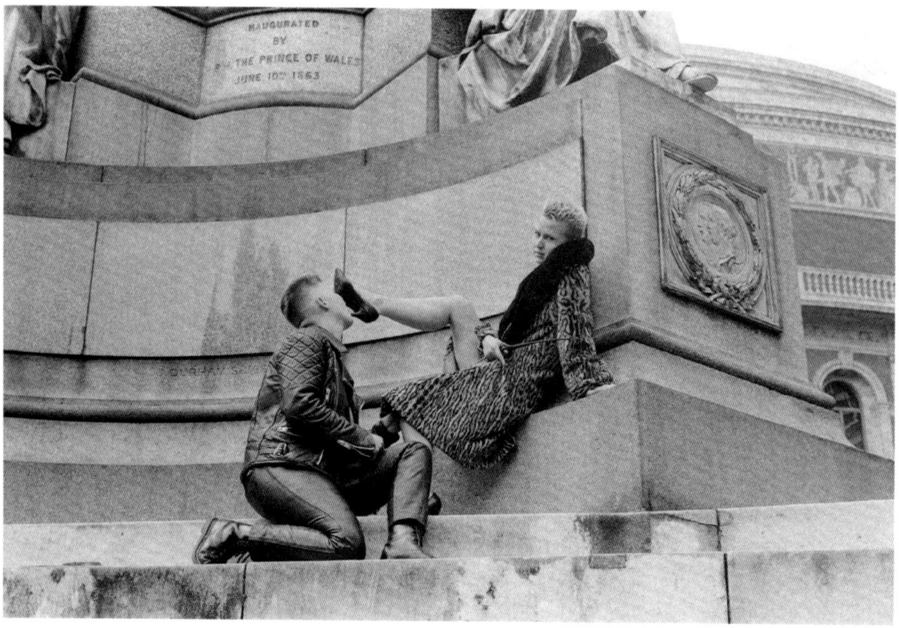

Born in London in 1953, Jill Posener trained as a stage manager at the London Academy of Music and Dramatic Art, and in 1973, began working at the pioneering Kings Head Theatre in Islington, London. She bought her first SLR camera to document the productions there. With encouragement from American queer playwright Robert Patrick, she wrote *Any Woman Can*, a reflection on her own coming out, first produced in 1974. In 1976 she became the first woman to join the Gay Sweatshop, England's first professional gay theatre company. As Posener's interest in social commentary increased, she began focusing on photography, joining the National Union of Journalists (NUJ) in the late 1970s, and working as a freelancer in alternative and mainstream media. In 1982, *Spray It Loud*, her book of graffiti images, was published, followed by a second collection, *Louder Than Words* in 1986. In the late 1980s Posener moved to San Francisco where she met Susie Bright, the editor of the lesbian erotica magazine *On Our Backs*, known for its influence in shaping the aesthetic and narrative of US lesbian culture at the time. Posener became the photo editor at the magazine. In 1996 she collaborated with Bright on a landmark collection of lesbian erotic photography, *Nothing But the Girl: The Blatant Lesbian Image*.

Posener lives in California. In 2010, she founded a non-profit organisation providing free veterinary care for homeless and low-income pet owners.

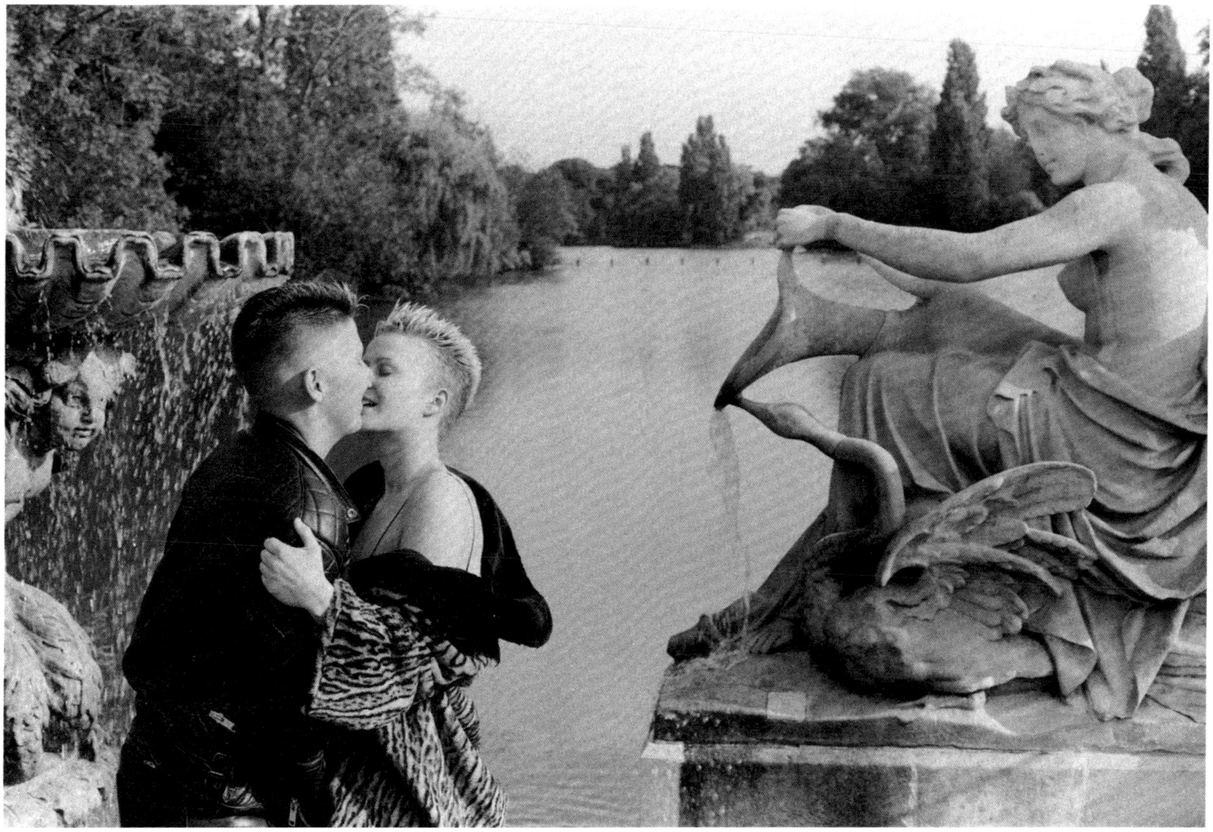

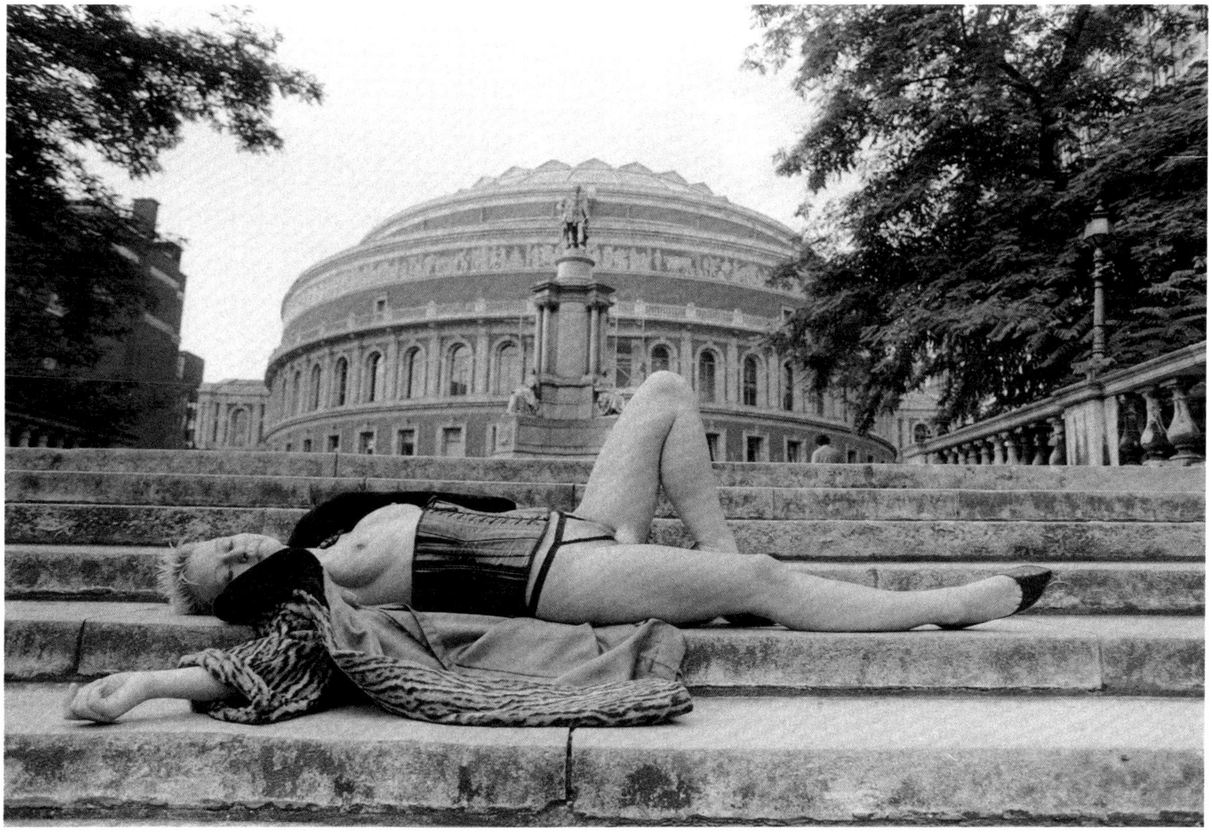

A Dirty Girls Guide to London 1987. 5 of 7 photographs 25.5 × 30.5 (each)

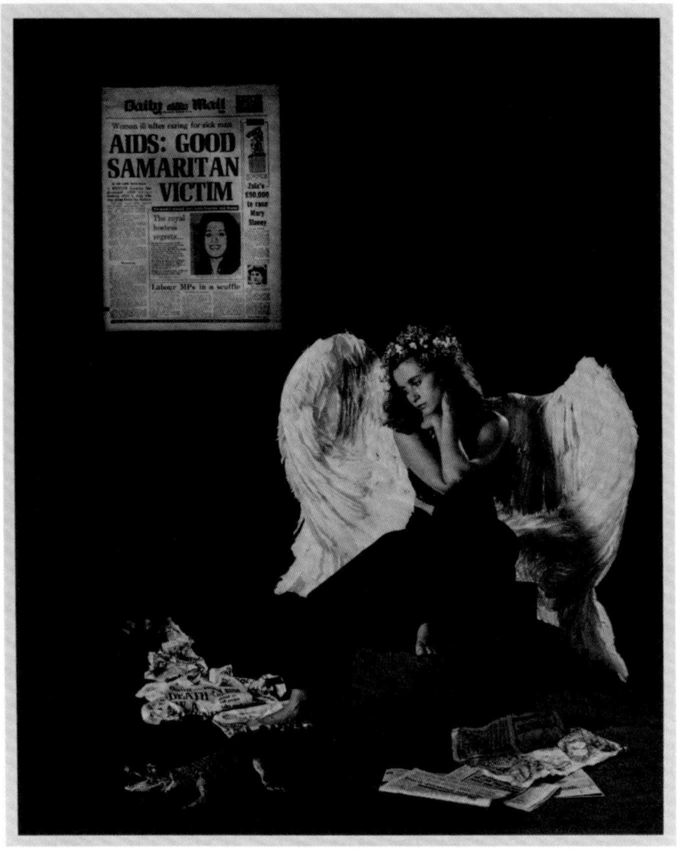

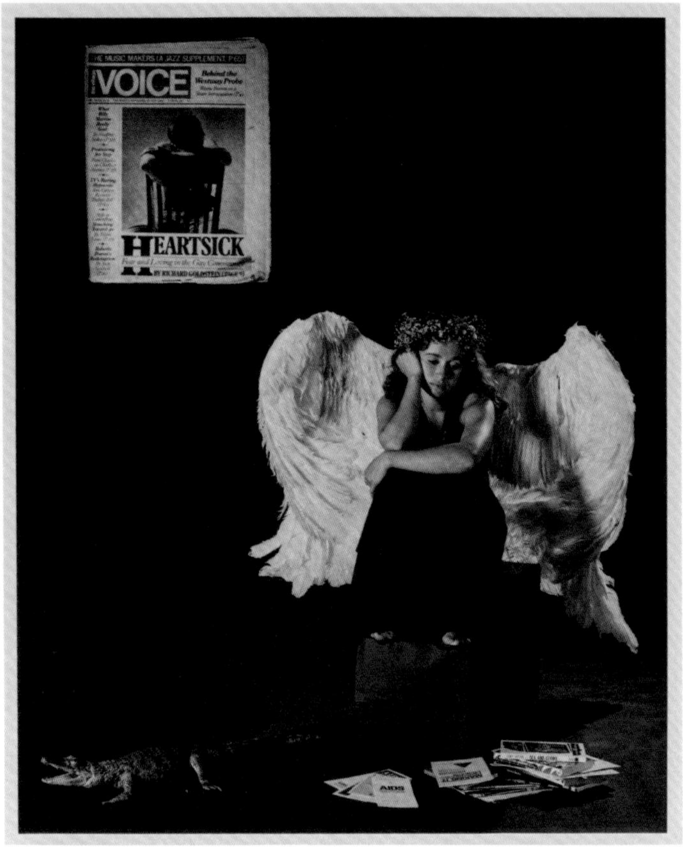

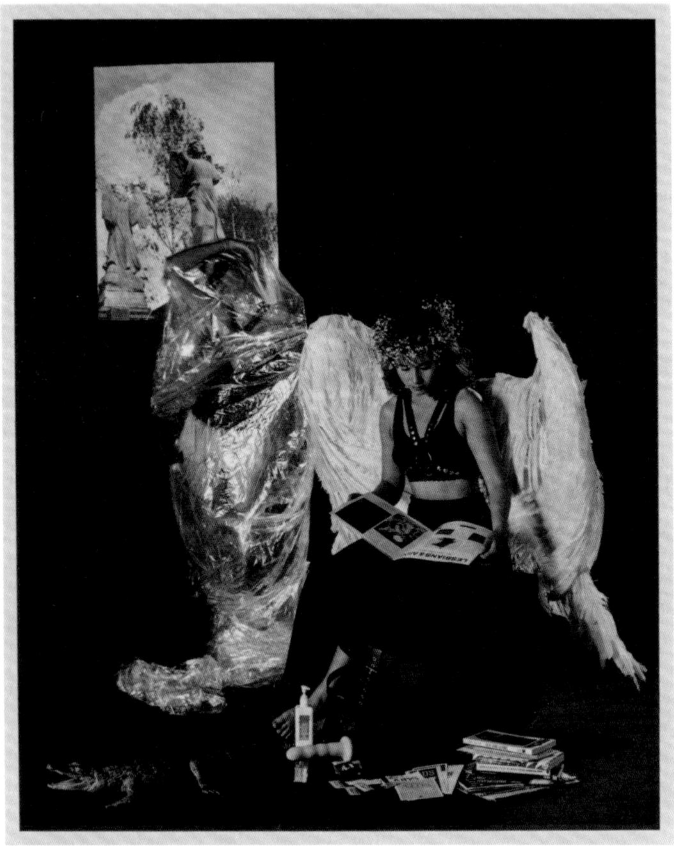
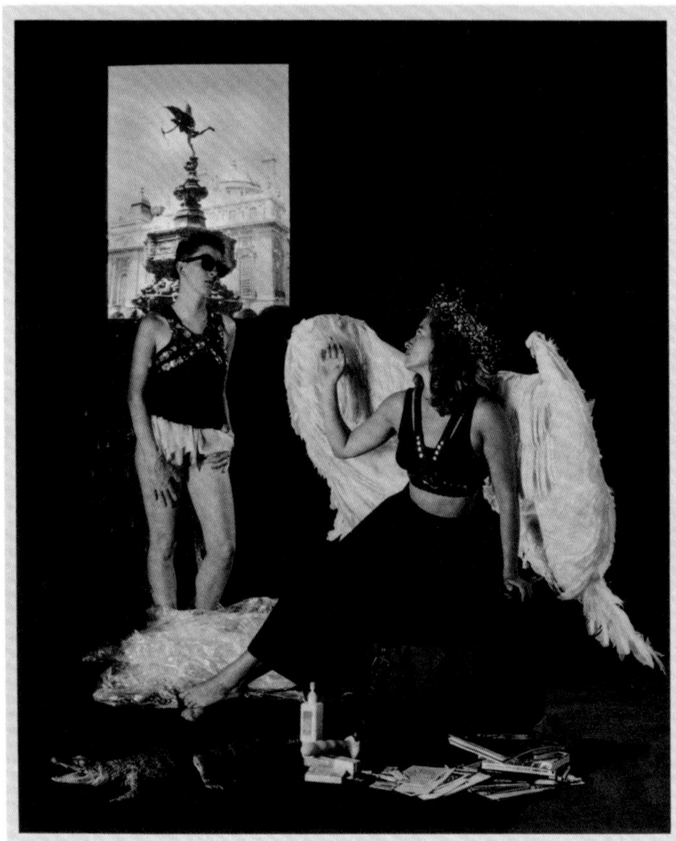

Untitled #1–#5, from the series *Angelic Rebels, Lesbians and Safer Sex* 1989.
Gelatin silver prints on paper 50.8 × 40.6, 48.1 × 37.8 and 47.9 × 37.8

Photographer, writer, editor and performance artist Tessa Boffin (1960–93) studied photography at the Polytechnic of Central London under the tutorship of Simon Watney. One of the few lesbian sex-positive photographers working in the UK in the 1980s, Boffin addressed the exclusion of lesbians from safe sex campaigns through her work and dismantled the misguided notion that lesbians were immune from HIV/AIDS. Her work combined historical figures with fantasy in order to combat the challenges of lesbian representation.

In 1987–8 Boffin undertook an MA in critical theory at the University of Sussex. With Sunil Gupta she co-curated the groundbreaking exhibition *Ecstatic Antibodies: Resisting the AIDS Mythology* (Battersea Arts Centre, 1990), and with Jean Fraser she co-edited the 1991 anthology *Stolen Glances: Lesbians Take Photographs* (accompanying the touring exhibition of the same name). Both remain central texts in relation to queer and lesbian visibility in the UK.

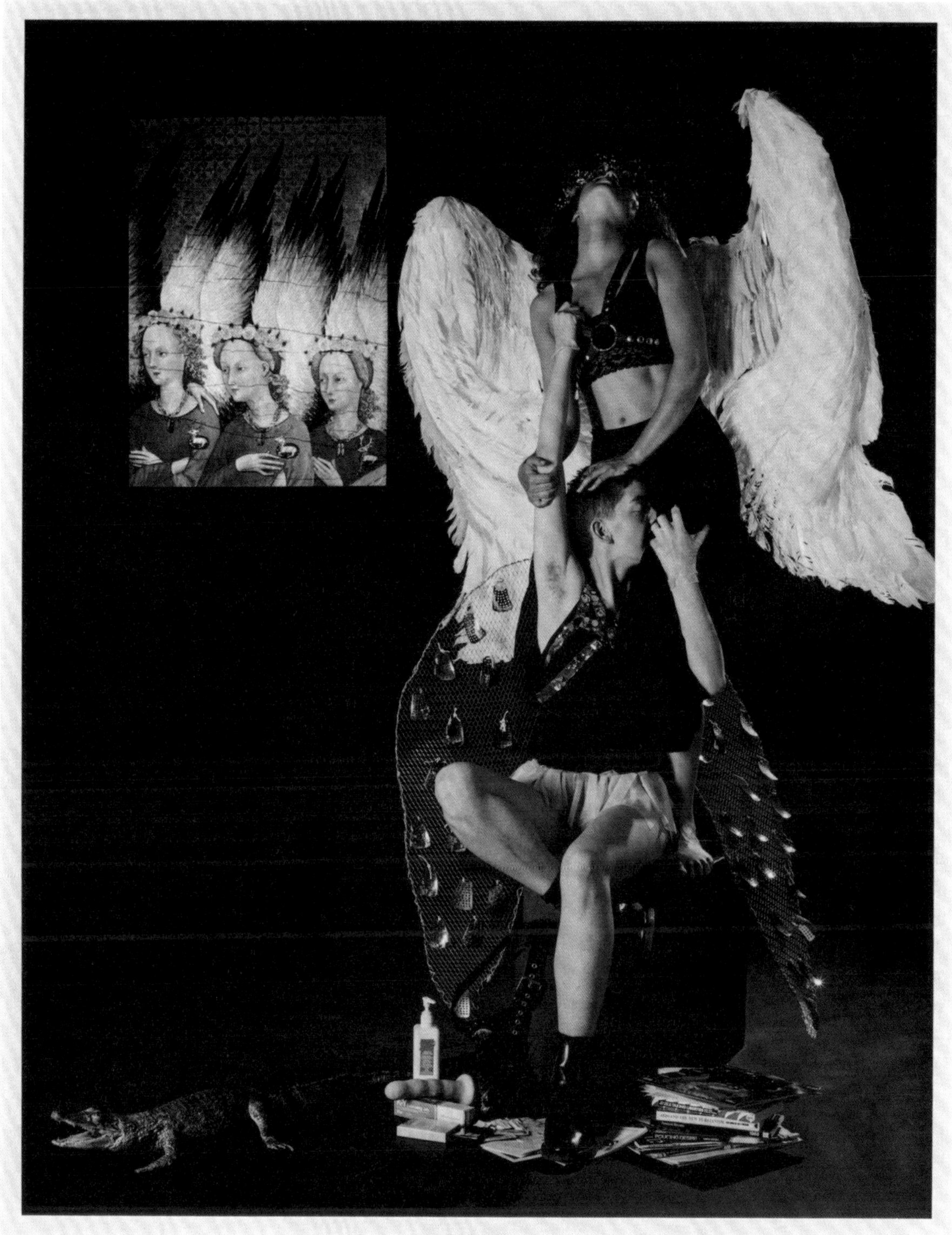

TESSA BOFFIN

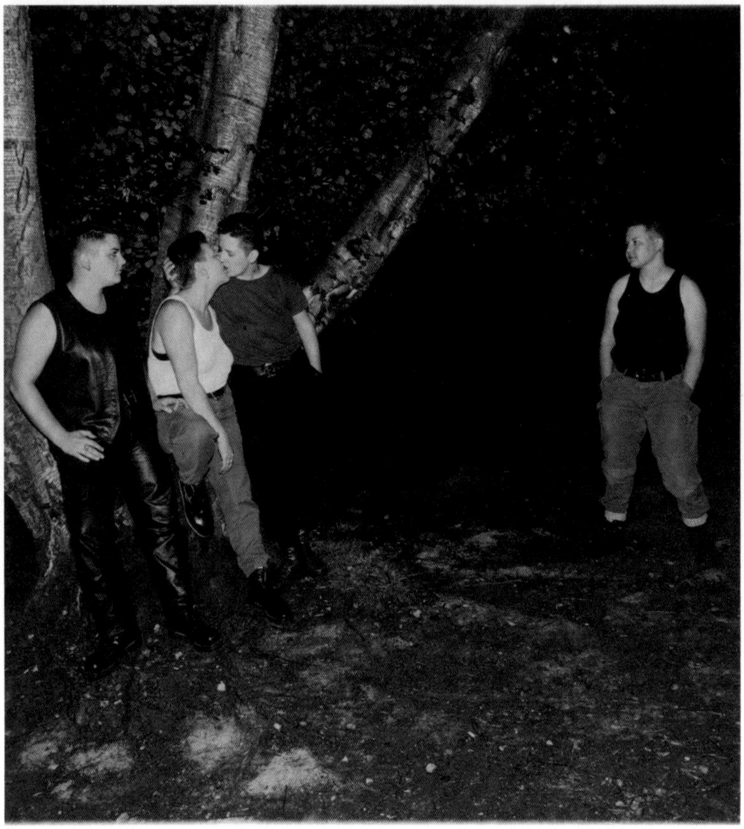

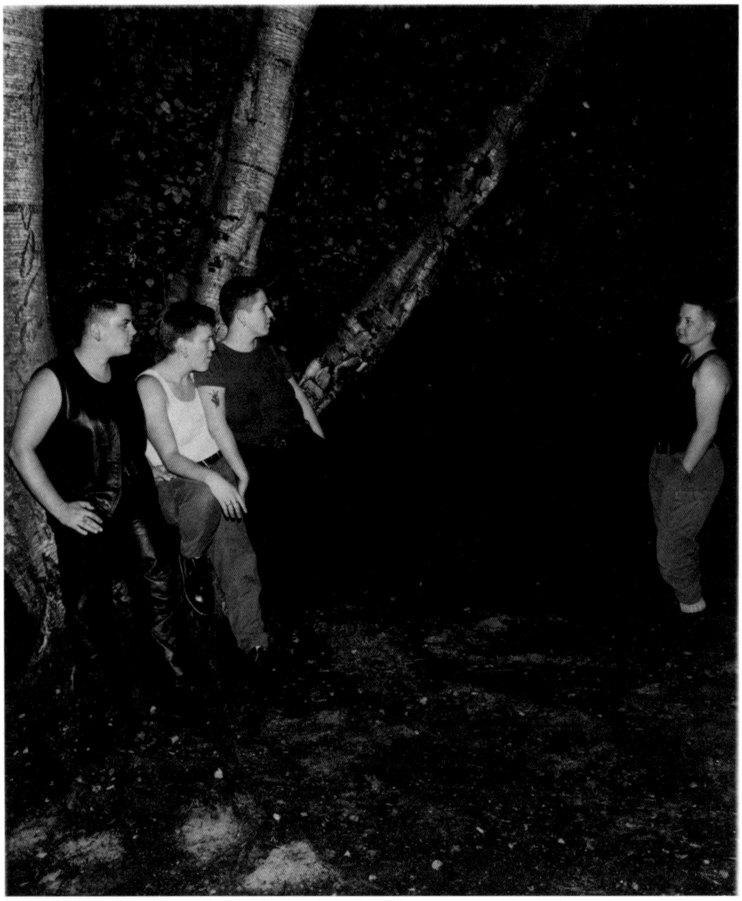

Cruising 1988. Photographs 30 × 24 (each)

Del LaGrace Volcano, formerly Della Grace, is a photographer and activist whose forty-year career has been defined by a working practice informed by the core feminist principles that 'the personal is political' and that 'processes of production are as important as the final product.'

Born in California in 1957, Volcano studied at the San Francisco Art Institute from 1979–81 and obtained a Masters in photographic studies from the University of Derby in 1992. The four C's: Connection, Collaboration, Consent and Care form the scaffolding that intentionally subverts mainstream conventions and provides a visual voice to those who, like the artist, live without the cultural safety nets non-queers take for granted. Their intention is to give a visual voice to those who have been vilified, neglected and erased. Works such as *Linda and Snake, London* 1983 (p.162), are part of their strategy of resistance to challenge the homophobic hetero-normative culture of the Thatcher era.

Celebratory images of queer subcultural movements have been a core part of the artist's practice throughout their career, and are demonstrated in their portraits of members of the lesbian SM Sex & Performance sadomasochistic nightclub Chain Reaction, active in London in the late 1980s until the early 1990s. The photographs of queer women 'cruising' on Hampstead Heath present us with a tender display of solidarity with gay male subculture and give visibility to the 'Rebel Dykes' who insisted on reclaiming their sexuality from the patriarchal gaze.

Volcano has published a number of foundational photographic monographs on gender, sexuality and the queer body, including *Love Bites* (Gay Men's Press, 1991), *The Drag King Book* (Serpent's Tail, 1999), *Sublime Mutations* (Konkursbuchverlag, 2000) and *Femmes of Power: Exploding Queer Femininities* (Serpent's Tail, 2008), in collaboration with leading queer and trans-academics such as Jack Halberstam, Paul Preciado, Jay Prosser, Ulrika Dahl and Mojisola Adebayo.

Their work has widely published in art, academic and feminist art publications since the mid 1990s. In line with their queer feminist, anti-capitalist, anti-racist methodology they make a point of exhibiting in both alternative/queer community venues along with mainstream museums and art spaces.

Their most recent solo exhibition, *Bodies of Resistance*, was at the Tampere Art Museum in Finland in 2023. They now live and work in Sweden.

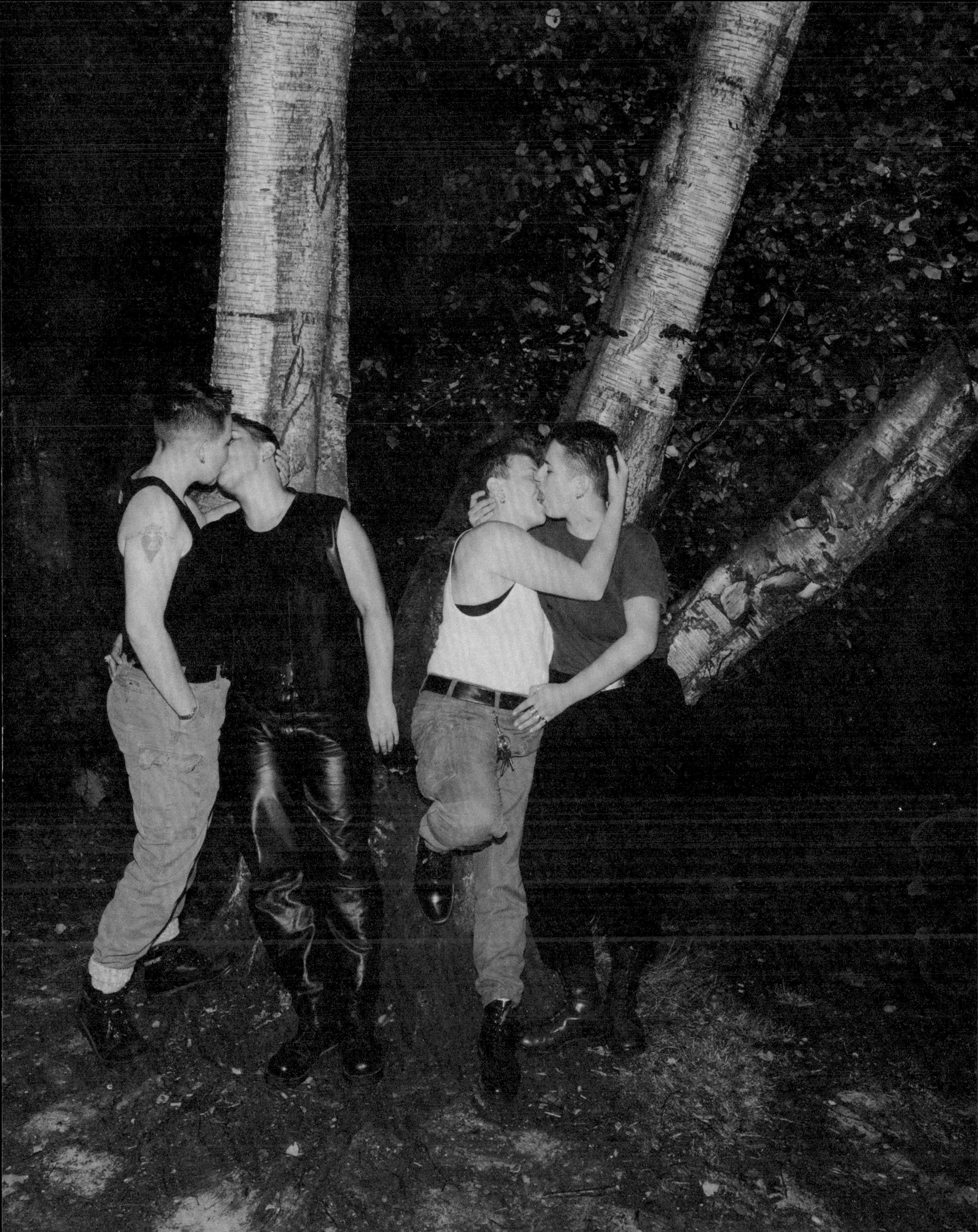

DEL LAGRACE VOLCANO

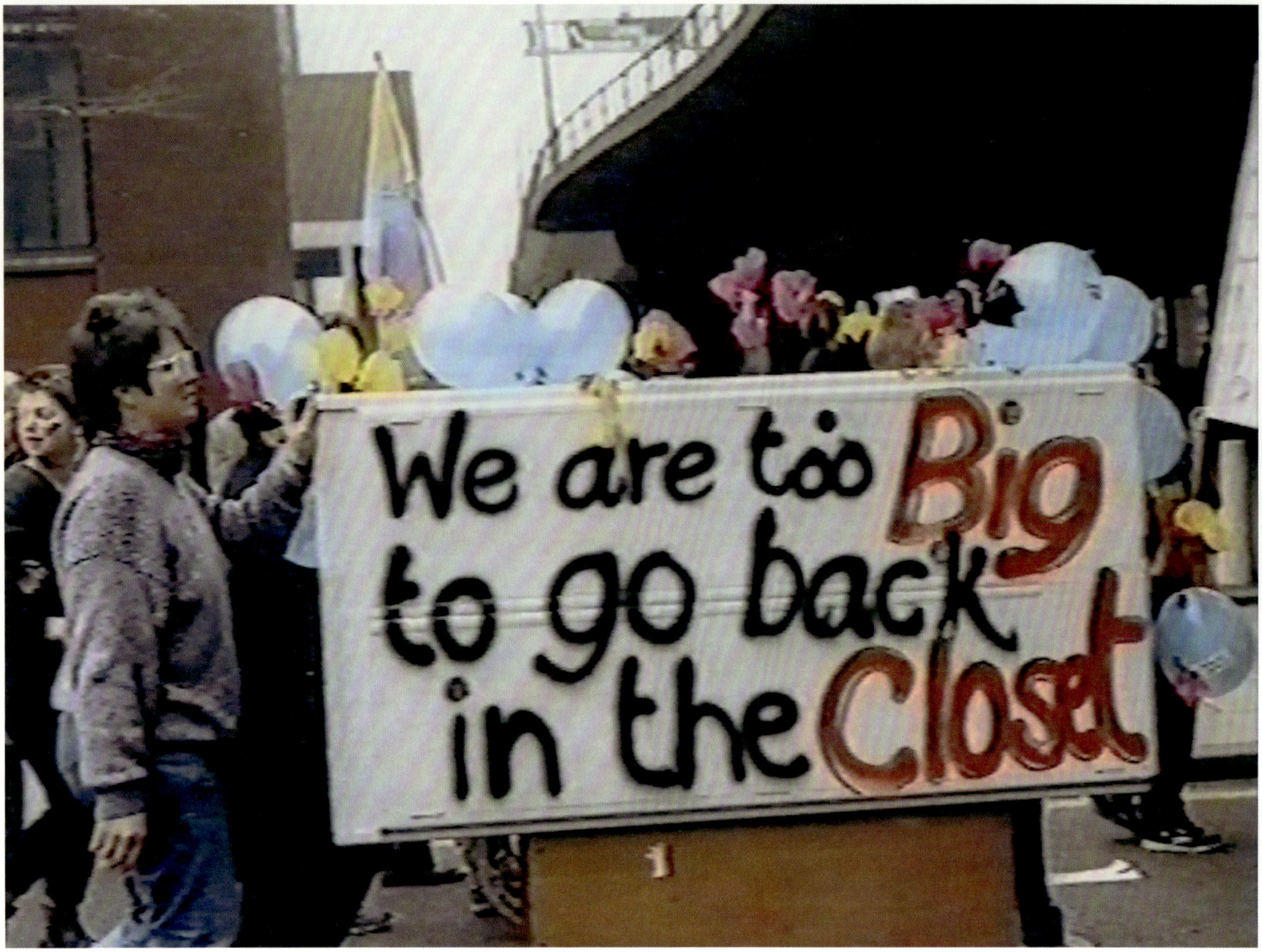

Video 28 1988. Video, shown digitally; colour, sound. 22 min

Vera Productions, now Vera Media, is a community film production collective based in Hillside, south Leeds. The collective was established following the Workshop Declaration of 1982, when the trade union ACTT (now BECTU) agreed to support non-commercial and grant-funded film and video 'workshops' comprising of at least four members working collaboratively. The agreement enabled feminist collectives such as Video Vera in Leeds, Red Flannel films in Cardiff and W.I.T.C.H. in Liverpool to produce films that addressed feminist experiences and conditions local to their communities, and through the voice of their communities, and to facilitate film and video workshops and screenings. *Video 28* 1988 records the widespread protests and campaigns against the passing of Section 28 of the Local Government Act in 1988 and its prohibition of 'the promotion of homosexuality,' which encouraged overt discrimination against the LGBTQ+ community.

VERA PRODUCTIONS

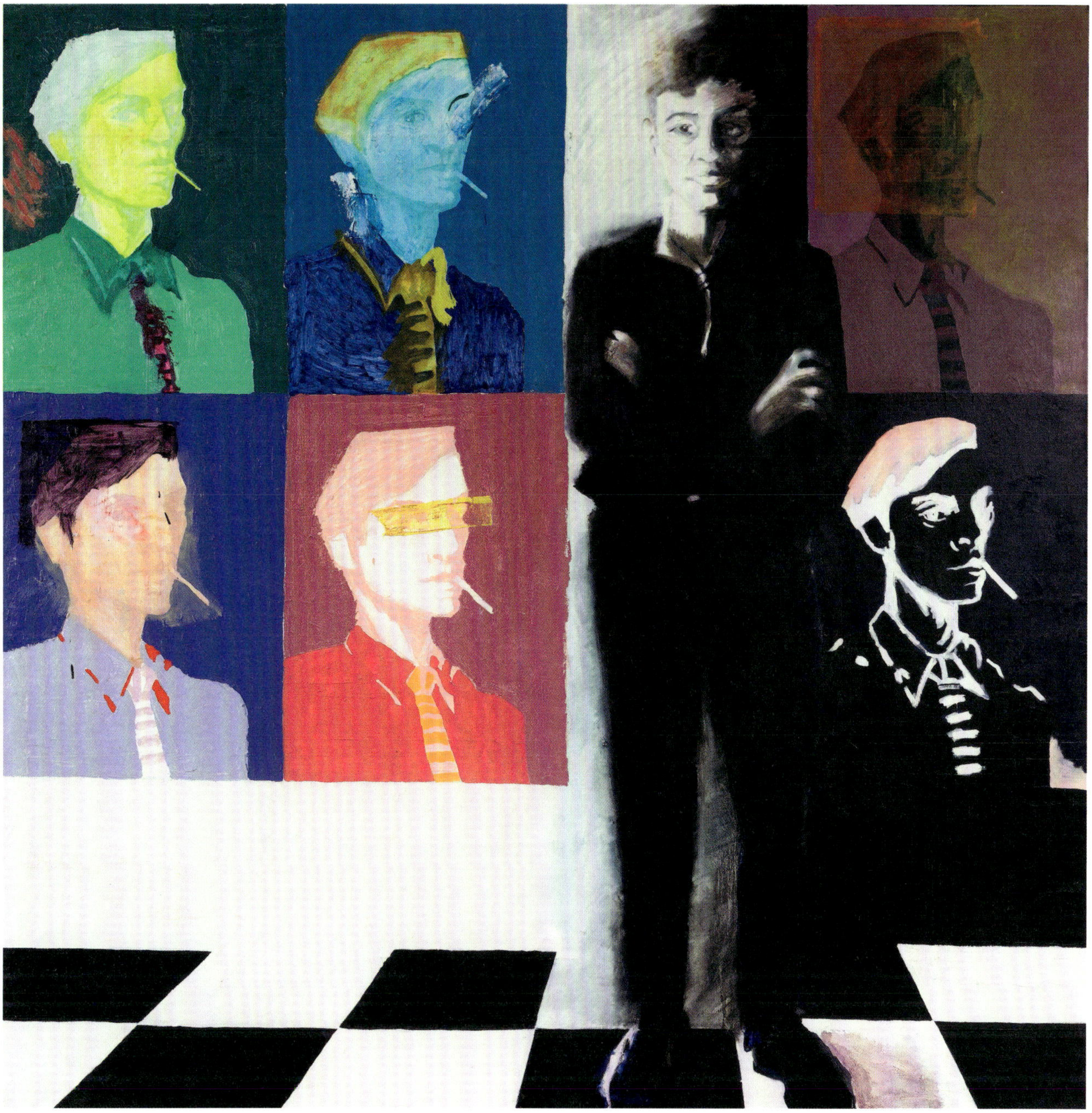

Soul Identified as Flesh 1987–8. Oil paint on canvas 182.8 × 182.8

Veronica Slater (b.1958) grew up in Sussex. She received a BA in fine art painting from Camberwell School of Arts and Crafts in London in 1980, and later an MA in fine art from the University of Northumbria, graduating in 1989. Slater is a multi-disciplinary artist, working across painting, installation and film-making. A member of the housing co-op Livin' Brix, Slater's political involvement in the 1980s manifested in her practice as she sought to address questions around LGBTQ+ identity within the hostile environment of the time, for instance by reinserting lesbians into the art historical canon by reworking the style of Warhol. Slater describes making art during the 1980s as being a 'cultural sniper' (as coined by Jo Spence), inserting oneself into pockets of resistance and visibility. Her work was included in the groundbreaking 1988 touring exhibition *Along the Lines of Resistance*.

Slater lives and works in Brighton. A solo exhibition of her work was held at Phoenix Art Space in Brighton in 2021.

VERONICA SLATER

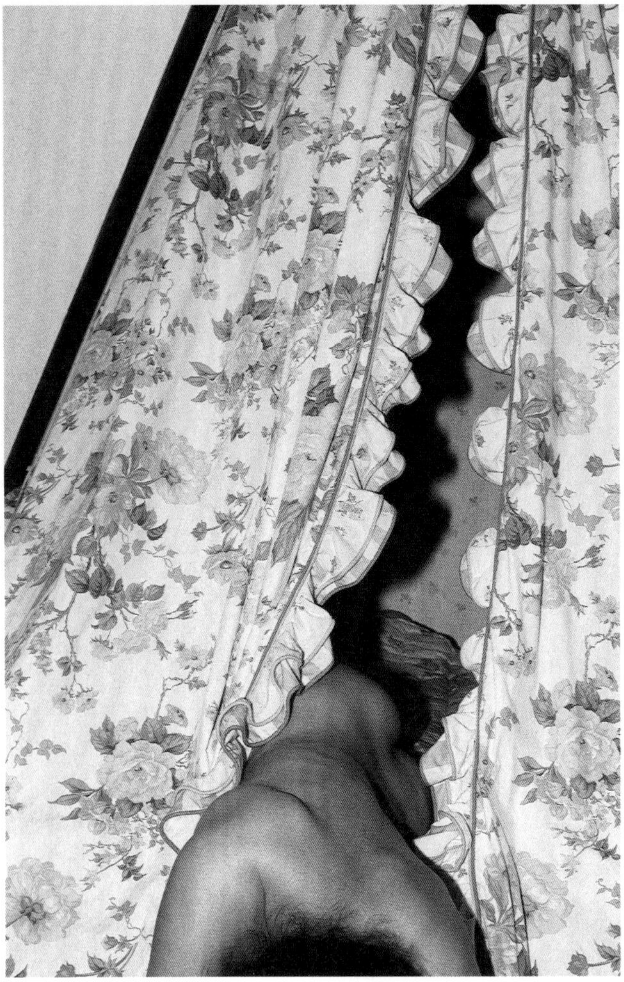
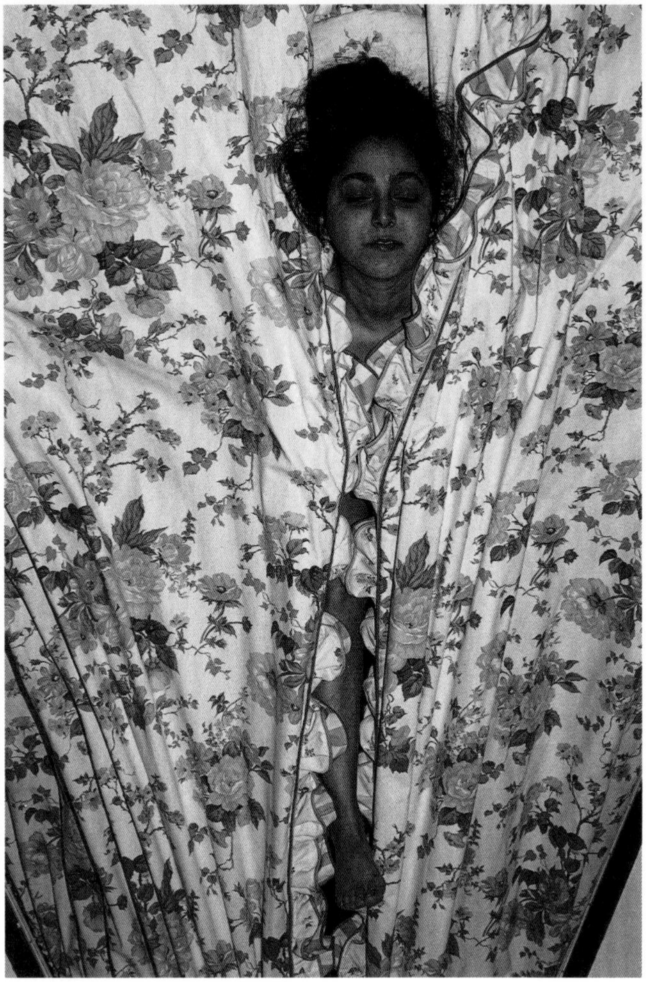
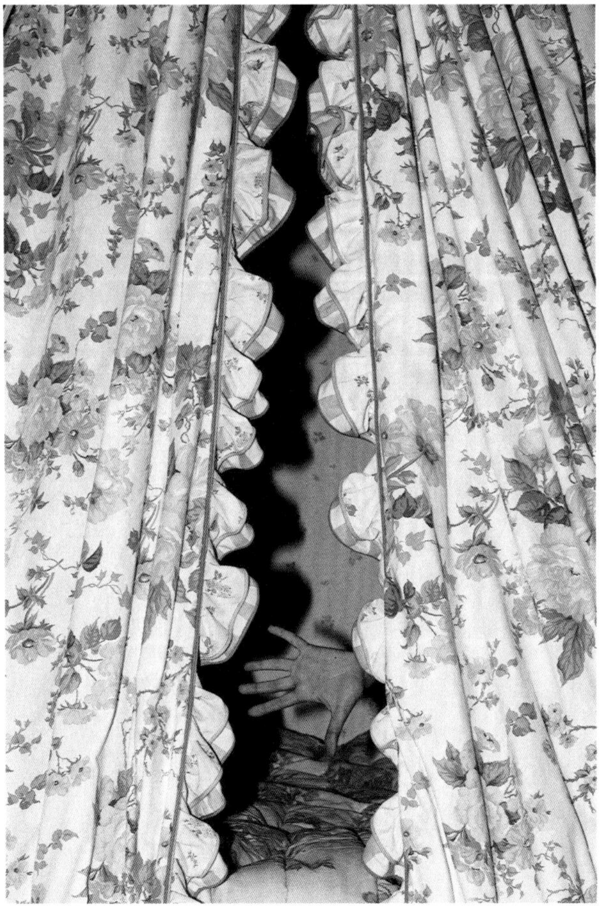

Poulomi Desai was born in London in 1965. At the age of just thirteen she co-founded the Hounslow Arts Cooperative Theatre and on leaving school she became involved with anti-fascist groups and the anti-apartheid movement. A self-taught artist with a background in street theatre, Desai works with performance and photography. Research and learning are integral to her practice and she often works collaboratively. As a curator, Desai is responsible for two long-overdue exhibitions. In 2010 she organised the first retrospective by the influential artist Chila Burman. *Chila Burman's Royal Academy Summer Exhibition*, held at Usurp Art Gallery & Studios, London, featured works created over forty years, many of which had not been seen before. Then in 2017, she curated *We Are the Lions*, the first comprehensive exhibition about the 1976–8 Grunwick strike.

Desai has undertaken significant work as an activist, co-founding *Shakti*, the first South Asian LGBTQ+ campaigning organisation, in 1987, and the Naz Foundation International, the first HIV/AIDS charity in India. She lives in London and works internationally.

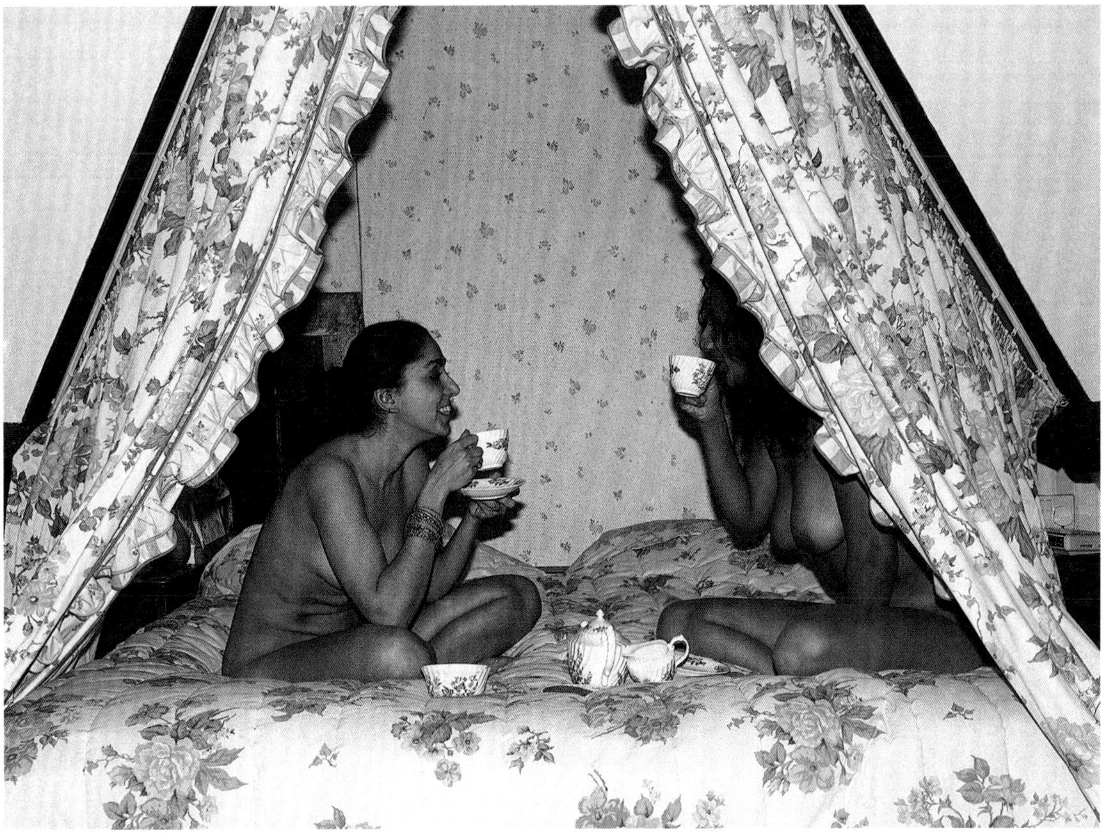

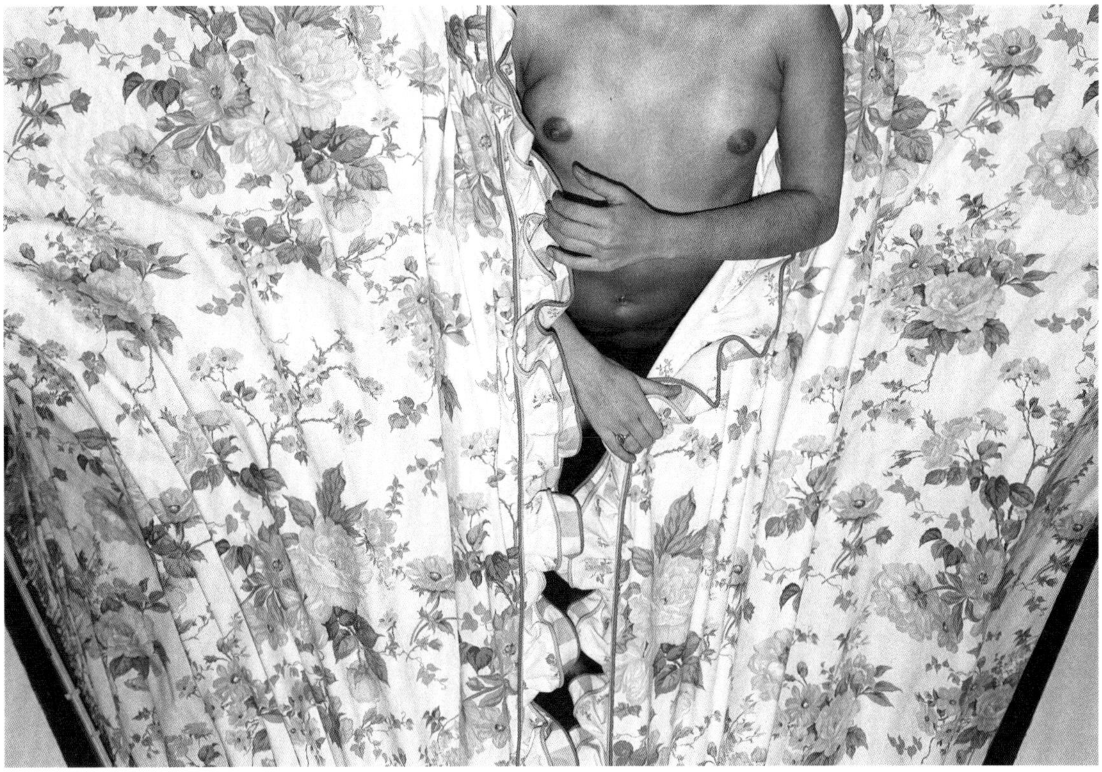

Our Asian Lesbian Gay Black bodies, our tea, our chintz 1989. 5 photographs 25.4 × 20.3 (each)

POULOMI DESAI

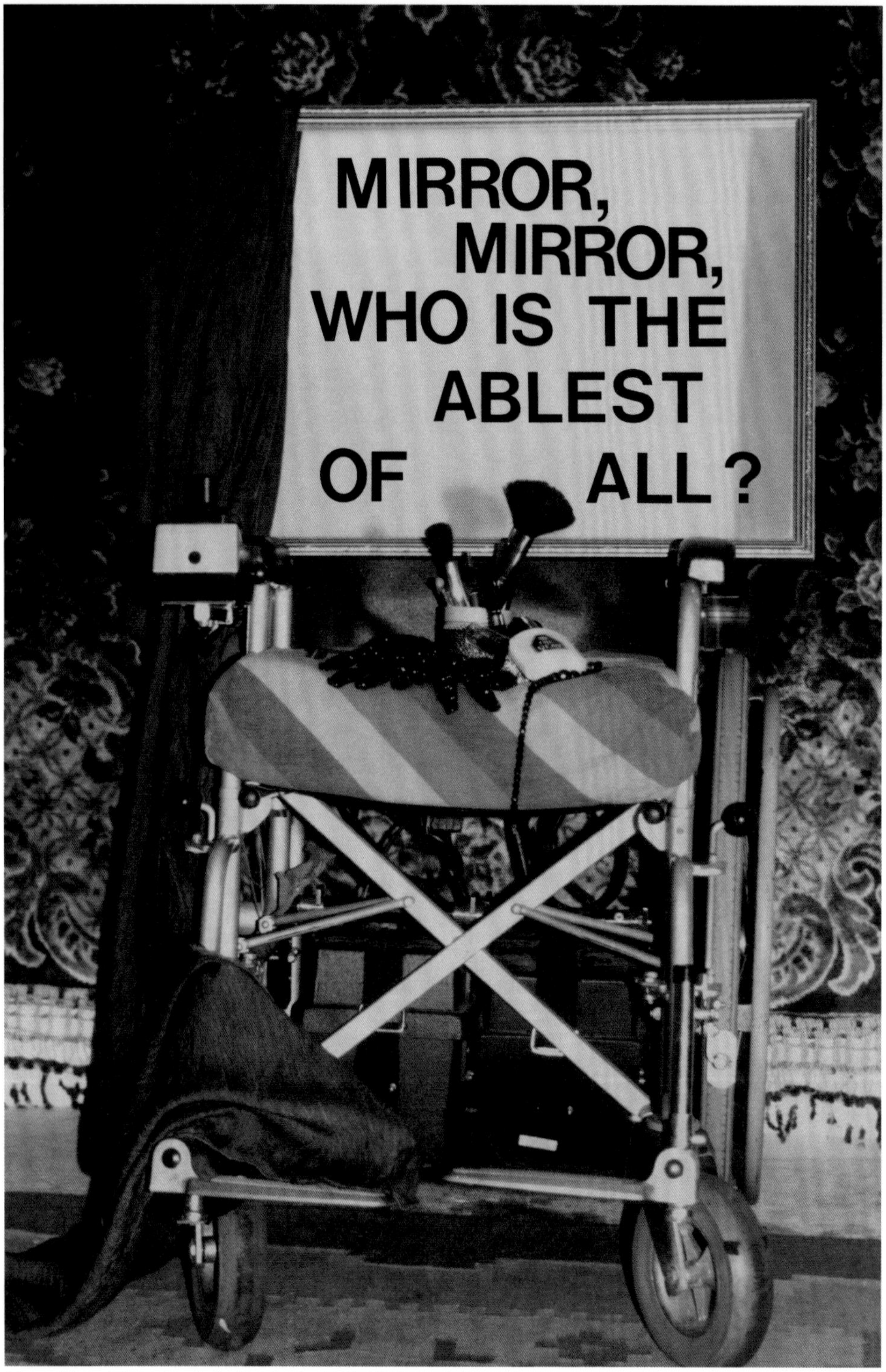

Mirror Mirror I, from the *Reflection Series* 1991. Photograph 29 × 19

Born in Lahore, Pakistan, Samena Rana (1955–92) moved to England with her family at the age of nine to receive medical treatment following a car accident. She developed an interest in photography while travelling in Pakistan after finishing her schooling and on her return to London she enrolled at the Sir John Cass School of Arts to study the subject. However, Rana left the course before graduating, owing to the lack of accessibility offered to disabled students. This experience ignited her activism and she developed her practice with SHAPE, a photography studio based at Battersea Arts Centre. Rana invented her own technique of taking photographs by adjusting the camera so that the trigger mechanism could be placed in her mouth. Her work considers issues of identity, disability and diaspora, as in the *Reflections Series*, which explores the construction of identity and challenges societal expectations around ideas of disability and beauty. Rana fought significantly for the rights of disabled photographers and her activism and work influenced institutions such as the ICA to adapt their darkrooms to meet the needs of all artists.

SAMENA RANA

With a practice encompassing painting, sculpture, printmaking, mixed media and moving image, Nancy Willis (b.1953) explores through her work ideas around mourning, vulnerability and suffering through love, and often considers her lived experience as a woman with a disability, as in her series of self-portraits from the 1980s. Her art creates a space in which complex emotions can be explored without fear of judgement or shame. Willis was a notable activist in the Disability Arts Movement in the 1980s and 90s, fighting for the rights of disabled people, especially women. In 1988 she organised the Disabled Women Artists Convention at the Women Artists Slide Library in London. Willis worked closely with the National Disability Arts Collection and Archive, gifting many of her works to them.

Willis has won a number of prestigious awards, including the Arts Council Innovate Award (2003), and her film *Elegy for the Elswick Envoy*, commissioned by Channel 4, was named Best Documentary at several film festivals internationally. She lives and works in London.

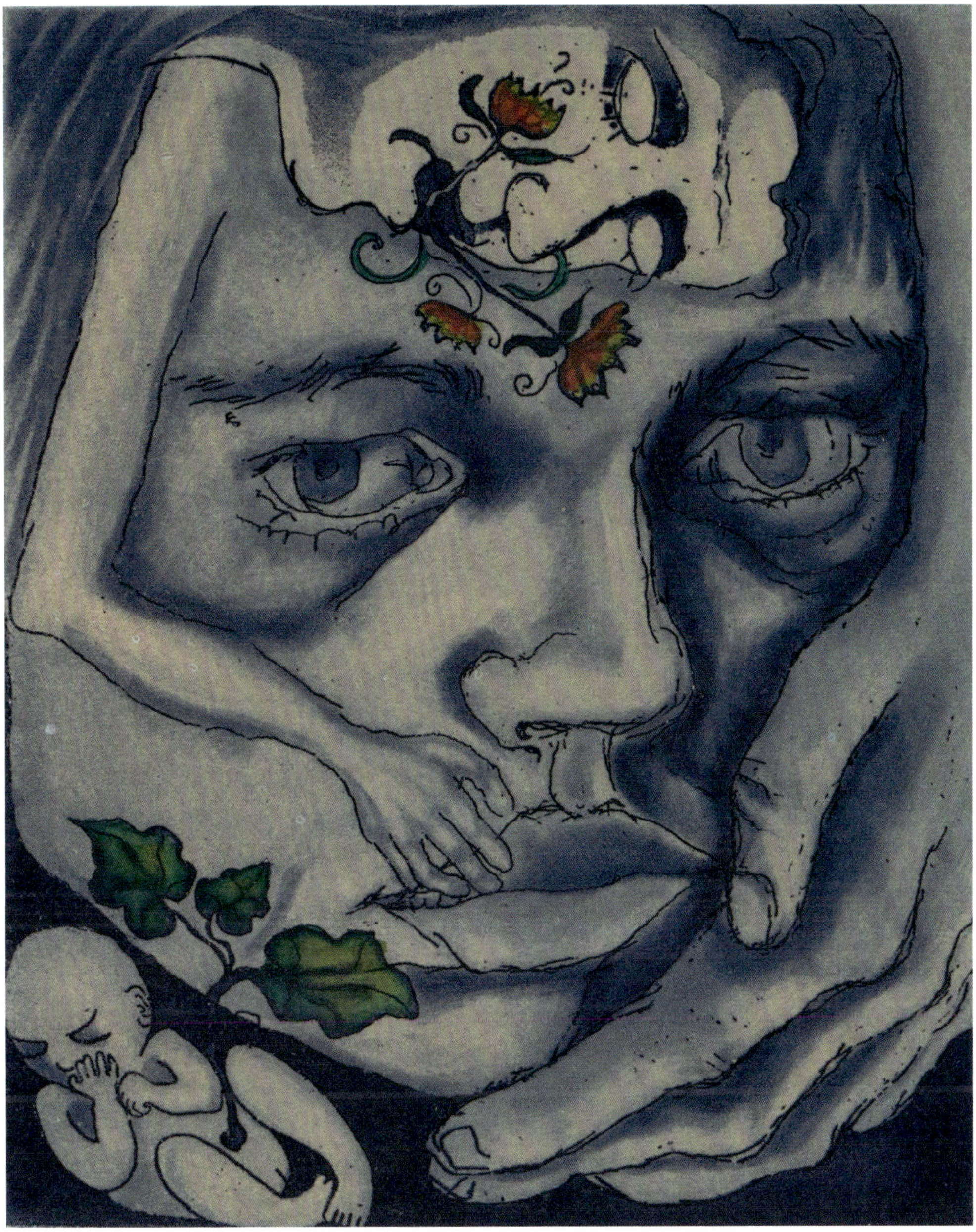

Self-portrait with Lost Baby 1988. Etching with hand-colouring on paper 28 × 24

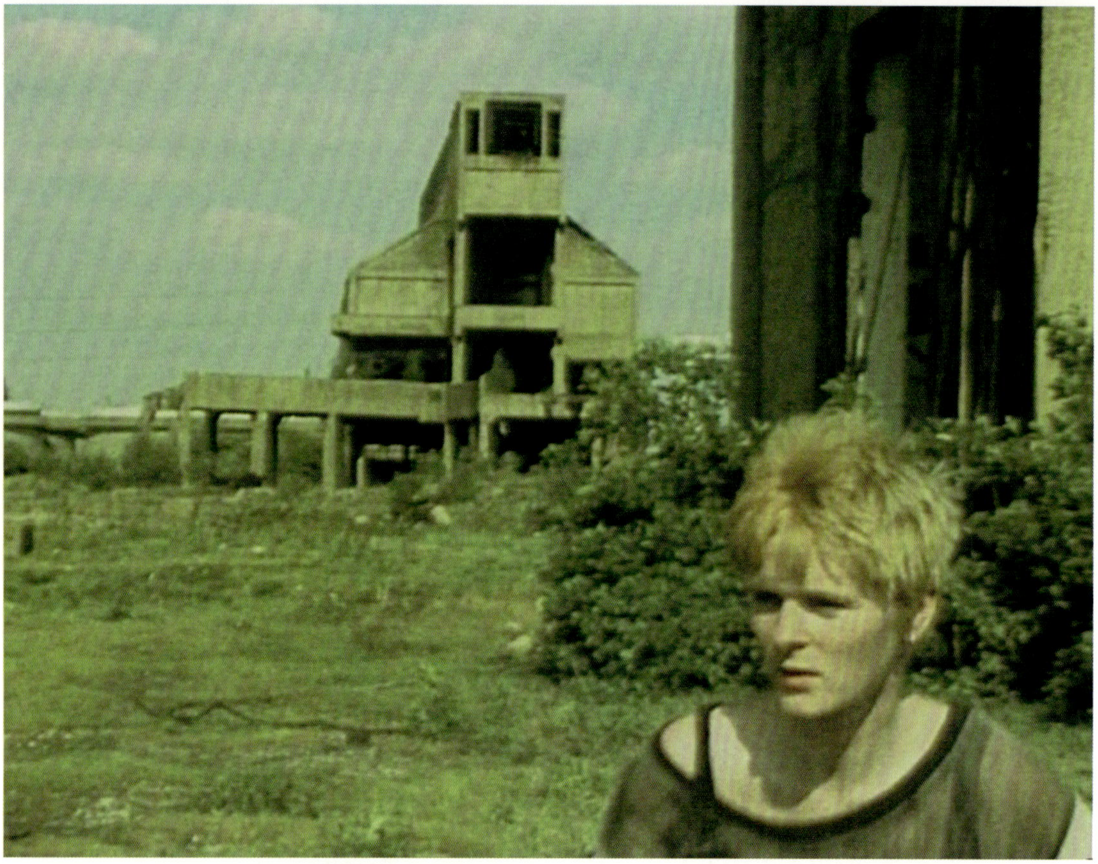

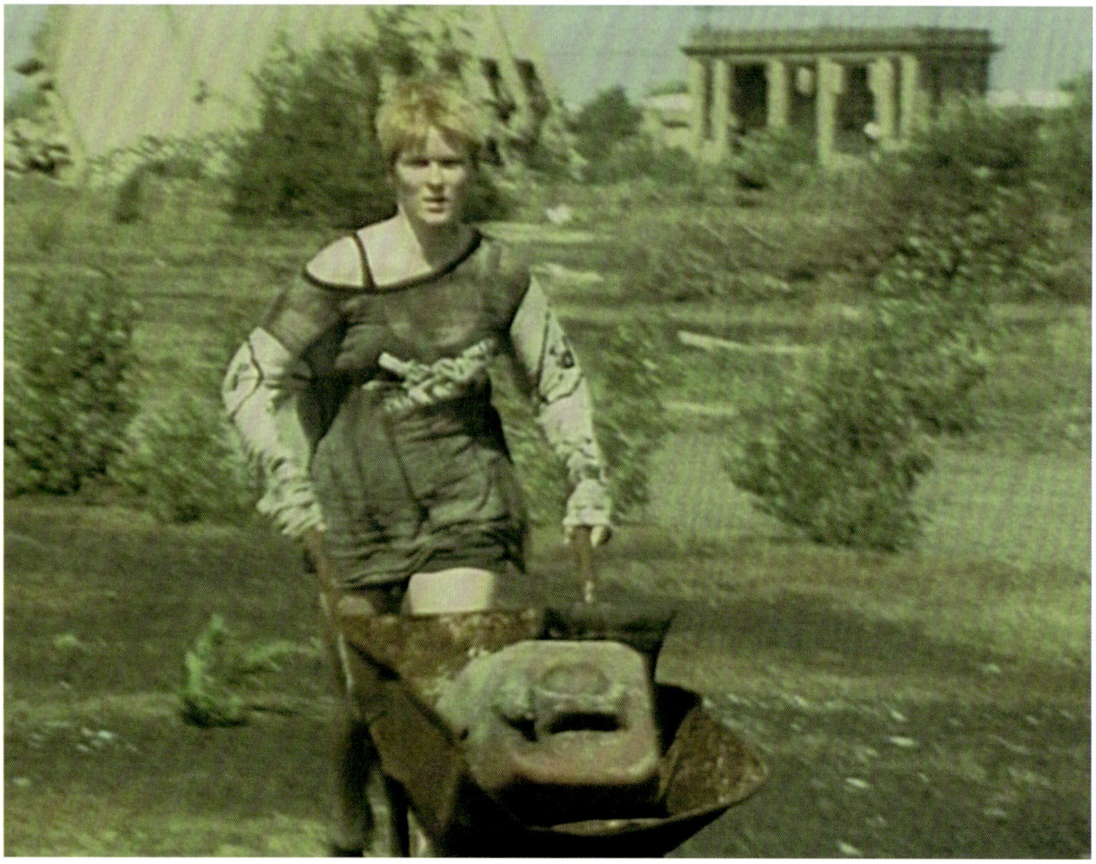

Two Little Pigeons 1990. Super 8 film, shown as digital video; colour, sound. 4 min, 38 sec

Vivienne Dick (b.1950) grew up in Donegal, Ireland, and attended University College Dublin in the 1960s. After living for a time in France and Germany, and travelling in India and Mexico, the artist settled in New York's East Village and became embedded in its artistic community and 'No Wave' film scene. Sliding between documentary, fiction and performance, Dick's work explores issues to do with social and gender politics, philosophy and ecology.

In the early 1980s, Dick relocated to London where she became a member of the London Filmmakers' Co-operative. Films from this period include *London Suite* 1989 and *Two Little Pigeons* 1990. Acting like a coda to *London Suite*, the short *Two Pigeons* presents a lyrical and affectionate portrait of London life at the end of the 1980s, contrasting scenes of workers relaxing in the park with a tea ritual between friends in the derelict shell of Beckton Gas Works.

In 2021 a retrospective of Dick's work was shown at Jeu de Paume, Paris, and in 2017, the Irish Museum of Modern Art, Dublin held a major survey of her work.

The artist currently lives and works in Dublin.

VIVIENNE DICK

Melanie Friend (b.1957) worked as an independent photojournalist in the 1980s and 90s, reporting for print and broadcast media, and was a member of Format Photographers Agency from 1986 to its closure in 2003. Her journalistic photographic work was underpinned by the contemporary political and social climate. Having received a BA in English from the University of York in 1978, Friend went on to study for a BA in photography at the Polytechnic of Central London, graduating in 1988, and then an MA in photography at the London College of Printing in 2000. Friend's photographic practice often documented political events and activism, with a wide body of work recording the Greenham Common Peace Camp. In 1988 Friend exhibited her powerful series *Mothers' Pride* as part of her degree show at the Polytechnic of Central London, and then at the Spectrum Women's Photography Festival in London later that year. The series consisted of photographs of teenage mothers around the UK, with an accompanying text drawn from interviews with the women. It sought to challenge and dispel the problematic perception of teenage mothers perpetuated by the Thatcher government through empowering portraits of the women with their children.

Friend's later documentary photography often references landscapes and war. A touring exhibition of her work *The Home Front* opened at the Impressions Gallery, Bradford, in 2013 and has since been shown at seven further venues.

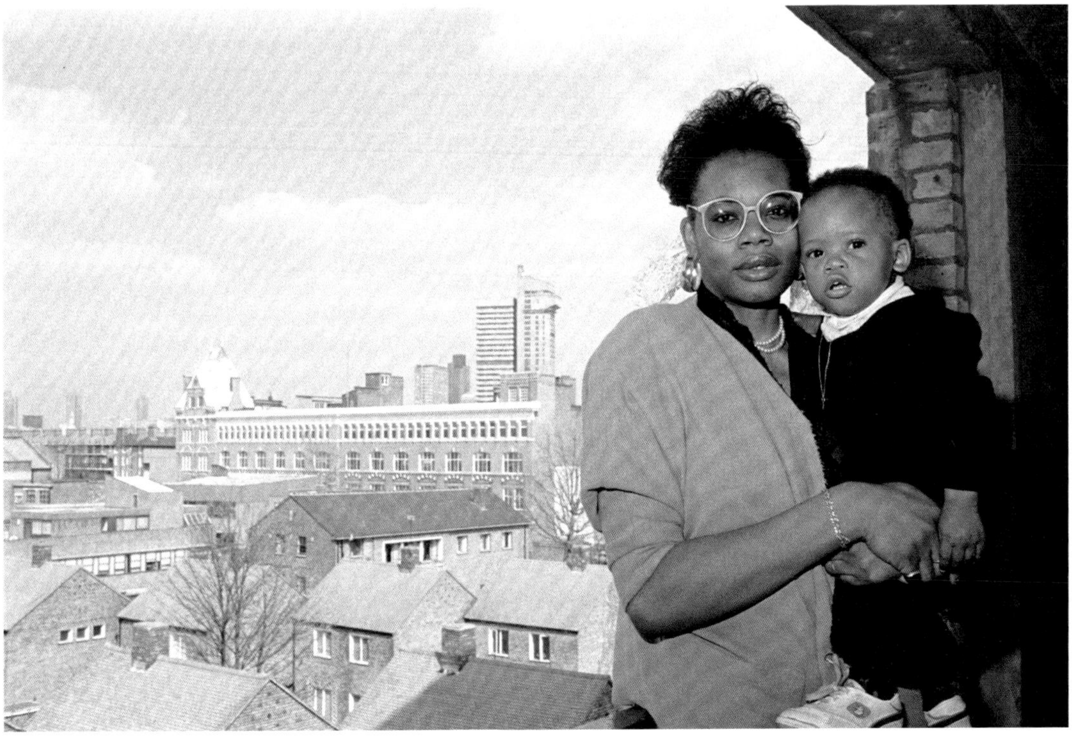

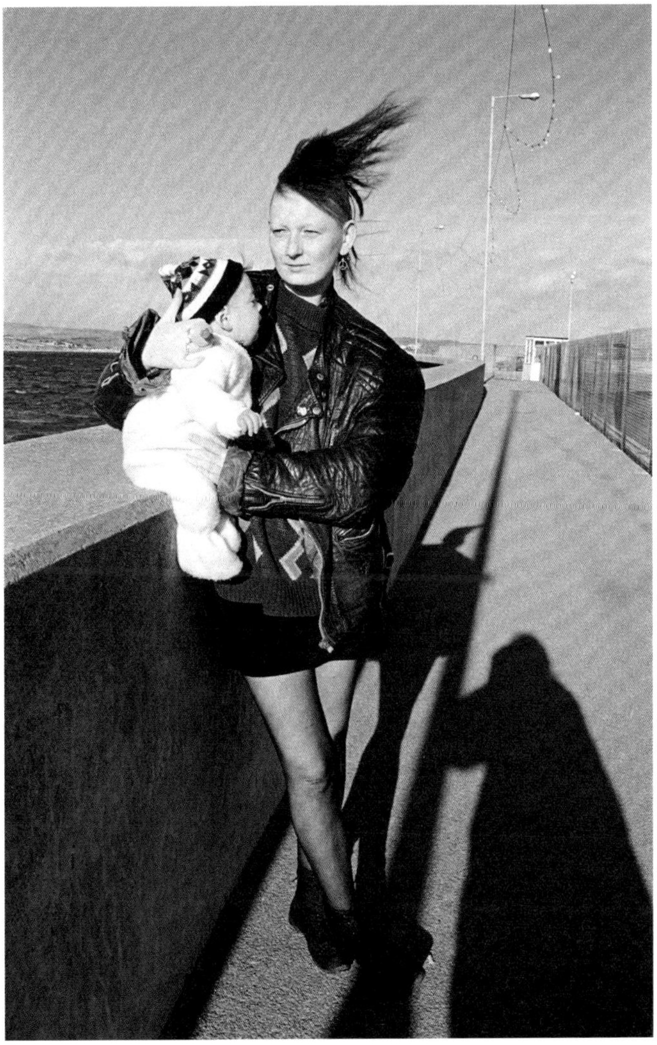

Jeana with her 18-month-old son and Fiona with Dominic, from the series *Mothers' Pride* 1988. 2 of 8 photographs. Various sizes

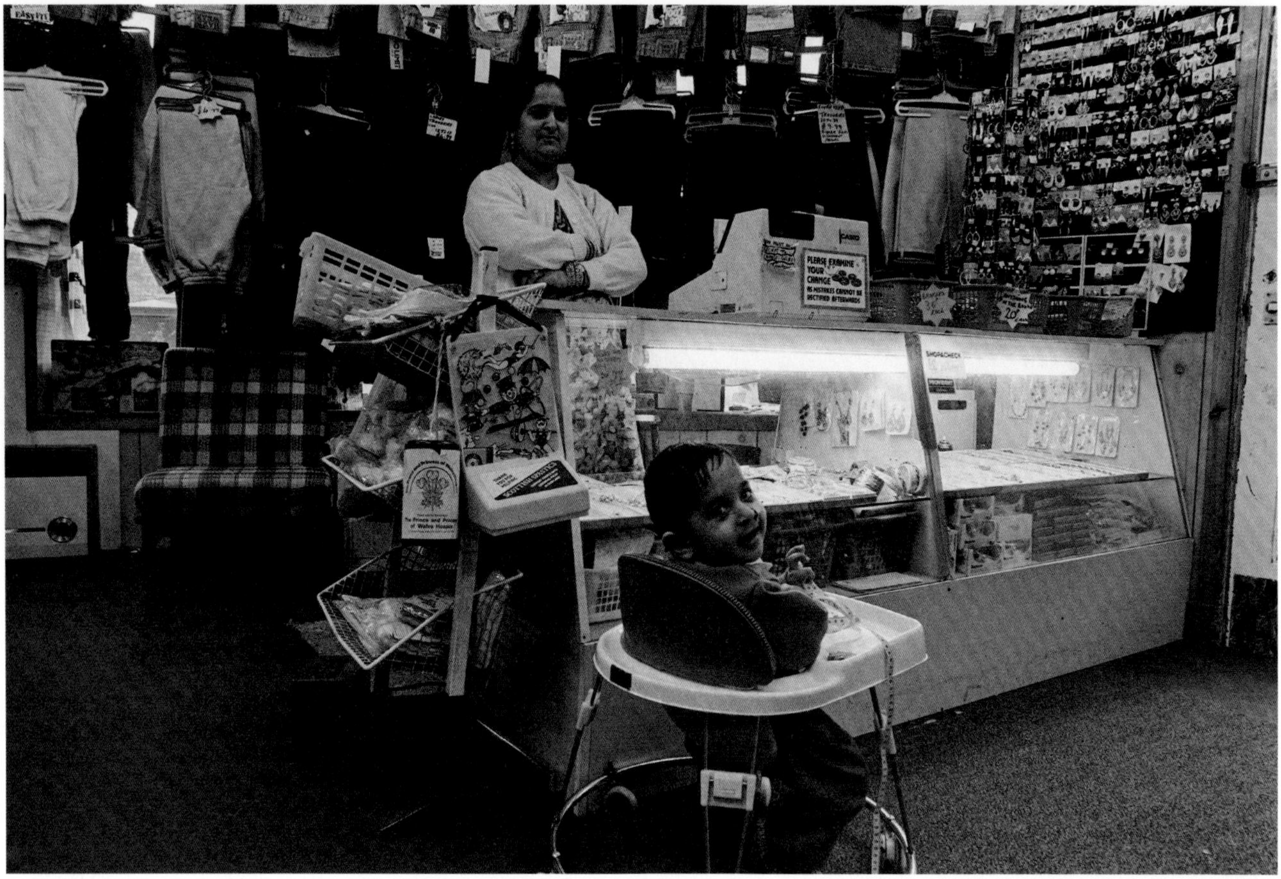

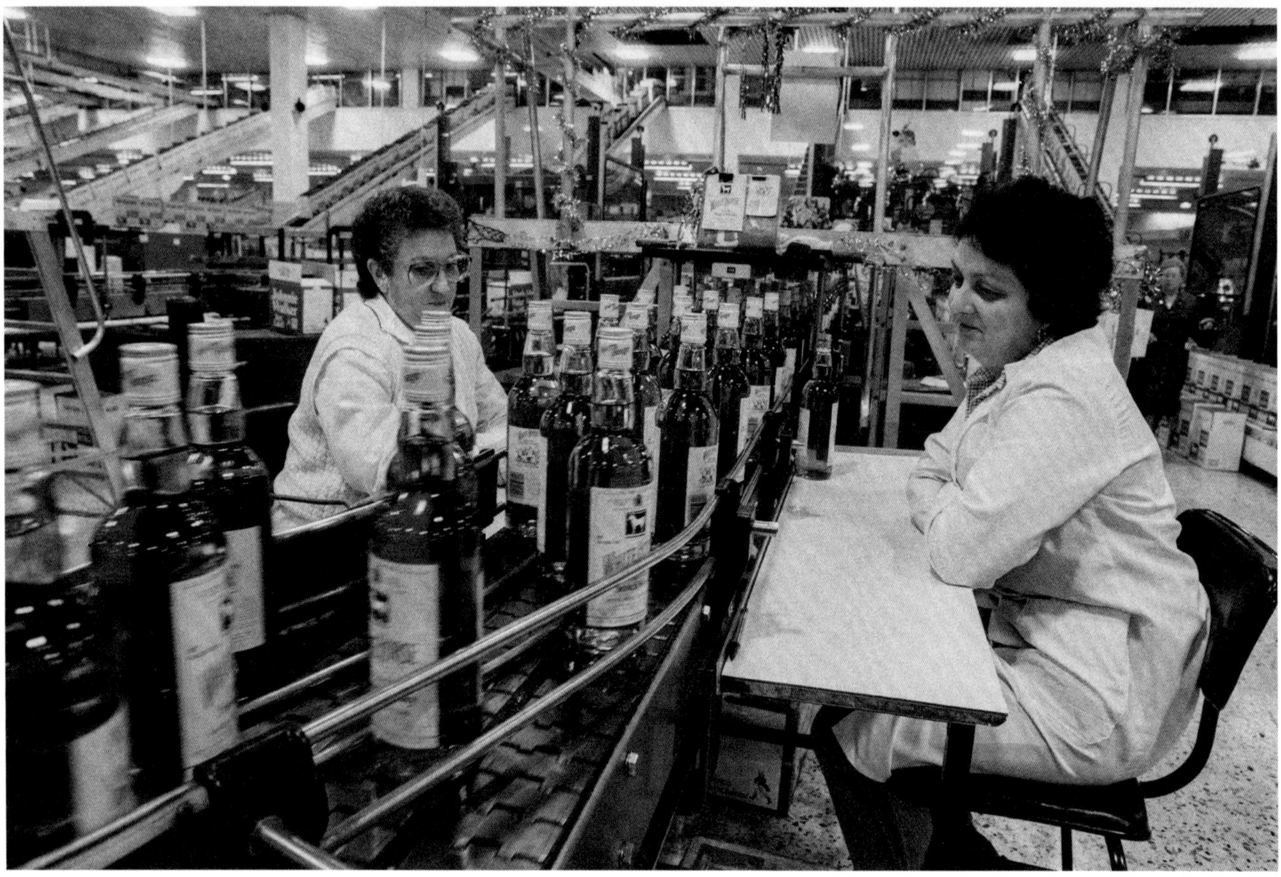

To Let You Understand 1988. 7 of 10 photographs 21 × 29.7 (each)

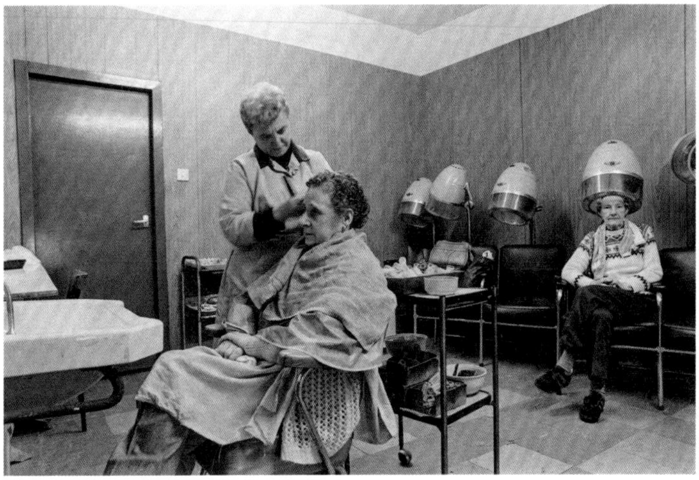

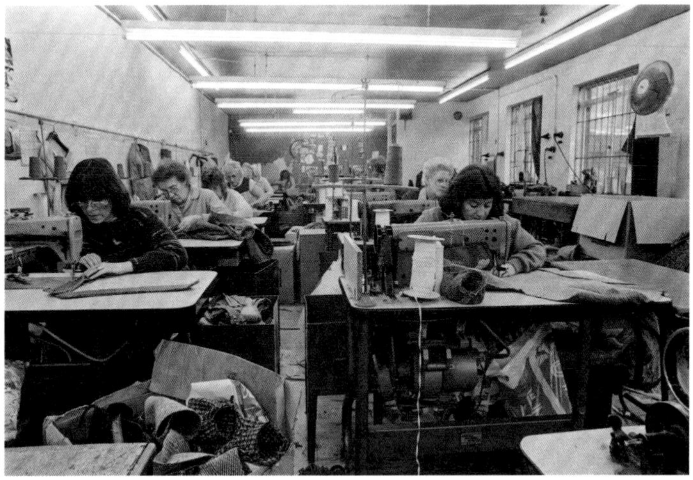

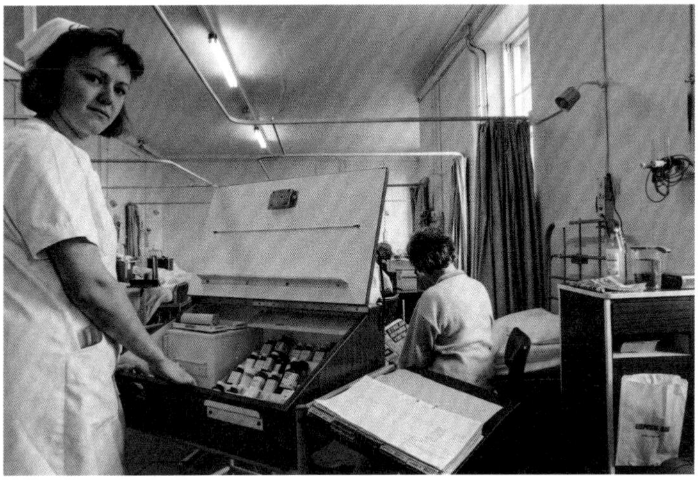

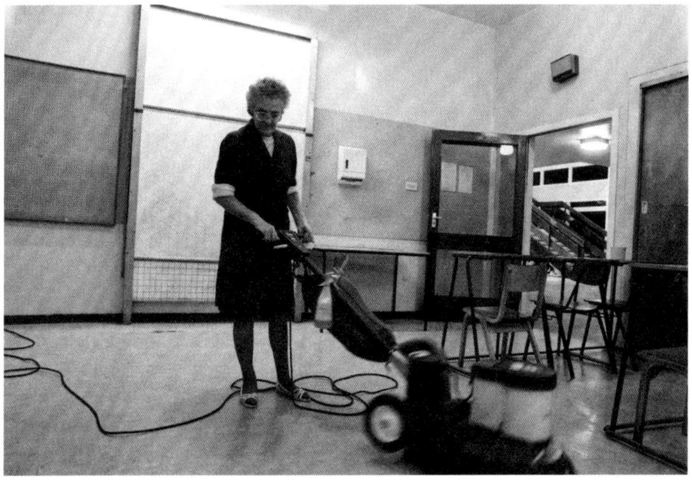

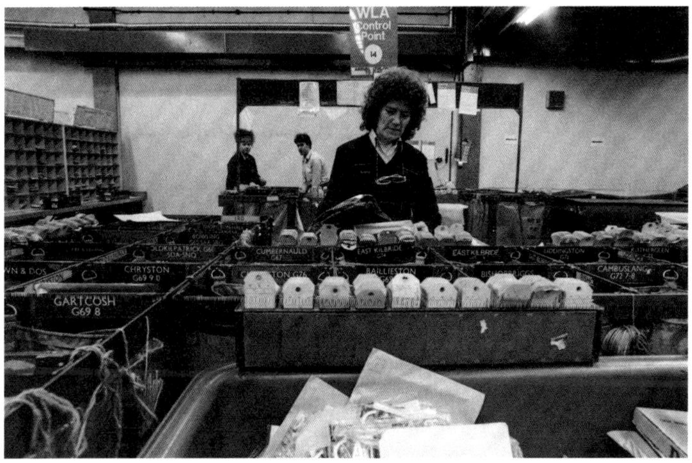

Born in Salford, Franki Raffles (1955–94) moved to London as a child with her family. After leaving school, she studied philosophy at the University of St Andrews. While Raffles was at university, she became actively involved in the Women's Liberation Movement, and after leaving university, she lived on the Isle of Lewis where she began to work as a photographer. In 1983 she moved to Edinburgh and, working with community groups, charities and arts organisations, she used her camera to raise social awareness regarding gender inequality and the threat of male violence against women. Raffles travelled around the world, photographing women at work and in their everyday lives. For the series *To Let You Understand* 1988, Raffles asked women in Scotland about their lives and working conditions under a Conservative government.

A retrospective of Raffles' work was held at Glasgow School of Art in 2017.

FRANKI RAFFLES

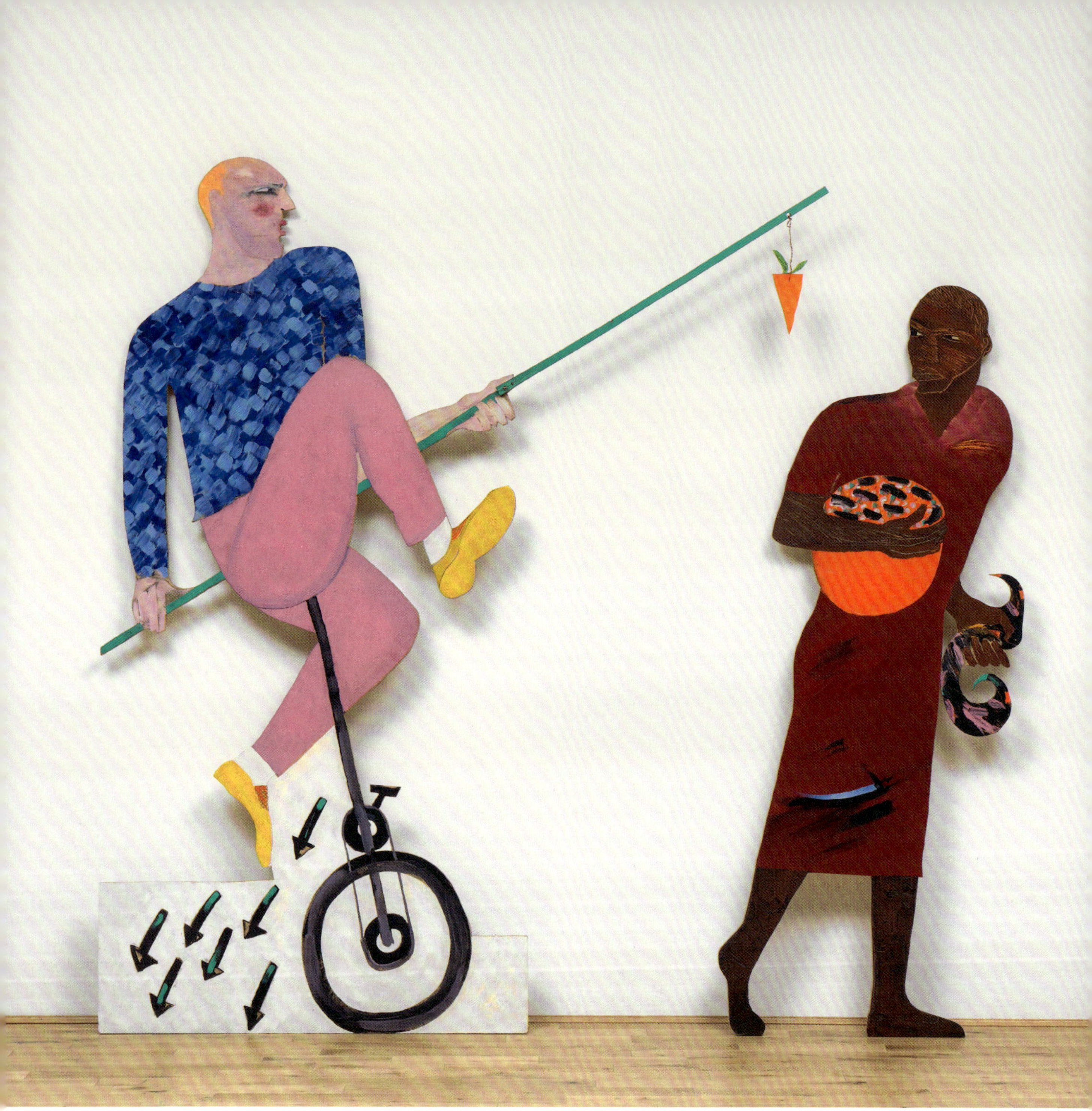

The Carrot Piece 1985. Acrylic paint on plywood, wood, cardboard and string 241 × 123 (man); 206 × 73 (woman)

LUBAINA HIMID

Born in Zanzibar, Tanzania in 1954, Lubaina Himid moved to London as a child. She studied theatre design at Wimbledon College of Arts and went on to graduate from the Royal College of Art in 1984. Himid's practice encompasses painting, printing, drawing and poetry and interrogates histories of colonialism and imperialism, the European art canon and the art world's exclusion of Black women. Himid has always sought to highlight the work of Black and Asian women artists working in the UK and in the early 1980s she began curating and publishing. *Five Black Women* (Africa Centre, 1983), *Black Woman Time Now* (Battersea Arts Centre, 1983) and *The Thin Black Line* (ICA, 1985) were key exhibitions in the Black Arts Movement that have had a profound and lasting impact on British art. The fight for recognition is mirrored in Himid's art, which often depicts Black women together, occupying the very spaces from which they have historically been excluded.

In 2017, Himid won the Turner Prize, and in 2018 she was both elected a Royal Academician and awarded a CBE. A solo exhibition of her work was held at Tate Modern in 2021–2. She lives and works in Preston.

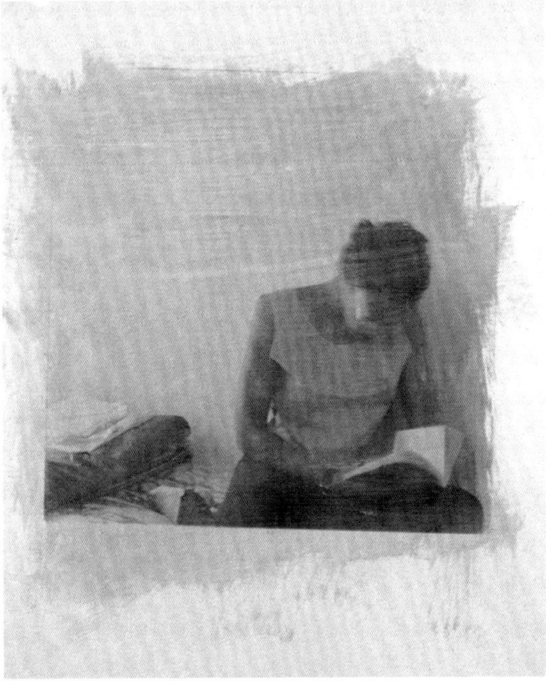

Villaroel, Barcelona

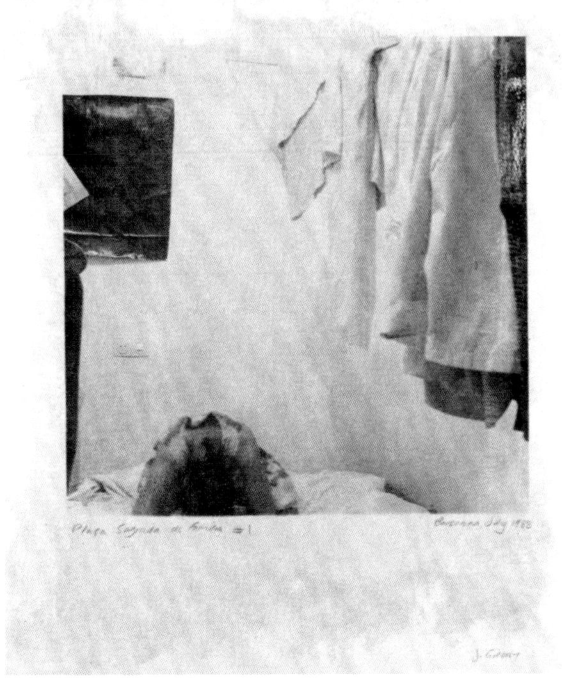

Plaza Sagrada Familia #1, Barcelona

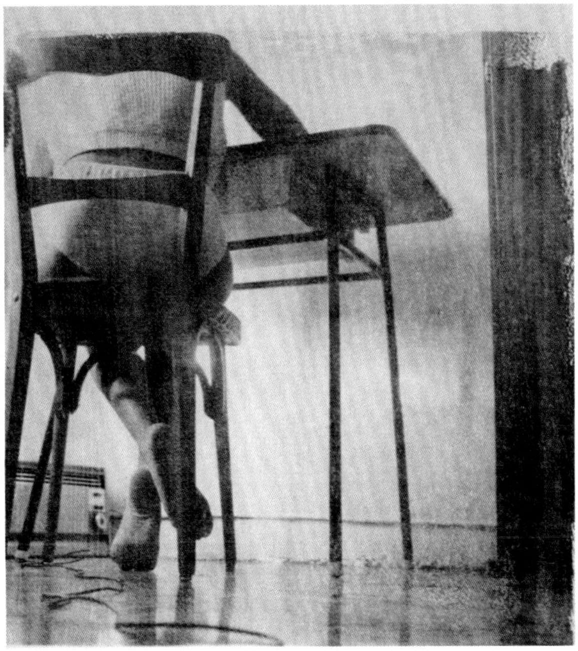

Hotel Normandia #2, Andorra La Vella
from the series *Women and Spaces* 1988
4 of 5 photographs; gelatin silver prints on watercolour paper
47 × 38 (each)

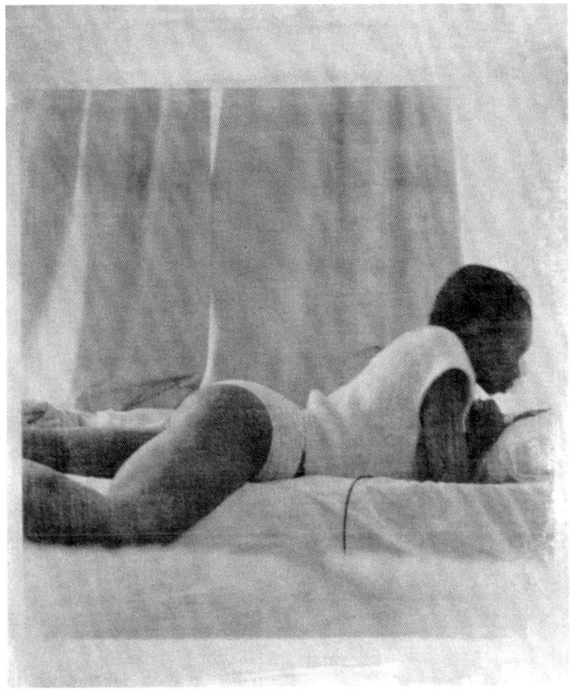

Hotel Normandia #1, Andorra La Vella

Joy Gregory was born in Oxfordshire in 1959 to Jamaican parents. She studied photography at Manchester Polytechnic and the Royal College of Art, London. In her practice, Gregory utilises film, video, analogue and digital photography and Victorian print processes. Her work considers notions of difference in society, particularly in regard to both race and gender, and often challenges cultural and historical beauty standards. *Autoportraits* 1990, for example, comprises a series of self-portraits of the artist made in response to the lack of presentations of Black women's beauty. It was published at the time in *Ten.8*'s *Critical Decade: Black British Photography in the 80s* (vol.2, no.3), accompanied by Stuart Hall's essay on representation. Gregory is associated with the Black British photography movement, alongside artists such as Sunil Gupta and Roshini Kempadoo, who were also considering notions of cultural difference through their photography. Gregory has worked closely with Autograph, the Association of Black Photographers, with whom she continues to associate to this day. More recently, Gregory has exhibited in *A Tall Order*, at Rochdale Art Gallery, and undertook a commission at William Morris Gallery in 2022. Gregory is editor of the book *Shining Lights: Black Women Photographers in 1980s–90s Britain* (published 2024) in which her work also features.

JOY GREGORY

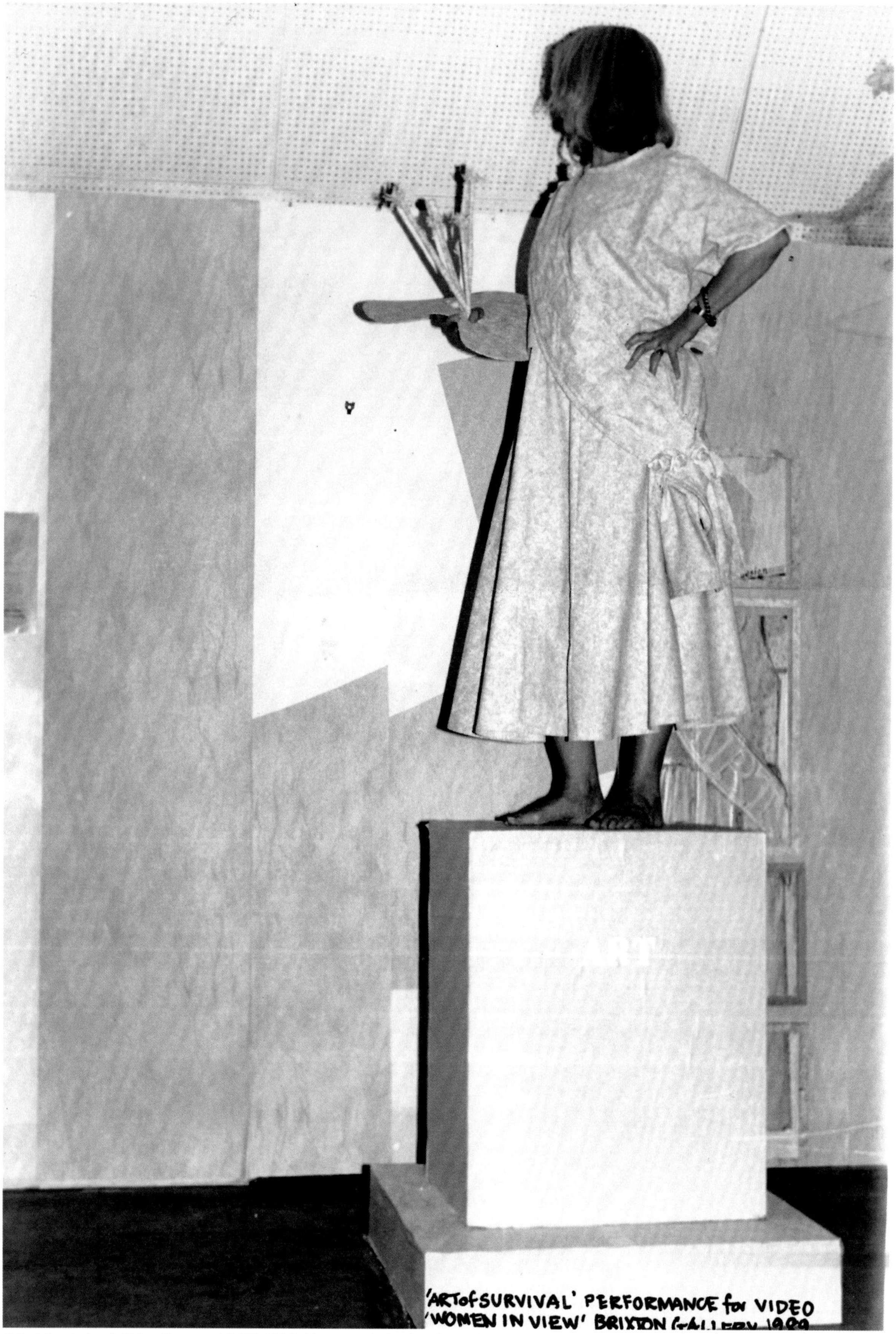

Art of Survival – A Living Monument 1987. Skirt, blouse, sash, handmade textile, paint palette and textile brushes. Various dimensions

ARTISTS STATEMENT

ART OF SURVIVAL - A Living Monument

Monuments commemorating artists are all too few, and the recognition of living art difficult. Here and there we see the heroic form of a dead artist, or a tasteful symbolic representation of FINE ART made of permanent materials and erected with due ceremony in the best possible place.

The living artist is too busy creating to wait until death for recognition.

A NEW WORK, therefore has been declared. The artist has become A LIVING MONUMENT.

It is now becoming customary to appreciate that this MONUMENT is constructed entirely of impermanent materials, and appears without ceremony, or with undue ceremony in the worst possible places - a LIVING MONUMENT to THE ART OF SURVIVAL.

signed, the artist

(or monument),

Kate Walker

copyright 1987

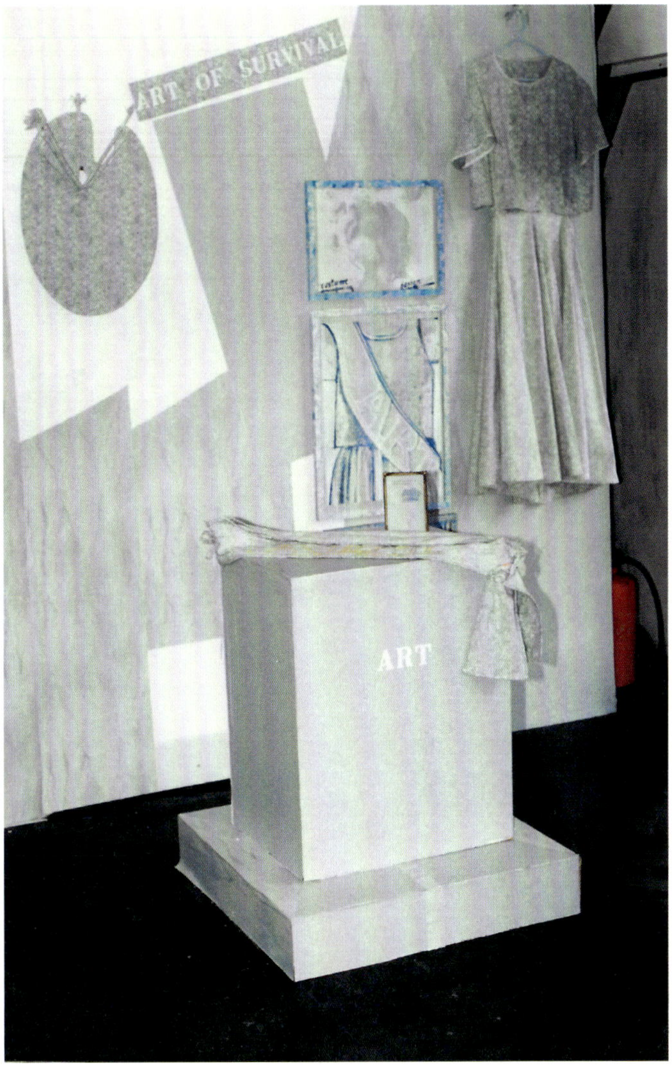

Born in Leeds, Kate Walker (1938–2015) attended Leeds College of Art and Sidney Webb College in London. Walker was an important figure within feminist art in the UK.
In 1974, inspired by the American feminist art project *Womanhouse*, she co-organised as part of the South London Art Group (S.L.A.G.) the immersive installation *A Woman's Place* at 14 Radnor Terrace, which was the site of the South London Women's Centre. In the same year, she showed a major installation and performance as part of the exhibition *Sweet Sixteen and Never Been Shown*, at the Women's Free Art Alliance, London. Walker was a founding member of the *Postal Art Event*, which started in 1975 when she and her friend Sally Gollop began to exchange artworks in the post (pp.64–5). The project expanded and by May of the following year, over a dozen women were exchanging homemade artworks by post. This culminated in the exhibition *A Portrait of the Artist as a Housewife* (also known as *Feministo*) at the ICA in 1977. In 1978–80 Walker co-organised, with Monica Ross and Su Richardson, the touring project *Fenix* which had multiple iterations across the UK and internationally (p.66).

Like many of her women artist peers, Walker found it difficult to gain a teaching position at an art school, despite her hugely varied and influential career, though she did go on to hold teaching jobs at Portsmouth Polytechnic, Brighton Polytechnic, Dartington Hall, and the men's prison HMP Belmarsh. In the 1990s Walker made the decision to stop making work.

Her 1987 work *Art of Survival – A Living Monument* saw the artist stood atop a plinth, dressed in a handmade costume with an artist's palette and brushes, all made from cloth printed with a pattern to look like granite. She performed the role of a monument to women artists. The work has been re-visited for the *Women in Revolt!* exhibition, with kind permission from the artist's family.

KATE WALKER

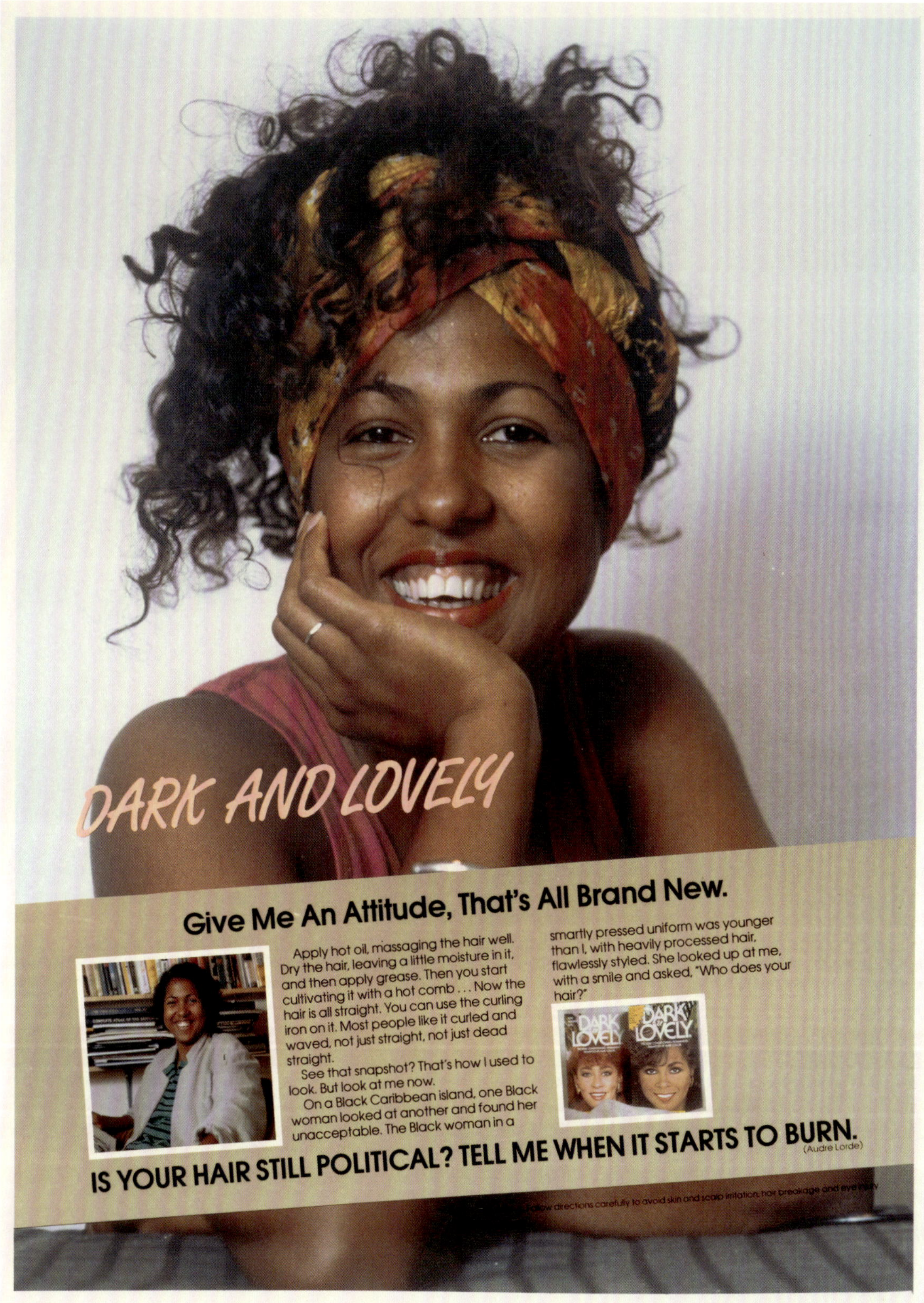

Untitled, from the series *Presence* 1990. 1 of 4 photographs 38.5 × 30

Roshini Kempadoo was born in Sussex in 1959 but spent her formative years in Guyana and other Caribbean countries. In England, she completed an MA in photographic studies at the University of Derby and a PhD at Goldsmiths College. Kempadoo describes herself as a photographer, media artist and scholar and is active in all fields, making and exhibiting art and working as a professor at the University of Westminster School of Arts, London. She characterises her artworks as 'factual and fictional re-imaginings of everyday experiences, histories and memories by Caribbean persons and its diaspora'.

Between 1983 and 2003 Kempadoo was part of Format Photographers Agency where she specialised in documenting Black communities, women's groups and trade union activity. In the late 1980s she was instrumental in founding the Association of Black Photographers (now Autograph ABP) and was actively involved in developing the photography magazine *Ten.8*. More recently, she has exhibited in *Life Between Islands: Caribbean-British Art 1950s – Now* (Tate Britain, 2021–2), and *Thirteen Ways of Looking* (Herbert Art Gallery, Coventry, 2020). She published the monograph *Creole in the Archive: Imagery, Presence and Location of the Caribbean Figure* in 2016.

Kempadoo lives and works in London.

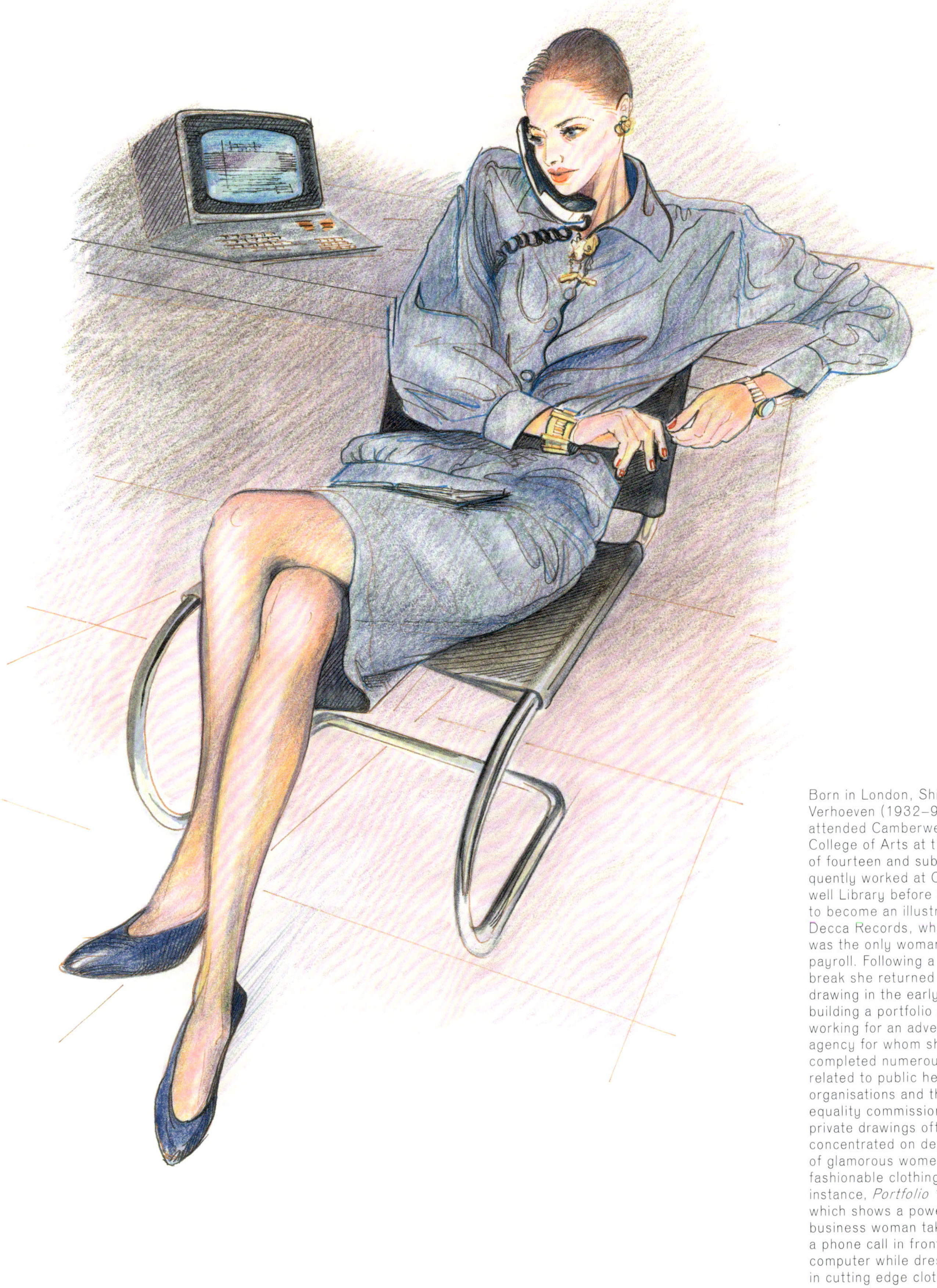

Born in London, Shirley Verhoeven (1932–99) attended Camberwell College of Arts at the age of fourteen and subsequently worked at Camberwell Library before moving to become an illustrator at Decca Records, where she was the only woman on the payroll. Following a career break she returned to drawing in the early 1980s, building a portfolio and working for an advertising agency for whom she completed numerous jobs related to public health organisations and the racial equality commission. Her private drawings often concentrated on depictions of glamorous women in fashionable clothing. For instance, *Portfolio* 1989, which shows a powerful business woman taking a phone call in front of her computer while dressed in cutting edge clothing of the late 1980s.

Portfolio 1989. Pen and coloured pencil on paper 32 × 29.5

SHIRLEY VERHOEVEN

WHAT IS THE STRATEGY?

TOWARDS BREAKING THE CYCLE

AMRITA DHALLU

> in order not to re/re/invent the wheel it is perhaps important to outline the chronology of the work and exhibitions of the black woman artist … not as a list but as a series of events and coincidences, of opportunities lost and taken, of careers made and destroyed.
>
> Lubaina Himid[2]

I first came across *Passion: Discourses on Blackwomen's Creativity*, edited by Maud Sulter, in my early twenties. It was published in 1990 by Urban Fox Press, a platform which was established in the previous decade and co-run with Lubaina Himid. The book held my hand as I embarked upon my first years as an institutional curator. It was not intentionally handed to me; I stumbled across it while working at the Stuart Hall Library at Rivington Place. I immediately felt cheated – that I had been left in the dark about this published space of community and collaboration. This was my artistic lineage. Painters, sculptors, photographers, poets, actors, directors, scriptwriters, agitators, rebels. They were all there and had dared to envision a new world.

This living archive of radical women of African, Caribbean and Asian descent confirmed my conviction that I was part of a continuum of artists, yet they had been invisible to me. This publication became a reparative balm. Published at the tail end of the 'critical decade' of the 1980s,[3] *Passion* is an anthology which urgently seeks to represent a sprawling network of diasporic feminist practitioners, and to confront the amnesia around the ongoing contributions of women artists of colour within British cultural spaces.

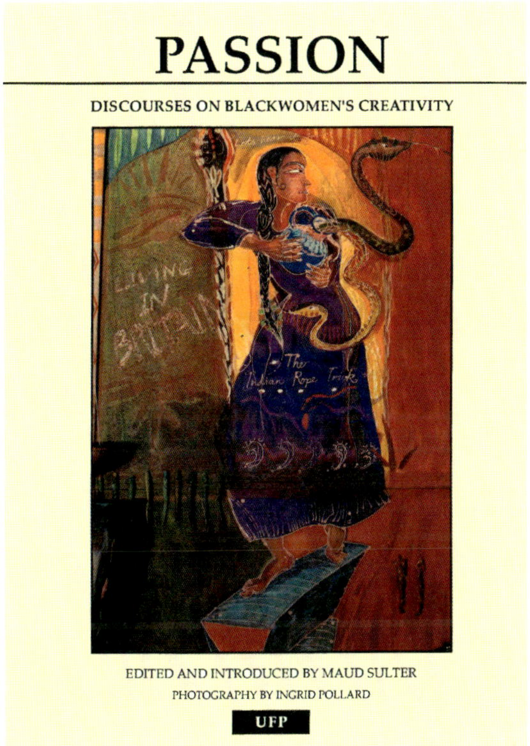

Maud Sulter's *Passion: Discourses on Blackwomen's Creativity*, published in 1990, featuring artwork by Nina Edge (see p.249).

After months of trawling through those pages, rereading the testimonies of each artist, I travelled to Preston to explore the Making Histories Visible archive at the University of Central Lancashire and to meet its instigator, Lubaina Himid. Her fervent advice resonated with calls from the archive, from *Women of Colour Index* reading groups and from *Passion* itself: a chorus of voices urging me to seek out my peers and learn everything I could about their practices and creative desires. In response, I created a network of emerging diasporic artists, curators, teachers and writers.[4] Worlding was a key tool embraced by Black women artists: to create the community that you seek.[5] *Passion* is a call to action, documenting the key strategies of Black women artists during the 1980s: archive, write and curate *with* passion, because your life depends on it.

Central to *Passion* was Maud Sulter's edict: 'we must break the cycle of reinventing the wheel'.[6] This sentiment reverberates throughout the book, as if the artists are speaking to one another and echoing each other's concerns

1 The title of this piece comes from Lubaina Himid, 'Mapping: A Decade of Black Women Artists 1980–1990.' This question formed part of the interpretation for Lubaina Himid's monographic exhibition at Tate Modern in 2021. It referred to the acts of debating and strategising that are central to Himid's work, where women 'are working out complicated futures together'. See Lubaina Himid's exhibition guide, https://www.tate.org.uk/whats-on/tate-modern/lubaina-himid/exhibition-guide, accessed 6 Aug. 2023.
2 Lubaina Himid, 'Mapping: A Decade of Black Women Artists 1980–1990', in Maud Sulter (ed.), *Passion: Discourses on Blackwomen's Creativity*, Hebden Bridge 1990, p.64.
3 Elizabeth Robles, 'Reframing Art History', in Nick Aikens and Elizabeth Robles (eds.), *The Place is Here: The Work of Black Artists in 1980s Britain*, Berlin 2019, p.91.
4 This diasporic network was funded by Artquest and hosted by Camden Arts Centre in 2018–19. *The PEER FORUM* network includes Kobby Adi, Danielle Brathwaite-Shirley, Tamar Clarke-Brown, Priya Jay, Georgia Lucas-Going, Hamed Maiye, Zarina Muhammad, Zeinab Saleh, Ebun Sodipo and Rosa-Johan Uddoh. We were mentored by artists Helen Cammock, Imran Perretta and Morgan Quaintance and curators Amanprit Sandhu, Nisha Matthew and Rahila Haque.
5 During this era, 'Black' was used as a self-defining political marker that aligned artists of African and Asian descent due to shared histories of colonial subjugation.
6 Maud Sulter, 'Preface', in Sulter 1990, p.10.

for the future. Reading this anthology crystallised a strong desire within me to avoid repeating this cycle again and again. However, in order to ensure that Sulter's words have a lasting influence, we must understand the obstacles that have consistently been imposed upon Black women's creativity. What was preventing their legacies from reaching future generations, causing the archive to unravel at the seams? What happened when this dialogical, diasporic feminist art world clashed with British institutional structures? In reviewing the artists' reflections, we must attend to the pain and loss associated with making these histories visible in spaces that are predicated on the erasure of their experiences, in the service of building a nation's image.

We must also ask when our encounters with these radical practices will shift from being happy accidents to intentional acts of sharing counter-histories and knowledges. How can we embed feminist insurgency into the structures of our cultural institutions?[7]

> We were not a movement, or a group or a sisterhood or even close friends but instead a fluid set of women who were not prepared to be herded into a single way of expressing ourselves.
>
> Lubaina Himid[8]

Curating was an essential strategy for the artists who initiated independent spaces to support and sustain one another's creative practices in hostile and austere urban landscapes. Reflecting on the impact of *The Thin Black Line*, the ICA's groundbreaking 1985 exhibition of Black and Asian women artists, Himid expressed the need to create spaces that enabled the multiplicity of diasporic feminist creativity, particularly in the face of these artists' exclusion by institutional fields of power. Organised by Himid, *The Thin Black Line* featured the work of eleven artists: Brenda Agard, Sutapa Biswas, Sonia Boyce, Chila Kumari Singh Burman, Jennifer Comrie, Claudette Johnson, Ingrid Pollard, Veronica Ryan, Marlene Smith, Maud Sulter and Himid herself. Despite proposing to take over the main gallery spaces, including in-between spaces such as the stairwell and concourse, Himid was only given the corridor space for this historic exhibition.

By curating exhibitions such as this, as well as *Five Black Women* (Africa Centre, London, 1983) and *Black Woman Time Now* (Battersea Arts Centre, 1983–4), and by establishing the independent publishing house Urban Fox Press and gallery spaces such as Elbow Room in London (1986–8), Himid seized the means of production. She used curatorial strategies which allowed for free expression, 'unleas[hing] a torrent of energetic and optimistic women into the exhibiting world who would go on to influence the way museums, collections and educators think about creative communication with audiences'.[9]

> It remind[ed] me of all the gatherings with so many different women coming together at our houses, at galleries, at event spaces. That sense of a cornucopia of Black women bursting out into what was a very white space, and submerging it with images of our realities. The daring and the energy really came across to me.
>
> Claudette Johnson[10]

7 Sonia Boyce and Dorothy Price, 'Dearly Beloved or Unrequited?: To be "Black" in Art's Histories', *Art History: Journal of the Association for Art History*, vol.44, no.3, June 2021, pp.468–80, p.477.

8 Lubaina Himid, 'Letters to Susan', in Lubaina Himid (ed.), *Thin Black Line(s)*, exh. cat., University of Central Lancashire, Preston 2011, p.12.

9 Ibid.

10 Claudette Johnson discussing *The Thin Black Line* with Marlene Smith in: 'Finding the Room Next to Mine: Marlene Smith in Conversation with Claudette Johnson', in Nana Adusei-Poku (ed.), *Reshaping the Field: Arts of the African Diasporas on Display*, London 2022, p.185.

11 Amber Esseiva, 'Black Girl: A Plot and a Promise', in Adusei-Poku (ed.) 2022, p.209.
12 Waldemar Januszczak, 'Anger at Hand', *Guardian*, Arts Section, 27 Nov. 1985, p.23.
13 Marlene Smith quoted in Himid 2011, p.22.
14 Maud Sulter, 'Call and Response', *Art History: Journal of the Association for Art History*, vol.44, no.3, June 2021, pp.598–602, p.601.
15 Lubaina Himid, 'Afterward', in *The Thin Black Line*, Hebden Bridge 1989, p.12.
16 'Interview with Lubaina Himid', in Amrita Dhallu (ed.), *Now Let Us Shift*, London 2019, p.5, https://chisenhale.org.uk/wp-content/uploads/Chisenhale-Research_Now-let-us-shift-1.pdf, accessed 6 Aug. 2023.
17 Quoted in Robles 2019, p.98.

As curator Amber Esseiva reminds us, 'whether the institution is newly founded or centuries old, we are entering into a structure that is somewhat predetermined, despite all promises; that it is designed to function in ways that are not always revealed'.[11] While collaborating with Lubaina Himid on her 2021–2 solo show at Tate Modern, I witnessed her instinct to subvert cultural infrastructure, and her determination to create embodied, nourishing spaces within the museum. She tasked us with creating curved structures to house delicate tin metal squares, painted vibrantly with text lifted from health and safety manuals. This spatial gesture aimed to reveal the invisibilised histories of labour and capital embedded in the architecture of the buildings that represent British culture.

I feel the same intention in Himid's acts of curating the work of Black and Asian women artists in other spaces. More than an exhibition, *The Thin Black Line* was also a spatial intervention: a rupture, a deep fissure in the façade of the white cube containing the impenetrable frame of the British art canon, through which a feminist counter-history burst. Rather than embrace the exhibition's 'torrent' of energy, however, the art establishment feared it: critics labelled the exhibition 'barely controlled fury'[12] and the artists 'cultural terrorist[s]'.[13]

> Being written out of history can happen to you. There is no safety in collusion with those who want to oppress our art and suppress our voices. They will turn their weapon on you, and who will be there to help you if your contemporaries no longer exist?
> Maud Sulter[14]

Despite Himid's call to develop a strategy for the 1990s,[15] this group of ferocious artists were largely forced into obscurity, their legacies suppressed through the 'wilderness years'. As she explains:

> The 1990s were quite difficult because although we were making and showing work in galleries both here and in the US, it wasn't really acknowledged in a public way. No one was buying or collecting it and, although some very eminent art historians – notably Griselda Pollock – were writing about the work, the impact was quite hidden. Many artists died, gave up or became embroiled in pointless arguments with mainstream organisations.[16]

I hold these words in mind when examining Himid's *Thin Black Line(s): Moments and Connections* 2011 (p.290). In this cartographic interpretation of the 1980s, which mimics the London Underground map, art spaces, exhibitions and peer groups intersect with the thin black line of women artists. Rather than conceiving of this period of art as a linear moment in time, Himid presents it as an expansive network, one that art historian Ella Spencer-Mills interprets as 'infinite possibilities for movement through and across a vast array of routes'.[17] While we observe an unimpeded circulatory system of diasporic feminist creativity, it immediately becomes enmeshed with the institutional and ideological powers that enforced what Himid saw as 'opportunities lost and taken, of careers made and destroyed'.

Moments and Connections visualises the insistent processes of worlding led by Black and Asian women artists in the 1980s and its associated labour: curating exhibitions, publishing books and magazines, initiating archives,

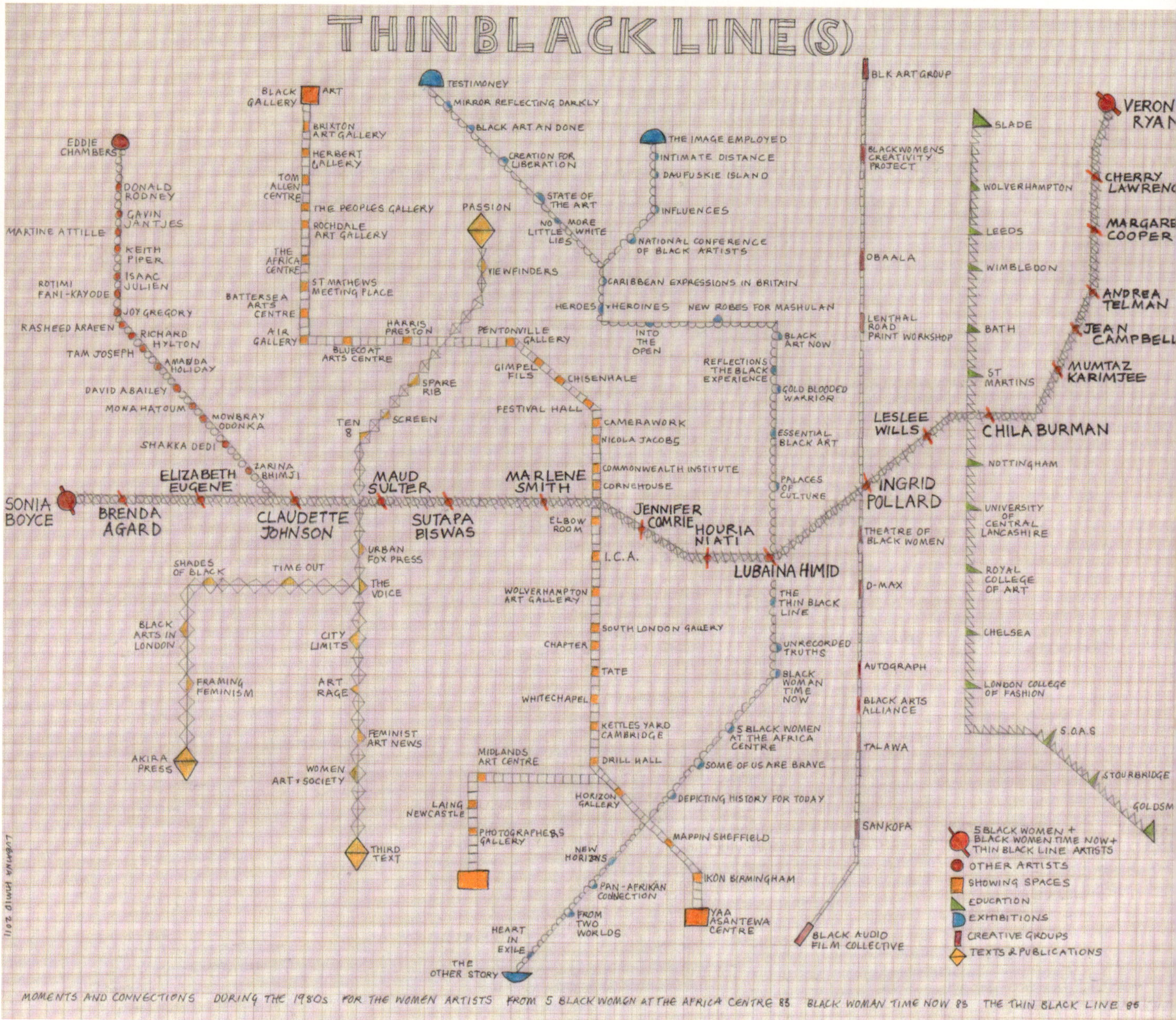

Lubaina Himid *Thin Black Line(s): Moments and Connections* 2011. Coloured pencil on paper 62 × 74.7

sitting on acquisitions panels and advisory boards. This would lead to exhaustion and burnout, as Sutapa Biswas and Marlene Smith described in 1988:

> Our energies are diffused because we have to work simultaneously on many different fronts. We must make our images, organise exhibitions, be art critics, historians, administrators, and speakers. We must be the watchdogs of art establishment bureaucracies; sitting as individuals on various panels, as a means of ensuring that Black people are not overlooked. The list is endless.[18]

Black women artists imagined and established their own art world and the generous discourse around it, however, as Himid observed, while 'having a multiplicity of histories should have been a strength … we left it to those that made the stuff and remained ignorant about what the real agenda of the dominant institutions might be'.[19]

> We created something, named it, and then allowed it to be un-named and thus de-funded.
>
> Lubaina Himid[20]

To build diasporic feminist cultural spaces, one must seamlessly merge a deep understanding of the past (as shaped by colonial histories) with both a drive to capture the present and the desire to reach future generations. Black and Asian women artists, particularly those who were instrumental in establishing public curatorial and publishing platforms, were therefore engaged in the act of building and *re-building. Over and over.*

If we return to Sulter's provocation about 'break[ing] the cycle of reinventing the wheel', it is clear why we still find ourselves in a loop of rediscovering a transnational legacy of diasporic feminist creativity. The sturdy support offered to me by *Passion* has not been allowed to integrate into the cultural infrastructure within which I work. This is not because they are incompatible with one another; rather, it is due to the lack of consistent critical and curatorial support systems for these artists. We must break the pattern of reigniting these institutional strategies once again at the turn of every new decade.

I find myself considering the feminist practice of refusal – the limits around one's willingness to simply accept and comply.[21] Is *this* the strategy? We must consider the practice of refusal so that we do not face yet another decade in the pernicious cycle of building up and tearing down supportive structures for diasporic feminism. The words of Audre Lorde echo and rebound: *For the master's tools will never dismantle the master's house.*[22] If the museum is the master's house, then perhaps we must refuse to shrink ourselves down into spaces that cannot hold us as we shift and change.[23]

I am taken back to a 2018 performance by the British artist Rosa-Johan Uddoh. Standing in the central space of Tate Britain, in front of the cold, hard whiteness of Henry Moore's reclining nude, she called on the audience to 'face your institution and sing!'[24] Now is the time to audaciously sing along with her, to bring about Sulter's vision of a 'passionate future':[25]

I've got to make like Lubaina
And set myself free!
Get myself my own big building, reject complicity!
Get on, get out and archive your lives, for the library![26]

18 Quoted in Adelaide Bannerman, 'Introduction', in David A. Bailey, Ian Baucom, and Sonia Boyce (eds.), *Shades of Black: Assembling Black Arts in 1980s Britain*, Durham, NC 2005, p.263.
19 Lubaina Himid, 'Inside the Invisible: For/Getting Strategy', in David A. Bailey, Ian Baucom, and Sonia Boyce (eds.), *Shades of Black: Assembling Black Arts in 1980s Britain*, Durham, NC 2005, p.42.
20 Ibid., p.41.
21 This idea emerged from a conversation between writer Lola Olufemi and historian and co-founder of the Organisation of Women of African and Asian Descent (OWAAD) Stella Dadzie, in relation to the legacies of Black feminist organising in the UK. See https://www.youtube.com/watch?v=WgTLHmT5hDY, accessed 6 Aug. 2023.
22 Audre Lorde, 'The Master's Tools Will Never Dismantle the Master's House', in *Your Silence Will Not Protect You*, London 2017, p.91.
23 Himid 2005, p.42.
24 Rosa-Johan Uddoh, 'Her Master's Tools', in *Practice Makes Perfect*, London 2022, p.65.
25 Sulter 2021, p.602.
26 Uddoh 2022, p.66.

The author would like to thank her dear friend and colleague Zoe Bromberg-McCarthy who has generously supported, critiqued and edited this text.

EXHIBITED WORKS

The works listed here are those featured in the Tate Britain exhibition. Works are listed alphabetically by artist, and chronologically within. Measurements of works are given in cm, height before width and depth. Page references to works illustrated are given at the end of the entries. All information was correct at the time of printing

BRENDA AGARD
1961–2012

Untitled from the series *Portrait of Black Women* 1985, reprinted 2023
2 photographs
40.5 × 30.5 (each)
The Brenda Agard Estate
p.232

LYNDA AGARD
b.1964

Portrait of Brenda 1985, reprinted 2023
Photograph
21 × 25
The Brenda Agard Estate

SAM AINSLEY
b.1950

Warrior Woman V: The Artist 1986
Acrylic paint on canvas with cotton binding
346.5 × 217.5
National Galleries of Scotland. Purchased 1987
p.179

SIMONE ALEXANDER
b.1964

Beyond the Nursey Door (When You Are Queen) 1987
Oil paint on canvas
180 × 120
Courtesy Simone Alexander
p.233

BOBBY BAKER
b.1950

An Edible Family in a Mobile Home 1976, remade 2023
Prefabricated house, newspapers and magazines, chicken wire, wire cabling, biscuits, fruitcake, coconut cake, chocolate cake, fairy cakes, savoury snacks, boxes of raisins, meringue, icing, napkins, enamel bath, sink, toilet, fridge, cooker, chest of drawers, television, radios, Swiss cuckoo clock, wooden cot, chair, double bed, duvet, pillows, dressmaker's dummy, tablecloth skirt, teapot, cake stand, Perspex, fabric, wooden stool
304 × 760 × 580
Presented by Daily Life Ltd. in Partnership with Tate, Whitworth and Idle Women. Supported using public funding by the National Lottery through Arts Council England

Documentation of An Edible Family in a Mobile Home 1976, reprinted 2023
5 photographs
29.7 × 42 (each)
Courtesy of the artist, Daily Life Ltd. and Andrew Whittuck
p.114

An Edible Family in a Mobile Home, at Bobby Baker's prefab Acme house in Conder Street, London, E1 1976, reprinted 2023
Photograph
29.7 × 42
Courtesy of the artist, Daily Life Ltd. and Andrew Whittuck.
p.115

ANNE BEAN
b.1950

Heat 1974–7
9 chemically altered and distressed gelatin silver prints from the performance *Elemental (Heat)*, on painted wood, glass and painted card
81.5 × 66.5 × 2.5 (overall)
England & Co. Gallery, London
p.76

Shouting 'Mortality' as I Drown 1977
Two sets of 9 photographs mounted on paper
39.5 × 27 (each)
England & Co. Gallery, London
p.77

ZARINA BHIMJI
b.1963

In Response to the F-Stops Exhibition (For the White Feminists) 1986
9 copper-toned photographs and printed texts
270 × 330 (overall)
Courtesy of the artist
p.239

JENNIFER BINNIE
b.1958

Woman 1983
Oil paint on canvas with decorated branch
220 × 88 × 6
Courtesy of the artist
p.156

GINA BIRCH
b.1955

3 Minute Scream 1977
Super 8 film, shown as digital video; colour, sound
2 min, 50 sec
Courtesy of the artist
p.128

SUTAPA BISWAS
b.1962

Kali 1983–5
Video; colour and sound (stereo)
23 min, 24 sec
Tate. Presented by the artist 2012 and 2017, accessioned 2018
p.225

Housewives with Steak Knives 1985
Oil paint, acrylic paint and pastel on paper, mounted on canvas
246 × 222 × 2.5
Bradford District Museums and Galleries, CBMDC
p.224

TESSA BOFFIN
1960–93

Untitled #1– #5 from the series *Angelic Rebels, Lesbians and Safer Sex* 1989, reprinted 2022
5 photographs; gelatin silver prints on paper
50.8 × 40.6; 47.9 × 37.8; 48.1 × 37.8
Courtesy of Hales London and New York, the Estate of Tessa Boffin and the Gupta+Singh Archive
pp.266–7

SONIA BOYCE
b.1962

Rice n Peas 1982
Pastel on paper
137 × 102
Private collection
p.226

CHILA KUMARI SINGH BURMAN
b.1957

Splatter 1979
Poster paint on paper
88.6 × 63.2
Courtesy of the artist
p.149

Splodge 1979
Poster paint on paper
71.2 × 50.8
Courtesy of the artist

If There is No Struggle, There is No Progress – Uprisings 1981
Etching, lithograph and paint on paper
61.2 × 81.2
Tate. Presented by Tate Members 2014

Militant Women 1982
Photo-etching and aquatint on paper
40.6 × 99.5
Tate. Presented by Tate Members 2014
pp.216–17

Solidarity with Sisters 1981
Screenprint on paper
71 × 81
Courtesy of the artist

Three Mug Shots in a Row 1982
Photo-etching and aquatint on paper
16.8 × 81.5
Tate. Presented by Tate Members 2014
pp.216–17

Triptych No Nukes 1982
Etching, aquatint and screenprint on paper
105.5 × 195.5 × 1.3
Tate. Presented by Tate Members 2014

SHIRLEY CAMERON
b.1944

Rabbits – the Pregnant Bunny Girl, Mrs Rabbits and Woman as Animal 1974, printed 2023
7 photographs
29.7 × 42 (each)
Courtesy of the artist
p.79

SHIRLEY CAMERON
b.1944
EVELYN SILVER
b.1949

The Collapsible Cruise Missile – Brides Against the Bomb 1983
Wood
186.5 × 43 × 103.5
Courtesy of Shirley Cameron and Evelyn Silver

THALIA CAMPBELL
b.1937

Replica of a banner originally made by Thalia Campbell, Lucy Campbell and Hannah Tyrell for the march from Cardiff to Greenham Common, 27 August to 5 September 1981 c.1981
Cotton, nylon and coloured marker pen
156 × 205
Lent by Amgueddfa Cymru – Museum Wales. Donated by Thalia Campbell, 2019
p.184

Thatcher's Thugs 1984
Mixed fabrics
177 × 119
Thalia Campbell designs courtesy of The Peace Museum, Bradford
p.185

HELEN CHADWICK
1953 –96

In the Kitchen 1977
12 photographs;pigment prints
41 × 30.5 (each)
Courtesy of Richard Saltoun Gallery, London and Rome
p.113

JUDY CLARK
b.1949

Cycle 1973
Wood, Perspex contraceptive pills, menstrual blood
68.7 × 67.6 (overall)
Arts Council Collection, Southbank Centre, London
p.102

JENNIFER COMRIE
b.1960

Conflict 1985
Photocopy, pastels, graphite, metal needle, and cotton thread on paper
73.5 × 54
Arts Council Collection, Southbank Centre, London
p.220

CAROLINE COON
b.1945

Ari Up, lead singer of The Slits 1977, reprinted 2023
Photograph
20.3 × 25.5
Courtesy the artist and Stephen Friedman Gallery

BLACK and WHITE UNITE: An anti-racism demonstration outside National Front leader Martin Webster's house, 1977. From Right to Left: Mykaell Riley (Steel Pulse), Mick Jones (The Clash), Glen Matlock (The Sex Pistols), Andy Bowen (Steel Pulse) and Paul Simonon (The Clash) 1977, reprinted 2023
Photograph
25.5 × 20.3
Courtesy the artist and Stephen Friedman Gallery London and New York
p.130

In the dressing room, Cardiff, June 1977. Ari Up, lead singer of The Slits, 'teasing' her hair as Paul Simonon (The Clash bassist) looks on 1977, reprinted 2023
Photograph
20.3 × 25.5
Courtesy the artist and Stephen Friedman Gallery London and New York

Post House Hotel, Cardiff, June 1977. The Slits-Viv Albertine (guitar), Palmolive (drummer), Tessa Pollitt (bass) and Ari Up (lead singer) – in hotel reception waiting to be taken to the gig 1977
Photograph
20.3 × 25.5
Courtesy the artist and Stephen Friedman Gallery London and New York
p.131

Ari Up in her Silver Jubilee knickers Sussex University, Brighton, 15th June 1977 1977, reprinted 2023
Photograph
20.3 × 25.5
Courtesy the artist and Stephen Friedman Gallery London and New York

Punk fans on the first Rock Against Racism march, from Trafalgar Square to the concert in Victoria Park in Hackney in April 1978. The concert featured The Clash, Steel Pulse, Tom Robinson Band, X-Ray Spex, Jimmy Pursey (from Sham 69), and Patrik Fitzgerald 1978, reprinted 2023
Photograph
25.5 × 20.3
Courtesy the artist and Stephen Friedman Gallery London and New York
p.131

Between Parades 1985
Oil paint on canvas
122 × 152
Private collection. Courtesy Stephen Friedman Gallery London and New York
p.145

EILEEN COOPER
b.1953

Figures on a Ladder 1979
Charcoal and pastel on paper
137 × 101.5
Courtesy of the artist
p.125

SUE CROCKFORD
1943–2019

A Woman's Place 1972
16mm film; shown as digital video; black and white, sound
32 min, 24 sec
Estate of Sue Crockford
p.81

STELLA DADZIE
b.1952

Motherland c.1984
Watercolour, gold foil and sand on card
60.5 × 41.5
Courtesy of the artist
p.243

JOANNA DAVIS
b.1945
LIS RHODES
b.1942

Ironing to Greenham 1983
16mm film, shown as digital video; colour, sound, 1 min
Cinenova Distribution
p.183

Goose and Common 1983
16mm film, shown as digital video; colour, sound
1 min
Cinenova Distribution

No.8 Bus 1983
16mm film, shown as digital video; colour, sound
1 min
Cinenova Distribution

POULOMI DESAI
b.1965

Nothing Between Denial and Acceptance 1983, reprinted 2023
2 photographs
42 × 29.7 (each)
Courtesy of the artist
p.151

Our Asian Lesbian Gay Black bodies, our tea, our chintz 1989
5 photographs
25.4 × 20.3 (each)
Courtesy of the artist
pp.272–3

VIVIENNE DICK
b.1950

Two Little Pigeons 1990
Super 8 film, shown as digital video; colour, sound
4 min, 38 sec
Courtesy of the artist and LUX, London
p.276

NINA EDGE
b.1962

Snakes and Ladders 1985
Batik on paper mounted on board, ceramics, string, wooden plinths and handwritten text on paper
250 × 177 × 65
Courtesy the artist
p.249

Chips on Her Shoulders, Her Arms Fell Off 1986
Permanent marker and oil crayon on cartridge paper on gold board
40.2 × 26.7
Courtesy of the artist
p.248

Paki Ride Home on a Piece of Spit 1986
Permanent marker and oil crayon on cartridge paper on gold board
40.2 × 26.7
Courtesy of the artist
p.248

Searching for Flowers in the Tandoori Garden 1986, remade 2023
Digital print on board.
40.5 × 26.5
Courtesy of the artist
p.248 (earlier iteration)

Trying Not to Offend My Parents 1986
Permanent marker and oil crayon on cartridge paper on gold board
40.5 × 26.5
Courtesy of the artist
p.248

MARIANNE ELLIOTT-SAID (AKA POLY STYRENE)
1957–2011

Germ-Free Adolescents 1977
Comic book cuttings, felt-tip pen, pill packet and glue tube on paper
21 × 29
Courtesy of the Poly Styrene Estate and Archive
p.148

CATHERINE ELWES
b.1952

Chevelure 1977
Photograph
25.5 × 18
Courtesy of the artist
p.78

Menstruation 1 1979
Photographs and text on paper
85 × 60
Courtesy of the artist
p.100

ROSE ENGLISH
b.1950

Study for a Divertissement: Diana and Porcelain Lace Veil 1973
5 photographs; C-prints on paper
25 × 20 (one photo); 14 × 11 (4 photos)
Courtesy of Richard Saltoun Gallery, London and Rome

Study for a Divertissement: Jo and Porcelain sheet with breasts, yoni and coverlet with hands 1973
2 photographs; C-prints on paper
13.5 × 11 (each)
Courtesy of Richard Saltoun Gallery, London and Rome
p.74

Study for a Divertissement: Porcelain Dancer 1, 3 and *4* 1973
Porcelain and enamel
22.9 × 17.8 × 2.5; 22.9 × 15.2 × 1.9 and 22 × 11.5 × 2
Courtesy of Richard Saltoun Gallery, London and Rome
p.74

Small Porcelain Pieces (Collage) 1973
Two collages; C-prints on paper
35 × 40 (each)
Courtesy of Richard Saltoun Gallery, London and Rome
p.75

AILEEN FERRIDAY
b.1943

Moira 1–4 1975
4 photographs; gelatin silver prints on paper
25.6 × 21; 22.9 × 27.4; 23.2 × 22.3; 25.6 × 21.1
Arts Council Collection, Southbank Centre, London
p.117

ROSE FINN-KELCEY
1945–2014

Flags (documentary footage featuring 'Here is a Gale Warning' and 'Fog') 1971
16mm film; shown digitally; colour and black and white, silent
5 min, 43 sec
Courtesy of the Estate of Rose Finn-Kelcey and Kate MacGarry

Here is a Gale Warning 1971, remake 2023
Black bunting and silver tissue
114 × 209
Courtesy of the Estate of Rose Finn-Kelcey and Kate MacGarry
p.2

Divided Self (Speakers' Corner) 1974–2011
Gelatin silver print on aluminium
51.2 × 77.8
Courtesy of the Estate of Rose Finn-Kelcey and Kate MacGarry
p.73

FORMAT PHOTOGRAPHERS
1983–2003

(MELANIE FRIEND)
b.1957

Greenham Common protest 1984, reprinted 2023
Photograph
40.6 × 30.5
Format Photographers Archive, Bishopsgate Institute
p.174

Greenham Common 1985, reprinted 2023
Photograph
30.5 × 40.6
Format Photographers Archive, Bishopsgate Institute
p.177

Join the Scottish Anti-Racist Movement 1980s, reprinted 2023
Photograph
25.4 × 20.3
Format Photographers Archive, Bishopsgate Institute
p.25

(SHEILA GRAY)
b.1948

Jayaben Desai at the Grunwick Strike 1976, reprinted 2023
Photograph
40.6 × 30.5
Format Photographers Archive, Bishopsgate Institute

Jayaben Desai, leader of the strike at the Grunwick photo processing lab 1976, reprinted 2023
Photograph
30.5 × 40.6
Format Photographers Archive, Bishopsgate Institute
p.202

Picket of a 'pro-life' meeting at the Royal Albert Hall, London 1990, reprinted 2023
Photograph
20.3 × 25.4
Format Photographers Archive, Bishopsgate Institute

(PAM ISHERWOOD)
b.1949

Angry, Manhating, Lesbian, & Proud 1980s, reprinted 2023
Photograph
40.6 × 30.5
Format Photographers Archive, Bishopsgate Institute
p.29

Lesbian Liberation 1981, reprinted 2023
Photograph
40.6 × 30.5
Format Photographers Archive, Bishopsgate Institute

'Brides Against the Bomb' (performance by Shirley Cameron and Evelyn Silver at Greenham Common Women's Peace Camp) 1983, reprinted 2023
Photograph
40.6 × 30.5
Format Photographers Archive, Bishopsgate Institute
p.173

Picket outside Conservative Party Conference in Blackpool 1983, reprinted 2023
Photograph
20.3 × 25.4
Format Photographers Archive, Bishopsgate Institute
p.211

Lesbians Against Pit Closures 1984, reprinted 2023
Photograph
20.3 × 25.4
Format Photographers Archive, Bishopsgate Institute

Greenham Common Women's Peace Camp, Bailiffs removing women 1985, reprinted 2023
Photograph
30.5 × 40.6
Format Photographers Archive, Bishopsgate Institute
p.172

Lesbian Strength March, London (Denise Saunders and Femi Otitoju) 1985, reprinted 2023
Photograph
30.5 × 40.6
Format Photographers Archive, Bishopsgate Institute
p.255

Demonstration against police violence 1980s, reprinted 2023
Photograph
25.4 × 20.3
Format Photographers Archive, Bishopsgate Institute

Disability Rights March 1980s, reprinted 2023
Photograph
20.3 × 25.4
Format Photographers Archive, Bishopsgate Institute
p.253

Gay Pride 1980s, reprinted 2023
Photograph
30.5 × 40.6
Format Photographers Archive, Bishopsgate Institute

Gay Pride March 1980s, reprinted 2023
Photograph
40.6 × 30.5
Format Photographers Archive, Bishopsgate Institute

Lesbian Strength 1980s, reprinted 2023
Photograph
30.5 × 40.6
Format Photographers Archive, Bishopsgate Institute

Pride March 1980s, reprinted 2023
Photograph
30.5 × 40.6
Format Photographers Archive, Bishopsgate Institute
p.255

Pride March 1980s, reprinted 2023
Photograph
20.3 × 25.4
Format Photographers Archive, Bishopsgate Institute

Women Rise and Fight, Safety is Our Right 1980s, reprinted 2023
Photograph
25.4 × 20.3
Format Photographers Archive, Bishopsgate Institute

Protest against domestic violence and the murder of Vadana Patel by her husband in a police station 1991, reprinted 2023
Photograph
20.3 × 25.4
Format Photographers Archive, Bishopsgate Institute

(JENNY MATTHEWS)
b.1948

Women for Peace 1983, reprinted 2023
Photograph
30.5 × 40.6
Format Photographers Archive, Bishopsgate Institute
p.172

Miners' Strike Supporters 1984, reprinted 2023
Photograph
25.4 × 20.3
Format Photographers Archive, Bishopsgate Institute
p.171

(MAGGIE MURRAY)
b.1942

Demonstration with children from Market Nursery, Hayward Gallery, London 1979, reprinted 2023
Photograph
20.3 × 25.4
Format Photographers Archive, Bishopsgate Institute
p.91

Britain's Toy Factory Strike for Higher Pay 1983, reprinted 2023
Photograph
30.5 × 40.6
Format Photographers Archive, Bishopsgate Institute
p.80

Greenham Common Peace Camp 1983, reprinted 2023
Photograph
30.5 × 40.6
Format Photographers Archive, Bishopsgate Institute
p.174

Greenham Common Peace Camp, Reflect the Base action 1983, reprinted 2023
Photograph
30.5 × 40.6
Format Photographers Archive, Bishopsgate Institute

Women of Greenham Common Peace Camp invade the base to dance on the nuclear missile silos at dawn on New Year's Day 1983, reprinted 2023
Photograph
40.6 × 30.5
Format Photographers Archive, Bishopsgate Institute
p.176

Support for Miners – March on Parliament, London 1984, reprinted 2023
Photograph
20.3 × 25.4
Format Photographers Archive, Bishopsgate Institute
p.170

Women Against Pit Closures demonstration, London 1984, reprinted 2023
Photograph
25.4 × 20.3
Format Photographers Archive, Bishopsgate Institute
p.170

Poll Tax protest, Islington Town Hall, London 1990, reprinted 2023
2 photographs
25.4 × 20.3; 20.3 × 25.4
Format Photographers Archive, Bishopsgate Institute

Poll Tax protest, Parliament Square 1990, reprinted 2023
Photograph
25.4 × 20.3
Format Photographers Archive, Bishopsgate Institute

(JOANNE O'BRIEN)
b.1955

Miss World Contest, Royal Albert Hall, London 1970, reprinted 2023
3 photographs
20.3 × 25.4
Format Photographers Archive, Bishopsgate Institute

Black People's Day of Action, 2 March 1981, reprinted 2023
Photograph
25.4 × 20.3
Format Photographers Archive, Bishopsgate Institute

Greenham Common, Peace Camp Activist 1983, reprinted 2023, reprinted 2023
Photograph
30.5 × 40.6
Format Photographers Archive, Bishopsgate Institute
p.177

Afia Begum solidarity march, 4 May 1984, reprinted 2023
Photograph
20.3 × 25.4
Format Photographers Archive, Bishopsgate Institute

Coal Miners Strike Demonstration, London 1985, reprinted 2023
Photograph
25.4 × 20.3
Format Photographers Archive, Bishopsgate Institute

Picket outside the Daily Mail Ideal Home *exhibition, Olympia, London* 1988, reprinted 2023
Photograph
20.3 × 25.4
Format Photographers Archive, Bishopsgate Institute

Police at a protest 1980s, reprinted 2023
Photograph
20.3 × 25.4
Format Photographers Archive, Bishopsgate Institute
p.210

Stop the Murders 1980s, reprinted 2023
Photograph
25.4 × 20.3
Format Photographers Archive, Bishopsgate Institute
p.210

(RAISSA PAGE)
1932–2011
Dancing on the Silos at Dawn on New Year's Day 1983, reprinted 2023
Photograph
30.5 × 40.6
Format Photographers Archive, Bishopsgate Institute
p.172

Police accost a miner, Cresswell, Nottinghamshire 1984, reprinted 2023
Photograph
20.3 × 25.4
Format Photographers Archive, Bishopsgate Institute

(ANGELA PHILIPS)

Demonstration against the Miss World Contest, Royal Albert Hall, London 1970, reprinted 2023
Photograph
20.3 × 25.4
Format Photographers Archive, Bishopsgate Institute

Reclaim the Night demonstration, International Women's Day 1979, reprinted 2023
Photograph
20.3 × 25.4
Format Photographers Archive, Bishopsgate Institute

(BRENDA PRINCE)
b.1950

Embrace the Base, Greenham Common 1982, reprinted 2023
Photograph
30.5 × 40.6
Format Photographers Archive, Bishopsgate Institute
p.23

Greenham Common Women's Peace Camp 1982, reprinted 2023
Photograph
30.5 × 40.6
Format Photographers Archive, Bishopsgate Institute
p.172

Femi Otitoju at the Lesbian Strength March 1983
Photograph
30.5 × 40.6
Format Photographers Archive, Bishopsgate Institute

Protesting the death of Colin Roach in police custody 1983, reprinted 2023
Photograph
25.4 × 20.3
Format Photographers Archive, Bishopsgate Institute

Dot Hickling in striking miners community kitchen, Hucknall and Linby Colliery, Nottinghamshire 1984/85, reprinted 2023
Photograph
20.3 × 25.4
Format Photographers Archive, Bishopsgate Institute

Women's picket at Bevercotes Colliery 1985, reprinted 2023
Photograph
20.3 × 25.4
Format Photographers Archive, Bishopsgate Institute
p.171

Mass picket at Orgreave Coke Works, Nottinghamshire 1985, reprinted 2023
Photograph
20.3 × 25.4
Format Photographers Archive, Bishopsgate Institute

Staff of the London Lesbian and Gay Centre, Cowcross Street 1985, reprinted 2023
Photograph
20.3 × 25.4
Format Photographers Archive, Bishopsgate Institute

Stop Clause 27 1987, reprinted 2023
Photograph
40.6 × 30.5
Format Photographers Archive, Bishopsgate Institute
p.254

Elsa Beckett and partner, founder members of 'Gemma' 1980s, reprinted 2023
Photograph
20.3 × 25.4
Format Photographers Archive, Bishopsgate Institute
p.253

Justice for Black People 1980s, reprinted 2023
Photograph
20.3 × 25.4
Format Photographers Archive, Bishopsgate Institute
p.211

Kath Gillespie-Sells and her son Daniel at a Gay Pride march 1980s, reprinted 2023
Photograph
40.6 × 30.5
Format Photographers Archive, Bishopsgate Institute

Mandy and Michelle Tomlinson, Ollerton Colliery, Nottinghamshire 1980s, reprinted 2023
Photograph
20.3 × 25.4
Format Photographers Archive, Bishopsgate Institute
p.170

Pride March 1980s, reprinted 2023
Photograph
20.3 × 25.4
Format Photographers Archive, Bishopsgate Institute

Thatcher Government Promotes Prejudice, Discrimination, Hatred, Violence 1980s, reprinted 2023
Photograph
30.5 × 40.6
Format Photographers Archive, Bishopsgate Institute
p.252

(SUZANNE RODEN)

Demonstration against police violence 1980s, reprinted 2023
Photograph
25.4 × 20.3
Format Photographers Archive, Bishopsgate Institute
p.211

(VAL WILMER)
b.1941

Selection of photos from Grunwick Strike 1976, reprinted 2023
4 photographs
30.5 × 40.6 (each)
Format Photographers Archive, Bishopsgate Institute
p.80

Campaign against the government immigration bill 1981, reprinted 2023
Photograph
25.4 × 20.3
Format Photographers Archive, Bishopsgate Institute
p.210

CHANDAN FRASER
b.1950

Women's Liberation Conference 1970
Women's Liberation March 1970–1
18 photographs
Dimensions variable
Courtesy of the artist and Four Corners
pp.19, 30–1, 33, 42–3, 60

MELANIE FRIEND
b.1957

Mothers' Pride 1988
8 text and photographic panels
50 × 70 (each)
Courtesy of the artist, with participant consent
p.277

CAROLE GIBBONS
b.1935

Goddess 1972
Oil paint on canvas
100 × 125
Courtesy of the artist
p.59

PENNY GORING
b.1961

Shock-A-Lolly Dolly 1985
Fabric, stuffed textile ragdoll
14 × 43 × 76
Courtesy the artist and Arcadia Missa, London
p.163

JOY GREGORY
b.1959

Roses and Razor Blades 1982, remade 2023
Photograph
30.5 × 25.4
Courtesy of the artist
p.143

Roses and Razor Blades (solarised paper negative) 1982, remade 2023
Photograph
25.4 × 20.3
Courtesy of the artist
p.143

Hotel Normandia #1, Andorra La Vella
Hotel Normandia #2, Andorra La Vella
Plaza Sagrada Familia #1, Barcelona
Plaza Sagrada Familia #2, Barcelona
Villaroel, Barcelona
From the series *Women and Spaces* 1988
5 photographs; gelatin silver prints on watercolour paper
47 × 38 (each)
Courtesy of the artist
p.281

HACKNEY FLASHERS
founded 1974

Women at Work 1975
21 photographs mounted on board
37.8 × 49.3
Courtesy of Richard Saltoun Gallery, London and Rome
pp.84–5

Who's Holding the Baby? 1978, printed c.1980
23 panels; gelatin silver prints, ink, typed text, photo-mechanical prints and collage on paper and cardboard
77 × 51.5 (each)
Museo Nacional Centro de Arte Reina Sofía, Madrid
pp.122–3

MARGARET HARRISON
b.1940

Banana Woman 1971
Watercolour, coloured graphite and graphite on paper
51.8 × 63.7
Tate. Purchased 2008

Dumped On 1971
Crayon and graphite on card
76 × 57.5
Tate. Purchased 2008

Little Woman at Home 1971
Graphite and watercolour on paper
63.6 × 51.8
Tate. Purchased 2008
p.67

Greenham Common (Common reflections) 1989–2013
Installation concrete, mirrors, clothes, children's boots, pram, soft toys, photographs and plastic bags, wire netting and barbed wire
282 × 440 (overall)
Collection les Abattoirs, Musée – Frac Occitanie Toulouse
pp.186–7

MONA HATOUM
b.1952

Roadworks 1985
Video; shown digitally, colour, sound
6 min, 45 sec
Courtesy of the artist and LUX, London
p.221

SUSAN HILLER
1940–2019

Ten Months 1977
10 framed works; photographs and text
24.3 × 57 (photos);
13.5 × 41.5 (text frames)
Arts Council Collection, Southbank Centre, London
pp.104–5

LUBAINA HIMID
b.1954

Dog Years 1981–3
Acrylic paint on wood
170 × 66 × 1.5
Collection of Richard Bliss
p.223

The Carrot Piece 1985
Two pieces; acrylic paint on plywood, wood, cardboard and string
241 × 123 (man);
206 × 73 (woman)
Tate. Purchased using funds provided by the 2014 Outset/Frieze Art Fair Fund to benefit the Tate Collection 2015
p.280

AMANDA HOLIDAY
b.1964

Red Riding Hood 1987
Pastel on paper
189 × 214
Courtesy of the artist
p.237

BHAJAN HUNJAN
b.1956

Tribute to Late Balwant Kaur and Gurdip Kaur – Victims of Domestic Violence 1986
Acrylic paint and paper on canvas
56 × 76 × 2
Courtesy of the artist
p.228

The Affair 1987–8
Acrylic paint on canvas
122 × 91.5
Tate. Presented by Tate Patrons 2023
p.229

ALEXIS HUNTER
1948-2014

The Marxist's Wife (still does the housework) 1978/2005
20 laser prints on archival paper in 4 framed panels
109.5 × 36 (each panel); 109.5 × 159 (overall)
Courtesy of Richard Saltoun Gallery, London and Rome
p.112

JANIS JEFFERIES
b.1952

Double Labia 1980
Dyed sisal
220 × 101 × 94
Courtesy of Richard Saltoun Gallery, London and Rome
p.109

CLAUDETTE JOHNSON
b.1959

Untitled (with wool and leather) 1982
Pastel, gouache paint, silver paper, leather and wool
76 × 45
Courtesy of the artist and Hollybush Gardens, London
p.195

Untitled (woman with earring) 1982
Pastel and wax carbon on paper
76 × 45
Private collection
p.214

WILMA JOHNSON
b.1960

The Maypole 1982
Oil paint on canvas
96 × 82
Phil Robbins - Asylum Studios UK
p.156

MUMTAZ KARIMJEE
b.1950

Justice for Black People 1980s
Photograph
25.4 × 20.3
Courtesy of the artist

End State Racism 1980s
Photograph
25.4 × 20.3
Courtesy of the artist
p.210

Beedi Makers from the series *My Mothers My Sisters* 1980s
Photograph; 20.3 × 25.4
Courtesy of the artist
p.212

In Search of an Image 1987
13 framed photographs and printed text
111.1 × 111.1 (overall)
Courtesy of the artist
pp.262–3

Stop the Clause protest 1988
5 photographs
30.5 × 40.6 (each)
Courtesy of the artist
pp.254 and 255

TINA KEANE
b.1940

Clapping Songs 1981
Slide tape, transferred to video; shown digitally
8 min
Courtesy of the artist and LUX, London
p.108

RITA KEEGAN
b.1949

Love, Sex and Romance 1984
12 photocopies and screenprints on paper
28.9 × 20.1 (each)
Tate. Purchased 2022
pp.240–1

Red Me 1986
Oil paint on canvas
72.5 × 64.7
UK Government Art Collection
p.242

MARGARET HARRISON
b.1940

KAY HUNT
1933–2001

MARY KELLY
b.1941

Women and Work: A Document on the Division of Labour in Industry 1973–5
Video on 2 monitors, colour, audio and photographs, gelatin silver print on paper; and works on paper, ink
Dimensions variable
Tate. Purchased 2001
pp.82–3

MARY KELLY
b.1941

Ante Partum 1973
Super 8 film, shown as digital video; black and white, silent
1 min, 30 sec
Brighton and Hove Museums – Presented by The Contemporary Art Society and Valeria Napoleone
p.103

ROSHINI KEMPADOO
b.1959

My Daughter's Mind 1984–5
12 parts; photographs and prints on paper
47.5 × 67 (each)
Courtesy of the artist
pp.246–7

Untitled from the series *Presence* 1990
4 photographs
38.5 × 30 (each)
Courtesy of the artist
p.284

SANDRA LAHIRE
1950–2001

Edge 1986
16mm film, shown as digital video; 8 min
Cinenova Distribution
p.155

LORAINE LEESON
b.1951

'Women Beware of Man Made Medicine' East London Health Project 1977–80
Offset lithograph on paper
62.3 × 44.2
Originally produced and distributed in conjunction with East London Trade Councils, health workers' unions and the Women's Health Information Collective
p.106

'Things That Make You Sick' East London Health Project 1980
Offset lithograph on paper
62.3 × 44.2
Originally produced and distributed in conjunction with East London Trade Councils, health workers' unions and the Women's Health Information Collective
p.107

LENTHALL ROAD WORKSHOP
1975–90

Women Reclaim the Night c.1980
Print on paper
50 × 74
Courtesy of Lenthall Road Workshop
p.230

Rolling Sisters c.1983
Print on paper
45 × 65
Courtesy of Lenthall Road Workshop
p.231

Tangled Roots 1986
Print on paper
42.4 × 29.6
Courtesy of Lenthall Road Workshop

Claudette Johnson screenprinting at Lenthall Road Workshop 1980s
Photograph
20 × 24
Courtesy of Lenthall Road Workshop

Joy Kahumbu, Amanda Kahumbu, Mo Ross, Sonia Johnson, Donna Keane and Louisa Jean-Baptiste 1980s
Photograph
20 × 25
Courtesy of Lenthall Road Workshop
p.230

Mo Ross and Dona Keane at Lenthall Road Workshop 1980s
Photograph
20 × 24
Courtesy of Lenthall Road Workshop

Young Women's Printing Workshop 1980s
Photograph
20 × 24
Courtesy of Lenthall Road Workshop

Sue and Rebecca at Lenthall Road Workshop photographed by Ingrid Pollard 1980s
Photograph
14 × 11
Courtesy of Lenthall Road Workshop

Black Lesbian Poster 1984
Printed paper
40.5 × 53.2
Private collection

LINDER
b.1954

Untitled 1976
Printed papers on paper
13.6 × 21
Tate. Purchased 2007

Untitled 1976
Printed papers on paper
17.2 × 18.5
Tate. Purchased 2007

Untitled 1976
Printed papers on board
27.1 × 19.5
Tate. Purchased 2007

Untitled 1976
Printed papers on paper
27.9 × 19.6
Tate. Purchased 2007
p.126

Untitled 1976
Printed papers on paper
37 × 30
Tate. Purchased 2007
p.152

Ludus Concert with Meat Dress, Hacienda, Manchester 1982
Video, shown digitally; colour sound
38 min, 53 sec
Courtesy the artist and Modern Art, London
p.137

ALISON LLOYD
1957–2024

Jake 1976, printed 2023
5 photographs; medium to follow on paper
18 × 13 (each)
Courtesy of the artist

Romilly Crescent, Cardiff, at the window, Evening Performance 1978–9
Photograph
9 × 13
Courtesy of the artist
p.118

Romilly Crescent, Cardiff, Looking at Herbie 1978
Polaroid photograph
10.5 × 8.5
Courtesy of the artist
p.118

Romilly Crescent, Cardiff, Watching 1978
Polaroid photograph
10.5 × 8.5
Courtesy of the artist
p.118

SUPPORT THE MINERS, Solidarity will win! 1984
4 photographs
130 × 90 (each)
Courtesy of the artist
p.171

LONDON WOMEN'S FILM GROUP
founded 1972

WOMEN'S STREET THEATRE GROUP
founded 1970

Amazing Equal Pay Show 1973–4
16mm film, shown as digital video; black and white, sound
48 min
Courtesy of the BFI National Archive
p.86

ROSY MARTIN
b.1946

Transforming the suit: what does a lesbian look like? Part I: The Patriarch The Capitalist The Boss 1987
Colour photographs and text mounted on card
76.2 × 60.8
Courtesy of the artist
p.261

Transforming the suit: what does a lesbian look like? Part II: What do Lesbians Look Like? 1987
Colour photographs and text mounted on card
76.2 × 60.8
Courtesy of the artist
p.261

Transforming the suit: what does a lesbian look like? Part III: An Alter Ego 1987
Colour photographs and text mounted on card
76.2 × 60.8
Courtesy of the artist
p.261

Transforming the suit: what does a lesbian look like? Part IV: Mother of Three 1987
Colour photographs and text mounted on card
76.2 × 60.8
Courtesy of the artist
p.261

Transforming the suit: what does a lesbian look like? Part V: The Madonna 1987
Colour photographs and text mounted on card
76.2 × 60.8
Courtesy of the artist
p261

Unwind the Lies That Bind 1988
7 photographic prints, mounted on aluminium
170 × 60 and 80 × 57
Courtesy of the artist
p.260

RITA MCGURN
b.1940

Untitled [Bessie figure] 1974–85
Acrylic, wool and cotton yarns, stuffed with polyester and other synthetic fibre
157 × 84 × 29
Courtesy of the McGurn family
p.127

Untitled [crochet rug] 1974–85
Acrylic, wool and cotton yarns
Diam. 135
Courtesy of the McGurn family
p.127

Untitled [Figure in black bikini] 1974–85
Acrylic, wool and cotton yarns, stuffed with polyester and other synthetic fibre
196 × 64 × 31
Courtesy of the McGurn family
p.127

Untitled [Louise Brooks figure] 1974–85
Acrylic, wool and cotton yarns, stuffed with polyester and other synthetic fibre
152 × 64 × 36
Courtesy of the McGurn family
p.127

Untitled [pair of cushions] 1974–85
Acrylic, wool and cotton yarns, stuffed with polyester and other synthetic fibre
48 × 50 × 15 (each)
Courtesy of the McGurn family
p.127

RAMONA METCALFE
b.1962

Impulse 1987
Video, shown digitally; colour, sound
1 min
Cinenova Distribution
p.180

JACQUELINE MORREAU
1929–2016

If Mary Came to Greenham
1983
Oil paint on board
202 × 81
On loan from Herbert Art Gallery and Museum, Coventry. Gifted by the Estate of Jacqueline Morreau through the Contemporary Art Society, 2018/19
p.181

THE NEO NATURISTS
founded 1980

CHRISTINE BINNIE
b.1955

JENNIER BINNIE
b.1958

WILMA JOHNSON
b.1960

Art School Performance on the Roof of St. Martins 1981
2 photographs
12.5 × 21.5 (each)
The Neo Naturist Archive
p.157

Christine Binnie in Wrought Iron Body Paint 1981
4 photocopies
29.5 × 21 (each)
The Neo Naturist Archive

Christine Binnie Flashing in Soho 1982
Photograph
24.5 × 18
The Neo Naturist Archive
p.158

Flashing (*British Museum*)
1982
Photograph
28 × 21
The Neo Naturist Archive
p.158

The Neo Naturist Sermon, Porridge and Black Roses at the Faerie Fair, Lyng 1982
11 photographs
13 × 9 (each)
The Neo Naturist Archive
p.157

Pink Punk Performance, The Fridge, Brixton 1982
4 photocopies
21.5 × 28 (each)
The Neo Naturist Archive
pp.156–7

Sexist Crabs, Oxford University Summer Performance 1983
Photograph
25 × 21.5
The Neo Naturist Archive

Sexist Crabs Performance, The Zap Club, Brighton 1983
4 photographs
9 × 12.5; 25 × 21.5; 13 × 21.5; 10 × 15
The Neo Naturist Archive
p.157

Centrepoint, Walking and Swimming Experiment 1984
12 photographs
11 × 15 (each)
The Neo Naturist Archive
p.158

Existentialists Performance, The Fridge, Brixton 1985
Photograph
24.5 × 17
The Neo Naturist Archive

Neo Naturist Cheerleading Performance, Heaven 1985
3 photographs
21 × 24.5 (each)
The Neo Naturist Archive

Neo Naturists Manifesto, International Times 1985
Newspaper
33.5 × 31
The Neo Naturist Archive

HOURIA NIATI
b.1948

No to Torture (*After Delacroix 'Women of Algiers'*) 1982–3
Oil paint on canvas
183 × 273.5
Courtesy of the artist
p.178

ANNABEL NICOLSON
b.1946

Fire Film 1981
Super 8 film, transferred to digital; colour, sound
10 min
Courtesy of the artist and LUX, London
p.182

RUTH NOVACZEK
b.1956

Tea Leaf 1986
16mm film, shown as digital video; colour, sound
8 min, 13 sec
Cinenova Distribution
p.154

MOWBRAY ODONKOR
b.1962

Onward Christian Soldiers
1987
Acrylic paint on paper
152 × 182
Arts Council Collection, Southbank Centre, London
p.222

HANNAH O'SHEA
b.1939

Stills from 'A Visual Time Span' (*A Visual Diary*) c.1975
2 photographs; vintage silver bromide prints
51 × 38 and 40.5 × 50.5
England & Co Gallery, London
p.72

PRATIBHA PARMAR
b.1955

Reframing AIDS 1987
Video, shown digitally; colour, sound
35 min, 59 sec
Courtesy of the artist and Kali Films
p.259

Sari Red 1988
Video, shown digitally; colour, sound
13 min, 26 sec
Courtesy of the artist and Kali Films
p.235

SYMRATH PATTI
b.1961

Tetley Bitter Men 1983
Photograph; gelatin silver print
48.3 × 68.5
Courtesy of the artist

Sketches for a Memorial–Yaadgari 1986
Collage and acrylic paint on paper
59.5 × 84.2
Courtesy of the artist
p.234

Woman in Red 1986
Acrylic paint and traces of pastel pigment on paper
113.5 × 81
Courtesy of the artist
p.234

INGRID POLLARD
b.1953

Deny: Imagine: Attack: Silence
1991
4 sets of framed gelatin silver photographic prints, Xerox prints and hand-painted mount card
61 × 56; 85 × 47;
76 × 40; 48 × 64
Courtesy of the artist
p.257

JILL POSENER
b.1953

Born Kicking, London 1983, reprinted 2023
Photograph
40.6 × 50.8
Courtesy of the artist
p.160

Fiat Ad, London 1979, reprinted 2023
Photograph
40.6 × 50.8
Courtesy of the artist
p.161

Macho Bore, London 1983, reprinted 2023
Photograph
40.6 × 50.8
Courtesy of the artist
p.160

Renew His Interest, London 1980, reprinted 2023
Photograph
40.6 × 50.8
Courtesy of the artist

Squat Against Nuclear Family
1982, reprinted 2023
Photograph
40.6 × 50.8
Courtesy of the artist
p.161

To Volvo A Son, London 1982, reprinted 2023
Photograph
40.6 × 50.8
Courtesy of the artist
pp.161

A Dirty Girls Guide to London
1987, reprinted 2023
7 photographs
25.5 × 30.5
Courtesy of the artist
pp.264–5

ELIZABETH RADCLIFFE
b.1949

Cool Bitch and Hot Dog 1978
Wool, linen, papier mâché, metal buckle and nylon glove on plywood
180 × 83 × 50
Courtesy of the artist
p.119

FRANKI RAFFLES
1955–94

To Let You Understand 1988, reprinted 2023
10 photographs
21 × 29.7
Franki Raffles Estate, courtesy of University of St Andrews Library and Edinburgh Napier University
pp.278–9

SAMENA RANA
1955–92

Mirror Mirror I and *II* from the *Reflection Series*, no.11 and 12 1991
2 photographs
29 × 19 (each)
Private collection
p.274

Self-portrait 1991
Photograph
23 × 23
Private collection

SU RICHARDSON
b.1947

Selection of Postal Art items
1975–6
Various mediums and dimensions
Courtesy of Richard Saltoun Gallery, London and Rome
pp.64–5

Bear it in Mind 1976
Dungarees, jeans, coat hanger, gloves, ink on paper and other materials
150 × 45 × 4
Tate. Presented by Tate Patrons 2022
p.63

LIZ RIDEAL
b.1954

'Think Pink' (*aka – booth wank at NPG*) 1985
7 strips of uncut, no negative photo-booth photos
20.5 × 28 (overall)
Courtesy of the artist
p.150

ROBINA ROSE
b.1951

Birth Rites 1977
16mm film shown as digital video; colour, sound
53 min
Cinenova Distribution, with support from FINE Neonatal UK Ltd
p.101

MONICA ROSS
1950–2013

'fly away Susy!' 1976
Graphite rubbing on paper
3 sections; 51 × 76 (each);
148.5 × 76 (overall)
MonicaRossArchive.org
p.62

I papered that wall myself
1976
Graphite or charcoal rubbing on paper
157 × 106
Alice Ross

Selection of archival and Postal Art items 1976–8
Various
MonicaRossArchive.org

Fenix box 1978
Cardboard box and paper collage, containing 1 A3 paper *Fenix* publication
47.6 × 33.5 × 4
MonicaRossArchive.org

Stop She Said 1982–3
Slide tape transferred to U-matic video, shown digitally; colour, sound
7 min, 18 sec
MonicaRossArchive.org

Morning at Blue Gate 1983
Graphite, grey and black paint, cut-outs made of paper, cotton and wool strings, black metal mesh fragment
55 × 71
MonicaRossArchive.org
p.191

ERICA RUTHERFORD
1947–2008

Erica Rutherford (*'Red Stockings'*) 1970
Gouache on paper
83.2 × 67.9
Lent by the National Portrait Gallery, London

The Bed 1973
Acrylic paint on canvas
122 × 127.2
Susana Rutherford
p.70

LESLEY SANDERSON
b.1962

Fuck the British Movement
1984
Graphite on paper
67.5 × 54
Courtesy of the Artist
p.244

Time for a Change 1988
Oil paint on canvas
183 × 168
Courtesy of the Artist
p.245

MAUREEN SCOTT
b.1940

Mother and Child at Breaking Point 1970
Oil paint on board
91.5 × 91.5
Courtesy of the artist and Bethlem Museum of the Mind
p.58

SEE RED WOMEN'S WORKSHOP
1974–90

7 Demands 1974
Screenprint on paper
29.5 × 63.3
Courtesy of See Red Women's Workshop

Protest 1974
Screenprint on paper
65 × 51
Courtesy of See Red Women's Workshop
p.42

Right on Jane (See Red Calendar) 1977
Printed paper
78.7 × 53.7
Courtesy of the Women's Art Library, Special Collections and Archives, Goldsmiths College

Bite the Hand 1978
Screenprint on paper
64 × 45
Courtesy See Red Women's Workshop
p.87

Tough – My Message to the Women of Our Nation… 1979
Photostencil, print on paper and plastic laminate
79 × 53
Courtesy See Red Women's Workshop
p.142

Our Body 1980
Screenprint on paper
51 × 76
Courtesy of See Red Women's Workshop
p.88

Black Women Will Not Be Intimidated 1980–1
Screenprint on paper
79 × 53
Courtesy of See Red Women's Workshop
p.209

YBA Wife – Is There Life After Marriage? 1981
Screenprint on paper
61 × 43
Courtesy of See Red Women's Workshop
p.141

Lesbians Are Coming Out 1982
Screenprint on paper
64 × 46
Courtesy of See Red Women's Workshop
p.256

Support the Women's Peace Camps 1983
Screenprint on paper
74 × 50.5
Courtesy of See Red Women's Workshop
p.175

GURMINDER SIKAND
1960–2021

Woman Strangling a Demon I 1990
Watercolour, ink, gouache and wax crayon on paper
35.5 × 32.1
Courtesy of the Estate of Gurminder Sikand
p.238

Faces 1990
Watercolour, ink, gouache and wax crayon on paper
29 × 41.5
Courtesy of the Estate of Gurminder Sikand

SISTER SEVEN
1981–4

Sister Seven touring show posters 1981
9 posters; printed paper, laminated
45.7 × 33 or 33 × 45.7
Sisterseven.org
pp.188–90

MONICA SJÖÖ
1938–2005

Selection of posters, flyers and publications
Courtesy of the Monica Sjöö Estate and Alison Jacques, London
p.8

Phallic Culture 1970
Oil paint, part on canvas, on board
121.9 × 121.9
Courtesy of the Monica Sjöö Estate and Alison Jacques, London
p.61

Wages for Housework 1975
Oil paint on board
183 × 122
Courtesy of the Monica Sjöö Estate and Alison Jacques, London

VERONICA SLATER
b.1958

Soul Identified as Flesh 1987–8
Oil paint on canvas
182.8 × 182.8
Courtesy of the artist
p.271

PENNY SLINGER
b.1947

Bride and Groom – Ceremonial Cutting of the Cake 1973
Photograph
20.3 × 12.7
Courtesy of the Artist, Richard Saltoun Gallery London and Rome, and Blum & Poe, Los Angeles/New York/Tokyo

Open Invitation – Ready for Consummation 1973
Photograph
25.4 × 20.3
Courtesy of the Artist, Richard Saltoun Gallery London and Rome, and Blum & Poe, Los Angeles/New York/Tokyo

Wedding Cake – Open Secret 1973
Photograph
25.4 × 20.3
Courtesy of the Artist, Richard Saltoun Gallery London and Rome, and Blum & Poe, Los Angeles/New York/Tokyo
p.69

Spirit Impressions – 2, 3, 4 and *5*
4 photocopy prints
48.3 × 29.2 and 48.3 × 29.9 (no.3)
Courtesy of the Artist, Richard Saltoun Gallery London and Rome, and Blum & Poe, Los Angeles/New York/Tokyo
p.68

MARLENE SMITH
b.1964

Good Housekeeping III 1985, remade 2023
Chipboard, household plaster, wire mesh, J-cloths and gouache
213.4 × 304.8
Courtesy of the artist
p.218

Art History 1987
Plastic flowers, vase and framed images
80.7 × 72 (overall)
Lent by Sheffield Museums Trust
p.219

JO SPENCE
1934–92

Beyond the Family Album 1978–9
Gelatin silver prints, C-prints and press cuttings
204 × 83 and 74 × 50 (each)
MACBA Collection. MACBA Foundation. Work purchased thanks to Terry Dennett
pp.110–1

JO SPENCE
1934–92
TERRY DENNETT
1938–2018

Untitled 1988
2 photographs
14 × 20 (each)
Private collection
p.27

MAUD SULTER
1960–2008

The Alabama Branch of My Family Tree 1988
Mixed media, folded card and burnt paper
29.7 × 42.2
The Estate of Maud Sulter
p.215

SUZAN SWALE
b.1946

Hegemony 1982
Newspaper, acrylic paint and Letraset lettering on card
50.6 × 63.2
Courtesy of the artist
p.159

ANNE TALLENTIRE
b.1949

Forbidden Heroines 1987
Video, shown digitally; black and white, silent
7 min, 56 sec
Courtesy of the artist and Hollybush Gardens, London
p.258

SHANTI THOMAS
b.1949

Self-Portrait 1984
Oil paint on canvas
60 × 60
Courtesy of the artist
p.250

Juggling c.1987
Oil paint on canvas
89 × 89
Private collection
p.251

MARTINE THOQUENNE
b.1956

Faster Princess 1982
Super 8 film, shown as digital video; colour, sound
10 min
Cinenova Distribution
p.153

COSEY FANNI TUTTI
b.1951

Woman's Roll 1978
30 framed photographs; black-and-white silver bromide prints
21 × 29.7 (each)
Courtesy of the artist and Cabinet Gallery, London
pp.98–9

Incognito 1979–2021
7 photographs; C-type prints
30.5 × 30.5 (each)
Courtesy of Sara Burn
p.144

White leotard 1979
Lycra; size 10
Courtesy of the artist and Cabinet Gallery, London

GEE VAUCHER
b.1945

International Anthem No.2 Domestic Violence 1979
Printed magazine cuttings on card
34 × 27.5
Courtesy of the artist
p.124

International Anthem No.2 Domestic Violence 1979
Gouache on cardboard
37 × 38 × 3
Courtesy of the artist

VERA PRODUCTIONS
founded 1982

Video 28 1988
Video, shown digitally; colour, sound
22 min
Cinenova Distribution
p.270

SHIRLEY VERHOEVEN
1932–99

Portfolio 1989
Pen and coloured pencil on paper
32 × 29.5
Courtesy the Estate of Shirley Verhoeven
p.285

CHRISTINE VOGE
b.1948

Erin Pizzey, Pioneer of the Protection of Women and Children Subjected to Domestic Violence 1978
Photograph; gelatin silver print on paper
23 × 29.7
Arts Council Collection, Southbank Centre, London

Untitled 1978
Photograph; gelatin silver print
19.9 × 29.6
Arts Council Collection, Southbank Centre, London

Untitled 1978
Photograph; gelatin silver print
29.7 × 20.1
Arts Council Collection, Southbank Centre, London
p.120

Untitled (*Three children and woman*) 1978
Photograph; gelatin silver print
29.8 × 20.3
Arts Council Collection, Southbank Centre, London
p.121 (top left)

Untitled (*Two women*) 1978
Photograph; gelatin silver print
19.9 × 29.3
Arts Council Collection, Southbank Centre, London
p.121 (bottom)

Untitled (*Woman*) 1978
Photograph; gelatin silver print
29.3 × 20.1
Arts Council Collection, Southbank Centre, London
p.121 (top right)

DEL LAGRACE VOLCANO
b.1957

Snake and Linda, London 1983
Photograph
19.5 × 29
Courtesy of the artist

Snake and Linda, London 1983
Photograph
27.5 × 35
Courtesy of the artist
p.162

Chain Reaction 1988
3 photographs
50 × 40 or 40 × 50
Courtesy of the artist

Cruising 1988
3 photographs
30 × 24
Courtesy of the artist
pp.268–9

Untitled 1980s
Photograph
28 × 21
Courtesy of the artist
p.162

WAGES FOR HOUSEWORK CAMPAIGN (FORMERLY POWER OF WOMEN COLLECTIVE)
founded 1972

All Work and No Pay 1975
Video, shown digitally; colour, sound
30 min, 19 sec
BBC © copyright content reproduced courtesy of the British Broadcasting Corporation. All rights reserved
p.129

KATE WALKER
1938–2015

Selection of archival and Postal Art items 1974–7
Estate of Kate Walker
p.64

Art of Survival – A Living Monument 1987
Skirt, blouse, sash, handmade textile paint palette and textile brushes
Various dimensions
Estate of Kate Walker
pp.282–3

LAI NGAN WALSH
b.1949

THE WOMEN AND THE LAW COLLECTIVE

Who Takes the Rap – Immigration 1986
Video, shown digitally; colour, sound
38 min
Cinenova Distribution
p.236

JILL WESTWOOD
b.1960

Hermetic-Female Triptych c.1982
3 photographs; colour Polaroids
11.5 × 9 (each)
Courtesy of the artist
p.147

Sovereign-Female-Subaltern-Male c.1982
Photograph
21 × 15
Courtesy of the artist

Alpha-Female Triptych 1983
3 photographs
8.5 × 12.5 (each)
Courtesy of the artist
p.138

Potent-Female c.1983
Photograph
25 × 20
Courtesy of the artist
p.146

Transparent-Female c.1983
Photograph
30 × 40
Courtesy of the artist
p.147

CHRISTINE WILKINSON
b.1951

Reflections 1983
Hand-coloured mezzotint
8.2 × 11.7 (image)
Christine Wilkinson
p.116

NANCY WILLIS
b.1953

Self Portrait II and *IV* 1983
2 works; pastel on paper
79.4 × 60.1
Courtesy of Imperial Health Charity Art Collection

Self-portrait with Lost Baby 1988
Etching with hand-colouring on paper
28 × 24
Courtesy of the artist
p.275

Her name is 'Rosie' 1990
Bronze
10 × 5 × 5
Courtesy of the artist

W.I.T.C.H. (BLACK WOMEN'S MEDIUM PROJECT)

A Tribute to Black Women (*They don't get a chance*) 1986
Video, shown digitally; colour, sound
22 min
Cinenova Distribution
p.227

ACKNOWLEDGEMENTS

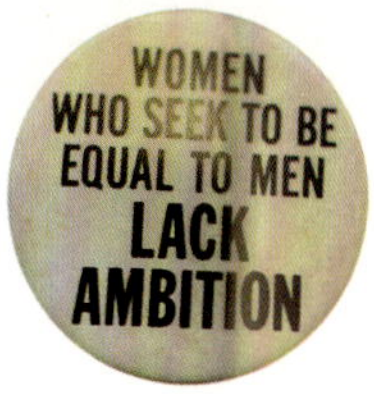

This exhibition and publication are built on the generosity and collaboration of a wide range of people, those who lived and worked through the 1970s and 1980s, and those who love and care for their mothers, sisters, lovers and friends' estates. We are deeply indebted to the curators, writers, archivists and activists who have spent years preserving and sharing their knowledge – without them this project would simply not be possible.

Our heartfelt thanks go of course to the artists who have welcomed us into their homes and studios, and who have been incredibly generous and patient with us, and to the archives who have shared their holdings with us, notably: the Black Cultural Archives, the Women's Art Library, Glasgow Women's Library, the Feminist Library, Bishopsgate Institute and Cinenova.

Advisors Althea Greenan, Griselda Pollock and Marlene Smith along with Stella Dadzie, Juliet Jacques, Suzanne Scafe and Lucy Whitman have reviewed and interrogated our work, challenging our assumptions and greatly enriching the project.

Lucy Reynolds has worked with great care to help us deliver all moving-image selections for the exhibition and has spearheaded its accompanying film programme, working with Cinenova, LUX, the BFI and the BBC, as well as directly with artists and their estates.

Writers Alice Correia, Stella Dadzie, Amrita Dhallu, Zuzana Flaskova, Rachel Garfield, Juliet Jacques, Dorothy Price, Ash Reid and Amy Tobin have provided rich new bodies of research to the accompanying publication.

Exhibition designers Varv Varv have worked with rigour and sensitivity to the material, realising their vision for the exhibition with Dylan Atkins and MCD Heritage.

Roland Brauchli has worked with his usual style and intuition to realise the publication we dreamed of under the careful and infinitely patient eye of Emma Poulter.

Lubaina Himid generously supported the production of our *Women in Revolt!* podcast. Her support has given us the time and freedom to construct an invaluable set of stories that will reach far beyond the gallery walls. We are also thankful to podcast producer Rosie Oliver who has worked with meticulous care on the series.

Julie Weir, Leah Divine and Ben Duke at Sony have worked with us to produce the *Women in Revolt!* compilation record with huge enthusiasm and generosity.

A great many conservators, printers and framers have expertly supported the delivery of the works in the show, including Archetype, Darbyshire, Sarah Glenn, Metro Imaging, Julia Nagle Studio, Keith Oliver, Pendragon, Amelia Rampton, Zenzie Tinker and Sophie Younger.Indefatigable Tate colleagues across all departments have helped to realise the exhibition at Tate. Special thanks to: Shareen Adler, Giulia Calvi, Juliette Dupire, Zuzana Flaskova, Inga Fraser, Amy Griffin, Mikei Hall, Elliot Higgs, Roz Hill, Bill Jones, Alma Jongstra, Sabrina Kaïci, Carolyn Kerr, Kwai Lau, Wendy Lothian, Hannah Marsh, Sam McGuire, Alexandra Nichols, Kiko Noda, Kristine Omandap, Toyin Omirin, Pierre Bouvier Patron, Bella Probyn, Lydia Riley, Francisca Roserio, Charlotte Sanguinetti, Sophie Sarkodie, Andy Shiel, Gates Sofer, Liam Tebbs, Alex White, Dale Wilson, and to all of our Tate colleagues in front of house, security, reception, catering, retail, cleaning and maintenance, whose work is critical to all we do.

Additional thanks to: Lucy Askew, Poppy Bowers, Rachel Browning, Laura Castignini, Niamh Coghlan, Stefan Dickers, James Finch, Darren Fox, Marina Geogriou, Emma Gillespie, Minna Haukka, the Henry Moore Foundation, Olivia Heron, Dominique Heyse-Moore, Michael Hill, Eleanor Jones, Derek Jordan, Steve Macleod, Milo Miller, Kate Mollison, Jenny Noble, Lola Olufemi, Alona Pardo, Adele Patrick, Charlotte Procter, Helena Reckitt, Jonathan Ruffer curatorial grant, Salmon Creek Farm, Cliodhna Shaffrey, Evie Slater, Polly Staple, Clarrie Wallis, Michael White and all of the staff at the Prince and Princess of Wales Hospice.

Personal thanks to Bruce Adams, Laura Aldridge, Luke Barker, Pascal Brannan, Nicholas Byrne, Blair Govan, Anthea Hamilton, Andrew Morgan, Joe Scotland, David Wostenholm and Bruce, Bunny and Annie.

And finally, to Andrew Smith, for his love and care of my mum and me when we needed it most.

RESOURCES

The Women's Art Library Collections, Goldsmiths, University of London, Dixon Road, London, SE14 6NW, https://www.gold.ac.uk/make/

Black Cultural Archives, 1 Windrush Square, London, SW2 1EF, https://blackculturalarchives.org/

Glasgow Women's Library, 23 Landressy Street, Glasgow, G40 1BP, https://womenslibrary.org.uk/

Panchayat Collection, Tate library and Archive, Tate Britain, Millbank, London, SW1P 4RG, https://www.tate.org.uk/research/panchayat-collection-research-resource

National Disability Arts Collection and Archive, https://the-ndaca.org/about/

The Feminist Library, The Sojourner Truth Community Centre, 161 Sumner Road, Peckham, London, SE15 6JL, https://feministlibrary.co.uk/

Feminist Archive North, Special Collections, Brotherton Library, University of Leeds, Woodhouse Lane, Leeds, LS2 9JT, https://library.leeds.ac.uk/special-collections/collection/705

Feminist Archive South, Special Collections, Art and Social Sciences Library, University of Bristol, Tyndall Avenue, Bristol, BS8 1TJ, https://feministarchivesouth.org.uk/

Bishopsgate Institute, 230 Bishopsgate, London, EC2M 4QH, https://www.bishopsgate.org.uk/

Cinenova, https://cinenova.org/

Lux, Waterlow Park Centre, Darmouth Park, Hill, London, N19 5JF, https://lux.org.uk/

Key feminist magazines/ journals (UK) 1970–90

Against the Clause, photocopy-based artwork celebrating Lesbian, Gay and heterosexual defiance, and the Community CopyArt Project (1988).

Banshee: Journal of Irish Women United (1975–7).

Beaumont Bulletin, produced by the Beaumont Society (1968–ongoing).

Feminist Art News (FAN), formalised version of the Women Artists Newsletter (1980–93).

Feminist Review, triannual peer-reviewed academic journal (1979–present).

FOWAAD!, publication of the Organisation for Women of Asian and African Descent (OWAAD) (1979–80, seven issues).

MAMA: Women Artists Together, single-edition journal produced in Birmingham by the Mama Collective (1977).

Mukti, magazine of the Mukti Collective (1983–7, seven issues).

Outwrite, an 'Internationalist Feminist publication', produced by a collective of women offering news by and for women (1982–8).

Polareyes: a journal by and about black women in photography (1987).

Red Rag: A Magazine of Women's Liberation (1972–80).

Shocking Pink, a groundbreaking feminist magazine (1981–2 and 1987–92).

Shrew, the newsletter of the London Women's Liberation Workshop (1969–78).

Spare Rib, the largest and most widely distributed feminist publication in the UK (1972–1993).

Speak Out, publication of Brixton Black Women's Group (1980–5).

We Are Here: Black Feminist Newsletter, small publication founded after the conference of the same name that took place in London in May 1984–6 (ten issues).

Women's Artists Slide Library Newsletter (1983– 2002). This began as *The Women's Artists Slide Library Newsletter*, before becoming the bimonthly *The Women Artists Slide Library Journal*, then the quarterly magazine *The Women's Art Magazine*, and then finally *MAKE, the magazine of women's art*.

Women's Report, bimonthly newspaper started by members of the Women's Lobby who were set up to support anti-sex discrimination legislation (1971–9).

Key women-only group exhibitions (UK) 1970–90

First Feminist Art Show, Woodstock Gallery, London, 1971.

Exhibition on Womanpower, Swiss Cottage Library, London, 1973.

A Woman's Place, S.L.A.G (South London Art Group), London, 1974.

Who's Holding the Baby?, Centreprise, London, 1975.

Sweet Sixteen and Never Been Shown, Women's Free Art Alliance, London, 1975.

Feministo/Portrait of the Artist as a Housewife, ICA, London (and touring), 1977.

Fenix (aka *Phoenix*), UK touring exhibition, 1978–80: Bluecoat Gallery, Liverpool (1978); Darlington Hall Gallery (1980); Bristol Arts Centre (1980); ICA, London, as part of *Issue: Social Strategies by Women Artists* (1980).

Women's Images of Men, ICA, London, 1980.

About Time, ICA, London, 1980.

Issue: Social Strategies by Women Artists, ICA, London, 1980.

Women's Work 1–7, Brixton Art Gallery, London, 1981–7.

Four Indian Women Artists, Indian Artists (UK) Gallery, London, 1981–2.

Sister Seven, UK-touring exhibition, 1982.

Five Black Women, Africa Centre, London, 1983.

Black Woman Time Now, Battersea Arts Centre, London, 1983.

Women's Performance, Rochdale Art Gallery, 1984.

Artists with Disabilities: Coming into View, Coming into Reach, Norwood Library, London, 1984.

The Thin Black Line, ICA, London, 1985.

Testimony: Three Black Women Photographers, Camerawork, London, 1986.

Mirror Reflecting Darkly, Brixton Art Gallery, London, 1985 and 1986.

Numaish: An Exhibition of 5 Asian Women's Work, People's Gallery, London, 1986.

Jagrati: *An Exhibition of Work by Asian Women Artists*, Greenwich Citizen's Gallery, London, 1986.

Some of Us Are Brave, All of Us Are Strong, The Black-Art Gallery, London, 1986.

Off the Map, curated by Irish Women Artists' Group, Chisenhale, 1987.

Against the Clause: photocopy-based artwork celebrating Lesbian, Gay and heterosexual defiance, printed at Community CopyArt Project, 1988.

Along the Lines of Resistance: contemporary feminist art show, Cooper Gallery, Barnsley, 1988–9 and South London Gallery, 1990.

Passion, Elbow Room, London, 1989.

Ecstatic Antibodies, Battersea Arts Centre, London, 1990.

In Focus, Horizon Gallery, London, 1990.

INDEX

Page references in *italics* indicate pages on which works appear.

CREDITS

Copyright Credits

Unless stated otherwise all works are © the artist

© Bobby Baker and Andrew Whittuck. All rights reserved, DACS/Artimage 2023.
© Anne Bean courtesy Jane England Gallery
© Zarina Bhimji. All Rights Reserved, DACS/Artimage 2023
© Sutapa Biswas. All rights reserved, DACS/Artimage 2023
Courtesy of the Estate of Tessa Boffin and the Gupta+Singh Archive
© Sonia Boyce. All Rights Reserved, DACS 2023
© Joanne O'Brien/Format Photographers Archive, Bishopsgate Institute
© Chila Kumari Singh Burman. All rights reserved, DACS 2023
© Estate of Helen Chadwick courtesy Richard Saltoun Gallery London and Rome
© Caroline Coon/Camera Press. Courtesy the artist and Stephen Friedman Gallery, London All rights reserved, DACS 2023
© Stella Dadzie
© Nina Edge. All rights reserved, DACS 2023
© the Estate of Rose Finn-Kelcey. Courtesy the Estate and Kate MacGarry
© Courtesy of the designer (Jenny Fortune) pp.12, 30
© Chandan Fraser. Courtesy the artist and Four Corners
©Melanie Friend/Format Photographers Archive, Bishopsgate Institute pp.25, 174, 177
© Carole Gibbons Courtesy of 5b, Glasgow
© Sheila Gray/Format Photographers Archive, Bishopsgate Institute
© Joy Gregory. All rights reserved, DACS 2023
© Mona Hatoum. Courtesy Kunstmuseum St. Gallen p.221
© Estate of Susan Hiller. All Rights Reserved, DACS 2023 Courtesy Lisson Gallery
© Lubaina Himid, courtesy the artist and Hollybush Gardens, London
© The Estate of Alexis Hunter. All rights reserved, DACS 2023
© Pam Isherwood/Format Photographers Archive, Bishopsgate Institute
© Janis K. Jefferies courtesy Richard Saltoun Gallery London and Rome
© Claudette Johnson, courtesy the artist and Hollybush Gardens, London All Rights Reserved, DACS/Artimage 2023
© Mary Kelly 2023 Courtesy the artist and Pippy Houldsworth Gallery, DACS 2023
© Loraine Leeson. All Rights Reserved, DACS 2023
© Lenthall Road Workshop
© Linder. All rights reserved, DACS 2023 Courtesy the artist and Modern Art, London
© Linder. Courtesy the artist and Modern Art, London
© Jenny Matthews/Format Photographers Archive, Bishopsgate Institute
© Courtesy of the Mukti Collective pp.206, 213(fig.8)
© Maggie Murray/Format Photographers Archive, Bishopsgate Institute
© Raissa Page/Format Photographers Archive, Bishopsgate Institute
© Angela Phillips/Format Photographers Archive, Bishopsgate Institute
© Ingrid Pollard. All rights reserved, DACS 2023
© Courtesy of Poly Styrene Estate and Archive
©Brenda Prince/ Format Photographers Archive, Bishopsgate Institute
© Susan Richardson. All Rights Reserved, DACS 2023 Courtesy Richard Saltoun Gallery London and Rome
© Suzanne Roden/Format Photographers Archive, Bishopsgate Institute
© Hannah O'Shea, courtesy England & co, London
© See Red Women's Workshop.
© Gurminder Sikand Courtesy of Tim Youngs.
© Monica Sjöö Estate. Courtesy: Monica Sjöö Estate; Alison Jacques, London p.8
© Monica Sjöö Estate. Courtesy: Museum Anna Nordlander p.38
© Penny Slinger. All Rights Reserved, DACS 2023 Courtesy Richard Saltoun Gallery London and Rome
© Estate of Jo Spence
© Jo Spence Memorial Archive London pp.110–11
© Jo Spence, Hackney Flashers pp.84–5
© Estate of Maud Sulter. All rights reserved, DACS 2023. Digital image by Birmingham Museums Trust
© Anne Tallentire Courtesy the artist and Hollybush Gardens, London
© Courtesy the Estate of Shirley Verhoeven
© Gee Vaucher
© Christine Wilkinson
© Val Wilmer/Format Archive
© Courtesy the artist Sarah Wilson p.13

Photo Credits

Photo ©Elssie Ansareo. Azkuna Zentroa – Alhóndiga Bilbao pp.186–7
Photo © Amgueddfa Cymru – National Museum Wales p.185
Photo © Arts Council Collection, Southbank Centre, London pp.102, 117, 120–1, 220, 222
Photography by Matthew Barnes, Glasgow p.59
Photo by Jason Bevan p.159
Photo © Tim Bowditch p.163
Photo by Phyllis Christopher p.223
Image courtesy of Cinenova pp.95, 101, 153, 155, 180, 183, 227, 236, 270
Image courtesy Crossroads and BBC Archives p.129
Photo © Crown copyright: UK Government Art Collection p.242
Image reproduced by kind permission of Culture Coventry Trust, Herbert Art Gallery and Museum, Coventry p.181
Photo © Prudence Cuming pp.61, 62, 191, 228–9, 233, 274
Photo courtesy of Stella Dadzie/Black Cultural Archives pp.17, 44–5, 47, 89(figs 4, 5), 210(fig.2), 212–13(figs 3, 9, 10)
Photo by Andrew Dunkley pp.188–90
Courtesy of Feminist Library p.31(fig.9), 212(fig.1), 213(fig.7)
Image courtesy of Feministo to Fenix artists Kate Walker, Monica Ross, Su Richardson and Suzy Varty p.66
Photo courtesy of Glasgow Women's Library pp.31(fig.10), 42(fig.2), 173(fig.3), 210(fig.4)
Photo by Jack Hems p.215
Photo: Krister Hägglund p.38
Photos courtesy of Bhajan Hunjan pp.204, 205
Photo by Keith Hunter p.127
Photos from the archive of Andrew Hurman (www.brixton50.co.uk) pp. 35, 41
Photo by Andy Keates p.224
Photograph by Graham Lester George. Courtesy of Tim Youngs p.238
Photo © Lisson Gallery pp.104–5
Photo: Rosy Martin in collaboration with Jo Spence pp.260–1
Photo by Frances McLean p.86
Photo © Michael Ann McMullen, Hackney Flashers p.94
Photo © 2022 Bernard G Mills All rights reserved p.271
Provided by MonicaRossArchive.org pp.31(fig.12), 42(fig.4), 43(fig.9), 90(fig.2)
Photo: Stefan Rohner p.221
Photo © Richard Saltoun Gallery London and Rome pp.63, 64–5, 68–9, 74–5, 84–5, 112, 113
Photo © Scottish National Gallery of Modern Art p.179
Photo © Sheffield Museums Trust p.219
Photo © Denise Swanson artworksphotography.co.uk pp.214, 226
Photo by: Keith Sweeney. Post production Jason Brown pp.248–9
Photo © Tate Images, 2023 pp.82–3, 216–17, 290
Photo © Tate Images, 2023: Lucy G pp.268–9
Photo © Tate Images, 2023: Joe Humphries pp.216–17, 246–7, 284
Tate Images, 2023, Jai Monaghan p.67
Photo © Courtesy of the University of St Andrews Libraries and Museums pp.278–9
Photo by Todd-White Art Photography p.145
Photo by Ben Westoby p.275
Photo by Ben Westoby. Courtesy Modern Art Oxford p.195
Courtesy of Lucy Whitman p.130(fig.4)
Photo courtesy Christine Wilkinson p.116
Photo © Andrew Wittuck pp.114–15
Courtesy Women's Art Library, Goldsmiths, University of London p.90(fig.3)

We take copyright very seriously and are very grateful for the many kind consents granted to us for use of the artworks and archival material illustrated here. Owing to the nature of some of the content (badges, pamphlets, self-published magazines, posters etc), much of which is anonymously-authored, it has been impossible to seek copyright consent in many cases. We apologise for any unauthorised reproduction, and warmly invite rights holders to be in touch with us to help fill some copyright gaps. Please email copyright@tate.org.uk. Thank you